Communicating as Professionals

4th Edition

Communicating as Professionals

Raymond Archee

Myra Gurney

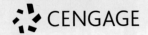

Communicating as Professionals
4th Edition
Raymond Archee
Myra Gurney

Portfolio manager: Fiona Hammond
Senior content developer: Kylie Scott
Project editor: Ronald Chung/Alex Chambers
Cover designer: Cengage Creative Studio
Text designer: Rina Gargano (Alba Design)
Editor: Jade Jakovcic
Permissions/Photo researcher: Helen Mammides
Indexer: Julie King
Proofreader: Andrew Liston
Art direction: Linda Davidson
Typeset by KnowledgeWorks Global Ltd.

Any URLs contained in this publication were checked for currency during the production process. Note, however, that the publisher cannot vouch for the ongoing currency of URLs.

This fourth edition published in 2024.

Acknowledgements
Part openers: Shutterstock.com/YummyBuum

For product information and technology assistance,
in Australia call **1300 790 853**;
in New Zealand call **0800 449 725**

For permission to use material from this text or product, please email
aust.permissions@cengage.com

National Library of Australia Cataloguing-in-Publication Data
ISBN: 9780170465632
A catalogue record for this book is available from the National Library of Australia.

Cengage Learning Australia
Level 5, 80 Dorcas Street
Southbank VIC 3006 Australia

For learning solutions, visit **cengage.com.au**

Printed in Malaysia by Papercraft.
1 2 3 4 5 6 7 27 26 25 24 23

Brief contents

PART ONE

PART TWO

PART THREE

Contents

PART ONE

PART TWO

PART THREE

Writing skills in professional life 314

Preface

Welcome to the fourth edition of *Communicating as Professionals*, which is presented as an upgraded set of readings on what we see as the most critical and immediate areas in communication theory and practice, those of importance to professional practitioners in the third decade of the 21st century. We still define 'professionals' as people who apply technical experience or scientific theory to their work, who need to keep upgrading their knowledge and who adhere to guidelines of ethical practice. For such people, an understanding of communication theory and practice is essential.

The new book is addressed to students undertaking professional studies, especially in the social and technical sciences, such as health and medicine, education and training, engineering and planning, building and design, and the computer sciences. It will also be useful to professional graduates of these courses wishing to maintain their competence in communication as part of their profession.

We have updated each of the previous edition's chapters by considering the implications of new technology on that chapter's theme, added recent references and changed many of the previous discussion questions and exercises to reflect recent issues and events. The landscape of communication practice has significantly changed over the past decade, thus we have written two entirely new chapters titled 'Visual communication' and 'Professional communication and ethics' to address omissions of the previous edition. 'Visual communication' signifies the increasing importance of images and video to communication, especially in the online sphere. The new chapter on ethics positions personal, research and professional ethics as central to being a communication professional.

The updated 'Mediated communication' chapter informs students about the latest developments in email, social media, videoconferencing, forums, chat, texting and blogs, and discusses the main issues that arise from the use of these communication technologies – privacy, copyright, censorship, cyberbullying, plagiarism, online dating and e-learning. We have not addressed artificial intelligence (AI) because the arrival of ChatGPT occurred after we had finalised writing the new edition of this book. We do predict that AI will will revolutionise all aspects of our lives for many years to come. The book is not just a new 'how-to' guide, it suggests best practice in using traditional and electronic methods of communication, and it gives theoretical and historical reasons for doing so. We have also introduced each chapter with a scenario which contextualises the chapter's contents in a professional setting.

The book has three sections. In Part 1, 'Perspectives on professional communication', we open the discussion on what exactly communication is and does, how it works, what its pitfalls are and how theorists can help the professional to steer through the hazards and uncertainties involved in communicating with other professionals, with clients and governments, and with the public.

Chapter 1 deals with theories and models of communication, notions of communication as a transmission of messages or a transaction of meanings, or both. We include an analysis of communication dimensions, such as interpersonal, group, intercultural and mediated modes. Chapter 2 focuses on language as the prime channel of communication and explores the potential of speech and writing to act as channels of information and persuasion, not only as they benefit students working their way through tertiary courses, but also graduates facing life in organisations and the public sphere. The challenges of detecting language vagueness and incompetence, distortions of meaning, 'sloganeering' and 'doublespeak', and examples of these tricks of language, add spice to this chapter. Chapter 3 pays attention to implied or non-verbal communication as it exists in person-to-person, mediated, public and even written communication. Chapter 4 deals with intercultural, or global, communication as it applies to relations between students of different ethnic groups working and studying together; professionals of different nations; between families and members of a multicultural society; and in relationships within the work organisations most of us belong to. Chapter 5 looks at mediated communication and the internet as the most predominant and pervasive change to human communication since the invention of the printing press. We deal with the major technologies and the major issues which have ensued from our near-universal use of the internet and mediated channels in professional settings. In Chapter 6 we examine the importance of visual communication in the education and training of both students and professional graduates. Chapter 7 discusses three kinds of ethics as absolutely essential to being a professional and human being in the 21st century.

In Part 2, 'Communication in organisations', we deal with communication as a basic interpersonal tool, in social and professional settings, in one-to-one relationships, and in groups and teams, especially those in which people work together contributing different kinds of expertise.

Communication competence, emotional intelligence and credibility, assertiveness and active listening are the topics of Chapter 8. The effects of values, attitudes and self-esteem on interpersonal communication are emphasised and the interpersonal impacts of new technology are explored. Active listening skills are analysed and illustrated. In Chapter 9, groups and teams involved in creative problem-solving, goal-directed activities and conflict resolution are discussed. Meetings (formal and informal) are considered, especially their potential for sharing expertise and the control by competent chairpersons of wasteful squabbling. In Chapter 10 the importance of oral presentations, verbal reports and interviewing skills both in student life and the workplace are discussed. The interview is seen as a specific communication event, with a rationale and structure of its own. Guidelines and techniques for successful interviewing are suggested, with special attention given to employment and negotiation interviews. This chapter also considers student seminars, group presentations and public speeches as essential skills in student and professional life.

Part 3, 'Writing skills in professional life', targets some important areas and shows that, even in the computer age, writing skills are essential. Chapter 11 considers general strategies of student and professional writing, form and style in writing, notions of 'good' and 'effective' writing and some guidelines for readability. Chapter 12 addresses organisational writing: letters of application, résumés, emails sent within and outside the organisation, and formal reports written for information or for advocacy. Of special interest to technical students is the discussion and illustration of technical writing as a craft, technical and laboratory reports, and technical articles. Chapter 13 concerns itself with workplace research methods (surveys, ethnography, interviews, focus groups and experiments) and writing (research reports and papers), and the accepted practices of referencing, structure and style.

This three-part structure of the book does not mean that all the theory is dealt with in Part 1 and the skills in Parts 2 and 3. Rather, the seven chapters of Part 1 deal with concepts that are common to the other parts and are necessary to the development of competence. Parts 2 and 3 take up and apply these concepts to the development of skills in conversations, discussions, meetings and different genres of professional writing, especially online writing.

Features of the book designed to help the student include the following:

- New learning objectives at the beginning of each chapter summarise the important concepts to be covered.
- Scenarios, exhibits, figures and diagrams presented throughout each chapter place communication concepts in a real-world context.
- New reflection exercises are for individual readers of the book to think about existing individual experiences, attitudes and ideas related to the chapter content.
- New margin definitions of key terms have been added to assist with possibly unknown concepts and terms.
- Each chapter contains a number of case studies designed to engage the student or class in a discussion of the application of a communication theory to a familiar workplace or classroom situation. The authors stress that there is not usually a 'correct' answer to the questions posed – rather, comments and insights are given at the end the book.
- Discussion questions and exercises at the end of each chapter help to sum up the chapter by providing activities that relate concepts to situations in the classroom or laboratory familiar to the student. These activities can be undertaken individually or in groups and are valuable tools in problem-solving.
- References and suggested websites are also provided for each chapter.

The first edition of *Communicating as Professionals*, published in 2004, grew from the text *Communicating!: Theory and Practice*, fourth edition, published in 1997. The second, third and now fourth editions are a response to some of the feedback about its predecessor from academics throughout the country. Its 13 chapters can be seen as 13 readings from the two authors, each on what we consider to be a basic area of study for a typical communication course offered to professional students at universities, TAFE and independent colleges.

Background

The two authors of this book are specialists in the aspects of communication covered here with over 50 years of combined experience teaching and researching these topics. Some overlapping treatment of theories and skills has occurred because topics are examined from more than one perspective, which is the whole point of communication.

Finally, in developing contemporary and engaging examples to illustrate sometimes controversial issues and ideas, questions asked and examples given may occasionally be provocative or challenging. We also understand that the language used in some of these examples is outdated. The authors and publisher of this book do not endorse such language but have made the decision to include the examples for their educational value in professional communication and to encourage conversation about using language for a more inclusive future.

Ray Archee (Western Sydney University)
Myra Gurney (Western Sydney University)

Guide to the text

As you read this text you will find a number of features in every chapter to enhance your study of communication and help you understand how the theory is applied in the real world.

PART OPENING FEATURES

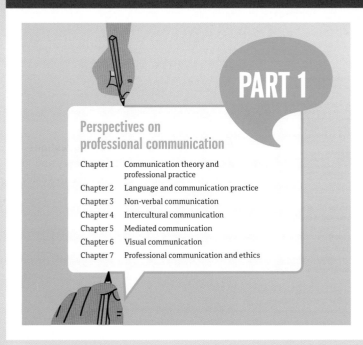

Part openers give an outline of the chapters in each part.

CHAPTER OPENING FEATURES

Chapter 1
Communication theory and professional practice

Learning objectives

After reading this chapter, you should be able to:
- define a range of meanings for *communication* and explain why they are relevant to professional practices
- describe the core elements of communication models
- explain the concept of communication as an action through the transmission approaches
- explain the concept of communication as a transaction, and explain the notion of the social construction of reality
- evaluate the differences between transmission and transaction approaches to understanding communication
- consider the role of ethics in communication.

Confusing messaging hampers our ability to prepare for rising flood waters

Echuca is on edge. Our near neighbours in Rochester are bracing for a second peak. We were awake as the rain pelted our roof at 4 a.m. on Saturday morning. We are tired, emotional and fragile. Processing information and making decisions is getting harder as the preparation and anticipation takes a mental toll.

The authorities urge us to be proactive. Now, more than ever, information needs to be clear, concise and consistent.

...

Despite the best intentions of Emergency Victoria, the flood information flow is confusing and inconsistent. Government agencies and apps must be on the same message – the same bloody message.

The problem is conflicting information. The messaging at the live updates and community meetings does not always equal that of the Victorian Emergency app or

Identify the key concepts you will engage with through the **Learning objectives** at the start of each chapter.

Gain an insight into how communication theories relate to the real world through the **Opening vignette** at the beginning of each chapter.

FEATURES WITHIN CHAPTERS

Introduction

During the 2022 eastern Australian floods that affected northern NSW, Victoria and southern Queensland, unpreparedness and **communication** failures – in particular telecommunications and mismanaged rain gauge warnings – led to at least 23 deaths and property displacement for tens of thousands of people. In Victoria, mixed messaging between communication authorities added to the already existing anxiety and stress. These are examples of the importance of understanding the complexities of communication, especially in a professional or public context.

This chapter presents some definitions of communication, introduces communication theory and attempts to place communication in realistic professional situations. A comparison is also undertaken of two models of, or ways of, conceptualising communication: the transmission and transaction models. Transmission emphasises the links in a communication chain, especially the source and the receiver, and compares the importance of the message itself and the medium by which it is transferred. The transaction model gives more importance to the sharing and co-creation of meaning in communication, and tries to account for individual differences and the impact of social uncertainties and contexts in the

Communication
In its simplest form, it involves an exchange of representations of meaning between two or more people. It is also the transmission of messages; social interaction through messages; the reciprocal creation of meaning in a context; and the sharing of meaning through information, ideas

Each chapter opens with an **Introduction**, giving you a clear idea of what the chapter will cover.

 CASE STUDY 2.5   Medical jargon and the COVID-19 pandemic

During the COVID-19 pandemic, the need for the use of plain language regarding health messaging became obvious as governments and health professionals attempted to explain complex medical phenomena, often resorting to jargon terms. The following excerpts come from an article on this topic written at the start of the pandemic, in February 2020.

Why health officials need to speak plainly on the COVID-19 virus

Between plain English and medical jargon, doctors tend to use the latter, part of their second nature developed through years of training. But in times of public health crises, such as the 2019 Novel Coronavirus ... speaking plainly can spell the difference between panic and calm. Or worse, life and death.

...

The US-based Center for Disease Control and Prevention has a 42-page document listing 'frequently used terms in public health materials and their common, everyday alternatives in plain language sentences'. The primer cites how 'incubation period' can be communicated more plainly. . . . Instead of just using the term, health workers can say that after the virus enters a person's body, 'it takes from

two to 14 days for that person to show the first signs of being sick'. Infectious diseases can also be translated simply as 'sicknesses caused by germs', the CDC primer said.

A 22 January WHO report said that four of the five patients who died of the novel coronavirus at that time had 'underlying comorbidities', a medical jargon also commonly used by health officials during press conferences. Simply put, those who died also had an existing sickness when they caught [COVID-19] ...

From 'Why health officials need to speak plainly on Wuhan coronavirus,' C. V. Esguerra, 2020, February 4, *ABS-CBN News.* https://news.abs-cbn.com/amp/spotlight/02/04/20/why-health-officials-need-to-speak-plainly-on-wuhan-coronavirus

Discussion

1   What impact do you think the use of medical jargon has had on communicating clearly during the COVID-19 pandemic? Do you agree that plainer terms could have been used?

2   Does plainer language in medicine or law mean that some important subtle meanings may be lost?

3   Is jargon always a bad thing? What helpful functions might it have?

After you have discussed this case study, refer to the 'Comments on case studies' section at the end of the text.

Case studies with discussion questions explore the communication theory and concepts by applying them to real-world examples.

Reflection question: Identify and remedy these common blocks to effective group work or teamwork:

1   The problem or task was not stated clearly.
2   The needed information was not available.
3   There were inadequate communication patterns within the group or team.
4   Hasty judgements were made and there was poor selection of alternatives.
5   The group or team atmosphere was critical, tense, competitive and evaluative.
6   Members did not realise the scope of the problem and did not pose relevant questions.
7   The group or team was insufficiently motivated to reach a thoughtful decision.

Engage with communication theory and the issues raised in the text by considering the **Reflection questions** throughout the chapters.

[V]oice can be difficult to talk about for several reasons. For one thing, you can't point to it exactly. It's just there, *among* all the words. For another, it's made up of a myriad of things: the words you choose (and the words you avoid), the sentences you write, the amount and kind of detail you use, what you're talking about, what your point is, how you organise your writing, who you're talking to. Almost every choice you make as a writer plays a part in creating the voice of the copy – the sense we get, when we read it, of living speech.

There was **chaos** during the meeting and, therefore, no decision was reached.
There was **ferment** during the meeting and, therefore, no decision was reached.
There was **bewilderment** during the meeting and, therefore, no decision was reached.
There was **turmoil** during the meeting and, therefore, no decision was reached.

Quotes from key sources and communication **examples** highlight and illustrate concepts and theory.

Hearing versus listening

Hearing and listening have been defined quite differently. **Hearing** is the physical reception of sound involving an automatic reaction of the senses and the nervous system. It is the physiological sensory process by which auditory sensations are received by the ears and transmitted to the brain. Whereas, **listening** involves a conscious effort to pay attention – a voluntary act involving our higher mental processes to make meaning from sound. The word listen is derived from two Anglo-Saxon words: *hlystan*, which means hearing, and *hlosnian*, which means to wait in suspense. Thus, listening is a

Hearing
The physiological sensory processes by which auditory sensations are received by the ears and transmitted to the brain.

Important **Key terms** are marked in bold in the text and **defined in the margin** when they are used for the first time.

END-OF-CHAPTER FEATURES

At the end of each chapter you will find several tools to help you to review, practise and extend your knowledge of the key learning objectives.

STUDY TOOLS

DISCUSSION QUESTIONS AND GROUP ACTIVITIES

For discussion topics and activities in addition to those that follow, please refer to the case studies presented throughout this chapter.

1 Which of the four definitions of communication seems to be the most useful and appropriate in relation to your work as a student?

2 Which forms of communication are most important in your profession? Give some examples and situations in which communication competence is important for you as a professional.

3 Discuss one recent case involving professional life in which poor communication has had serious results.

4 What do you understand by *whistleblowing* among professionals? (You may need to do some research on this one.)

5 Examine and discuss the ethics involved in a recent case of whistleblowing in your profession.

6 Communication theorist Marshall McLuhan said, 'The medium is the message' (1967, p. 15). He meant that the choice of medium can transform a message and its meaning. Discuss this idea.

7 We discussed that the choice of media is as important as the message itself. If you were asked to give advice on plagiarism and how to avoid it to the 500 students in Stage 1 of your course, how would you communicate your message? Discuss the advantages and disadvantages of each of the following forms of media to communicate this message to your particular audience:

    a   word-of-mouth communication in small group briefing sessions

    b   an email announcement to all students

    c   an article in the weekly student newspaper

    d   a speech to the whole group in a large lecture hall with accompanying PowerPoint slideshow

    e   a continuous video, set up in the student cafeteria

    f   an interactive, self-paced tutorial on the faculty's website.

Discussion questions and group activities at the end of each chapter encourage further exploration of the content and challenge your comprehension of important topics.

WEBSITES

Macquarie Dictionary https://www.macquariedictionary.com.au

Racial Hatred Act 1995 https://humanrights.gov.au/our-work/racial-hatred-act-what-racial-hatred-act

The Australian Style Manual (online version) https://www.stylemanual.gov.au

The Diversity Council of Australia has a range of useful online resources related to inclusive writing https://www.dca.org.au

The Plain English Foundation is a useful Australian organisation with resources for writing and speaking clearly https://www.plainenglishfoundation.com/home

REFERENCES

Allan, K., & Burridge, K. (2006). *Forbidden words: Taboo and the censoring of language*. Cambridge University Press.

Australian Institute of Family Studies. (2022). *LGBTIQA+ glossary of common terms*. https://aifs.gov.au/resources/resource-sheets/lgbtiqa-glossary-common-terms.

Bump, P. (2023, January 18). Why 'woke' replaced 'politically correct'. *The Washington Post* https://www.washingtonpost.com/politics/2023/01/18/woke-cancel-desantis-academics

Carrington, D. (2019, May 17). Why the Guardian is changing the language it uses about the environment. *The Guardian*. https://www.theguardian.com/environment/2019/may/17/why-the-guardian-is-changing-the-language-it-uses-about-the-environment

Carroll, L. (1871/2010). *Through the looking glass*. William Collins.

Chan, G. (2014, March 24). George Brandis: 'People have the right to be bigots'. *The Guardian* https://www.theguardian.com/world/2014/mar/24/george-brandis-people-have-the-right-to-be-bigots

Davey, M. (2018, August 13). Doctors should avoid saying 'cancer' for minor lesions – study. *The Guardian*. https://www.theguardian.com/society/2018/aug/13/doctors-should-avoid-saying-cancer-for-minor-lesions-study

Foucault, M. (2002). *The archaeology of knowledge* (A. M. S. Smith, Trans). Routledge. (Original work published 1969)

Gillard, J. (2012, October 10). Transcript of Julia Gillard's 'misogyny speech'. *Sydney Morning Herald*. http://www.smh.com.au/opinion/political-news/transcript-of-julia-gillards-speech-20121010-27c36.html

Gray A. J. (2011). Worldviews. *International psychiatry: Bulletin of the Board of International Affairs of the Royal College of Psychiatrists, 8*(3), 58–60.

Grosscup, B. (2011). Cluster munitions and state terrorism, *The Monthly Review, 62*(11) http://monthlyreview.org/2011/04/01/cluster-munitions-and-state-terrorism

Hall, E. T. (1959). *The silent language*. Doubleday.

Hawkes, G. (2022, July 29). The Manly pride jersey furore is not as simple as a choice between inclusivity and homophobia. *The Conversation*. https://theconversation.com/the-manly-pride-jersey-furore-is-not-as-simple-as-a-choice-between-inclusivity-and-homophobia-187859

Hodge, R., & Kress, G. (1979). *Language as ideology*. Routledge.

Hudson, K. (1978). *The jargon of the professions*. Macmillan.

Extend your understanding with the suggested **Websites** and extensive **References** relevant to each chapter.

END-OF-BOOK FEATURES

CASE STUDY 2.5 Medical jargon and the COVID-19 pandemic

Jargon is common in all professional areas as a way of both 'short cutting' conversations about complex, professionally specific concepts and identifying the users as members of a group or 'discourse community'. However, in a public health emergency, as has been the COVID-19 pandemic, public health officials urgently had to find ways of explaining complex phenomena to ordinary citizens in order to minimise death, serious disease and overwhelmed public hospital systems. Clear, unambiguous language was required. The case study proposed more general descriptions such as 'co-morbidities' being recast as 'existing serious illnesses' or similar. Many jargon-heavy professions argue that specialised language is necessary to be able to capture the nuances of the concept, but in the case of a need for mass communication, simpler language is important.

Comments on case studies from the authors provide you with further information and knowledge to gain a deeper understanding of the background and context of the provided case studies.

Guide to the online resources

FOR THE INSTRUCTOR

Cengage is pleased to provide you with a selection of resources
that will help you to prepare your lectures and assessments,
when you choose this textbook for your course.
Log in or request an account to access instructor resources at
au.cengage.com/instructor/account for Australia or
nz.cengage.com/instructor/account for New Zealand.

MINDTAP

Premium online teaching and learning tools are available on the *MindTap* platform – the personalised eLearning solution.

MindTap is a flexible and easy-to-use platform that helps build student confidence and gives you a clear picture of their progress. We partner with you to ease the transition to digital – we're with you every step of the way.

MindTap for Archee & Gurney's Communicating as Professionals 4th edition is full of innovative resources to support critical thinking, and help your students move from memorisation to mastery! Includes:
* Archee & Gurney's *Communicating as Professionals* 4th edition eBook
* Concept check quiz, reflection activities, case studies, communication examples and more!

MindTap is a premium purchasable eLearning tool. Contact your Cengage learning consultant to find out how MindTap can transform your course.

INSTRUCTOR'S GUIDE

The **Instructor's guide** includes suggested solutions to all the questions from the text.

COGNERO® TEST BANK

A **bank of questions** has been developed in conjunction with the text for creating quizzes, tests and exams for your students. Create multiple test versions in an instant and deliver tests from your LMS, your classroom, or wherever you want using **Cognero**. Cognero test generator is a flexible online system that allows you to import, edit, and manipulate content from the text's test bank or elsewhere, including your own favourite test questions.

POWERPOINT™ PRESENTATIONS

Use the chapter-by-chapter **PowerPoint slides** to enhance your lecture presentations and handouts by reinforcing the key principles of your subject.

ARTWORK FROM THE TEXT

Add the **digital files** of graphs, tables, pictures and flow charts into your learning management system, use them in student handouts, or copy them into your lecture presentations.

FOR THE STUDENT

MINDTAP

MindTap is the next-level online learning tool that helps you get better grades!

MindTap gives you the resources you need to study – all in one place and available when you need them. In the *MindTap Reader*, you can make notes, highlight text and even find a definition directly from the page.

If your instructor has chosen *MindTap* for your subject this semester, log in to *MindTap* to:
• Get better grades
• Save time and get organised
• Connect with your instructor and peers
• Study when and where you want, online and mobile
• Complete assessment tasks as set by your instructor

When your instructor creates a course using *MindTap*, they will let you know your course key so you can access the content. Please purchase *MindTap* only when directed by your instructor. Course length is set by your instructor.

About the authors

Ray Archee is an academic at the Western Sydney University and has taught professional writing, research methods and communication subjects for over 35 years. Ray has been a school teacher, a computer journalist who authored the first Internet column in any Australian periodical (*Your PC,* in *1994*), and consultant to business in technology-related areas. He has a PhD (Charles Sturt University) in computer-mediated communication, an MA in Psychology (USyd) and a Graduate Diploma in Adult Education (ITATE). He is also a part-time luthier who plays and builds jazz, acoustic and Flamenco guitars. His current research interests include mediated communication, intercultural communication and higher education. Ray was one of the original co-authors of *Communicating!: Theory and Practice* (1997), and the first, second and third editions of *Communicating as Professionals*.

Myra Gurney has taught in the tertiary education sector for over 25 years and is currently an academic in the School of Humanities and Communication Arts at Western Sydney University, where she teaches units in professional communication theory and practice, professional and academic writing skills and communication research. She has a BA (Hons) in English Literature and Australian History and a Diploma in Education from the University of Sydney, an MA in Communication and Cultural Studies from UWS, a Diploma in Book Editing and Publishing from Macleay College and a PhD from Western Sydney University in which she is examined the discursive characteristics of the climate change debate in Australia.

Myra and Ray have collaborated for several years on a variety of grants, courses and projects related to e-learning and have won awards for their course and curriculum design, including a 2011 Australian Learning and Teaching Council citation for outstanding contribution to student learning.

Acknowledgements

The authors and Cengage Learning have been assisted and encouraged by a number of academic colleagues who have reviewed the outline and selected chapters of the text. We express our gratitude to: Grant Meredith, Federation University; Sharon Hebdon, Holmesglen Institute; Angela Feekery, Massey University; Susan Leslie, Western Sydney University; Ki Pyung Kim, University of South Australia; Dr Carol Crevacore, Edith Cowan University and a number of anonymous reviewers. The authors, of course, take full responsibility for any of the book's shortcomings.

We would like to thank and remember Terry Mohan who passed away but was an inspiration to all the past authors for decades. We also need to thank Helen McGregor and Shirley Saunders who have retired from academia, since some of their hard work and expertise still exists in this new edition.

PART 1

Perspectives on professional communication

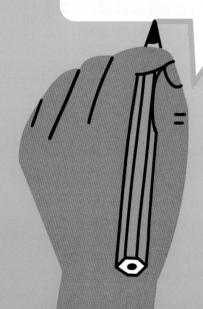

Communication theory and professional practice

Confusing messaging hampers our ability to prepare for rising flood waters

Echuca is on edge. Our near neighbours in Rochester are bracing for a second peak. We were awake as the rain pelted our roof at 4 a.m. on Saturday morning. We are tired, emotional and fragile. Processing information and making decisions is getting harder as the preparation and anticipation takes a mental toll.

The authorities urge us to be proactive. Now, more than ever, information needs to be clear, concise and consistent.

...

Despite the best intentions of Emergency Victoria, the flood information flow is confusing and inconsistent. Government agencies and apps must be on the same message – the same bloody message.

The problem is conflicting information. The messaging at the live updates and community meetings does not always equal that of the Victorian Emergency app or the Bureau of Meteorology.

We are unsure and frustrated. Which number is the peak? Which agency knows best? Why does the Vic Emergency app – the supposed sacred source of truth – not reflect the information provided by local authorities?

Source: Extract from K. Burke (2022, October 23). Confusing messaging hampers our ability to prepare for rising flood waters. *The Guardian*.

Introduction

During the 2022 eastern Australian floods that affected northern NSW, Victoria and southern Queensland, unpreparedness and **communication** failures – in particular telecommunications and mismanaged rain gauge warnings – led to at least 23 deaths and property displacement for tens of thousands of people. In Victoria, mixed messaging between communication authorities added to the already existing anxiety and stress. These are examples of the importance of understanding the complexities of communication, especially in a professional or public context.

This chapter presents some definitions of communication, introduces communication theory and attempts to place communication in realistic professional situations. A comparison is also undertaken of two models of, or ways of, conceptualising communication: the transmission and transaction models. Transmission emphasises the links in a communication chain, especially the source and the receiver, and compares the importance of the message itself and the medium by which it is transferred. The transaction model gives more importance to the sharing and co-creation of meaning in communication, and tries to account for individual differences and the impact of social uncertainties and contexts in the process. Additionally, there are some references to cultural and gender factors in communication, which are further examined in later chapters. Lastly, the dimensions of communication in the personal, social and public spheres are discussed, and how they relate, overlap and sometimes need to be reconciled with each other.

Communication
In its simplest form, it involves an exchange of representations of meaning between two or more people. It is also the transmission of messages; social interaction through messages; the reciprocal creation of meaning in a context; and the sharing of meaning through information, ideas and feelings.

Why study communication?

The field of communication studies is large. Whole university programs relate to it. These days, communication professionals, such as journalists, public relations consultants, advertising account executives, film and television practitioners, and creative writers, combine tertiary study of communication theory with study of their professional practice. However, most other professions rely heavily on well-developed communication skills. Nurses, medical practitioners, accountants, managers, engineers, lawyers, builders, teachers, IT specialists and librarians are just some of the professionals for whom this book has been prepared.

In describing the duties of professional people, employers invariably emphasise communication skills (see Exhibit 1.1). Take, for instance, advertisements for executive placements. Typically, they ask for qualities such as:

- excellent communication and presentation skills
- the ability to liaise harmoniously with senior management and clients
- initiative
- team focus
- high-level oral, written and interpersonal skills
- the ability to lead and coordinate a team and liaise with specialists in other departments
- the ability to prepare proposals and submissions, etc.

It is generally accepted that professional people need to be good communicators. However, it should not be assumed that professional communication competence is easy and natural, or that it is a skill brought with you from high school or that can be picked up once in the job. Newspapers frequently provide stories of failed communication in business dealings, caused by such things as faulty written instructions to staff or misunderstood email briefings. Some of these failures are matters of personality clashes and deliberate conflict, but many more stem from inadequate attention to communication skills.

| Exhibit 1.1 | A typical job advertisement asking for professional communication skills |

WE ARE
Hiring

WHY WORK WITH US

We believe in the power of diversity and inclusion, in mutual respect and support. We are committed to ensure that our employees work in an environment that is inclusive and that everyone is treated with dignity and respect. We are constantly working on creating a workplace at which you can feel at home.

SALES MANAGER

- Strong communication skills.
- Creating and implementing a sales plan.
- Analysing sales data.
- Presentation skills.
- Management and leadership skills.
- Degree in Business Management.

ADMINISTRATOR

- To provide office support to either an individual or team and is vital for the smooth-running of a business.
- 3 years working experience.

APPLY ONLINE AT
www.website.com/job

APPLY IN PERSON AT
155, WESTPORT MAIN STREET, PSY

Defining communication

How do we arrive at a theory of *communication*? In **Exhibit 1.2**, we look at some of the definitions of *communication* that have been developed by communication analysts.

Exhibit 1.2	Definitions of communication
Communication is the transmission of messages	The sender encodes a message, which may be an instruction, request or demand. It is sent through a medium – say a spoken statement, email, letter, television or radio announcement – and it is decoded by the receiver. The intention of the sender and the 'packaging' of the message affect the efficiency of the communication
Communication is social interaction through messages	Communication is behaviour that helps people relate to each other. People interact or exchange ideas and experiences to develop understandings. Parties take turns at sending and receiving. All take responsibility for reaching agreement or understanding and the result is better relationships between people
Communication is the reciprocal creation of meaning in a context	Here *meaning* is emphasised rather than *message*, reminding us that it is through language and other *symbolic* forms that we generate meaning. We make sense of the world by relating to each other. Individuals may begin with different meanings for the same thing and then negotiate a closer understanding. Perhaps they never agree on the meaning of a concept or idea, but they may have narrowed the gap between themselves. Meaning relates to context or the setting in which meaning is generated. Thus, time, place, emotional atmosphere and culture can all affect meaning

Exhibit 1.2	Definitions of communication (*Continued*)
Communication is the sharing of meaning through information, ideas and feelings	Sharing implies an intention to contribute, not merely an incidental coming together or interaction. This definition also tries to analyse the components of a communication. It says that meaning consists of: • information (perception of facts; e.g., dark clouds signal that rain is coming) • ideas (concepts, opinions and attitudes; e.g., commitment to a safe workplace) • feelings (e.g., love, admiration, distrust, anger)

These four definitions of communication describe the process with different emphases. But merely defining communication does not guarantee effective communication. The capacity of people, groups, political parties, governments and nations to communicate and build constructive relationships is very limited indeed. Communication breaks down all the time between all sorts of people, including those who are highly educated and highly articulate. Meanings differ from one person to another, even when they are looking at the same object, listening to the same speech or reading the same report. Additionally, symbolic forms like words and images may be accompanied by non-verbal expressions like laughter, frowning or angry outbursts of emotion, all adding to and complicating the search for meaning in a situation. In fact, it may be more appropriate to speak of narrowing the communication gap rather than achieving perfect communication between people.

Reflection question: Consider your own profession. What criteria determine how your clients and colleagues define your *professionalism*?

CASE STUDY 1.1   What is meant by *professional* in *professional communication*?

The term 'professional' can have different meanings depending on the context, but in general, it refers to someone who is engaged in a particular occupation, activity, or field of expertise and conducts themselves with a high level of skill, competence, and integrity. Examples of **professionalism** may differ slightly between different professions, but in general, the idea refers to how staff are expected to behave in a workplace in interactions with colleagues and clients.

> **Professionalism**
> Measured by both internal and external examples of communication behaviours that include non-verbal behaviours, interpersonal behaviours as well as profession-specific behaviours.

Some common characteristics of professionals include:

1   Expertise: a professional is knowledgeable and skilled in their area of work. They have acquired the necessary education, training and experience to perform their jobs competently.

2   Ethical standards: professionals adhere to a set of ethical guidelines and principles specific to their field. They act with honesty, integrity, and respect towards their clients, their colleagues and the public.

3   Responsibility: professionals take their responsibilities seriously and are accountable for their actions and decisions. They prioritise their duties and commitments to meet the expectations of their role.

4   Communication: effective communication is a hallmark of professionalism. Professionals can articulate their ideas clearly, listen actively and interact respectfully with others. Professionals can speak and write with confidence with a diverse range of clients.

5   Appearance and behaviour: a professional often maintains an attractive and appropriate appearance and exhibits behaviour that is courteous and respectful in both formal and informal settings.

6   Reliability: professionals are reliable and consistent in delivering their services or completing tasks. They respond to their clients, meet deadlines and keep their promises.

Discussion

In small groups, read through the different criteria above as they may be relevant in the profession that you are studying.

1   What are the expectations of 'professionalism' expected in your professional area? Give specific examples for each of the criteria listed above.

2 How might these differ between different professional areas?

3 Can you think of recent examples of 'non-professionalism' that have been highlighted in the media in different organisations? What is the potential impact for the credibility or status of that organisation?

After you have discussed this case study, refer to the 'Comments on case studies' section at the end of the text.

Not only are there several definitions that are attached to the word *communication*, but there are also different ways that we use the words *communicate*, *communication* or *communicating*. **Exhibit 1.3** displays some typical uses.

Exhibit 1.3	Examples of typical uses of the words *communicate*, *communication* or *communicating*
Communication with the advance party has been cut off for four days. We're hoping they're safe	The mobile phones are out of range, the satellite phones are not charged, the advance party is stranded or captured. There is no contact. Technical transmission of the message has broken down. Transmission is responsible for a lot of failures in communication
I can't seem to communicate with my patient. I'm sure she's not taking the medication I prescribed last week	Perhaps the doctor gave her patient instructions too rapidly or in highly scientific terms that they couldn't follow. Perhaps the patient is experiencing side effects from the medication that she is not communicating to the doctor. Transmission is not the problem here; the message is being delivered, but the patient has no confidence in either the prescription or the doctor. There has not been enough interrelating or exchanging of information and experiences between these two
There was good communication between group members, despite our different backgrounds. In three hours, we had planned a new approach to the project. Everybody was ready to back it	Here there is a shared aim: to cooperate. Hence, there is a willingness to reveal information and diminish any differences in feelings that might have been brought to the situation. So, meaning is shared and information can be conveyed confidently and with respect for individual views
I simply can't communicate with my staff anymore. Nobody wants to do any work!	Perhaps this manager's approach to his staff is outdated or his ideas unworkable. But more likely his feelings of superiority or contempt are transmitted unintentionally but strongly. As a result, his staff decline to share meaning with him
Communication between the old and the young is as bad now as it ever was	Here we seem to be discussing attitudes, ways of thinking, the effects of experience and the intolerance of differences; that is, ideas and feelings. If ideas and feelings are out of touch, information is distorted and meanings cannot be shared
Jean is a resourceful, pleasant and helpful executive, but when she writes a letter, memo or report, her style is overly formal and brusque. She just can't communicate in writing with her junior staff	Jean may use the channel of speech well to convey meaning, but her lack of training and practice in written communication means she conveys information, attitudes and feelings clumsily. Meaning is not shared

Different modes of communication

As shown in **Exhibit 1.4**, communication involves the sharing and exchange of representations of meaning between two or more people. However, there are different modes or channels through which we might convey a message, which can be used deliberately or unintentionally. While we will discuss each of these in more detail in later chapters, they include:

| Exhibit 1.4 | Communication as the sharing and exchange of meaning |

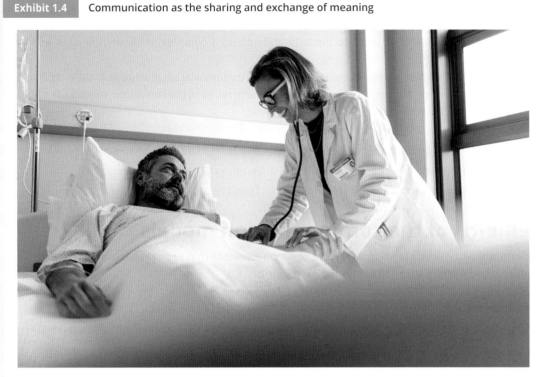

Shutterstock.com/Jacob Lund

- **Verbal communication**: the use of written or spoken words in which meaning is embedded or encoded between two or more people to convey meaning.
- **Non-verbal communication**: communication sent by any means other than written or spoken words, and can include body and facial gestures, vocal characteristics, and use of artefacts, such as furniture, modes of dress or adornments. Non-verbal elements can exist in both written or spoken language and in graphic communication.
- **Graphic communication**: conveyance of meaning or ideas using visual symbols or codes, such as images, shapes, lines, colour, page placement and so on.

It is important to remember that communication may involve all of these modes in any combination.

The role of theory in understanding communication

In this book, theory refers to the concepts or ideas that attempt to explain communication effects or performance. Any study of a subject, even if it is only a matter of collecting data, involves taking up a theoretical position, and the models that we will outline illustrate how our understanding of communication has evolved over the past century.

According to Dr Richard Denniss (2012) from the Australia Institute, a **model** can be defined as follows:

Verbal communication
The use of written or spoken words in which meaning is embedded or encoded between two or more people to convey meaning.

Non-verbal communication
Communication sent by any means other than written or spoken words; can include body and facial gestures, vocal characteristics, and use of artefacts, such as furniture, modes of dress or adornments.

Graphic communication
Conveyance of meaning or ideas using visual symbols or codes such as images, shapes, lines, colour, and page placement.

Model
A simplified representation of a more complex phenomenon.

> A model, be it a model car or an economic model, is a simplified representation of a more complex mechanism. A model is typically smaller, simpler and easier to build than a full-scale replica. A model sheds light on the main features of the reality it seeks to represent. (p. 1)
>
> Source: The Australia Institute

A variety of models have been developed to graphically map or explain how human communication works. The problem with models, whether they are real (e.g., model planes) or academic (e.g., economic or climate change models), is that they are a simplified version of something that is inherently complex. For this very reason we should be careful with the way that we use them. However, that is not to say that models are not useful as ways to initially understand a complex phenomenon such as human communication.

While no single theory or model adequately explains all communication phenomena, the ones discussed in this chapter have been chosen because they most closely relate to the communication skills addressed in this text. These communication theories will help you:

- choose appropriate channels of communication
- narrow the communication gap between a communicator and their audience
- understand some of the reasons for cultural differences in communication
- understand why people get different meanings from the same message.

Elements of the communication models

All communication *events* or *encounters* have common elements that need to be defined before exploring the different models. These are summarised in **Exhibit 1.5**.

Exhibit 1.5	Elements of a communication encounter
Element	**Definition**
Sender/source	The originator of a thought, emotion or information that is sent as part of a communication encounter
Receiver/recipient	The person or group for whom the message is intended
Message	Written, spoken, unspoken or visual elements or content of a communication to which meaning is assigned. Can be intentional (composing an email) or unintentional (sweating when nervous), verbal ('hello, nice to meet you') or non-verbal (a smile or handshake to greet a friend)
Encoding	The choice and combination of elements of communication (words, images, colour, fonts, vocal characteristics, non-verbal gestures) into an organised pattern or code
Decoding	The deciphering or interpreting of the encoded elements by the receiver(s) of the message
Channel	A medium, or pathway via which a message is carried. Channels can include any of the five senses: sight (images or words on a page), sounds (spoken words or music), touch (handshakes, hugs, textures), smell (fragrances), taste (sweet, spicy). A channel can also include an electronic medium, such as a telephone, the internet or a television broadcast
Feedback	The response to a message. Can be direct (replying to an email request or question, or raising your eyebrows in response to an unusual request) or indirect (ignoring repeated phone calls)
Context	The environment or situation (physical, historical or psychological) within which the sender, receiver and message are encoded and decoded
Noise	Any physical or environmental (static on a phone line), semantic (misuse or misunderstanding of language), psychological (prejudice or negative attitude) or physiological (hearing impairment) distortion or interference with the encoding or decoding of a message

Communication as a transmission of information

An early way of thinking about communication was that it was simply a matter of a message being sent and received between one person (the sender) and another (the recipient or destination). In other words, the focus was on the message being transmitted or transferred. This section will explore the **transmission models of communication**, including Shannon and Weaver's model, Schramm's circular model and Berlo's SMCR model.

Transmission models of communication
Early models of communication whereby a message is simply sent by one person (sender) and received by another (the recipient or destination).

Shannon and Weaver

The earliest attempt to model or describe the communication process was developed by theorists Claude Shannon and Warren Weaver (1949), who were engineers working for the Bell Telephone Labs in the US. While Shannon and Weaver were actually trying to model *transmission* rather *human communication*, their model has since become influential as a starting point for thinking about communication as a *process* or series of *linear steps* (see **Exhibit 1.6**). In this model, communication is shown as taking place when a message is sent and received.

In 1948, Harold Lasswell similarly described the process as follows:

* who (sender)
* says what (message)
* in what channel
* to whom (receiver)
* with what effect.

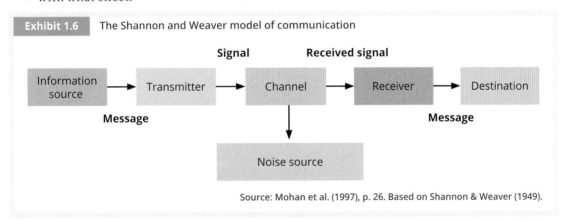

Exhibit 1.6 The Shannon and Weaver model of communication

Source: Mohan et al. (1997), p. 26. Based on Shannon & Weaver (1949).

The following example of two people speaking on the telephone demonstrates this model of communication.

> Alex telephones Rihanna. He speaks into the mouthpiece and an electrical simulation of his voice is transmitted via a series of signals and networks. His telephone encodes his voice as a signal through the channel of the telephone network to the phone receiver in Rihanna's office, where it is decoded and the message reaches its destination: Rihanna.

The model seems to suggest that communication is linear and straightforward, and that it moves only in one direction. So, in terms of **Exhibit 1.6**, Alex is the information source, and the arrows point from the information source (Alex) to the destination (Rihanna). Rihanna, of course, will reply, and when she does, the roles will be reversed; Rihanna becomes the information source and Alex the destination.

This transmission model can also be applied to a conversation in a room, even if there are multiple sources and destinations. The voices, if they can be heard above the din, are still being transmitted into the atmosphere of the room, by speech, which is the channel. The signals are the voices themselves, and the receivers are the hearing and mental processes of the listeners, who are the destinations. This model could similarly be applied to a public speech in a large hall, a lecture in a classroom, or to mediated communication on television, radio or the internet.

The notion that ideas, facts or commands are actually conveyed as messages from one person or party to another is common. A message-centred view of communication is part of Western culture, implicit in such statements as:

- 'Am I getting through to you?'
- 'I think he's getting the message at last.'
- 'Let's see if we can push this idea at the meeting.'

The transmission model, with its emphasis on conveying a message, is also used to explain the success or failure of communication. **Exhibit 1.6** includes the concept of *noise* in the channel. Nothing spoils a telephone conversation more than a loud buzzing interference in your ear. According to this model of communication, noise is anything that distorts the signal, and it is the signal that conveys the intended message.

But is a technical system of telephone communication comparable to what happens when human beings attempt to communicate with each other? Shannon and Weaver's model was highly mechanistic, as can be seen by the labels they applied. Let's consider how this model may apply to another communication situation.

Source and receiver

We might pursue the notion of transmission by examining another telephone conversation between two partners in a small service-industry business, who have different skills, points of view, personal needs and approaches to business. The following scenario illustrates how points of view and unspoken needs on the part of both sender and receiver can impact on a communication encounter to the point that it may become a conflict.

> Michael telephones his business partner Kathy. They briefly chat about business figures and issues, taking it in turn to lead and then follow, and then Michael tells Kathy he wants the company to relocate to a city 1000 kilometres away. He believes that labour is cheaper and transport better organised there. Kathy knows her family will be upset at the idea, and reminds Michael of the business advantages of their present location. The partners become angry with each other, and there are accusations of short-sightedness and selfishness. However, they agree to drop the subject for the moment, until they feel calmer.

At first, Michael could be considered the source of the communication, and Kathy the receiver. Michael has a message for Kathy and uses a particular medium, the telephone, to quickly communicate his exciting business idea. Kathy is immediately alarmed by the message. Michael's information (the facts relating to the benefits of the move) is clear, but his ideas (the value of land in the other city, the demand for their product there) and his feelings (elation, pride) are not shared by Kathy. Kathy takes the initiative, arguing against Michael's case, giving him reasons why he is wrong, at which point, Kathy becomes the source and Michael the receiver.

Message

Shannon and Weaver mention the message at two stages of their model: as it relates to the source and the transmitter, and as it links the receiver and the destination. A message has content (its basic idea), it has structure or shape (the way the idea or information is ordered), and it has a code or codes. The structure might be a narrative, an argument or an explanation. It might involve repetition, quotations or humour. The code might be language, pictures, body movements or music, or all of these.

Consider the different ways in which the same message can be treated by three different sources; for example:

- a scientist announcing a breakthrough in AIDS research in a medical journal
- a journalist reporting the research for readers of a Sunday newspaper
- a science teacher presenting the research to a Year 12 biology group.

Each will select a structure and code to convey the content effectively to the particular audience.

Medium/channel

In the previous example, Michael used his mobile phone as the medium/channel because he wanted the message conveyed quickly and confidentially. He could have sent Kathy a text message or an email, but these would lack the immediacy of the telephone call. He could hardly have dictated a letter and had it delivered to his business partner's address, nor could he have published the news in a press release and faxed it to Kathy. He also could have arranged a face-to-face meeting with her in the office or over lunch to discuss his proposal. These various options show that the choice of medium is an important part of the communication. Additionally, depending on which choice is made, it may put the receiver at a disadvantage; for example Kathy may have been busy in her own office or may have been attending a meeting.

According to the transmission model, choosing the medium of communication is as important as constructing the message itself. Each medium has its own strengths and weaknesses. The telephone is fast but uses only the senses of speech and hearing, and phone reception may be poor. A couriered letter is too formal and may not reach Kathy if she is out of the office, and an email is too informal and Kathy might not check her email regularly. Even though a face-to-face meeting over lunch may have been the best channel, it may take longer to arrange if they are both very busy.

Note that the term *channel* refers to the sensory base for conveying, or transmitting, a message. For example, speech and body language are the channels for the media of conversation, interviews and public addresses; and musical instrumentation, singing and speech are the channels for opera, musical comedy and rock.

Arguably, the more channels used in a medium, the greater the depth of communication achieved. In our example, speech is the only channel available to Michael.

Feedback

In the transmission model, **feedback** is the response to our message – the way we test the effectiveness of our communication. Not all communication involves feedback. For example, a letter lost in the post, a telephone message given to an answering machine that fails to record, a message in a spaceship lost beyond the galaxy, all contain messages but are not communication until they reach their destinations. For the source, it is only when there is a response that the feedback circuit is complete.

Noise

One of the distinctive elements of Shannon and Weaver's model is the concept of *noise*; that is, any element that interferes with the process of communication. In the early version of their model, the noise to which they referred was *mechanical* (i.e., actual physical interference with the signal). Later versions of the model expanded this to include *semantic noise* (i.e., breakdown of meaning between source and receiver as a result of the misuse or misinterpretation of language) and *psychological noise* (i.e., emotional barriers between parties to the communication). **Exhibit 1.7** summarises the concept of noise and ways in which they can be controlled.

Feedback
Consists of all of the verbal or non-verbal messages that a person sends out either consciously or unconsciously in response to another person's communication, which enables the sender to evaluate whether the message has been interpreted as the sender intended.

Exhibit 1.7 Types of noise and how to control them

Type of noise	Definition	How to control
Environmental or mechanical	Noise that occurs as a result of environmental sounds: e.g., loud music, people talking, cars honking or poor reception of a mobile phone. Perhaps the easiest form to detect and control	Change mobile phone providers or buy a more updated phone; get a better antenna; ask the venue to turn down the music or rearrange the room furniture; ask the speaker to provide written notes for their talk or ask them to speak more slowly
Physiological	Noise that occurs as a result of a physiological impairment: e.g., hearing or sight loss, memory impairment. Harder to overcome as it relates to a physical inability to either detect or understand a message due to impaired senses	While a hearing aid or other devices may help, senders must consider any sensory impairment and assist a reader or listener; for example, with closed captions on a device or other accessibility functions
Semantic	Semantics is the study of the meaning of words (see Chapter 2). This noise is due to a failure to understand words or the context in which they are being used; e.g., jargon, technical language, slang, sarcasm; may be either misinterpreted, or deemed confusing, inappropriate or unprofessional, which may impact on your credibility and ability to persuade your audience of the validity of your ideas or sincerity of your intentions	The sender must choose their words carefully to ensure that the receivers understand them as intended. This takes into consideration the receivers' level of education and vocabulary and the context within which words are spoken
Psychological	Preconceived notions, attitudes, biases or prejudices about either the speaker, the message itself or perhaps the organisation from which the message is being sent, and emotional arousal (e.g., anger, anxiety or confusion) that interferes with how a person 'hears' a message	Try to frame or shape your message to suit the audience. Consider word choice, how arguments are organised or relevant examples, to address what you believe are the attitudes, biases, prejudices or preconceived notions held by audience in relation to the subject

 CASE STUDY 1.2 Identifying noise in communication

Here are some passages of text that have been extracted from recent publications, each of which includes an example of a form of noise. Classify each one as either environmental/mechanical, semantic or psychological. Make sure you can explain your choice.

1 You will hear from us as soon as we have investigated your claims.

2 The estate will be divided equally between his brother and his wife's three sisters.

3 Joe did not enjoy the catch up with his friends as the restaurant they chose had both poor acoustics and a loud house band.

4 We trust that in future you will not fall behind in your instalments.

5 Peter did not trust the surgeon after he broke both his hands.

6 After her mother related a poor experience when trying to make a policy claim with Acme Car Insurance, Melinda will not get a quote to use their insurance services even though their rates are usually cheaper.

7 We need to achieve conceptual communication criteria with a view to bringing about a dynamic parameters analysis. Overall capabilities implementation is compatible with the modular facilities interface.

After you have discussed this case study, refer to the 'Comments on case studies' section at the end of the text.

Encoding
The packaging or translation of an idea into a form that allows it to be communicated.

Decoding
The interpretation, translation or unpacking of a message that has been received.

Schramm's circular model

Schramm's (1954) circular model (see **Exhibit 1.8**) introduces the concepts of **encoding** – the packaging or translating of an idea into a form that allows it to be communicated – and **decoding** – the interpretation, translation or unpacking of a message. For example, if we want to communicate the idea of danger we could use the word danger in a loud voice, the colour red in a flashing light or a loud sound like a siren. This reminds us that communication is symbolic and that it is carried out using signs and symbols. These signs or symbols are mainly language-based, but can also be non-verbal, visual and aural signs that have meaning assigned to them within a culture or between cultures. So, the message, usually in words, is encoded into language and decoded by the receiver, who encodes a response that is conveyed back to the original encoder. The process is circular and continuous and is a process of interactivity with two or more parties encoding messages in words or other symbols, interpreting these symbols, and encoding responses. This is a useful model because it links the notions of circularity and feedback.

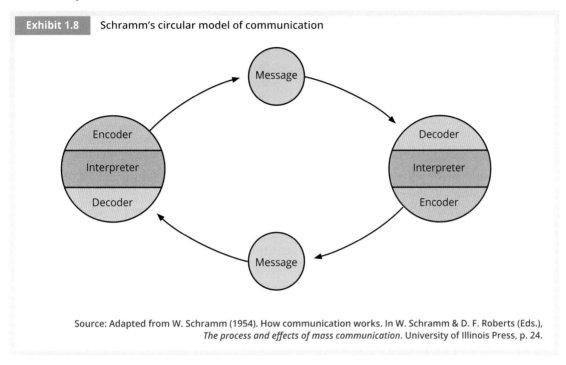

Exhibit 1.8   Schramm's circular model of communication

Source: Adapted from W. Schramm (1954). How communication works. In W. Schramm & D. F. Roberts (Eds.), *The process and effects of mass communication*. University of Illinois Press, p. 24.

In professional life, we communicate to achieve results. Too often words are ignored because the message is poorly expressed, threatening, too technical or poorly timed; does not consider biases or attitudes of the receiver; or is communicated via the wrong channel or medium. It is important that the source tests the effectiveness of their message. In the case of Michael and Kathy, Michael receives very strong, negative feedback from Kathy.

Opportunities for feedback vary according to the form of communication, social context and emphasis on transmission or transaction involved. In a face-to-face conversation we can immediately begin to appreciate what people think of our ideas through their words, gestures and expressions. However, not all forms of communication offer such immediate feedback opportunities. For example, if you wanted to provide feedback to a television station manager regarding an inappropriate remark you heard in a program, this contact may be delayed or the complaint may never be passed on.

At the same time, it is not easy to get people to give you feedback. For example, university lecturers are often anxious to measure the success of their lectures or tutorials. They may seek feedback by asking the lecture group to write a summary of what has been said, give their opinions on the points made, give examples of the points made from their own experience, or conduct a 'buzz session' in which they chat informally in pairs about what has been said and then criticise or support it. They may also issue subject evaluation forms in which students comment on their experiences of studying the subject.

Berlo's SMCR model

The final transmission model that we will discuss was devised in the 1960s by David Berlo from Michigan State University. Berlo's SMCR (sender, message, channel and receiver) model expanded on Shannon and Weaver's model by more clearly identifying the components of each of the stages, as shown in **Exhibit 1.9**.

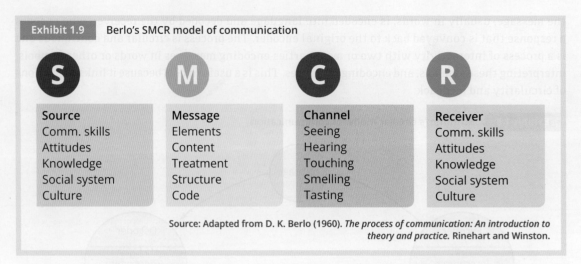

Exhibit 1.9 Berlo's SMCR model of communication

S	**M**	**C**	**R**
Source	**Message**	**Channel**	**Receiver**
Comm. skills	Elements	Seeing	Comm. skills
Attitudes	Content	Hearing	Attitudes
Knowledge	Treatment	Touching	Knowledge
Social system	Structure	Smelling	Social system
Culture	Code	Tasting	Culture

Source: Adapted from D. K. Berlo (1960). *The process of communication: An introduction to theory and practice.* Rinehart and Winston.

Berlo argued that at each stage of the process, different factors may impact upon how the message was sent and how it was understood.

Source/receiver

Both the source (sender) and the recipient (receiver) are influenced by the same factors, which in turn impact upon how the message was encoded and how it might be decoded. These factors are:

- *Communication skills*: the relative ability of the sender and receiver to speak, read or write.
- *Attitudes:* the speaker's/listener's point of view or attitude towards the subject of the message or even towards the receiver of the message.
- *Knowledge:* how much a speaker or listener knows about a subject.
- *Social system:* the values, beliefs or opinions of the society that each message participant is influenced by.
- *Culture:* cultural factors that shape or influence how either the sender or receiver chooses or interprets a message.

Message

A message can be delivered in a number of ways. It can be verbal or non-verbal, use spoken or written words, images, symbols or be sent electronically via SMS. How these are combined or organised, however, may affect the final message. These factors are:

- *Elements:* the letters in words, non-verbal gestures or colours, images or graphics.
- *Structure:* the way the elements are assembled (e.g., the order of information).
- *Content:* the information, ideas or feelings being conveyed.
- *Treatment:* the way in which the message is presented; for example, humour, a series of verbatim quotes or graphic layout.
- *Code:* how particular elements are combined and communicated; for example, music, text or graphics.

Channel

A message can be sent or received through any of the five senses. Think of how a mother might express her affection to her child – she might say she loves them (sound), give them a hug (touch) or make their favourite dessert (taste). We often have positive associations with certain smells, such as freshly baked bread or a grandmother's perfume.

By more specifically identifying particular human characteristics, Berlo's model is more nuanced and complex than that of Shannon and Weaver. However, it still focuses on component parts communicating in a linear fashion.

Summary of the transmission model of communication

The value of the transmission model of communication lies in its emphasis on the elements in a communication process. The model reminds us that:

- sources or senders should think carefully about the effect they wish to achieve before communicating
- sources or senders should structure their message carefully, using codes likely to be familiar to their receivers
- the choice of channel or medium can be vital to the success of a communication
- the elements of skills, attitudes, knowledge, social system and cultural awareness all play a part in the sending and receiving of messages. Overlooking the importance of any one of these elements in the receivers can disrupt communication
- various types of noise can interfere with the process of communication
- feedback evaluates communication and allows a sender to adjust their message to the needs of the receiver.

Despite the many things that the transmission model reveals, there are also several criticisms. Critics say that it is reductionist and places too much emphasis on the message and the channel of communication. They point out that elements of a communication cannot be reduced or isolated and still make sense because communication is a 'big picture' that is greater than the sum of its parts.

Criticisms also focuses on the way in which the model assumes that communication is *linear*, with the sender being the active participant who determines the meaning, while the receiver is the passive target. From this point of view, communication between two people involves simultaneous sending and receiving, and not just of words and language but also non-verbal signals, such as body language.

Critics also suggest that the use of an analogy between the mechanical and the human is simplistic and misleading. You can explain the workings of an internal combustion engine by discussing its parts in isolation, and can show that when one of these parts breaks down the whole structure is endangered. However, human communication is not mechanical and cannot be broken down in this way.

Furthermore, critics argue that by placing too much emphasis on the parties to the communication and the elements within them, the model completely ignores the central issue in communication – meaning. They also claim that the model ignores the way in which meaning is created, sustained and shared between two or more parties. Chandler (1994) argues that the transmission model relies too heavily on the *conduit metaphor* of communication, whereby 'the speaker puts ideas (objects) into words (containers) and sends them (along a conduit) to a hearer who takes the idea/objects out of the word/container.' This assumes that meaning is *extracted* rather than *constructed*.

 CASE STUDY 1.3 Purpose in communication

A ward supervisor at a hospital wishes to prevent time wasting at morning tea breaks. She tries out a number of noticeboard messages and asks you to pick the one most likely to produce worker cooperation. The messages are:

1 Nursing staff are asked to respect the morning tea privilege. Ward sisters to note.

2 Morning tea is taking too long. Staff late back to work will lose this privilege.

3 Boys and girls, we know you like to chinwag at morning tea break but give *us* a break and cut *yours* down to the allocated 15 minutes provided.

4 A short respite from the morning's nursing duties between 10.30 and 10.45 a.m. is provided. Staff are inclined, however, to presume on the hospital's generosity in the granting of this privilege, with the result that many do not resume normal duties for up to half an hour after the commencement of the break. Patients may be inconvenienced as a result. It is desired that staff take cognisance of the need to cooperate in this regard.

5 Staff are asked to limit their morning tea break to the 15 minutes provided between 10.30 and 10.45 a.m.

Communication as a negotiated transaction

Transaction models of communication
View communication as a two-way interactive process within social, cultural and relational contexts, with meaning evolving and being negotiated.

Transaction models of communication, which evolved in the 1960s, acknowledge that when we communicate with one another, we are simultaneously reacting to what the communication partner is doing or saying. Even as we talk, we are also interpreting our communication partner's non-verbal and verbal responses and then adapting our own to accommodate these. Meaning is understood not as a fixed entity but as something that is negotiated in an active interaction between the sender and receiver, who are themselves changed by the experience. In these models, messages are seen as dynamic – generated within a social or cultural context and evolving through negotiation with the audience or receiver.

The place of meaning

A favourite saying in communication studies is 'Meanings are in people, not in words'; that is, meaning is in the *interpretation* of words, not the words themselves. Even simple terms like 'good relations', 'a positive environment', 'maximum productivity' and 'organisational loyalty' can mean very different things to different people within an organisation. In the first place, people interpret meanings in context; that is, in a social situation at a certain time, between particular individuals or groups. Outside the given context, meanings may vary considerably.

Furthermore, meanings do not remain constant even to each person using the words in similar situations or contexts (Chapter 2 discusses this idea in greater detail). For example, in an interview, you may be subject to a number of different cues or indicators of meaning. You may be sensitive to:

- the interviewer's smile as you are invited to sit down (a positive cue)
- the interviewer's enthusiastic tone while reading through your letter of application and résumé (a positive cue)
- the drumming of fingers as the interviewer looks up with a frown at the wall clock (a negative cue)
- the interviewer's stifled yawn while listening to your hesitant account of your recent retrenchment from another job (a negative cue).

From this composite experience of speech, gesture, movement and facial expression, you may emerge from the interview room saying to yourself, 'I don't think I'll get that job. The supervisor thought I was too inexperienced'. That is the meaning you assign to the interview. Note that much of the meaning in this interview arose from non-verbal cues and their interpretation. We analyse this means of communication more closely in Chapter 3.

Further examples of the dynamic (or constantly changing) nature of meaning are:

- a sudden change of mind for no apparent reason
- a sudden insight into a problem long after it has been unsuccessfully explained to us
- two completely different interpretations of the same set of words by two people; for example, a letter or email to staff or students.

So, there is no guarantee that identical inputs will lead to the same result, or that the same message will generate identical meanings for all parties, or even for a single individual, on different occasions. We are not like computers or telephone systems that can be programmed to give predictable results. Such systems are called *closed* or *deterministic*. Human systems are not deterministic, but rather spontaneous and discretionary. In other words, they respond not only to clearly articulated facts, agreeable attitudes and pleasant feelings, but also to moods, distractions and impulses, all of which can change from moment by moment.

This is not to say that our behaviour is chaotic and completely unpredictable; people usually act fairly consistently. Most of us try to make sense of our experiences and use sign systems (mainly language) to keep us from communicating too idiosyncratically. (We discuss this further in Chapter 2.)

The model shown in **Exhibit 1.10** introduces the notions of *social context* and the mutual interpretation of meaningful messages in an atmosphere of *shared experience* in a *common language*. You can see how communication could fail where some or all of these ingredients are missing. A shared social context, shared experience and a common language are likely to produce better communication between strangers meeting in the city, or for a group working together for the first time (e.g., as a jury), than where some or all of these are missing.

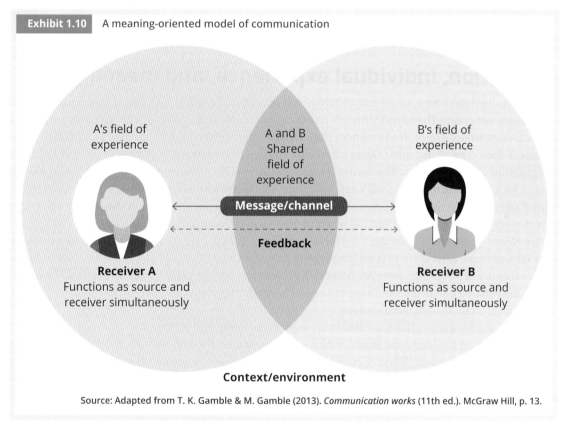

Exhibit 1.10   A meaning-oriented model of communication

A's field of experience

A and B Shared field of experience

B's field of experience

Message/channel

Feedback

Receiver A
Functions as source and receiver simultaneously

Receiver B
Functions as source and receiver simultaneously

Context/environment

Source: Adapted from T. K. Gamble & M. Gamble (2013). *Communication works* (11th ed.). McGraw Hill, p. 13.

We might illustrate this concept of meaning creation by observing two solicitors in an interview. They are both women in their twenties who are negotiating on behalf of their clients for an out-of-court settlement of a damages suit. The stages in their meeting might go like this:

1 Before the meeting, each has been briefed about the case, the arguments of the other side and the claim she will try to justify.

2 Each enters the meeting room, nervous of the other's reputation and determined not to be intimidated.

3 They chat amiably for a few minutes to get each other's measure. They are pleased that they get on well together.

4 They begin to bargain, and there is tension as each tries to get the advantage.

5 They respond to non-verbal cues, such as each other's appearance, voice and mannerisms.

6 Both are relieved when they break for coffee. There is a joke about the weather.

7 They become tense again when approaching the final point of the settlement.

8 When agreement is reached and each feels her client will be pleased, they relax together with some colleagues over drinks at the bar.

During this interview, each lawyer constructed her own *meaning* of the situation, and the meanings changed as the discussion proceeded. Perhaps the setting or environment was the central point, whereby the room itself generated feelings and meanings, with its austere lines and abstract, postmodernist wall hangings. For each, the meanings of *negotiate*, *conflict*, *compromise*, *satisfactory settlement* and *victory* all developed and changed as each stage of the discussion passed. Most of all, the relationship between the two lawyers changed subtly throughout the discussion, softening into camaraderie; but it just as likely could have hardened into dislike and mutual suspicion. Therefore, the transaction model of communication does not see communication as flowing from a source to a receiver and back. Rather, two or more parties respond to a phenomenon or to their environment and bring to it their own set of interpretations. They negotiate meanings and are themselves changed by the experience.

Perception, individual experience, and meaning

In communication theory, there is a debate about whether the world 'out there' is objectively real or whether we create the world through our consciousness, subjectively. The extreme version of subjectivism would claim, for instance, that a chair that we see by the window exists only if we believe it does. The philosopher George Berkeley (1685–1753) claimed that objects exist only in the imagination of the observer. The writer Samuel Johnson (1709–84), on hearing this theory, gave a chair a kick, hurt his toe, and said 'I refute it thus!' Berkeley was a subjectivist, and Johnson was a realist and an empiricist; that is, one who believes that facts are independent of theories and that one can produce evidence from the factual world to prove a point of argument.

Are things really there if we don't perceive or measure them? Is there thunder if there is no-one to hear it? Can ideas exist if there is no language to describe them? Perhaps you could attempt to argue that concepts like *patriotism*, *betrayal*, *friendship* or *greed* can only be constructed in language. However, Uluru, the Panama Canal and the Tower of London are definitely out there, even if you and I have never visited and seen them with our own eyes.

Whether you are a subjectivist, a realist or an empiricist, you do, to an extent, construct your own reality; that is, give meanings to facts and events, which are different from those given to them by other people. For example, if you were asked, 'What does your favourite chair means to you?', 'What kind of a chair is it?', 'How well built is it?' and 'What memories and emotions, if any, does it triggers in you when you look at it or sit in it?' To these questions there would be a diversity of answers, and hence a variety of meanings of *chair*.

Personal construction of reality

To further highlight the primacy of *meaning* rather than *message* in communication, consider what we mean by the *personal construction* of reality (see **Exhibit 1.11**), and why people have so many different opinions about films, television programs, football codes (and players), and even chairs! Constructivists are communication scholars who believe we give meanings to objects, people and ideas according to our cognitive systems; that is, our systems of mental processing. The meanings we give are based on our experiences and conditioning. These meanings, in turn, determine our communication.

Does this personal construction of reality produce great gaps of understanding between people? Can't we even agree that two plus two equals four? Or that water freezes at zero degrees Celsius at sea level? These two propositions may be difficult to deny, but think about the following statements:

Exhibit 1.11 The personal construction of reality

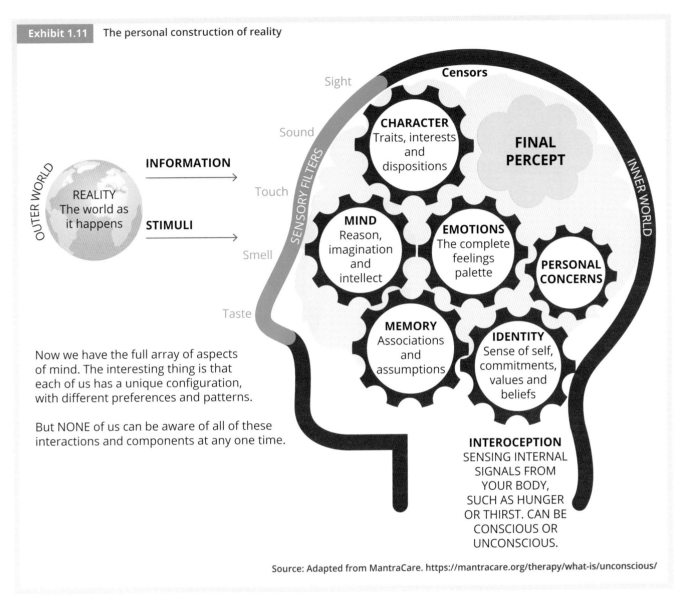

Source: Adapted from MantraCare. https://mantracare.org/therapy/what-is/unconscious/

- 'The 10.45 bus is late again! It's now 10.50.'
- 'Gee, that HR manager is arrogant!'

Is five minutes late today, always late? What is arrogance? Is one person's arrogance another person's firmness of purpose? Let's pursue this idea of individual experience. We experience the world around us through our sensory nerve endings. In other words, we experience sensory stimuli and then our brains attempt to process those **sensations** until they have meaning for us.

Objects in our world stand out because of their shape, colour, size, sound and smell. The act of interpreting these sensory stimuli is called **perception**, and it is important to our understanding about how we communicate and make meaning from the world around us. Try looking at an object in front of you. Are your eyes just a camera that records this sight? Apparently not. In fact, light waves are reflected off the thing you are looking at and impinge on the retina of your eye. Visual nerves send electrical impulses through the sensory apparatus to the cortex. These are recorded and decoded by the brain. Consider how we attempt to understand or make sense of visual illusions. Are the men in **Exhibit 1.12** the same height? What is impacting upon how we perceive this image?

In one sense, we are aware of our nerves and not aware of objects. The eyes are not a camera; our experience of the world is indirect and comes to us through our senses. It is as though we were sitting deep within a cave and had a friend at the cave's mouth using a mobile phone to report to us the state of the weather outside. The

Sensation
Occurs when our sensory receptors (eyes, ears, nose, etc), detect sensory stimuli (sights, sounds, smells).

Perception
The mental or cognitive process of selecting, organising and interpreting stimuli from the environment in order to gain information and make meaning.

Exhibit 1.12 Example of a visual illusion

surprising thing is that we do not merely receive all this information. We unconsciously select the bits we need and ignore those we don't need. If it were not so, our lives would be a miserable, frightening chaos. For example, if you were sitting listening to a lecture, you would be conscious not only of the lecturer's voice and the content of the lecture, but also of the temperature of the room, the buzz of whispered conversation around you, the pressure of your clothes on your body, and the tightness of your new shoes – all in equal degree! How much, then, of the lecturer's main points would you hear and remember?

In summary, therefore, there are some important things to remember about the process of perception and how it might impact the making of meaning in a communication event:

- To avoid overload and to make processing easier, our brains select, organise and interpret stimuli or sensory information.
- We often interpret stimuli by referring to previous experiences or categories, known as **schema**.
- Our perceptions are influenced by external factors or the context in which the sensations are received.
- Our perceptions are influenced by our individual differences, the nature of what is being perceived and the context in which the perception occurs.

Consider some of the influences in **Exhibit 1.13** in terms of choices that we make in the supermarket and, importantly, how producers and marketers take account of the characteristics of our perceptual faculties to influence our spending habits.

Schema
Cognitive or mental frameworks that help us organise and interpret information and the relationships between them.

Exhibit 1.13	Influences on interpersonal perception

	Influences	Example
Perceiver	Motives, personality, expectations, prior learning, self-concept, attitudes, past experiences	A nervous, introverted person might interpret their manager's request for an 'urgent meeting to discuss your future' as something to fear. This may be particularly so if they previously had a negative experience with their manager regarding performance feedback
Perceived	Physical characteristics, social attributes, past experiences, traditions	Society communicates positive and negative perceptions of people who are different or who do not fit the idealised 'norm'. An overweight person may be perceived as slovenly, or an older person may be perceived as slow or in cognitive decline
Context	Place or time, situational factors	Receiving a phone call from a family member in the middle of the night would make us feel more anxious than a phone call received during the day

 CASE STUDY 1.4 Supermarket sales tactics cleverly use the way our brains perceive and process sensory information

Ever wonder why you always seem to spend more than you intend when you do the weekly food shopping? Consumer research shows how supermarkets cleverly use their knowledge of psychology and the way our brains deal with the mass of sensory information to influence our spending habits. The points below have been adapted from a guide published by CHOICE:

- It's very common to locate the attractive fresh produce or the bakery at the supermarket entry. Does the deli section with its medley of colours and tasty offerings then follow? The sights and smells create a market-type atmosphere that aims to put you in the mood to shop as you are led through the labyrinth to the less interesting packaged dry goods and strategically placed impulse-buy items. Smell is a powerful sense that links to our memory, and freshly baked goods and fresh produce conjure positive associations. Fresh food also looks best in natural light, hence the positioning near the front entrance.

- More expensive items with higher profit margins tend to be placed in line of sight of the target customer, as shoppers are considered 'lazy' and will see those first. This is why manufacturers pay more for the eye-level space on the shelves. Cheaper or supermarket brands tend to be located on the higher or lower shelves.

- Where are the eggs? Probably nowhere near the milk or bread. Separation of popular staples is a common element of supermarket design. Why? So that you'll spend more time in store negotiating your way past all those flashy and tempting impulse-buy items.

- Items that are positioned in close proximity are perceived to be related. Positioning natural combinations like chips with dips or biscuits near coffee or tea may be logical, but it also increases the sales of both.

- Research shows that grocery shoppers are heavily influenced by in-store displays, particularly those at the end of aisles in the 'bargain bin'. Are they really discounted?

- Colours invoke our emotions and can encourage us to spend more money. Red is used because it stands out above all other colours. It also causes our body to release adrenaline and makes our heart beat faster. Blue is used as a trust symbol and green invokes the idea 'fresh'.

- Size and shape do matter. If a manufacturer wants their brand to stand out from their competitors, they will use either larger packaging or a different shaped bottle to catch the shopper's attention among the mass of colours and shapes on the shelves. Generic or supermarket brands are often similar in appearance, size, shape and package design to the leading brands to make it harder for shoppers to distinguish between them.

- A study published by the American Psychological Association showed that even the choice of in-store music influenced shoppers' wine selection. Over a two-week period in an English supermarket, either French or German music was played at a display of wines from these countries. When the music was French, sales of French wine increased, and when it was German, sales of German wine increased. When questioned, shoppers seemed unaware of the effect the music had on their wine purchasing.

Source: Adapted from J. Baldwin (2023, January 10). Supermarket psychology – tactics to get you to spend more. CHOICE.

Discussion

Which characteristics of the way that we perceive information from the environment are these display tactics using? Can you think of other clever ploys that shops use to appeal to people's senses and get them in the mood for shopping?

After you have discussed this case study, refer to the 'Comments on case studies' section at the end of the text.

Social construction of reality

It is not surprising that, with all this information around, we have different experiences from each other, and why we communicate about our experiences in different ways. What is not clear is whether these differences in perception are caused by innate psychological qualities or by *social conditioning*.

In their book *The Social Construction of Reality* (1975), Berger and Luckmann assert that we construct our world through experience and, especially, through language. They say we depend on relations within a group for our understanding of reality and that this reality changes when our group relations change. Knowledge can be rather unstable because it depends more on how groups perceive 'facts' than on any objective reality outside of human experience. For example, you might claim to be poor because you have little money, no job and you don't own a house or car. Someone from a developing country might say you cannot be poor because you are wearing shoes and do not seem to be hungry. Poverty, then, is defined in terms of the social group in which you experience reality; therefore, reality differs for members of different groups.

Frames of reference

Mental set or frame of reference
A set of beliefs, values or ideas upon which you base your judgement or interpretation; also known as a frame of reference.

Whether individual or social, we seem to construct our own meanings for what we see, hear, touch or smell. Our **mental set**, or **frame of reference**, may be personal or social or both. For the communication theorist and practitioner, it is imperative to assume that there could be a gap in the construction of meanings between us, even about the simplest of facts or opinions. As we all have mental sets, which could be personal, social or cultural, we need to take precautions when we are communicating to ensure that, despite our differences, we can share meaning.

Leeper and the three pictures

An experiment by Robert W. Leeper (1935) provides a rather convincing example of the observer's frame of reference in interpreting meaning. Leeper arranged for three sketches to be drawn, shown in **Exhibit 1.14**. Picture (A) depicted a young woman, picture (B) an old woman, and picture (C) combined the features of (A) and (B) to form an ambiguous picture. To one group of students, Leeper showed only picture (A), and to another group, only picture (B). Then both groups were shown picture (C). You may be surprised to learn that no-one in either group thought picture (C) was ambiguous. Those who had seen picture (A) of the young woman, thought that picture (C) was of a young woman. Those who had seen picture (B) of the old woman, thought picture (C) was of an old woman.

Exhibit 1.14	An exercise in perception

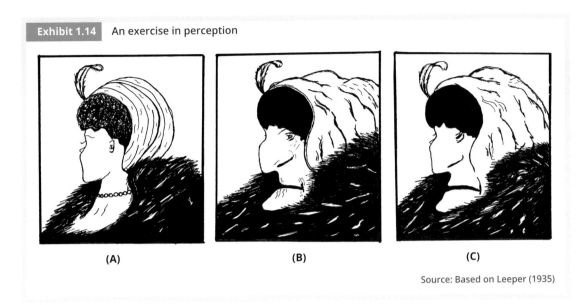

(A) (B) (C)

Source: Based on Leeper (1935)

It is too late for you to experience this experiment yourself, but try it on some other people, say two groups of four friends or colleagues. See if your results agree with those of Leeper.

What inference can we draw from this special case? Not, we suspect, that all old people would see picture (C) as that of an old woman and all young people would see it as that of a young woman. In fact, the groups seemed consistent in deriving their mental set from the picture viewed immediately before.

What is interesting in Leeper's pictures is the process of selection involved. For example, none of his test subjects saw picture (C) merely as that of a female person; they all saw it as either an old or a young woman. Leeper argued that we select perceptions and use them to give structure and meaning to our world, but that our worlds differ from one another. It is not difficult to understand how people's reports of the same incident, such as a fire or car crash, can vary so much.

What is the point of all this? The experiment conducted by Leeper shows that mental sets can distort communication. If we are communicating in writing, through speech or by mass media, then we must be aware of the fragility of the communicating process. That is why purposiveness in communication is so important.

 CASE STUDY 1.5   Crime, sex, immigration and climate change: how Australians get it wrong

More often than not, people, when asked to estimate the occurrence of things such as crime, they either make overestimations or underestimations. In its annual survey titled 'The Perils of Perception', Ipsos polling company explores the gap between people's perceptions about the world and the reality.

The uncomfortable truth about voters' perception versus reality

... The 2018 [Ipsos] survey zeroed in on three issues: migration, renewable energy and the economy. In each case, our perceptions are a long way from reality. The

survey questions on migration showed Australians vastly overestimate the proportion of the population born overseas. The average respondent guessed the share was 41 per cent, when the actual figure is 29 per cent.

...

Ipsos researchers have noticed that public perceptions are often most inaccurate on topics that are being widely discussed in the media, and on issues that are of concern to us. The tendency for Australians to overestimate our Muslim population is a classic example.

...

Another case in point is renewable energy and the response to climate change, a policy issue that has plagued both major parties. [The 2018] Perils of Perception survey asked respondents what share of energy consumed in

Australia comes from renewable sources, such as wind and solar. The average guess was 21 per cent, more than double the actual figure of nine per cent. In other words, voters have the impression that Australia is doing more to reduce greenhouse gas emission than we actually are.

Also, Australians underestimate the level of temperature change over the past two decades. The typical respondents said nine of the past 18 years were among the hottest on record globally when in reality it is 17.

…

Why are we so wrong, so often? We are often exposed to being misled by those around us, be it family members, friends, the media or politicians. But the cause of our collective misconceptions runs much deeper than the 'fake-news effect'. Our own internal biases are crucial. The Perils of Perception survey shows there is a systematic pattern to our errors. People the world over tend to think things are worse than they really are …

Source: Adapted from M. Wade (2018, December 30). The uncomfortable truth about voters' perception vs reality. *Sydney Morning Herald*.

Discussion

1 Think about some of the common misconceptions revealed by the Ipsos survey. To what extent can these be attributed to people's internal biases, prejudices or fears at any given time?

2 To what extent are these impacted by 'fake news' on social media platforms?

3 Can you think of recent examples where your own perceptions were challenged or changed by 'reality'? What might this tell us about how our brains process information and the brains role in communication?

After you have discussed this case study, refer to the 'Comments on case studies' section at the end of the text.

Communicating in society

Symbolic interactionists

Argue that meaning is not essentially personal but is instead created and sustained by interactions in the social group.

Symbolic interactionists are communication scholars who say that meaning is not essentially personal but is created and sustained by interactions in the social group. This is a sociological approach to communication as opposed to a psychological approach.

Symbolic interactionists define society in terms of a large group having a common culture; that is, a similar way of communicating. They say we create and sustain society through symbols – mainly language – and the use of these symbols defines 'normal' behaviour in society. Within any social group we engage in role-taking. This is a process by which we identify with someone else's opinions or feelings. Society has a set of unstated rules that apply to communication. We become part of society by understanding both ourselves and others, and by seeing ourselves and others playing the game.

So, our communication reflects the rules of society. For example, we take our turn in conversations; we stand in line to wait for buses; and we behave differently in the company of our friends, parents, teachers and supervisors. In each of these situations we communicate in symbols – either verbal or non-verbal. (We shall discuss symbols, signs and non-verbal cues in Chapters 2 and 3.) It is certainly true that for most of us, appearance, dress, accent, behaviour and attitudes are largely social in origin. Watching a crowd of business executives promenading in the city, school students visiting an art gallery, or youths skateboarding in a park, we are often struck more by the similarities in the behaviour of people when in groups than by the differences.

We are all conditioned by our family, peers, community, and national and cultural groups. This conditioning may not dominate our every thought and action, but it lends a certain stability and predictability to our actions as members of various communities (e.g., the student community, Catholic community, Chinese community or engineering community).

You might say, then, that each of us communicates as a result of our cognitive processes, and that these processes are conditioned to some extent by our *personal* and our *social* construction of reality. Although, the two may sometimes be counterintuitive. You may be shy and introverted but highly animated at rock concerts, or extroverted and aggressive in business but a passionate environmentalist known for your patient vigils in the branches of endangered rainforest trees.

Kress, who is suspicious of the 'nice friendly definition of communication as a sharing of meaning', reminds us that 'the processes of communication can have the effect of becoming devices of control, or means of instruction, or suppression'. He says, 'The processes of communication always take place in a specific social and cultural setting, never simply between you and me as individuals; and the structures of power, of authority, as well as the structures of solidarity, exert their influence on the participants' (Kress, 1988, p. 5). Kress would claim that many of our meanings for concepts in public life are in fact dominated by power structures in society, and we are not as free to choose our meaning as we think.

Communication and culture

When we talk about **culture** in regard to communication, we are not referring to the specialised sense of 'high' and 'popular' culture (whether we like Mozart or Bob Dylan, classical ballet or MasterChef). Instead, we are describing the learnt system of knowledge, behaviour, attitudes, values, rules and norms that are shared by a group of people and shapes their behaviour and worldview, and marks a national or ethnic group as distinctive. It is a component in communication as transaction and, therefore, in meaning. Culture can include factors such as the way we organise our lives, the things we believe and take for granted, the kinds of work we do and our attitudes toward it, our sports and sporting traditions, and our artistic activities. (See Chapter 4 for a detailed discussion of culture and its effects on communication.)

Culture
A learnt system of knowledge, behaviour, attitudes, values, rules and norms that is shared by a group of people and which shapes their behaviour and worldview.

Culture is dynamic and constantly changing. Some elements of Anglo Australian culture include bush literature; suburban life, with its emphasis on barbecues and backyard cricket; the beach; winning the Ashes from the 'Poms'; and arguing fiercely about which is the superior football code. This cultural self-image is that of a casual, tolerant, sceptical and democratic people. Do you think these descriptions still apply? Did they ever?

Some Aboriginal and Torres Strait Islanders share these cultural traditions, and others see them as part of the neglect and oppression that their culture has suffered since 1788. For First Nations Australians, a more important cultural dimension is their close relationship to the land, and they see themselves as belonging to the land rather than it to them. They place a high value on song and other oral traditions, and on kinship. If you are an Aboriginal and/or Torres Strait Islander, you may be in a good position to comment on the accuracy of these traditions to sum up the cultural profile of your people in the 21st century.

Communication and gender

An important feature of culture is gender differentiation. In society, the roles of men and women have always been distinguished, and those of women have usually been subordinated. It is interesting to view a film from the 1940s and compare it with a current film, just to observe the differences in the way men and women treat each other and the degree to which women are taken seriously as anything other than wives, mothers and caregivers. Further, it is now recognised that traditional views related to gender identity have broadened beyond the binary of male/female, and this is providing challenges and debates around policies and language as they attempt to take these broadening definitions into account. (See Chapter 11 for more on this topic.)

For some years now in most Western nations, there has been a democratic movement, supported by legislation, which aims to provide equal opportunity and treatment for all sections of society. The feminist movement, which had been in existence at least as far back as the turn of the 20th century, gained momentum in the 1950s in the US, UK and Australia. It took the form of debates, rallies and mass action to achieve equal pay and political and social rights for women, and to enable them to compete equally with men for jobs and for political office.

As a result of the feminist movement, over the past 50 years in particular, there have been significant increases in the proportion of women to men in many professions, such as architecture, medicine and engineering. Women are also gradually beginning to play a more prominent roles in politics. Australia elected its first female prime minister in 2010 and many other countries, such as Britain, New Zealand, Germany, India and Pakistan, have also had elected female leaders.

Despite this progress, in management and organisational work, women have detected the existence of a **glass ceiling**. This means that although their training and competence have earned them appointments to junior management positions, they are not represented equally in higher organisational ranks, higher political office, or on the boards of large corporations. Some feminist scholars have analysed the problem of discrimination as primarily linguistic. They say that women have an inferior status because language *constructs* them as inferior. We discuss how to write more inclusively, and why this matters, in Chapter 11.

Glass ceiling
A metaphor referring to the invisible barriers or obstacles that prevent some demographics, usually women, advancing beyond a certain level in a hierarchy. First coined around 1978 during the women's liberation movement.

Summary of the transaction model of communication

The transaction model foregrounds meaning rather than message – its creation and sharing, its subjectivity and unreliability, and the fact that there is always a gap between meanings attributed by different people to the same phenomena. According to this model, people create their individual meanings, as do social groups. We see the world through our own frames of reference as well as through the frames of reference of the society we belong to. Society is the way we organise our communication, lives and relationships.

Reflection question: How might issues of individual difference such as gender, culture and social status impact on differences in how a receiver might decode a message?

Evaluating the two models of communication

The approaches to communication discussed so far are:

1 the *transmission model*, which sees communication as the transfer of messages from a source to a receiver, using a channel and medium

2 the *transaction model*, which sees communication as the creation or negotiation of meaning in two or more parties responding to their environment and to each other.

Note that these models are attempts to explain typical behaviour; they are not developed theories of communication. They can only have value for us if they sketch the likely course of a communication event. Both models have value, and both have weaknesses. **Exhibit 1.15** compares the two approaches.

Exhibit 1.15	A comparison of two models of communication
Transmission models	**Transaction models**
Communication is a series of linear steps	Communication is dynamic, circular and unrepeatable
'Meaning' lies in the components of the message itself: words chosen and treatment	Meaning lies within the individual parties to the communication: education, attitudes, prior knowledge, motivations, etc. Shared experiences and common language are important
Any variation in the individual elements e.g., inappropriate channel, can impact on the clarity of the message	Communication is dependent on a wide range of factors, including contexts, psychological characteristics of the sender (encoder) and receiver (decoder) of a message
Communication describes the *production* of meaning and messages	Communication describes the *evolution* and *negotiation* of meaning

The transmission model uses mechanistic terms like *source*, *receiver*, *feedback* and *noise*, and it assumes that information moves in a linear way from A to B. This model has value in helping us to think carefully about how we might construct a message to deliver to particular people in various ways. But mechanistic terms can be applied to human communication only as analogies or metaphors. Human communication is not mechanical, closed or predictable. You may ensure that your message allows for feedback, but you cannot be sure of the exact content or value of the feedback, or of its meaning. There is no way of ensuring that the message received is the same as the message sent.

The transaction model also concentrates on meaning. It may be useful in analysing the complexities of conversations, interviews, negotiations or large meetings and is helpful in allowing us to understand that communication is not always predictable, and that the situation or context in which communication takes place can have a significant impact on how parties communicate. This model also has value in helping us to check that we have shared our intended meaning with others.

 CASE STUDY 1.6 Applying communication models to a case study

Read through the following case study of a communication encounter and, using Berlo's model, answer the discussion questions that follow.

Jane Seymour has to advise her seven staff members of a new policy that affects their working hours. Just before knock-off time on Friday, she calls her staff together and speaks to them.

'Look, I'll try not to hold you up too long ... I know you are keen to get away. I've been told to inform you that working hours for our department are going to be changed. In fact, this policy affects the whole company. You've probably noticed what a mess it is down at the gate at knock-off time. Because of these rush hour conditions, and considering all the problems that they create, it seems that the best solution is to get different departments to report and knock-off at different times. Because of the increased traffic on Mayer Road, there have been major traffic jams when all the staff try to get here by 8.30 and leave at 4.30. We have decided to change your knock-off time to 4.00 and have you start at 8.00 each morning. These new hours will come into effect from the last Monday in February. We appreciate your cooperation. Sorry to keep you so late. If there are no questions, have a good weekend and I'll see you on Monday.'

Discussion

1 Did Jane (sender) have a clear idea of what she wanted the staff (receivers) to think, feel or do?

2 Identify some elements of the message Jane delivered that might have hindered or helped the staff to have a clear idea of what they needed to do? Consider her language, the timing and the nature of the message.

3 What were possible differences within the staff group that might have impacted how they 'heard' or responded to the message?

4 Did Jane choose the best channel to deliver her message? What other channels might she have chosen?

5 Did Jane allow for enough feedback? What could have gone wrong?

After you have discussed this case study, refer to the 'Comments on case studies' section at the end of the text.

The role of ethics in professional communication

Ethical communication is fundamental to responsible thinking, decision-making and the development of relationships and communities within and across context, cultures, channels and media. Moreover, ethical communication enhances human worth and dignity by fostering truthfulness, fairness, responsibility, personal integrity and respect for self and others.

Source: National Communication Association (2001)

Ethics
Can be broadly defined as a set of principles of right and moral conduct, which may be socially and culturally determined.

The definition of **ethics** is abstract, complex and sometimes problematic, but generally relates to questions of right or wrong, honesty, accuracy of information and integrity. Ethics can be broadly defined as a set of principles of right and moral conduct, which are sometimes socially and culturally determined. So, when thinking about communication skills, there are other important issues besides competence (e.g., the ability to write, speak and generally interact with others effectively), and they relate not only to the language of professionals but also to the ethics of communication in the professional workplace.

These days, the boundaries of business ethics are usually set out in an organisation's mission statement and by codes of conduct within which most professions are supposed to act. However, we often seem to hear about businesses large and small that have been caught out acting unethically and sometimes illegally. Phillip Lewis (1985, p. 383) wrote that 'business ethics is more than just virtue, integrity or character. It involves the application of what is morally right and truthful at a time of ethical dilemma'. In other words, it can be measured by how businesses and professionals behave and respond to challenges that arise during crises, and their application of ethical business behaviour.

In this book we are interested in the ethics of professional communication, and while we will discuss this in more detail in Chapter 7, we present some initial principles to consider in the following.

Communication code of ethics

The following is a list of some of the hallmarks of good and ethical communication:

- *Good communication is clear.* It uses language and other symbols to explain simply, describe exactly and persuade logically. It avoids vagueness, inaccuracy and distortion of facts.
- *Good communication is honest.* It does not lie but presents all necessary and relevant information.
- *Good communication is democratic.* It should not lead to disadvantage for any ethnic, gender, religious or social group in the society.
- *Good communication is sincere.* It uses persuasion and advocacy with facts and judgements, which do not, either overtly or covertly, appeal to bias, prejudice or ignorance.
- *Good communication respects its audience.* It makes its message clear to them in language they understand. It is thorough and balanced. It does not 'talk down to' or patronise its audience.
- *Good communication is logical.* It employs no tricks of persuasion, omissions deliberately designed to deceive, or details designed to distort or manipulate.

It is worth considering how these points affect the specific ways in which professionals communicate with each other, members of other professions and non-professionals such as clients or the general public. How might these differences be explained by the complexity of professional practice or by the desire to guard professional secrets? Are they explained by the need to maintain market advantage or to mask professional uncertainties? What obligations do professionals have to their profession, employers, colleagues, clients and society as a whole? Does the need to consider professional ethics impose too many restrictions on successful business practice?

Reflection question: In your profession, is there a conflict between your personal ethics and professional practices?

Summary

There are varied definitions of communication; some emphasise the transfer or transmission of knowledge, others the mutual creation of meaning, and yet others emphasise the building of understanding and cooperation. You will benefit by understanding communication processes and strategies, by developing skills in language use, and by being clear about their purpose in communicating. Whether seen as transmission or transaction, communication takes place within a social, cultural and ethical setting. It is influenced by the communicator's personal and social construction of reality and by the meanings they, and others, give to the world around them. The role of individual and professional ethics in shaping and determining meaning is also highly significant. The chapters which follow examine in more detail specific dimensions of communication that range from intrapersonal, interpersonal, group and intercultural to mediated, and all these dimensions, or settings, strongly influence the meanings conveyed and received.

STUDY TOOLS

DISCUSSION QUESTIONS AND GROUP ACTIVITIES

For discussion topics and activities in addition to those that follow, please refer to the case studies presented throughout this chapter.

1   Which of the four definitions of communication seems to be the most useful and appropriate in relation to your work as a student?

2   Which forms of communication are most important in your profession? Give some examples and situations in which communication competence is important for you as a professional.

3   Discuss one recent case involving professional life in which poor communication has had serious results.

4   What do you understand by *whistleblowing* among professionals? (You may need to do some research on this one.)

5   Examine and discuss the ethics involved in a recent case of whistleblowing in your profession.

6   Communication theorist Marshall McLuhan said, 'The medium is the message' (1967, p. 15). He meant that the choice of medium can transform a message and its meaning. Discuss this idea.

7   We discussed that the choice of media is as important as the message itself. If you were asked to give advice on plagiarism and how to avoid it to the 500 students in Stage 1 of your course, how would you communicate your message? Discuss the advantages and disadvantages of each of the following forms of media to communicate this message to your particular audience:

   a   word-of-mouth communication in small group briefing sessions

   b   an email announcement to all students

   c   an article in the weekly student newspaper

   d   a speech to the whole group in a large lecture hall with accompanying PowerPoint slideshow

   e   a continuous video, set up in the student cafeteria

   f   an interactive, self-paced tutorial on the faculty's website.

8   We define feedback as the response to a message. Without it, we cannot be sure we have communicated effectively. But how do we get feedback? Form groups of four or five and discuss specific methods of seeking feedback in the two situations below. Compile the list on a whiteboard or paper and then compare your list to those of other groups.

   a   Your lecturer keeps giving you poor marks for written assignments but few comments. You would like to improve your assessments.

   b   Promotion is coming slowly to you in the firm. Despite having finished a higher degree and having won two company awards for creative designs, you have remained in the same position for three years while watching contemporaries surge ahead of you.

9   Test the claim that 'Meanings are in people, not in words'. Write brief definitions of the terms in the following list, then in small groups compare your definitions with those of other group members:

   • company loyalty

   • climate crisis

   • sustainable development

   • globalisation

   • border protection

   • professional integrity

   • crisis management

   • spin doctoring.

10 On separate sheets of paper, write one-sentence definitions of *professionalism*, *loyalty*, *quality*, *productivity* and *transparency*. Then, in small groups, exchange your definitions and discuss the varieties of meaning. Note the differences of perspective and emphasis.

11 Write a sentence containing a statement of fact, as you see it. For example, the following example leans into a stereotype to attempt to state a fact: 'Redheads are bad tempered'. Exchange your statement for a partner's sentence and see if you can agree on its meaning.

WEBSITES

Communication Theory, Wikibooks.org

https://en.wikibooks.org/wiki/Communication_Theory

Wikipedia – Communication Theory

http://en.wikipedia.org/wiki/Communication_theory (Wikipedia)

REFERENCES

Baldwin, J. (2023, January 10). Supermarket psychology – tactics to get you to spend more. CHOICE.

Berger, P. L., & Luckmann, T. (1975). *The social construction of reality: A treatise in the sociology of knowledge*. Penguin Books.

Berlo, D. K. (1960). *The process of communication: An introduction to theory and practice*. Rinehart and Winston.

Burke, K. (2022, October 23). Confusing messaging hampers our ability to prepare for rising flood waters. *The Guardian*.

Chandler, D. (1994). *The transmission model of communication*. http://visual-memory.co.uk/daniel//Documents/short/trans.html.

Denniss, R. (2012). The use and abuse of economic modelling in Australia. *Technical Brief no, 12*. http://australiainstitute.org.au/wp-content/uploads/2020/12/TB-12-The-use-and-abuse-of-economic-modelling-in-Australia_4.pdf

Gamble, T. K., & Gamble, M. (2013). *Communication Works* (11th ed.). McGraw Hill. https://www.sagepub.com/sites/default/files/upm-binaries/52575_Gamble_(IC)_Chapter_1.pdf

Kress, G. R. (Ed.). (1988). *Communication and culture: An introduction*. UNSW Press.

Lasswell, H. D. (1948). The structure and function of communication in society. In L. Bryson (Ed.), *The communication of ideas* (pp. 37–51). Harper and Row.

Leeper, R. (1935). The role of motivation in learning: A study of the phenomenon of differential motivational control of the utilization of habits. *The Pedagogical Seminary and Journal of Genetic Psychology, 46*(1), 3-40. https://doi.org/10.1080/08856559.1935.10533143

Lewis, P. (1985). Defining 'business ethics': Like nailing Jello to a wall. *Journal of Business Ethics, 4*(5). 377–383. https://doi.org/10.1007/BF02388590

McLuhan, M. (1964). *Understanding media: The extensions of man*. Sphere Books.

Mohan, T., McGregor, H., Saunder, S., & Archee, R. (1997). *Communicating! Theory and practice* (4th ed.). Harcourt Brace.

National Communication Association (2001). *Credo for communication ethics*. https://www.natcom.org/sites/default/files/pages/1999_Public_Statements_NCA_Credo_for_Ethical_Communication_November.pdf

Schramm, W. (1954). How communication works. In W. Schramm & D. F. Roberts (Eds.), *The process and effects of mass communication*. University of Illinois Press.

Shannon, C. E., & Weaver, W. (1949). *The mathematical theory of communication*. University of Illinois Press.

Wade, M. (2018, December 30). The uncomfortable truth about voters' perception vs reality. *Sydney Morning Herald*.

Language and communication practice

Learning objectives

After reading this chapter, you should be able to:
- explain why language is not a neutral medium, and how meanings are in people not in words
- define and provide examples of linguistic concepts, such as denotation, connotation, euphemism and doublespeak
- explain how language choices may shape and reflect social attitudes and behaviours
- understand how words have the power to impact thoughts and actions in particular contexts.

Language like this should be put to the torch

'They leapt from mountain peak to mountain peak or far out into the lower country, lighting forests six or seven miles in advance of the main fires. Blown by wind of great force they roared as they travelled. Balls of crackling fire sped at a great pace and in advance of the fires consuming with a roaring explosive noise all that they touched. Houses of brick were seen and heard to leap into a roar of flame before the fires had reached them.'

The fires described here are not the Black Saturday fires of 2009, but the Black Friday fires of 1939. The writer is Justice Leonard Stretton, who conducted the inquiry into Black Friday. When Jack Rush, QC, quoted these passages to the current commission, he intended to suggest to the chief of the Country Fire Authority that last summer's fires were not without precedent, and to ask why its warnings on February 6 'did not prepare people for the sort of fire that could be anticipated on February 7' ...

The matter, of course, has nothing to do with the efforts of CFA firefighters. It concerns CFA management and more particularly what managers call 'communication' ...

One CFA manager variously described the business of telling the public as 'messaging'; 'communicating the likely impact'; providing 'precise complex fire behaviour information', 'to communicate more effectively in a timely manner not just that it is a bad day, but other factors as well'. He spoke of his task as 'value-adding' and as 'populating the template' or 'populating the document' and of the 'document' as an 'iterative type document'. He talked a great deal about 'learnings', 'big learnings' and even 'huge learnings'. 'Of course the learnings from these fires', one said, 'the scientists will come out and give us an outcome of what sort of messaging and where we can go to better inform communities about what they should do.'

Commissioner Ron McLeod asked the CFA chief if it might not have been more useful to have told people what firefighters in the Yarra region had been told: 'That they were liable to face a fire that could not be stopped, that had a flame height of 35 metres.' He wondered if more 'explicit terms' might have 'added a bit more substance and bit more meaning' with 'implications ... for people who might in other circumstances have chosen to stay as their preferred option'.

In reply, the chief could not escape the limits of his professional idiom: 'My view of the world is that for those people who are in that environment the weather conditions were very plain to understand. We very clearly communicated the fuel conditions. I think the bit – if you think about it in terms of the fire triangle – was we had not communicated the likely outcome, if that is the judgement.'

Stripped of jargon, we presume he meant to say the only thing they messed up was the bit about the fire. They neglected to tell people in concrete language – the only kind we understand – that any fire on February 7 was likely to be one they could not fight, and might not survive. If instead of 'fire activity with potential to impact' we had dangerous, unpredictable fires, fires like the one Stretton described, the CFA's 'messagings' might have persuaded more people to get out of the way. If instead of 'wind events' and 'weather events' ... the experts and the authorities ... had said the wind will blow a tremendous gale of searing air through forests so dry they will explode into fires that no one can stop; and that the wind will very likely suddenly blow just as hard from another direction and send these firestorms into the midst of people who just minutes before thought they were safe – or something like this – perhaps more people would have recognised the danger.

Source: D. Watson (2009, September 19). Language like this should be put to the torch. *The Sydney Morning Herald*. The use of this work has been licensed by Copyright Agency except as permitted by the Copyright Act, you must not re-use this work without the permission of the copyright owner or Copyright Agency.

Introduction

In developing contemporary and engaging examples to illustrate sometimes controversial issues and ideas, questions asked and examples given may occasionally be provocative or challenging. We also understand that the language used in some of these examples is outdated. The authors and publisher of this book do not endorse such language but have made the decision to include the examples for their educational value in professional communication and to encourage conversation about using language for a more inclusive future.

Professionals are regularly required to write or speak persuasively and informatively and, therefore, it is important that they are aware of how language functions. This knowledge allows them to appreciate and master the complexities of this aspect of the communication process. As illustrated above in Don Watson's critique of the language used by the Victorian Country Fire Authority (CFA) during the 2009 Black Saturday bushfires, understanding the implications of the language used in a professional (and personal) context can have significant ramifications.

Part 1 of this text keeps language at the fore in defining communication, analysing effects of communication, and illustrating communication weaknesses and fragility. In Parts 2 and 3, the emphasis will be on language in practical professional contexts – in writing for the world of work and in using the voice to instruct, persuade and to entertain. This chapter explores meaning, or the study of **semantics**. We distinguish between denotation and connotation, euphemism and doublespeak, and jargon and slang. We also examine the differences between written and spoken modes of language, as well as the debates around inclusive or non-discriminatory language and 'political correctness'.

Semantics
The linguistic study of the meaning of words.

Why study language?

Language helps form the limits of our reality. It is our means of ordering, classifying and manipulating the world. It is through language that we become members of a human community, that the world becomes comprehensible and meaningful, that we bring into existence the world in which we live.

Source: Spender (1994), p. 3

Language
A system of words (visual symbols or oral sounds) structured by grammar (rules or conventions) and syntax (patterns in how words are arranged) common to a group of people.

Most human communication uses **language** as its primary channel. However, as argued by Australian linguist Dale Spender (1994), writers and speakers must understand that language is not merely a *vehicle* for meaning; rather, it has multiple functions. The words that we choose, whether consciously or unconsciously, can reveal much about how we *see* the world. Additionally, Spender argues, the very words that we use help *create* the world in which we live. Our personal word choices also act as markers of our social and cultural identity. These are complex but important notions. In this chapter, we explore some of these issues as they relate to language and, especially, to semantics, or the production of meaning.

As a starting point, let's consider some basic principles:

- Words are symbols.
- Language is not fixed.
- Meanings are in people, not in words.
- Words create and label experience.
- Language is culture bound.
- Language is context bound.

Words are symbols

The first thing that we need to remember is that words, whether they are the sounds made when we speak or the squiggles on the page made when we write, are merely symbols or *codes* that have evolved to *represent* the spoken and written language. In themselves, they have no meaning. They are given meaning by those who use them and by the manner and context in which they are used. In other words, they are human inventions.

Symbol
A mark, sign, visual image, gesture or word that signifies, or is understood as representing an idea, object, concept or relationship.

A **symbol** can be defined as a mark, sign, visual image, gesture or word that signifies, or is understood as representing an idea, object, concept or relationship. For example, consider how a flag (i.e., a symbol) can be used to represent and communication the ideals, values or history of a nation (see **Exhibit 2.1**). Consider another example, what do you think of when you see or hear the word 'heart'? It may conjure up ideas of romantic love, of courage in the face of adversity, or the need to maintain a healthy diet and exercise regime to minimise the risk of heart disease.

Language is not fixed

A second important point is that language never remains static; it evolves and changes according to where, how, by whom and for what purpose it is used. Looking at texts from the past reveals how those writers or speakers saw the world. Even dictionaries regularly update their lists of words to reflect new usage and recent invention.

English is a complex language that has evolved as a hybrid of Latin, French and Anglo-Saxon. It regularly borrows from other languages; for example, think *café* from French, *karaoke* from Japanese, *zeitgeist* and *kindergarten* from German, *avatar* from Sanskrit, *spaghetti* from Italian. New words and phrases are constantly being invented to capture new phenomena, while existing words take on new meanings; such as *friend*, *tweet* and *spam* in the context of social media. Sometimes we invent new words, and at other times we repurpose existing words and use them in new ways. Over time some words take on new meanings while others fall from use. The evolution of the internet has produced a raft of new words, such as *blog*, *wiki*, *trolling* and *flaming*, to name a few. In the context of social media, the word *friend* has a secondary meaning, as does the word *virus* in the context of problems that may occur when we use a computer connected to the internet. In all of these examples, the context shapes how each word is used and understood.

| Exhibit 2.1 | Athletes often wrap themselves in their national flag to symbolise their national pride |

Fairfax Photos/Craig Golding/SMH

Meanings are in people, not in words

As we discussed in Chapter 1, meanings do not exist in isolation from those who use the words. **Meaning** can change from one context to another, one moment to another, and from one speaker or writer (i.e., sender) to another. In other words, the meaning of a word lies in how the sender uses a word and how a receiver makes sense of the symbol or sound. This, in turn, can be shaped by the context in which a word is used, and perhaps by the sender's and receiver's individual experiences, education, culture, attitudes and biases and familiarity with the topic.

Meaning
In language, occurs when those in the communication process interpret a symbol.

Words create and label experience

Words give us the tools to create, understand and communicate about our world by naming and labelling what we experience. According to Hodge and Kress (1979, p. 5), 'whatever has a name can become familiar, and is easier to classify and remember'.

Words are powerful and can fix and shape perceptions of people, events and experiences, and evoke emotions, both positively and negatively. Consider how our language around mental illness and disability has evolved in recent decades. In the not so recent past, people who suffered from mental health issues of any sort were broadly labelled 'hysterical', 'lunatics', 'insane', 'demented' and 'moronic'. These labels both shaped and reflected narrow and negative understandings and views of mental illness, lumping what we now know as a complex series of conditions into one broad category, with largely negative connotations. We will discuss this more in the later section on non-discriminatory language.

Language is culture bound

As many travellers have discovered, the same word can have different meanings in different cultures. Also, translation research has shown that there are words in some languages that do not have English equivalents. While we will discuss culture and its broader significance to professional communication in more detail in Chapter 4, the place of language in how culture impacts, shapes and determines an

Worldview
'A collection of attitudes, values, stories and expectations about the world around us which shape and inform our actions. It can be expressed and informed by ethics, religion, philosophy, scientific beliefs etc.' (Gray, 2011).

Context
The environment or situation (physical, historical or psychological) within which the sender, receiver and message is encoded and decoded.

individual's **worldview** is significant. According to Guy Deutscher (2010, p. 1), 'a nation's language ... reflects its culture, psyche, [identity] and modes of thought'.

American ethno-linguists Edward Sapir and Benjamin Whorf noted that in different cultures there exist several words for key concepts that do not have parallel translations in other languages. They proposed what became known as the Sapir-Whorf hypothesis (Sapir, 1929; Whorf, 2012), arguing that language evolves to reflect the culture in which it is used, and that the linguistic choices, in part, determine a particular culture's ways of thinking and what is actually observed in nature.

While we discuss this in more detail in Chapter 4, English as spoken in the US versus Australia and the UK offers many examples. For example, in the US, deep-fried, thinly sliced potatoes are called *fries*, while in Australia and the UK they are called *chips*. Australians and the British walk on the *pavement* or *footpath,* put *petrol* in their car and load their groceries into the *boot.* In contrast, Americans walk on the *sidewalk,* put *gasoline* in their car, and load their groceries into the *trunk.*

Language is context bound

The meanings that people attach to particular words or phrases are also greatly influenced by the context in which they are used. **Context** refers to the other words or information that surround communication and that may shape or impact how they are interpreted. These might include the items shown in **Exhibit 2.2**.

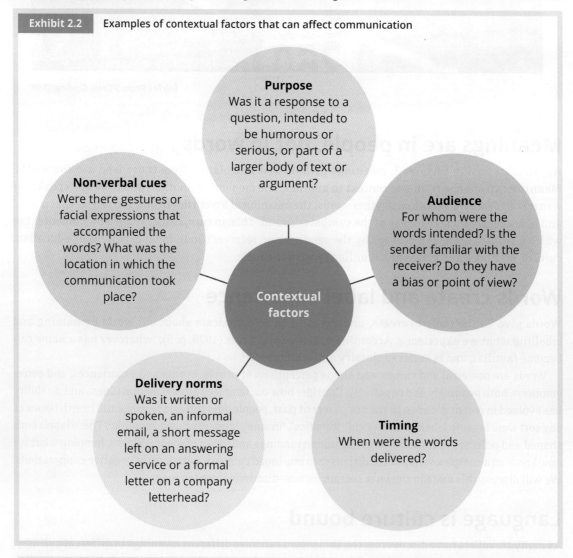

Exhibit 2.2   Examples of contextual factors that can affect communication

Purpose
Was it a response to a question, intended to be humorous or serious, or part of a larger body of text or argument?

Audience
For whom were the words intended? Is the sender familiar with the receiver? Do they have a bias or point of view?

Non-verbal cues
Were there gestures or facial expressions that accompanied the words? What was the location in which the communication took place?

Contextual factors

Delivery norms
Was it written or spoken, an informal email, a short message left on an answering service or a formal letter on a company letterhead?

Timing
When were the words delivered?

Reflection question: Can you think of examples of words where the meanings may differ depending on the context, the audience or culture?

Language and meaning

It is no exaggeration to say that *meaning* is an elusive concept that can change from one user to the next, and from one context to another. Think of the variety of meanings the verb *means* itself can have. It is more slippery even than the word *communicate*. But as you can see in **Exhibit 2.3**, perhaps we could classify most uses of the verb *means* as 'designates', 'signifies', 'indicates' or 'expresses'.

Exhibit 2.3	Different meanings of the word *means*
Expression	**Meaning**
Sodium chloride *means* 'salt'	Sodium chloride denotes 'the same substance as' or 'is a word more or less synonymous with' salt
Brenda *means* mischief	Brenda 'intends to cause' mischief
Bill *means* the University of Technology	Bill 'is referring to' the University of Technology
Mozart *has no meaning* for me	Listening to Mozart's music 'arouses no specific emotion' in me
Life *has no meaning* for me now	Life 'has no interest or purpose' for me now
I *mean* what I say	I 'am determined to do' what I say
I know what I *mean* but I can't think how to say it	I know what I 'intend to convey' but I can't think how to say it
In Spanish 'espejo' *means* 'mirror'	In Spanish, 'espejo 'translates as' or 'is the equivalent of' mirror

The problem with all these approaches to meaning is that most meanings of a communicated message differ between the source or sender and the receiver or destination. Not only do senders and receivers often miss each other's meanings, meaning is so complex and difficult to pin down that there is no perfect fit between our private experience (our *intrapersonal* communication) and our linguistic expression of it to others (our *interpersonal* communication). In this section, we'll discuss some linguistic concepts that can affect meaning, including denotation, connotation, euphemisms and doublespeak. We'll also look at how language can be used to persuade or convey personal perspectives of reality.

Denotation and connotation

English is rich in synonyms; that is, words similar in meaning to each other. Words have both denotative and connotative meanings. **Denotation** is the literal or straightforward meanings of a word. Denoting is pointing. It is meant to be objective and unemotional; for example, 'keep left', 'if there is a fire do not use the lift', 'disabled parking only', 'see you at the pub at 6 p.m.'. Denotation is using a word literally, as when we point at a dog and say, 'That is a dog'. In contrast, **connotation** is the subjective meaning we give to a word, a meaning or meanings that may depend on our emotions or attitudes, our culture, our age group, our profession or our personal memories. Connotations can be positive if they enhance the reader's attitude to the topic, or negative if they diminish this attitude.

A word may have both denotative and connotative meanings. For example, *greasy* is a word that might denote a well-oiled car engine, but it contains negative connotations if applied to food containing a lot of fat that is bad for your health or to a person who is believed to be deliberately insincere. The denotation of the term *politics* are the activities of people who represent electorates in parliament and help to run a democratic nation. But what if it is used in the following way: 'If the minor parties would only stop playing politics with this bill, we might get some important legislation through'? Here, *politics* has a different connotation, implying the use of power plays, deceit, special pleading and intimidation. In addition to having different denotative and connotative meanings, words can also have positive and negative connotations, as shown in **Exhibit 2.4**.

Denotation
The literal or straightforward meanings of a word.

Connotation
A subjective meaning of a word, that may depend on individual emotions or attitudes, culture, age, experiences or profession.

Exhibit 2.4	Examples of positive and negative connotations		

Example of word use	Positive connotation	Negative connotation
Grandpa is *thrifty*	spends money wisely	cheap, a tightwad
Jan is *strong-willed*	determined	stubborn, obstinate
She is tall and *slender*	slim	skinny, anorexic
John is *mature*	experienced	old, doddery
Liz has a healthy *self-esteem*	confident of abilities	conceited, arrogant
Mark is a *private* person	self-contained, quiet	secretive, introverted
Guy is *fussy*	particular, attentive to detail	obsessive, controlling

It is important to be aware of the differences between denotation and connotation when writing. For example, if you wanted to avoid inflaming a sensitive situation when writing a staff email, you would need to choose your words carefully. Equally, it is important to be aware of the possible intended purpose of word choice when reading or listening to emotionally charged statements. For example, if a newspaper uses strongly connotative words in its headlines, this is a signal that the publication is politically aligned, either to the left or the right. While we will discuss these strategies in our chapters on professional writing, consider Case study 2.1.

CASE STUDY 2.1   A shutdown, a lockout or industrial action: when is a 'strike' a 'strike'?

In February 2022, the selective choice of the emotive word 'strike' caused considerable staff and reader backlash against the editor of the *Sydney Morning Herald* (SMH) when he insisted on using the word in a headline reporting a planned industrial action by Sydney rail unions.

The background is that the NSW rail union had planned a limited industrial action to progress a log of claims with the state government. On the day of the planned action, the minister in charge called for the entire network to be shut down at short notice, leaving workers who had turned up for work locked out, and resulting in chaos for commuters.

In his Twitter feed, the *SMH* editor wrote: 'Sydney hit by snap train strike ... 'This is industrial bastardry of the worst form', quoting the NSW Employee Relations Minister (but not referencing him in his tweet).

What follows are excerpts of a report by rival publication the *Daily Telegraph* on the fallout.

Sydney Morning Herald editor versus staff over use of the word 'strike'

The backlash on Twitter was swift and came not just from the general public but also from current and former Nine staffers.

...

'This is NOT a Sydney strike', responded one of over a thousand primarily angry respondents.

...

Regular SMH columnist Jenna Price concurred on her Twitter site: 'Can someone explain to me why the stopped trains are being described as a strike? Isn't it a lockout? Why is the RTB Union being blamed?'

...

In an internal workplace chat that followed his strike tweet, four of [the editor's] staff rejected his advice and usage of the term 'strike'.

Having pluckily explained to her boss prior to his tweet that the action was 'not technically a strike', breaking news reporter Sarah McPhee was put in her place by [the editor]: 'It's a strike,' he said ...

Hours later McPhee pushed back: 'I would be leaning towards using shutdown', she wrote. Transport reporter Tom Rabe said he preferred the term 'industrial action'. Sydney editor Michael Koziol added he was also anti 'strike': 'my support for "shutdown" over strike'.

Source: Adapted from A. Sharp (2022, February 27). *Sydney Morning Herald editor v staff over use of the word 'strike'. Daily Telegraph.*

Discussion

1   List the different connotations of the various words for 'industrial action' being debated among the *Sydney Morning Herald* journalists: 'strike', 'shutdown', and 'lock out'.

2 How might the choice of any of these, especially in a newspaper headline, impact how readers react or interpret the message?

3 Can you think of other examples in news reporting where particular words or descriptors are used to deliberately 'frame' a news story either positively or negatively?

4 The account above was published in a rival news outlet and written by a 'gossip' columnist. How might that have impacted the language used in the article?

After you have discussed this case study, refer to the 'Comments on case studies' section at the end of the text.

Euphemism

Our discussion of denotation and connotation leads us to **euphemisms**, another area of language usage that is important to understand in professional communication. A *euphemism* is a non-offensive or indirect word that is used to cover other words that may be considered offensive, brutal or painful. They are commonly used by journalists, medical practitioners, lawyers and counsellors, all of whom have to write and speak about subjects that society regards as distasteful or taboo, such as body parts and functions, sex, lust, anger, drunkenness and murder.

Allan and Burridge (2006, p. 39) describe euphemisms as 'linguistic fig leaves' and argue that they serve numerous functions. To spare the feelings of relatives, we speak of someone 'passing away' rather than 'dying'. Wealthy people might be soothed to hear of the 'economically non-affluent' rather than 'the poor'. Company directors may wish to report to their shareholders that the company has suffered a 'negative cash flow' rather than 'a loss of profits'.

If your child's teacher writes 'Michael is experiencing difficulties in paying attention to new concepts in the classroom and is not always conscious of the needs of less able members of the class', you might privately translate the report as, 'I'm being told Michael is lazy and a bit of a bully'. Or if they write 'April needs to seek opportunities elsewhere', you are possibly being told, 'April is a wasting her time at school and would be better off leaving and getting a job'.

Disguising contentious, controversial, anti-social or taboo activities by euphemism is a common strategy. In Australia, a case in point is the long running debate around 'euthanasia' or 'voluntary assisted dying', as discussed in Case study 2.2.

> **Euphemism**
> A non-offensive or indirect word that is used to cover other words that may be considered offensive, brutal or painful.

 CASE STUDY 2.2 The contested language of the euthanasia debate

Read the following commentary from a *Sydney Morning Herald* article and consider how the different terms have impacted attempts to legislate for assisted dying.

Language as a battlefield: How we got from euthanasia to voluntary assisted dying

Right to die, euthanasia, dying with dignity, assisted suicide: the language around this debate is enormously loaded, and shapes the way we feel about it.

As a society, we are hesitant to talk about death, which is considered a taboo subject ... If it were a train, this debate would have set off from Euthanasia Central, stopped at Voluntary Euthanasia and Assisted Suicide, moved on to Medically Assisted Death and Assisted Dying, before arriving at Voluntary Assisted Dying, the form of words that our parliamentarians have settled on (and which some would further reduce to the neutral acronym VAD).

...

[When fact-checking] claims ... that 80 per cent of Australians 'support euthanasia laws', that support varies significantly depending on how the question is framed, and what language is used. Use the word 'suicide', for instance, and support plummets.

...

In Australia, this ethical battleground is still colloquially referred to as 'the euthanasia debate', but you will rarely hear the major proponents of 'the right to choose to die' invoke that phrase. That's because euthanasia is sometimes considered to be a negative word, despite its neutral origins ... They frame euthanasia as something done to someone by someone else (a doctor, a family member). And that something is killing, which most religious and moral codes strictly forbid.

...

There is ... significant social stigma attached to the term 'suicide' [according to a government report].

'For this reason ... "assisted suicide" is not an appropriate term.' Suicide, they argue, connotes a violent death, usually carried out by someone suffering from depression or a mental illness that might feasibly have been treated. By contrast, 'voluntary assisted dying' is about a decision made by a terminally ill person in full command of their mental faculties. 'It's not about someone choosing to end their life because they want to end their life,' as prominent supporter Andrew Denton puts it. 'It's about someone who is already dying choosing to end their suffering.'

Discussion

1 Consider how different terms for *euthanasia* may have shifted support for the voluntary assisted dying legislation? Why do you think this has occurred?

2 What are some examples of the arguments for adoption of the different terms?

3 In linguistics, this choice of particular euphemistic language is referred to as *framing*. How is this debate an example of the power of language to shape attitudes? Can you think of other examples?

After you have discussed this case study, refer to the 'Comments on case studies' section at the end of the text.

Doublespeak

Doublespeak
A term given to words, phrases or euphemisms deliberately designed to obscure, distort or distract reactions to an unpalatable, uncomfortable idea, action or concept.

Doublespeak is a term given to phrases or euphemisms deliberately designed to obscure, distort or distract understanding of, or reaction to, an unpalatable action, idea or concept. For example, it has often been used to hide horrendous crimes against human rights and life. The term implies hypocrisy – we are hiding the atrocities by using polite or vague phrases. No-one has written more powerfully about doublespeak than George Orwell (1946/1968, p. 362):

> In our time [1946], political speech and writing are largely the defence of the indefensible. Things like ... the dropping of the atom bombs on Japan, can indeed be defended, but only by arguments which are too brutal for most people to face, and which do not square with the professed aims of political parties. Thus, political language has to consist largely of euphemism, question-begging and sheer cloudy vagueness. Defenceless villages are bombarded from the air, the inhabitants driven out into the countryside, the cattle machine-gunned, the huts set on fire with incendiary bullets: this is called *pacification*. Millions of peasants are robbed of their farms and sent trudging along the roads with no more than they can carry: this is called *transfer of population* or *rectification of frontiers*. People are imprisoned for years without trial, or shot in the back of the neck or sent to die of scurvy in Arctic lumber camps: this is called *elimination of undesirable elements*.
>
> Source: Orwell, G. (1946/1968). Politics and the English language. In *Collected essays*. Secker & Warburg.

Orwell wrote that paragraph over 70 years ago, yet doublespeak continues undiminished. Perhaps the most chilling example in recent times has been the term *ethnic cleansing*. This term was used in the 1990s Bosnian war to convey the notion of purifying a society by forcibly removing and massacring people whose religion and race did not suit those with power – in other words, committing *genocide*.

 CASE STUDY 2.3   Warspeak

For decades, major global and regional powers have waged war against those they accuse of fighting immorally – that is, those who use terrorism to harm civilians at home and abroad. Paradoxically, these righteous 'wars on terror' are being fought in an era in which the distinction between war waged only against soldiers, and war against soldiers as well as civilians has virtually collapsed ...

...

The discourse of 'warspeak' has also been used to sanitise the destructive power of cluster munitions. For the US public and media, the terminology 'collateral damage' effectively masks the death and destruction of cluster munitions to civilian life. Within US military and corporate circles, the approved 'techno-speak' for cluster munitions starts with 'soft-targets' – a euphemism for human bodies – and ends with 'explosive remnants of war' or unexploded ordnance, meaning hazardous munitions remaining on or in the ground that, with the slightest disturbance, kill or maim civilians. Cluster munitions are delivered by 'strike packages', 'platforms', and 'weapons systems' (aircraft). Aircraft do not launch munitions but fly 'sorties', provide 'air support', 'visit a site', and do 'kinetic targeting.' They drop 'force packages', 'ordnance', and 'antipersonnel devices', often in a 'routine limited-duration protective reaction' (air raid), causing an 'airburst' (warhead or cluster munitions set to explode above the ground to maximize effect). 'Incontinent ordnance delivery' means that a bomb missed its target and may have caused 'collateral damage' or 'regrettable by-products' (civilian casualties). 'Assets' (targets) are not destroyed but 'visited', 'acquired', 'taken out', 'serviced', or 'suppressed.' Cluster munitions do not kill, they 'eliminate', 'neutralize', 'degrade', 'hurt', 'smoke', 'blow away', 'suppress', 'impact', 'cleanse', 'attrit', or 'terminate with extreme prejudice.'

...

According to warspeak advocates, cluster munitions are essential in 'precision bombing' to win 'clean', 'high-tech', or 'robo' wars. Yes, air war enthusiasts admit, 'accidents' do happen, missiles 'go astray', but then 'war is hell', 'a dirty business'. Cluster munitions are 'nasty' but necessary weapons ...

From B. Grosscup (2011, April). Cluster munitions and state terrorism. *The Monthly Review*, 62(11).

Discussion

1 Discuss some of the examples of warspeak given in the article. Why do governments and military organisations need to use warspeak to describe the tactics and strategies of war?

2 Do you agree that the use of warspeak is a way of distancing the military and governments from the reality of the impact on civilian populations of weapons such as cluster bombs and unmanned drones?

3 How do other related phrases and titles coined in recent years such as 'coalition of the willing', 'war on terror', and 'regime change' work to construct the way the broader public understand their meaning?

After you have discussed this case study, refer to the 'Comments on case studies' section at the end of the text.

Reflection question: How does euphemism differ from doublespeak?

Using language persuasively

Connotations do not have to be avoided in your persuasive writing, but they should be used consciously and intentionally. We might say that every time we write or speak, we are seeking to impose our version of the world and our reality on our respondents. The problem is that some words are supposedly being used to denote objective facts when instead they are used to dodge reality and avoid accusations or value judgements. That is, words are often presented as though they are denotations when they are actually heavily connotative.

A continuing debate in Australia is over the treatment of asylum seekers, also referred to as *illegal immigrants*, *queue jumpers* or *boat people*. Someone's choice of terminology can reveal their attitude to the people concerned as either positive or negative. The term *asylum seekers* has a positive connotation suggesting distress and the need for compassion. *Illegal immigrants* has a negative connotation that implies unruly incursions by possibly dangerous elements. *Queue jumpers* implies that people are unfairly usurping others who are waiting in an orderly manner for their asylum claims to be processed. *Boat people* is a more neutral term with elements of denotation (describing the way in which the people have arrived), and also connotation (indicating that these people are possibly part of an unofficial invasion and need to be controlled, if not turned back).

Often words are taken out of one discourse, say that of computing or physical science, and applied in a general business or social discourse. Some examples include *a higher profile*, a *spectrum of views*, *downshifting*, *outsourcing*, *mainstreaming*, *interactive*, *targeted*. Often the desire behind the use of this language is to suggest that ideas are objective and scientific. To say 'our downsizing strategies will focus on the age context' may seem more scientific than 'we are dismissing several of our older workers'. Also, using the latter phrase would remind the reader of the human aspects of the action and the consequences for those who have lost their jobs and for their families.

Consider the example of language use in the ongoing debate over Australia's policy response to the threat of human-induced climate change discussed in Case study 2.4.

💬 CASE STUDY 2.4 Fear of a burning planet: the semantics of climate change

Shutterstock.com/JP Phillippe

The war of words over climate change during the last decade or so, is indicative of how important language choices are to marshalling public opinion. In May 2019, for example, *The Guardian* announced that it was changing its inhouse style guide to recommend that 'climate emergency', 'global heating' and 'climate crisis' be used as opposed to the rather passive 'climate change' (Carrington, 2019). In Australia, much of the politics of climate change policy has been played out via the choice of particular key words or phrases: 'carbon tax' versus 'carbon price' for example. Consider this summary of the language debate.

Fear of a burning planet: the semantics of climate change

Language has always been central to the politics of climate change. In the past few months, a number of local, state and national governments have declared a 'climate emergency'. At the same time, governments … have frequently used language to downplay the state of the planet or water down reports.

Once upon a time, we all talked about 'global warming'. In the late 1980s, as consensus began to crystallise around the reality of a heating planet, global warming became the dominant term scientists used to explain what was happening. …

While climate change is still the dominant term, there's plenty of debate around whether it is the most useful. Scientists are divided. Some like 'anthropogenic' or 'human-induced', others favour 'climate disruption'.

There's now a growing linguistic tide turning in favour of terms like 'climate crisis', proponents of which argue is necessary to cut through stagnant politics and reinforce just how urgently action is needed to stop the world from burning …

…

On the flip side, some are worried that even climate change has become a far too toxic, partisan term … arguing it was overly politicised at a time when consensus was desperately needed.

Language has also been central to governmental efforts to fortify inaction … In Australia, that would be watering down language, to muzzling reports [about the impact on the Great Barrier Reef] or just not mentioning climate at all.

…

Australia's semantics of denial puts it more in line with the [former] Trump administration. Since 2017 the US administration has removed a quarter of all references to climate change from government websites. The Department of Energy started calling fossil fuels 'molecules of freedom' …

As the climate crisis worsens, the battle to control the narrative is only going to intensify. But that battle is as much linguistic as political.

From K. Napier-Raman (2019, August 16). Fear of a burning planet: The semantics of climate change. Crikey.com.

Discussion

This article discusses the way in which different sides of a debate use certain words or phrases, with positive and negative connotations, to frame and argue their points of view. How effective are these strategies? Does it matter which words we use?

After you have discussed this case study, refer to the 'Comments on case studies' section at the end of the text.

Language and 'reality'

> 'When *I* use a word,' Humpty Dumpty said in rather a scornful tone, 'it means just what I choose it to mean – neither more nor less.'
> 'The question is,' said Alice, 'whether you *can* make words mean so many different things.'
> 'The question is,' said Humpty Dumpty, 'which is to be master – that's all.'
>
> Source: Carroll (1871/2010)

We've argued that meanings do not exist in the *words* but rather in the *minds* of the senders and receivers of a communication exchange. It is important, therefore, for those senders and receivers to understand the impact of their personal perspectives on how they interpret and use language. In the introduction to his book *The New Doublespeak*, Bill Lutz (1996) puts it like this:

> ... something happens when we perceive reality and then interpret that reality by means of language. And that's what we do with language: interpret reality as we, each one of us, see and experience reality. Thus, the language each of us uses is not reality but a representation of reality, a personal interpretation of the world as we know it. In this sense distortion is inherent in the very act of using language ... It is precisely because each of us sees and experiences the world differently that language becomes our most important means for coming to some kind of agreement on our individual experiences, on how we see the world.
>
> Source: Lutz (1996), p. 7

So, while there's no arguing that reality exists 'out there' – we all see rain on the window or cars on the highway – the words that we choose to describe that reality will both reflect how we experience these phenomena and also how we wish others to see it.

What's in a name?

Differing versions of reality can sometimes be a problem of labelling, as Lutz illustrates:

> I like my coffee hot; my wife says my coffee is scalding. I say the handle of the pot is too hot to touch; my wife grabs it with her bare hand. I say the shirt is red; my wife says it is orange. I say the car is small; the salesman calls it mid-sized. What passes for a mountain in the Midwest is called a foothill in the West.
>
> Source: Lutz (1996), p. 9

In addition, the extent to which our word choice is a deliberate and conscious act is also a matter of debate. Hodge and Kress (1979) note that naming or labelling a phenomenon can have the effect of shaping how we think about that phenomenon. Naming leads to familiarity with, and easier classification and memory of, what is named, and 'only what has a name can be shared'. So, labelling *asylum seekers* as *boat people*, *illegal immigrants* or *queue jumpers*, may very well have the effect of corralling the way in which many people think about them and about the issue. Hodge and Kress go on to say:

> Language fixes a world that is so much more stable and coherent than what we actually see that it takes its place in our consciousness and becomes what we think we have seen. And since normal perception works by constant feedback, the gap between the real world and the socially constructed world is constantly being reduced, so that what we do 'see' tends to become what we say.
>
> Source: Hodge & Kress (1979), p. 5

Metaphors

In a similar vein, Lakoff and Johnson (1980) argue that our 'reality' can also be influenced by the **metaphors** we use, and that these metaphors help structure the way we interpret our experiences. They use the example of the metaphor of *time* as a *resource*, and this is exemplified by a range of expressions that we use when describing time in our lives.

Metaphor
A metaphor is a figure of speech that describes an object or action in a way that isn't literally true but helps explain an idea or make a comparison.

You're *wasting* my time.
This gadget will *save* you hours.
I don't *have* the time *to give* you.
How do you *spend* your time these days?
That flat tyre *cost me* an hour.
Is that *worth* your while?

Source: Lakoff & Johnson (1980), p. 8

They point out that this way of thinking about and *talking* about time reflects the way that the concept of work has developed since the Industrial Revolution. It reflects our economic system, which measures concepts such as *productivity* and *value* according to how long it takes to do things because we are paid by the hour, a cost which is subsequently passed on to the consumer.

This way of thinking about time is by no means universal to all cultures (see Hall, 1959), and is relatively recent in the scale of human existence. However, in Western industrialised society it is all-pervasive, and because we conceive of time as a limited resource and associate it with an economic value system, the language we use both reflects and largely controls this. Thus, we understand and experience time as the kind of thing that can be spent, wasted, budgeted, invested wisely or poorly, saved or squandered. In fact, because our lives are so governed by our economic system, it is difficult *not* to think of time in this way. We will discuss this further in Chapter 4 in relation to how this is impacted by our culture.

Reflection question: To what extent do you agree that language and thought are closely connected, as argued by Sapir and Whorf? If we don't have words, can we conceptualise new concepts?

Speaking versus writing: same language, different rules

The most important aspect of these characteristics is that the language used may operate differently because of the different modes in which it is used, as well as the different ways listeners and readers cognitively process spoken versus written language. While we will expand on these in our later chapters on oral presentations, verbal reports and interviews (Chapter 10) and professional writing techniques (Chapter 11), **Exhibit 2.5** summarises some of these differences.

Exhibit 2.5	Differences between written and spoken language	
Characteristic	**Spoken language**	**Written language**
Universality	Everyone can speak	Problems with literacy may exclude some individuals or groups
Permanence	Unless recorded, speech is ephemeral and transient	Writing allows for repeated reading to aid understanding
Availability of feedback	Audience can offer immediate feedback and so speakers can rephrase and adapt to their needs	Audience is unseen and, in the absence of immediate feedback, writers must minimise vagueness and ambiguity
Complexity	Speakers tend to use phrases rather than full sentences	Requires greater skill, more careful organisation, and compact and structured expressions to be effective
Formality	Likely to use more informal, including colloquial, language and less rigid constructions	Likely to be more formal
Non-verbal cues	Repetition, intonation and other paralinguistic cues help listeners	Sentences, paragraphs, punctuation are visual cues that aid readers

Reflection question: What are some of the differences that you note when you are speaking to a work colleague compared to writing them an email?

Language and discourse

Spender (1994) says it is through language that we become members of a human community; although, she might have said 'of a number of human communities'. In politics and professional work, word meanings are incorporated into speeches, conversations, meetings, seminars, reports and submissions, press releases, feature articles, debates and editorials. These we classify as **discourses**; that is complete spoken and/or written texts created *within social and cultural contexts*.

Discourse is a tricky concept and has been defined in a number of ways. Motion and Leitch (2008), for example, observe that, at its simplest level, discourse is a collection of statements that construct our sense of reality. In a more sophisticated sense, influential French philosopher Michel Foucault (1969/2002) argued that language does more than merely carry meaning and knowledge, it also has a role in the creation and maintenance of power. Along these lines, discourse was further defined by du Gay (1996) as:

> ... a group of statements which provide a language for talking about a topic and a way of producing a particular kind of knowledge about a topic. Thus the term refers both to the production of knowledge through language and representations and the way that knowledge is institutionalised, shaping social practices and setting new practices into play.
>
> Source: du Gay (1996), p. 43

Discourse
A group of statements that provide a language for talking about a topic and a way of producing a particular kind of knowledge about a topic.

Therefore, the way we talk about things, the word choices, the metaphors, the euphemisms, and so on, that make up our language, can serve a strategic purpose; that is, encourage people to think about things in a certain way – as well as provide a mechanism to constrain argument and thought. The earlier case studies on the evolving discourses of climate change and euthanasia are examples of this in practice.

Discourse can be classified under many headings, including political, religious, educational, sporting or academic. We all inherit a number of these discourses. A devout Christian politician might make election speeches borrowing from religious rhetoric and containing moral appeals. An ex-military officer working in human resource management might use terms from military discourse, such as *reinforcement*, *risk management*, *attrition rates* or *liaison with hostile elements*. This tendency to mix discourses is called *contestation* and is common to all of us. By listening closely to the speeches of a politician, you might be able to detect the mixture of discourses that 'construct' the person in his or her public sphere.

Generally, language relates to specific audiences or readers and specific settings or contexts. When you write or speak about an aspect of your profession in a sales address, a project proposal, a radio talk or a television documentary program, your discourse is shaped by the concepts and, therefore, the vocabulary of your profession, as well as the needs, levels of understanding and expectations of your receiver. However, in recent years, academics have noted what eminent UK linguistics professor Norman Fairclough (1992) refers to as a 'weakening of the boundaries' between traditional discourses and those of marketing and management. He says that there has been:

> an upsurge in the extension of the market to new areas of social life: sectors such as education, health care and the arts have been required to restructure and reconceptualise their activities as the production and marketing of commodities for consumers.
>
> Source: Fairclough (1992), p. 6

The impact of this is that in many quite different contexts, we now hear the language of the market and of management. Australian writer and academic Don Watson (2003) has been highly critical of the impact of this contestation on public language, describing it as a 'decay'. He argues that:

> the curse has spread through the pursuit of business models in places that were never businesses ... [universities, libraries, galleries, museums, welfare agencies and all levels of government] speak of *focusing on the delivery of outputs* and matching decisions to *strategic initiatives* ... In an education curriculum or the mission statement of a fast food chain you will hear the same phrases. Military leaders while actually conducting wars sound like marketing gurus, and politicians sound like both of them. If one day in the finance pages you encounter *critical deliverables*, do not be surprised if it turns up the next day when you're listening to the football.
>
> Source: Watson (2003), pp. 13–14

It is this type of language to which Watson was referring in the article that opened this chapter.

Writers and speakers, therefore, will often choose a particular discourse, or mixture of discourses, depending on their audience and their rhetorical or persuasive purpose. Imagine a member of parliament summing up his reasons for asking you to vote for him at the coming election:

> Ladies and gentlemen, you can see the government is on a sticky wicket when it asks you to trust it with another term. Nothing that this treasurer has said or done since he took office offers the average fair-dinkum bloke in the street a fair go! And Australians want a fair go! A fair go for their womenfolk, for their kids and for their future. This is the greatest country on Earth, and we have made it that way. With God's help, we'll keep it that way, and I know He'll guide us wisely when election day comes.

In this piece of fictional rhetoric, the speaker is mixing a number of discourses, perhaps in an attempt to appeal to different groups in the electorate. The cricketing metaphor that introduces the discussion is a male-oriented reference and so it is an example of both sporting and sexist discourse (the term 'their womenfolk' is the most overt use of sexist discourse). The reference to a 'fair go' for the 'fair-dinkum bloke' appeals to perceived Australian virtues of egalitarianism and mateship. The same politician would want to be televised holding up a glass of beer in a public bar – whether he drinks it or not. This is the discourse of *populism*, which extols the virtues of the normal and the ordinary, and despises the 'elite'. This is the extreme appeal to patriotism that takes the form of asserting the superiority of one's country over all others. It is often, as here, linked with the discourse of *misogyny* or hatred of women. Finally, the politician uses the discourse of religion, colonising it, you might say, to support his emotional appeal.

> **Reflection question:** Is there a discourse or way of speaking/writing that is particular to your profession? Does your profession use obscure terms and titles that outsiders find difficult to understand? If so, how does this help those in your profession to communicate?

New words for new meanings

Modern life and technology continue to throw up new words to denote new ideas, relationships, jobs and inventions. Consider some of the terms used in computing that did not exist 20 years ago because the technology they refer to was not yet available. Terms like *flame wars*, *net surfing*, *emoticon* and *encryption* come to mind.

Recent additions to the *Macquarie Dictionary* (2023) include the following new words, some of which reflect changes in modern communications:

- *Cancel culture:* the attitudes within a community that call for or bring about the withdrawal of support from a public figure, usually in response to an accusation of a socially unacceptable action or comment.
- *Eco-anxiety:* feelings of distress and fear brought on by the effects of climate change
- *Woke:* aware of and actively attentive to important facts and issues (especially issues of racial and social justice). Has also been co-opted as a slur.
- *Virtue signalling:* the action or practice of publicly expressing opinions or sentiments intended to demonstrate one's good character or the moral correctness of one's position on a particular issue. As with 'woke', has been used as a slur.
- *Crowdfunding:* the practice of obtaining needed services, ideas or content from a large group of people, especially the online community, rather than traditional financiers such as banks or government grants.
- *Gig worker:* a person who works temporary jobs typically in the service sector as an independent contractor or freelancer rather than in a regular salaried position.

From pop culture comes:

- *Cougar:* a middle-aged woman seeking a romantic relationship with a younger man.
- *Bromance:* a close, non-sexual friendship between men.

And the following two reflect the changing nature of parent–child relationships:

- *Helicopter parent:* a parent who is overly involved in the life of his or her child.
- *Boomerang child:* a young adult who returns to live at his or her family home, especially for financial reasons.
- *Bank of mum and dad:* parents who lend adult children money to fund property purchases.

Source: Macquarie Dictionary (2023)

It is difficult to predict the lifespan of a word. Perhaps some disappear because they are no longer needed to describe a thing or procedure that has itself disappeared. Others, like *radar*, become well embedded in the language and even extend their original meanings.

Technical terminology, jargon and buzzwords

The terms *technical terminology* and *jargon* overlap in meaning. Both refer to a restricted use of language by a professional, administrative, trade, religious or social group. The former, however, consists of terms that have exact denotations and positive connotations. **Jargon** may have the same meanings but often involves incomprehensible, longwinded statements meant to make the speaker or writer seem important and eminent, or that are determined to hide rather than divulge information. **Buzzwords** are similar to jargon but are used because they are fashionable. They begin to be used and repeated, almost subconsciously, within corporate and political meeting rooms, then tend to spread into the broader public discourse with little thought to either their effect or what they actually mean. Recent examples include *new normal, synergy, unprecedented, let's take this offline, pivot* and *low hanging fruit.*

Chapter 11 discusses the importance of clarity and simplicity in writing and in using language that your readers will understand and relate to. While this is often taken to imply that we should not use technical terminology and jargon, it is not necessarily true. Kenneth Hudson (1978) distinguishes between the two:

> Every profession necessarily has its own terminology, without which its members cannot think or express themselves. To deprive them of such words would be to condemn them to inactivity. If one wished to kill a profession, to remove its cohesion and strength, the most effective way would be to forbid the use of its characteristic language. On the other hand, there are people, possibly many people, whose supposedly technical language does not stand up to close examination. It is bogus, existing only to impress the innocent and unwary, and interfering with the process of communication instead of improving it.
>
> Source: Hudson (1978), p. 1

In deciding whether professionals are using language to exclude the public from their 'secrets' and hence protect their control of information, one test is to ask whether a particular term can be expressed in a simple, direct, familiar way without distorting its meaning. Another is to ask whether the term helps to interpret a wide range of activities and technical initiatives that call for new terms or even new metaphors. Information technology regularly borrows and repurposes words and creates new technical terms. Terms such as *virus, bookmark, address, mouse, crash, homepage* and *icon* would be familiar to most computer users, or even non-users.

This distinction between technical terminology and jargon is important because if jargon is language designed to exclude non-experts, it can lead to obscurity and subterfuge, and deliberate miscommunication, even within the profession. Consider the impact of medical jargon on the public health communication challenges during the early stages of the COVID-19 pandemic, discussed in Case study 2.5.

Jargon
Communications that involve incomprehensible, longwinded statements meant to make the speaker or writer seem important and eminent, or that are determined to hide rather than divulge information.

Buzzwords
Communications that are similar to jargon but are used because they are fashionable. They begin to be used and repeated, almost subconsciously, within corporate and political meeting rooms, then tend to spread into the broader public discourse.

CASE STUDY 2.5   Medical jargon and the COVID-19 pandemic

During the COVID-19 pandemic, the need for the use of plain language regarding health messaging became obvious as governments and health professionals attempted to explain complex medical phenomena, often resorting to jargon terms. The following excerpts come from an article on this topic written at the start of the pandemic, in February 2020.

Why health officials need to speak plainly on the COVID-19 virus

Between plain English and medical jargon, doctors tend to use the latter, part of their second nature developed through years of training. But in times of public health crises, such as the 2019 Novel Coronavirus … speaking plainly can spell the difference between panic and calm. Or worse, life and death.

…

The US-based Center for Disease Control and Prevention has a 42-page document listing 'frequently used terms in public health materials and their common, everyday alternatives in plain language sentences'. The primer cites how 'incubation period' can be communicated more plainly … Instead of just using the term, health workers can say that after the virus enters a person's body, 'it takes from two to 14 days for that person to show the first signs of being sick'. Infectious diseases can also be translated simply as 'sicknesses caused by germs', the CDC primer said.

A 22 January WHO report said that four of the five patients who died of the novel coronavirus at that time had 'underlying comorbidities', a medical jargon also commonly used by health officials during press conferences. Simply put, those who died also had an existing sickness when they caught [COVID-19] …

Source: Adapted from C. V. Esguerra (2020, February 4). Why health officials need to speak plainly on Wuhan coronavirus. *ABS-CBN News*.

Discussion

1   What impact do you think the use of medical jargon has had on communicating clearly during the COVID-19 pandemic? Do you agree that plainer terms could have been used?

2   Does plainer language in medicine or law mean that some important subtle meanings may be lost?

3   Is jargon always a bad thing? What helpful functions might it have?

After you have discussed this case study, refer to the 'Comments on case studies' section at the end of the text.

Slang

Slang is very informal language that is mainly used for verbal conversation. It is friendly, colourful, creative, irreverent, funny and sometimes vulgar. It emphasises the human side of life, and it usually brings a smile to our lips. The use of slang in persuasive speech or writing depends on its suitability for the reader or audience concerned. Apart from a tendency to offend readers with its inappropriate tone, slang's main disadvantage is a tendency to drop out of usage. We can often tell a person's age by the slang they use. Have you heard anyone lately using these terms: *cobber*, *sheila*, *walloper* or *egghead*? How much longer do you think *nerd*, *geek* and *cool* will last?

Swear words are a form of slang that exist in all languages, evolve and change over time, and broadly reflect linguistic strategies for dealing with social and cultural taboos (Hughes, 1998). In the Australian context, Amanda Laugesen (2020) notes that:

Bad language has been used in all sorts of ways in our history: to defy authority, as a form of liberation and subversion, and as a source of humour and creativity. It has also been used to oppress and punish, notably Indigenous Australians and women.

Source: A. Laugesen (2020). *Rooted: An Australian history of bad language*. NewSouth Publishing.

Of course, while the use of swear or cuss words is not appropriate in professional communication, every profession has its list of slang terms. Often, they include terms, often meant to be kept within the 'club' of professional members, that are personal and abusive and which help to relieve the tensions of professional life. In professional speeches and writings, slang should be used carefully. At its best, it relieves tension with humour; at its worst, it offends.

Inclusive or non-discriminatory language

The civil rights movement in the US, the feminist movement and the commitment to the rights of people with disabilities and disadvantaged minority groups, foreshadowed awareness regarding the use of language that discriminates during the 1970s and after. Strictures were aimed at the use of language that isolates, ridicules or insults minorities, emphasises their disadvantage or focuses on their difference. The assumption was that definition is not neutral and the way we define things indicates the power we have over them. This has led to the introduction of more **inclusive language**, or non-discriminatory language.

To some extent, this shift in language was prompted by the view that the way we describe the world and reality forms our meaning of it, and this may lead to actions and behaviour that perpetuate and exacerbate discrimination. In other words, the claim is that language that exhibits raw racism, sexism or bigotry, actually hurts minority groups.

In *The dictionary of bias-free usage*, Rosalie Maggio (1991) says:

> [Discriminatory language can also] powerfully harm people, as amply illustrated by bigots' and tyrants' deliberate attempts to linguistically dehumanize and demean groups they intend to exploit, oppress, or exterminate. Calling Asians 'gooks' made it easier to kill them. Calling blacks 'niggers' made it easier to enslave and brutalize them. Calling native Americans 'primitives' and 'savages' made it okay to conquer and despoil them. And to talk of 'fishermen', 'councilmen', and 'longshoremen' is to clearly exclude and discourage women from those pursuits, to diminish and degrade them.
>
> Source: Maggio (1991), p. 3

Maggio says discriminatory language communicates inaccurately about what it means to be, for example, male, female or transgender; black or white; young or old; or heterosexual or homosexual. She lists the biases of racism, sexism, ageism, classism, ethnocentrism, anti-Semitism and homophobia.

Today, there is increasing recognition of the importance of language when referring to people's sexuality and gender. In Australia, the Australian Institute of Family Studies (2022) explains this change as follows:

> There is a great deal of diversity within and across LGBTIQA+ [lesbian, gay, bisexual, trans/transgender, intersex, queer and other sexuality, gender, and bodily diverse people] communities; LGBTIQA+ people are not a homogenous group. There is also a wide range of terms and language related to bodies, gender, sexual orientation, sexual attraction, sexual behaviour, and legal and medical processes. Sexual orientation, gender identity and variations of sex characteristics are different concepts, and it is acknowledged that related language constantly evolves. Understanding and using the language/terminology associated with lesbian, gay, bisexual, transgender, intersex, queer, asexual and other sexually or gender diverse (LGBTIQA+) people helps to ensure that services and organisations are inclusive and respectful.
>
> Source: Australian Institute of Family Studies (2022). LGBTIQA+ glossary of common terms. CC BY 4.0.
> https://creativecommons.org/licenses/by/4.0/

Chapter 11 will discuss strategies for using inclusive language. Also discussed is the eternal debate about so-called 'political correctness' versus 'freedom of speech', which will be touched on next.

Inclusive language
Language that is free from words, phrases or tones that reflect prejudiced, stereotyped or discriminatory views of people or groups. Also known as non-discriminatory language.

'Political correctness' and 'woke'

The focus on the power of connotation in the use of words has led to, or been accompanied by, many improvements in social equality for minority groups. Some critics, however, claim that this process has gone too far, and that academics, journalists and other writers are now afraid to speak plainly about contentious political or social issues in case they offend a strong interest group. They label the ban on certain words and terms as **political correctness**.

Australian radio talkback commentators frequently rail against political correctness, claiming it inhibits freedom of speech, panders to minority interest groups and even conceals favoured treatment of these groups. Such commentators are themselves sometimes accused of racism and sexism. Describing the evolution of the term from ironic epithet to pejorative slur, Allan and Burridge (2006) conclude that:

> The end result of all this was the label *political correctness* had turned into a powerful rhetorical stick to beat your political opponents with; a way of bringing contumely on someone you didn't like; an effective strategy to short-circuit serious debate.
>
> Source: K. Allan & K. Burridge (2006). *Forbidden words: Taboo and the censoring of language*. Cambridge University Press, p. 94.

Political correctness
'Conformity to current beliefs about correctness in language with regard to policies on sexism, racism, ageism etc.' (*Macquarie Dictionary*, 2023).

Historically, the use of 'political correctness' has been most common in two areas of fierce debate – racism and sexism. Where does criticism of or factual comment on racial, social or religious groups end and outright bias and bigotry begin? If so-called 'ordinary citizens' perceive themselves to be disadvantaged by 'favoured treatment' offered to 'minority groups', at what point will their public statements about these matters turn from criticism to abuse, and even vilification? More recently, fierce debates have ensued over public recognition of gender diversity and its intersection with particular religious and ideological beliefs (Hawkes, 2022). In particular, the term **woke** has tended to replace 'political correctness' as the favoured term to criticise those whose socially progressive or 'elitist' views, which some people view as extreme, self-righteous or overly sensitive. Originating in the US among African American communities, the term was originally used positively to reference awareness of, and attention to, social and racial injustice among marginalised groups. It gained wider usage to more broadly describe individuals who are socially conscious and politically engaged.

As with 'political correctness', the term has morphed further to be co-opted as a criticism of those who seek to draw attention to issues relating to race, gender and sexuality (Bump, 2023). During the 2019 -2020 Australian bushfires, then deputy prime minister Michael McCormack, dismissed links between climate change and the unprecedented bushfires in Queensland and NSW, using a radio interview to slam 'woke capital city greenies' (McIllroy & Tillett, 2019). Similarly, sometimes the term *political correctness* is used ironically by people to complain about what they see as a restriction of their freedom of expression, or their 'free speech'. Case study 2.6 explores this in more detail.

Woke
Being very aware of social and political unfairness.

 CASE STUDY 2.6   'Not now, not ever': Julia Gillard's 'misogyny speech'

Shutterstock.com/Christopher Penler

The following is an edited excerpt from former prime minister Julia Gillard's (2012) famous 'misogyny speech'. This speech was made in response to a motion in the Australian parliament accusing her of sexism by the then Liberal opposition leader (and later prime minister) Tony Abbott. The speech was both lauded and condemned at the time, but has since has been seen as a landmark strike, calling out the invidious sexism and misogyny that many women are subjected to in their workplaces.

> Thank you very much Deputy Speaker and I rise to oppose the motion moved by the Leader of the Opposition. And in so doing I say to the Leader of the Opposition I will not be lectured about sexism and misogyny by this man. I will not … Not now, not ever …

Let's go through the Opposition Leader's repulsive double standards, repulsive double standards when it comes to misogyny and sexism.

He has said, and I quote, in a discussion about women being under-represented in institutions of power in Australia ... 'If it's true, Stavros, that men have more power generally speaking than women, is that a bad thing?'

And then a discussion ensues, and another person says, 'I want my daughter to have as much opportunity as my son.' To which the Leader of the Opposition says 'Yeah, I completely agree, but what if men are by physiology or temperament, more adapted to exercise authority or to issue command?'

I was also very offended on behalf of the women of Australia when in the course of this carbon pricing campaign, the Leader of the Opposition said 'What the housewives of Australia need to understand as they do the ironing ...' Thank you for that painting of women's roles in modern Australia. And then of course, I was offended too by the sexism, by the misogyny of the Leader of the Opposition catcalling across this table at me as I sit here as prime minister, 'If the Prime Minister wants to, politically speaking, make an honest woman of herself ...', something that would never have been said to any man sitting in this chair. I was offended when the Leader of the Opposition went outside in the front of Parliament and stood next to a sign that said, 'Ditch the witch.'

I was offended when the Leader of the Opposition stood next to a sign that described me as a man's bitch. I was offended by those things. Misogyny, sexism, every day from this Leader of the Opposition. Every day in every way, across the time the Leader of the Opposition has sat in that chair and I've sat in this chair, that is all we have heard from him.

Source: J. Gillard (2012, October 10). Transcript of Julia Gillard's 'misogyny speech'. *Sydney Morning Herald*. The use of this work has been licensed by Copyright Agency except as permitted by the Copyright Act, you must not re-use this work without the permission of the copyright owner or Copyright Agency.

Discussion

1 Why is labelling a woman a 'witch' or a man's 'bitch' an example of misogyny? Consider the literal meaning of these words and why they might be chosen to apply to women.

2 How does Tony Abbott's comment that 'the housewives of Australia need to understand as they do the ironing ...' reflect how he and others saw the role and place of women in society more broadly?

3 Read some of the contemporary reactions to the speech by journalists and commentators (see https://en.wikipedia.org/wiki/Misogyny_Speech). Was this an example of 'political correctness gone mad' as some had claimed?

After you have discussed this case study, refer to the 'Comments on case studies' section at the end of the text.

Perhaps, from the perspective of the impact of language on public and social consciousness, the final word should go to Allan and Burridge (2006). They contend that while the term political correctness has negative connotations:

... there is [also] the emphasis on the role of PC [politically correct] language as a form of public action. By drawing attention to form, it forces us to sit up and take notice ... PC language deliberately throws down the gauntlet, and challenges us to go beyond the content of the message and acknowledge the assumptions on which our language is operating.

Source: K. Allan & K. Burridge (2006). *Forbidden words: Taboo and the censoring of language.* Cambridge University Press, p. 97.

The *Racial Hatred Act 1995*

In 1995 the Australian Parliament passed the *Racial Hatred Act 1995* (Cth). This was 'an act to prohibit certain conduct involving the hatred of other people on the ground of race, colour or national or ethnic origin ...'

In part, the Act states:

18c (1) it is unlawful for a person to do an act, otherwise than in private, if:
    (a) the act is reasonably likely, in all the circumstances, to offend, insult, humiliate or intimidate another person or a group of people; and
    (b) the act is done because of the race, colour or national or ethnic origin of the other person or of some or all of the people in the group.

Source: *Racial Hatred Act 1995* (Cth)

Supporters of the legislation drew attention to the dangers of inciting people to hate minority groups in the community. They argued that messages that insult and vilify racial or religious groups, whether painted on walls; written in books or magazines; or spoken on radio, television or in public speeches, have led to persecution of and discrimination against such groups, which cannot be tolerated in a democracy.

Many opponents of the legislation, while agreeing that racial vilification is undemocratic and evil, believed that freedom of speech was the more important principle of democracy to preserve (see **Exhibit 2.6**). They said the best way to oppose racial vilification and prejudice is to educate the vilifiers, and that you cannot identify and educate those people if you refuse to let them express themselves. You might say that parliament, in passing this Act, was accepting, by extension, the theory of linguistic relativity.

Exhibit 2.6	People protested against the *Racial Hatred Act 1995,* claiming it violated freedom of speech

Fairfax Photos/Andrew Meares

In 2014, when proposing an amendment to article 18C of the *Racial Discrimination Act 1975* (Cth), then Liberal Attorney-General George Brandis quipped in *The Guardian*, 'people have the right to be bigots, you know' (Chan, 2014) referring to a judgement of defamation against columnist Andrew Bolt. Read Case study 2.7 and see if you agree. What are the arguments for and against?

 CASE STUDY 2.7   Political correctness versus freedom of speech: do people have the right to be bigots?

The fine distinction between freedom of speech and racial discrimination was the subject of a controversial 2011 Federal Court ruling against columnist Andrew Bolt. The decision stoked widespread debate about the extent of the limits of freedom of speech, especially as it impacted on discussing issues of race and culture. The following presents the view of one journalist.

The Bolt decision will have implications for us all

No doubt the Federal Court would like us to see its judgment against columnist Andrew Bolt ... as a call for decent standards in journalism, rather than as a landmark ruling against freedom of speech.

But in reality it will not be seen that way because it is a slap in the face for free expression. It limits the kinds of things we can discuss in public and it suggests there are lots of taboo areas where only the meekest forms of reporting would be legally acceptable.

Justice Mordy Bromberg ruled in favour of nine fair skinned Aborigines who claimed that two articles written by Andrew Bolt two years ago were inflammatory, offensive and contravened the *Racial Discrimination Act*.

...

Bromberg makes it clear that Bolt and the Herald Sun lost their case because Bolt got his facts wrong and because he went out of his way to distort and inflame and provoke. So it is important to work out exactly what was being argued about.

The lead applicant, Pat Eatock, claimed that Bolt had insinuated that she and the other applicants were not genuinely Aboriginal and that they were only pretending to be Aboriginal so that they could grab benefits that are only available to Aboriginal people. Under the *Racial Discrimination Act* she needed to prove that at least some fair skinned Aboriginal people were offended or insulted by Bolt's comments. Not a difficult thing to do. And she had to prove that Bolt made those offensive comments because she was of a particular race or colour or ethnic origin. Again, a pretty easy thing to prove, given Bolt's entire argument was about the colour of her skin and her ethnic origin.

...

Bolt tried to argue that because he didn't incite racial hatred, he was entitled to a measure of protection under the law. The judge thought otherwise. He found that the *Racial Discrimination Act* is actually about promoting racial tolerance and human dignity and equality.

...

Bolt did not get an exemption under the Act because of 'the manner in which those articles were written' and because 'they contained errors in fact, distortions of the truth and inflammatory and provocative language'.

I think the ruling is dangerous because it asserts as indisputable fact that Bolt's articles were not reasonable and were not written in good faith and do not classify as 'fair comment'. The judge clearly believes they were not written with a genuine public interest in mind.

... Although those of us that don't like Bolt's writing might think we understand his motives, we really don't have a clue whether Bolt honestly held these views. Perhaps he was being courageous, rather than reckless, in seeking to talk openly what many would say quietly. I don't share his views but I can see some merit in the argument that true racial tolerance is only achieved when we can ventilate unpopular views openly and have a robust discussion about them. In any case do we really want to silence debate on irksome and uncomfortable topics? ...

Source: A. Dodd (2011, September 28). The Bolt decision will have implications for us all. *ABC News*. Reproduced with permission of Dr Andrew Dodd, Director of the Centre for Advancing Journalism at the University of Melbourne.

Discussion

1   The author of the *Racial Discrimination Act 1975 (Cth)*, former Attorney-General Michael Lavarch, wrote in defence of the Act that 'history tells us that overblown rhetoric on race fosters damaging social stereotyping, and this in turn can contribute to societal harm, well beyond any deeply felt personal offense' (Lavarch, 2011). What does this position say about how he and the judge in the Bolt case see the impact of language on public perceptions?

2   Do you agree with Dodd that while we may disagree with a particular perspective, all views should be able to be expressed openly without fear of legal retribution? Should the feelings of those at whom a published argument is directed be considered when deciding if what is said is 'racist' or 'discriminatory'?

3   In Australia, does 'freedom of speech' exist legally and is it absolute? What are some arguments for and against?

After you have discussed this case study, refer to the 'Comments on case studies' section at the end of the text.

Summary

This chapter has dealt with some aspects of language theory relevant to professional communication. The focus has been on semantics, the branch of linguistics concerned with the communication of meaning. In any work group where people are writing emails, letters or reports; making phone calls; or conducting meetings, interviews or negotiations, there needs to be awareness of language's potential for both getting to the truth and avoiding it. The nature of meaning as it facilitates communication in professional work has also been analysed, along with the relevant strengths and differences between writing and speaking. Some impacts on how we use and understand language have also been explored, including the concept of discourse as it impacts and constructs the way we see the world.

Some of the tricks of facile communication in politics and the media, where 'spin doctors' and extremists use their expertise in the emotional or connotative meanings of words to win arguments without presenting evidence, have been examined. Watson's (2003, p. 118) advice is useful here: 'When the words are suspicious, go after them, insist they tell us what they mean. Go after the *meaning* of the words. And if the speakers say they are the kind who call things as they see them, that they don't mince words, and call a spade a spade if not a bloody shovel, go after them even harder. They're often the worst liars of the lot.'

Finally, the discussion of inclusive and non-discriminatory language explored how reforms in this area of language use have sought to raise awareness of the power of language to shape social attitudes, and to exclude and marginalise particular groups in the community on the basis of their sexuality, ethnicity or disability.

STUDY TOOLS

DISCUSSION QUESTIONS AND GROUP ACTIVITIES

For discussion topics and activities in addition to those that follow, please refer to the case studies presented throughout this chapter.

1   In each of the following sentences substitute another word or phrase for the italicised word:

   a   He *means* more to me than a meal ticket.

   b   I *mean* to qualify for the Olympics in 2012.

   c   What do you *mean* 'unqualified at present'?

   d   What actually is the *meaning* of this painting?

   e   The formula H_2SO_4 *means* sulphuric acid.

   f   My lotto prize *means* I can tell the boss what to do with his job tomorrow.

   g   I *mean*, why can't you go to the movie with me tonight?

   h   Here comes Shari looking angry, and I *mean* angry.

2   Read the following excerpt. What words or expressions in your profession or organisation have you noticed have become commonly used in recent years? Which ones are colleagues or bosses resorting to disguise or soften negative events or news?

> During a 2011 conference call, for example, TriQuint Semiconductor Inc. CEO Ralph Quinsey talked about 'cloudier near-term visibility' rather than simply discussing his company's failure to plan ahead. The same year, Lennox International Chief Financial Officer Bob Hau used 'headwinds' to suggest the impact of markets is as fickle as the weather. And in 2005, Marty Singer, chief executive of Pctel, a provider of wireless security services, called his failure to execute on a plan merely a 'hiccup'.
>
> **Source: K. Suslava (2019, April 22). 'You're unallocated!' and other BS companies use to disguise reality. Originally published in *The Conversation*.**

3   Don Watson (2003, p. 118) wrote, 'When the words are suspicious, go after them, insist they tell us what they mean.' What do the following words or phrases *mean*?

a	friends of the Earth	h	chattering classes
b	virtue signalling	i	woke
c	black-armband historians	j	war on terror
d	surgical strike	k	smart bomb
e	pro-choice	l	pro-life
f	collateral damage	m	intelligent design
g	clean coal	n	greenwashing.

4   Research published by the *British Medical Journal* in 2018 argued that the word 'cancer' should be dropped from some medical diagnoses because 'it can scare people into invasive treatments they do not need'. Read through the extract below. What do you think of when you hear that a friend or relative has been diagnosed with cancer? Do you agree with the suggestion that the word should be dropped? Can you think of any other medical-type labels that could be replaced?

> Medical technology is now so advanced that early abnormal cell changes and lesions, sometimes described as 'pre-cancers', can be detected at much smaller sizes than could ever have been found clinically. However, for some types of cancers, these early changes or lesions will never go on to cause harm in the patient's lifetime. But identifying these changes can cause distress and prompt patients to undergo treatment to get rid of them.
>
> 'The use of more medicalised labels can increase both concern about illness and desire for more invasive treatment', the analysis said. 'For decades cancer has been associated with death. This association has been ingrained in society with public health messaging that cancer screening saves lives. This promotion has been used with the best of intentions, but in part deployed to induce feelings of fear and vulnerability in the population and then offer hope through screening. Although the label needs to be biologically accurate, it also needs to be something patients can understand and that will not induce disproportionate concern' ...
>
> **Source: Davey (2018), *The Guardian***

5   For the following words, classify each as either a technical term, jargon or slang. Explain your choices.

    a   swiping   e   hacker

    b   emoji   f   megabytes

    c   encryption   g   docudrama

    d   doomscrolling   h   gig economy.

6   Try translating the following sentences and phrases into plain English:

    a   'In this new period of strategic growth we are maximizing synergies and pushing the envelope' (Watson 2003, p. 37).

    b   'Given the within year and budget time flexibility accorded to the science agencies in the determination of resource allocation from within their global budget, a multi-parameter approach to maintaining the agencies' budgets in real terms is not appropriate' (p. 47).

    c   'I would like to progress discussion with Indigenous people to set in process the parameters of reconciliation' (p. 56).

    d   'Knowledge management caters to the critical issues of organizational adoption, survival and competence in face of increasingly discontinuous environmental changes … Essentially it embodies organizational processes that seek synergistic combination of data and information processing capacity of information technologies and the creative and innovative capacity of human beings' (p. 128).

Watson 2003, pp. 37, 47, 56, 128

7   The following article cites a study that argues that remote workers in the US are put off by colleagues who overuse jargon. Is this your experience?

Are you guilty of just checking in on a team player, circling back and touching base, or demanding 110 per cent ASAP? These are the workplace jargon phrases that make employees cringe, especially in the – ahem – 'new normal' of hybrid work.

A survey commissioned by Slack and carried out by OnePoll quizzed more than 2000 remote and hybrid workers in the US on how they feel about jargon in the workplace – virtual or otherwise. About two thirds of respondents, 65 per cent, said they find it off-putting when colleagues use jargon, and more than 50 per cent said they have at least one colleague they don't like working with because of their communication habits.

The vast majority, however – a massive 89 per cent – admitted to using jargon themselves. Of those, 43 per cent said they use that language in order to maintain 'office norms'. The same amount said they used it in order to sound more intelligent or professional.

Some 55 per cent said they have caught themselves using the very same phrases they're sick of, and 78 per cent have stopped themselves mid-sentence to avoid doing just that. A massive 83 per cent admitted to going back and editing messages they have already sent, in order to delete jargon and buzzwords.

The jargon terms that caused the most offence include classics like 'circle back', 'touch base' and 'keep me in the loop'. Perhaps a newer entrant is the pandemic special buzzword of the 'new normal'. Shudder.

Source: S. Palmer-Derrian (2022, February 18). Let's circle back: The 14 most despised workplace phrases. Smart Company.

8   A report from the UK at the start of the COVID-19 pandemic urged journalists to stop using military metaphors such as *battling*, *fighting* and *struggling* when reporting illness. Some tweeters argued:

Message received from emergency doc friend 'Will the media and others please stop using terms like battling and struggling. It is unfair on sick patients who have no say in the matter. And it's ok to be scared.'

Another tweeted:

Please, please stop using this language about fighting through. It really upsets those of us who've known cancer. It implies that those who lost didn't fight hard enough.

Source: Excerpts from J. Parkinson (2020, April 9). Coronavirus: Why do we talk about 'fighting' illness? BBC.

What do you think? Why are these common metaphors used for dealing with illness and do they mispresent the nature of the experience of serious illness?

9   Do a Google search on the use of the terms 'political correctness' and 'woke' and the debates about them over the past year. Summarise, with examples, how the terms were used and in what context. Do you agree with the idea of using these terms as a way of drawing language users' attention to the way that language operates?

10 While some people might deride language changes as 'PC gone mad', the following extract uses examples of how adopted language changes have altered social perspectives on disability.

> In the second half of the 20th century, we came to accept that in certain cases we should avoid deliberately hurtful language. While many deride political correctness for going too far, its initial aim to establish non-hateful language was, and still is, admirable.
>
> In the early 20th century, 'moron' was a medical term for someone with a mental age of between eight and 12. 'Mongol' was a person with Down syndrome, and also was indirectly a slur on people from Mongolia, some of whose features were supposed to resemble those with Down syndrome. 'Retarded' described someone mentally, socially or physically less advanced than their chronological age.
>
> Words like 'deaf', 'blind', 'dumb' and 'lame' are not only descriptions of physical ability and disability, but are commonly used in negative ways. For instance, 'deaf as a post', 'blind Freddie'. We have now moved away from such language. Especially unacceptable are nouns like 'retard' or adjectives like 'demented'. In their place we have the principle of people first. The person and the disability are separated.
>
> Source: R. Sussex, Professor Emeritus, The University of Queensland (2017, December 17). From 'demented' to 'person with dementia': How and why the language of disability changed. This article was originally published on *The Conversation*. CC BY ND.

Can you think of other examples where terms for disability or illness that were once widely used have been replaced by different terms? How might this have altered perceptions of the people or affliction in society?

WEBSITES

Macquarie Dictionary https://www.macquariedictionary.com.au

Racial Hatred Act 1995 https://humanrights.gov.au/our-work/racial-hatred-act-what-racial-hatred-act

The Australian Style Manual (online version) https://www.stylemanual.gov.au

The Diversity Council of Australia has a range of useful online resources related to inclusive writing https://www.dca.org.au

The Plain English Foundation is a useful Australian organisation with resources for writing and speaking clearly https://www.plainenglishfoundation.com/home

REFERENCES

Allan, K., & Burridge, K. (2006). *Forbidden words: Taboo and the censoring of language*. Cambridge University Press.

Australian Institute of Family Studies. (2022). *LGBTIQA+ glossary of common terms*. https://aifs.gov.au/resources/resource-sheets/lgbtiqa-glossary-common-terms.

Bump, P. (2023, January 18). Why 'woke' replaced 'politically correct'. *The Washington Post* https://www.washingtonpost.com/politics/2023/01/18/woke-cancel-desantis-academics

Carrington, D. (2019, May 17). Why the Guardian is changing the language it uses about the environment. *The Guardian*. https://www.theguardian.com/environment/2019/may/17/why-the-guardian-is-changing-the-language-it-uses-about-the-environment

Carroll, L. (1871/2010). *Through the looking glass*. William Collins.

Chan, G. (2014, March 24). George Brandis: 'People have the right to be bigots', *The Guardian* https://www.theguardian.com/world/2014/mar/24/george-brandis-people-have-the-right-to-be-bigots

Davey, M. (2018, August 13). Doctors should avoid saying 'cancer' for minor lesions – study. *The Guardian*. https://www.theguardian.com/society/2018/aug/13/doctors-should-avoid-saying-cancer-for-minor-lesions-study

Deutscher, G. (2010). *Through the language glass: Why the world looks different in other languages*. Metropolitan Books.

Dodd, A. (2011, September 28). The Bolt decision will have implications for us all. *ABC News*.

du Gay, P. (1996). *Consumption and identity at work*. Sage.

Esguerra, C. V. (2020, February 4). Why health officials need to speak plainly on Wuhan coronavirus. *ABS-CBN News*.

Fairclough, N. (1992). *Discourse and social change*. Polity Press.

Foucault, M. (2002). *The archaeology of knowledge* (A. M. S. Smith, Trans). Routledge. (Original work published 1969)

Gillard, J. (2012, October 10). Transcript of Julia Gillard's 'misogyny speech'. *Sydney Morning Herald*. http://www.smh.com.au/opinion/political-news/transcript-of-julia-gillards-speech-20121010-27c36.html

Gray A. J. (2011). Worldviews. *International psychiatry: Bulletin of the Board of International Affairs of the Royal College of Psychiatrists, 8*(3), 58–60.

Grosscup, B. (2011). Cluster munitions and state terrorism, *The Monthly Review, 62*(11). http://monthlyreview.org/2011/04/01/cluster-munitions-and-state-terrorism

Hall, E. T. (1959). *The silent language*. Doubleday.

Hawkes, G. (2022, July 29). The Manly pride jersey furore is not as simple as a choice between inclusivity and homophobia. *The Conversation*. https://theconversation.com/the-manly-pride-jersey-furore-is-not-as-simple-as-a-choice-between-inclusivity-and-homophobia-187859

Hodge, R., & Kress, G. (1979). *Language as ideology*. Routledge.

Hudson, K. (1978). *The jargon of the professions*. Macmillan.

Hughes, G. (1998). *Swearing: A social history of foul language, oaths and profanity in English*. Penguin.

Lakoff, G., & Johnson, M. (1980), *Metaphors we live by*. University of Chicago Press.

Laugesen, A. (2020). *Rooted: An Australian history of bad language*. NewSouth Publishing.

Lavarch, M. (2011, April 9). Free speech has limits. *The Australian*. http://www.theaustralian.com.au/national-affairs/opinion/free-speech-has-limits-in-the-law/story-e6frgd0x-1226036205910

Lutz, W. (1996). *The new doublespeak*. Harper & Row.

Macquarie Dictionary. (2023). Political correctness. *Macquarie Dictionary Online*. https://www.macquariedictionary.com.au

Maggio, R. (1991). *The dictionary of bias-free usage: A guide to non-discriminatory language*. Oryx.

McIlroy, T. & Tillett, A. (2019, November 11). NSW, Qld bushfires: Coalition dismisses climate link to crisis. *Australian Financial Review* https://www.afr.com/politics/federal/raving-inner-city-lunatics-deputy-pm-lashes-bushfire-climate-link-20191111-p539ar

Motion, J., & Leitch, S. (2008). The multiple discourses of science-society engagement. *Australian Journal of Communication*, *35*(3), pp. 29-40.

Napier-Raman, K. (2019, August 16). Fear of a burning planet: The semantics of climate change. *Crikey.com*. https://www.crikey.com.au/2019/08/16/climate-change-semantics

Palmer-Derrian, S. (2022, February 18). Let's circle back: The 14 most despised workplace phrases. *Smart Company*. https://www.smartcompany.com.au/people-human-resources/remote-work/workplace-jargon-employees-hate

Parkinson, J. (2020, April 9). Coronavirus: Why do we talk about 'fighting' illness? *BBC*. https://www.bbc.com/news/uk-politics-52216542?fbclid=IwAR3kCnJE-mqBHYO_944HpTEBlTXcXVdRn_V-WMDMJdoKzMNj2tJ39cBcALg

Racial Hatred Act 1995 (Cth).

Orwell, G. (1946/1968). Politics and the English language, in *Collected essays*. Secker & Warburg.

Sapir, E. (1929). The status of linguistics as a science. *Language*, 207–214.

Sharp, A. (2022, February 27). *Sydney Morning Herald* editor v staff over use of the word 'strike'. *Daily Telegraph*.

Spender, D. (1994). *Man-made language* (2nd ed.). Pandora.

Suslava, K. (2019, April 22). 'You're unallocated!' and other BS companies use to disguise reality. *The Conversation*. https://theconversation.com/youre-unallocated-and-other-bs-companies-use-to-obscure-reality-109129.

Sussex, R. (2017, December 7). From 'demented' to 'person with dementia': How and why the language of disability changed. *The Conversation*. https://theconversation.com/from-demented-to-person-with-dementia-how-and-why-the-language-of-disability-changed-85172

Watson, D. (2003). *Death sentence: The decay of public language*. Random House Australia.

Watson, D. (2009, 19 September). Language like this should be put to the torch, *Sydney Morning Herald*, p. 7.

Whorf, B. L. (2012). *Language, thought, and reality: Selected writings of Benjamin Lee Whorf* (J. B. Carroll, S. C. Levinson, & P. Lee, Eds.). The MIT Press.

Non-verbal communication

Learning objectives

After reading this chapter, you should be able to:

- define *non-verbal communication*
- explain how verbal and non-verbal communication are related
- list the three key characteristics of non-verbal communication
- describe the main functions of non-verbal communication
- outline the main categories of non-verbal communication
- identify examples of non-verbal cues in interpersonal communication
- explain the impact of good and poor non-verbal communication in professional settings
- analyse your own non-verbal behaviours in professionally critical settings, such as job interviews and workplace encounters
- explain why it is important to be aware of the intercultural dimensions of non-verbal behaviour.

Effect of face masks on interpersonal communication during the COVID-19 pandemic

The COVID-19 pandemic has severely affected the way people communicate with each other. Precautionary measures to limit the spread of the virus necessitated a shift in the communication paradigm when it comes to greetings and handshakes. The situation required people to adopt salutations that do not involve physical contact, such as the 'peace sign', the 'hand on chest' and the 'namaste'. In addition, emphasis on personal spaces and social distancing markedly increased, with telecommunication witnessing a huge rise, as business meetings, conferences, and educational activities shifted to virtual communication via social applications, such as Zoom, Cisco Webex, Skype, and Microsoft Teams.

Face-to-face communication, specifically, was majorly affected by the pandemic. The need for face masks, as an important protective measure to decrease the spread of the virus, had a huge toll on interpersonal communication. Facial expressions and gestures play a major role in facilitating interpersonal communication, comprehension, and the delivery of intended messages. As such, wearing face masks hindered the ability of seeing and understanding people's expressions during conversations, and decreased the impact of communicated material ...

Source: N. Mheidly, M. Y. Fares, H. Zalzale & J. Fares (2020). Effect of face masks on interpersonal communication during the COVID-19 pandemic. *Frontiers in Public Health, 8*.

Introduction

As discussed in the opening article excerpt, the COVID-19 pandemic highlighted the importance of non-verbal signals to effective human communication. Various restrictions that limited people's physical and spatial interactions, as a way of minimising transmission of the virus, had numerous unforeseen professional and individual consequences. For example, wearing face masks impacted upon hearing impaired people who rely on lip reading as their main way of communicating.

Non-verbal communication has many facets, but it is broadly defined as the sharing of meaning in ways other than with words. According to Kendon et al. (1981, p. 3), the study of non-verbal behaviours 'most frequently refers to ways communication is effected between persons when in each other's presence'. Further, 'studies of non-verbal behaviours are most often concerned with the parts that these play in establishing and maintaining interaction and interpersonal relationships'.

While non-verbal behaviour is often primarily associated with the study of 'body language', it is much more than this. Non-verbal communication also includes how people use sound, time, space and objects to arouse or accentuate meaning, either deliberately or unintentionally. Non-verbal communication may exist in the *speaker* (dressing in black for a funeral, crossing arms with an angry facial expression, or fidgeting nervously), the *listener* (slumping in a chair looking bored, drumming fingers in impatience, laughing, or sitting forward clapping continuously), or the *setting* as perceived by an onlooker (a crowded, noisy shopping centre at lunchtime; a nightclub with deafening music and flashing lights; a dimly lit restaurant with soft background music; or a cathedral during a Sunday morning service). All of these socially shared cues work to create or enhance meaning.

Research by Mark Knapp (1992) suggests that 65 per cent of social meaning is carried by non-verbal cues. Therefore, as professional communicators, we must understand how this impacts our efforts to communicate ideas, opinions, attitudes and policies, and how we understand and interpret the ideas, opinions and attitudes of those with whom we communicate.

This chapter overviews the different modes or categories of non-verbal communication, emphasising the importance of eye behaviour, facial expression, gesture and posture, space, time, touch and paralanguage. Examples of these modes are then discussed in relation to real-world professional situations, such as interview behaviour. Non-verbal communication in specific types of interpersonal communication modes, such as group interactions, negotiation and conflict management, and oral presentations, are covered in Chapters 8, 9 and 10. Finally, some general observations about cultural differences in non-verbal communication are introduced (a more complete treatment of intercultural communication is presented in Chapter 4).

How are non-verbal communication and verbal communication related?

According to Mark Knapp (1992, p. 15) :

> The average person actually speaks words for a total of only 10 to 11 minutes daily – the standard spoken sentence taking only about 2.5 seconds. In a normal two-person conversation, the verbal components carry less than 35 per cent of the social meaning of the situation; more than 65 per cent of the social meaning is carried on the nonverbal band.
>
> Source: M. L. Knapp (1992). *Essentials of non-verbal communication*. Holt, Rinehart & Winston.

If Knapp is correct, the impact of the non-verbal band is significant. But how might this work? It is important to understand that it is difficult to neatly distinguish between verbal and non-verbal messages because the two modes do not exist in isolation but are interrelated and often clustered. People shift back and forth between them, often subconsciously. Too often speakers are unaware of how their non-verbal behaviours may be alternatively complementing or contradicting their intended meaning. Also, how an individual displays or interprets these behaviours is dependent on various factors related to the individual and the context within which the communication occurs.

So, what are the functions of non-verbal communication in a verbal interaction such as an interview, a public speech or a conversation? Some of these functions are summarised in Exhibit 3.1.

Exhibit 3.1	Functions of non-verbal communication

Functions	Example
Emphasising, reinforcing and complementing	• People who stand behind a politician giving an interview and regularly nod their heads in agreement with what is being said • We may speak with a serious tone about something important, bang our fist on the table to demonstrate anger and frustration, point a finger when giving directions or smile when telling a funny story
Contradicting	• A friend asks, 'Have you got time for a chat?' You say yes, but then keep checking your watch • You ask, 'Are you ok with that?' and your colleague frowns as they say, 'Yes, that's fine'
Regulating or repeating	• We might throw up our hands to stop the other person speaking, or purse our lips and lean forward, hoping to get a chance to have our say • We use eye contact, gestures and pauses to regulate taking turns in a conversation
Substituting	• You ask a friend 'How is your new job?' and they just roll their eyes • When we don't know what to say to express our sorrow at the death of a friend or a relative, an embrace often suffices • We may stretch our hands in a wide gesture to indicate size or distance

So, is verbal or non-verbal communication more powerful? Research by University of California professor Albert Mehrabian illustrates the relative importance of verbal and non-verbal messages in a communication encounter (see **Exhibit 3.2**). Mehrabian's formula states that for the communication of attitudes, the loading is 7 per cent verbal cues (i.e., word meanings), 38 per cent vocal cues (i.e., paralanguage, or how the words are said) and 55 per cent facial cues (Mehrabian, 1981, p. 77). While the interpretation of Mehrabian's research has been challenged (e.g., Oestreich, 1999), the relative importance of non-verbal cues has not.

Exhibit 3.2	The relative importance of verbal and non-verbal messages in a communication encounter

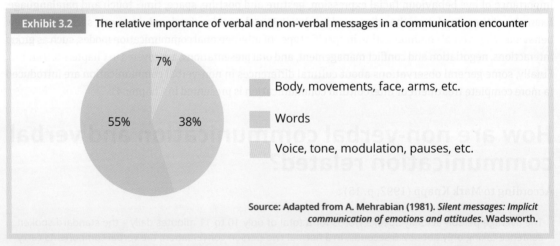

Source: Adapted from A. Mehrabian (1981). *Silent messages: Implicit communication of emotions and attitudes*. Wadsworth.

However, too often we remain unaware of the messages that our bodies, our voices or the space around us send to others. We simply act and react without considering how actions modify, reinforce, distort or detract from messages.

> **Reflection question:** Can you remember a time when your attitude in a professional setting – whether positive, negative or neutral – was communicated more by how you delivered a message than by what you actually verbalised?

Key characteristics of non-verbal communication

Knapp (1992) warns against some of the myths surrounding the subject of non-verbal communication. This warning is appropriate, as many professed 'experts' offer quick advice on how we can use non-verbal codes or formulae to take advantage of clients or rivals. For this reason, we need to understand some of the overriding characteristics of non-verbal communication. In particular:

- non-verbal cues should not be considered in isolation
- non-verbal communication is culture-bound
- non-verbal communication is unavoidable.

Non-verbal cues should not be considered in isolation

Non-verbal behaviours or cues are part of the total system of human communication and need to be understood as such. In fact, Knapp (1992) insists that verbal and non-verbal systems are heavily interrelated and interdependent. Non-verbal movements, just like verbal symbols, may have different meanings depending on their social context and the personal mannerisms of the communicator. For example, there could be any number of reasons why a person looks at their watch, coughs, rubs their eyes or crosses their arms or legs. All non-verbal behaviours should be interpreted within the specific context in which they occur and in relation to the other cluster of cues that are present.

Non-verbal communication is culture-bound

While some non-verbal behaviours are believed to be universal – for example, facial expressions indicating fear, surprise, sadness and happiness (Ekman, 2004) – each culture seems to have unique ways of expressing and interpreting emotions, which need to be taken into consideration. Consider the multiple meanings of the 'ok' sign formed with your forefinger and thumb. In Australia, you might just want to let people know that you're alright, but in France you are may be saying that you or someone else is worthless, in Venezuela and Brazil the sign may have sexual connotations, while in Turkey it may be considered an insult towards gay people. Therefore, awareness of the possible multiple meanings of gestures in different cultural settings is vital. We discuss this aspect further toward the end of this chapter and in Chapter 4.

Non-verbal communication is unavoidable

Since the time of Charles Darwin, many aspects of human behaviour have been argued to have biological and evolutionary origins. For example, evolutionary psychologists have suggested that certain physical characteristics that we associate with dominant males, such as physical height, broad shoulders and protuberant chins, have evolved to attract females because they suggest physical strength, fitness and, thus, ability to protect against threats.

While most adults can become reasonably well schooled in controlling negative aspects of their non-verbal behaviour, there are usually 'leakages' of contradictory expressions or actions. For example, while I might affect a poker face to hide my annoyance, you may be able to spot my emotions via my gestures, such as a tapping foot, a sharp tone in my voice or pursed lips. Even when we purposely avoid communication by shutting our office door, avoiding eye contact or not speaking when we encounter a colleague, we are sending a signal that can be interpreted.

Lastly, an even more subtle type of non-verbal cue can be found in *micro-expressions*. Micro-expressions are often undetectable changes of facial expressions or body movements that are claimed to reveal the real emotions that people are feeling, especially when they lie (Ekman, 2009). So even if you are a master at concealing non-verbal signs, your *micro-expressions* may still betray you!

Reflection question: Considering the key characteristics of non-verbal behaviour. Why do you think people are more inclined to believe non-verbal cues when they contradict verbal statements?

The different categories of non-verbal communication

Non-verbal communication comprises a number of major interacting systems or categories, as shown in **Exhibit 3.3**. These will be discussed in greater detail in the following sections.

Exhibit 3.3	The categories of non-verbal communication

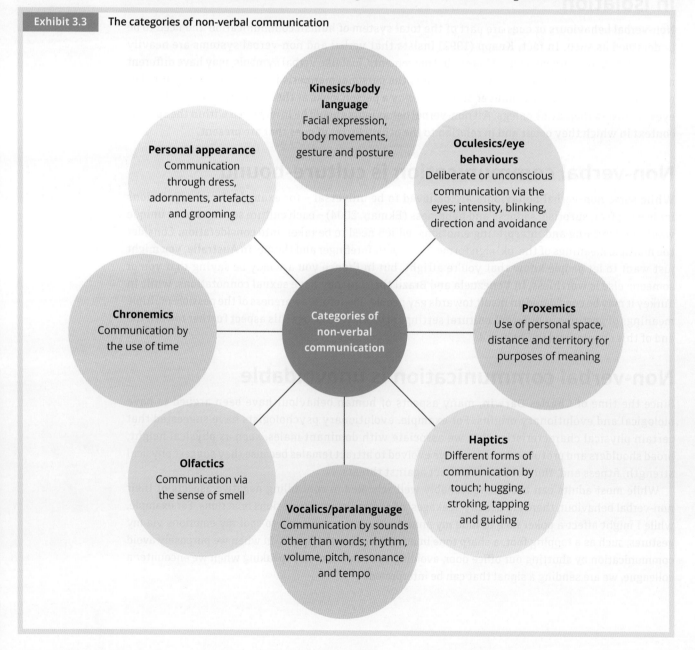

Kinesics/body language
Facial expression, body movements, gesture and posture

Personal appearance
Communication through dress, adornments, artefacts and grooming

Oculesics/eye behaviours
Deliberate or unconscious communication via the eyes; intensity, blinking, direction and avoidance

Chronemics
Communication by the use of time

Categories of non-verbal communication

Proxemics
Use of personal space, distance and territory for purposes of meaning

Olfactics
Communication via the sense of smell

Haptics
Different forms of communication by touch; hugging, stroking, tapping and guiding

Vocalics/paralanguage
Communication by sounds other than words; rhythm, volume, pitch, resonance and tempo

Kinesics and body motion

Kinesics is the study of body motion. In the context of non-verbal communication, **kinesics** refers to body movements, such as gestures, postures and facial expressions.

Gesture and posture

You might know someone who fits the following description: 'If their hands were tied behind their back, they couldn't utter a word'. Such people might use gestures that are merely nervous, meaningless movements of the hands and arms. Others use their hands very descriptively. Watching such a person talking in the distance, we may feel we know what they are saying without hearing a word.

Similarly, people use posture differently. For example, some people sit and stand differently, which is sometimes due to differing levels of interest and confidence, as shown in Exhibit 3.4.

Kinesics
Body movements, such as gestures, postures and facial expressions.

Gestures
Movements of parts of the body, especially the hands and arms.

| **Exhibit 3.4** | Gestures and body postures add additional meaning to verbal communication |

Shutterstock.com/TZIDO SUN

Shutterstock.com/Juice Verve

Shutterstock.com/ViDI Studio

Shutterstock.com/CREATISTA

Gesture and posture are discussed together because it is difficult to imagine one happening without the other. **Gestures** usually refer to movements of parts of the body, especially the hands and arms, while **posture** refers to the disposition of the whole body. In public speaking, we may move quickly from one gesture to another but retain a fairly stable posture. Or we may lean forward from a relaxed sitting position, stare fixedly at our companion and make chopping signs with our right hand to drive home a point we wish to make.

Posture
The disposition of the person's whole body.

Eaves and Leathers (2017, p. 80) discuss functional (positive) and dysfunctional (negative) uses of bodily cues (gestures and posture):

- Bodily cues that communicate a sense of openness and confidence are desirable. Examples are individuals who 'unbutton their coats, uncross their legs, and move up towards the edge of the chair'. In contrast, crossed arms, crossed legs and related gestures often communicate inaccessibility and defensiveness.
- Nervous gestures take many forms and are usually unintentional. We all get nervous at times but there may be ways to control our nerves by not allowing them to be expressed in unintentional non-verbal cues. Tugging at clothes or ears, playing with objects on the table, twiddling, fiddling and fidgeting or any extraneous movement that serves no purpose, will probably be interpreted by our audience as signs of nervousness or lack of confidence. Hand-to-face gestures, like covering the mouth, and nose- and head-scratching, are signals that the communicator lacks confidence or is tense.

Source: M. Eaves & D. G. Leathers (2017). *Successful nonverbal communication: Principles and applications* (5th ed.). Taylor and Francis.

They argue that these are generally agreed on in Western social contexts. What do you think?

Facial expression

Facial expression
Movements of the face that communicate value judgements about, and interest in, the things and people around us.

The second important focus in kinesics concerns **facial expression**. The most important function of the face in communication is to provide information about emotion, as it is the main channel that we use to decipher the feelings of others (see **Exhibit 3.5**). The face is estimated to be able to create 250 000 expressions (Ruben & Stewart, 2006), and, generally, we all learn to read both the obvious emotion conveyed by our companions as well as the more subtle, perhaps contradictory, feelings.

| Exhibit 3.5 | Facial expressions communicate emotions both consciously and unconsciously |

Alamy Stock Photo/dpa picture alliance

The face communicates value judgements about things and people. It communicates how interested we are in other people or in the activities going on around us, as well as our degree of involvement in a situation. But just as importantly, the face communicates the amount of control we have over our emotions. In business situations, we often 'mask' our facial expressions. Watch a salesperson diplomatically handling a fractious customer, or a public speaker, such as a politician, being subjected to abusive shouts from the audience and maintaining a cool demeanour. In some cultures, such as Japanese culture and to a lesser extent British culture, self-control is greatly valued, and emphasis is placed on not revealing emotions (Morris, 2002). The great British 'stiff upper lip', the 'inscrutable Japanese' and the 'poker face' are examples of references to this attempt to publicly mask emotions.

According to Blum (1998, p. 34), research findings indicate the following:

- The face can twist and pull into 5000 expressions, all the way from an outright grin to the faintest sneer.
- There is a distinct anatomical difference between real and feigned expressions – and in the biological effect they produce in the creators of those expressions.
- We send and read signals with lightning-like speed and over great distances … We can tell in a blink of a second if a stranger's face is registering surprise or pleasure – even if he or she is 50 metres away.
- Smiles are such an important part of communication that we see them far more clearly than any other expression. We can pick up a smile at 100 metres – the length of [an American] football field.
- Facial expressions are largely universal, products of biological imperatives. We are programmed to make and read faces.
- Culture, parenting and experience can temper our ability to display and interpret emotions.

Source: D. Blum (1998). Face it! *Psychology Today, 31*(5), pp. 36, 64.

Ekman et al. (1987) studied the ability for people from several cultures, including remote tribes in New Guinea with little or no exposure to Westerners or to modern media, to accurately read emotions on the faces of Western people in photographs shown to them. His findings indicated that the basic emotions of anger, disgust, fear, happiness, sadness and surprise were universally recognised across cultures. According to Blum (1998, p. 36):

Show photos of an infuriated New Yorker to a high-mountain Tibetan or a miserable New Guinea tribeswoman to a Japanese worker, and there's no translation problem. Everyone makes the same face – and everyone gets the message.

Source: D. Blum (1998). Face it! *Psychology Today, 31*(5), pp. 36, 64.

Exhibit 3.6	Techniques for putting on a 'false face'	
Technique	**Description**	**Example**
Qualifying	Adding another facial expression to the original in order to modify its impact	A boss who gives a subordinate a look of surprise, immediately followed by raised eyebrows in a look of concern, may be trying to modify the impact of initial amazement by switching to a questioning mode to find out more details
Modulating	Changing the intensity of a facial expression to communicate stronger or weaker feelings than those actually being experienced	We may communicate slight surprise, facially, when in fact we feel quite shocked
Falsifying	Showing facial emotion when no emotion is felt, or masking emotion with a blank expression	A person might display no surprise at a fellow player's poker hand, even if they are pleased or horrified

Source: P. Ekman (2004). *Emotions revealed: Understanding faces and feelings*. Phoenix.

Ekman (2004) claims that it is fairly easy for people to 'put on a false face', thus limiting the power of non-verbal cues of this kind. He refers to three techniques – qualifying, modulating and falsifying. Exhibit 3.6 summarises each of these.

What this all indicates is that facial expressions can be difficult to interpret accurately. For professionals, it is important to be sensitive to the needs of colleagues and try to develop awareness of the meanings of non-verbal cues, such as facial expression. A bit of pretence can of course be beneficial. The advice given in the song 'Put on a happy face' can be a good way of getting people to listen when you rise to begin a public speech. It's certainly more advisable than mounting the podium with an expression that mirrors your terror.

Reflection question: How difficult is it to control your facial expressions? What strategies or techniques do you use?

Oculesics and eye behaviour

Oculesics
The study of eye behaviour, focusing on how people use their eyes to communicate.

Oculesics, the study of eye behaviour, focuses on how we use our eyes to communicate. Most people agree that eye behaviour is one of the most powerful means of non-verbal communication. In Western culture there is a tradition that the eyes are the 'windows to the soul'. In nearly all cultures, terms equivalent to 'the evil eye' or 'the divine eye' can be found. It is not surprising, then, that Westerners tend to believe that eye-contact avoidance denotes shiftiness and deviousness. Westerners tend to respect people who 'look you in the eye'. The eyes are also seen to communicate most directly on our behalf.

Eyes regulate the flow of communication (see **Exhibit 3. 7**). Seeking eye contact with a colleague at a party informs her that you wish to speak to her. In a different situation you may wish to use your eyes to signal that you are not receptive. So, if the lecturer is gazing around the room wanting to pick on someone to answer a difficult question, the best way to avoid being called upon is to look away. Additionally, eye contact provides signals for turn-taking. We may be looking away from our colleague while we are speaking, and when coming to the end of our utterance we may glance at them to indicate it is their turn to speak.

Exhibit 3.7	Eyes regulate the flow of communication

iStock.com/RelaxFoto.de

How long should you look at people's eyes when conversing with them? One researcher on Western communication reactions has produced the following statistics:

> In a typical two-person conversation, people look at each other about 61 per cent of the time, and their gaze coincides (mutual gaze) about 31 per cent of the time. Mutual gaze lasts on the average only about one second, while each individual gaze is usually about three seconds long. The same person will look more when listening (75 per cent of the time) than when speaking (41 per cent of the time).
>
> Source: Forgas (1996), p. 157

We are not suggesting you set out to measure your own eye-contact activity, but if the above statistics are valid for Western contexts, they suggest that there is an implicit set of rules by which we moderate our polite interactions. This is part of any culture.

In an oral presentation to a professional group, it is normal and advisable for the speaker to distribute eye contact fairly evenly around the audience, scanning the room for non-verbal cues of interest, uncertainty or boredom. In turn, the audience is expected to look at the speaker most of the time. If they don't, the speaker may feel that either the material or its presentation needs revision.

We might summarise the communicative functions of' 'eye behaviour' as follows:

- indicating degrees of attentiveness, interest and arousal
- helping to initiate and sustain relationships
- influencing attitude change and persuasion
- regulating interaction
- communicating emotions
- defining power and status relationships.

Reflection question: Have you experienced a time when you misinterpreted someone's eye behaviour? Why did you make the error and what did you learn from it?

 CASE STUDY 3.1 Non-verbal behaviours: what do they tell us about relationships?

The photograph in Exhibit 3.8 shows former German Chancellor Angela Merkel and other leaders looking intently at former US president Donald Trump during a G7 meeting in 2018, while others study her actions.

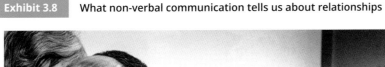

Exhibit 3.8   What non-verbal communication tells us about relationships

Alamy Stock Photo/Bradley Cooper

Discussion

1   How many different types of non-verbal behaviours can you identify in this photograph?

2   How do you interpret the following:

a   German Chancellor Angela Merkel and others leaning in toward President Trump.

b   Trump's crossed arms, seated position and facial expression.

c   The non-verbal behaviour of other participants in the picture? Consider their stance, facial expressions and eye behaviours in particular.

3   What difference does context make? Does knowing more about the two leaders and the context of the exchange impact your interpretation?

After you have discussed this case study, refer to the 'Comments on case studies' section at the end of the text.

Proxemics and spatial communication

The anthropologist Edward T. Hall (1969, pp. 110–118) pioneered the study of space and territory as aspects of human interaction. He named the study **proxemics**. Hall claimed that people segment their social life into four zones, shown in Exhibit 3.9, and described in the following:

Proxemics
The study of how people use personal space to communicate.

- *Intimate zone:* (approximately 0 to 46 cm) is reserved for loved ones. Handholding, embraces and whispering are important here.
- *Personal zone:* (approximately 46 cm to 1.2 m) we interact with friends and acquaintances. There will be more touching and lower vocal volume. Physical contact is possible at the 'close phase' of this zone but there is also a 'small protective sphere or bubble that an organism maintains between itself and others'.
- *Social zone:* (approximately 1.2 to 3.6 m) we are at ease with casual acquaintances in interviews, conversations or, say, card games. Physical contact is not appropriate and business discourse at the far end of this zone has a formal character.
- *Public zone:* (over 3.6 metres), we interact with strangers in a public place. Lecturers and their students, rock singers and their audiences operate at this level.

Exhibit 3.9	Personal space zone distances

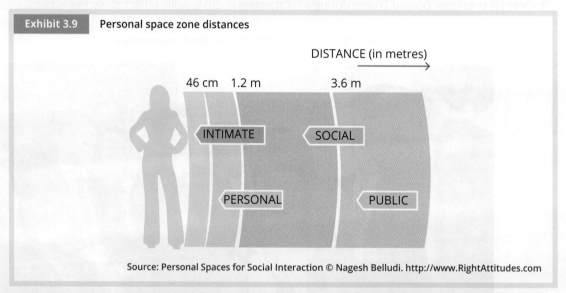

Source: Personal Spaces for Social Interaction © Nagesh Belludi. http://www.RightAttitudes.com

It is important to note that these zones or distances most specifically apply to middle-class adults in Western cultures and are not necessarily typical of people from other cultures, age levels or classes. However, while specific zone distances may vary, all cultures will have 'rules' that govern how they perceive and use personal space. Hall has written extensively about this as it applies across different cultures.

Of course, we cannot always control our social distance, especially if we live in cities or work in crowded offices or factories, or if we go to universities and institutes with huge enrolments. But, as a rule, our behaviour changes according to the social distance we are experiencing. For example, in a crowded lift, we would be in the intimate zone with strangers; so we may turn away from them, if possible, and avoid eye contact. Sharing a seat in a bus or train, we are again in either the intimate or the personal zone of others and will probably turn away from them or avoid their gaze. If a stranger in either of these situations uses the social distance to be familiar, we are likely to be offended or at least feel uncomfortable. Of course, in either of these settings, we may strike up an acquaintance with the person we are thrown together with. This may happen if we like the look of each other, or if an incident gives us something to discuss (e.g., a long train delay). But such occasions are the exception rather than the rule.

CASE STUDY 3.2 How behaviour changes with social distance

In the photograph shown in Exhibit 3.10, a crowd of people are engaged in a relaxed but animated discussion. Consider the social dynamics shown in relation to the social distance between the different individuals.

Exhibit 3.10   Our behaviour changes according to the social distance we are experiencing

Getty Images/Thinkstock

Discussion

1   A number of people in the crowd are engaged in animated conversation. What characteristics of their non-verbal behaviour can you point to that may indicate how they feel about each other and about the event they are sharing?

2   Many people in the crowd are in each other's personal zones, either facing or sitting beside each other. Do they appear comfortable in these zones, or can you imagine them being more comfortable in the social zones? Give details of each case.

3   Are we likely to make exceptions to our usual 'rules' of personal space when in a crowd of people such as this? Are there other situations (e.g., a crowded lift or bus) when these rules are also broken? What strategies do we use to overcome any discomfort?

4   The manner in which we organise and use space is also a means of communicating non-verbally. Can your group give personal examples of how they do this in their own lives? Are there cultural differences between members of your group that might explain any differences?

5   During the COVID-19 pandemic, deliberate 'social distancing' became an important public health measure designed to minimise transmission of the virus. Can you give examples of how this has impacted your interactions and relationships either with friends or with strangers in public?

After you have discussed this case study, refer to the 'Comments on case studies' section at the end of the text.

Reflection question: If you are on a night out in a crowded venue, how do other partygoers signal their need for personal space?

The manner in which we organise and use space is also a means of communicating non-verbally. The physical distances we create among ourselves are psychologically, socially and culturally determined and have an important effect on communication. Spatial arrangements communicate information about the way we live and feel. The size of a house or office will communicate something about the wealth or importance of its occupants. Offices on the top floors of buildings are generally considered to be more prestigious than those on lower levels. A large Australian public company for whom a colleague once worked provided office furniture of different sizes and quality according to the status of the staff member whose office was being furnished – larger, leather, padded and swivel chairs, for example, were only available for general managers and above.

We place distance between ourselves and others according to the kinds of relationships we have or are striving to achieve – particularly in Western cultures. No matter how crowded a bus, train or lift, people always try to keep apart from each other. Even if a railway carriage is practically empty, strangers entering it will occupy seats as far from each other as possible. What constitutes a comfortable personal distance varies greatly from culture to culture, person to person and situation to situation, and also depends on our relationships with the people concerned.

In the office you may also notice peculiarities of positioning. Furniture may be arranged in specific positions to create a particular working atmosphere. People may sit in particular seats around a boardroom table when they are called to meetings. We may have our favourite chair in the break room and feel annoyed if someone else occupies it. A manager may wish to make visitors to her office more at ease by inviting them to sit around a low coffee table in comfortable chairs, rather than in a chair positioned in front of her oversized desk. On the other hand, a school principal wishing to discipline a student in his office may make the student stand away from the desk while the principal remains seated behind it. In **Exhibit 3.11**, what is the impact of the extremely long table?

Exhibit 3.11   Russian president Vladimir Putin meeting with French president Emmanuel Macron to discuss Russia's invasion of Ukraine in 2022

Alamy Stock Photo/Russian Look Ltd.

CASE STUDY 3.3 Crowd behaviour in the public zone: 2021 US Capitol invasion

Most political or social demonstrations occur in the public zone, with demonstrators often separated from authorities by barriers. When this public zone is invaded, rioting is more likely. Amplified speeches, shouted slogans and displays, and sharing social and personal zones may lead to violence as tempers flare and insults are traded. Consider the photos in **Exhibit 3.12**, which show scenes from the 6 January 2021 invasion of the US Capitol building.

Exhibit 3.12 Crowd behaviour in the 2021 invasion of the US Capitol building

AAP Photos/AP/STRMX

Getty Images/AFP/SAUL LOEB

Exhibit 3.12 Crowd behaviour in the 2021 invasion of the US Capitol building (*Continued*)

Getty Images/Kent Nishimura

Discussion

1   Why are people more likely to engage in anti-social behaviour in a crowded public space?

2   Identify examples of various costumes, flags and other artefacts that the protesters are using, and explain why they may have been chosen for this particular context.

3   Why is the image of the protester placing his feet on House Speaker Nancy Pelosi's desk significant in relation to the overall message conveyed by these photos?

After you have discussed this case study, refer to the 'Comments on case studies' section at the end of the text.

Haptics and touch communication

Haptics
The study of how people use touch to communicate.

Haptics is the study of how we use touch – a powerful non-verbal communication signal – to communicate a variety of feelings, including anger, interest, trust, warmth, love or fear. For example, parents convey their feelings towards newborn babies using touch and also use other non-verbal signals, such as facial expressions and tone and pitch of voice (paralanguage). We humans crave touch from a young age to make us feel better. When a child scrapes their knee, they turn to their parents for a hug, and this is often a more immediate and effective communication channel than mere words. In fact, some of our primary emotions, like love or pity, are communicated through touch.

Touching behaviour is partly a matter of individual style and is linked to people's personalities. There are some people for whom touching comes naturally and contributes positively to their effectiveness as communicators. The hand on your shoulder from such an individual may be a friendly, reassuring communication signal. However, the same action from someone else may be interpreted as insincere or presumptuous, or even a signal of superior power and, therefore, patronising.

As with eye contact, there are certain accepted patterns of touching behaviour. The degree of touching acceptable in any social group varies according to age, social situations and cultural background. In some cultures, it is accepted behaviour for men to embrace and kiss each other in public, whereas in other cultures such behaviour would arouse disapproval, embarrassment or ridicule. In Western society, touching is subject to implicit norms. Between those who are closely associated, touching is both accepted and expected, but among strangers it is not encouraged. In fact, we all give out non-verbal bodily signals that indicate whether we wish or do not wish to be touched.

Greeting gestures, such as handshaking or cheek-kissing, involve touch and are subject to social and cultural norms (see **Exhibit 3.13**). Different handshakes can signal different interpretations; we've all heard of someone who has been derided for having a 'wet fish' or a 'bone-crusher' handshake. Among Western men in particular, the style of handshake is indicative of status, power and even masculinity. These days, most women shake hands in business, although some older female colleagues tell tales of the confusion on both sides about who should first extend their hand when meeting a male in a business transaction and how soft or firm the grasp should be.

| **Exhibit 3.13** | Greetings are subject to social and cultural norms related to touch |

Shutterstock.com/kittipong053

Shutterstock.com/Barock

The #MeToo movement that began in 2017 drew further attention to the issue of sexual harassment in the workplace, in particular via inappropriate touching behaviours as well as by other means of verbal and non-verbal communication. In the wake of this, managers and senior staff in an organisation are expected to model and enforce sexual harassment policies and to educate staff about appropriate behavioural standards (Atwater et al., 2021). In general, we need to be aware of how our non-verbal communication, especially touch, may be interpreted by others in the workplace, and consider adjusting our natural inclinations accordingly.

Reflection question: We know that norms of touching and greeting behaviours have evolved quite significantly since the last century. Can you give examples, from the experience of your family culture or by talking with older relatives, of the shift in these cultural and social norms?

CASE STUDY 3.4   Are we living through a crisis of touch?

The pleasure of being touched and held, and of touching others, is crucial not only for newborns, but also for everyone throughout life. This is because it releases a flood of pleasure-producing and stress-reducing hormones. It can even calm the stress response we feel after tragedy, loss or fear.

However, awareness of the problematic power of touch has been amplified in recent times. The #MeToo movement has drawn attention to issues related to unwanted touching behaviours in professional and social settings, and the prevalence of sexual harassment and assault in the workplace (Atwater et al., 2020; Khubchandani et al., 2019). Additionally, lockdowns during the initial years of the COVID-19 pandemic meant that we were kept at a physical distance from our friends and family, and new rules in relation to touch-free greetings were widely encouraged.

These changes have had an impact on professions, such as those in health care, where touch is an important aspect of communication. Davin et al. (2019, p. 559) noted:

> In health professional practice we use four of the five senses regularly: sight, hearing, smell and touch. Of these four, touch (i.e. tactile perception) is arguably the most problematic and open to misinterpretation. Yet … the appropriate use of touch is central to effective and compassionate care. It is a nuanced and complex behaviour defying rigid regulatory guidelines as well as being highly context specific, as it borders the edges of intimacy with vulnerable patients and their (at times vulnerable) clinicians. It is therefore important that learners, clinicians and educators review the role of touch. We need to consider its benefits, cultural significance and potential dangers, and what is considered acceptable professional behaviour, in order to meet the needs of patients.

Source: L. Davin, J. Thistlethwaite, E. Bartle & K. Russell (2019). Touch in health professional practice: A review. *The Clinical Teacher, 16*(6), 559–564. © 2019 John Wiley & Sons Ltd and The Association for the Study of Medical Education.

Discussion

1   Why is touch such an integral part of healthcare practice? Consider particular contexts, such as aged care, physiotherapists or emergency rooms.

2   What are some of the benefits of touch in a healthcare context?

3   What are some of the potential problems associated with touch?

4   What steps should a healthcare professional take to overcome these potential problems?

5   How has the #MeToo movement impacted our awareness of workplace situations where touch may be problematic?

After you have discussed this case study, refer to the 'Comments on case studies' section at the end of the text.

Vocalics and paralanguage

Paralanguage
Refers to aspects of vocal sounds that are non-verbal or 'wordless', used either consciously or unconsciously, to convey emotions.

Vocalics
The study of paralanguage and communication via sound.

Much like our facial expressions, we use our voice both deliberately and unconsciously to convey our feelings and emotions (see **Exhibit 3.14**). **Paralanguage** ('para' means *beyond)* refers to aspects of vocal sounds that are non-verbal or 'wordless', and **vocalics** is the study of paralanguage and communication via sound. Our voice can give insight into our thoughts, emotions, self-confidence and the nature of our attitudes to and relationships with others. We often speak quickly if we are excited, raise our voice if we are angry or lower our voice during times of intimacy.

We also use vocal cues to regulate conversations, signalling when we want to talk or when we are finished; for example, we tend to lower the volume and pitch of our final words as we finish talking. We also use vocal cues to signal understanding or agreement during a conversation, such as 'sure', 'uh huh' and 'okay'. Absence of speech can also be powerful. Pauses and silence can be indicators of respect, disagreement, desire to avoid conflict, or a sign that someone is considering what has just been said.

Exhibit 3.15 summarises examples of paralinguistic qualities. Keep in mind that most of these do not occur in isolation but in clusters. The context in which they occur also needs to be considered – in a noisy bar or shopping centre, you may have to raise your voice in order to be heard, while in a church or hospital, lower tones are expected as a mark of respect or consideration.

We will discuss the best uses of the cues in **Exhibit 3.15** in the context of a formal speech presentation in Chapter 10.

Reflection question: Listen to several news presenters on television or radio. What vocal characteristics do they use to communicate a range of different emotions? Consider their pitch, tempo, volume and vocal inflections.

Exhibit 3.14 Martin Luther King's particular vocal qualities, cadences and delivery made his speeches memorable

Alamy Stock Photo/Glasshouse Images

Exhibit 3.15 Examples of different vocal or paralinguistic cues

Paralinguistic quality	Description	Interpretation
Pitch	How high or low (deep) a voice might be	• Low-pitched voices tend to be associated with strength, sexiness and maturity, and high-pitched voices with helplessness, tension and nervousness • Expresses emotional states, e.g., anger, annoyance, patience or tolerance • Indicates whether you are making a statement or asking a question, or whether you are expressing concern or conviction
Tempo	Speech rate or pace, i.e., how quickly or slowly we speak	• Rapid speech may be difficult to understand or may convey nervousness or being unsure, while slow speech may convey tentativeness or lack of confidence • An overly deliberate speaking pace may indicate condescension or boredom
Volume	How loudly or softly a person speaks	• Loud voices can be interpreted as aggressive or overbearing, while soft voices can be heard as timidity or uncertainty • Speakers need to modulate the volume at which they speak depending on the location and the context
Tone	The emotion or attitude conveyed to the listener about the topic via the sender's volume, inflection, emphasis and pitch	• Tone can be indicated by choice of words or choice of vocal cues • It may be enthusiastic, friendly, sincere, ironic, sarcastic, hostile, etc. • The same words but using different tones or inflections convey totally different meanings: sarcasm, teasing, urgency or sadness

Olfactics and communicating via smell

Olfactics
The study of how smell is used consciously or unconsciously to communicate.

Olfactics is the study of the role of smells in communication. The sense of smell is an important, if poorly understood, factor of human communication. Smells have been shown to affect us at a primal level. While scientists have long known that animals can communicate via body odour, more recent research indicates that certain human emotional states, such as stress and sexual attraction, are also communicated via smell (Chen & Haviland-Jones, 2000).

Smell is closely linked in the brain receptors to memory and emotion (Hackländer et al., 2019); for example, the smell of baking, flowers, furniture polish or a particular perfume can evoke an immediate unprovoked memory of childhood or some past emotionally charged experience.

Our sense of smell is also closely related to our sense of taste and is primarily responsible for creating flavour and the relative attractiveness of foods, although we don't all perceive these in the same way. Smell can also alert us to dangerous substances, such as rotting food.

As noted by Hall (1969), smell also has an important cultural dimension. While in Western cultures in particular, we mask our body odours with deodorants and use a variety of artificial scents in perfumes and cologne to make ourselves appealing to others, other cultures perceive smell quite differently. According to anthropologist Marybeth MacPhee (1992, p. 89), 'Odour control manifests as both the American ideal of self-control and as individual expression, or release'.

Reflection question: What memories (good or bad) from your life are automatically revived by particular smells?

Chronemics and time communication

Chronemics
The study of how people interpret and perceive time when they communicate.

Chronemics, the study of how we use time to communicate, is an important, if often neglected, aspect of non-verbal communication – especially in the workplace (Ballard & Seibold, 2006). Early studies by Hall (1959) made the distinction between the way in which high- and low-context cultures conceive of and apply an understanding of time when they communicate. In Western contexts, the language that we use to discuss time is indicative of the perspective of time as a commodity: we *use* time, we *waste* time, we *make up* time, we *time* our day, and so on.

In professional and personal settings, we judge people by how they use time. Be five minutes late for an interview and your reliability may be questioned. Be 10 minutes early and you may be thought insecure. Turn up on time at a party and your hosts may think you are too keen to make an impression; be one hour late and they may be insulted. For social appointments, some people keep others waiting to demonstrate power or superior attractiveness. There may be a 'waiting game' where people jostle for power in a relationship, using time as the weapon. In business, executives sometimes keep visitors waiting to impress them with their importance. In interviews, pausing and silences can be powerful weapons to demonstrate disapproval, superior power or intimidation. Many factory workers are required to 'clock in' when they arrive at work and 'clock out' when they leave, while company executives are excused from such close time monitoring. Regularly checking your watch or the time on your phone during a meeting or conversation can be interpreted as rude or lacking in interest.

Are there different concepts of time in different cultures? It would appear so. In Western cultures, professional conduct usually favours a fairly conscientious attitude to punctuality and promptness of response. So, phone calls and emails are returned within hours, not days. Applicants are in the waiting room five minutes before the appointment time. For other cultures, such as many in Latin America or the Middle East, a strict time schedule is less important than interpersonal relations, and so people will stop to talk to someone, take a phone call or answer an email even if they have a scheduled appointment. (Chronemics in intercultural communication is discussed further in Chapter 4.) Our work and personal time has traditionally been organised to meet the expectations of the modern workplace, although this has significantly changed as a result of the need to work and study from home during the COVID-19 pandemic (Galanti et al., 2021; Parker et al., 2020).

Reflection question: Do you get anxious when you are running late or annoyed when another person is late for an appointment? Consider your own attitude to time and the extent to which this may cause problems with either work colleagues or friends.

Personal appearance and use of artefacts

Despite the saying 'you can't judge a book by its cover' being true, the role **artefacts**, such as clothes and personal adornments (e.g., jewellery, tattoos, makeup and hairstyles), are important aspects of non-verbal communication. They are all social inventions developed to communicate notions of attractiveness, authority, dominance, status or group identification. Judges and academics wear gowns and wigs, bikers wear leather, business professionals wear suits, and doctors and scientists wear white coats. While some of these conventions of dress have a specific function, they are all serve to communicate a shared identity, group affiliation, status, rank, wealth or some other implied aspect of the individual's personality or worldview. Exhibit 3.16 summarises some of these.

Artefacts
Personal adornments, such as choice of jewellery, hairstyles and tattoos, chosen to communicate some aspects of the wearer.

Exhibit 3.16	Common messages conveyed by clothing or artefacts

Implied message	Example
Group identification	Uniforms (police, military, school), sporting insignia, tattoos, piercings, hairstyles
Wealth/status	Brand name clothes/accessories, jewellery, insignia, titles
Dominance/physical toughness	Shoulder pads, body piercing, leather clothing, heavy boots, large desks/offices/cars
Religious affiliation	Clerical collars, crucifixes, turbans, yarmulkes, veils, burkas, hijabs

An interesting example of how these can be appropriated as a form of non-verbal communication can be seen in the phenomenon of campaigning politicians donning hard hats and fluoro vests (as shown in Exhibit 3.17), normally required for construction sites, to signal authenticity and connection with working constituents (Keane, 2016). Others deliberately choose headwear to signal some aspect of their preferred identity – former prime minister Scott Morrison was fond of a baseball cap to signal his football loving 'suburban dad' persona, while former National Party leader Barnaby Joyce favoured the famous Australian Akubra, an insignia of his connections to his rural roots (Napier-Raman, 2021).

In recent years the norms of traditional business dress have become less regimented; however, women in the business world have traditionally adopted the clothing styles of businessmen as a way of signalling legitimacy and equality (Gilpin, 2008). In the case of female broadcast journalists and politicians, such as Australia's first female prime minister Julia Gillard, the focus on their dress, hair and jewellery is often disproportionate to that of their male counterparts (Goodall, 2013; Williams, 2020). This is illustrative both of different norms that have been applied to men and women, and of the importance of appearance and dress in personal communication and impression management.

While the norms of beauty and attractiveness change over time and are rooted in culture, physical appearance and dress have been shown to influence first impressions and, in particular, willingness to initially interact with strangers. We are more willing to converse with those we perceive to be physically attractive and avoid those we feel are physically unattractive (Richmond et al., 2008). These issues will be further discussed in Chapter 4 on intercultural communication and Chapter 8 on interpersonal communication.

Reflection question: Consider how norms about personal appearance in business or other professional settings have changed in recent years (e.g., the acceptability of tattoos or wearing 'business attire'). Are there still rules or norms that remain in place? Which ones have changed?

Exhibit 3.17 Politicians regularly don 'hi-viz' workwear to signal their connection with working constituents

Newspix/Sam Ruttyn

Non-verbal communication in professional situations

In an interview, participants tend to be closer and more intimately connected than in other situations, such as meetings. This may be why research suggests that non-verbal communication is relevant to success in interviews.

One research study tested the success of engineers applying for jobs (Forbes & Jackson, 1980). It revealed the following:

1 Eye behaviour was the most reliable indicator of success. Direct eye contact (rather than gaze avoidance and wandering eyes) was much more in evidence among successful applicants than among unsuccessful applicants. Short-term eye contact suggests lack of self-confidence. Looking directly at the interviewer conveys more assertiveness, confidence and initiative.

2 Smiling was also an indicator of success (although, insincere smiles were detected easily) and frowning was a feature of rejected applicants.

3 Head movements, usually in the form of nodding, were also features of successful applicants.

4 High-immediacy behaviour sums up success here. It is characterised as sustained eye contact, smiling, attentive posture, direct body-orientation, animated gestures and close proximity to the interviewer. On the other hand, what are known as *adaptor gestures*, such as handwringing, hand-to-face movements and fidgeting, indicate lack of self-confidence.

This is not to suggest that verbal communication skills are not extremely important in interviews. Some studies even caution against placing too much emphasis on non-verbal aspects, especially given the stressful nature of job interviews (Millar & Tracey, 2019). Researchers fairly consistently find that successful applicants exhibit conciseness of expression, answer questions fully and frankly, and keep to the point.

Perhaps you may have found the points about non-verbal communication cues interesting, but may be asking what value this knowledge is to you in your work. Can one change personal non-verbal habits built up over a lifetime? We all have non-verbal habits or behaviours, developed over time, which might irritate people. For example, think of your friends, the ones you really care about. List their non-verbal 'faults'; that is, those areas of behaviour that they might be able to improve if it were vital to do so. Perhaps you are aware of some of your own habits when giving an oral presentation. This might include saying 'um' every three sentences, tugging at your ear, moving around the podium too much (or not moving at all), rocking back and forward on the spot, failing to look at the audience, or mispronouncing certain key words.

The insights into meaning provided by non-verbal cues might help us manage the impressions we leave on those we have contact with in professional life. If we consider the range of non-verbal behaviours – eye contact, facial expression, dress and appearance, gestures and posture, spatial relations, touching and vocalic or paralanguage messages – there may be alterations we can make to our behaviour that will help us create positive impressions.

You may find Exhibit 3.18 useful in evaluating your own or other people's non-verbal cues in a Western context. It applies best perhaps to people's behaviour in an interview or speech presentation.

Exhibit 3.18	Common perception of non-verbal cues	
Type	**Positive**	**Negative**
Eye behaviour	• Sustained eye contact	• Looking away from questioner when answering • Keeping eyes downcast • Excessive blinking or eye flutter
Gestures	• Relaxed, spontaneous, unrehearsed and related to verbal points made • Arms spread expansively out from body	• Hand-to-face gestures • Throat clutching • Fidgeting • Tugging at clothes or fiddling with jewellery • Extraneous head movements
Posture	• Open and relaxed • Frequent and forceful postural shifts • Leaning forward when smiling	• Constricted position • Body rigidity • Crossed arms or legs • Arms and hands kept close to body
Voice	• Conversational style • Appropriate variation in pitch, rate and volume • Volume sufficient to convey competence and dynamism	• Flat, tense and nasal • Too fast, too slow, dull or monotonous • Too many pauses • Ahs and ums, and repeated words

 CASE STUDY 3.5   Non-verbal communication in a police interview

Read the following extract from Australian author Helen Garner's 2014 book *This House of Grief* about the trial of Robert Farquharson, a man who was charged with killing his three children by driving his car into a dam in country Victoria, Australia. The extract describes the police interview with the suspect, and Garner spends much of the narrative focusing on various aspects of his non-verbal behaviour. Read the extract and complete the questions that follow.

The bare, fluro-lit room is empty but for a small, stocky man in a lime-green Adidas t-shirt. He sits sideways on a chair with his back slumped against the wall and one arm resting on the table. His short brown hair is wavy, thinning

and going grey. His eyes are set deep, fatty sockets. He appears not to have shaved. His head is bowed. The slack curve of his spine gives prominence to the plumpness of his belly and chest. There is something piteous about his deflated posture. But when the door opens he straightens up and turns to face the two detectives, who enter briskly with notebooks, pens and paper cups of coffee, and sit with their backs to the camera ...

At the first mention of the fact that his boys died on Sunday night, Farquharson closes his eyes for a second in a moment of private pain. Then he sighs and launches once more on his story.

When he speaks, he keeps his eyes on the melamine tabletop. He has an anxious hangdog look, like a schoolboy. Now and then he flicks a glance at his questioners from under his brow. When he relates the events, he illustrates his account with eager movements of his small, well-shaped, very clean hands. Sometimes he rubs one bare forearm, or audibly scratches his thigh or his armpit. At certain moments, when the questions come in a rush, he blinks rapidly, or licks his lips. His whisks his fingertips across his face, and glances at them. Once he presses his palms together, then wipes them on his trousers. When he speaks of his love for his sons, his over-protective attitude towards them, he shakes his head and clasps his hands. When he explains that his marriage ended because his wife, though she still *loved* him, was no longer *in love* with him, he distinguishes between these two states by flexing his bent wrists and knotted fingers to left and right. At the mention of his ex-wife's new man, his jaw takes on a grey, tense look.

Source: H. Garner (2014). *This house of grief: The story of a murder trial.* Text Publishing, pp. 139–140.

Discussion

1   How many examples of different non-verbal signals or cues can you identify in this passage?

2   How do these create a sense for the reader of how Farquharson is feeling?

3   Would any of the cues give the jury (who watched the video during the trial) a sense of whether Farquharson was innocent or guilty of the crime? Explain your reasoning.

4   In isolation or out of context, are the non-verbal signals described possibly misleading?

After you have discussed this case study, refer to the 'Comments on case studies' section at the end of the text.

Intercultural dimensions of non-verbal behaviour

As we have highlighted already, non-verbal cues are a powerful influence in interpersonal communication. Not surprisingly, differences in non-verbal communication cues between cultures can nullify well-prepared negotiations, and even destroy developing business relationships. Exhibit 3.19 retraces some of the areas discussed previously, but this time in the context of intercultural comparisons. (Chapter 4 discusses intercultural communication in more detail.)

Exhibit 3.19   Non-verbal behaviour and cultural variations

Non-verbal behaviour	Possible intercultural misinterpretation
Body language	In some cultures the open body position (leaning forward with uncrossed arms and legs, arms away from the body) suggests acceptance of new ideas. The closed positions (leaning back, hands behind head, arms and legs crossed/close together, or hands in pockets) suggest defensiveness and shutting others out
Head movements	Most cultures share the habit of shaking the head for 'no' and nodding the head for 'yes'. But some have other signs, which, if not identified, can lead to confusion and embarrassment
Facial expression	Some cultures are demonstrative and expressive; others value the suppression and control of emotion to indicate the desired characteristic of self-control
Eye contact	In some cultures it is considered rude to engage a gaze or stare. Inferiors or juniors lower their eyes in the company of superiors or elders; people of different genders do not make eye contact. While in other cultures, people in a conversation gaze intently at each other, and regard wearing sunglasses as rude
Display of emotion	In some cultures men do not (usually) cry and women are discouraged from showing anger. In others, anger is never shown in public by anyone, and emotional control is considered both polite and dignified
Gestures	Head nodding and 'thumbs up' and 'OK' signs vary in meaning between different cultures, and should be used sparingly
Space	Distance between people interacting in formal and informal situations differs culturally. There can also be differences within cultures (e.g., between men and women, or younger and older people)
Touch	Some claim touching is associated with power: more powerful people touch less powerful people more often than vice versa. The nature and conventions of touching between people of the same sex and people of different sexes can be completely different from culture to culture

Exhibit 3.19 Non-verbal behaviour and cultural variations (*Continued*)

Non-verbal behaviour	Possible intercultural misinterpretation
Time	In some cultures, punctuality is evidence of dependability, but in others they are more spontaneous and 'unreliable'. Some act slowly in negotiations to get to know the other party better and won't close a deal before they are comfortable with the relationship. Meetings have different lead times, in some two weeks' notice is needed for meeting appointments; in others a date two weeks ahead would be forgotten
Other non-verbal symbols	Clothing and colours are two other non-verbal variables. Certain styles and colours of clothing may be considered more professional and more credible, or may be even more prescribed and related to specific occupational groups. For example, company badges may be worn to indicate rank within the organisation. In some cultures, brides wear white and mourners black. In others, people wear pink or red to weddings and white for mourning. Purple flowers might be for the dead, and red ink might be used to record deaths but never to write about the living

While drawing your attention to some variations in behaviour, the complexity of cultural norms and customs means that in all cultures there will be individual and regional variations and differences between the young and old, radical and conservative, and poor and wealthy. In countries subject to a lot of immigration and mixing of cultures, like Australia, generalisations about cultural behaviour will be difficult to make, and possibly misleading. This makes the task of 'culture reading' more complex, and it emphasises the need for vigilance and tolerance.

If you travel, you will need to be particularly sensitive to all of these codes. But how do you learn about them? There are guidebooks on customs, but good general advice is to be sensitive to the presence of cultural stereotypes. It is wise to be courteous, polite, respectful and considerate. These qualities will usually translate well in any culture.

 CASE STUDY 3.6   Mary's crisis: it's often not what you say, but how you don't say it!

Mary McDonald has worked for ten years as the office manager of a company that specialises in IT solutions for small business. Her department is considered one of the most productive in the whole company, and she is well liked by everyone with whom she works. She has always had an 'open door' policy and has encouraged staff to communicate with her on work and personal issues.

Because of developments in new technologies, the company plans to reorganise the section. Any staff changes will be made on the basis of seniority. Mary and her boss agree that the changes will benefit the organisation, improve working conditions for current employees and result in additional job opportunities. This reorganisation will mean a lot of initial work, and Mary's boss has asked her to avoid discussing any of the planned changes until all the details are finalised.

Many of Mary's co-workers have noticed that whenever they make suggestions about improving work processes, Mary avoids eye contact, runs her hands through her hair and walks away mumbling, 'Let's talk about this later'. She also seems increasingly stressed and preoccupied, with the door to her office now closed more often than not. When staff knock on her office door to ask her opinion about a day-to-day problem, her tone of voice is more clipped and impatient. She no longer asks them to have a seat when they come in, and she now speaks to them briefly from behind her desk and then resumes working on her computer. To make matters worse, Mary's administrative assistant unknowingly 'leaked' to a colleague that 'some big changes are going to be happening around here'.

The staff begin to talk, and rumours spread about sackings. Other staff also notice that Mary seems 'less friendly' and no longer joins them on Friday after work for a drink. Lateness and absenteeism rise sharply, and the department becomes much less productive. Mary begins to spend more and more time counselling her staff and in writing reports for their Human Resources files.

Mary becomes very dissatisfied with her job. The boss picks up the signals and calls Mary into his office for a discussion about her future with the company.

Source: Adapted from M. Galvin, D. Prescott & R. Huseman (1992). *Business communication: Strategies and skills*. Holt, Rinehart & Winston, p. 548.

Discussion

1 What were some of the poor non-verbal signals Mary emitted that contributed to the crisis?

2 Were there any other ways to interpret her behaviour? What was the importance of context in the ways that her staff interpreted the cues from her behaviour?

3 How could she have avoided the problems by being more conscious of her non-verbal behaviours?

After you have discussed this case study, refer to the 'Comments on case studies' section at the end of the text.

Summary

Non-verbal communication may reinforce verbal communication via gesture and posture cues, it may communicate the emotional content of the message via voice or facial expression, or it may contradict what is actually spoken or written. It also sets up positive or negative cues or signals, which express or reflect liking or disliking, dominance or submission, and degrees of responsiveness.

In most transactions language is central, and the relative importance of non-verbal cues will vary from one situation to another. How we really feel about an issue is largely conveyed non-verbally, despite what we may say. Ultimately, professionals need to be able to use words and non-verbal cues effectively in their professional work.

Non-verbal communication must be considered within a cultural and social context. We can think of communication as clusters of codes, verbal and non-verbal, that apply in any specific situation and enable the participant to read non-verbal meanings.

While the non-verbal operates alongside the verbal, it has characteristics different from those of language. It can usually be decoded more immediately and automatically than verbal communication. It also appears that non-verbal messages are less likely to be stage-managed than verbal messages; that is, they are more likely to be sincere and spontaneous. Thus they can often give the speakers away, revealing attitudes and emotions they may wish to hide. A number of studies have suggested that non-verbal messages have more credibility than verbal ones, simply because they seem less easy to manipulate. Finally, appreciation and understanding of non-verbal communication are essential to professional communication competence.

STUDY TOOLS

DISCUSSION QUESTIONS AND GROUP ACTIVITIES

For discussion topics and activities in addition to those that follow, please refer to the case studies presented throughout this chapter.

1   How do 'body language' and 'non-verbal communication' differ? Why do we need to understand the distinction?

2   Why do we need to consider both verbal and non-verbal cues or behaviours when communicating with other people and when interpreting what others say or do?

3   What are the most important characteristics of non-verbal communication that professionals need to remember?

4   Name at least three of the categories of non-verbal communication. Which of these are the most important?

5   Which types of non-verbal cues that we have outlined do you most rely on in your own interpersonal communication? Can you explain why?

6   In a job interview or negotiation, which are the most valuable non-verbal cues to maximise the likelihood of success?

7   Explain your own best strategies for using your own non-verbal behaviours in two different professional situations.

8   Mention three ways in which you might use non-verbal communication in a speech to the class to reinforce a point you are making.

9   Closely watch fellow classmates giving their oral presentations. What kinds of non-verbal behaviours show how nervous they are?

10 Give two additional non-verbal cues or signals that might contradict a statement you have just made to your lecturer when you are not satisfied with an answer they have given to a question you have asked.

11 Indicate how you might signal to a friend non-verbally that their joke is in bad taste and is offending your other companions.

12 Conduct a classroom discussion about some myths of non-verbal communication you have encountered. For example, are crossed arms always a sign of defensiveness? Can you always tell when people are lying?

13 Make a study of the eye-contact and eye-avoidance behaviour of people you encounter in public places. Be careful to conduct your observations discreetly so as to not offend or upset others. Some settings you might consider are classrooms, lifts, escalators, footpaths, traffic jams, street crossings, parks, trains, buses and cinema foyers.

14 Observe some people in conversation (e.g., in a café) and make a list of bodily cues that convey confidence and cues that convey nervousness. This exercise can be conducted in class in small groups of three, where roles of speakers and observer are rotated. Observers may then compare their lists and the small groups can report their findings to the larger class.

15 Test Hall's (1969) theory of social distance for yourself. Spend time among a group of friends or colleagues in a workplace, at a university or sports gathering, or in a crowd at a shopping centre. Observe (discreetly) the social distances that apply. Write about your observations, especially about any breaking of the rules you note. Have these changed as a result of the COVID-19 pandemic?

16 Enter an occupied elevator and turn and face the people in it and smile. How do they react?

17 Go to a crowded area like a cafeteria at lunchtime. Place a notebook or jacket on a table then sit at another table nearby. Observe and record people's reactions.

18 Keep a 'touch diary' for one day of this next week and write up your findings for the group. Consider the touching behaviour of your friends with each other – men and men, men and women, women and women, family members, people of higher and lower status, strangers. Try to decide what feelings are conveyed by what kinds of touching and to what extent touching reinforces, contradicts, regulates or substitutes for verbal communication.

19 If you work in nursing or other healthcare professions, how important is touch to the outcomes of the patient? What are some of the 'rules' around this?

20 Try presenting the following speech to your group. Take it in turns, adopting different tones: the first speaker could adopt a tone that is enthusiastic and committed; the second, sceptical and ironic; the third, outraged; and the fourth might treat the whole thing as a complete joke.

> The boss told us today that the firm is to start a new flexitime program next week. The new system will control arrival and finishing times more closely and make sure people are supervised at all times during the day. In return it will give us a guaranteed two days a month off-duty, which we would take when it suited the firm.

21 Imagine you have been asked to write a short manual of 'dos' and 'don'ts' for the use of non-verbal communication in any one of the following situations (write about 300 words):

   a a nurse or doctor interviewing a patient in an emergency room to talk about their health symptoms

   b a senior manager conducting an interview to select a new member of staff

   c a salesperson making a sales presentation to a small number of potential clients gathered in the company's reception room

   d a staff member going to an interview with a senior person in the organisation to ask for a promotion or transfer

   f a teacher, interviewing a student in relation to their poor grades to discover where they need help.

22 Use your knowledge of non-Western cultures to draw attention to differences in non-verbal communication between one or more of these cultures and a Western culture. Consider especially eye behaviour, touching, gesture and posture, and social distance.

23 Watch a recording on YouTube or the internet of a television interview or speech and write an analysis of the non-verbal cues used by one or more of the participants. Consider their gestures and posture, eye-contact patterns, touching and territorial behaviour, and paralanguage. Make use of **Exhibit 3.15**.

WEBSITES

About nonverbal communications, by Adam Blatner, 2009 http://www.blatner.com/adam/level2/nverb1.htm

CNN: Coronavirus has stolen our most meaningful ways to connect, by Bianca Nobilo, 2020, *CNN* https://edition.cnn.com/interactive/2020/06/world/coronavirus-body-language-wellness/

Exploring Nonverbal Communication http://nonverbal.ucsc.edu

National Communication Association http://www.natcom.org

Top 10 Nonverbal communication tips, by Kendra Cherry, 2020, *VeryWell Mind* http://psychology.about.com/od/nonverbalcommunication/tp/nonverbaltips.htm

REFERENCES

Atwater, L. E., Sturm, R. E., Taylor, S. N., & Tringale, A. (2021). The era of #MeToo and what managers should do about it. *Business Horizons*, 64(2), 307–318. https://doi.org/10.1016/j.bushor.2020.12.006

Ballard, D. I., & Seibold, D. R. (2006). The experience of time at work: Relationship to communication load, job satisfaction, and interdepartmental communication. *Communication Studies*, 57(3), 317–340. https://doi.org/10.1080/10510970600845974

Blum, D. 1998, 'Face it!' *Psychology Today*, 31(5), 32–39.

Chen, D., & Haviland-Jones, J. (2000). Human olfactory communication of emotion. *Perceptual and Motor Skills*, 91(3), 771–778.

Davin, L., Thistlethwaite, J., Bartle, E., & Russell, K. (2019). Touch in health professional practice: A review. *The Clinical Teacher*, 16(6), 559–564. https://doi.org/10.1111/tct.13089

Eaves, M., & Leathers, D.G. (2017). *Successful nonverbal communication: Principles and applications* (5th ed.). Taylor and Francis.

Ekman, P. (2004). *Emotions revealed: Understanding faces and feelings*. Phoenix.

Ekman, P. (2009). *Telling lies: Clues to deceit in the marketplace, politics and marriage* (3rd ed.). WW Norton.

Ekman, P., Friesen, W. V., O'Sullivan, M., Chan, A., Diacoyanni-Tarlatzis, I., Heider, K., Krause, R., LeCompte, W. A., Pitcairn, T., & Ricci-Bitti, P. E. (1987). Universals and cultural differences in the judgments of facial expressions of emotion. *Journal of Personality and Social Psychology*, 53(4), 712–717. https://doi.org/10.1037//0022-3514.53.4.712

Forbes, R. J., & Jackson, P. R. (1980). Nonverbal behaviour and the outcome of selection interviews. *Journal of Occupational Psychology*, 53(1), 65–72. https://doi.org/10.1111/j.2044-8325.1980.tb00007.x

Forgas, J. (1996). *Interpersonal behaviour: the psychology of social interaction*. Pergamon Press.

Galanti, T., Guidetti, G., Mazzei, E., Zappalà, S., & Toscano, F. (2021). Work from home during the COVID-19 outbreak: The impact on employees' remote work productivity, engagement, and stress. *Journal of occupational and environmental medicine, 63*(7), e426–e432. https://doi.org/10.1097/JOM.0000000000002236

Galvin, M., Prescott, D., & Huseman, R. (1992). *Business communication: Strategies and skills*. Holt, Rinehart & Winston.

Garner, H. (2014). *This house of grief: The story of a murder trial*. Text Publishing.

Gilpin, S. S. (2008). Disadvantaged women dress for success: A study in empowerment and censure. *American Communication Journal, 10*(2). http://ac-journal.org/journal/2008/Summer/2DressforSuccess.pdf

Goodall, J. (2013). Cracking the dress code: Get rid of those bloody jackets! *Griffith Review, 40*, 31-41.

Hackländer, R. P., Janssen, S. M., & Bermeitinger, C. (2019). An in-depth review of the methods, findings, and theories associated with odor-evoked autobiographical memory. *Psychonomic Bulletin & Review, 26*(2), 401-429. https://doi.org/10.3758/s13423-018-1545-3

Hall, E. T. (1959). *The silent language*. Doubleday.

Hall, E. T. (1969). *The hidden dimension*. The Bodley Head.

Keane, B. (2016, May 17). Let them eat fake: Pollies in hi-vis evoke Marie Antoinette *Crikey.com.au*. https://www.crikey.com.au/2016/05/17/fluoro-vests-as-costumed-campaign-theatrics

Kendon, A., Sebeok, T. A., & Umiker-Sebeok, J. (Eds.). (1981). *Nonverbal communication, interaction, and gesture: selections from Semiotica* (Vol. 41). Walter de Gruyter.

Knapp, M. L. (1992). *Essentials of non-verbal communication*. Holt, Rinehart & Winston.

Khubchandani, J., Kumar, R., & Bowman, S. L. (2019). Physicians and healthcare professionals in the era of #MeToo. *Journal of Family Medicine and Primary Care, 8*(3), 771–774. https://doi.org/10.4103/jfmpc.jfmpc_228_19

MacPhee, M. (1992). Deodorized culture: Anthropology of smell in America. *Arizona Anthropologist, 8*, 89–102.

Mehrabian, A. (1981). *Silent messages: Implicit communication of emotions and attitudes*. Wadsworth.

Mheidly, N., Fares, M. Y., Zalzale, H., & Fares, J. (2020). Effect of face masks on interpersonal communication during the COVID-19 pandemic. *Frontiers in Public Health, 8*, 582191. https://doi.org/10.3389/fpubh.2020.582191

Millar, R., & Tracey, A. (2019). The employment interview. In O. Hargie (Ed.), *The handbook of communication skills* (4th ed, pp. 477–510). Routledge.

Morris, D. (2002). *Peoplewatching*. Random House.

Napier-Raman, K. (2021, March 29). Memo to ScoMo: Stop playing dress ups and start leading the nation. *Crikey.com.au*. https://www.crikey.com.au/2021/03/29/scott-morrison-stunts-dress-up

Oestreich, H. (1999). Let's dump the 55%, 38%, 7% Rule. *Transitions, 7*(2), 11–14.

Parker, K., Horowitz, J. M., & Minkin, R. (2020). How the coronavirus outbreak has – and hasn't – changed the way Americans work. *Pew Research Center*. https://www.pewresearch.org/social-trends/2020/12/09/how-the-coronavirus-outbreak-has-and-hasnt-changed-the-way-americans-work

Richmond, V. P., McCroskey, J. C., & Hickson, M. (2008). *Nonverbal behavior in interpersonal relations* (6th ed.). Pearson.

Ruben, B. D., & Stewart, L. P. (2006). *Communication and human behaviour* (5th ed.). Allyn & Bacon.

Williams, B. (2020). It's a man's world at the top: Gendered media representations of Julia Gillard and Helen Clark. *Feminist Media Studies, 22*(4), 780–799. https://doi.org/10.1080/14680777.2020.1842482

Intercultural communication

Interpersonal exchange between an Australian and a Chinese businessman

Mr Clarke: G'day, mate. I'm Robert Clarke. My friends call me Bob. Here's my card.

Mr Lau: Hello, Mr Clarke. I am William Lau. Very glad to meet you. How was your trip? (The two men exchange business cards.)

Mr Clarke: Call me Bob. Good, thanks. (He reads the card, which says 'Lau Wing-Leung'.) Oh, it's Wing-Leung! Nice to meet you. I'll call you tomorrow, Wing-Leung, OK?

Mr Lau (smiles): Yes, I will expect your call. (Both men depart.)

Source: R. Scollon & S. W. Scollon (2001). *Intercultural communication: A discourse approach*, 2nd ed. Blackwell Publishers.

Meetings like this take place every day all over the world, in offices, airports, restaurants and the street. But this ordinary exchange between members of different cultures has unforeseen problems that create tension and uneasiness, ultimately leading to intercultural miscommunication. The reasons for this lie in the rules and regulations of the participants' own cultures.

Mr Lau prefers initial business meetings to be formal and polite; thus the use of the titles 'Mr Clarke' and 'Mr Lau' is a natural sign of respect for the occasion. The Australian, Mr Clarke, is uncomfortable with using formal titles, and wishes to show his friendship by using first names. Mr Clarke correctly distinguishes Mr Lau's surname on his business card and then rashly uses his given name. In Chinese culture, the decision to use given names is complex and is influenced by kinship, past relationships and current situations. Mr Lau feels uncomfortable at being addressed as Wing-Leung and so smiles (an acceptable form of displaying embarrassment in Chinese culture). Mr Clarke, however, feels secure in his cultural sensitivity and his egalitarian gesture of goodwill. Mr Clarke also wants to show he is considerate of Chinese culture and so avoids Mr Lau's English name (William) in favour of his Chinese name. Mr Clarke is surprised when his follow-up telephone call receives a cooler reception from Mr Lau than he expected.

Introduction

This chapter will show that when practising intercultural communication to achieve our goals as students and professionals, it is essential to consider a range of perspectives. It is important to be sensitive to the possible effects that differences between cultures have on communication. Researchers explain these effects as relating to high-context and low-context cultures, power distance, individualism–collectivism, masculinity–femininity, and non-verbal cues, such as tone of voice, appearance and use of space. Since culture can be defined to include attitudes, expectations, family roles, history, language, non-verbal communication, socialisation, traditions and worldview, intercultural communication has a very broad meaning. To practise intercultural communication effectively requires us to be adequately informed about our own culture and the recipient's culture. It is important to understand how to use and interpret verbal and non-verbal signals, and to be open to evaluating our own understanding and emotional impacts upon others in intercultural, and indeed any, communication contexts.

The short dialogue in the opening discussion illustrates the problems faced in intercultural communication. First, real cultural differences are encountered on a daily basis in the real world; second, problems must be recognised and identified for what they are; and third, these issues must be dealt with in order to communicate successfully. In this example, both parties make intercultural 'mistakes' even though both men try to be culturally sensitive. Mr Clarke's partial knowledge of Chinese culture leads to him making the situation more awkward, and if Mr Lau wished to be addressed as William Lau, then perhaps his business card should have indicated this. Both men's expectations of the other are influenced by their own cultural norms, which they cannot escape. To overcome the miscommunication, both men need to be aware of the complexities of the other person's culture. They also both need to be open-minded and not react emotionally, which is not an easy task.

What is intercultural communication?

The study of intercultural communication is a relatively young field, which forms a subcategory of communication research, and is also included in many other disciplines, such as psychology, political science, education, international studies, linguistics, sociology and anthropology. The starting point is usually said to be the book *The Silent Language* (1959) by the anthropologist Edward T. Hall, who studied Hopi and Navajo Indians, as well as other cultures. Hall developed several key concepts with which he attempted to explain the problematic nature of non-verbal communication in non-Western cultures. In particular, Hall popularised the field of *proxemics*, or the study of interpersonal distance, and its effects on communication in different cultures. Hall's main contribution to the field was to highlight the role that culture plays in influencing human behaviour. His concept of 'social distance', or 1.2 metres, was also extensively used as the safe distance to be standing apart from others in public during the pandemic.

By the 1970s, intercultural communication was firmly a part of communication studies, with specialised courses, numerous books and special divisions established by the International Communication Association, and the Speech Communication Association in the US. In 1983, Gudykunst edited the first theoretical book, *Intercultural Communication Theory*, which was then followed by several key chapters in communication handbooks of the time. Modern research into intercultural communication still focuses on describing the processes involved, rather than attempting to develop general theories. One of the major challenges is defining the term **intercultural communication**; and an equally difficult task for communication researchers, and one fundamental to the field, has been to define what is meant by *culture*.

Intercultural communication occurs whenever someone travels overseas, but also occurs in one's home country and on the internet. Usually, it is differing worldviews that cause the most tension, conflict and problems. Given Australia's colonial past, and its geographical isolation from the rest of the world, Anglo-Australians are particularly oblivious to recognising situations where intercultural communication is

Intercultural communication
Occurs whenever the groups or individuals who are creating shared meanings originate from disparate cultural backgrounds.

Ethnocentrism
Perception of other cultures from the viewpoint of only one's own culture.

occurring, but they are not alone. Since the beginning of the COVID-19 pandemic, with its border closures and travel restrictions, **ethnocentrism** has become more prevalent all around the world (Bizumic et al., 2021).

> **Reflection question:** Have you ever been in a situation where differing worldviews have caused tension in communication?

The importance of intercultural communication

Many consultants, distinguished authors and writers of textbooks discuss the need to understand other cultures because we live in a 'global village'. In 1870 Jules Verne wrote *Around the World in Eighty Days* – now astronauts can make the trip in under 80 minutes, while internet users do it in a mere eight seconds. The media has given us a taste for other cultures, and the cost of modern air travel is within the budget of many people, so we are travelling overseas more regularly than ever before. Holiday travel, business trips, family reunions and conferences in other parts of the world are now commonplace for business travellers and tourists, with the big trip overseas a rite of passage for many young people. The closeness of South-East Asia means that Indonesia, Thailand, Singapore, Vietnam and Malaysia are favourite destinations for many Australians and New Zealanders, while Japanese citizens frequently holiday on the Great Barrier Reef, Uluru and Sydney. We also need to understand global cultures because we are increasingly interacting with them in person or through social media, telephones or videoconferencing.

But there is another reason why intercultural communication is important. Australians live in one of the most multicultural societies in the world. Officially, Australia's population comprises a large mixture of ethnicities, with the 2021 Census (Australian Bureau of Statistics [ABS], 2021) showing 27.6 per cent of people born overseas, up from 22.2 per cent at the 2006 census (ABS, 2006). If you add second- and third-generation migrants, who were born in Australia, and the large number of tourists, overseas students and short-stay visitors, then this figure is much higher. Australians are frequently communicating with people whose cultures originate in other parts of the world. However, many of us are totally unaware of our own uniquely different cultural backgrounds when we ourselves communicate. Our deeply held cultural norms or attitudes may not be conscious, and we only become aware of them when other people break certain 'rules', disappoint us or even offend us. The situation is similar with subcultures within the one culture, such as fans of football or particular music styles, or people from different age groups or generations, who all have their own ways of communicating and behaving.

Culture and communication

Culture is one of the most used but also misunderstood concepts of all time. It is used by politicians, academics, managers, schoolteachers and students repeatedly, often as an explanation for behaviour that differs from one's own. Linguists, anthropologists, sociologists and organisational theorists have variously attempted to define *culture* and the related term, *subculture*. While we all seem to have some idea of what is meant by *culture*, defining it precisely has proven extremely difficult. Informally, the word *culture* refers to a way of thinking and acting that is somewhat related to people speaking a common language. But this is not always true; for example, the English-speaking communities of Australia, New Zealand, Canada, the UK and the US speak the same language yet have distinct cultures. Culture also encompasses traditions, family roles, expectations, attitudes and non-verbal communication.

There is another meaning of *culture*, which refers to activities of an artistic or intellectual nature, such as attending the ballet, the opera or art galleries. This meaning of *culture* is used when academics discuss artefacts of *high culture* and *low culture*, such as chamber music (high culture) versus pop songs (low culture). However, this second meaning of culture is seldom used when discussing intercultural communication.

Many researchers break up *culture* into a series of constituent and sometimes overlapping parts, in order to better understand how culture affects communication and how communication can affect culture. One of the overlooked aspects in such approaches is the impact that communication technologies, such as the internet, have had on intercultural communication. In order to best understand culture, it is useful to break it into four main dimensions:

1 history and worldview, including values, beliefs and religion

2 socialisation, including education, enculturation and personal growth

3 language

4 non-verbal communication.

It is these (and other) aspects of specific cultures that affect the quality and outcomes of intercultural communication. The following will focus on the effects of these four dimensions on intercultural professional activities. Many of the examples will compare Western cultures with other cultures since much of the research in this area is from a Western perspective.

The effect of history and worldview

All of us have a worldview; that is, our perspective on how we stand in relation to everyone else. For example, Australians may ask themselves 'Who am I as an Australian?' or 'Where do I stand as an Australian with respect to people living in other countries?' People from many countries display ethnocentrism by evaluating other cultures from their own culture's value system. Past evidence of ethnocentrism in Australia can be found in the so-called White Australia policy (1901–1958, with lingering remnants until 1973), and the terrible treatment of First Nations Australians, which is still ongoing.

Many cultures respect their history – but some more than others. For example, it has been said that Anglo-Australians have mixed emotions regarding their convict past (Williams, 2015), often preferring to concentrate on sporting prowess and a relaxed way of life. Many East Asian cultures, on the other hand, have a deep regard for their country's or culture's heritage and past. This is seen in religion, art and respect for ancestors, elders and family. For example, anyone who visits Korea will almost certainly be told that Korea has a 5000-year-old history. A long and continuous history forms an important part of the worldview of most of the East Asian cultures, much of the Middle East and many European nations.

In general, Anglo-Australian professionals desire short negotiations or a quick decision, and they emphasise expediency in order to keep up with political, social and technological change. Work happens now, and the organisation needs a decision in order to move on to the next project. Work is linear and tied to the immediate present or not-too-distant past (i.e., last week). In comparison, an historically centred Japanese professional may need a slower-paced meeting or series of meetings. Work may be an ongoing part of a person's social life, family context and employment, and decisions are likely to be influenced by the effect on a person's reputation and the good of the company, including its future growth potential. Thus, an Anglo-Australian might view a Japanese person as ponderously slow and overly careful, while the Japanese person may view the Australian as rushing headlong into a decision and ignoring a range of important factors.

 CASE STUDY 4.1 The Ugly Australian

While one of the authors of this book was travelling in Europe when they were younger, they discovered a certain term used to describe Australians who congregated together overseas – the *Ugly Australian*. The origin of the term is unimportant, yet it fairly accurately described some young Australians who lived together in Earl's Court, London, and who took Viking bus tours and inhabited European camping grounds. The antisocial behaviour included drinking to excess, singing loudly, vomiting and sometimes baring their buttocks through the windows of moving vehicles. The strange thing was that the behaviour of the Ugly Australian was usually quite normal at home, with the ugly behaviour only manifesting itself overseas. According to some reports, this bad behaviour continues to be observed in recent times (Oliver, 2019).

Discussion

1 Why do some young Australians behave in 'ugly' ways on their first trip overseas? Is this behaviour isolated to overseas locations?

2   In the classroom, break up into small groups. Students should discuss the 'ugly' behaviour of people when travelling internationally. Groups could try to describe attitudes, behaviours and incidents that are often seen in settings such as an overseas pub or camping ground. If you have never travelled overseas, think about similar local behaviour you may have witnessed.

After you have discussed this case study, refer to the 'Comments on case studies' section at the end of the text.

The effect of socialisation

Socialisation
The process by which we learn, are educated and grow as people.

Socialisation is the process by which we learn and grow into socially responsible human beings. Beginning at birth, we learn ways of behaving from our parents, siblings, friends, teachers and the media. In totalitarian countries, the government also plays a part in dictating the guidelines by which children are raised and encultured. *Enculturation* is the term for the process of bringing up a child informally without institutional input. There is yet another term, *acculturation*, which is used by anthropologists to describe the way in which a dominant culture imposes itself on a weaker culture, so that members of the latter eventually lose most of their culture. Because of the loss of culture, acculturation has strong negative connotations for most researchers.

The socialisation process has been described as consisting of several overlapping stages (Appelrouth & Edles, 2007). The first stage is called primary socialisation and occurs when a child learns the dominant attitudes of a culture. Children carefully observe the behaviour being enacted around them and typically model that behaviour unless told otherwise. Gender roles, family roles and individual roles develop at this stage. An individual learns how to relate to older and younger people, higher status and lower status people, and what is expected of their gender.

The secondary stage occurs when the child enters adolescence, goes to high school and joins various groups, where they learn group roles, leadership roles and friendship rules. Attitudes to authority, study and work are developed. If the child is good at school, then achievement becomes a part of the child's identity. A person's identity as a functioning human becomes more defined in this secondary stage of socialisation, which can last well into adulthood.

The secondary stage may be mixed with organisational socialisation, whereby the young adult enters the workforce and joins an organisation. Here, the rules, etiquette, norms and procedures of organisations are learnt and added to existing knowledge and skills. Along the way, cultural rituals may have already taken place, including such events as circumcision, tattooing, body piercing, baptism and other religious ceremonies.

It should be noted that the processes of socialisation differ from country to country because of local conditions and variations. Apart from the language differences, going to a school in China is a very different experience from going to a school in Melbourne; and attending university in Dubai is different to attending university in Sydney. Where there is similarity between family life, institutions and organisations, there is usually much less difference between cultures. Typically, large language differences also equate with cultural dissimilarities. The more divergent the languages, the more extreme the cultural differences.

The ability to write effectively is highly valued by all cultures and is seen as a sign of education. However, the writing of persuasive essays, articles and books is aligned with culturally derived audience expectations. The structure and style of a good essay differs around the world according to culture. In Australia, we immediately state the aim of the essay, whereas some cultures may find this direct style is disrespectful to the reader, so an essay may cover related peripheral topics and established ideas in a circular fashion. International students may need to unlearn their own cultural writing knowledge and relearn a new approach to writing and reading in order to adapt to the cultural expectations of the university they are attending. John Swales (1990) identified discourse communities amongst a range of disciplines, and this has led to comparisons with speech communities (and hence culture). These various communities use different vocabularies, structures and styles of writing.

A typical East Asian way of writing includes long sentences, uses coordinating conjunctions and writes around a topic (University of Adelaide, n.d.). This style is similar to Middle Eastern students who may also repeat and elaborate their ideas (Rass, 2015). While research into this topic is minimal, the consensus is that a student will use their original, culturally derived skills in order to write English essays. These often need to be heavily corrected in order to be judged acceptable – even though this judgement of overseas students is clearly ethnocentric.

Language and culture

Language is probably the single most important dimension of a speaker's culture. When asked what distinguishes culture, a Chinese person will usually point to the Chinese language, even though their place of residence may be Hong Kong, Taiwan or other parts of the Chinese diaspora. But an English-speaking Westerner will seldom say that English is what distinguishes their culture. In fact, many people claim to have quite distinct cultures, even though they share English as their mother tongue (Gelman & Roberts, 2017). One need only compare middle-class Australian, upper-class English and African American cultures who share a mother tongue with distinct linguistic variations (discussed in more detail in Chapter 2).

Language may be used for many reasons, but there is general agreement that language has at least two main functions: an information function and a relationship function. Scollon and Scollon (2001) stress that language usually serves both functions in any context, but that different cultures give different weightings to the importance of one function over the other. For example, Japanese culture places great importance on the use of language to convey subtle aspects of feeling and relationships, while Western culture emphasises its use to convey information. A European exception to this is the Polish language, in which subtle forms of nouns and verbs are used to convey highly personal aspects of a relationship.

Some business research highlights the importance of establishing intercultural rapport in order to build good relationships. Cohen and Kassis-Henderson (2012) concluded that knowing the same language is not enough to create effective teams across national boundaries. Western culture's emphasis on understanding a culture and timely information was not as important as the trust and rapport that initial interactions needed to establish. Showing care, goodwill and friendliness is of paramount importance to newly initiated relationships.

Language subtleties

There is a tradition in parts of Asia of communicating without language, strongly influenced by Confucianism and Zen Buddhism. Richard D. Lewis (2005) developed a professional model that extended Hall's theories to include three overlapping categories: linear-active, multi-active and reactive types that all individuals (not cultures) identify with. While all individuals possess characteristics of all three categories, people have a dominant category that epitomises their behaviour. A summary description of these styles of behaviour can be found at https://redtangerine.org/agile-around-the-world/the-lewis-model. The reactive category epitomises many East Asian cultures, where there is a tendency to believe that nothing important can be communicated solely through verbal language. This is in stark contrast to the linear-active category type which comprise mainly Western traditions of language usage, where the effective use of language is seen as highly beneficial and is often the basis on which students pass exams, managers are promoted and politicians are elected. In intercultural meetings, the inscrutable silence of an East Asian person is often misinterpreted as a negotiation trick or a device to gain extra bargaining power, whereas it may simply be an indication of contemplation or reflection.

CASE STUDY 4.2   The Meaning of Tingo

British author Salman Rushdie famously observed that 'the history of a culture can be determined by its untranslatable words'. Adam Jacot de Boinod has a unique book called *The Meaning of Tingo*, which is both amusing and instructive. The book cites countless examples of single words from various languages that are impossible to translate without using a great many words in English. In an interview with the BBC, he started looking at foreign language dictionaries for examples of words for which there were no direct equivalents in English. He goes on to explain:

> *The Meaning of Tingo* [is] about all the world's most extraordinary, telling, thought-provoking, culturally informative, funny, wacky and bizarre words. *Tingo* itself is from Easter Island, and it means to borrow objects from a friend's home one-by-one until there is nothing left.
>
> I picked up, just out of sheer curiosity, an eleven hundred page Albanian to English dictionary, and found within minutes that there were 27 words for moustache and 27 words for eyebrow.
>
> Among [many] interesting words [he found] *nakhur*, a six letter Persian word meaning a camel that won't give milk

until her nostrils are tickled. *Gurfur* is a uniquely telling word. It's an Arabic word and it means the amount of water scooped up with one hand. And then of course Hawaiian is just a godsend because it's got *ohkullanockanocka*, meaning a day spent in nervous anticipation of a coughing spell ...

I am very fond of *areodjarekput*, an Inuit word meaning to exchange wives for a few days only. And *cigerci*, a Turkish word for a seller of livers and lungs. It tells us what a great diversity there is in this world and we should be celebrating that diversity.

Source: Adapted from A. Phillips (2006). The meaning of Tingo: One man's favourite words from 254 languages. *Voice of America* (voanews.com).

Discussion

From some of the examples above, how might they illustrate the relationship between language, culture and its worldview?

After you have discussed this case study, refer to the 'Comments on case studies' section at the end of the text.

Language relativity and the problems of translation

Edward Sapir and Benjamin Lee Whorf were two American ethno-linguists who noted that in different cultures there exist several words for key concepts that do not have parallel translations in other languages. Sapir and Whorf proposed the theory that language evolves to reflect the culture in which it is used, and that the linguistic choices in part determine a particular culture's ways of thinking and what is actually observed in nature. Sapir said:

> No two languages are ever sufficiently similar to be considered as representing the same social reality. The worlds in which different societies live are distinct worlds, not merely the same world with different labels attached ... We see and hear and otherwise experience very largely as we do because the language habits of our community predispose certain choices of interpretation.
>
> Source: Sapir (1929/1958), p. 69

Whorf, who was Sapir's protégé, analysed the concept in this way:

> ... the world is presented in a kaleidoscopic flux of impressions which has to be organized by our minds – and this means largely by the linguistic systems in our minds. We cut nature up, organize it into concepts, and ascribe significances as we do, largely because we are parties to an agreement to organize it this way – an agreement that holds throughout our speech community and is codified in the patterns of our language.
>
> Source: Whorf (1940), pp. 213–214

Few researchers have been able to convincingly demonstrate the strong Sapir–Whorf hypothesis, namely that language determines cognition; although some research appears to support the weak versions of the hypothesis that language influences thinking (see Kashima & Kashima, 1998).

From the point of view of intercultural communication, the significance of the Sapir–Whorf hypothesis is that, between cultures and languages, there may be impenetrable barriers of understanding simply because one language has been developed to deal with situations and information quite different from those of another language.

Fortunately, few linguists agree completely with the hypothesis. Rather than *linguistic determinism* – that language determines thought and that people can think only about objects, events and processes through the symbolised language that they speak – they prefer to discuss *linguistic relativity* – that language influences thought but does not determine it. Thus, although some terms in one language are virtually untranslatable, most ideas can be translated from one language to another.

 CASE STUDY 4.3 Communicating public health information to culturally diverse communities

The COVID-19 pandemic required governments to inform and educate Australians about important public health measures designed to minimise the spread of the virus: social distancing, mask wearing, vaccination and government mandated lockdowns. As Australia is a highly multicultural community, a range of strategies needed to be adopted to ensure that this information was available to culturally and linguistically diverse communities. However, a report from the ABC noted that:

An expert panel of doctors and politicians warned the Federal Government of a 'missed opportunity' to prevent coronavirus outbreaks in high-risk groups like migrant communities, several weeks before a spike of cases in Victoria. Community representatives ... identified migrants and refugees as among those at a higher risk of contracting the virus and passing it on without realising it.

[A spokesman for the] Multicultural Youth Advocacy Network Australia (MYAN) ... said the coronavirus crisis had exposed a gap in the way governments engaged with culturally and linguistically diverse Australians, with translation issues predating the pandemic.

In Victoria, one poster about using face masks when leaving home featured information in both Farsi and Arabic — two entirely different languages, which share a similar alphabet [See Exhibit 4.1].

Source: Adapted from S. Dalzell (2020, August 13). Government coronavirus messages left nonsensical after being translated into other languages. *ABC News.*

Exhibit 4.1 An example of poor translation in COVID-19 health related messaging

Source: Reproduced by permission of the Australian Broadcasting Corporation – Library Sales

Discussion

The reasons for the problem in the case study are complex but include not checking translations and technical wording. In small groups, discuss the following:

1   What are some of the issues related to communicating complex health or government information to multi-lingual communities?

2   As we know, not all literal translations are easy to understand. What strategies should governments and health officials adopt to ensure important information is clearly communicated?

3   Are there other communication strategies that should be used? Why?

After you have discussed this case study, refer to the 'Comments on case studies' section at the end of the text.

The relationship between language and experience, also discussed in Chapter 2, is important to understand when looking at language within any one culture.

The effect of non-verbal communication

Chapter 3 discussed non-verbal communication, especially in relation to professional activities, such as discussions, meetings, interviews and speeches. As that chapter indicated, the more conscious we are of our own and other people's non-verbal cues as they relate to verbal messages, the more we will maximise effective communication and narrow the 'communication gap'.

This chapter highlights the role played in cultural and national differences by non-verbal communication. Needless to say, the professional person who travels internationally is constantly confronted with differences in manner, social behaviour, workplace protocols and negotiation techniques. These may cause embarrassment, or even be intimidating, and may reduce the clarity of communication necessary for effective practice.

Non-verbal communication can be conceptualised as any form of communication that does not use the written or spoken word. It is more than just body language, since it includes use of time, space, furniture and clothing. Non-verbal communication accompanies verbal communication. Try imagining a nod or smile that was not a reaction to some verbal signal, or a rude hand sign that did not accompany a swear word. Non-verbal communication is integrally related to language use and, as such, forms a distinctive part of intercultural communication.

Chapter 3 defined specific areas of non-verbal communication and made some generalisations about cultural differences in non-verbal behaviour. This chapter analyses more closely the potential for this form of communication to help or hinder effective communication between cultural and language communities, especially in professional contexts.

Kinesics

Kinesics is what we commonly call *body language* and refers to those movements of our body that communicate meaning. Our eyes and face convey a wide range of meanings in interpersonal meetings (see **Exhibit 4.2**). In the opening vignette of this chapter, Mr Lau uses a smile to convey his embarrassment, but this smile is interpreted incorrectly by Mr Clarke. According to psychologists, smiles are universally recognised in every culture in the world. But while smiles may be easily recognised, their true purpose may not be understood, as is the case with Mr Lau, who uses a smile to mask his embarrassment.

Some Asian people smile or even laugh more easily than Westerners in response to minor embarrassments or anxieties. Westerners sometimes misinterpret this behaviour as agreement and are, therefore, ignorant about the source of subsequent difficulties. One interpretation of this so-called nervous smiling or laughter, as with Mr Lau, is that Asian people are trying to preserve the interpersonal harmony of the situation. Many Australians have no such need, since their culture reinforces individualism rather than collectivism and group welfare. Thus, in any given social situation, an Anglo-Australian who smiles or laughs is usually expressing emotion, not unconsciously covering up an awkward situation.

| Exhibit 4.2 | Our eyes and face help to convey meaning when we communicate in person. What meanings do these facial expressions convey to you? |

Shutterstock.com/Cast Of Thousands

Shutterstock.com/Cast Of Thousands

Shutterstock.com/Prostock-studio

Shutterstock.com/metamorworks

The accepted form of greeting new acquaintances, colleagues or friends is also very different around the world. In the West, shaking hands is the most common form of greeting, with the cheek kiss commonplace between friends. In Asia, the bow is a very commonplace greeting between people from all walks of life. However, bowing is not the same in each country, with Japanese and Korean people exhibiting more frequent and deeper bows than Chinese people. Shaking hands is also practised, especially in Japan where there is considerable Western influence as more and more Westerners make contact with previously traditional companies and institutions. Even within Anglo-Australian culture, the practice of handshaking has changed, particularly with respect to women, whose hands were seldom shaken 30 years ago. In France, Italy, Spain and Latin American countries, the handshake between men and women often gives way to kisses on both cheeks. This level of familiarity is not normally practised in Asian or English-speaking countries, but given the multicultural nature of Australia, it is becoming more popular with younger people.

Proxemics

Proxemics studies the use of space: both interpersonal space and the space within rooms, buildings, precincts and cities. The use of space varies enormously between different cultures and is a constant source of confusion in intercultural communication. The leading researcher in this field was Edward T. Hall (see Chapter 3), who was the first scholar to categorise the interpersonal distances used by Americans. Obviously, none of our family and friends use any one distance all the time with us. Everyone constantly moves in and out of different spatial zones. Hall was depicting an average distance, but the problem with Hall's zones is that they really only apply to Anglo-Americans during the 1950s. If we were to examine Latin American or Japanese cultures, we would find that their relative distances are typically smaller than Hall's four interpersonal zones. Mediterranean Europeans, Asians, females and equal-status professionals (e.g., a group of doctors or lawyers) also tend to stand nearer to each other than Hall's categories would have us believe (Aliakbari et al., 2011; Beaulieu, 2004; Uzzell & Horne, 2006).

Hall's categories are useful for describing relationships, which may be symbolically represented by distance between people. The categories are also able to explain the discomfort experienced. For example, when an Anglo-Australian's interpersonal space is violated by a member of another culture, say an Italian, who expects a smaller interpersonal distance, the Italian keeps moving closer to feel comfortable while the Anglo-Australian unconsciously backs away. Similarly, in population-dense, crowded areas of Asia, such as Hong Kong and Bangkok, the overcrowding a farmer from outback Australia feels will not be experienced to the same degree by the locals.

Proxemics may also be applied to furniture; for example, the way it is arranged around a room reflects cultural attitudes towards family life. Space is a scarce resource in Japanese homes, hence much furniture is hidden from sight or arranged around the edges of a room to allow for a multiplicity of room functions. Western furniture tends to be organised around the middle of rooms, endowing each room with a single function. In most Australian living rooms, for example, the furniture is arranged around the television set, which is on the same level as the seated family members. The television screen constitutes the room's main focus, while in other cultures the television may be disguised in a closet or lowered on to the floor level, giving it a less conspicuous status. Similar intercultural analyses can be made about differences in the location of the computer, both at work and in the home.

The study of proxemics extends to examining organisational distribution of rooms, staff, hardware and office furniture. Indications of a culture's prevailing attitudes and values towards users or owners of a space might include the position of the director's office on the top floor, the arrangement of chairs at a business meeting or in a classroom, or the use of space in an apartment complex or even a whole city. The sense of strangeness that is often termed *culture shock*, and which occurs when we travel to exotic locations, is due, in part, to these intercultural differences in the use of space.

Chronemics

English-speaking Westerners generally regard time as an inflexible entity, with only a small degree of latitude. When businesspeople make appointments in Australia, they are normally expected to be on time, give or take five minutes. Other cultures are much more flexible about time, with businesspeople sometimes being up to 45 minutes late for meetings.

It is important to be aware of cultural norms regarding the use of time because many people make judgements about others' attitudes, credibility and reliability based on 'being on time'. In Western contexts if time 'rules' are broken by being late or using the set time inefficiently, professionals may be judged to be incompetent or unreliable. In such cases, people usually apologise if they are more than five minutes late for an appointment, as a sign of respect with a view to restoring any damage to their reputation.

As professionals in global contexts, we need to be aware of the variety of expectations and uses of time throughout the world. For example, Western people comprehend action through its changing aspects, while Indian people tend to comprehend time as an attribute. Thus, many Indians consider that action is an unchanging aspect, an attribute of existence. Westerners tend to regard action as an active phenomenon while Indians tend to look upon it statically.

Haptics

The term *haptics*, in its broadest sense, relates to the sense of touch. The study of haptics forms a part of psychology that has developed from our sense of touch. We rely on our sense of touch to do everyday tasks such as using a touch-tone phone, finding second gear in a manual car, or playing a musical instrument like a guitar or a piano, which all rely heavily on the tactile cues we receive. Much research comprises finding the best way to use these tactile cues and so become a better driver or guitar player.

Haptics is also applied to compare different cultures. Anglo-Saxons are a low- to non-contact culture, particularly in the professional setting (Hall, 2005). Anglo-Australians, the British and Americans tend not to touch each other in normal conversation and Asian cultures are somewhat similar. On the other hand, African, Mediterranean, Arab, Russian and South American cultures are high-contact cultures. It is common for Latino friends to kiss each other on the cheek to say hello, and to touch or grab the arm or hand of their friend while talking. It is common for Latinos to hug, to shake hands and touch the arm, or to place a hand on the other's shoulder while communicating. The cross-cultural result of this difference in the use of touch is that Anglo-Australians often feel that high-contact cultures touch to a degree that is uncomfortable, threatening or insulting to them. Italians and Latinos may feel that Australians are cold, unfriendly or rejecting. As professional communicators, we need to be aware of these culturally sensitive differences in touch behaviour.

Vocalics/paralanguage

Vocalics, also called *paralanguage* or *paralinguistics*, is the study of how people use tonal variation in their voice to emphasise certain words or phrases. Paralinguistic behaviour is always concurrent with language usage and includes vocalisations (e.g., *um* and *ah*), volume, speed, intonation, rhythm, pronunciation, use of pauses, and vocal accent or timbre. One challenge for intercultural communicators is that non-native speakers will often accompany a new language, such as English, with the paralanguage that is more suitable for the speaker's native language, thus giving a mistaken impression of the speaker's meaning or emotional state of mind.

It is difficult to comprehend this problem without actually seeing it in action. A good example comes from the BBC's longest selling training DVD, the instructional video *Crosstalk: A study of cross-cultural communication* (Gumperz et al., 1979), which depicts the speech and intonation patterns of an Indian speaker using the English language to ask questions of a British clerk. The paralanguage, which expresses questioning behaviour in Hindi, sounds very aggressive when heard by native English speakers, and so the rhythm and intonation of the voice communicate the wrong message, even though the words are quite meaningful and acceptable. Westerners hearing the paralanguage ignore the meaning of the words and erroneously perceive the speaker as agitated. So they may respond in either a conciliatory or equally irritable tone. The Indian speaker receives an unexpected response to his questions and thinks all Westerners are rude (see Kandiah, 1991).

There are no rights or wrongs in these intercultural communication incidents. We could blame the person speaking to us for not using the correct paralanguage, or we could blame ourselves for misinterpreting the exact meaning. Similarly, we could blame either Mr Lau or Mr Clarke (from the start of this chapter) for their cultural insensitivity. But blame is not the appropriate action in many cases. Understanding all possible cultural factors in such meetings is an impossible task unless one is born and raised in all possible cultures. It is perhaps better to withhold judgements that are based on non-verbal communication until we have confirmed these judgements by using language. Thus, if you are feeling irritation about the non-verbal responses of another person, you should investigate whether your feelings are justified or merely a response to paralanguage that is different from yours.

Other non-verbal communication

The way in which we dress, the hairstyles we adopt, and the make-up and jewellery that we choose to wear are all indicators of our status and our socioeconomic class. Dress and appearance are important signifiers of our social identities, but we are constrained by the acceptable limits of our culture (see Exhibit 4.3). We can think of dress and appearance as a sort of uniform that we choose to adopt in order to belong to a particular group of people in society. Thus, some professional people wear suits in the workplace. In fact, such people are called *suits* by some students and non-professionals. Even within the business subculture of businesspeople, there are classification systems based on the limited alternatives of business attire. Someone wearing a designer-label suit instead of an off-the-rack suit may indicate that they have a particular status within the company. In some workplaces professional women have a wider palette of attire to choose from, including choices of hairstyles, make-up, accessories and jewellery. Even the choices of shirt colour, shoes or briefcase can be signifiers of the professional status of the individual. Hairstyles, tattoos and body piercings are yet another area of wide variability across cultures and at different periods in time.

Exhibit 4.3	The ways in which we dress or adorn our bodies can be important identifiers of social and cultural identity

Shutterstock.com/Paravyan Eduard

Shutterstock.com/Oleg Znamenskiy

Shutterstock.com/wong yu liang

CASE STUDY 4.4 Customs of other cultures

It is an obvious fact that different cultures can have very different customs. However, what is often perplexing is how to act appropriately when we are with someone from another culture. The following intercultural scenarios have been written by S. Paul Verluyten (n.d.) of the University of Antwerp. They outline some communication scenarios involving university students, where cultural differences have been experienced.

Scenario 1

In 1991, I was a student at a university in Pennsylvania, US. I lived on campus and I shared a room with a girl from India. Many times at night, while we were studying, she asked me: 'Petra, do you feel like drinking a Coke?' And I replied 'yes' or 'no'. But invariably, her next question always was: 'Could you get me one?' So whether I wanted something from the vending machine or not, I went four floors downstairs, and brought her what she wanted. It didn't bother me, it just surprised me that someone would ask for this on [a] regular basis instead of helping herself. (Petra K., Czech Republic)

Scenario 2

Valentina and I went looking for my cousin Paola on campus where she was taking her classes. There we met Yuko and a Japanese friend of hers. Since Yuko lived in the same house as Paola, and they were also in the same class, I asked her whether she had recently seen Paola. She said no. I gently asked her to say to Paola that we were looking for her, if she happened to meet her. I noticed that after this request Yuko and her friend stood there instead of continuing their walk, but I did not pay much attention and walked away. After fifteen minutes we came back the same way. From afar, I noticed that Yuko and her friend were still standing exactly in the same place as before. They were still waiting for Paola! (Raffaella P., Italy)

Scenario 3

In my class there are some thirty Americans, and four Indonesians including me. When the professor asks questions in class, none of the Indonesians will raise their hands and volunteer for an answer, even if they know it. Typically, only the Americans participate in the classroom discussion. The professor called one of us one day and asked why we were not participating in the discussions. He attributed our passiveness to a lack of interest in the subject. (Omar H., Indonesia)

Scenario 4

I met a Hungarian girl the first week I got here in Europe. When we introduced ourselves she kissed me on the cheek. It felt strange to me that someone I did not know would show so much affection. We met on two more occasions, and each time she kissed me. Sometime later I arrived back from a long vacation and met her again. I gave her a big hug, but she froze like a statue. The rest of the conversation seemed a little uncomfortable, although the next day things were back to normal. (Brad D., US)

Scenario 5

Kei, a Chinese friend I met in England, announced that she was coming over to Spain for a visit, and I wanted to introduce her to my parents also. I liked the idea of her visit, but I was worried about the behaviour she might exhibit in front of my fairly conservative parents. After her arrival she had her first meal with me alone, and again she did not mind burping or farting in front of me, and even if she used to say 'Excuse me' I found it terribly rude. Thinking of a polite way to express my dissatisfaction without hurting her, I started shaking my legs like one does when one is nervous or upset. Kei said: 'Ana, don't shake your legs like that, don't you know this is really impolite?' (Ana S., Spain)

Source: Adapted from S. P. Verluyten (n.d.). *Selected intercultural incidents*. Retrieved 20 August 2011, http://www.bsu.edu/web/00jjzhao/abc-intl/paul.htm

Discussion

Break up into small groups, choose one scenario per group, and discuss the possible causes of intercultural conflict.

After you have discussed this case study, refer to the 'Comments on case studies' section at the end of the text.

Theories of culture

Two theories of culture are often discussed in relation to professional communication. These are Hall's theory of high- and low-context cultures, and Hofstede's six dimensions of culture, which will be discussed in more detail in the following.

Hall's high- and low-context cultures

In his book *Beyond culture* (1976), Hall divided all cultures into high-context or low-context categories. He maintained that all behaviour, including verbal and non-verbal communication, was either significantly affected by the cultural context (high-context) or minimally affected by such context (low-context). Americans, Australians, the British, Scandinavians, Swiss and Germans all come from low-context cultures, and they react directly to verbal and non-verbal messages. However, for people from Mediterranean, Korean, Vietnamese, Japanese, Chinese, Middle Eastern and Latin American cultures, the context of the message is just as important as the message itself, and in some cases more important. Some researchers have said that Hall's two categories are really a continuum of context and there are middle-of-the-road cultures that seem to fit both high- and low-context definitions. African cultures are examples of these.

High- and low-context cultures differ in their approaches to power hierarchies, social relationships, work ethics, business practices and time management. The dominant values of high- and low-context cultures are significantly diverse (see Exhibit 4.4) and may be the source of many intercultural problems and conflict.

Exhibit 4.4	Dominant values of high-context and low-context cultures
High context (group orientation)	**Low context (individual orientation)**
Harmony with nature	Mastery over nature
Fate	Personal control over the environment
Being	Doing
Past or present orientation	Future orientation
Tradition	Change
Focus on relationships	Time dominates
Hierarchy/status	Human equality
Elders	Youth
Cooperation	Competition
Formality	Informality
Indirectness/ritual	Directness/openness
Spiritualism/detachment	Practicality/efficiency

Knowledge of high- and low-context cultures is important to our understanding of how culture can influence one's own and other people's style of communication. For example, the dominant style of communication in the Australian (low-context) culture has the following characteristics:

1 Most information is explicitly stated; for example, an apology needs to be clearly articulated. In a high-context culture the same message can be communicated through a variety of non-verbal gestures, such as a smile, a sigh, a shrug or a frown.

2 Directness and openness is preferred, with some degree of freedom of emotional expression. Spontaneity and casualness characterise informal relationships. Within this context, successful communication mainly requires an understanding of the explicit norms of behaviour. In such low-context cultures, success also requires knowledge of implicit norms and expectations.

3 Challenging the status quo, within reason, is expected of others. Polite questioning of the boss or authority figures suggests one is perceptive, has personal power and may help bring about change. Independence, self-determination and personal confidence are highly prized, whatever the level of employment. As a contrast, in high-context Japan, subordinates tend to defer to the boss's decision. Of course, in all cultures, personal dynamics affect what is regarded as the rule.

4 Non-verbal communication cues, such as posture, gestures and facial expressions, are very useful communication tools and are encouraged. For example, eye contact is perceived to be important in validating recognition and communicating interest. It is also seen as assertive and shows that one has nothing to hide. The exact opposite is true of high-context cultures where expressions of emotion are often hidden from view.

Hofstede's cultural dimensions

Probably the most extensive intercultural study was performed by Dutch researcher Geert Hofstede (1984), who studied employees of the multinational company IBM. Hofstede surveyed 117 000 participants from 53 separate cultures and then re-surveyed 29 000 of these people several years later to check on the validity and reliability of his findings. He theorised that people have mental ways of behaving, like internal programs, which are developed during childhood and then reinforced by the culture.

Through statistical analysis and reasoning, Hofstede identified six dimensions of culture (as shown in Exhibit 4.5), which initially included power distance, uncertainty avoidance, individualism–collectivism and masculinity–femininity, and later also included long-term–short-term and indulgence–restraint after subsequent research. These dimensions are discussed in the following sections.

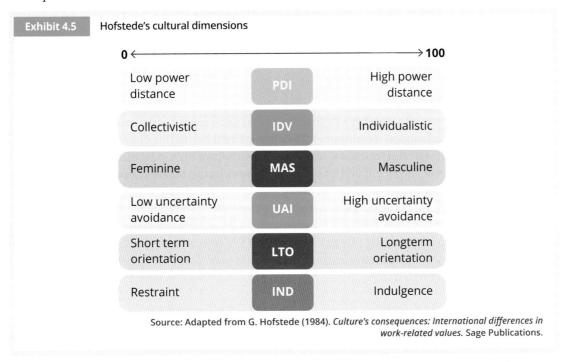

| Exhibit 4.5 | Hofstede's cultural dimensions |

0 ⟷ 100

Low power distance	PDI	High power distance
Collectivistic	IDV	Individualistic
Feminine	MAS	Masculine
Low uncertainty avoidance	UAI	High uncertainty avoidance
Short term orientation	LTO	Longterm orientation
Restraint	IND	Indulgence

Source: Adapted from G. Hofstede (1984). *Culture's consequences: International differences in work-related values.* Sage Publications.

Power distance

Power distance refers to the fact that in various cultures people react differently to status differences and social power. Some cultures, for example, New Zealand, Denmark, Israel and Austria, have low power distance indexes (PDIs) and minimise inequalities in terms of job status, social class or wealth. Managers in these cultures typically want to be 'one of the group' and be addressed by first names. Decisions may be questioned and challenged in these cultures, resulting in flat organisational structures with relatively few hierarchical levels. In contrast, in Arab countries, Guatemala, Malaysia and the Philippines, which have high PDIs, individuals have rightful places in society and authority figures should not be challenged. Interestingly, although China was not represented in the survey, Hong Kong recorded higher PDIs than Japan.

Uncertainty avoidance

Uncertainty avoidance refers to how certain cultures adapt to change and cope with uncertainties in their societies. How much a culture avoids uncertainty becomes a measure of cultural anxiety or fear with respect to unpredictable events. In places such as Sweden, Denmark and Hong Kong, the cultures seem to have low uncertainty avoidance indexes (UAIs), meaning that they cope very easily with unexpected problems and also have a relatively small number of rituals and rules that govern social conduct and human behaviour. These cultures, according to Hofstede (1984), are more tolerant of dissent and social deviance, and encourage new ideas and innovation in work. High-UAI countries include Greece, Guatemala, Portugal, Uruguay and Japan. These cultures promote or even demand consensus in terms of social goals, and they disapprove of any deviant behaviour. Australia has a relatively low UAI, appearing near the middle of the whole range of this dimension.

Individualism–collectivism

Individualism–collectivism refers to the extent to which a culture values individual autonomy as opposed to collective teamwork. Australia, Belgium, the Netherlands and the US have high scores on the individualism index (IDV), which translates into an individualistic culture that looks after family but little else. Privacy, independence and the self are all-important characteristics of these cultures. Decision-making is based on the individual, with competition being the norm in terms of job selection and promotion. Low-IDV regions include Hong Kong, Indonesia, South Korea, Thailand and Mexico. These all have a strong collectivist orientation, which values the group over the individual. Such cultures have a 'we' consciousness and emphasise belonging to a group or many groups.

Masculinity–femininity

Masculinity–femininity refers to whether a cultures prefers assertiveness and achievement (masculinity) or nurturance and social support (femininity). The alternative label for this dimension is *achievement–nurturance*. The cultures of Austria, Italy, Japan and Mexico have high masculinity indexes (MASs) and strongly believe in achievement and ambition. In these cultures, business and professional people tend to judge others according to their level of performance and the amount of material goods that they possess. People in high-MAS cultures also believe in ostentatious shows of manliness or machismo. Low-MAS cultures, such as Chile, Portugal, Sweden and Thailand, adhere less to external achievement and shows of manliness and more to things like quality of life and empathy for the less fortunate. The term *feminine* is somewhat misleading because these cultures prefer equality between the sexes and less prescriptive gender-based roles.

Long-term–short-term

This dimension is a newer finding from Hofstede's 1988 research (Hofstede et al., 2010). *Long-term orientation* means valuing persistence and thrift, having a sense of shame and observing status rules. *Short-term* means valuing personal stability, protecting your 'face' and respect for tradition. Asian countries were found to be long-term oriented, while Western countries were seen as medium- or short-term oriented. China, Hong Kong, Taiwan, Japan and Korea were the most extreme long-term cultures, while Brazil, India, Thailand and Bangladesh were seen as medium-term countries. All of Africa, the US, Canada and the UK are seen as short-term oriented cultures. Thus savings, use of credit facilities, loans and mortgages are reflected in this dimension, with Asians having more savings than other countries.

Indulgence–restraint

This dimension conceptualises wellbeing or happiness as being permitted or encouraged by certain countries, but frowned upon or controlled by others (Hofstede et al., 2010). Indulgent cultures include North and South America, most of Western Europe, and parts of sub-Saharan Africa. Restraint cultures are found in Eastern Europe, Asia and most of the Muslim world. The middle ground can be found in Mediterranean European countries. It appears that freedom of speech, involvement in sports, and more open sexual norms are significant differences between low and high scores on this dimension. Australia would align itself with the US as being at the high end, or more indulgent, than many neighbouring countries.

Reflection question: Can you think of an example of how someone from a high-indulgence culture might behave when on holidays in another country?

Patterns of dimensions

One of Hofstede's most controversial findings was that there were patterns to how the six dimensions appeared around the world. Hofstede suggested climatic, geographic and economic reasons for these cultural differences. Climate, measured by latitude, was shown to correlate with certain PDI scores and masculinity–femininity scores. For example, people who live in warmer climates had high PDI scores and masculine behaviour. People who live further from the equator tend to have lower PDI scores and a more feminine outlook on life (Basabe et al., 2002).

Exhibit 4.6 contains a summary of points of difference between mainstream Australian cultural values and those of other cultures. The statements below are open to questioning and the reader is invited to discuss the behaviours for any known exceptions.

However, one should view Hofstede's findings with some scepticism because his sampling methods were not random. Most of his participants were male and of a particular social class, and all worked for one large multinational company, IBM. Hofstede's results may simply be a descriptive map based on gender, level of education and organisational factors. Some of the data were also collected more than 30 years ago and cultures have changed since then due to developments in media, global travel and information technology.

'You talkin' to moi?' Mediated communication with other cultures

Most professionals would agree that the internet has enabled us to communicate more effectively with our professional colleagues, both locally and overseas. The ease, speed and convenience of email, online collaboration platforms, chat systems, instant messaging (IM) and videoconferencing have revolutionised our professional practices. But there is one area of concern that gets overlooked – the way that online communication affects intercultural communication. Does our Western, informal and very direct use of mediated communication technologies conflict with the way other cultures use these technologies? Or has the whole world become a homogeneous community, each country indistinguishable in terms of their online communication behaviour?

Five thousand years of civilisation cannot be changed by a mere three decades of internet usage. Enthusiasm for mediated communication can sometimes be naive and misplaced when it comes to communicating with members of other cultures, or even our own. With vastly increased opportunities for communication to take place, there is presumably an equivalent increase in the amount of possible miscommunication occurring between cultures and within cultures. However, it is difficult to confirm the extent of this because any research that has studied the intersection of communication technology and intercultural relationships is still ongoing and transforming. Yum and Hara (2005) tested the notion that it

Exhibit 4.6	A comparison of intercultural behaviours in Australia and other cultures	
Behaviour	**In Australia**	**In other cultures**
Legal contracts	Contracts are legally binding and enforceable by law	Contracts may not always be regarded highly. They may not be enforceable under international law. *Caveat emptor* ('let the buyer beware') may be the response
Social customs	Australians tend to be forgiving of violations of their own social customs by foreigners	Other cultures may be more unforgiving than Australians, e.g., a gift may be seen as a bribe in some cultures; informal attire may be viewed as disrespectful
Use of space	Australians prefer lots of personal space	Other cultures may not require the same amount of personal space
Use of time	Australians prefer to be on time and quickly get down to business in a meeting	Other cultures may view time flexibly, and start meetings slowly, with social discourse
Friendships	Australians try to make friends very quickly and regard their business acquaintances as possible friends	Other cultures may not make friends easily. They may view all business acquaintances with a degree of social distance
Class systems	Class is not a predominant issue in Australia	Other cultures may have a strict social hierarchy that cannot be violated
Dress	Formal business attire is important in many settings	While important, dress expectations may not be the same in other cultures
Religion	Many Australians are not deeply religious and lack knowledge of other religious beliefs	Other cultures are likely to be more religious than their Australian counterparts
Practicality	Most Australians are practically oriented. If something has no practical value, it is usually thrown out	Other cultures retain practices that have little practical value but are integral to their heritage
Efficiency/materialism	Efficiency is usually measured in terms of costs and benefits	Other cultures may not see profits as the main measure of success. Enjoyment or satisfaction may be more highly regarded
Change	While resistant to change, Australians will accommodate it eventually	Other cultures may be totally resistant to any kind of change or very flexible
Competition	Australians will entertain competition in business	Other cultures may not be accustomed to competition at all, e.g., state-controlled monopolies
Formality	While ostensibly formal in their dress, Australia is among the least formal cultures in the world	Other cultures may have strict rules governing dress, language usage and behaviour
Equality of opportunity	Australians still have a long way to go, but are closer to equal opportunity than many other cultures	Many other cultures openly practise discrimination based on age, sex, religion and ethnicity
Written communication	Using a standard written document is usually seen as the best medium. Reports, memorandums and letters have a standard recognisable format	Written communication is not universally seen as the medium of business. The content or the writing style of Western documents may be offensive to some cultures, e.g., most Japanese documents are apologetic and place the writers in inferior positions to the readers. Thus, Western documents are seen as too bold or direct

Source: Adapted from N. Sprinks & B. Wells (1997). Intercultural communication: A key element in global strategies. *Career Development International, 2*(6), pp. 287–292.

is the gradual revelation of self in mediated communication settings that leads to the development of trust in others. They found that Korean, Japanese and US students believed that self-disclosure in mediated communication enhanced relationships, but only the US students thought that such self-disclosure was related to trustworthiness. Limited online social cues (i.e., contextual features) perhaps meant that the high-context East Asian students could not trust their fellow respondents the way the US students did.

In the light of online communications between cultural and national groups ever increasing, this section discusses the importance of being competent at intercultural communication using electronic channels of communication.

Worldview

For many anthropologists and sociologists, a person's worldview is an important determinant of their communication expectations. Because work happens in the immediate present, Australian or other English-speaking organisations emphasise fast decisions and negotiations, before moving on to the next project. Thus, when we use email, we prefer fast turnarounds and equally quick decisions. This expectation may be totally at odds with East Asian partners, who may feel pressured to make premature decisions due to the demands of the technology, or may simply defer answering demanding emails.

On the internet, our true identities are most often hidden, unless we choose to reveal who we really are. Celebrities, politicians, CEOs and professionals all have email addresses that disguise their real identities. However, in many cultures, understanding the identity of the other person is imperative to understanding how to act towards that person. The status of that person, their role in the organisation, their decision-making power and their personality are all, to some extent, important considerations that are usually totally absent in mediated communication.

Context

If Hall's (1959) high-context and low-context categories are also applicable to online communication, this may explain why mediated communication technologies are problematic for some cultures. Low-context cultures, such as in the US, the UK and Australia, do not always use social contexts as a way of determining the most appropriate way of replying to messages. But in high-context cultures, such as those of Japan, Russia and Latin America, the context conveys as much information as, or even more than, the exact meaning of the message being discussed. When we receive an email message, participate on a forum or peruse a bulletin board, we are not usually looking for context, and the argument, ideas and prose style of the message are more important than who the authors are. This is exactly the opposite approach to that of someone from a high-context culture, whose whole upbringing requires a clear, unambiguous social structure in order for any communication to occur. Without the context, the high-context person may be lost for words.

Language

Probably the most obvious feature of intercultural mediated communication is the strong likelihood that Australians will be writing in English, which will be a foreign language for many international colleagues. Difficulties with English grammar will lead to mistakes, which may give us a less than favourable impression of our overseas colleagues. Moreover, while we might proclaim the wonders of email, our informal manner of writing email messages may contribute to the interpretation burden on our non-English-speaking partners, so the use of English colloquial expressions should be avoided at all costs.

Our use of language has other problems. Given that language has an informative function and a relationship function, what happens when we use mediated communication with a foreign colleague who is attuned to the social functions of the language, not the information provided? Westerners do not normally ask about family and health in business meetings or professional online communication. We tend to get to the point very quickly, express our individual viewpoints, and expect a prompt reply that affirms or contradicts our conclusions. We do not expect our local colleagues to talk about the weather, their health or their fathers' or mothers' wellbeing. Could it be the case that online we are tacitly seen by many of our overseas partners as rude and uncaring, devoid of humanity and only worried about individual gain?

Non-verbal (mis)communication

A person's use of non-verbal communication is a highly visible feature of their cultural identity. A person's body language, their use of personal space and their appearance are obvious differences when we physically encounter people from other cultures. Less obvious differences are their speech patterns, and features such as tone of voice, vocal inflections, rhythmic phrasing, accent and word choices, which are strong indicators of their culture, class and socioeconomic group. Apart from the simplest devices, such as emoticons, paralinguistic features are usually completely missing in online communication. Thus, when professionals communicate solely via technology, their relationships can be entirely based on the written word.

Using mediated communication, we create a persona via the keyboard, with eventual problems occurring when there is a considerable mismatch between our screen identity and our real selves. Synchronous chat systems are especially prone to this kind of distortion and exaggeration because we are severely limited in the kinds of non-verbal emotion we can portray. Attempts at linguistic subtlety, such as sarcasm or irony, may simply be viewed as criticism.

Humour

Humour is often used by Westerners as a way of breaking the ice in tension-filled situations or achieving group cohesion and is sometimes used in online communication. Unfortunately, humour is not a universally accepted way of doing business, with many cultures having very specific ideas about what is humorous and what is not. Humour may even be viewed as disrespectful in certain situations. In China, it is disrespectful to make fun of one's colleagues or superiors; in Slovakia, humour is inappropriate until after a meeting; in Denmark, sarcasm is a preferred method of joke-making; in Mexico, jokes about one's family are totally off-limits. Any attempt at levity in intercultural exchanges is highly risky behaviour and probably should not be attempted when using mediated communication technologies for professional endeavours.

Problems and solutions

The complex problems discussed so far are not easy to solve. One solution is to try to adopt the other person's style of online writing, their way of thinking or joking, and to undervalue your own natural tendencies, although this solution is misguided and bound to fail. A better solution is to be less extreme in your own cultural inclinations and more sensitive to the possible alternative explanations inherent in electronic messages.

If given the choice of a videoconferencing meeting, an email or a text message, people from high-context cultures would probably choose the slower medium, since it allows for a more deliberate, more considered reply or series of replies. Thus, we can model our collaborative partner's potential responses by leaving the discussion open, by asking open-ended questions and by not necessarily asking for a decision as soon as possible. Mediated communication is usually devoid of non-verbal communication, but we can add bracketed actions (laughs), ellipses (...) and emoticons (e.g., :-)) to our email. If in doubt, one should always courteously ask for clarification, perhaps using an offline medium. Communication theory extols the virtues of two-way communication. Withholding judgement and sensitively questioning overseas colleagues about their points of view is the only way to fully understand their online ideas.

Communication competence

One of the key concepts that this book encourages is the notion of communication competence. Thus, a variety of ways of communicating appropriately have been presented, both in writing and in speech, to achieve our professional goals in the most efficient way. This notion of communication competence is very much a Western idea, which probably originated from the Greek philosophers such as Socrates and Aristotle. In East Asia, it is Confucius whose writings and ideas have had such a great influence, not only on China, but also on Japan, Korea and other South-East Asian nations. Confucianism is not about communicating with your audience or persuading anyone to change their mind, but about individual and group spiritual enlightenment.

In our society, high personal credibility is quite often linked with communication competence. In some communication contexts, such credibility is not demonstrated by behaviour that is dynamic or energetic, but rather by being quiet, reserved and respectful of others, and by fitting in with the norms of the group, family or institution. Additionally, some cultures see competence as non-verbal, rather than verbal expression. Santilli et al. (2011) found differences between Brazilian and US students when they ranked an instructor's non-verbal communication. The Brazilians associated the instructor's non-verbal behaviours with higher competence than their US counterparts. Brazil is a high-context culture and as such would be more dependent on contextual cues for information about an instructor.

Communication competence is a necessary part of many Western university students' degrees, and an expected skill in the real world. But this is not necessarily the case in other countries, whose cultures and work ethics may depend more on kinship ties and traditional values of family, respect and honour, and may prefer non-verbal communication to verbal communication.

Summary

Understanding intercultural communication is important, particularly in Australia, which is one of the most multicultural countries in the world. Culture can be broken up into four overlapping dimensions – worldview, socialisation, language and non-verbal communication. Not recognising differences between these dimensions is responsible for a substantial amount of conflict and misunderstanding in professional settings.

The work of seminal researchers, Edward T. Hall and Geert Hofstede, has been described and explained in order to assist with comprehension of the complexity of intercultural communication research findings. This chapter concludes with a reminder that this book is itself a culturally derived artefact, and that not all cultures aspire to be communicationally competent.

STUDY TOOLS

DISCUSSION QUESTIONS AND GROUP ACTIVITIES

For discussion topics and activities in addition to those that follow, please refer to the case studies presented throughout this chapter.

1   On the internet, look up a well-known brand such as Coca-Cola or McDonald's, or a product such as jeans or sneakers. Search for these products both locally and internationally on US, Australian and Japanese sites. For example, look up Nike shoes in Tokyo, Hawaii and Perth.

   a   How are the websites presented differently?

   b   What colours are predominantly used in different countries?

   c   Why do different countries create different-looking websites for the same product?

2   When you are on a trip in a foreign country, how much about that country's culture should you know? Conversely, how much of a culture should a new immigrant know when he or she arrives in a country? What are the appropriate kind of clothes to wear for a formal meeting in another country?

3   Are there any cultural practices that are reprehensible in your culture? Are there any Australian cultural practices that may be difficult for a foreigner to understand? How would you deal with this in terms of intercultural communication?

4   If someone comes to your home country to live, should they entirely give up their own culture? If not, how much should they retain? For example, should a new immigrant to Australia be required to learn English? Why, or why not? What are possible implications for implementing such a requirement for each of the following?

   a   The immigrant.

   b   The Australian government.

   c   Education providers.

5   Are there any universal cultural values that transcend particular cultures?

6   Ask your class members if they know of words for *surfing or barbecue* in languages other than English. Ask them if they have more than one word for particularly important concepts in their own cultures. Share these with the whole class and identify similarities and differences across cultures. Discuss whether such differences might affect communication and professional practice.

7   Use the internet to study intercultural differences on the Usenet via Google's 'Groups', on Facebook or a chat channel.

8   Culture can also be applied to companies and organisations. Describe the culture of the organisation you work for or the institution you are studying with. Use categories introduced in this chapter to structure your description. Explain which categories were most useful or valuable for your investigation.

9   What are some words in your own language that have meanings that only really apply to your culture? Are there any swear words that are not very translatable?

10 The word 'like' is overused by many people when they speak English, especially those under the age of 25. Why is it the case that Australians, Americans and British people, as well as those from the United Arab Emirates are all using this 'discourse filler'? What does the research say?

WEBSITES

Hans Köchler (2012). Unity in diversity: The integrative approach to intercultural relations, UN https://www.un.org/en/chronicle/article/unity-diversitythe-integrative-approach-intercultural-relations

Nina Evason (2016). Communication (Australian Culture). SBS Cultural Atlas https://culturalatlas.sbs.com.au/australian-culture/australian-culture-communication

SBS Cultural Atlas https://culturalatlas.sbs.com.au

Tom Cox (2021). Understanding intercultural communication in business https://preply.com/en/blog/b2b-intercultural-communication-in-business

United Nations Hub https://www.un.org/en/academic-impact/inter-cultural-dialogue

REFERENCES

Aliakbari, M., Faraji, E., & Pourshakibaee, P. (2011). Investigation of the proxemic behavior of Iranian professors and university students: Effects of gender and status. *Journal of Pragmatics*, *43*(5), 1392–1402. https://doi.org/10.1016/j.pragma.2010.10.021

Appelrouth, S., & Edles, L. D. (2007). *Sociological theory in the contemporary era*. Sage Publications.

Australian Bureau of Statistics. (2006). *Census*. ABS. https://www.abs.gov.au/statistics/people/people-and-communities/cultural-diversity-census/2021

Australian Bureau of Statistics. (2021). *Cultural diversity: Census*. ABS. https://www.abs.gov.au/statistics/people/people-and-communities/cultural-diversity-census/2021

Basabe, N., Paez, D., Valencia, J., Gonzalez, J. L., Rimé, B., & Diener, E. (2002). Cultural dimensions, socioeconomic development, climate, and emotional hedonic level. *Cognition & Emotion*, *16*(1), 103–125. https://doi.org/10.1080/02699930143000158

Beaulieu, C. (2004). Intercultural study of personal space: A case study. *Journal of Applied Social Psychology*, *34*(4), 794-805. https://doi.org/10.1111/j.1559-1816.2004.tb02571.x

Bizumic, B., Monaghan, C., & Priest, D. (2021). The return of ethnocentrism. *Political Psychology*, *42*(S1), 29–73. https://doi.org/10.1111/pops.12710

Cohen, L., & Kassis-Henderson, J. (2012). Language use in establishing rapport and building relations: Implications for international teams and management education. *Management & Avenir*, *55*, 185-207. https://doi.org/10.3917/mav.055.0185

Dalzell, S. (2020, August 13). Government coronavirus messages left nonsensical after being translated into other languages, *ABC News*. https://www.abc.net.au/news/2020-08-13/coronavirus-messages-translated-to-nonsense-in-other-languages/12550520

Gelman, S. A., & Roberts, S. O. (2017). *How language shapes the cultural inheritance of categories*. https://www.pnas.org/doi/10.1073/pnas.1621073114

Gumperz, J, Jupp, T., & Roberts, C. (1979). *Crosstalk: A study of cross-cultural communication, video recording*. National Center for Industrial Language Training in association with the BBC.

Hall, B. J. (2005). *Among cultures: The challenge of communication*. Wadsworth/Thomson Learning.

Hall, E. T. (1959). *The Silent Language*. Doubleday.

Hall, E. T. (1976). *Beyond culture*. Anchor Press/Doubleday.

Hofstede, G. (1984). *Culture's consequences: International differences in work-related values*. Sage Publications.

Hofstede, G., Hofstede, G. J., & Minkov, M. (2010). *Cultures and Organizations: Software of the Mind* (3rd ed.). McGraw-Hill.

Kandiah, T. (1991). Extenuatory sociolinguistics: Diverting attention from issues to symptoms in cross-cultural communication studies. *Multilingua*, *10*(4), 345–379. https://doi.org/10.1515/mult.1991.10.4.345

Kashima, E. S., & Kashima, Y. (1998). Culture and language: The case of cultural dimensions and personal pronoun use.

Journal of Cross-Cultural Psychology, *29*(3), 461–486. https://doi.org/10.1177/0022022198293005

Lewis, R. S. (2005). *When cultures collide: Leading across cultures*. Nicholas Brealey International.

Oliver, A. (2022). Sheer stupidity and diplomatic damage from ugly Aussies abroad. *The Interpreter*, https://www.lowyinstitute.org/the-interpreter/sheer-stupidity-and-diplomatic-damage-ugly-aussies-abroad

Phillips, A. (2006, April 25). *The Meaning of Tingo: One man's favourite words from 254 languages*. Wordmaster. https://learningenglish.voanews.com/a/a-23-2006-04-25-voa4-83127927/117185.html

Rass, R. A. (2015). Challenges face Arab students in writing well-developed paragraphs in English. *English Language Teaching*, *8*(10), 49–59. http://dx.doi.org/10.5539/elt.v8n10p49

Santilli, V., Miller, A. N., & Katt, J. (2011). A comparison of the relationship between instructor nonverbal immediacy and teacher credibility in Brazilian and US classrooms. *Communication Research Reports*, *28*(3), 266–274. https://doi.org/10.1080/08824096.2011.588583

Sapir, E. (1929/1958). 'The status of linguistics as a science', in Mandelbaum, D. G. (Ed.), Culture, language and personality: selected essays, University of California Press, Berkeley.

Scollon, R., & Scollon, S. W. (2001). *Intercultural communication: A discourse approach* (2nd ed.). Blackwell Publishers.

Sprinks, N., & Wells, B. (1997). Intercultural communication: A key element in global strategies. *Career Development International*, *2*(6), pp. 287–292. https://doi.org/10.1108/13620439710178684

Swales, J. (1990). *The concept of discourse community. Genre analysis: English in academic and research settings*. Cambridge UP.

University of Adelaide. (n.d.). Essays in different academic cultures. https://www.adelaide.edu.au/english-for-uni/essay-writing/essays-in-different-academic-cultures#essay-writing-in-french

Uzzell, D., & Horne, N. (2006). The influence of biological sex, sexuality and gender role on interpersonal distance. *British Journal of Social Psychology*, *45*(3), 579–597. https://doi.org/10.1348/014466605X58384

Verluyten, S. P. (n.d.). *Selected intercultural incidents*. Retrieved 20 August 2011, http://www.bsu.edu/web/00jjzhao/abc-intl/paul.htm

Williams, M. (2015, June 8). Stain or badge of honour? Convict heritage inspires mixed feelings. *The Conversation*. https://theconversation.com/stain-or-badge-of-honour-convict-heritage-inspires-mixed-feelings-41097

Whorf, B. L. (1940). Science and linguistics, *Technology Review*, *42*(6), 213–214, 229–231, 247–248.

Yum, Y. O., & Hara, K. (2005). Computer-mediated relationship development: A cross-cultural comparison. *Journal of Computer-Mediated Communication*, *11*(1), 133–152. https://doi.org/10.1111/j.1083-6101.2006.tb00307.x

Mediated communication

After reading this chapter, you should be able to:

- define mediated communication and how it has affected all of us
- explain the different types of mediated communication, their differences and limitations
- describe some of the major issues of mediated communication – privacy, copyright, plagiarism, censorship, e-learning, cyberbullying and online dating
- explain some of the major theories about mediated communication – social presence, social identity, and hyperpersonal models.

Choice of medium is imperative

Carla, a management consultant, had just won a prestigious business award. She was looking forward to the ceremony at the Opera House, but there was a problem regarding bringing guests. Carla had been sent an email from Sharon, the events officer, asking who she wanted to register as guests for the event.

Monday, Sharon wrote: I sent you a reply regarding your email yesterday and I haven't heard back from you. The RSVP has closed. All attendees MUST be registered and if you don't get back to me by COB today, I'm afraid your guests won't be on our list.

Monday, Carla replied: I would like my husband and brother to be registered as guests, please. Thank you.

Tuesday, Sharon wrote: Thanks for getting back to me. However, I can't accept RSVPs via email – what I'll do is reopen the RSVP page for the next half an hour ONLY. Please ensure you go on ASAP to register your husband and brother.

Wednesday, Carla wrote: I was not online after your last email, and have not been able to register my guests.

I am extremely angry and frustrated by this whole process and have decided not to attend the event. I am also going to write to the Awards Council to complain about you and their entire registration system.

There are two assumptions inherent in this electronic exchange of information. The first involves Sharon and Carla's understanding of what 'registering' means. Sharon assumes that Carla has the same meaning; that is, logging in and filling out an online form. Carla assumes that it means just registering names. By its very nature, email is brief, and the assumption is not clarified by either party. The second problem occurs when Sharon commits the fatal mistake of assuming that Carla would be online and gives her a 30-minute deadline via email. A better alternative would have been to ring Carla and politely ask if she could register her guests via the online system within half an hour. The fact that Carla missed the email and missed the deadline, makes her feel like a failure. Her resultant emotions are a mix of guilt and anger. The difficulty may have been avoided if the RSVP system was able to be manually changed by Sharon. But the whole problem would never have occurred if the phone had been used instead of a series of enigmatic emails.

Introduction

In this chapter we overview the range of communication tools that are mediated by other mediums – computers, programs, networks, mobile phones and other devices. We will introduce you to familiar (and perhaps not so familiar) ways of accessing technology. We will also give advice on how to use these ways of communicating with colleagues, friends and acquaintances. However, as the example above shows, email is not only subject to the problems inherent in everyday offline communication, it also brings its own demands, limitations and unique difficulties, which add complexity and confusion. The internet, its services and programs, and the smartphone are essential communication tools of the 21st century and supply a myriad of opportunities for communication. But are we also suffering from communication overload? What are the major problems that these new mediums bring? And every time we use a different medium, are we also selecting tacit protocols of that medium? These rules, when violated, may produce irritation, or in some cases cause offence, resulting in total communication breakdown. In many cases, careful choice of the appropriate medium is the most important consideration.

What is mediated communication?

We accept that most communication is, in fact, **mediated** by paper, air, wires and electro magnetic waves. In previous years, communication that was mediated by computer technology used to be called 'computer mediated communication', or CMC. But the wealth of alternate mediums and various software applications complicates the simplistic notion that computers are, in fact, handling all the communicating, or doing all the mediating.

Mediation
Anything that intervenes or acts between two agents.

The notion that a computer is somehow the conduit of the messages we send and receive does not truly represent the complex nature of the electronic processes that we all now use. In the 21st century, communication is accomplished by our mobile phones, laptops, tablets, voicemail, Facebook pages, networked games and email. Granted, computer chips are at the heart of most of these channels, but the CMC of the 1980s was almost child's play compared with the number of mediums we use today. An umbrella term for all of these new communication channels is **mediated communication**.

In his book *Understanding Media* (1964), the Canadian media theorist Marshall McLuhan (**Exhibit 5.1**) introduced the enigmatic phrase 'the medium is the message'. Many commentators have tried to explain this phrase by saying that the medium is actually more important than the message itself. How you say something and in what medium is just as important, or even more important, than the message itself. As we saw in Chapter 3, non-verbal communication is in some ways more significant than the accompanying verbal content, and if faced with a choice most people respond more readily to the non-verbal medium.

Mediated communication
Any form of communication between two or more people that occurs via a computer or device connected to the internet or other electronic network.

However, McLuhan's catchphrase meant more than this. He was indicating that while we might use a new technology or medium, we tend to be unaware of the changes that any new innovation is causing. There are unintended effects of all new mediums that may bring about wide-ranging changes in interpersonal communication, employment and society. We believe that technology has changed the way in which we think about ourselves so much that we really do feel lost when our network connections crash or when our computers are infected with a virus.

For university students, access to the internet has replaced printing departments at educational institutions in many countries. Few students use pen and paper in class or at home. One of McLuhan's avid supporters, Neil Postman (1990), has also stated that 'technology giveth and technology taketh away', meaning that every new technology or innovation has its benefits, but what we do not see is the destruction and mayhem that this causes in the long term. Progress is a Faustian bargain in many ways, Postman said. In the US, the obliteration of parts of American community life was a direct result of the federal highway system of the 1950s circumventing small townships that depended on the passing traffic. McLuhan and Postman warn us that mediated communication may also bring about widespread changes that we may never recover from.

| Exhibit 5.1 | Canadian media theorist Marshall McLuhan introduced the phrase 'the medium is the message' |

AAP Photos/AP/John Lindsay

Reflection question: How much mainstream media do you consume (e.g., respected newspapers, reputable magazines, non-commercial television) compared to social media sites? That is, are you really an informed citizen or a target of big business and propaganda?

Types of mediated communication

There are many different things that can be thought of as mediated communication. Radio, television and newspapers are traditional mainstream media; blogs, podcasts and YouTube are contemporary mediums; Facebook and Instagram are social media; and email, text messaging and chat are electronic media, and the list goes on.

We would like to leave traditional media exactly where they are – older, one-way, audience-based communication channels owned by large corporations (or sometimes smaller community-based organisations). Telephony is also a much older medium and should not be included in any discussion of new technology. This leaves the newer mediums, which we have placed into the following typology:

- *Interactive* mediums, such as email, text messaging, chat and forums.
- *Non-interactive* mediums, such as blogs, podcasts and YouTube.
- *Social* mediums, such as Facebook, TikTok, Instagram, WeChat and Twitter.
- *Videoconferencing* mediums, such as Zoom, Teams, Skype and other videoconferencing apps.

All of these mediums may be accessed through a standard computer, smartphone, smartwatch, tablet, smart TV or game console. The main differences between mediums lie in their ability to support one-way or two-way communication, and whether it is necessary that a critical mass of people are dedicated users. Obviously, a blog can be interactive, but it need not be – a blogger can still keep writing online with 'reply' turned off. But email cannot really work without a two-way exchange of messages; one-way email is simply an announcement. Similarly, a Facebook account requires a large number of friends to be a part of a social network for it to be functional. The sociability is not an optional aspect of your Facebook or Instagram account; it requires the participation of others for the thing to work. Twitter is a hybrid medium these days because Twitter calls itself a news medium, with most of the world's mainstream media contributing to major hashtags and setting the online agenda for many current issues. Videoconferencing is special because it looks very much like face-to-face communication at a distance but has some important limitations.

The interactive mediums

Interactivity is at the heart of communication, with two-way communication usually ranked higher than one-way communication because of the value of feedback in the process. The interactive mediums, such as electronic mail, chat and text messaging, are the most used forms of mediated communication in the world. Using only the ASCII keyboard characters, these mediums are the oldest, the most fundamental and the most akin to direct writing and speaking. Keyboards are a necessity for the interactive mediums (other than videoconferencing), so computers, smartphones, tablets and games consoles are the most used interfaces. We will now overview the main interactive mediated communication modes.

Electronic mail or email

Email is the most basic, and probably the most relied upon, form of mediated communication in the world. Even before the internet, email existed on local networks that you had to connect to via a modem. An electronic mail message resembles the old-fashioned paper memorandum in many ways: the sender, receiver, subject and date headers are identical to both. However, email is uniquely different. Messages are usually short in length, very direct and informal in tone. The body of an email message is usually restricted to the 256 ASCII characters on the keyboard. The formality and pleasantries of letter writing are missing, so email can sound abrupt and harsh, depending on the message content. The formal greeting and the ending of a letter are often omitted, replaced by an idiosyncratic substitute. Email can very usefully 'quote' a received message in the reply message. It can also be saved and/or forwarded to others. The ability to transfer attachments (e.g., documents, pictures, videos or sound files) is an important add-on.

An email *server* is a remote computer located on the internet that is dedicated to one particular function; that is, serving or supplying messages to people who have the right credentials to accept their messages. Email is sent around the world and stored on these servers using a special email protocol. Electronic mail services can be accessed in two ways – through a 'client' or computer program or through a Web-based interface such as Outlook Web or Gmail services.

An email *client* is a local program for a Windows or Mac computer or a smartphone. Microsoft Outlook is a familiar client for many people. The user operates the email client by logging into the email server to transfer part or all of the remote mailbox to the local personal computer, Mac, tablet or smartphone. The user can opt to delete or keep all the messages on the server, once they have all been sent to the local device. That is, you can have two copies of your email – one on your local hard disk, and the original one on the server. Most users tend to download then delete messages on email servers since they become too numerous to keep track of, and duplicates are a nuisance when they are downloaded again and again.

Another useful way of accessing your email is to use a Web-based service, since it allows a user to bypass the mailbox (spam included) from being downloaded to their local machines. It is much safer from viruses and malware, and it does not take up a great deal of space on your hard drive. The web service logs in the same way as a client, but instead of downloading the mailbox, it shows only the headers of the messages. Typically, users select the important messages to read, save anything significant locally and delete the spam. Savvy users often leave the email on the web server forever, or until they are required to delete it. Thus, they have a record of all correspondence, and they do not have to look after it, since web servers are backed up regularly, unlike local hard drives. Web-based services can be used for organisational email and also for the very popular and free Gmail and Yahoo! Mail services.

Most people make a choice based on how they wish to receive their email. Some professionals use both methods – usually the 'client' for work and the public access web service for personal email. But many people are confused about the exact mechanisms of these two methods. The internet actually runs on *client-server* applications, so understanding the difference will help sort out some problems and issues that crop up from time to time.

In terms of email clients (or programs), there are several reliable and robust programs that can be downloaded free of charge. An example is Postbox Express (https://www.postbox-inc.com), which has a simple and elegant interface, and works on both Mac and PC platforms. Another example is Mozilla Thunderbird (https://www.thunderbird.net/en-US), which is made by the same company that produces the Firefox browser and has just about every feature you would want in an email client. For a different style of email, Spike (https://www.spikenow.com) is a client that looks a bit like WhatsApp and Outlook.

Avoiding some of the pitfalls of email

The normal *salutation* for an email to someone you do not know very well is 'Dear Robin'; do not use 'Sir' or 'Madam'. Use 'Hi Sally' for friends but not for superiors. If you are emailing your boss in Australia, then their first name by itself is usually all right. Kaitlin Sherwood has an excellent introduction to many aspects of using email at http://www.webfoot.com/advice/email.top.php. (This webpage looks old-fashioned, but it is the most popular guide, and answers all the right issues, without any adverts interrupting the page.) Some important email etiquette points are outlined in Exhibit 5.2.

Exhibit 5.2	Email etiquette
Valedictions	These are the closings before you sign your name. 'Yours faithfully' used in letters is too formal, but 'Regards' or 'Warm regards' has gained a lot of popularity. Australians often say 'Cheers'
Email signatures	These are the extra bits that follow your name. Be considerate and only list the most important aspects, such as job title, telephone/fax number and maybe your contact address. You may also add your videochat link, WhatsApp handle, preferred gender pronouns, and awards you may have won. But omit inspirational quotes – these are no longer trendy
Forwarding messages	Never forward someone's message to others without their consent. Just because you have this function in your inbox does not give you permission to use it
Deadlines and time	Never give someone a short deadline or assume the receiver will read the message as soon as you send it. The chapter introductory scenario shows the folly of this. If an email is not returned quickly it may be because the person is on holidays, has work commitments, is unwell or has computer problems, for example
Assumptions	Never assume that the email you sent was actually received. Email often gets completely lost or delayed, especially if the recipient has internet filtering software installed
Reply to all	Be very careful which button to hit when you reply. 'Reply to all' is not merely annoying, it could cost you your job if you inadvertently express a personal grudge to the wrong person
Proofread	Read your email before you send it. Some of the strangest messages have been sent due to typos that were not detected by email senders
Respect	Respect all senders of email messages (within reason), and respond in a timely fashion and a helpful and respectful way

CASE STUDY 5.1   Communication breakdown: Emails are the culprit

Emails were a godsend when they replaced 'snail mail' (i.e. the traditional letter), but now they are starting to become a burden. Several Australian companies have started banning internal and external emails after they were found to cause stress and conflicts and cause work to slow down. [A major company] has banned emails between employees to promote and encourage face-to-face communication.

…

'My staff are very energetic and tech savvy, being part of a start-up. People were emailing on weekends, public holidays and any day of the week with ideas. While the ideas were good, it was starting to get tiresome,' he said. 'People felt compelled to respond and we found confusion and implied tones of voice became irritating and bred a bit of conflict between people.'

…

Emails with clients could also lead to misunderstandings … 'We had a dispute with a client once and it erupted over email. I went to see them and said the same thing to them from the emails word for word and it solved the issue. Emails lead to a lot of finger pointing,' he said. He also said the work duplication was a waste …

Other companies … have banned employees from reading emails during their leave.

…

The Australian Psychology Society had found one of the causes of work-related stress was 'checking work emails at home'. American psychologists, Justin Kruger and Nicholas Epley found 'people overestimate both their ability to convey their intended tone when they send an e-mail as well as their ability to correctly interpret the tone of messages others send to them'. In their research they found the reason for this is 'egocentrism', a social phenomenon where people have difficulty detaching themselves from their own perspectives and understanding how other people will interpret them.

'Of course, there's nothing new about text-based communication, people have been writing letters for centuries,' Epley said. 'But what's different in this medium is … the ease with which we can fire things back and forth. It makes text-based communication seem more informal and more like face-to-face communication than it really is.'

…

Source: S. Tan (2015, March 27). Communication breakdown? Emails are the culprit. *Sydney Morning Herald*.

Discussion

The article excerpts above outline some of the problems associated with reliance on email as the major form of both internal and external communication in business, to the extent that some businesses have taken to prescribing and enforcing how email should be used. Consider your own email use.

1   What are the advantages of email over face-to-face communication?

2   Have you experienced communication breakdowns over a poorly written, misunderstood or misinterpreted email?

3   Do you find yourself checking your email constantly, either while you are working on your PC or via the email app on your phone? If so, why? If not, how do you avoid this?

4   How does the 'mediation' factor improve or cause problems in your workplace communication?

After you have discussed this case study, refer to the 'Comments on case studies' section at the end of the text.

Chat and instant messaging

Talking to others using a keyboard has taken place on the internet ever since it began. The talk command was a basic command of most mainframe operating systems and all Unix servers. When invoked, the screen would split into two halves, and the other person could see you typing messages, letter by letter. However, the word 'chat' is normally reserved for specialised client-based applications that allow you to write quick text exchanges seemingly in real time. Chatting is synchronous, or takes place in real time, whereas email is termed asynchronous, or takes place in delayed time.

The first internet chat system, called Internet Relay Chat (or IRC), was invented by a Finnish student Jarkko 'WiZ' Oikarinen in 1988. The system was a command line Unix client-server program that allowed a user to join a channel of other users or to chat to a single person. IRC eventually became a Windows and a Mac application and had up to 200000 users daily in the 1990s (see Exhibit 5.3). IRC came to public attention in 1991 when live reports of the Gulf War were sent via the medium. The beauty of IRC was the fact that its functionality and many of its features became standards for later programs.

Exhibit 5.3 Screenshot of the IRC client showing a text-based discussion

```
<TomS> Bubba and Stephan probably worship Oprah
<AliceA> he's probably got Alzhiemers disease anyway and is bound to lose
money for the company- then everyone would be in shit wouldnt they!!
<PatA> John is also to conservative! New innovations such as the
computers would be out of his league and by the sound of him he would not
be willing to adjust to change.
<Jacky> why don't we see if any of them want to go?
<JulieP> okay why don't you go ask them jacki
<TomS> John lives alone therefore is more flexable time wise
<Kathy6> Jacki what do you mean???????
<TomS> just a thought
<AliceA> I dont think that anyone wants to lose their job- more so if
they have financial commitments such as a family
<AliceA> pat are you still there? You need to be more vocal about this
<Kathy6> Tim I think his flexibility might decrease with age but hey maybe
he's a yoga freak
>
```

The public successor of IRC was a program called ICQ (short for I Seek You) introduced in 1996, which removed the ability to join channels, concentrating on the interpersonal messaging and allowing user profiles to be searched worldwide. ICQ called itself an instant messaging service and was originally Israeli, then sold to America Online and most recently to a Russian conglomerate. ICQ has lost favour in the UK and the US but is still popular in Eastern Europe and Russia.

In about 2000, MSN Messenger made instant messaging mainstream by encouraging everyone to find friends and chat to them. In many ways, Messenger was the first social networking application since it necessitated a critical mass of friends to work. Messenger quickly overtook ICQ but was replaced by Hotmail and now Facebook, and the dedicated apps like WhatsApp, Viber and Signal.

One of the most neglected aspects of chat systems is the very useful feature of transferring files using the chat protocol. It has been suggested that criminal and deviant elements of society, for example, hackers, terrorists and paedophiles, have used this feature in order to escape detection.

The scholarly research into asynchronous mediated communication is well established, but the notion that chat is also a worthy academic pursuit is not shared by the research community. Chat is thought to be ephemeral, trite, trivial and simply not professional enough for ongoing study. The study of the telephone was similarly regarded by communications researchers in the early 20th century. Research on chatting and instant messaging tends to focus on the interpersonal and intimate nature of the medium, its discourse structures or the use of the medium for workplace purposes.

Messaging apps on mobile phones are definitely here to stay, with billions of messages being sent and received every day around the world (see **Exhibit 5.4**). According to statista.com (2023), WhatsApp is by far the most popular followed by WeChat (China), then Facebook Messenger (Facebook), QQ (China), Snapchat and Telegram. These apps usually include text, audio and video capabilities, meaning that one app can accommodate any form of communication medium, as long as a user has Wi-Fi or data available to them. Most generations of user tend to use the same apps, except for the youngest generation that wants to use a different application. If such a new application exists, then the upcoming generation may completely switch programs.

This has arguably occurred with the use of Discord (est. 2015), a VoIP and messaging social media platform available for desktop computers and mobile phones. Discord is currently infamous for its alternative right-wing activities, and an underage sexual exploitation issue from its supposed anonymity and non-regulated content reputation.

Exhibit 5.4 Messaging apps on mobile phones allow billions of messages sent and received every day

Shutterstock.com/A1.VIEWS

Texting (SMS)

Text message, or SMS, is the most widely used data application in the world with around 27 billion SMS or MMS messages sent every day (see **Exhibit 5.5**). SMS is exactly the same as chatting or messaging but uses a phone network instead of the internet. It is also more flexible insofar as it does not depend on an internet connection, or on being attached to a networked computer. One can send and receive an SMS message from virtually anywhere. SMS is often used by professionals and tradespeople, while WhatsApp is popular for social use.

Even though the protocols for SMS began in the 1980s, the first SMS message was not sent until 1992 on the Vodaphone network in the UK. The text read: 'Merry Christmas'. Notably, the ability of ordinary mobile phones (not smartphones) to use SMS was not originally thought to be a selling point of mobile phones. No marketing gurus, sales staff, engineering staff or early pioneers predicted that this service would be popular; there was no promotion, and no advertising of this medium. SMS was an accidental success that took everyone in the industry by surprise. SMS was only planned to be an add-on that would take up some spare bandwidth in the network.

In the US during the 1990s, SMS was not able to be fully implemented because the different network companies, such as AT&T, Sprint and Verizon, used different standards, so users of one network could not use SMS to reach users of other networks. It took 10 years for a single standard to be reached, and so SMS was enjoyed all over Europe, South-East Asia and Australia, but not in the USA for a long time.

Some commentators have stated that the popularity of SMS was the impetus for the creation of a new way of communicating using emoticons and highly abbreviated words and acronyms. This is incorrect. These keyboard shortcuts were already being used by chat users on the internet several years earlier. The popularity of SMS was largely due to the consumer using a medium in new and innovative ways, and most of these consumers were a generation of young people who still use SMS in preference to voice

Exhibit 5.5   SMS is popular worldwide

Shutterstock.com/DC Studio

messages. While email used to be eschewed in favour of text, the smartphone has meant that sending emails is now just as convenient as sending an SMS. Thus, advertising has now gone from sombre images of business-suited men, to bright, colourful pictures of teenagers using their preferred mediums.

One of the most controversial aspects of texting is the attachment of self-produced sexually explicit images and video (or 'nudes') via SMS and chat messages. The term for this behaviour is 'sexting', and it has become a problem because even consensual, self-produced erotic images involving underage teenagers are illegal. Cyberbullying is often discussed at the same time as sexting in both the popular and academic literature because people use and distribute other peoples' 'nudes' to intimidate, harass or bully them.

Forums

The old phrase for forums or discussion groups was 'computer conferencing'. In the early days of the internet, there were two main applications that were a must-have for internet users: electronic mail and the Usenet. Chat was always possible but was never a mainstream method of electronic communication. The Usenet (or usernet) began life in 1979 when two US students wrote a program to exchange messages on three servers in North Carolina. The idea took off and the content of the messages was dubbed 'news' and the channels or groups were called 'newsgroups'. A special set of protocols was then created for the news. In the 1980s and early 1990s, the Usenet was a large set of text-based computer conferences that circled the globe every few days. Various Usenet moderators at the large universities would choose which groups would be allowed to be accessed by the local users. Unix programs and eventually Windows/Mac clients were written to access the newsgroups.

Before the Web, the Usenet was the only way to put up public messages for global consumption and was mainly the province of computer and engineering students. Nine hierarchies were created that allowed for a logical method of categorising the content of the news messages. The hierarchies were:

1 *comp.** – computer-related discussions (e.g. comp.software)
2 *humanities.** – fine arts, literature, philosophy (humanities.classics, humanities.design.misc)

3 *misc.** – miscellaneous topics (misc.education, misc.forsale, misc.kids)

4 *news.** – discussions and announcements about news (meaning Usenet, not current events)

5 *rec.** – recreation and entertainment (rec.music, rec.arts.movies)

6 *sci.** – science-related discussions (sci.psychology, sci.research)

7 *soc.** – social discussions (soc.college.org, soc.culture.african)

8 *talk.** – talk about various controversial topics (talk.religion, talk.politics)

9 *alt.** – the anarchistic hierarchy of everything else (alt.binaries).

The last hierarchy, *alt.*, is where all the binaries, or programs, were sent, and where all the controversial content (e.g., pornography and copyright violations) were posted. Indeed, it was the flawed Usenet research of a graduate student, Martin Rimm, in 1995 that provided the content for Philip Elmer-DeWitt's now infamous *Time* magazine 'Cyberporn' article. The internet and the Web were unknown to most politicians of the time, and the *Time* article mistakenly stated that 83 per cent of all images on the internet were pornographic. Subsequently, the US government legislated the *Communications Decency Act* in 1996, which made it a criminal offence for any service provider or any author to insert a link on to a webpage or email that could possibly lead to a minor accessing pornography. The punishment was US$100 000 or up to two years imprisonment. Internet outrage led to a blue ribbon being placed on every participating website in the US. Part of this Act was blocked a few months later by the Supreme Court on constitutional grounds.

The reaction of the Australian government was to copycat American laws, with similar legislation being passed in 1999 and 2007, which were amendments to the *Broadcasting Services Act 1992*; however, the regulations governing internet censorship of sexual content were never repealed, leading to Australia having some of the most draconian internet laws in the world. We will discuss this issue later in the chapter.

Today, Google Groups (https://groups.google.com) is the largest set of conferencing forums in the world. Google Groups is the place to find content related to any special interest you can think of. The news articles themselves might be queries, replies, technical documents, stories, reviews, pictures or even programs. Each article's 'life' is about a week. The articles range from the highly informative and technical to the most trivial and even offensive. Rec, misc and alt groups vary enormously in their content and tone. A query in Google Groups into the rec.* hierarchy about what others have experienced will usually garner a number of replies within hours, and you will then have your own custom review of your intended purchase.

In 2020, Google changed all new and current users to a new interface and phased out the default classic hierarchy of newsgroups. Newsgroups tend to be organisationally oriented and are still being used, especially in high-tech firms. Most ordinary people tend not to use these bulletin boards, preferring the newer, image centric social media platforms. The classic groups can still be accessed by changing settings in the user profile.

The non-interactive mediums

Non-interactive mediums are those that are mainly one-way communication applications, and include blogs, YouTube and podcasts. All these mediums have added the ability for others to make comments, or respond in kind, but the majority of the content has one-to-many appeal that is similar to the traditional mass media like radio, television or magazines.

Blogs

Blogs gained notoriety when several political blogs appeared in the early 2000s. Andrew Sullivan's blog (Andrew.Sullivan.com, now *The Daily Dish*) gained readership in 2001, especially after the 9/11 terrorist attacks. Blogging became mainstream in 2002, when several blogs covered comments by Senator Lott, then Republican Senate Majority Leader. No traditional media reported Lott's implied advocacy of racial segregation but, largely due to the blog reports, Senator Lott was forced to step down as leader. While blogs were seen as reliable, they were more often seen as alternative sources of news and opinion, generally in opposition to the traditional media. However, online blogging was becoming a normal news source and has begun to be taught by major journalism schools across the US. Blogs are also now seen as a non-fiction source of creativity and writing style. For example, the website https://effectiveideas.org offers five prizes of $100 000 for recent, influential blogs, presumably by emerging writers. Blogs are often evaluated according to quality, presentation and social media integration.

Blogs have increasingly gained credibility and prestige as media outlets, with political consultants, news services and politicians using blogs to pursue their own activities. Some bloggers have become celebrities in their own right and have moved over to more traditional media or had guest spots on radio or television. Blogs were an important source of current news during the December 2004 tsunami and Hurricane Katrina. *The Guardian* newspaper in the UK redesigned its website in 2005 to include a daily digest of blogs. *The Huffington Post* began its life as a blog in 2005 and the *BBC News* also launched a blog for its editors in 2006. No-one knows for certain, but there are an estimated 600 million blogs worldwide (Wise, 2023).

The typical way to search for blogs is to use a search engine such as Google and add the word 'blog' to the end of the query. Other search tools such as Technorati (http://technorati.com) are also useful but cannot discern between an Australian blog and an overseas one, especially because many Australians are using a .com site. The Australian Index (http://theaustralianindex.com), shows that Australian blogs mainly relate to food, music, fashion, craft, sports and culture.

YouTube is often seen as a social media platform but began its life in 2005 as a 'vlog' or video blog. The comments attached to many videos are not the core purpose of YouTube, which is really just a blog using videos, not text.

YouTube

YouTube has completely changed the nature of communication, entertainment, advertising, education, DIY instructions and politics (see **Exhibit 5.6**). It was started by three disgruntled PayPal employees in February 2005, who give conflicting accounts of exactly who came up with the idea. In December of the same year, Nike uploaded a soccer video of Ronaldinho on the site, and it ended up being viewed one million times. By July the following year, YouTube was estimated to be showing 100 million clips per day. Both Google and MySpace tried without success to launch their own versions, and eventually YouTube was sold to Google in 2006 for $1.65 billion. By 2010, YouTube was still not making any profit, and advertising, while disliked, has since become the key way that YouTube turns a profit.

Exhibit 5.6	YouTube revolutionised video communication and entertainment

Shutterstock.com/PixieMe

The original policy about video content on YouTube was simple: no obscenity and no copyright violations. In the beginning, these two rules were fiercely policed. Infringements were strictly enforced with dubious videos lasting only a few days. Additionally, several media corporations have successfully sued YouTube for breaches of copyright. Thus, potential uploaders are shown a screen with the message 'Do not upload any TV shows, music videos, music concerts or advertisements without permission, unless they consist entirely of content that you created yourself'. Despite this warning, there are still hundreds of unauthorised clips of copyrighted material. YouTube does not view videos before they are posted online, and it is left to copyright holders to issue a takedown notice pursuant to the terms of the US *Digital Millennium Copyright Act 1998*. However, copyright owners can choose not to complain, with many copyright violations left unchallenged by their rightful owners. YouTube can host the clip and make money from it without the owner objecting. Obviously, some copyright owners believe that the free advertising and exposure that YouTube engenders is a worthwhile trade-off. Exhibit 5.7 provides some revealing statistics about YouTube.

Exhibit 5.7   YouTube statistics

One billion hours of YouTube content is viewed each day

Females outnumber males in terms of users

YouTube is more popular with users **35 years or younger**

70% of videos are viewed on a mobile phone

Videos with more comments are more popular

27% of users use YouTube for news content

YouTube is by far most popular in the US

YouTube has a bigger audience than Netflix

Sources: YouTube Press; Statista; Think with Google; Backlinko; Channel Meter

As with much of the internet, YouTube used to be the place for young adults searching for music videos and skateboard tricks, but with a changing demographic audience in the millions, it is now the domain of politics, news, business and technical communicators. US President Joe Biden has a regular YouTube video, as do many other world leaders, but the usual comments section has been turned off for obvious reasons. In Australia, the Labor Party has used YouTube for campaigning since 2007 (allowing ratings but no comments). All the other major political parties have a YouTube presence, notably the Liberals, whose videos are also available on their own secure site.

In terms of business, YouTube has become a new frontier of marketing and self-promotion for companies of all descriptions. Corporations and sole businesses alike have set up channels that reflect the company brand and allow engagement with others. As a result, highly creative videos are being produced that resemble trailers of soon-to-be-released films, video testimonials are shot to give added credibility, products and services are being more fully explained, and mass media advertisements on YouTube are lasting much longer than through other channels. One of the most interesting offshoots is the huge number of technical and how-to videos that explain and review processes of all manner of products and software. In the past, if you wanted to know how to operate a certain mobile phone or how to perform a task using Photoshop, you needed to buy a manual. Not anymore. Instructions for performing a task with any given product are usually available on YouTube. In fact, there are videos of users unwrapping, or 'unboxing', popular cameras, mobile phones and computers and then reviewing the packaging!

Podcasts

Podcasts – a term combining 'iPod' and 'broadcasts' – are technically any form of video or audio file that is available for download via the Web. Podcasts were not normally thought of as being streamed (i.e. playing as they are being downloaded); however, modern browser technology allows any podcast file to be played, given bandwidth considerations. Thus, the term 'podcast' would seem to be inaccurate, since most users are streaming these files nowadays and no-one is doing the broadcasting!

The original word 'podcast' came from Aled Williams of *The Guardian* in 2004, but even then, the alternate terms 'webcast' or 'netcast' would have been more appropriate since iPods were just one device capable of receiving the files. Webcasts of lectures were once provided under the name of downloadable files. In the age of YouTube, the notion of podcasts will probably fade into obscurity.

The social mediums

The social mediums (see **Exhibit 5.8**) are the most recent forms of mediated communication, since they rely on universal access to the internet and a critical mass of users who populate or congregate around a user's account or profile. Such social networking would not have been possible when the Web first started. At that time, slow networks, limited bandwidth and a specialist kind of user meant that one's wider circle of family, friends and acquaintances were not online to befriend. Many of the social mediums have been associated with Web 2.0, which is shorthand for an upgrade of the original World Wide Web – not in terms of the network, but in the philosophy behind website sharing, interoperability, user-centred design and collaboration.

| Exhibit 5.8 | Various social networking sites |

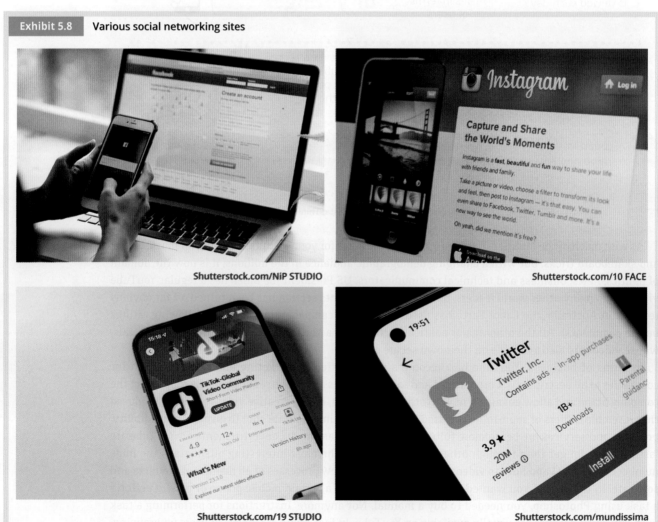

Shutterstock.com/NiP STUDIO

Shutterstock.com/10 FACE

Shutterstock.com/19 STUDIO

Shutterstock.com/mundissima

Facebook and Meta

Facebook (see **Exhibit 5.9**) is the medium that most people over the age of 35 think of when social media is mentioned. It offers chat, blogging, a marketplace classifieds section, text messages, voice calls and video calls, all from one account. In 2023, Facebook has the status of the most visited social media website in the world (Google is most popular website; Socialmediatoday.com, 2023). Facebook has over 2.963 billion active users (Datareportal.com, 19 February 2023) and is most popular in India and the USA.

| **Exhibit 5.9** | Facebook is the most visited social media website |

Shutterstock.com/chrisdorney

Facebook was launched in February 2004 by Mark Zuckerberg and his colleagues as a way for Harvard College students to own a home page and invite friends to view ideas and photos. The idea spread to other colleges across the US, and then to high schools, and later to anyone in the world. By 2008, Facebook was attracting large amounts of advertising revenue and became the third-largest US Web-based company, after Google and Amazon, edging out eBay in fourth place.

Being on Facebook is like being at a huge virtual party, where you get to share your life with, and the lives of, anyone who is willing to be your 'friend'. Thus, people start to make the acquaintance of friends of friends, and then friends of friends of friends – their social circle widens as users go searching for new people to get to know. Facebook users can have thousands of friends and can spend hours a day catching up on these friends' activities. But is it real friendship? Debatin et al. (2009) concluded that Facebook allows its users to maintain superficial social relationships with large numbers of people, and young adults trade potential threats to their privacy for daily gossip and trivia.

Facebook has a number of features that have boosted its popularity. Privacy has become an important aspect of the internet, so Facebook allows its users to customise their level of privacy. However, many people tend not to change the privacy setting too far from the default (Debatin et al., 2009). The hugely popular photos and videos section allows users to upload an unlimited number of media files, unlike hosting sites like Photobucket and Flickr.

Facebook is not generally seen as a professional communication tool but rather as a personal social media platform. However, sharing Facebook posts and photos with friends has become more commonplace with baby boomers (78%) than other age groups (Yaqub, 2023).

Cambridge Analytica scandal

Facebook changed its name to Meta in 2021, partly to distance itself from its association with Cambridge Analytica, a company that collected huge amounts of personal data belonging to 87 million Facebook users without their consent, between 2010–2016. Cambridge Analytica has been accused of interfering in democratic elections of Ted Cruz and Donald Trump in 2016 by sending out biased memes to Facebook users who voted in marginal seats. The propagandist memes depicted Democrat candidate, Hillary Clinton, as corrupt and anti-American, thus persuading certain Facebook users in key states to vote Republican, biasing the election. Cambridge Analytica was also accused of interfering in the UK Brexit election but was cleared of any wrongdoing.

In 2018, founder Mark Zuckerberg was called before Congress and apologised for allowing privacy violations of Facebook users' data and fined US$5 billion. Public interest in privacy and social media's undue influence led to a Twitter hashtag #DeleteFacebook. Facebook suffered in the public eye but has not suffered that much financially, remaining the number one social media platform for millions of users. The name change to Meta reflects its attempts to usher in the metaverse, the new world built upon virtual reality.

We are constantly aware that our classrooms are full of students who are checking their Facebook pages via smartphones and laptops, but only a few years ago they were messaging their friends on WhatsApp or Telegram. We suspect that even newer students may not wish to emulate their parents by adopting Facebook. In a few years' time, Facebook may be replaced by another internet phenomenon supposedly revolutionising communication.

Instagram

Instagram (see Exhibit 5.10) is a video and photo sharing social media service founded in 2010 by Kevin Systrom and Mike Krieger, and bought by Facebook in 2012. In the beginning, the platform was an app for only Apple iPhone users, but has been universally available to all mobile phone users since 2016. There is currently a desktop application as well, but this is not very popular.

In terms of usability, Instagram is probably the most mobile-friendly of all the image and video sharing applications because it has been designed for phones, not laptops. The majority of users are reportedly

| Exhibit 5.10 | Instagram is often used by companies to improve brand recognition |

Shutterstock.com/Hadrian

below the age of 35 and interested more in image and video sharing than keeping in touch with long-lost friends or reading the news of the day. The images and videos stand by themselves (with some optional text), thus Instagram has become the place for highly original photos and standout videos, not just ordinary snapshots. Instagram competes directly with YouTube, but encourages followers and friends, as opposed to YouTube's mainly public offerings. Instagram is the would-be photographer's gallery, with many users posting technically proficient, Photoshopped images to create artistic collections of their visual skills. The Instagram app also includes a suite of image filters that can enhance original images.

Instagram is a worldwide app with over 80 per cent of users residing outside the US (Ruby, 2023). Apart from personal users, many industries and companies use Instagram to boost sales, establish brand recognition and find new customers. Education, art, tourism, hospitality, fashion, entertainment, health, real estate, retail and service industries have a strong presence on Instagram. The old saying that a picture is worth a thousand words rings true in the Instagram space.

Researchers of Instagram and other social media platforms suggest that the self-promotional showcase of Instagram with teenagers can lead to body dysmorphism (Lee, 2021; Verrastro et al., 2020), where the user sees only beautiful images of others and believes that their own bodies have a range of 'defects' such as being too fat, too skinny, too tall, or too short. Additionally, social comparison theory (Festinger, 1954) would predict that there may be emotional consequences to constantly viewing strangers' positive posts, especially when a young viewer's identity is still evolving. There are numerous research findings that suggest that frustration, resentment, eating disorders and even depression are possible negative consequences of making social comparisons on social media (Jang & Niang, 2020; Reer et al., 2019).

TikTok

TikTok is a short video hosting service which allows users to upload a short 15 second video and then choose music to add to the background (see **Exhibit 5.11**). The video can be slowed down or sped up or edited with filters. Other sounds may be added alongside the background music. When logging on to TikTok, users are presented with a range of videos that are curated for them using proprietary AI that analyses users' past selections, searches and interactions. TikTok also allows users to store draft videos before publication if the user wishes to keep the video private.

Exhibit 5.11   TikTok is the fastest growing social media platform

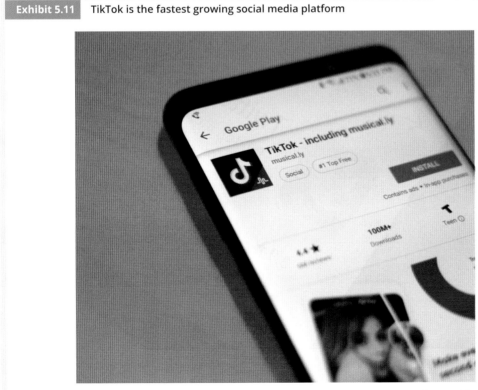

Shutterstock.com/Ricky Of The World

TikTok is the only major social media platform that does not come from American founders, instead being owned by Chinese company ByteDance and called *Douyin* in China. Established in September 2016, it took one more year for Apple and Android versions to be released to the world, with no desktop version available. Strangely, both TikTok and Douyin have near identical interfaces on mobile phones, but zero access to each other's content, being housed on completely different web servers. TikTok is the fastest growing social media platform on the internet and was supposedly more popular than Google in 2021 (Tomé & Cardita, 2021).

One of TikTok's claims to fame is that it is available in more than 75 languages and has been downloaded more than two billion times as of 2022. Celebrities such as Tony Hawk, Jimmy Fallon, Jennifer Lopez, Jessica Alba and Justin Bieber have started using the app, bringing their fan bases with them. However, Tik Tok is not universally popular, with security concerns causing the platform to be banned from many government-issued devices in Australia, the UK and US (Al-Khouri et al., 2023).

Twitter

Twitter (see **Exhibit 5.12**) was created by Jack Dorsey, Biz Stone, Noah Glass and Evan Williams in 2006. The concept of Twitter is simple: a user registers on twitter.com and creates a profile that can be used on Twitter via the Web or smartphones/tablets via the Twitter app. The user follows any number of other users, including friends, colleagues, celebrities, politicians and news sites. Whenever the followed people create messages or tweets, the messages appear on the user's main Twitter page, or feed. Depending on the number of followed people, a user will see a scrolling list updated every few minutes of the day, and users can reply, Retweet, Quote Tweet, or like.

Twitter currently allows a maximum of 280 characters (4000 for Twitter Blue paid subscribers) per tweet, plus up to four photos, a video and URL to be sent to a user's followers. Tweets may also be placed in several hashtag groups for public consumption. Users can choose who will see their tweets, with the default setting being public; but most users tend to send tweets to only their specified groups. Twitter currently has 230 million active users sending 500 million tweets per day. It is the favoured platform for

Exhibit 5.12   Twitter is the favoured social media platform for journalists

Shutterstock.com/mundissima

journalists and news outlets and has become very popular with academic researchers because of the app's intentional ease of data collection.

People either love Twitter or hate it. It really is a question of who you are and where you reside, with most Twitter users residing in the US. Australians' usage of Twitter is much lower than most other social media platforms, with only 2.6 per cent of Australians saying that Twitter is their favourite platform (Tong, 2022). However, if you know enough people using Twitter, and you need to contact those people all at once, then a Twitter account is a must-have for social networking. Additionally, if you work in advertising, media or public relations, then Twitter allows you to stay in touch with dozens of contacts spread throughout the world.

Many traditional journalists, editors and media personnel use Twitter daily for work purposes, but prefer Facebook for personal reasons. Thus, most students do not use Twitter, unless is it work related. Some commentators have also noticed that Facebook posts tend to be positive in nature, with accompanying photographs, celebrating an individual's life, hobbies and relationships, while Twitter posts are often negative. We see a good deal of Twitter posts that can be categorised as highly critical in nature and pessimistic in their content. A good example is the ABC program *Q and A*, where Twitter comments display some agreement but more disagreement with the speakers in the television program. Use of Twitter in conference settings also tends to be critical in nature as opposed to congratulatory. Previous lack of graphics and non-verbal details used to encourage anonymity, so-called 'deindividuation' and judgemental comments. More recently, Twitter abounds with images and videos because it has become a 'news medium' not just a social medium.

CASE STUDY 5.2   Content analysis of Twitter

In 2009, Pear Analytics analysed the content of 2000 tweets sent during a two-week period and categorised the messages into six classes: pointless babble (40 per cent), conversations (38 per cent), pass-along messages (9 per cent), self-promotion (6 per cent), spam (4 per cent) and news (4 per cent). On Twitter, researcher and social networking commentator Danah Boyd (2009) responded to these figures, saying that the analysis of words alone does not convey the social functions of language inherent in Twitter posts. The pointless babble category consists of social communication (e.g., hello, thank you) rather than information. Such social (or phatic) communication is not meant to convey anything except respect, trust and honesty. All communication has at least two main functions: informational and socio-emotional. These two functions are often conflated in the one sentence and can be interpreted differently by various audiences and researchers.

In 2018, Twitter reported that it had found 50 000 Russian accounts that used tweets to publish pro-Trump information for the previous two years to both confuse voters and control discussions surrounding the 2016 federal election. In 2020, a Carnegie-Mellon study found that about half of the Twitter accounts calling for an end to lockdowns were most probably bots. Analysis of 200 million tweets that used the word COVID-19 found that 82 per cent of the top re-tweeters were automated bots (Kim, 2020).

Discussion

1   Open up Twitter and locate a hashtag you wish to analyse.

   a   Copy a segment of the tweets so that you have a fairly representative sample across the board of around 100 tweets or so. Place the tweets into Excel, in the first column.

   b   Add a label in the Excel sheet next to each tweet identifying if the tweet is mainly pointless babble, conversation, retweets, self-promotion, spam, news or some other kind of content.

   c   Sort the sheet/document by the second column that labels the content type. This will allow you to see what the most popular content labels really are in your sample of tweets.

   d   Compare your results with other people in the class. Were the Pear Analytics results confirmed?

2   Twitter has recently been accused of not removing programmed accounts, known as 'bots', that have undue influence over public opinion and elections. Does this make Twitter untrustworthy?

After you have discussed this case study, refer to the 'Comments on case studies' section at the end of the text.

Videoconferencing

Videoconferencing is the medium that most closely resembles face-to-face communication. It has long been seen as the holy grail of mediated communication, depicted in imaginings of communications in the future in countless films, TV programs, comics and cartoons. Nowadays, the Dick Tracy videophone watch is a real product, and the video chat imagined in 1927's *Metropolis* has been available for several years on our mobile phones.

Videoconferencing came of age through the early years of the COVID-19 pandemic, when lockdowns prevented students and staff from attending face-to-face classes. Zoom videoconferencing, Microsoft Teams, GoToMeeting, RemotePC Meeting and many other programs were the only ways that education, health, business, government and ordinary people could continue to operate during the pandemic. This software demonstrated that we could simulate ordinary face-to-face communication, with many institutions and industries now continuing to use videoconferencing because it saves travel time, reduces carbon pollution and protects us from becoming sick, and because many workers are choosing to continue working remotely.

But surprisingly, we do not see too many people choosing video sessions over SMS and ordinary telephony. Why has the promise of such a rich communication medium not been taken up with more enthusiasm by a media-hungry workforce? Why is videoconferencing not more popular in these days of cheap internet deals and fast bandwidth outside of business meetings and applications? It may be that once people have tried videoconferencing, they are disappointed – it is not the same as having a coffee with a friend at the local café. Additionally, there are unexpected problems with videoconferencing that may make it less desirable than other mediums.

One of the main problems with all videoconferencing systems is that eye contact plays an underestimated and often unconscious role in turn-taking and relationship maintenance. Videoconferencing systems have cameras that tend to give the impression that the speaker is trying to actively avoid looking at the audience because they are looking at the screen at other participants and not the camera itself. Some systems have embedded cameras in the middle of monitor, reducing but not eliminating the problem. Webcams or cameras are often positioned on top of or off to the side of laptops and computers, and sometimes fail to show more than the speaker's shoulder or background.

A second issue with videoconferencing is the stress that being on camera places on most people. People often feel embarrassed, unattractive, ugly, not dressed properly or nervous when they find themselves in front of a camera. Many people are simply camera shy, and thus instead of enhancing a meeting, videoconferencing may actually impair the communication process. Hence our experience is that most students use videoconferencing with their cameras turned off. The smiling faces on the Zoom image in Exhibit 5.13 are forced and unnatural, and their eye gaze is manipulated to be straight at the viewer. From our own experience, such happy direct gaze videoconferencing is very rare. Most of the time we see a majority of black screens.

For the rest of us, using a combination of email, SMS, forums and Facebook will probably allow us to communicate with most people in our personal and professional lives.

 CASE STUDY 5.3   The case for turning off your Zoom camera

'Good morning team! If we could all turn our cameras on for this meeting, that'd be great.' It's a line that's become a common refrain in the remote work era – but one that many employees dread.

Platforms such as Zoom were a blessing when COVID-19 lockdowns hit, allowing many people to work from home. But [after] two and a half years that same technology had become something of a curse, too. These days, millions of workers spend hours each day on video calls, exhausting themselves trying to decode colleagues' body language or distracted by their own image on screen.

Having a camera on can often be seen as a sign of engagement; proof an employee really is committed to their work. But experts also suggest turning off cameras could, along with mitigating the annoyance of always appearing on screen, improve worker wellbeing – and make meetings more efficient, to boot.

...

There's also an element of micro-management: bosses who ask workers to switch webcams on are shifting controlling office behaviours to the virtual world. 'It's the closest to what we know: if you're a manager, you're used to the old way of work, which was you can kind of roam the halls to see if people are at their desks working,' explains [one manager].

But, as workers well know, leaving cameras on for everything can take a toll and exacerbate Zoom fatigue: a tiredness linked to factors like fixating on your own on-camera appearance and the cognitive strain of trying to pick up on non-verbal cues that are much easier to interpret in person.

...

Turning cameras off can eliminate these distractions and allow workers to be more engaged in the meeting. And being out of vision might even enable employees to work more productively, by multi-tasking as they listen ...

Source: B. Lufkin (2022, June 22). The case for turning off your Zoom camera. *BBC Worklife*.

Discussion

1 From the perspective of effective communication, what are the problems created when meeting participants, either in a workplace or maybe a classroom, do not turn on their cameras?

2 Are there other reasons for employees or students not turning on their cameras?

3 Have you suffered from 'Zoom fatigue'? How does this impact your participation in a meeting or online class? Why?

4 Do you agree with the research cited in the case study that employees or students should be able to leave their cameras off so that they can multi-task while they listen to the meeting discussion?

After you have discussed this case study, refer to the 'Comments on case studies' section at the end of the text.

Exhibit 5.13   The promise of Zoom

Shutterstock.com/fizkes

Major issues of mediated communication and the internet

If you agree with McLuhan's (1964) and Postman's (1990) arguments that new technology brings both useful and possibly harmful effects, then we should end this chapter by discussing some of the challenging issues that have arisen since the advent of the internet and its various mediums of communication. Most electronic mediums have created issues that never existed beforehand. A short list of such problems would include privacy, copyright, plagiarism, censorship, pornography, e-learning, cyberbullying and online dating, and. We will spend the next section of this chapter outlining some of these challenges.

Privacy

In comparison with the tragedy of the Russian invasion of the Ukraine and the horrors of the COVID-19 pandemic that has now killed millions of people, privacy breaches are generally minor setbacks for the average individual. But privacy is probably the number one issue affecting every person who uses any form of mediated communication today. Ironically, this was mainly due to the events of 9/11 and the Bush government's reaction to them. It passed a massive amount of legislation to allow government agencies to surveil ordinary American citizens on a magnitude never before seen. Sanctioned searches, wiretaps and data collection have been commonplace occurrences in post-9/11 America. The *Patriot Act* legislation, which passed through Congress without any real debate or objection, was intended to prevent future terrorist acts. At the time, this was deemed more important than preserving individual rights, fundamental liberties or privacy. It is possible to surveil every piece of digital communication that anyone sends or receives on a computer, landline or mobile phone. Thus, any person's online and offline purchases, voice conversations, website accesses, forum posts and emails can and may be collected and stored.

While Australia has not been so blatantly affected, the subject of privacy has become highly controversial. There are no constitutional bases for protecting the privacy of Australians. There are several sets of guidelines that are normative suggestions for how organisations should behave, but in Australia we have no guarantee of privacy (see http://www.privacy.gov.au). For example, in Australia, the National Driver Licence Facial Recognition Solution is facial feature mapping current photographs taken for licence renewals throughout the country to be stored in a national police database for comparison with CCTV footage of criminals. However, new licence holders are not informed of this process, and there is no ability to opt out. Unfortunately, the recognition software is not 100 per cent accurate, sometimes matching the wrong person to the video footage (Taylor, 2019).

Is privacy dead?

Google, Facebook and Amazon analyse our internet browsing habits and interests; credit card companies know our behaviours so well that they send us queries when unusual purchases occur; mobile phone providers knows all the numbers we call and SMS; and our key passes record every place we visit in our workplaces. We are being watched so much that many internet security experts believe that individual privacy simply does not exist, saying that privacy is dead and we should get over it. Others believe that we can achieve a degree of privacy, whereby we decide what is revealed about us, if we are careful and sensible.

Schneier (2006) says that the typical response to complaints about government snooping, such as, 'If you have nothing to hide, you have nothing to fear!', is difficult to respond to, unless we say, 'I have nothing to hide, and I do not want to show you!' Many commentators say that the problem is that those in power tend to abuse that power, and if an honest person is surveilled long enough, then someone will find fault with that person's life. We believe privacy is an undeniable human right which needs protecting at all costs. Privacy is essential to our sense of dignity and respect as human beings. This basic human right is codified in the United Nations Declaration of Human Rights, in Article 12 (see https://www.un.org/en/about-us/universal-declaration-of-human-rights).

Email, especially corporately owned email, is not private, nor is Web browsing on a company computer. Most companies in the Western world have special software filters in place that detect keyword instances and supposedly protect the system from hackers, spam and intruders. Such filtering software can be easily bought for either home or corporate settings. Parental control programs such as Net Nanny, Symantec Norton Family and Qustodio Parental Control, and network management control programs such as

Solarwinds and Datadog, all work in similar ways, by intercepting data to and from the local computer, tagging keywords and producing reports that list possible violations. These programs can be set to block certain websites and activities that are suspicious. They also often slow down the computer experience for a user. The Australian government produced a parental program called NetAlert in 2007, and the $84 million program was bypassed by a 16-year-old student in half an hour (Arthur, 2007), exposing the problems inherent in this type of approach to internet censorship and privacy.

The Optus cyberattack, revealed in September 2022, shows how vulnerable our personal information is. Millions of Australians had their Medicare and licence details, name, date of birth, email address, residential address and passport number revealed (Smith, 2022). This data breach permits the possibility of multiple scams and identity theft targeting unsuspecting Optus customers, for years to come.

> **Reflection question:** What can you do to protect yourself, your family, and loved ones from the large internet companies, such as Google, Amazon, eBay and Meta, and our own institutions and companies that are surveilling us and collecting data on our personal lives? Hint: there are answers to this question!

Copyright

The word 'copyright' derives from copyright law, which was first granted to the publishers of British books in 1709. Initially the law applied only to book copy. Over time, the word has extended to other creative works, including maps, performances, paintings, sound recordings, films and computer programs, and the copyright is now granted to the author or creator of the original work. Copyright does not protect ideas, only the concrete expressions of ideas. Copyright is also a Western concept, with the word having no equivalent in many languages, such as Chinese or Japanese. China, in fact, had no copyright legislation until 1990, and Japan's *Rights of Broadcasting and Wire Transmissions* dates from 1986.

The rise of the internet and the Web in the mid-1990s has led to the global publication of books, articles, comments, graphics, sound files, videos and photographs that anybody can download, store and copy, both freely and anonymously. Placing any article, photograph, music composition or graphic on any website means that anyone can download it and do with it as they please, and you are powerless to stop it. Locating breaches of individual copyright worldwide is an almost pointless task for the average person. We might find parts of this book on a website in China, or a booklet in Taiwan, but how can we really prevent this from occurring? What recourse do we have in Australia to affect citizens of other countries? It has become almost accepted that once you publish on the Web, you give up some rights of authorship for the ability to reach an audience in the millions. Thus, the notion of authorship is devalued because copyright law is so difficult to enforce on an international playing field.

Different countries have their own copyright laws. For example, downloading already copied music files is legal in Canada, the Netherlands, Spain, Panama and (only for domestic use) in Russia. There is no copyright law in Afghanistan, Laos or the Marshall Islands.

In 2006, the Australian Government rushed new laws through Parliament, which govern copyright and intellectual property on the internet in Australia. The *Copyright Act 1968* had been criticised for being founded too much on paper-based technologies, but the 2006 amendment equated online material with printed material. The new amendments did not consider the extensive variations in content of online publishing, nor the many differences between printed text and websites. Few other Western democracies have sanctioned such copyright laws, which many critics believe reflects ill-advised, short-term thinking by the Australian Government.

One of the main problems is the fact that the Web inherently asks all users to infringe copyright by enabling the downloading of a copy of every article, graphic and picture on a website at the click of a button. All Web browsers have a menu item for exactly this purpose. In fact, browser technology has such tools built in – click on the right mouse button while using Firefox or Chrome and you will be given a 'Save Target As' menu choice. The ease of copyright infringement makes it very tempting for people to save artistic and creative works.

Many Web users still believe that anything they see is *freeware*; that is, publicly, freely available and, therefore, not copyright protected. Nothing could be further from the truth. In the US prior to March 1989, all copyright-protected works, on the internet and otherwise, required a visible copyright notice on the work before distribution took place. Today, in both Australia and the US, this notice is not necessary, although it is still used by many people either through ignorance or to enlighten others' misunderstanding. Copyright of a work exists and attaches to any work as soon as it is made into any tangible shape or form that can be perceived, reproduced or communicated. Any viewable file, including electronic mail, Web images or any other form of internet content, is protected under international copyright laws.

If you want to copy and use any materials that are taken from another source for commercial purposes, including websites, you would be wise to ask permission of the author. The rule of thumb is that personal use (with acknowledgement) is fine, but commercial use always necessitates permission from the author.

Plagiarism

Plagiarism
When someone copies an original work and then passes it off as their own.

A term related to copyright is **plagiarism**, which is when someone copies an original work and then passes it off as their own. It does not matter if the copy this is done for monetary gain or not, omitting the acknowledgement to the original author means that the copier is using the work unethically and immorally.

Plagiarism is a Western concept that began with the Romantic movement in the 18th century. Before then, literature, art and music were seen as public material that others were freely able to borrow from as a means of inspiration. Many artists were actively encouraged to copy the masters, and even today, many forms of music and musical instruments are taught by imitation. In the new millennium, plagiarism is unethical, not illegal, and is usually regarded as extensively practised by high school and college students. Sally Brown (2015) states that teachers regard the internet as a limitless place for plagiarism in student academic writing, while students see the internet as a copyright-free space, not regulated by legal or proprietary rights. In most universities, plagiarism is punished by failure and/or expulsion from units and courses.

Proving plagiarism was previously a difficult task given the number of scholarly articles and brazen 'cheater' sites on the Web. However, identifying plagiarism is now a simple process with the development of plagiarism software that can detect keywords in essays and assignments and compare student work with its own extensive database of previous student work and the Web. The program *Turnitin* works by requiring students to upload their assignments to a web server and returning a percentage score for how many times the program can find a match in its own databases and on the internet. The instructor can nominate what length of keyword phrase the computer matches, with four words being the default. Every time *Turnitin* matches the same four words in a row, those words in the assignment are highlighted, and after a few seconds the assignment then becomes a part of the program's database. Obviously, the assignment's references will be always matched, so these need to be omitted from the submission. The student can see the score and the assignment's exact matches with other material. The instructor can also view the results and identify the students who have plagiarised and those who have not. While not 100 per cent foolproof, this program is extremely useful in deterring students who may feel the urge to plagiarise others' work.

Reflection question: How much do you plagiarise other people's ideas without giving full credit?

Censorship

In 2002, the Electronic Frontiers Australia organisation concluded that there existed no other democratic country in the world that had internet censorship laws as restrictive as Australia's. The original 1999 legislation would have made ISPs responsible for banning adult content on overseas websites or risk heavy fines. Due to public outcry, the amended and passed 2000 legislation established a complaints-based system. In this, Australian sites that have complaints lodged against them, and are deemed 'objectionable' or 'unsuitable for minors', can have take-down notices applied to them. This process does not apply to websites that are hosted overseas. Instead, the overseas site is placed on a blacklist that is filtered, but providers are currently not required by law to implement the filtering system.

The result of this legislation was that thousands of Australian companies set up .com websites instead of .com.au sites, and hosted them overseas for fear of reprisals from the Australian Government. Adult content was not stopped in any way, but Australian e-commerce was constrained from the start.

In 2022, almost every country in the world, including those that have long traditions of free speech, practises some form of censorship of the internet and the Web. Many parts of Asia, Africa and the Middle East filter the internet to remove unwanted aspects, such as pornography, political viewpoints and popular culture. Australia and the US filter all websites seen by K–12 schools, while content related to Nazism or holocaust denial is censored in France and Germany. Most countries block child pornography, hate speech and sites that encourage theft of intellectual property. In March 2022, the European Union decided to censor *Russia Today* and *Sputnik News*, the main propaganda websites for reporting the Russia–Ukraine war. The European Union's ban was to prevent its own citizens from seeing the fake news seen in Russia.

Censorship of pornography is not a very media-worthy topic these days, with most of the debate occurring 20 years ago. We seem to have become complacent and accepting of internet censorship, and more interested in checking out our friends' activities on social media. However, Australia was on the verge of passing legislation that would have technically placed a firewall around the entire country. In 2011, the Australian government was trying to introduce a blacklist of sites that would be totally banned from viewing by Australians of all ages. The blacklist included illegal paedophile and terrorist sites that we all abhor, but it also was to include content that was not determined. Most hardcore or X-rated material was not supposed to be banned. But some of the potentially banned topics on webpages and forums were information on anorexia, euthanasia, small breasts, female orgasm (but not male orgasm) and any site that was refused classification. The small breasts category was to ban images of women who may be perceived as underage children. The legislation was shelved in 2013 but resurrected in 2019 when a law was passed that required social media platforms to censor themselves for allowing images of abhorrent/violent material such as the Christchurch massacre, where 50 people were murdered.

 CASE STUDY 5.4 Find your own case study

We all have access to cameras that reside on our mobile phones, and we all consistently use them whenever a humorous scene occurs in our lives. While taking photographs is not an illegal activity, and we all take photographs of strangers and passers-by, there are special classes of people who deserve to be asked for their consent – namely children and the elderly.

Social media possess remarkable potential for supporting professional relationships and providing valuable information to consumers. However, the laissez-fair use of social media by professionals who post images and videos can cause concern among educators, employers and professional bodies. When using social media, professionals must protect a person's rights to privacy and confidentiality and always consider the possible effects on clients, employers, the profession and themselves.

One such breach of privacy occurred in 2015 when a nurse apparently took an explicit photograph of a patient who was under anaesthetic, but luckily did not post it on social media sites. Unfortunately, there have been instances of such photos making their way online.

Discussion

1 Use Google to locate some articles on the abusive or inappropriate use of images or information in your selected profession – nursing, business, or computer science – and the results of social media posting for the people or organisations involved.

2 Create your own case study by summarising the main points of one of these incidents.

3 Identify and explain any form of abuse or breach of privacy involved in your chosen incident.

After you have discussed this case study, refer to the 'Comments on case studies' section at the end of the text.

E-learning

E-learning is the use of mediated communication technologies and the Web to instruct and deliver resources to students, usually as part of higher education qualifications or training courses. Over the past two decades, e-learning has become the standard way of supporting students, and in some cases is the sole medium of instruction. E-learning suits those students who prefer to work and study or live in remote areas, and is being used by an ever-increasing proportion of students with a disability or who originate from non-native speaking cultures. However, e-learning is not always successful, with a large number of professional and corporate organisations reducing the face-to-face, human element of instruction. Learning management systems employing e-learning have become the excuse for institutions short-changing students in terms of face-to-face hours, and enrolling them in larger class sizes.

In Australia and many other countries, financial pressure from diminishing funding resources for higher education has driven the search for more efficient methods of program delivery. Thus, both educational institutions and private enterprise have installed any one of dozens of course management systems, such as Moodle, Blackboard and Edmodo, for easy, user-friendly ways of providing online material for education and training purposes.

In the Australian higher education sphere, courses have been transformed into blended learning websites, whereby the traditional face-to-face mode is supplemented or replaced by teacher materials that are placed on an e-learning site. References, notes, exercises and other support materials are placed online for value-added student learning. The system often includes email, chat, quiz creation modules, assignment drop boxes and administration tools. For the vast majority of academics, the management system allows them to create unit-specific websites without having to understand the intricacies of Web authoring. Normally technology-resistant academics are celebrating their new-found expertise as e-learning exponents, and while face-to-face hours have been reduced, students are supposedly consoled by the management system as a substitute for missing teaching time. Whole reprographics departments have been eliminated from many institutions and companies that now use third-party vendors for printing that was previously done in-house.

Thousands of previously traditional courses have changed into partly or wholly online courses for the unaware new student. The net educational effect of this significant change to education and training has yet to be calculated. While students still pass courses, and evaluation surveys still show student satisfaction, the full effect on learning, communication and collaboration is uncertain.

One of the most compelling criticisms of e-learning comes from constructivist theorists (relying on the work of Jean Piaget and Lev Vygotsky) who believe that people learn by being in a social context and slowly discovering concepts, principles and facts for themselves. Social constructivist instructors insist that individuals make meanings out of experiences with others, and by interacting with the environment they study in. However, with online education, the social environment is less and less present, and mediated communication technologies are not sufficient for significant interaction. Genuine learning thus suffers as more courses use increasing amounts of e-learning, requiring less and less class time with instructors and fellow students.

In 20 years of e-learning, we have seen average class times at some Australian universities go from three or four hours contact per unit to 90 minutes. While e-learning forums are sometimes useful, the missing time is usually never reclaimed by students using Web-based resources. Institutions could examine how many hours students use within the management system, in order to confirm that missing face-to-face instruction is being replaced for good reasons, but this is not a priority evaluation. Students are simply being short-changed in the new millennium compared to students of previous eras.

Nicholas Carr (2010), in his book *The Shallows: What the internet is doing to our brains*, claims that the Web has changed the way in which students think and act around information for learning. Carr believes that learning online allows for too many distractions. This makes deep learning difficult and leads to the search for shallow concepts. The internet encourages us to scan information, and our screens have allowed us to only develop greater visual-spatial intelligence, but the cost has been weakened higher-order cognition, which includes better vocabulary, reflection, inductive problem solving, critical thinking and imagination. Many critics have rebutted Carr's theories, but most educational research shows that online learning is only equal to classroom learning, and in many cases, significantly worse.

> **Reflection question:** What do you think of e-learning? What is your experience of online teaching right now? Is it better or worse in terms of learning? Is the convenience of e-learning worth the learning effects?

Cyberbullying

Cyberbullying refers to when individuals or groups deliberately and repeatedly engage in hostile behaviour toward another via information and communication technologies (e.g., mobile phones and other devices that are used to send textual or graphical messages; Belsey, 2019). Cyberbullying may be sexual in nature, threatening, labelling, ridiculing or simply spreading lies. Cyberbullies can overwhelm victims by co-opting others to gang up on a victim, often via Facebook or by revealing the victim's personal details. In the media, cyberbullying has been associated with teenage girls more than boys because males tend to act out their aggression. However, anyone can be the victim of cyberbullying, which has only developed because of the near universality of the internet and mobile phones.

Certain characteristics of mediated communication technologies encourage the use of cyberbullying rather than ordinary bullying behaviour. Internet users can retain some degree of anonymity by using pseudonyms in forums, chat rooms and other programs. Many electronic forums and chat rooms lack supervision by a moderator, allowing anything to be stated without any controls in place. If the victim is being cyberbullied on their mobile phone, then the fact that the victim is inseparable from their phone makes them an instant target. Therefore, a cyberbully can invade the walls of the victim's home, where traditional bullies could never reach them.

Many governments of Western countries admit that up to 25 per cent of all children have been cyberbullied at some stage in their life (Peebles, 2014) but are at a loss as to how to deal with the situation, which often goes unnoticed by parents and schools until a child displays distressed or depressive behaviour. By that time, the damage has usually been done and, in the extreme, can end in suicide. In Australia, the *Online Safety Act 2021* (Cth) compels social media companies and websites to take down posts that are judged to involve bullying with 24 hours or risk fines of up to $111 000 for individuals or $555 000 for companies. For this to happen, a victim first needs to ask the company to remove the content, then report it to the police and then the e-Safety Commissioner.

The problem with making cyberbullying a criminal offence is that in order to be found guilty, a cyberbully must be judged to be 'criminally responsible' for the offence; that is, they must be found to be of a mindset to commit a crime and know they are doing so (Kift et al., 2009). In Australia, the age of criminal responsibility is 10, meaning a child under 10 cannot be held responsible, and children aged 10 to 14 must be proven to be responsible beyond reasonable doubt. Some states and territories are currently attempting to increase this age to 14, with ACT and Tasmania most likely to make this change.

> **Reflection question:** Have you ever sent or received nude or explicit photos? What was your reaction to these at the time? Do you think sexting should be criminalised, and if so, in what circumstances?

Online dating

A Monash University report called The Future of Dating (2021) concluded that online dating is the major way that couples meet in the 21st century with around 29.4 per cent of Australian couples meeting on a dating site. That percentage is predicted to climb every year until 2040 when more couples will meet online than offline. Dr Marie Bergström (2021), in her book *The New Laws of Love*, says that the whole concept of love has changed from being based on chance encounters with people who you meet, to being 'scientifically' matched with your supposed soulmate via a paid dating site. In the West, traditional courtship is attached to ordinary social activities, such as attending school or university, drinking in bars, going to parties, and socialising with work colleagues. Before the internet there were personal ads and bricks and mortar agencies to find true love, but dating sites are now the special location external to ordinary socialisation.

The middle-aged person (40–50) who has recently divorced or separated is probably the typical user of dating sites. But there are also many senior clients (50+) who find themselves looking for new partners. Surprisingly, dating sites also cater for a continual stream of younger unattached males and females (under 35), who wish to experiment with affairs, love and sex and may not wish to experience breaking-up in front of their friends or social circle. Bergström recounts women who purposely avoid hooking up with men from the same college or university because they do not want to accidentally run into their partner while studying. It is as if romance has been compartmentalised from other aspects of people's lives such as family, friends, school and work.

CASE STUDY 5.5   The Ashley Madison affair

The number one digital risk for any company is data breaches. Millions of customer records are being archived on networked servers around the world, and these records are open to data attacks and possible theft by criminals who are intent on obtaining money for their efforts. While most of the successful kidnap and ransom schemes are never revealed, there have been a few incidents that have been exposed and are now in the public domain.

One of the most famous data hacks targeted online dating and social networking service Ashley Madison in 2015. The Ashley Madison website (see **Exhibit 5.14**) claims to offer paid users the chance to 'hook up' with others looking for extramarital affairs. In July 2015, a group calling itself the Impact Team stole 60 gigabytes of Ashley Madison's user data and threatened to release it if the company did not shut its website down. Ashley Madison refused, and a month later 25 gigabytes and then 10 gigabytes were released on the internet.

The result of this was public shaming of millions of males, and a few thousand females who were looking for affairs. There were two reported suicides, and numerous hate crimes related to this incident. The fallout allowed other parties to sort through the huge amount of data and locate prospective email addresses to harass victims even further. For example, among the data there were 1200 Saudi Arabian email addresses

| Exhibit 5.14 | The Ashley Madison website |

exposed, putting those users in a grave situation given that in Saudi Arabia adultery is punishable by death.

Data analysis by experts found that fewer than 12 000 of the 5.5 million female addresses were used regularly, less than 1 per cent. This leads to the conclusion that the vast majority of females on the site were fake accounts, or that 99 per cent of the males were being contacted by bots or other employees, pretending to be interested women. The whole site is a huge scam, yet despite this information being easily located in a web search, the Ashley Madison website is still currently active.

Discussion

Fake information on websites is not isolated to simple lies, false events or Photoshopped images, but can extend to entire websites such as online dating sites.

1   What other forms of lying occur on the Web apart from the obvious ones seen in this case study?

2   Are all dating site profiles honest and use current dating profiles? Why do you think this is?

3   Have you or someone you know ever used a dating site? What happened?

After you have discussed this case study, refer to the 'Comments on case studies' section at the end of the text.

Theories of mediated communication

There are no generally accepted theories of mediated communication technologies or the internet, to our knowledge. While there are several competing computer-mediated communication hypotheses and approaches, the changing landscape of hardware innovation, networking upgrades and software invention makes this whole area challenging to describe, let alone theorise about. Many 'theories' created at a particular time have limited application a few years later, as the mediums change and as users rapidly adapt to, and then become bored with, particular technologies. Any mediated communication theories seem destined to have a time limit or are only applicable to a restricted number of users in a particular context. We will describe three of the early theories, which still have some relevance to mediated communication today.

Social Presence Theory

Social Presence Theory is one of the first mediated communication theories, espoused by Short et al. (1976) in their book *The Social Psychology of Telecommunications*. Their theory argues that all mediums have a degree of **social presence**, or awareness of the other person in the communication. Ordinary face-to-face communication has 100 per cent social presence. But if you compare telephone, videoconferencing and email, then you can place these three mediums on a spectrum of social presence according to the reality of the other person in the medium. Videoconferencing would have more social presence than the telephone, which in turn would have more social presence than an email message. The theory really measures the amount of non-verbal communication able to be transmitted by a particular medium, with videoconferencing having both visual and audio channels available, telephone restricted to audio, and email restricted to mainly textual features of language.

Social presence
A communicator's awareness of the presence of the person or people with whom they are interacting.

As computer-mediated communication has evolved, the concept of social presence has changed. Social presence can also mean the way individuals represent themselves in their online environment. A person's social presence can include their availability and willingness to engage and connect with others in an online community. Social presence can be demonstrated by the way messages are posted (e.g., length, frequency and openness) and how those messages are interpreted by others (e.g., positive, negative or critical). Social presence can be defined as how participants relate to one another, which in turn affects their ability to communicate effectively. This latter view considers social presence and mediated communication in their own right, not as a limited substitute for face-to-face meetings. For further discussion of this concept in relation to interpersonal communication, see Chapter 8.

Traditional curriculum designers never consider social presence in course design. Face-to-face courses, with their traditional lectures and tutorial groups, are always in the same place at the same time, and students are expected to communicate with each other. This is generally what constructivist theorists call social learning. We do not call it social presence. However, in the online classroom, the lack of social presence is exactly what course designers need to work against in order to create a sense of connectedness between students and instructors.

Tu and McIsaac (2002) concluded that while social presence positively influences online instruction, sheer frequency of participation was not the same as high social presence. In both a quantitative and qualitative analysis of 51 volunteers' interactions, they found that social context was a learnt skill set rather than a prescriptive set of actions. In online contexts, the existence of social presence is important and should not be left to chance. By providing social support from the beginning, by building online trust and by promoting informal relationships, the online instructor can provide a strong sense of social presence, increase interaction between participants and build stronger communities.

This notion of social presence appears to be largely correlated to the availability of non-verbal channels of communication. The more non-verbal communication, the higher the social presence.

Social identity model of deindividuation effects (SIDE)

Deindividuation
A state in which people lose their sense of individuality due to the anonymity that is afforded by being part of a group, and the merging of the self with the group that dilutes their sense of personal responsibility.

Deindividuation theory comes from psychology and refers to a state in which people lose their sense of individuality due to the anonymity that is afforded by being part of a group, and the merging of the self with the group that dilutes their sense of personal responsibility (Festinger et al., 1952). Young Australians often act in erratic ways when in groups while travelling overseas (see Chapter 4). The explanation is that when people are relatively anonymous, they stop being individuals and become less accountable, resulting in erratic, sometimes anti-social behaviour.

Psychological studies of deindividuation have examined instances where widely accepted social norms have been violated, often resulting in horrendous acts of cruelty. History is littered with examples, including the treatment of Jewish people in the Nazi concentration camps, the treatment of prisoners of war in Abu Ghraib prison in Iraq, and the behaviour of the Ku Klux Klan lynch mobs. In his famous 1971 prison study, Stanford psychology professor Philip Zimbardo (2007) concluded that a loss of the sense of the individuality of others can lead to a loss of control, causing affected persons to behave impulsively and in ways that they would not behave in normal social situations.

However, while some critics have pointed out that there is little empirical support for the deindividuation theory, historical evidence and case studies show that the predicted psychological processes do often occur in crowd behaviour. In a study of crowd behaviour of the mob who invaded the US Capitol on 6 January 2021, Paulus and Kenworthy (2022) concluded that the crowd dynamics were largely the results of social influence processes, deindividuation, poor decision making and emotional contagion spurred on by the rhetoric of former president Donald Trump.

The social identity model of deindividuation effects (SIDE) model (Lea & Spears, 1991) modified the theory and applied it to computer-mediated communication settings. The early research showed that flaming behaviour and other forms of disinhibition regularly occurred in computer conferencing groups. This was originally thought to be an instance of deindividuation, but later the concept of 'social identity' was proposed, which brings in the social and intergroup interaction of the setting. The SIDE model, thus, can account for both crowd behaviour and computer-mediated communication contexts. The model argues that anonymity and the social context have cognitive and strategic consequences for an individual.

Cognitively, the individual anonymity leads to a lack of identity for a person, who then seeks out the group identity as his or her own way of expression. That is, a person starts to acquire the shared identity of the group. Strategically, a group is more powerful if it is more unified. In a group situation, there will always be oppositional groups who may have more power. For example, crowds may be confronted by armed police. By giving up individual norms and acquiring the crowd's rules, the individual and the group grow stronger and can act more forcefully to achieve a task.

SIDE is useful in explaining the effects of anonymity and social isolation in a variety of contexts. The research to date using SIDE has particularly focused on crowds and collective action, online teams, online relationships and virtual communities, knowledge sharing, and, more recently, on the social effects of surveillance.

Hyperpersonal model of interpersonal communication

The **hyperpersonal** model of interpersonal communication, developed by Walther (1996), proposed that mediated communication is so valuable to us because it extends the ordinary limits of face-to-face communication. This means that users of mediated communication have more choices to select from, and some of these choices outweigh the advantages of mainstream or traditional channels. For example, email is faster than the mailing a letter, but instant messaging is faster than email, as long as the receiver is paying attention to their messaging app.

The hyperpersonal model also allows users to more carefully control their individual representation of themselves to other people. These people are also controlling their own image, thus creating a relationship that is unique to the specific medium or platform that is being used. This is probably most true for social media platforms such as Facebook, Instagram and TikTok, where users curate their profiles and revise their posts making sure to present an optimised sense of their identity. This better-than-life representation is often displayed in dating site profiles, where all the males drive nice cars and have 'good physiques', and all the females are fun loving and 'slim'.

We see some merit in this model because it is equally applicable to organisations, which strategically organise their public profiles using advertising and mediated communication channels. Self-representation in the corporate world is the province of public relations and brand image creation that can create trust in companies or lose clients if the wrong messages are conveyed.

Our experience shows that reciprocal and regular online communication between two people can expedite the time that it takes for people to develop mutual trust in each other, and this occurs because of the hyperpersonal nature of the online interaction. It is believed that when we read we tend to sub-vocalise the sentences by using our own silent voices. In intense chat sessions, online interactants can begin to use their imagination to 'hear' the other person talking in the chat messages or even emails, and in the absence of face-to-face interaction, they also begin to assemble missing characteristics of the other online person (See Suler, 2003). What sometimes occurs is that an idealised persona is created, and if that other person is the right age and gender, strong feelings of trust and intimacy can develop that would have ordinarily taken months to develop in real life.

Hyperpersonal
A model of mediated communication suggests CMC can become 'hyperpersonal' because it extends the limits of face-to-face interaction, allowing communicators more choices and additional levels of control.

Summary

Mediated communication is the way that most people in the West communicate in writing, learning, news and talking to friends, family, colleagues and peers. Social media, in particular, has become a major way to stay in touch with others; however, like all technologies, it has impacted not only the manner in which we communicate but also how we think and behave in relation to interpersonal communication.

The chapter started by categorising all electronically mediated communication into four basic types: interactive, non-interactive, social and videoconferencing. Email, chat groups, forums, blogs, YouTube, Facebook, Instagram, TikTok, Twitter and videoconferencing were described and explained. The major issues of the internet that should be understood are related to privacy, copyright, plagiarism, censorship, e-learning, cyberbullying and dating sites.

Lastly, three theories of mediated communication have been outlined: Social Presence Theory, the social identity model of deindividuation effects (SIDE) model, and the hyperpersonal model of interpersonal communication.

Computers and mediated communications tools were predicted to free us of the tyranny of paper, filing cabinets and indexing systems, as far back as the 1960s. The electronic office or paperless office was described for the general public in a *Bloomberg Business Week* article in 1975 (Lorenz, 2014), and we can report that this has now occurred, but 50 years later than predicted. Paper is no longer used in institutions such as universities and colleges, mostly because printing is an expensive activity. However, this is not true of certain professions such as law, government and aviation, for example. Pharmacists still store paper medical scripts because prescriptions sent via SMS sometimes fail to show up!

Paper and print will probably continue to be used for many years to come, alongside mediated forms of communication. One reason is that paper is remarkably archival, while hard drives are not. Paper does not need constant care or maintenance, unlike computers and networks. Ironically, most digital storage media break down or fail after about 10 years. In terms of communication, the real skill is choosing the right medium, identifying what the audience expects, and using the medium's unique qualities to successfully say what you want to say. Perhaps telephone calls are an underused solution to many of the problems of mediated communication?

STUDY TOOLS

DISCUSSION QUESTIONS AND GROUP ACTIVITIES

For discussion topics and activities in addition to those that follow, please refer to the case studies presented throughout this chapter.

1   Do you think that we have an excessive dependence upon electronic forms of communication today? Interview someone who grew up without the internet and the Web. What do they think? How were their social lives different? How did they communicate with their friends, complete their university assignments and entertain themselves?

2   What kinds of problems have you experienced with email?

3   Do you prefer email or SMS for certain activities? Please explain.

4   What challenges do you think people with disabilities might face when using the internet?

5   Investigate blogs that talk about an interest of yours. Locate such blogs and describe the writers' viewpoints and focus.

6   What are some famous uses of Twitter?

7   Find the most boring video you can on YouTube. What makes it so boring? How could it be improved?

8   Do you understand the implications of having a Facebook or Instagram account? Have you read the Facebook or Instagram terms and conditions in relation to content ownership? Who owns the content you produce and upload?

9   Think about some of the material on your Facebook or Instagram site. Is there material such as photos or posts that might potentially embarrass you in the future? Are there opinions, photos or posts that you would prefer a potential future employer had not to read? Is it ethical for an employer to check an interviewee's social media sites?

10 Have you ever used Zoom or Skype or WhatsApp for videoconferencing? If not, get the software and attempt to contact someone you know. Describe the experience after five minutes has elapsed. Are you bored? Which software do you prefer? Why?

11 Recall or research an incident that is related to a major issue described in this chapter that has occurred to you (or another). Is this an ongoing issue, or has it been resolved? You might choose issues such as copyright (e.g., as it applies to downloading music), censorship or privacy.

12 Is the migration of newspapers and books from a paper-based to an online form merely a more convenient way of accessing the same material? Do we read differently online to the way we read hard copy text? Do you have an e-reader, such as an Amazon Kindle or iPad to read newspapers or books? If so, what do you notice about the difference in the reading experience compared to hard copy texts?

13 Locate a news or magazine article that is presented both online and in a hard copy. How are they presented differently? Are they merely different versions of the same thing? Consider the following:

   a   How is the layout different and does this affect how you read the story?

   b   Are there any other differences, such as the prominence of the story, images used, or articles and advertisements that accompany the story?

   c   Is there a difference in the substance (level of detail) or the writing (language used) between the two? Give examples.

   d   Do you have different approaches to reading the text? Are you more likely to just scan the online text?

   e   What is your preferred method of accessing your daily news and why? How does this compare with others in your group?

14 How can you prevent yourself from identity theft in the event that an organisation storing your information is hacked? Are there any ways to protect your personal information from theft?

WEBSITES

Amazon http://www.amazon.com

Australian Government eSafety Commissioner: Cyberbullying https://www.esafety.gov.au/key-issues/cyberbullying

eBay Australia http://www.ebay.com.au

Facebook http://www.facebook.com

Australian Privacy Principles, Office of the Australian Information Commissioner https://www.oaic.gov.au/privacy/australian-privacy-principles

Zoom http://www.zoom.us

Twitter http://www.twitter.com

Wikipedia http://www.wikipedia.com

YouTube http://www.youtube.com

Digital Futures Project (US) https://www.digitalcenter.org/digital-future-project

REFERENCES

Al-Khouri, C., Lowrey, T., & Long, C. (2023, April 4). TikTok to be banned from Australian government devices. *ABC News*. https://www.abc.net.au/news/2023-04-04/tiktok-ban-australian-government-devices/102183478

Arthur, C. (2009, August 30). Are web filters just a waste of everyone's time and money? *The Guardian*. https://www.theguardian.com/technology/2007/aug/30/guardianweeklytechnologysection.internet1

Belsey, B. (2019, February 25). Cyberbullying. https://cyberbullying.ca/2019/02/25/cyberbullying-involves-the-use-of-information-and-communication-technologies-to-support-deliberate-repeated-and-hostile-behaviour-by-an-individual-or-group-that-is-intended-to-harm-others

Bergström, M. (2021). *The new laws of love: Online dating and the privatization of intimacy.* John Wiley & Sons.

Brown, S. (2015). *Learning, Teaching and Assessment in Higher Education: Global Perspectives.* Palgrave-Macmillan.

Boyd, D. (2009). Twitter: 'Pointless babble' or peripheral awareness + social grooming? https://www.zephoria.org/thoughts/archives/2009/08/16/twitter_pointle.html.

Carr, N. (2010). *The shallows: How the internet is changing the way we think, read and remember.* Atlantic Books Ltd.

Debatin, B., Lovejoy, J. P., Horn, A. K., & Hughes, B. N. (2009). Facebook and online privacy: Attitudes, behaviors, and unintended consequences. *Journal of computer-mediated communication*, 15(1), 83–108. https://doi.org/10.1111/j.1083-6101.2009.01494.x

Festinger, L., Pepitone, A., & Newcomb, T. (1952). Some consequences of de-individuation in a group. *Journal of Abnormal and Social Psychology*, 47(2, Suppl), 382–389. https://doi.org/10.1037/h0057906

Festinger, L. (1954). A theory of social comparison processes. *Human relations*, 7(2), 117–140. https://doi.org/10.1177/001872675400700202

Jiang, S. & Ngien, A. (2020). The effects of Instagram use, social comparison, and self-esteem on social anxiety: A survey study in Singapore. *Social Media + Society*, 6(2), 2056305120912488.

Kift, S., Campbell, M., & Butler, D. 2009, Cyberbullying in social networking sites and blogs: legal issues for young people and schools. *Journal of Law, Information and Science*, 20(2), 23–70.

Kim, A. (2020, May 22). Nearly Half of the Twitter accounts discussing 'reopening America' may be bots, researchers say. *CNN*. https://edition.cnn.com/2020/05/22/tech/twitter-bots-trnd/index.html

Lea, M., & Spears, R. (1991). Computer-mediated communication, de-individuation and group decision-making. *International Journal of Man-machine Studies*, 34(2), 283-301.

Lee, M. (2022). Exploring how Instagram addiction is associated with women's body image and drive for thinness. *The Social Science Journal*, 1–14. https://doi.org/10.1080/03623319.2022.2092380

Lorenz, T. (2014, December 4). 40 years ago, this is what people though the office of the future would look like. *Business Insider*. https://www.businessinsider.com/40-years-ago-this-is-what-people-thought-the-office-of-the-future-would-look-like-2014-12

Lufkin, B. (2022, June 22). The case for turning off your Zoom camera. *BBC Worklife*.

McLuhan, M. (1964). *Understanding Media: The Extensions of Man*. McGraw-Hill,

Monash University News. (2021). Rise of the ebabies: Kids born to Aussie couples who met online will be in the majority by 2038. https://www.monash.edu/news/articles/rise-of-the-ebabies-kids-born-to-aussie-couples-who-met-online-will-be-in-the-majority-by-2038

Online Safety Act 2021 (Cth). https://www.legislation.gov.au/Details/C2021A00076

Paulus, P. B., & Kenworthy, J. B. (2022). The crowd dynamics and collective stupidity of the January 6 riot: Theoretical analyses and prescriptions for a collectively wiser future. *Group Dynamics: Theory, Research, and Practice*, 26(3), 199–219. https://doi.org/10.1037/gdn0000184

Peebles, E. (2014). Cyberbullying: Hiding behind the screen. *Paediatric Child Health*, 19(10): 527–528.

Postman, N. (1990, October 11). *Informing ourselves to death*. Speech to the German Informatics Society. https://web.williams.edu/HistSci/curriculum/101/informing.html

Reer, F., Tang, W. Y., & Quandt, T. (2019). Psychosocial well-being and social media engagement: The mediating roles of social comparison orientation and fear of missing out. *New Media & Society*, 21(7), 1486–1505.

Ruby, D. (2023). 71+ Instagram statistics for marketers in 2023 (data and trends). https://www.demandsage.com/instagram-statistics/#:~:text=As%20of%202022%2C%20around%2087,position%20with%20119.45%20million%20users.

Short, J., Williams, E., & Christie, B. (1976). *The social psychology of telecommunications*. John Wiley & Sons.

Schneier, B. (2006, 18 May). The eternal value of privacy. *Wired magazine*. http://www.wired.com/politics/security/commentary/securitymatters/2006/05/70886

Smith, P. (2022, December 22). Inside the Optus hack that woke up Australia. *Australian Financial Review*. https://www.afr.com/technology/inside-the-optus-hack-that-woke-up-australia-20221123-p5c0lm

Statista Search Department. (2023, February 25). Most popular global mobile messenger apps as of January 2022, based on number of monthly active users [Infographic]. *Statista*. https://www.statista.com/statistics/258749/most-popular-global-mobile-messenger-apps

Suler, J. (2003). The Online Disinhibition Effect. http://www-usr.rider.edu/~suler/psycyber/disinhibit.html

Taylor, J. (2019, September 29). Plan for massive facial recognition database sparks privacy concerns. *The Guardian*. https://www.theguardian.com/technology/2019/sep/29/plan-for-massive-facial-recognition-database-sparks-privacy-concerns

Tan, S. (2015, March 27). Communication breakdown? Emails are the culprit. *Sydney Morning Herald*. https://www.smh.com.au/technology/communication-breakdown-emails-are-the-culprit-20150326-1m8sr2.html

Tomé, J., & Cardita, S. (2021, 21 December). In 2021, the Internet went for TikTok, space and beyond. *Cloudflare*. https://blog.cloudflare.com/popular-domains-year-in-review-2021/

Tong, K. (2022, April 27). How relevant is Twitter to most people? ABC News. https://www.abc.net.au/news/2022-04-27/how-relevant-is-twitter-to-most-people/101018420

Tu, C. H., & McIsaac, M. (2002). The relationship of social presence and interaction in online classes. *The American Journal of Distance Education, 16*(3), 131–150. https://doi.org/10.1207/S15389286AJDE1603_2

Walther, J. B. (1996). Computer-mediated communication: Impersonal, interpersonal, and hyperpersonal interaction. *Communication Research, 23*(1), 3–43. https://doi.org/10.1177/009365096023001001

Verrastro, V., Liga, F., Cuzzocrea, F., & Gugliandolo, M. C. (2020). Fear the Instagram: beauty stereotypes, body image and Instagram use in a sample of male and female adolescents. *Qwerty-Open and Interdisciplinary Journal of Technology, Culture and Education, 15*(1), 31–49.

Wise, J. (2023, January 28). How many blogs are there in the world in 2023? *Earthweb*. https://earthweb.com/how-many-blogs-are-there-in-the-world

Yaqub, M. (2023, 20 April). What social media do baby boomers use 2022: The facts on baby boomers and social media. *Business DIT*. https://www.businessdit.com/baby-boomers-and-social-media/

Zimbardo, P. G. (2007, March 30). Understanding how good people turn evil, Democracy Now! http://www.democracynow.org/2007/3/30/understanding_how_good_people_turn_evil

Chapter 6

Visual communication

Learning objectives

After reading this chapter, you should be able to:

- explain the early origins of visual communication and the development of visual communication in Western culture
- explain why visuals are important in professional writing
- describe the range of visuals and when to use them
- recognise how visuals can be used to persuade, lie and misinform
- understand the basic principles of good layout, design and use of colour.

Good graphics can make us smarter, but reading them is the key

'In newspapers and magazines, infographics have traditionally been created within art departments. In all of those I'm familiar with, the infographics director is subordinate to the art director, who is usually a graphic designer. This is not a mistake *per se*, but it can lead to damaging misunderstandings ... Thinking of graphics as art leads many to put bells and whistles over substance and to confound infographics with mere illustrations.

'This error is at least in part the result of a centuries-long tradition in which visual communication has not been as intellectually elevated as writing. For too many traditional journalists, infographics are mere ornaments to make the page look lighter and more attractive for audiences who grow more impatient with long-form stories every day. Infographics are treated not as devices that expand the scope of our perception and cognition, but as decoration. As Rudolf Arnheim wrote, this tradition goes back to ancient Western philosophy, whose Greek thinkers such as Parmenides and Plato mistrusted the senses deeply ...'

Source: A. Cairo (2013). *The Functional Art*. New Riders, p. xxi

Introduction

Many chapters of the textbook so far have mainly been about communicating with words in professional settings. However, words are seldom used in isolation from other forms of communication. When we think, we outline or visualise; when we speak, we supplement our words with gestures and visual aids; and when we write, we choose different font types, font styles and layouts, and often add visual elements to enhance our communication. In daily life, mobile phones, tablets and laptops have become our companions to our working day, and these devices are full of apps, pages and platforms that include visual elements, such as buttons, icons and signs.

In this chapter we briefly explore some of the graphical elements that can be used to enhance communication. Specialist fields have emerged in visual design, animation, and in information and scientific visualisation. However, we believe that it is important to include a lively discussion of the variety of visuals we can possibly use and suggest that the chapter be seen as a stimulus to further investigation into this intriguing area. Understanding how visual communication works together with language to communicate is critical to professional communication, especially in today's multimedia world. Visual literacy is central to communicating in this volatile era of climate change, diseases, wars and technological change.

This chapter will also focus on the effects that visual elements generally have on people raised in Western countries such as the US, Australia, UK, and parts of Western Europe and South America. We make no claims about the visuals that appear for East Asian nations, such as Japan, China, Korea or Vietnam. Perception of visuals is different for citizens of different nations, with those from Western countries seeing more analytically and people from East Asian countries seeing more holistically. Perceptual differences in children as young as three-years old have been shown to exist when tested using picture books (Kuwabara & Smith, 2016). Accumulating evidence implies that Westerners tend to focus on individual elements of any visual groupings, while East Asians tend to focus on the relationships among objects in a visual scene (Nisbett & Miyamoto, 2005). Given our own background, we will discuss visuals from an analytical perspective – a necessarily biased worldview.

The origins of visual communication

The earliest existing instances of visual communication are cave paintings, petroglyphs (see Exhibit 6.1) and geoglyphs from 60 000 to 15 000 BCE. Arguably, these pieces of art were significant methods of communicating thoughts and information at the time they were created, even if we cannot always determine their true meanings from a modern perspective. The function of these artistic creations is thus subject to numerous theories. It is obvious that communication played a role in this work, but it is unclear if they were meant to deliver vital survival messages, tell narratives or maintain memories for future generations. The use of verbal language during this time is thought to have been virtually non-existent. These engravings, drawings and large geological exhibits are found all over the world, and so we can assume they were essential for communication.

| Exhibit 6.1 | Petroglyphs in northern Tasmania |

Getty Images/Werner Forman

Cuneiform

Writing itself is a form of visual communication, and the earliest forms include Sumerian **cuneiform** (about 3400 BCE; see Exhibit 6.2), Egyptian hieroglyphics (about 3100 BCE), and Chinese ideograms, which were precursors to the Chinese language (6000 BCE).

Exhibit 6.2	Sumerian cuneiform

Alamy Stock Photo/Elitsa Lambova

Sumerian cuneiform is particularly noteworthy because it was used for hundreds of years in Mesopotamia (Iraq) and the Middle East but was replaced by the Phoenician alphabet. By the time of the Greek civilisation, Sumerian cuneiform was an extinct language (i.e. no-one knew how to speak, read, write or understand it). Clay was plentiful in the Middle East and so Sumerian scholars used a wedge-shaped stylus to imprint about a thousand combinations of these indentations onto damp clay, which was then allowed to dry. The medium chosen, that is clay and a wedge-shaped stylus, in part dictated the format of the Sumerian writing, which was both symbolic of concepts and represented spoken words of the time. Cuneiform writing was not like English, which can be pronounced word by word. Cuneiform, due to its chosen medium, comprised some words and also some visuals, namely symbols of concepts like 'god' and 'king'. It was not until 1802 that the first cuneiform script was deciphered. This ancient form of writing could then be understood to be emulating contemporary reports which also use words and visuals.

Tables

The main visual elements used by contemporary authors are tables, graphs, photographs, diagrams, charts, maps and exhibits. All of these elements are important to writers, with tables and graphs being the most important to many of the physical sciences, and general writing for laypersons. However, mathematical (or data) tables are not a modern phenomenon. The earliest known mathematical table was discovered in the southern Iraqi city of Shuruppak, and dates back to the Sumerian era. The word 'table' resembles the piece of furniture because the original column plus row calculations performed in the trade of sheep and cattle were performed on four-legged tables in ancient markets and business offices. The word for the visual trading record became the same as the furniture item. Since ancient times, tables of logarithms, census tables, astronomical charts, and weather data have been created for centuries to keep records and allow comparisons across a range of fields.

Exhibit 6.3	Proportion of population born overseas.

Census year	Proportion of population born overseas (%)
1911	17.7
1921	15.7
1933	13.6
1947	9.8
1954	14.3
1961	16.9
1966	18.4
1971	20.0
…	…
2006	22.2
2011	24.6
2016	26.3
2021	27.6

Source: Australian Bureau of Statistics (CC BY 4.0). Australia's population by country of birth. https://creativecommons.org/licenses/by/4.0/

For example, Exhibit 6.3 comes from the Australian Bureau of Statistics and shows an increasing percentage of Australians who were born overseas. Note the simple table format (APA style), which we will discuss later in the chapter.

However, a table cannot generally stand by itself. The majority of visuals, including tables, necessitate expert comment that highlights various parts of the table, and also explains underlying meanings of the figures, sometimes adding citations for extra rhetorical weight or academic credibility. For example, Exhibit 6.3 does not reveal the countries of origin of those born overseas, the circumstances of their arrival or reasons for immigration, which would have varied considerably between 1911 and 2021. These omissions mean that the table may be misrepresenting what the statistics are telling us, especially considering that Aboriginal and Torres Strait Islander people were not included in the population count prior to 1971. The table 'lies' by what it omits from the numbers (note that the ABS website does give additional commentary on this particular table). A table (or graph) that is merely inserted as decoration is artifice, and a missed opportunity to add value to the analysis.

Graphs

While tables show exact figures, **graphs** show trends, often over time, or allow comparisons between a range of discrete measurements. Tables and graphs are sometimes interchangeable, but the two visuals have different strengths and weaknesses, thus student should not simply create a graph because it is easier to draw. Compared to tables, graphs have not been around for very long. Statistical line, area and bar graphs were invented in 1786 and the pie chart and circle graph in 1801 by Scottish engineer (and spy) William Playfair. One of Playfair's original bar charts is shown in Exhibit 6.4.

Exhibit 6.5a and Exhibit 6.5b show two different types of graphs created from data collected by the Australian Bureau of Statistics. Note again that without further description, the graphs do not give us a complete picture of how the information was collected or what may have been omitted.

Graphs or visuals
Show trends, often over time, or allow comparisons between a range of discrete measurements.

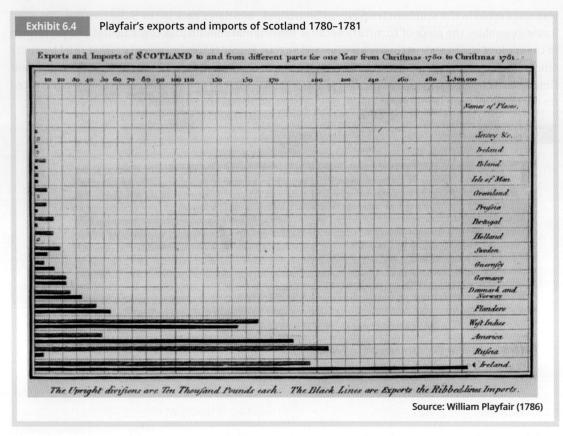

Exhibit 6.4 Playfair's exports and imports of Scotland 1780–1781

Source: William Playfair (1786)

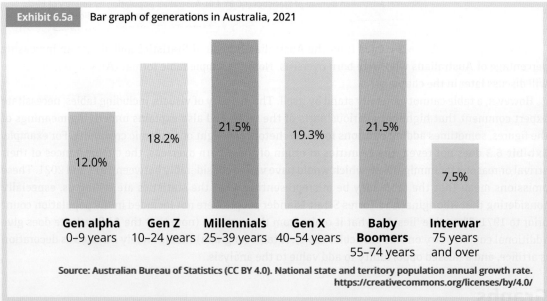

Exhibit 6.5a Bar graph of generations in Australia, 2021

Gen alpha	Gen Z	Millennials	Gen X	Baby Boomers	Interwar
12.0%	18.2%	21.5%	19.3%	21.5%	7.5%
0–9 years	10–24 years	25–39 years	40–54 years	55–74 years	75 years and over

Source: Australian Bureau of Statistics (CC BY 4.0). National state and territory population annual growth rate.
https://creativecommons.org/licenses/by/4.0/

While we would like words and argument to be the important ways to change society for the better, it is often photographs and video that make a real difference by attracting attention, going viral and producing lasting improvements for all of us; one need only think of 'tank man' from Tiananmen Square, the naked Vietnamese child running down the road in Vietnam, or the New York Twin Towers collapsing. Visuals have a mass impact because they are worth a thousand words.

One particularly important historical example can be seen to have been used by the famous English nurse, Florence Nightingale in the 19th century (see Exhibit 6.6). Florence Nightingale is probably best known for her heroic nursing during the Crimean War (1853–1856), and she was a brilliant advocate for a much wider range of health issues. Nightingale discovered that one in five soldiers died in the war, not

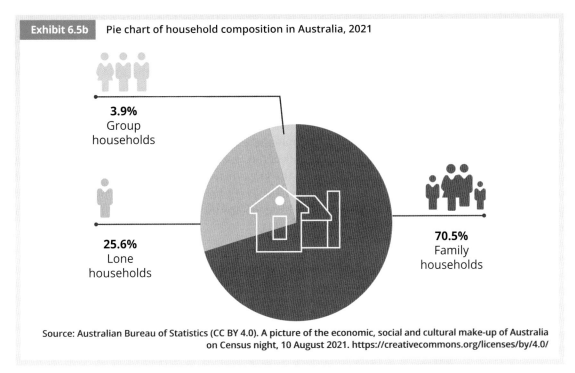

Exhibit 6.5b   Pie chart of household composition in Australia, 2021

3.9%
Group
households

25.6%
Lone
households

70.5%
Family
households

Source: Australian Bureau of Statistics (CC BY 4.0). A picture of the economic, social and cultural make-up of Australia on Census night, 10 August 2021. https://creativecommons.org/licenses/by/4.0/

from wounds they sustained but from dysentery and diseases like typhoid fever. Using collected data, she concluded that death rates of soldiers in hospitals with poor hygiene were much higher than hospitals that practised good ventilation and scrupulous cleanliness. Germ theory as an explanation of and death was not recognised at the time. The medical profession was divided on this subject, with some doctors fearing that simple hygiene measures would undermine their specialised profession.

Her success can be attributed to her ability to convincingly support her arguments with statistical evidence presented in numbers and graphs (see **Exhibit 6.6**). She argued that poor sanitary conditions were the cause of loss of life. Her reports are still considered to be some of the best written documents of their type, for their time.

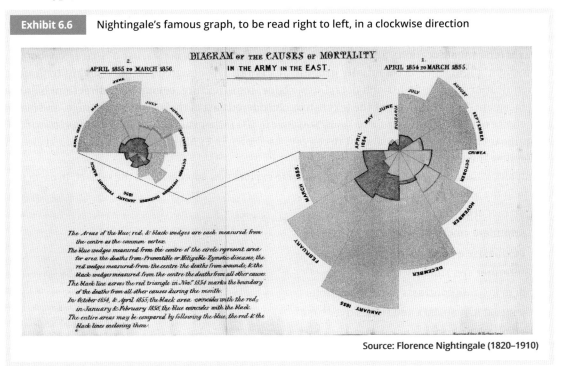

Exhibit 6.6   Nightingale's famous graph, to be read right to left, in a clockwise direction

Source: Florence Nightingale (1820–1910)

She is also famous for her 'coxcomb' graphics. In the unusual graph in Exhibit 6.6 it is somewhat challenging to see that preventable diseases are by far the greatest cause of mortality. The graph takes two stacked column charts for two separate years and transfers the columns into two unusual pie charts with expanded wedges. To understand the diagram, a reader must start with the 1854 coxcomb on the right. It needs to be read in a clockwise direction starting at 9 o'clock. Then the reader needs to study the left-hand, 1855 coxcomb.

Alberto Cairo (2019) argues that Florence Nightingale's choice of graph was no mere accident. Each wedge represents a month, but also depicts death from three separate causes. From Exhibit 6.7, disease is clearly the most prominent cause of death (the bulk of the wedge) with other causes and wounds being much less important (at the tip). The audience of the graph included the government's chief medical officer, who believed that diseases were inevitable outcomes of war. This is obviously not the case in this graphic. The visual allure of the peculiar graph almost demands that it be read because it is a puzzle to understand, but once solved, the conclusion is inevitable.

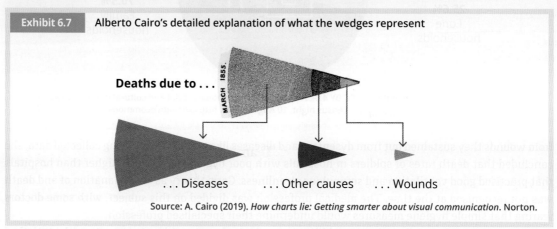

Exhibit 6.7 Alberto Cairo's detailed explanation of what the wedges represent

Deaths due to . . .

. . . Diseases   . . . Other causes   . . . Wounds

Source: A. Cairo (2019). *How charts lie: Getting smarter about visual communication.* Norton.

Why visuals are important in professional writing

The term visuals, or graphics, is commonly used to refer to sketches, drawings, graphs, charts, tables, boxes, borders, pictures, illustrations, cartoons, diagrams, symbols and maps. However, we often forget that written communication – alphabetical characters, punctuation marks, use of space, top–bottom or left–right alignment – is essentially **graphic or visual**. The design elements relevant to graphic communication include points and dots, lines, shape, tone, texture, colour, size, direction, balance and placement. Even the shape of the text can be considered part of the graphical message, and hence your choice of text font and size, say Times New Roman (11) rather than *Lucida Handwriting* (11), is significant to the message you want to convey. As shown in Exhibit 6.8, a choice of font style can impact how the actual text is interpreted.

Graphics attract the eye and stimulate the reader to explore new approaches to the subject. In particular they help the writer to:

- attract attention
- stimulate emotion
- emphasise a point
- interpret and simplify complex data
- demonstrate contrasts and comparisons
- suggest movements and trends over time
- emphasise physical appearance
- analyse concepts, processes and abstract relationships

Graphic or visual
Any visual representation of data; includes a variety of forms, such as drawings, photographs, line art, graphs, numbers, symbols, geometric designs and engineering drawings.

Exhibit 6.8   Font styles can subtly impact text meaning

A Yummy Apology
Aachen bold
Alex Brush
Aquarelle
Arial
Arial Black
BlackJack
Cafe ROJO
Calligraph
Comic Sans
Doctor Soos Bold
Edwardian
Elise
Freehand
fReeze!
Futura
Garamond
Grilled Cheese
Grinched

Harrington
Hiccups
Honey Script Light
Impact
Imperial
Inspiration
Kids
Kristen ITC
LaurenScript
Marker Felt
Monotype Corsiva
My Own Topher
Old London
Papyrus
Phyllis
Script
Team US
Will&Grace
Zephyr Regular

- capture events
- show what can not be seen by the untrained eye
- provide the summarised evidence for reports of all kinds.

Providing the summarised evidence for reports of all kinds is the most important of these for report writing. This is because tables and/or graphs in the results section of a report can convey information to the reader in a visual format that summarises the data you have collected. This gives you something to direct your readers' attention to when you describe and discuss your findings. Your results should be encapsulated by the table or graph, and those graphical details should be precisely discussed with as much detail as possible. This means that your results are shown twice – the first time, results are translated into a graphical image, and the second time, results are written about by unpacking that image.

Writing about graphics is a highly practised skill, and not something that most students learn in high school or even higher education. You are being asked to provide a narrative, description or analysis of numbers in rows or columns in a histogram. But first you have to spend some time creating the table or graph.

Using visuals to communicate

There is a huge range of visuals that you can choose to use in order to assist your reader to read your text, stay motivated and perceive extra meaning. However, a visual can only be effective when both the sender and the receiver share the same meaning for the viewed elements. When you are planning your visual communication ask yourself these key questions:

- Who are you trying to communicate with?
- Which messages would be best presented visually?

- What do you want to say in the visual?
- What does the visual need to do?
- What effect are you hoping to create?
- How will it relate to your text?
- What are common 'visual languages' that you and your audience share?

If you are an architect, for example, you may be quite skilled at architectural drawings, but your client may need a simplified version to appreciate the beauty of your design. If you are a scientist, a visualisation created by a computational program such as MatLab or Scilab may be very significant to you but would be confusing to community groups interested only in the basics of your research. Assuming that a visual designed for one audience is applicable to any audience is a common mistake that many writers or presenters make.

You also need to understand how the material will be reproduced or viewed because the quality of any visual may be significantly affected by printing capabilities, screen resolution or format. This is particularly important if you are using colour as a critical visual element.

In addition, you need to understand the functions of visuals. Some examples are shown in **Exhibit 6.9.**

Exhibit 6.9	Examples of functional visual solutions
Function	**Visual solution**
Record a direct observation – e.g., how an object is formed or developed, or to simplify it	You could do this through sketches, technical drawings or photographs
Generate ideas or help solve a problem	Concept maps, flow charts and fishbone diagrams are examples of visual problem-solving tools
Present information	Charts and graphs are frequently used to present data clearly and concisely
Highlight a particular piece of information	Bullet points and boxes help to focus readers on individual sections of a document
Affect your reader's emotions.	Photographs are ideal for evoking emotions
For occasional cosmetic reasons	Making your document more attractive to your audience can enhance your professional image, keep readers' attention and motivate them to accept your messages

Some tips for using visuals

Some documents may need a number of visuals, while others need none at all, but the majority may rely on a select few in order to make the information more interesting or to clarify meaning. It is important to select the most appropriate graphic design to assist in communicating the message as effectively as possible. Some key tips include:

- All visual representations should be explained and referred to in the body of the document. In reports, each graphic should be numbered (for example, Figure 1/Table 1), have an explanatory title and be kept as close as possible to the relevant text.
- Long excerpts of visual material can interrupt the flow of a report and may even distract a reader. In this case, such illustrations are better placed at the end of a report as appendices. Tables and graphs, in particular, can be incorporated in this way, as can material that you feel could be of interest to a reader but does not belong to any particular paragraph of the report. Try to make the visual as small as possible but not so small as to be unreadable. A maximum size of around half an A4 page is the rule of thumb.
- Make sure that the reader is led through the visual by providing clues to the direction and steps to take to work through the message. You can use numbers, shading, arrows or colour to achieve direction.
- Ensure that the tone of the visual is appropriate. Including a humorous cartoon in a serious news article may trivialise the significance of the message. Choosing a text font such as *Monotype Corsiva* for a formal report may appear amateurish rather than professional. Make sure that the

visual messages match the verbal message. Readers may perceive different messages from visual representations. It is a good idea to test different reactions to your visuals.

- Finally, the KISS (keep it short and simple) principle is usually a wise procedure to use. Keep the visual devices as simple and streamlined as possible. Avoid too many different text fonts, boxes and shadings. Do not use a graphic device unless it contributes to the message you want to convey. Each visual should be elegantly simple so that your message comes through loud and clear.

Selecting the best visual for the job

Your choice of visual to enhance a piece of written communication is largely dependent on a number of factors. These include:

- *The content of the message*: is it serious or light-hearted? Are readers likely to be familiar with the message or reading it for the first time?
- *The characteristics of the readers*: their age, ethnic or cultural background, level of education, attitude to the substance of the message or to the sender of the message.
- *The conventions of the medium in which the message will appear*: visuals used in a formal report for a company will differ to those in an instruction manual for a mass audience or a comic style layout for a high school audience. The format in which the text will be published, such as hard copy, projected presentation, a web page or liquid design for a mobile device, will also affect your choice of visuals.

Even taking these issues into considerations, different visuals have different purposes, as we will discuss in the following.

Tables

If you have a large quantity of complex information to convey, a **table** may be an effective option. A table is a mosaic of text, figures or concepts arranged in columns and rows (with or without grid lines) to permit easy comprehension, reference and comparison. Microsoft Word offers a variety of options for creating tables, including grid lines, shading, colour and patterns, so the process of developing tables becomes easier after a bit of experimentation and practice. There are some conventions that can help you to design tables that will effectively communicate your message, and these are explored in the following sections.

Table
An arrangement of information or data, typically in rows and columns, or possibly in a more complex structure.

Spot tables

A writer would use a spot table if it was important that the information be read as part of the text. These tables are inserted into the text at the appropriate place and usually consist of only a few lines. An example is given in Exhibit 6.10. In a formal report, the spot table is not given a figure number and, therefore, is not indexed.

Exhibit 6.10	Example spot table		
Years	Green Hill	Alston	Total vehicles
2014	671 283	1 012 345	1 683 628
2015	710 778	1 115 990	1 826 768
2016	785 667	1 556 965	2 342 632

Reference tables

Reference tables (see Exhibit 6.11) are used to display more complex material than spot tables and are positioned independently, either near the text to which they refer or in the appendix of a report. The information presented in a reference table is often also shown as a graph in an attempt to show trends or relationships. A reference table must be labelled and numbered so that it can be easily referred to, discussed and indexed.

| | Exhibit 6.11 | Example reference table |

Comparison of employment(a) by age and sex, 1971 and 2021

	Male 1971 (%)	Male 2021 (%)	Female 1971 (%)	Female 2021 (%)
15–19 years	53.0	42.4	49.8	47.9
20–24 years	88.1	73.3	57.8	74.4
25–29 years	94.2	82.2	38.4	78.2
30–34 years	94.9	85.7	38.0	76.5
35–39 years	94.8	86.7	43.1	76.8
40–44 years	94.5	85.7	45.0	78.1
45–49 years	93.6	84.2	42.9	78.4
50–54 years	91.9	81.7	36.4	75.8
55–59 years	88.4	76.3	28.5	68.0
60–64 years	76.0	61.7	16.3	51.1
65–69 years	35.5	35.3	7.8	25.2
70–74 years	19.1	16.9	3.7	10.1
75 years and over	8.9	0.6	1.5	2.6

a To compare employment, 2021 included 'Employed, worked full-time', 'Employed, worked part-time' and 'Employed, away from work'. 1971 included 'Employer', 'Own account worker' and 'Wage earner'.

Source: Australian Bureau of Statistics (CC BY 4.0). Employment in the 2021 Census (2022).
https://creativecommons.org/licenses/by/4.0/

The data in a table are arranged in rows (horizontal) and columns (vertical), so that a relationship can be shown by the figure at the junction of a row and a column. Usually, quantities are shown in columns, while the items being studied (the variables) are listed in the stub on the left-hand side of the table.

If you convert a column of figures to percentages, they should be placed to the right of the base figures. The column heads or box heads are usually separated from the items by a line, but shading can also be used to separate chunks of text.

Graphs and charts

While the information contained in graphs is often drawn from tables, graphs go a step further than tables in emphasising and interpreting trends, making predictions and demonstrating comparisons. Many computer programs include graphical functions, and programs such as Excel include the following basic types of graphs or charts, with variations:

- line graphs
- scatter and bubble graphs
- column charts (with a choice of cones, pyramids and cylinders)
- bar charts
- pie or doughnut charts
- area or surface charts
- stock charts, high–low charts, candle charts and others.

To learn how to use your computer application to create these types of graphs and charts, YouTube often has useful instructional videos.

Line graphs

Line and scatter graphs
Illustrate a relationship of one variable to another commonly drawn to show changes over time.

Line and scatter graphs illustrate a relationship of one variable to another. Line graphs may have single or multiple curves or lines (see **Exhibit 6.12**). The horizontal scale is the independent variable (often this is time). The vertical scale is the dependent variable; that is, the factor being measured.

Some points to remember about plotting a graph are:

- Scale intervals need to be balanced between the two variables, otherwise the information will be distorted and the graph will be biased.
- The width of the figure should be about one-and-a-half times the height.
- Quantity scales should begin at zero.
- If several curves or lines are used on the same figure, each should be clearly identified, for example by contrasting colour or noticeable differences in line make-up (e.g. dotted versus solid lines).
- Lines may be curved to suggest gradual change or plotted to particular points according to exact figures for certain dates.

| Exhibit 6.12 | Example line graph |

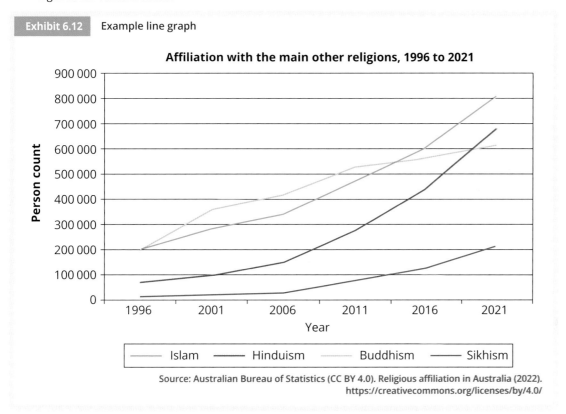

Affiliation with the main other religions, 1996 to 2021

Source: Australian Bureau of Statistics (CC BY 4.0). Religious affiliation in Australia (2022).
https://creativecommons.org/licenses/by/4.0/

Graphs are not meant to give exact figures, which is best left to tables. Rather they show movement or trends over time. Notice that the line graph clearly suggests the rise of non-Christian religions in Australia.

Column and bar charts

Column and bar charts compare sets of data. For column charts, the x-axis lists the different categories and the y-axis shows the value through the height of the column. In a bar chart, the axes are reversed. They provide a quick reference that emphasises the relationship referred to in the text. Excel will usually do a good job for most kinds of graphs, but custom bar charts are sometimes difficult or impossible to create. ClickCharts from NCHsoftware.com is useful for flow charts and has a freeware version, but does not possess custom capabilities for charting purposes.

Pie charts

Pie charts are most effective with audiences of high-school level or below. They are also commonly used by journalists and annual report writers, in order to reach the largest possible audience. If you wish to use a pie chart, simply start at 12 o'clock, with your largest percentage, then add the next largest percentage, then the third largest, and so on, always moving clockwise to add percentages.

Column and bar charts
Compare sets of data using rectangular bars where the length of the bar is proportional to the data value. A bar chart is oriented horizontally, whereas a column chart is oriented vertically.

Pie chart
Represents the data in a circular graph. The slices of pie show the relative size of sections of the data in proportion to the relative percentage of the whole data set.

Flow charts

Flow chart
A diagram of the sequence of movements or actions of people or things involved in a complex system or activity.

The **flow chart** is not designed to compare, but rather to indicate the flow or sequence of action or process (see **Exhibit 6.13**). It can be applied to movement of work in an office or workshop, to the procedures to be followed by people doing such things as completing their tax return paperwork, applying to enrol at a university or finding out how to arrange an overseas trip through a travel agency.

Exhibit 6.13	Example flow chart

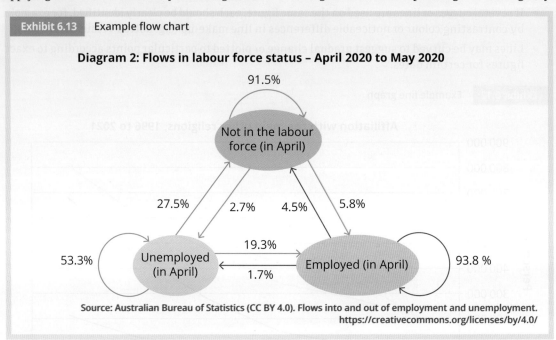

Diagram 2: Flows in labour force status – April 2020 to May 2020

Source: Australian Bureau of Statistics (CC BY 4.0). Flows into and out of employment and unemployment. https://creativecommons.org/licenses/by/4.0/

The accompanying text from the ABS may be dry but is necessary to explain the graphic.

This flow chart shows the proportions of people moving between employment, unemployment and not in the labour force from April to May 2020. Each status of workforce participation is represented as an oval connecting to each of the other statuses in the shape of a triangle. From the 'not in the labour force' status, 2.7 per cent have moved to the 'unemployed' status whereas 5.8 per cent have moved to the 'employed' status. 91.5 per cent have retained the 'not in the labour force' status. From the 'unemployed' status, 27.5 per cent have moved to the 'not in the labour force' status whereas 19.3 per cent have moved to the 'employed' status. 53.3 per cent have retained the 'unemployed' status. From the 'employed' status, 1.7 per cent have moved to the 'unemployed' status whereas 4.5 per cent have moved to the 'not in the labour force' status. 93.8 per cent have retained the 'employed' status. (ABS, 2020)

Organisation charts

Organisation chart
A graphic representation of the structure of an organisation showing the relationships of the positions or jobs within it.

Organisation charts (see **Exhibit 6.14** below) indicate the flow of command in an organisation and frequently appear on a website, company manual or annual report so that readers can clearly see the lines of responsibility for various positions. The function for developing organisation charts is available as part of many word-processing packages and is useful whenever you want to show lines and levels of authority and relationships.

Exhibit 6.14	Example organisation structure

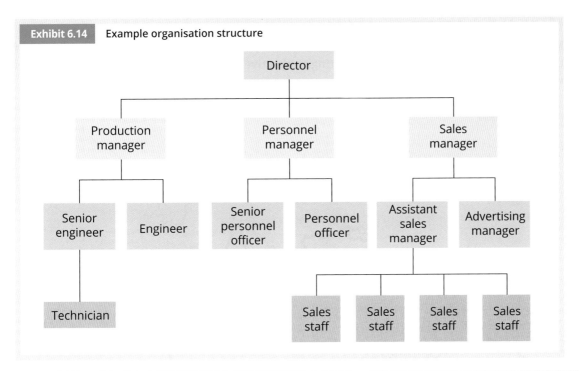

Exhibit 6.15	Example diagram

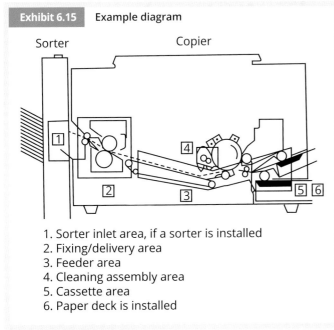

1. Sorter inlet area, if a sorter is installed
2. Fixing/delivery area
3. Feeder area
4. Cleaning assembly area
5. Cassette area
6. Paper deck is installed

Exhibit 6.16	Diagram from the WHO infodemiology conference booklet

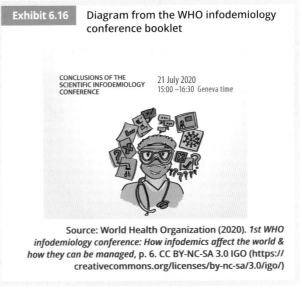

Source: World Health Organization (2020). *1st WHO infodemiology conference: How infodemics affect the world & how they can be managed*, p. 6. CC BY-NC-SA 3.0 IGO (https://creativecommons.org/licenses/by-nc-sa/3.0/igo/)

Diagrams and sketches

Diagrams are similar to flow charts in that they show information at various stages or a flow of activity or material through a system or process, as shown in Exhibit 6.15.

One of the nicest things about diagrams and sketches, especially when humans are depicted, is that they are often ambiguous in terms of ethnicity and other features. If you only have one person in the visual, choosing a photograph of a white male, for example, may be interpreted as racial and/or gender bias. A non-gendered blue doctor appears in Exhibit 6.16.

Maps and drawings

Maps and drawings can represent reality, but they can still be distorted or emphasised at the whim of the designer. **Exhibit 6.17** offers an interesting perspective on the physical size of Australia compared with Europe.

Exhibit 6.17	How big is Australia compared to Europe?

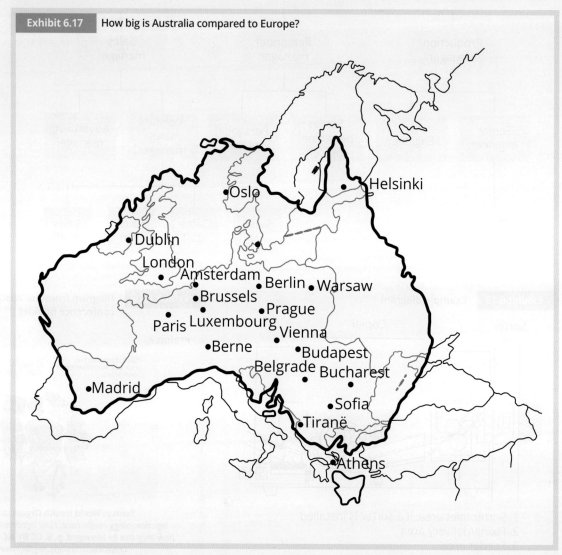

On the other hand, Minard's map of Napoleon's 1812 Russian campaign, shown in **Exhibit 6.18**, is considered to be the best statistical graphic ever drawn because of the extraordinary amount of information displayed. The size and location of the advancing French army is shown by the width and length of the upper band; the lower band depicts the dwindling number of retreating troops. Temperature is also shown at the bottom of the map.

| Exhibit 6.18 | Minard's map of Napoleon's Russian march |

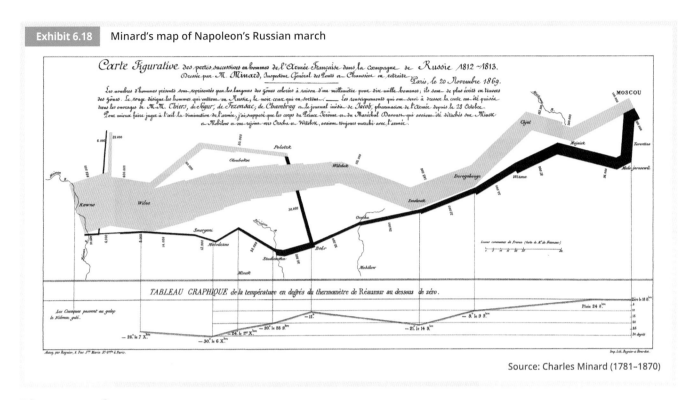

Source: Charles Minard (1781–1870)

Photographs

Photographs can powerfully and accurately depict the truth or a version of the facts. For example, the image of a wrecked car shown **Exhibit 6.19**, may be more effective at deterring people from drink driving than scientific written information.

| Exhibit 6.19 | Photograph of a wrecked vehicle |

Shutterstock.com/Dr. Norbert Lange

In another example, Exhibit 6.20 shows how photos can depict changes over time. The message of the effects of climate change is compelling when such visual evidence is presented.

Reflection question: Consider other examples of the most poignant and affective press photos that you have seen. What is it about how they are composed and the context in which they have been used that makes them so memorable?

Exhibit 6.20   Alaska's Columbia Glacier has retreated 6.5 km from 2009 to 2015

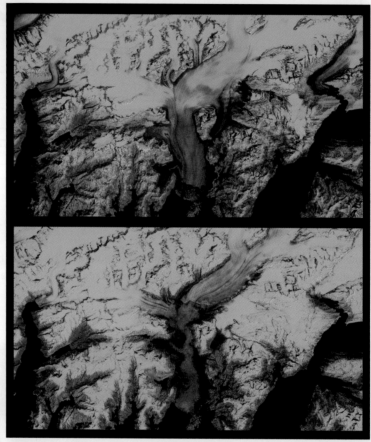

Alamy Stock Photo/ B.A.E. Inc

Creating tables and graphs

We prefer APA (American Psychological Association) format for tables and graphs. An APA table should be simple, elegant and highly comprehensible without needing specialist training. Garish borders, too many colours, nested cells and unnecessary complexity can detract from the table message. Exhibit 6.21 shows a typical example of an APA table.

Note the lack of vertical lines and the four horizontal lines (sometimes less), the use of indenting for the Y axis and the typical categories of demographic data. Table numbers and titles should be placed at the top of the table.

APA tables can also cater for mixed methods, and qualitative data (in words). Exhibit 6.22 summarises the study's quantitative and qualitative results, and provides example quotes from the study interviews.

Exhibits 6.23 and 6.24 demonstrate the APA styles for bar and line graphs.

Note that the use of colour has not been previously recommended, but this has changed in the most recent edition of the APA Style Guide 7 (2020).

Exhibit 6.21   Example APA demographic characteristics table

Baseline characteristic	Guided self-help		Unguided self-help		Wait-list control		Full sample	
	n	%	*n*	%	*n*	%	*n*	%
Gender								
Female	25	50	20	40	23	46	68	45.3
Male	25	50	30	60	27	54	82	54.7
Marital status								
Single	13	26	11	22	17	34	41	27.3
Married/partnered	35	70	38	76	28	56	101	67.3
Divorced/widowed	1	2	1	2	4	8	6	4.0
Other	1	1	0	0	1	2	2	1.3
Children[a]	26	52	26	52	22	44	74	49.3
Cohabitating	37	74	36	72	26	52	99	66.0
Highest Educational level								
Middle school	0	0	1	2	1	2	2	1.3
High school/some college	22	44	17	34	13	26	52	34.7
University or postgraduate degree	27	54	30	60	32	64	89	59.3
Employment								
Unemployed	3	6	5	10	2	4	10	6.7
Student	8	16	7	14	3	6	18	12.0
Employed	30	60	29	58	40	80	99	66.0
Self-employed	9	18	7	14	5	10	21	14.0
Retired	0	0	2	4	0	0	2	1.3
Previous psychological treatment[a]	17	34	18	36	24	48	59	33.3
Previous psychotropic medication[a]	6	12	13	26	11	22	30	20.0

Source: APA (2021). *APA Style*, Sample tables. https://apastyle.apa.org/style-grammar-guidelines/tables-figures/sample- tables

Note. N = 150 (*n* = 50 for each condition). Participants were on average 39.5 years old (*SD* = 10.1), and participant age did not differ by condition.
[a]Reflects the number and percentage of participants answering 'yes' to this question.

Exhibit 6.22   Example APA mixed methods table

Quantitative results	Qualitative results	Example quote
When the topic was more familiar (e.g., climate change) and cards were more relevant, participants placed less value on author expertise.	When an assertion was considered to be more familiar and considered to be general knowledge, participants perceived less need to rely on author expertise.	Participant 144: "I feel that I know more about climate and there are several things on the climate cards that are obvious, and that if I sort of know it already, then the source is not so critical … whereas with nuclear energy, I don't know so much so then I'm maybe more interested in who says what."
When the topic was less familiar (e.g., nuclear power) and cards were more relevant, participants placed more value on authors with higher expertise.	When an assertion was considered to be less familiar and not general knowledge, participants perceived more need to rely on author expertise.	Participant 3: "[Nuclear power], which I know much, much less about, I would back up my arguments more with what I trust from the professors."

Source: APA (2021). *APA Style*, Sample tables. https://apastyle.apa.org/style-grammar-guidelines/tables-figures/sample- tables

Note. We integrated quantitative data (whether students selected a card about nuclear power or about climate change) and qualitative data (interviews with students) to provide a more comprehensive description of students' card selections between the two topics.

Exhibit 6.23 Example APA bar graph

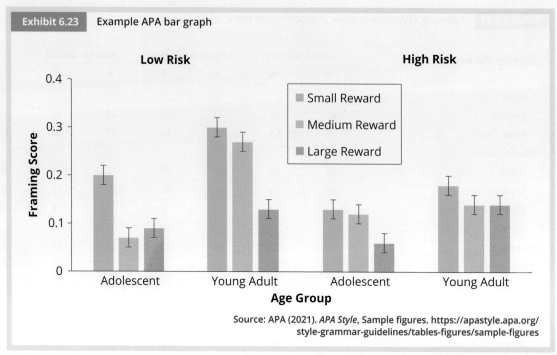

Source: APA (2021). *APA Style*, Sample figures. https://apastyle.apa.org/style-grammar-guidelines/tables-figures/sample-figures

Exhibit 6.24 Example APA line graph

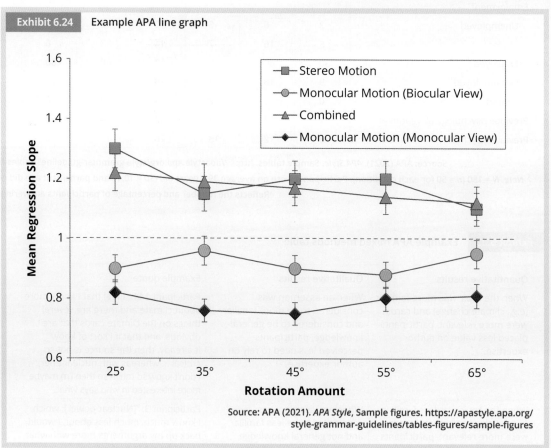

Source: APA (2021). *APA Style*, Sample figures. https://apastyle.apa.org/style-grammar-guidelines/tables-figures/sample-figures

CASE STUDY 6.1 Creating graphs with Excel or OpenOffice for Mac

Creating good looking and informative graphs from scratch has always been challenging for anyone who is new to this task. There are specialised programs, most of which cost money; but the majority of graph makers nowadays use just one program, Excel, which is both a spreadsheet and a graph making program. Excel is the easiest way to create a graph, but you also have to edit the final product, in Excel or Word, if you wish to ensure it is in APA style, or create custom headings, borders, shading and so forth. Another free alternative is OpenOffice for Mac.

Let's use the last five rows from the table in **Exhibit 6.21** and input these into Excel. You will need to insert the x-axis and y-axis headings and numbers manually. The following graph shows what it should look like. The graph is automatically created when you highlight all the Excel cells with headings, then click Insert/Column.

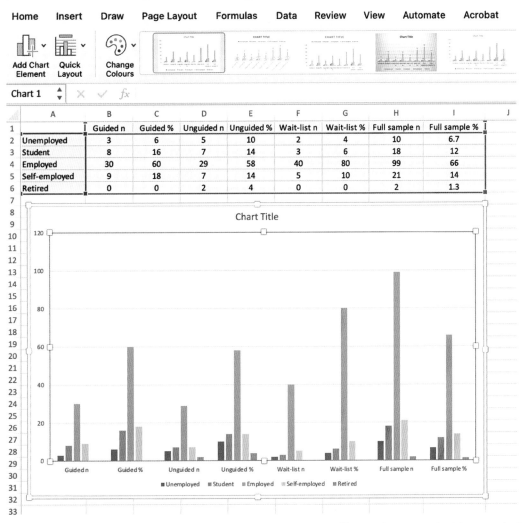

Depending on your version of Excel, if you click on the resultant graph you have created, your menu will change (in the Mac version), then you can click the menu icon to switch the rows and columns around and obtain a different view of your data.

You may like to play around with your choice of graph types to ensure your graph best presents your data.

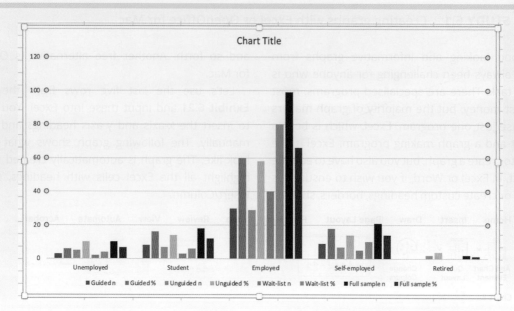

Discussion

1   Which is the better graph from the two outcomes? Why?

2   Which are better, raw scores or percentages? Why?

3   How would you structure the Excel data to ensure valid comparisons? (Hint: you can change the single table into two tables).

4   Do either of the two column graphs above really work with both kinds of scores on the same graph?

After you have discussed this case study, refer to the 'Comments on case studies' section at the end of the text.

Using visuals to persuade: bias, distortion and lies

Bad visuals have been around for decades. Darrel Huff's 1954 book *How to Lie with Statistics* became the biggest selling statistics book in history, selling over 1.5 million copies in English, and it has been translated into many other languages. The book has also been prescribed reading for generations of students since its release. Huff's book is worth a read and uses cartoons and visuals some of the time to illustrate issues around bias, distortion and outright lies told by advertisers, media groups, governments and corporations.

The most popular expert on bad charts in modern times is Alberto Cairo. His books and publications predominantly discuss charts, and also rely on the underlying statistical numbers and research procedures to unpack the trickery that can be found all around us. Cairo's most recent book. *How Charts Lie: Getting Smarter About Visual Information* (2019), is excellent, and it is organised into chapters that embody poor design, dubious data, insufficient data, concealment, confusion and misleading patterns.

We believe that whether the visual 'lie' is an honest mistake or an outright, intentional graphical lie, the same judgement must be made: we are viewing the absence of integrity, ethics and the truth. We believe all material that does this must be recognised for what it is, perhaps publicly admonished, or simply ignored. If Florence Nightingale's visuals could help save generations of people from sickness and death from poor hygiene, then bad visuals (and bad research) have the potential to wreck lives and produce ideas that undermine society.

Survey research has had a long history, but also a chequered reputation as being a somewhat dubious method of research analysis. In some cases, poor survey research has been responsible for unreliable findings including bad visuals. This is easily seen in the specialised field of election polling. In 1936, the incumbent American President, Theodore Roosevelt (Democrat) was up against Alf Landon (Republican). The conservative magazine, *The Literary Digest* (see **Exhibit 6.25**) had been

Exhibit 6.25   The *Literary Digest* front cover for its election issue, September 1936

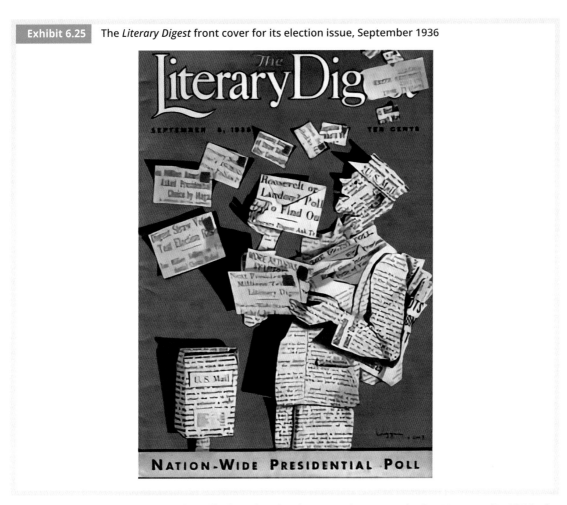

polling their own members and predicting the elections results correctly for 15 years. In 1936, the magazine mailed out 10 million survey cards asking how the recipient would vote, and received back 2.4 million responses. The straw poll results forecasted that Landon would win convincingly, but the eventual election had Roosevelt winning by a landslide. **Exhibit 6.26** shows the predicted and actual results in pie chart format.

Exhibit 6.26   Comparing the *Literary Digest* forecast, and the US election results for 1936

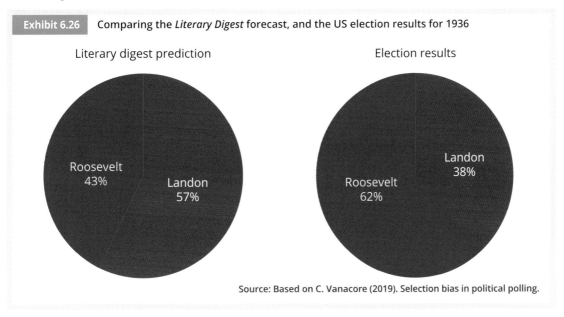

Source: Based on C. Vanacore (2019). Selection bias in political polling.

Exhibit 6.26 convincingly shows *The Literary Digest* polling prediction to be erroneous. Addresses from telephone directories, auto club membership data, and the magazine subscriber list were combined to produce a mailing list for the huge mailout. Telephones were a luxury at the time, only about 40 per cent of Americans could afford them. This was even more true for automobile owners (22 per cent) at the time. Thus, these lists did not accurately reflect the population as a whole and instead featured a higher proportion of middle- and upper-class voters, who would have voted Republican and a lesser proportion of lower-class voters, who would have voted Democrat. This sampling error has been the supposed cause of the faulty magazine poll that eventually caused the magazine to go out of business. It was also the reason that election polling was not trusted in American politics until the 1960s.

The 1936 election example has been used countless times to illustrate the sins of survey researchers who do not sample randomly, even if you obtain 2.4 million responses. Guess what? The assumption that telephone owners and automobile owners voted Republican at the time was not true. Lusinchi (2012) used results from a 1937 Gallup poll to reveal that more telephone and car owners backed Roosevelt. If the 1936 poll was full of only telephone and car owners, Roosevelt should have been predicted to win by *The Literary Digest*. The reason that the magazine poll was mistaken was that, of the 2.4 million responses, the Roosevelt supporters did not bother to vote. This is not biased sampling due to the survey design, but non-response bias of participants. The same issue exists today with online surveys where only those who are interested in the topic, or have an axe to grind, will go to the trouble of participating.

However, it took 75 years for the cautionary tale of the 1936 election to be set straight. When things go wrong in research, people tend to always blame obvious causes. In 1936 telephone and car owners were just scapegoats.

At the beginning of the COVID-19 pandemic in March 2020 the motto of 'flattening the curve' became a constant sign-off for the ABC 7 p.m. news and many other TV channels around Australia. The graphs similar to the one in **Exhibit 6.28** were shown on websites all around the globe. The problem was in how this graph was understood by ordinary citizens and health professionals alike.

The graph, at first glance, appears to be rational in stating that if a lot of people get sick too quickly (in the orange curve area) then the healthcare system capacity will be over-extended. This is obviously because of the limited numbers of hospital beds, doctors and nurses, respiratory equipment and personal protective equipment available. Thus, the doctors and nurses will also get sick and the entire health system will collapse, leading to deaths of many untreated COVID-19 patients who cannot find hospital places. The healthcare advice was to slow the rate of infection by staying home and avoiding infection, allowing the healthcare system (in green flatter curve area) to effectively be able to treat all those that need it.

To many people, even those who worked in health care, there was a poor understanding of what was meant by 'flattering the curve'. This was not helped by graphics such as the one shown in **Exhibit 6.27**, which does

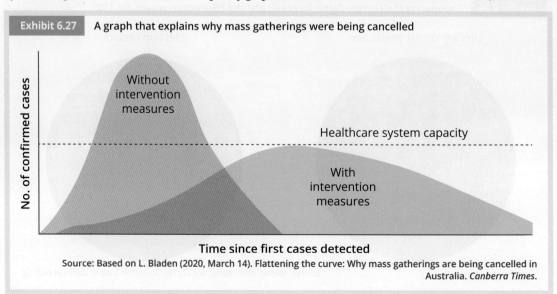

Exhibit 6.27 A graph that explains why mass gatherings were being cancelled

Without intervention measures

Healthcare system capacity

With intervention measures

No. of confirmed cases

Time since first cases detected

Source: Based on L. Bladen (2020, March 14). Flattening the curve: Why mass gatherings are being cancelled in Australia. *Canberra Times*.

not show anything that can stop an individual from getting sick or dying from COVID-19. This graph also does not give time frames or specific case numbers that will push the curve past the healthcare system capacity limit line. Thus, there is a lack of detail in the idea of 'flattening the curve' that some may find confusing.

Exhibit 6.28 is another graph displaying similar information; however, it provides more detailed information. It indicates how many days of physical distancing and how many cases will occur if the population complies with guidelines. This graph does not have a dotted line to denote health care system capacity, but it shows that about 1500 cases equals the breaking point. However, this graph also leaves questions; the curve only flattens for 80-90% compliance, but not 70%. Why is this the point of no return? What about 75%, or 72% compliance?

The issue with both these graphs is that they do not provide enough information for people to understand all of the contributing data that went toward infection and infection prevention. Therefore, it is possible for them to mislead or misrepresent the reality of the situation.

Reflection question: With hindsight, we can see that Exhibits 6.27 and 6.28 may not have presented accurate or complete information about the COVID-19 pandemic to the public. Why do you think graphs like these were used so often by the media and governments at the time? Do you think these graphs may have been effective in persuading people to follow recommended health guidelines? Why or why not?

| Exhibit 6.28 | How coronavirus spreads under different physical distancing scenarios |

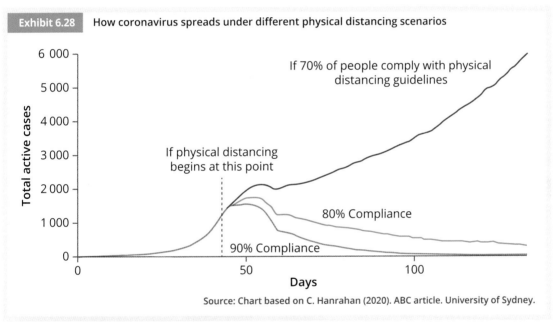

Source: Chart based on C. Hanrahan (2020). ABC article. University of Sydney.

Disinformation often relies on **confirmation bias**, or the tendency of people to look for information that confirms what they already believe. Governments of many countries have played upon this tendency, publishing photographs and stories meant to persuade their citizens to follow a desired set of behaviours or beliefs. Photographs published by the Soviet Union in the first half of the twentieth century demonstrate how some images were manipulated to convey information (see https://www.bbc.com/culture/article/20171110-the-early-soviet-images-that-foreshadowed-fake-news). Even now that images can be manipulated easily with image-editing software, the most common form of visual misinformation used today involves using photographs and videos from actual events of the past and presenting them as evidence for other unrelated events (Fazio, 2020). A well-known example of this is a black and white photograph showing British soldiers playing football during the First World War (**Exhibit 6.29**). This photograph has often been published as evidence of a football match played between British and Germans soldiers on Christmas Day in Flanders in 1914, but the photograph was actually taken in Greece in 1915 under entirely different circumstances (Doyle, 2021). Case study 6.2 further explores how photos have been used to shape public opinion.

Confirmation bias
The tendency of people to look for information that confirms what they already believe.

Exhibit 6.29   British soldiers playing football in Greece, 1915

Alamy Stock Photo/PA Images

 CASE STUDY 6.2   Worth a thousand words: how photos shape attitudes toward refugees

The power of images to affect social and political change has long been debated. In the case of contentious or politically sensitive issues such as war, governments of all persuasions have sought to control their preferred narrative by either suppressing or selectively publishing particular photographs. In Australia, the case of refugees is a case in point. Read this extract from an essay in *The Conversation*, which outlines research about the impact of particular photographs on Australian attitudes to the ongoing and contentious debate over refugee policy.

[In Australia in recent decades respective governments have sought] to suppress photographs of asylum seekers, seemingly from fear that such images will prompt empathy with them and undermine border security policy.

...

In August 2001, the MV Tampa rescued 438 mostly Afghan refugees from their sinking boat, around four hours from the Australian territory of Christmas Island.

...

Australian citizens' understanding of these remote events was necessarily highly mediated. A review ... examined visual representations of asylum seekers on the front pages of two prominent Australian newspapers at the time ... Their analysis showed the predominance of pictures of boats, mostly from a distance, as well as those depicting

asylum seekers as large groups (42%). In contrast, there was a striking lack of images showing asylum seekers with clearly recognisable facial features (only 2%).

AAP Images/WALLENIUS WILHELMSEN

The researchers concluded that the effect of this pattern was to dehumanise refugees and frame the refugee 'problem' as a potential threat that demanded mechanisms of security and border control... [It was reported that] that Defence Minister Peter Reith had explicitly instructed personnel, 'Don't humanize the refugees'.

...

Visual theorists express concerns about the ethical use of images of suffering. They argue that such images exploit their subjects by violating their privacy or showing them as abject and less-than-human. ... However, the complete suppression of images by the state also acts to erase the social experience of suffering. In this way, the absent image may be as powerful, and terrifying in its effects, as images of suffering.

...

Source: J. Lydon (2016, July 29). Friday essay: Worth a thousand words – how photos shape attitudes to refugees. *The Conversation*. CC BY ND.

Discussion

1 What are the characteristics of images that allow them to be used to either support or distort messages?

2 In the scenario described in the article, why might the government at the time feel it was important not to publish images that 'humanise' refugees?

3 Think of subjects such as climate change, animal cruelty, destruction during war or natural disaster. How might examples from one of these areas have altered perspectives on a controversial topic?

After you have discussed this case study, refer to the 'Comments on case studies' section at the end of the text.

Ugly, plain and unethical visuals

In advertising, we understand that beauty sells products and, conversely, that 'ugliness' or plainness does not sell. The assumption is that consumers all want to buy products that are associated with ideals of beauty and youth. When we view images of people who look better than us, we then wish to obtain these products because they might just make us look or feel better about ourselves. This theory has led to companies airbrushing or editing images to remove the 'imperfections' from models' faces and bodies in order to create the most perfect image possible. However, in 2023, beautiful images come at a cost. They are unethical because they employ subterfuge and deceit to make them perfect. If we want ethical photographs then we must rely on viewing 'imperfect', natural ones.

However, unlike photographs, charts do not display human beings in natural contexts in most cases. Graphs and tables represent human behaviour over time and compare human behaviour of different demographic groups. Technical communication visuals, particularly those that focus on accidents, injuries and deaths, need to be treated with special care and sensitivity.

Dragga and Voss (2001) have argued that plain pie charts used to summarise human fatalities and injuries are in fact a form of cruelty and disrespect to the victims (see Exhibit 6.30). That is, the

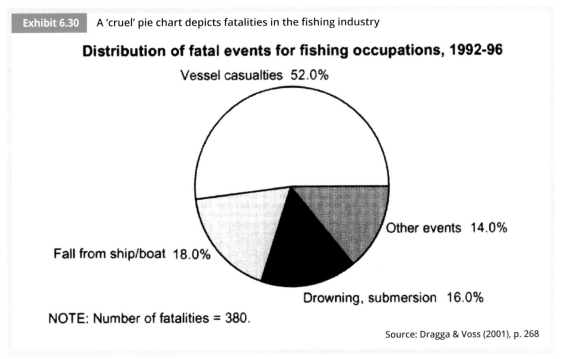

Exhibit 6.30 A 'cruel' pie chart depicts fatalities in the fishing industry

Distribution of fatal events for fishing occupations, 1992-96

Vessel casualties 52.0%

Other events 14.0%

Fall from ship/boat 18.0%

Drowning, submersion 16.0%

NOTE: Number of fatalities = 380.

Source: Dragga & Voss (2001), p. 268

plainness of the graphs undermines the seriousness of the statistics that are being stated. Additionally, plain visuals that are homogenised and devoid of any kind of shock value will not provide the impetus for meaningful change for law and policy makers. The solution is to provide the audience with extra information on the graph itself, so it cannot be viewed without understanding the tragedy of the statistics, hidden by the chart. **Exhibit 6.31** is an uncomfortable, uglier alternative to the sanitised previous version, with the addition of a quote and a list of unnatural causes of death. The graphic's author has made the chart more extreme by emphasising the horror of people dying from fishing accidents.

> **Reflection question:** Do you think the way that Exhibits 6.30 and 6.31 are presented make a difference to the impact of these statistics?

Exhibit 6.31	Semantic fusion using words to display human suffering assumed by statistics of fatalities in the fishing industry

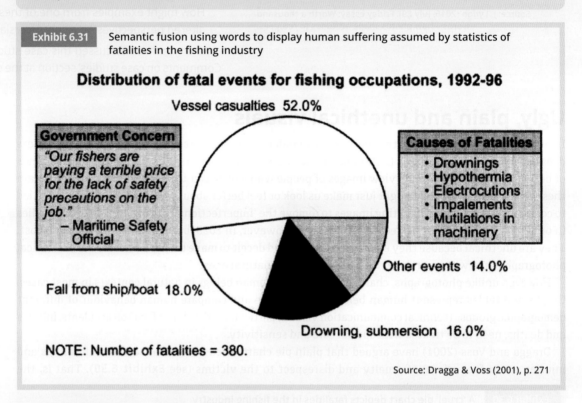

Source: Dragga & Voss (2001), p. 271

The problem of deepfakes

Deepfake
An image or video of a person in which their face or body has been digitally altered so that they appear to be someone else, typically used maliciously or to spread false information.

People have been creating fake photographs and films meant to fool us or entertain us for as long as there have been images and films. The Edison Manufacturing Company in the 1890s used real old footage interlaced with modern footage of soldiers to re-create the Spanish–American war. **Deepfakes** properly begin with *Video Rewrite* program in 1997 that allowed creators to display people mouthing brand new words that they did not really speak. In 2001 a computer vision algorithm was written that improved on the 1997 program (see Q5id, 2022).

This practice has become more evident because the widespread use of the internet has given these fakes a vast audience. However, there is a new kind of machine-made or synthetic fake, and it is becoming increasingly more difficult to recognise the difference between fact and fiction. The new deepfakes are much more compelling than photographs changed by editing software like Photoshop, or films and videos that employ specialised techniques.

On 29 September 2019, ZaoApp was released in China via the iOS Apple store. The ZaoApp was a face-switching application that used videoclips from a range of TV shows and films and a user's own selfies to make it seem that the user was part of the video. This process was so convincing that within only three days, the app was the most downloaded app in China. ZaoApp's terms of service originally allowed the app developers to retain the copyright once someone used the app and uploaded it to the internet. However, the terms of service were quickly updated allowing the user the right to control their faked videos, and allowing users to delete content, which would also be deleted on the app's databases (*The Guardian*, 2019).

The most recent issues concerning visual ethics surrounds the phenomenon of deepfakes and the many more apps that have copycatted ZaoApp (see Exhibit 6.32). A deepfake has come to mean any kind of media file where the image has been digitally altered to create juxtaposed images or voices that impersonate others. There now exists thousands of convincing audio or video files of someone famous (or non-famous) appearing to say or do something completely out of character. Users can use their own faces, or other people's faces to create pornographic images or videos, or simply appear to be in popular films. Individuals can be made to look older or younger, or change ethnicity. When celebrities or politicians have been the main characters of these deepfakes, the audio or video file goes viral on social media all over the world, causing reputational damage in some cases.

Exhibit 6.32   ZaoApp and similar apps have raised new issues about deepfakes

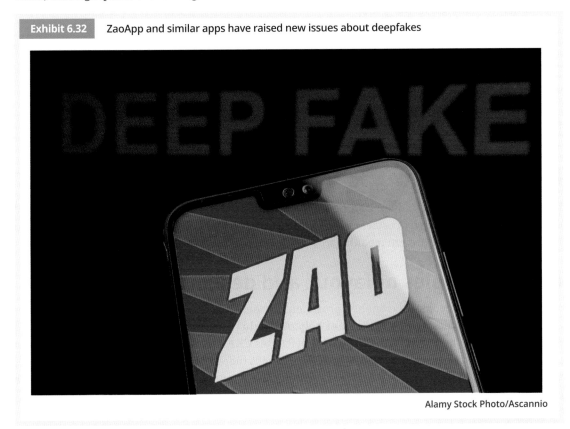

Alamy Stock Photo/Ascannio

At this point in time, the academic literature on the problems and ethics of deepfakes is growing, but policies and laws have not been forthcoming anywhere in the world. Case study 6.3 explores these issues further.

Reflection question: Think back to the first time you saw a deepfake. What was your reaction at the time?

CASE STUDY 6.3 Exploring deepfakes

The technology behind deepfakes is evolving very quickly. Numerous legal, social, and ethical issues are generated by the popularity and reach of deepfakes through widely accessible apps. Several questions arise from this technology that have not been answered as yet by any governments.

First, locate some famous deepfakes from YouTube or Reddit by searching for them on the web.

In groups, or individually, discuss the questions below, one per group, and take notes on possible answers. After 10–15 minutes, one person in each group should address the class in order to summarise the group discussion.

Discussion

1   Do legal interventions need to be made with this new technology? Should deepfakes be censored if they are too offensive?

2   If not, what is the most effective strategy for authorities to intervene and direct how online communities should produce deepfakes?

3   Should platform operators have any obligations for ensuring ethical deepfakes?

4   How does intellectual property fit into the discussion of this new technology?

5   Who owns copyright of deepfakes since they are hybrids of personal information and public information?

6   What is the best way to regulate deepfakes in democratic countries?

After you have discussed this case study, refer to the 'Comments on case studies' section at the end of the text.

Layout, design and use of colour

Layout, design and use of colour can be important in written communication. A well-designed document can make your work easier to read, while certain colours might make text and images hard to read, or even convey different meanings.

CRAP principles of layout and design

Non-experts can become reasonably proficient at designing a well-written document with accompanying graphics, with a little bit of help. A highly recommended text is *The Non-Designer's Design Book* (2014) by Robin Williams, which discusses CRAP (contrast, repetition, alignment and proximity) design principles. While the word CRAP sounds rude and inappropriate, it certainly attracts your attention and makes is very easy to remember these four principles in practice when you are creating a new document.

Contrast

Contrast
In graphic design, occurs when visual elements placed close to one another are noticeably different from each other.

Contrast is usually the most important visual element of a document. Contrast is what distinguishes white text on a black background, charts from body text and is also the reason why black and white PowerPoint themes never fail to work. Contrast also refers to varying colours, sizes, shapes and types of objects. The rule is that if elements are not similar, then they should look quite different. Colour contrast is also a useful consideration, with close colours used for similar elements and opposing colours useful for very different elements (see **Exhibit 6.33**).

| Exhibit 6.33 | This poster contrast oversized black quote marks and black and white photograph on a white background |

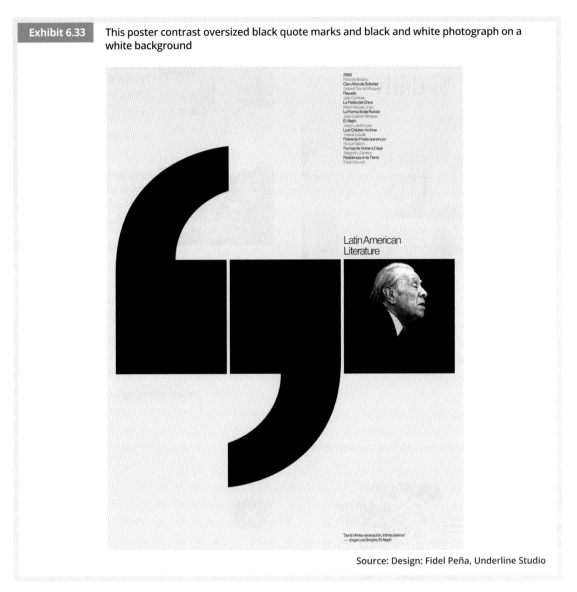

Source: Design: Fidel Peña, Underline Studio

Repetition

The principle of **repetition** refers to deliberately repeating graphical elements throughout the document, such as shapes, fonts, sizes, colours, line thicknesses, spatial relationships, textures and graphics. This process makes everything predictable and strengthens the unity of the document. Repetition of certain visual elements makes a reader feel safe that they are reading an organised document (see example in Exhibit 6.34).

Alignment

All elements on a page should be placed there with a reason and nothing left to chance. All the items should be connected in a purposeful way. Text should be left-aligned, and margins and corners of elements should connect with each other in kind of grid system. An example of **alignment** is shown in Exhibit 6.35.

Repetition
Refers to the reusing of graphic elements such as colours, patterns, fonts, images, textures and more throughout a piece of work to signify connection and consistency.

Alignment
Refers to the arrangement of elements on a page to create the sense of purposeful connection.

Exhibit 6.34 This screenshot of the Apartment Therapy website shows repetitive elements

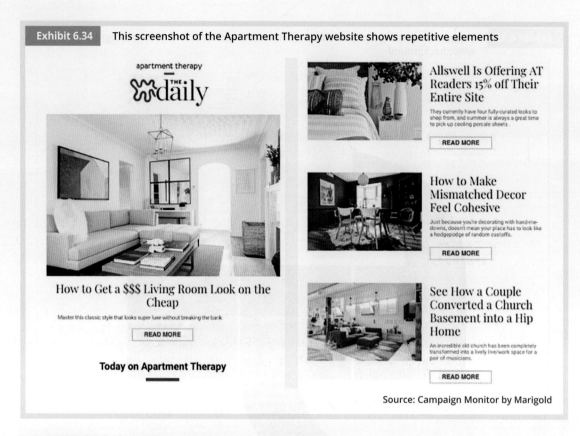

Source: Campaign Monitor by Marigold

Exhibit 6.35 Gridlines help to show alignment layout

Proximity

When several items are positioned close to each other (i.e. are in **proximity**), they are perceived as a group that are related to each other. When objects are not close to each other, those objects are not seen as a group. For example, images supporting text need to be close to each other. This process helps to manage information and imparts a clear structure to the document.

Obviously, the CRAP principles are seldom used in isolation from each other, with two or more principles seen in many examples of page layout and design (see Exhibit 6.36). Depending on the audience, the genre of the document, and the medium selected for distribution, your choices may be endless or very constrained by the medium. Paradoxically, it is old-fashioned paper that affords the layout artist the most freedom of choice in terms of design, texture, and size. Some web pages might look pretty impressive, but web designers are limited by the size of screens, placement of elements and speed of transfer in some locations. Web page designers also have to contend with at least two different devices owned by audiences: mobile phones, which use a portrait-oriented screen; and laptops, which have a landscape orientation. This means that web pages must either be designed twice, or a single design must cater for both devices. The most popular current solution is to use the middle half of a computer screen for text to serve mobile phone audiences and laptop owners. Graphics are usually placed before or after text on phones, and on the sides in the case of computer screens.

Proximity
Refers to the spatial relationship between elements of a design; things that are related should be located near each other, while those not connected should be situated further from each other.

Exhibit 6.36	Example of proximity (and repetition). The groups are numbered and close to each other on this pamphlet

Source: Red Fleece Editorial Newspaper by Stephanie Toole. Licensed under CC By-NC-SA.3.0 (https://creativecommons.org/licenses/by-nc-sa/3.0/)

The importance of colour

We all have our own favourite colours. People like different colours just as they like different foods. Colour also represents feelings, people and countries, and in different cultures, colours are symbolic. Therefore, one of the final aspects of visual communication, especially as it impacts layout and design, is the use of colour.

How we see colour

Roses are red and violets are blue, but we only know that thanks to specialised cells in our eyes called cones. When light hits an object – say, a banana – the object absorbs some of the light and reflects the rest of it. Which wavelengths are reflected or absorbed depends on the properties of the object. The physiology of how our eyes receive and our brains perceive colour is quite complex, but neuroscience strongly suggests that our perception of colour is controlled much more by our brains than by our eyes (Pappas, 2021).

While most people have similar colour receptors, we don't always *interpret* the meaning of the colour in the same way. For this reason, advertisers, interior decorators and graphic designers must be careful when choosing appropriate colours to accompany a message.

Symbolic and cultural meanings of colour

Colour symbolism is the use of colour as a representation or meaning of something that is usually specific to a particular culture or society. Colour means many different things to different people and cultures. Even in the modern English-speaking world, where superstitious beliefs have largely faded, many colours retain their ancient symbolic associations (Wolchover & Duffield, 2022).

In the Western world, the colour red, for example, is frequently understood as symbolising anger or aggression. It also holds the related meaning of excitement, danger and sexual potency. Some car insurance companies charge more for red cars because some owners of red cars are more aggressive and take more risks. Red lights mean stop or danger. In Western cultures, most people know that brides traditionally wear white, symbolising purity. In contrast, many Chinese brides wear red, symbolising luck. According to a study in the journal *Nature* (Hill & Barton, 2005), several soccer teams achieved greater match results while wearing predominantly red shirts than while playing in other colours, such as white and blue.

Artists and interior designers have long understood how colour can dramatically affect moods, feelings and emotions. Certain colours have been associated with physiological changes, including increased blood pressure, increased metabolism and eyestrain (Cherry, 2022). **Exhibit 6.37** summarises some of these general findings.

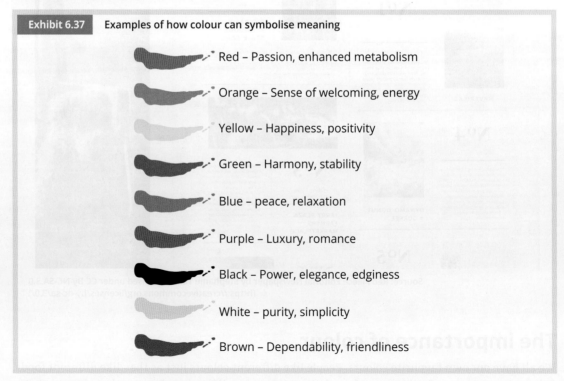

| Exhibit 6.37 | Examples of how colour can symbolise meaning |

Red – Passion, enhanced metabolism

Orange – Sense of welcoming, energy

Yellow – Happiness, positivity

Green – Harmony, stability

Blue – peace, relaxation

Purple – Luxury, romance

Black – Power, elegance, edginess

White – purity, simplicity

Brown – Dependability, friendliness

Using colour in professional documents

While this is a complex issue, our message here is to be aware of the inherent meaning and impact of different colours and colour combinations within a professional document or presentation. Many businesses and major corporates spend have spent a significant amount of money creating brand identity based around a particular colour palette (Snell, 2009). For example, think about how Coca Cola uses the colour red, or IBM uses the colour blue. Famous jewellery brand Tiffany is synonymous with a light blue colour while fast food giant McDonald's is easily identified by their 'golden arches'. There are many more examples.

In summary, here are some hints:

- Colours should relate to the topic in appropriate ways. What kind of image does the company want to project?
- Colours should be consistent throughout the document and enhance the company logo.
- Dark or textured backgrounds should be used sparingly as they can be hard to read.
- All colours should be tested as to what they will look like when produced in the final report form, as what you see on a screen may not be the same as the final colour if professionally printed.

CASE STUDY 6.4   Scary red or icky green? We can't say what colour coronavirus is and dressing it up might feed fears

The importance of colour choice in professional communication can be illustrated by the challenges of trying to visually convey important health information. For example, how do you visually represent an almost invisible virus, such as COVID-19?

Images of COVID-19 are now instantly recognisable, often vibrantly coloured and floating in an opaque background. In most representations, the shape of the virus is the same – a spherical particle with spikes, resembling an alien invader. But there's little consensus about the colour: images of the virus come in red, orange, blue, yellow, soft green, white with red spikes, red with blue spikes, and many colours in between.

In their depictions of the virus, designers, illustrators and communicators are making some highly creative and evocative decisions. Grey images of unfamiliar blobs, which are in reality what the virus looks like under an electron microscope, don't make for persuasive or emotive media content.

Research into the representation of the Ebola virus outbreak in 1995 revealed the image of choice was not the worm-like virus, but was instead teams of Western medical experts working in African villages in hermetically sealed suits. The early visual representation of the AIDS virus focused on the emaciated bodies of those with the resulting disease, often younger men.

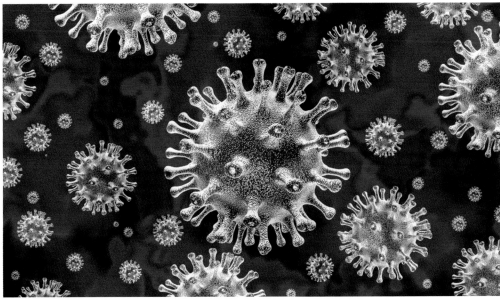

iStock.com/wildpixel

With symptoms similar to the common cold and initial death rates highest amongst the elderly, the coronavirus pandemic provides no such dramatic visual material. To fill this void, the vivid range of colourful images of the coronavirus have strong appeal.

While these images look aesthetically striking, the arbitrary nature of their colouring does little to solve WHO's concerns about the insecurity that comes with unclear facts about viruses and disease.

One solution would be to embrace the colourless sub-microscopic world that viruses inhabit and accept their greyness. Stripping the coronavirus of the distracting vibrancy of vivid colour – and seeing it consistently as an inert grey particle – could help reduce community fear and better allow us to continue the enormous collective task of managing its biological and social impact.

Source: Simon Weaving, Senior Lecturer, School of Creative Industries, University of Newcastle. Originally published on *The Conversation*, under CC BY ND License. Full article found at: https://theconversation.com/scary-red-or-icky-green-we-cant-say-what-colour-coronavirus-is-and-dressing-it-up-might-feed-fears-134380

Discussion

1   How does the colour used to represent the coronavirus in the media impact on the strength of the public health communication related to COVID-19?

2   Is the visual representation of the virus as 'alien' or 'spiky' a useful technique?

3   Can you think of other advertising or public health examples where colour has been used to create a particular emotional reaction?

After you have discussed this case study, refer to the 'Comments on case studies' section at the end of the text.

Summary

This chapter focuses on the Western interpretation of graphics and visuals in English-speaking countries and Western European nations. The origins of graphics are explored looking at Sumeria, Egypt and China. Florence Nightingale's outstanding graphs are used to exemplify her approach to mortality in the Crimean War. Reasons for using visuals in professional writing are explained. The huge range of possible visuals is shown and advice is given on their strengths and weaknesses. We demonstrated how visuals can be 'bad', with examples of how visuals can be used to lie, misinform or deliberately distort information. Ugly, plain and unethical visuals are exemplified, especially the most recent problem of deepfakes. The principles of good layout and design are summarised by a single acronym, CRAP. Colour is discussed in terms of its uses, connotations and meanings.

STUDY TOOLS

DISCUSSION QUESTIONS AND GROUP ACTIVITIES

For discussion topics and activities in addition to those listed below, please refer to the case studies presented throughout this chapter.

1   Why is important to distinguish a Western perspective as opposed to an East Asian perspective on visuals?

2   What are some of the oldest visuals and graphics in your culture? How old are they and what do they look like?

3   What are the origins of tables and graphs in Western cultures?

4   What is the APA format style for tables and graphs?

5   Find a recent graph and see if you can find hidden mistakes in the data.

6   Can you explain Florence Nightingale's coxcomb pie charts?

7   List six different kinds of visuals found in professional and scientific writing.

8   List three different reasons for employing visuals in your writing.

9   What is the APA 7 guideline for using colour in graphs?

10 What are tables good at showing? What are graphs good at showing?

11 OpenOffice from the Apache company still supplies a version of OpenOffice for Mac computers. Download a free copy and see what its spreadsheet can do that MS Excel cannot do.

12 When would you use a photograph in a business report?

13 Custom graphs are fairly difficult to produce without special software. Do some research to see if there are any free demos that can produce unusual graphs for a one-off special visual.

14 What would Dragga and Voss (2001) say about **Exhibit 6.18**, Minard's famous graph of the 1812 retreat that shows the devastating human loss. Check their article in the References.

15 There are lots of alleged comparison photographs from conspiracy theorists that claim climate change is untrue. Find some and explain why they are false claims.

16 What is the latest health advice about COVID-19? Are graphs and tables still being used to persuade us to get vaccinated or be careful?

17 Download a copy of ZaoApp to your phone. See if you can create your own personal deepfake and show some friends. What do you think?

WEBSITES

The Society for Technical Communication https://stc.org

The Australian Bureau of Statistics https://abs.gov.au

OpenOffice https://sourceforge.net/projects/openofficeorg.mirror

Seven best free graph drawing programs https://fixthephoto.com/best-graph-making-software.html

The authentic guide to the APA format of referencing and charts https://apastyle.apa.org

Alberto Cairo's website https://albertocairo.com

Florence Nightingale Museum in London https://www.florence-nightingale.co.uk

A brief history of graphic design https://uxdesign.cc/a-brief-history-of-graphic-design-90eb5e1b5632

How to lie with charts, a National Geographic website https://www.nationalgeographic.com/science/article/150619-data-points-five-ways-to-lie-with-charts

REFERENCES

American Psychological Association. (2020). *Publication manual of the American Psychological Association* (7th ed.). APA.

Australian Bureau of Statistics. (2020). *Flows into and out of employment and unemployment*. https://www.abs.gov.au/articles/religious-affiliation-australia

Bladen, L. (2020, March 14). Flattening the curve: Why mass gatherings are being cancelled in Australia. *Canberra Times*.

Cairo, A. (2013). *The functional art*. New Riders.

Cairo, A. (2019). *How charts lie: Getting smarter about visual communication*. Norton.

Cherry, K. (2022). Color psychology: Does it affect how you feel? *VeryWell Mind, 24*. https://www.verywellmind.com/color-psychology-2795824

Doyle, P. (2021, December 15). The Christmas Truce Football Match – a picture of a Greek kickabout is misappropriated yearly. *The Conversation*. https://theconversation.com/the-christmas-truce-football-match-a-picture-of-a-greek-kickabout-is-misappropriated-yearly-173468

Dragga, S. & Voss, D. (2001). Cruel pies: The inhumanity of technical illustrations. *Technical Communication, 48*(3), 265–274.

Fazio, L. (2020, February 15). Out-of-context photos are a powerful low-tech form of misinformation. *The Conversation*. https://theconversation.com/out-of-context-photos-are-a-powerful-low-tech-form-of-misinformation-129959

Hanrahan, C. (2020). ABC article. University of Sydney.

Hicks, S. M., Pohl, K., Neeman, T., McNamara, H. A., Parsons, K. M., He, J. S., Ali, S. A., Nazir, S., Rowntree, L. C., Nguyen, T. H. O., Kedzierska, K., Doolan, D. L., Vinuesa, C. G., Cook, M. C., Coatsworth, N., Myles, P. S., Kurth, F., Sander, L. E., Mann, G. J., Gruen, R. L., ... SARS-CoV-2 Testing in Elective Surgery Collaborators. (2021). A dual-antigen enzyme-linked immunosorbent assay allows the assessment of severe acute respiratory syndrome Coronavirus 2 antibody seroprevalence in a low-transmission setting. *Journal of Infectious Diseases, 223*(1), 10–14. https://doi.org/10.1093/infdis/jiaa623

Hill, R. A., & Barton, R. A. (2005). Red enhances human performance in contests. *Nature, 435*(7040), 293–293.

Kalish, H., Klumpp-Thomas, C., Hunsberger, S., Baus, H. A., Fay, M. P., Siripong, N., Wang, J., Hicks, J., Mehalko, J., Travers, J., Drew, M., Pauly, K., Spathies, J., Ngo, T., Adusei, K. M., Karkanitsa, M., Croker, J. A., Li, Y., Graubard, B. I., Czajkowski, L., ... Sadtler, K. (2021). Undiagnosed SARS-CoV-2 seropositivity during the first 6 months of the COVID-19 pandemic in the United States. *Science Translational Medicine, 13*(601), eabh3826. https://doi.org/10.1126/scitranslmed.abh3826

Kuwabara, M., & Smith, L. B. (2016). Cultural differences in visual object recognition in 3-year-old children. *Journal of Experimental Child Psychology, 147*, 22–38. https://doi.org/10.1016/j.jecp.2016.02.006

Lusinchi, D. (2012). *Social Science History 36*(1) (Spring) 23-54. https://doi.org/10.1215/01455532-1461650

Lydon, J. (2016, July 29). Friday essay: Worth a thousand words – how photos shape attitudes to refugees. *The Conversation*.

Macdonald, F. (2021, November 10). The early Soviet images that foreshadowed fake news. *BBC News*. https://www.bbc.com/culture/article/20171110-the-early-soviet-images-that-foreshadowed-fake-news

Nightingale, F. (1858). Notes on matters affecting the health, efficiency, and hospital administration of the British Army. Founded chiefly on the experience of the late war. Presented by request to the Secretary of State for War. Privately printed for Miss Nightingale, Harrison and Sons, London.

Nisbett, R. E., & Miyamoto, Y. (2005). The influence of culture: Holistic versus analytic perception. *Trends in Cognitive Science, 9*(10), 467–473. https://doi.org/10.1016/j.tics.2005.08.004

Pappas, S. (2021, July 8). How do we see colour? *Live Science*. https://www.livescience.com/32559-why-do-we-see-in-color.html

Q5id (2022). A quick history of deepfakes: How it all began. https://q5id.com/blog/a-quick-history-of-deepfakes-how-it-all-began

Snell, S. (2009, January 29). Colours in corporate branding and design. *Smashing Magazine*. https://www.smashingmagazine.com/2009/01/colors-in-corporate-branding-and-design

The Guardian. (2019, September 2). Chinese deepfake app Zao sparks privacy row after going viral. https://www.theguardian.com/technology/2019/sep/02/chinese-face-swap-app-zao-triggers-privacy-fears-viral

Vanacore, C. (2019). Selection bias in political polling. https://medium.com/@vanacorec/selection-bias-in-political-polling-9fd667e8e7f7

Williams, R. (2014). *The Non-Designers' Design Book*. Peachpit Press.

Wolchover, N., & Dutfield, S. (2022). The meaning of colours: How 8 colours became symbolic. *Pristupljeno, 9*, 2022.

World Health Organization. (2020). *1st WHO infodemiology conference: How infodemics affect the world & how they can be managed*.

Professional communication and ethics

What is an ethical act at university?

Farouk is a student who is studying his degree mostly online. He is enrolled in a subject that requires him to complete several online quizzes in order to pass. The quizzes are supposed to be completed individually and are marked automatically throughout the semester. Farouk sometimes attends classes in person when he has some time free from his part-time job. During one of these on-campus visits, he sees several of his classmates attempting the quizzes in groups in the computer labs. He believes that this is cheating and emails his instructor, who replies that it is impossible to control this type of behaviour. Farouk does not know what to do about this.

Online quizzes are used extensively in higher education in the 21st century, but are commonly open to collusion (or cheating) if students decide to work together to obtain the best possible marks for themselves. Multiple choice quizzes themselves are subject to internal errors and alternate answers that can make them unreliable assessment instruments. Instructors may be forced to use such quizzes because the institution demands self-marking 'objective' assessments that are not overly taxing to sessional instructors.

In terms of ethical behaviour, Farouk is powerless to change this situation and needs to decide if he can pass these quizzes by himself. Realistically, apart from examinations, all individual assessment items can be attempted with the help of fellow students, but this could be called academic misconduct. Farouk needs to understand these facts and make his own decision based upon his own set of ethical beliefs.

Introduction

The topic of professional ethics is important to address on its own, particularly in today's world, because:

- ethics is an important topic that many of us have never studied in detail
- the COVID-19 pandemic has exposed a multitude of ethical issues that Australians could not avoid and are still being resolved
- we are constantly being exposed to 'fake news', misinformation and propaganda that promote unreliable opinions and attitudes.

We need to understand that ethics is a broad-ranging topic that can apply to us personally, within our jobs, across our media consumption and within society as a whole.

Hopefully, this chapter will supply you with some new ideas and concepts, and a series of examples and tools so that you can better appreciate the complexity of a range of types of ethics. The exercises in this chapter should also assist you in making good decisions when confronted with ethical professional issues, which occur much more often than you might think.

Sociologist and ethicist Raymond Baumhart is famous for asking the question, 'What is ethics?' in classes and seminars during the 1960s. He is often quoted as receiving a range of responses, such as:

- 'Ethics has to do with my feelings and emotions.'
- 'Ethics has to do with religion.'
- 'Ethics has to do with what the law says.'
- 'Ethics is about the standards of behaviour that our society accepts.'
- 'I am not quite sure I know what the word means.'

The first four statements are incorrect, though the last statement of ignorance is probably true for many people. Many of us equate ethics with our feelings; but while emotions are involved, being ethical does not equate with merely having emotions. Just because you might dislike the government does not make the way you vote an ethical act.

Many religions recommend high ethical standards. However, if ethics were only about religion, then ethics would apply only to religious people. But ethics applies to everyone, from atheists and agnostics, to Buddhists, Muslims, Hare Krishnas and Christians; both adults and children. Religion can set high moral standards and can provide strong incentives for ethical behaviour, but religion is not the total picture.

Ethics should not be equated with the law. While the law often includes ethical standards, laws, like religion, can differ from what is ethical. For example, older Australian laws around sperm donor rights, censorship, divorce and removing children from Indigenous families have drastically changed. Does this mean that these old laws were originally ethical, and that changing them simply makes them more ethical?

Finally, being ethical is not the same as following societal norms. Many societies have a multiplicity of societal values (Velasquez et al., 1987). Americans were split in 2020 in terms of the validity of the Joe Biden victory, and Australia has a small but vocal group of anti-vaxxers. Which part of society do you follow? Some societies are vastly different to ours. Does an Afghani citizen automatically follow the Taliban government and adopt its ethics?

Ethics, first and foremost, begin with your own sense of fairness, honesty and justice. Ethics are a part of your character and identity; therefore, you need to describe what your ethics are, and attempt to uphold them most of the time.

The Ethics Centre (n.d.) defines ethics as 'the process of questioning, discovering and defending our values, principles and purpose. It's about finding out who we are and staying true to that in the face of temptations, challenges and uncertainty.'

This chapter will begin by exploring the origins of ethics, Ancient Greek philosophy and the concept of virtue. It then explores research ethics, professional codes of conduct, ethical issues in society and suggests some guidelines for becoming more ethical in the workplace and our personal lives.

Reflection question: Ethics is an important part of all our lives

Ethics and ethical decision-making are all around us if we care to look for them. They are a part of all our relationships, our grocery shopping, the decision-making in our jobs, in the news, in sport, and in our entertainment.

The film *Locke*, starring Tom Hardy (see **Exhibit 7.1**), is an ethical drama about a man who has walked away from his job, wife, friends and possibly his life because of a single night dalliance with a woman at a conference. The film depicts Ivan Locke and the dozens of mobile phone conversations he has within the claustrophobic confines of his BMW. He is in the process of minimising his losses using his phone because he wants to be at the birth of the baby he and his lover conceived nine months earlier. The woman is lonely and scared of the impending birth and he does not want her to be alone for this event. His ethical decision is starkly heroic because he is in danger of losing his entire life. The film is also quite funny at times. The title 'Locke' is also a reference to John Locke, the philosopher who theorised about human rights, the role of the state and ethics in the 17th century.

| **Exhibit 7.1** | Tom Hardy in a scene from *Locke* |

Alamy Stock Photo/AJ Pics

Watch the film or view the trailers on YouTube and reflect on the decisions of Ivan Locke. Is he acting ethically or not?

The origins of ethics

Many ethicists believe that the capacity to help others is one of the most fundamental characteristics of ethical behaviour. Thus, altruism, or sharing resources (e.g., food or drink) and assisting others when they are injured or sick, would all be viewed as moral or ethical acts.

Can a plant or an animal act in an ethical fashion?

While the recent books, *The Hidden Life of Trees* (2016) by Peter Wohlleben and *Brilliant green: The surprising history and science of plant intelligence* (2015) by Stefano Mancuso and Alessandra Viola, suggest that plants possess rudimentary brains via their root systems, it was the legendary mycologist Paul Stamets who discovered that these basic brains are interconnected in the wild through underground networks of *mycelia* (fungal threads). Paul Stamets (2005) believes mycelial networks from fungi or mushrooms are responsible for creating the topsoil that allow all plants to grow. These underground networks of fungal fibres connect all the plants in a forest, so that nutrients and water can be transported to the plants that need them to survive and grow. The mycelial network can act as a filter for polluted water and also allows plants to communicate with each other to launch chemical defences against competing microbes or insects.

Some anthropologists and biologists believe that altruistic behaviour, and therefore ethics, are a typical and natural part of the lives of animals such as bees, bats, birds, monkeys, dogs and other mammals. A good example can be seen in jungles when sounds of distress are made when a bird or mammal is attacked, or even threatened. In a thick forest, a flock of birds may start to screech loudly and fly away when a dangerous predator is sensed hunting on the ground. Other nearby bird species may hear these sounds and react similarly. Monkeys upon hearing these birds will also become excited and give off warning sounds, alerting still other species of animals to be on the lookout. In this way, a whole community of animal species are communicating fear and danger and acting ethically in order to assist others to survive a possible attack. Nearby humans who know the meanings of such sounds may also be warned of impending danger and thus become a part of the 'system'.

Dogs are often called our best friends because they display human qualities like loyalty, companionship and friendship, and have been known to save human lives in emergency situations. For over 15 thousand years, dogs have been domesticated and selectively bred to engender human qualities that we all admire in our 'best friends'. According to Benz-Schwarzburg et al. (2020) dogs can read our faces, listen to our voices, understand human emotions and our gestures, can socialise with humans, and even grieve for fellow dogs and humans.

In the book, *Wild Justice*, by Marc Bekoff and Jessica Pierce (2009), it was found that animals, such as coyotes and wolves, foster and learn a whole range of ethical behaviours such as altruism, tolerance, forgiveness, mutual benefit and fairness when young animals play with each other. There were structured rules and rituals to the way that young animals engaged in mock fights and tussles. These protocols included: use of head bows and crouching to initiate the play session; self-handicapping if one animal had a marked advantage in terms of size; apologies in terms of in-play bowing; and strong punishment for those animals who broke the rules, such as banishment from the pack. Bekoff and Pierce hypothesise that these rules and behaviours were also precursors to our earliest ancestors' notions of ethics that allowed us to develop and flourish as a species.

> **Reflection question:** Perhaps the ancient mycelial network was the first instance of complex ethical behaviour. What do you think?

Ancient Greek philosophy, virtues and the middle ground

Whenever the word ethics is mentioned, we tend to think of black and white issues of right and wrong, of morality and immorality, and information or disinformation. We also think of universal objective standards that can never be argued or debated.

However, for the ancient Greeks, although such ethical standards were discussed, they did not form the basis of their doctrines. Their ethical thought was focused on the ideal types of human life rather than universal principles of conduct; that is, rather than asking 'What actions are universally morally right?' they asked, 'What is the best sort of life for human beings to live?'(Prior, 2016, p. 20). Greeks conceptualised ethical virtues to be situated on a continuum from 'worthless' to 'ideal', and these concepts were not only moral notions, but also included many other aspects of their lives. A good example is the ancient Greek emotion *acedia*, which objectively means 'listlessness and yawning hunger, resulting in back and forth pacing'. This feeling is something similar to what many of us experienced during COVID-19 lockdowns. Ancient Greek citizens would add extra meaning, namely the negative concepts of 'depression and numbness'. Thus, identifying 'acedia' compels a descriptive and negative value to the emotions we experienced. The extreme opposite of acedia would be 'vigour', or 'happiness'. The virtuous and ideal middle ground is, arguably, 'relaxed', or 'composed'. Greek philosophy would recommend this middle choice in order to live a better life.

The earliest literature of the ancient Greek culture were Homer's two great poems, *The Iliad* and *The Odyssey* (800 BCE), whose influence upon later Greek thought was monumental. The poems were used for hundreds of years as Bible-like, primary texts for the education of young people. They were also used for their theology, for ethics and for how Greek culture should be lived and understood. The heroes, Achilles and Odysseus respectively, were flawed but virtuous characters who served as long-lasting models of how to behave (and sometimes, not behave) in society. Achilles, even though half god, possessed wisdom but not the wisdom that could assure him of a successful life. He violated many of the norms of good conduct in Greece, and this eventually led to disaster, but he was still admired and revered by many people. Odysseus is a very different hero, who spent ten years coming home from war by overcoming many obstacles along the way. Odysseus is a typical virtuous hero who strives and succeeds in his quests but lacks the critical perspective of life that epitomised Achilles, while Achilles lacks the practical knowledge to meet his needs.

The ideas of the ancient Greek philosophers, especially Plato, Aristotle and Socrates, represent the beginnings of Western philosophy, including such topics as ethics, democracy, rhetoric and success in life, or happiness. Ancient Greek philosophy has had substantial influence upon contemporary Western notions of the individual, society, government and our responsibilities to each other as human beings. Plato's four virtues are shown in Exhibit 7.2 and these were considered the most important character traits for individuals to attain success in life.

Exhibit 7.2 Plato's four virtues

Courage (or bravery)

Wisdom (or knowledge)

Moderation (or self-restraint)

Justice (or fairness)

Aristotle's detailed explanations of similar virtuous concepts can be summarised in Exhibit 7.3, which comprises a range of degrees of important concepts and how too much or too little of the concept can compromise the virtue and turn it into a vice. The table shows that Greek ethics or virtues could be applied to many human emotions and behaviours, and unlike modern-day conceptualisations of ethics, could be given a rank on a continuum from negative to positive. According to this value system, the apparent altruistic act of giving money to less fortunate people can be a virtue (or ethical) but could also be judged as being excessive or negligible (or vices), depending on the motives behind such charity, the recipients of the money, and the repercussions of the gifts. Giving money, or sponsoring an activity in the case of contemporary organisations, is not a simple judgement of good ethical behaviour. In fact, a Greek philosopher would question many of our so-called ethical values as being possibly self-serving or distortions of sensible, moderate behaviours.

Exhibit 7.3 Detailed continuums of five ethical concepts according to Aristotle

Ethical concept	Deficit (Vice)	Middle ground (Virtue)	Excess (Vice)
Bravery	Cowardice	Courage	Recklessness
Anger	Indifference	Firmness	Rage
Humour	Boorishness	Quick-wittedness	Buffoonery
Justice	Fickleness	Fairness	Prejudice
Wisdom	Ignorance	Knowledge	Fanaticism

Another use of the middle ground is the concept of compromise, often associated with union disputes, buying a car or house, or settling arguments or divorces. In many cases conflicts can be resolved by accepting the middle ground for the two parties, or the two alternatives in question. Typically, the two parties compromise so that the stress of the decision-making is alleviated, and life can continue without the anguish of conflict, or because a decision must be made by a certain deadline. A compromise may be the only alternative when decision-making is deadlocked and both parties stand to lose something by the conflict going unresolved. Compromises, however, are not always beneficial in the long term, with one or both parties feeling forced to make a decision, and both parties harbouring anger or dissatisfaction of some sort.

Reflection question: Think of an argument you had with a friend, parent, sibling or partner. It could be about money, going to see a concert, going on holiday, etc. In a factual way, write down the two sides of the argument and create a compromise solution for you and the other person. Did you adopt that middle ground in real life? If not, would it have worked if it was enacted? Can you think of two possible middle ground solutions?

Ethical considerations of choosing a job

Exhibit 7.4 lists the top ten companies that business students aspire to work for from Universum's 2020 survey.

Exhibit 7.4	Top Ten of 50 Dream Jobs 2020	
	1 Google	6 Goldman Sachs
	2 Apple	7 Ernst & Young
	3 Microsoft	8 Price Waterhouse Coopers
	4 Amazon	9 J P Morgan
	5 Deloitte	10 L'Oreal Group

Source: Based on Universum. (2020). World's most attractive employers 2020.

Over the 12 years that Universum has conducted this survey, Google has always been the #1 choice. In 2020 students were asked ten questions that related to their rankings. High future earnings, a friendly work environment and secure employment were the top three reasons for making their decisions. But where does a graduate student find out information about these companies? Are these companies popular because of their reputations or because of their ethical profiles?

Note that Facebook is not in the top ten, but much further down the list at #43, perhaps because of the negative publicity that has surfaced over the years, including the Cambridge Analytica data scandal. HSBC is also lower down the list and has been accused of money laundering in the media. However, Amazon features at #4 despite being accused of harsh employment practices and self-serving workplace policies fairly recently.

Professional ethics is not a popular topic and is seldom discussed in the media. Professional ethical behaviour often relies on individual accountability and may go unnoticed at the organisational level.

Cheney, Lair, Ritz and Kendall's book, *Just a Job? Communication, Ethics, and Professional Life* (2010) suggests that individual company managers and employees can be conceptualised as a community and that this community also comprises a culture that can be identified, evaluated and judged by anyone who has heard of the organisation. Everyone 'knows' Google, Apple, Microsoft, and Amazon because we use their products on a daily basis. Thus, we all tend to develop attitudes and values towards these big name companies without even considering if our values are correct or based upon ethical standards. In other words, we all tend to award companies an ethical rank without thought or research, and this is a mistake.

Graduate students rarely understand the reality of working full-time for any company. It is not the same as having a part-time job. Most young people do not fully know themselves when they graduate – they might yearn to find their dream job without realising that the culture of the company may not suit them. Many students will find jobs and often discover that the company or industry is not suited to their aspirations and so will need to change jobs or even re-train.

If graduates originally had some insight into the ethics of the company or industry, they possibly may have avoided wasting precious time by realising that their earlier dream job was just a fantasy.

An alternative list of top ten companies is provided by LinkedIn, which has listed the Top 10 Australian companies to work for in 2022, as shown in Exhibit 7.5.

Exhibit 7.5	LinkedIn top 10 Australian companies to work for in 2022

1 Commonwealth Bank	6 Telstra
2 Woolworths Group	7 WPP
3 NAB	8 Salesforce
4 Westpac Group	9 DXC Technology
5 ANZ	10 Alphabet

Source: Based on LinkedIn New Australia (2022, April 5). Top companies 2022: The 25 best workplaces to grow your career in Australia.

All of these companies were selected by Simplilearn because they placed great emphasis on employee well-being, equal opportunities, staff recognition, and development. Some of these companies had won multiple industry awards. Salary earnings were also highly competitive with the previous big name companies which can afford to layoff new staff because they have such a long line of would-be employees.

 CASE STUDY 7.1   Accessibility and the internet

Ensuring that you meet accessibility guidelines is, first and foremost, an ethical responsibility to provide all people with access to information and not disadvantage anyone by requiring that users do not have a vision or hearing impairment. Website accessibility is now also a legal responsibility in many parts of the world.

Read the following article from *The Guardian* about accessibility issues on the official Sydney Games website during the year of the Sydney Olympics.

Website 'discriminated against blind'

The official Sydney Games website may be fined for violating anti-discrimination laws, after a blind fan was unable to retrieve Olympic information from the site.

Australia's human rights and equal opportunities commission said www.olympics.com had discriminated against Bruce Maguire, 42, who has been blind since birth, in failing to conform to internationally recognised standards which enable the blind to navigate the web.

In a stinging 23-page verdict, the discrimination inquiry commissioner William Carter found that the Sydney organising committee for the Olympic Games (SOCOG), which is responsible for the site, had broken the law. He warned that it faced a fine and a compensation award if it did not upgrade its site before the Games begin on September 15.

But SOCOG remains adamant that a revamp of the site to be completely user-friendly for the blind is not possible. Its lawyers pleaded 'unjustifiable hardship', claiming the changes would cost A$2m and would take one employee 365 days to implement, although another estimate put the figure at A$40 000. 'IBM's advice to us is that it's not feasible to meet Mr Maguire's demands', said a spokesperson.

...

Source: P. Barkham (2000, August 30).
Website 'discriminated against blind'.
Copyright Guardian News & Media Ltd 2023.

Discussion

Read up on website accessibility for people with visual impairment. What are the current definitions of accessibility, from the World Wide Web Consortium (https://w3.org)?

1 What are some other famous breaches of accessibility guidelines around the world?

2 Do you think it is possible to make all websites accessible?

3 Do you think that university websites are totally accessible now?

4 What happened in the Maguire versus SOCOG case, in the end?

5 Download a screen reader, then close your eyes and see if you can navigate a website just by using the screen reader.

After you have discussed this case study, refer to the 'Comments on case studies' section at the end of the text.

Research ethics

Ethics was not really an issue for researchers until the revelation of the horrific experiments conducted on concentration camp victims during the Second World War by the Nazis. The Nuremberg Code and the Universal Declaration of Human Rights (UDHR) were developed after the Nuremberg trials in 1946, and developed into the Helsinki Declaration in 1964, with later revisions. Ethics guidelines have been subsequently devised for many areas of research practice and professional responsibility in many countries around the world.

Research ethics
The specific ethical principles that must be considered by all researchers, particularly when they are dealing with human beings.

In Australia and most other Western democracies, research conducted by research staff or postgraduates at a university or health organisation that involves human subjects, embryos or animals, or that presents any sort of ethical risk to living beings, must first be vetted and approved by the relevant official **research ethics** committee. This includes research that employs questionnaires, observation, interviews, focus groups and social media. Conceptual, theoretical or text-based research is mainly exempt from ethics scrutiny because it poses no ethical risks to humans. Likewise, journalistic, marketing, public relations or media projects, which often contain interviews with witnesses or commentators, are not subject to these constraints because they are not viewed as research. Additionally, media research is exempt because the public communication they produce, such as newspaper stories, are in the public domain. However, research that utilises social media messages, on platforms such as Twitter, Facebook, Reddit and YouTube, is subject to human ethics approval as these messages are identifiable. These message may appear to be public communication, but the authors of messages and videos will not have consented to be included in a research project.

The governing body for research ethics in Australia is the National Health and Medical Research Council (NHMRC; see https://www.nhmrc.gov.au). Researchers must fill out a lengthy online form located at the NHMRC website to apply for ethics approval for research involving data that comes from human beings or their bodily tissue. The NHMRC guidelines stipulate that all human research must conform to the principles shown in Exhibit 7.6.

Reflection question: Do you think that these research ethics principles shown in Exhibit 7.6 are similar (or not) to many of those espoused as virtues by the ancient Greeks, in particular, Plato (with the exception of bravery).

However, it should be noted that research ethics guidelines do not apply to most areas of the private sector. Many businesses and professional organisations have instead created their own codes of conduct to guide ethical behaviour.

The Universal Declaration of Human Rights

The UDHR was the first major achievement of the United Nations (UN), an organisation that was formed immediately after Second World War. Prior to the creation of this document, ethics and human rights were the province of individual nations and states, or totally non-existent in many countries. Today, many Australians might find it hard to believe that 75 years ago, citizens of every

Exhibit 7.6 Guiding principles for human research

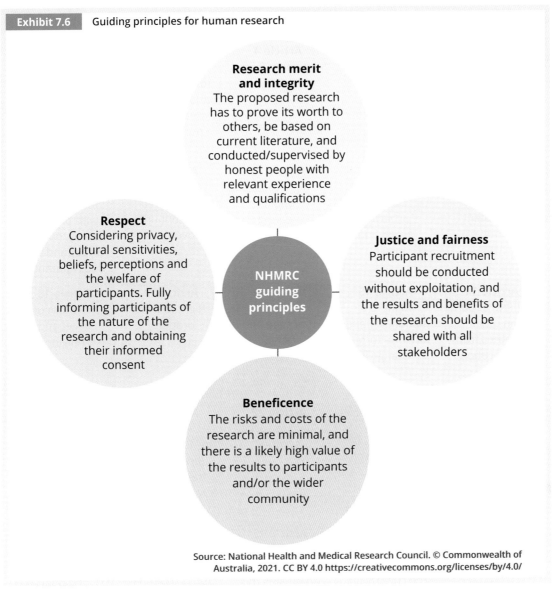

Source: National Health and Medical Research Council. © Commonwealth of Australia, 2021. CC BY 4.0 https://creativecommons.org/licenses/by/4.0/

country were treated inconsistently by their governments, whether they were democratically elected, kingdoms or communist. Ordinary citizens of any country could be detained, imprisoned, silenced or worse, for any reason, by their governments, and in many countries today, this is still a possibility. Before the UDHR people did not enjoy the freedoms that we all now take for granted in Australia and other countries. Unfortunately, these universal rights are not available to a large percentage of the world's population, still. The full version of the UDHR can be found at https://www.un.org/en/about-us/universal-declaration-of-human-rights, but Exhibit 7.7 provides a summary.

It should be noted that freedom of expression, or **freedom of speech**, appears in Article 19 in this list of human rights. The US government enshrines this right in its Constitution, but Australia does not. However, the meaning of freedom of speech is often wrongly interpreted as meaning that people can say whatever they what to say without censure. This is incorrect. Thus, a controversial Twitter post in Australia may not place you in prison, but you might lose your job or be sued if you defame another person. A journalist may be asked to retract a statement or an entire article, and in some cases be required to apologise to the general public for any offence that was caused. There are also some topics that are off limits – racism, ageism, sexism and slander will usually be censored.

The UN adopted the UDHR in 1948, but many member countries have breached these guidelines in the years since and may still be doing so. For example, Amnesty International (2022) claim that the

Freedom of speech
A principle in which people can express their ideas and opinions without being censored, retaliated against or legally sanctioned.

| Exhibit 7.7 | Summary of the Universal Declaration of Human Rights |

Article 1 Right to equality and dignity	**Article 2** Freedom from discrimination	**Article 3** Right to life, liberty, and personal security	**Article 4** Freedom from slavery	**Article 5** Freedom from torture, cruelty and degrading treatment or punishment	**Article 6** Right to recognition as a person before the law
Article 7 Right to equality before the law	**Article 8** Right to remedy by competent tribunal	**Article 9** Freedom from arbitrary arrest and exile	**Article 10** Right to fair public hearing	**Article 11** Right to be considered innocent until proven guilty	**Article 12** Freedom from interference with privacy, family, home, correspondence and reputation
Article 13 Right to free movement into and out of their country	**Article 14** Right to asylum in other countries from persecution	**Article 15** Right to a nationality and the freedom to change it	**Article 16** Right to marriage and family	**Article 17** Right to own property	**Article 18** Freedom of belief and religion
Article 19 Freedom of opinion and expression, and the receipt and retrieval of information	**Article 20** Right of peaceful assembly and association	**Article 21** Right to participate in government and free elections	**Article 22** Right to social security	**Article 23** Right to desirable work and to join trade unions	**Article 24** Right to rest and leisure
Article 25 Right to adequate living standard	**Article 26** Right to education	**Article 27** Right to participate in the cultural life of community	**Article 28** Right to a social order that articulates this document	**Article 29** Responsibility for community duties essential to free and full development	**Article 30** Freedom from state or personal interference in the above Rights.

Source: Adapted from United Nations (1948). Universal Declaration of Human Rights. https://www.un.org/en/about-us/universal-declaration-of-human-rights

US is violating human rights today in areas such as reproductive rights and excessive use of police force. They also claim that the Australian government continues to violate the rights of refugees and Aboriginal and Torres Strait Islander people.

Reflection question: Australia was a founding member of the UN in 1945 and is currently the twelfth largest contributor to its budget. Read through the articles that comprise the UDHR and determine which human rights the Australian Government may still be violating today, despite its UN involvement. Do you think the Australian Government's treatment of refugees or Aboriginal and Torres Strait Islander people is ethical?

Professional codes of conduct

Professional ethics are usually defined by codes of conduct that are specific to certain kinds of professions; for example, medical ethics, business ethics, computer ethics, legal ethics, and so on. In Australia and other democratic countries, almost every industry, professional association or sporting code has developed its own, customised code of conduct or practice that mandates certain behaviour for its practitioners and stakeholders. Schools, universities, companies and government departments are also free to create their own codes, which really amount to ethical guidelines that apply to students, employees or members of that profession or industry.

Australian Council of Professions

The Australian Council of Professions (ACoP) is the peak alliance of professional associations that represents about one million professionals, ranging from engineers and managers to librarians, architects, accountants and veterinarians. ACoP (2003) defines a **profession** as a group of people who adhere to ethical standards, are accepted by the public as having a specialised set of skills and knowledge, and are prepared to apply their skills in the interest of others. Thus, the fundamental basis of being a professional is complying with a specific code of ethics that governs the activities of each profession. Such professions are widespread in scope and cover most white collar and blue collar jobs. Sectors such as banking, insurance, retail, trades, education, manufacturing and service have continually developed such codes in line with the UDHR (UN, 1948).

Profession
A group of people who adhere to ethical standards, are accepted by the public as having a specialised set of skills and knowledge, and are prepared to apply their skills in the interest of others.

The ACoP's activities comprise typical advice regarding educational credentials and policy formation, but extend to a range of ethical issues in the professions. In September 2021, an ACoP round-table explored questions associated with artificial intelligence. Starting with past unethical disasters such as the Robodebt failure, Facebook scams and COVID-19 fake news in the media landscape, the ACoP asked how professionals should evaluate new advancing technologies that may save costs but create unexpected hardship for clients and citizens in a range of industries.

Professional codes of ethics are also developed for many highly visible communication and health professions. Examples include the medical profession (Australian Medical Association code of ethics), media industry (Media, Entertainment and Arts Alliance code of ethics), journalism (Australian Journalists Association code of ethics), advertising (Australian Association of National Advertisers code of ethics), and the public relations (Public Relations Institute of Australia code of ethics). Usually these codes of conduct are recommended, but seldom enforceable by law, except under special circumstances.

Australian Association of National Advertisers

The Australian Association of National Advertisers is the peak body for the advertising industry in Australia. Australia's current system of advertising self-regulation was established by the AANA in 1998. A sister organisation, Ad Standards (https:/adstandards.com.au) manages the complaints process of this system. A community panel of 21 members makes regular decisions about the hundreds of complaints that are submitted every year. In 2020, none of the top 10 complaints were upheld, while in the first 6 months of 2021, three advertisements relating to the top ten complaints were forced to be removed or be modified because they breached the standards around discrimination, vilification and health and safety issues. The advertisements were not deemed to be illegal but were subject to self-regulatory codes of ethics and behaviour (AdNews, 2021).

Nursing and Midwifery Board of Australia

The Nursing and Midwifery Board of Australia had a membership of over 400 000 members from across Australia in 2021. Members include practising nurses, registered nurses and midwives. The following summarises the Code of Professional Conduct for Nurses:

1 Nurses respect and adhere to their professional obligations under the National Law and abide by relevant laws.
2 Nurses provide safe, person-centred and evidence-based practice for the health and wellbeing of people and, in partnership with the person, promote shared decision-making and care delivery between the person, nominated partners, family, friends and health professionals.
3 Nurses engage with people as individuals in a culturally safe and respectful way, foster open and honest professional relationships, and adhere to their obligations about privacy and confidentiality.
4 Nurses embody integrity, honesty, respect and compassion.
5 Nurses commit to teaching, supervising and assessing students and other nurses, in order to develop the nursing workforce across all contexts of practice.
6 Nurses recognise the vital role of research to inform quality healthcare and policy development, conduct research ethically and support the decision-making of people who participate in research.
7 Nurses promote health and wellbeing for people and their families, colleagues, the broader community and themselves and in a way that addresses health inequality. (Nursing and Midwifery Board, 2018)

Source: Nursing and Midwifery Board (AHPRA). Code of Conduct for Nurses (updated June 2022).

CASE STUDY 7.2   An ethical dilemma in nursing

This case study involves discussion of suicide, which might be upsetting to some. Feel free to reach out to support services, or discuss with your convener alternatives to this content.

The patient Mr Lee is a 61 year old man with aggressive prostate cancer who is being cared for by the nursing team in the oncology department of a general hospital. Mr Lee was diagnosed with prostate cancer six years ago but refused medical and surgical treatment at the time. He chose to seek alternative treatment and did not follow up with the urologist over that period. Mr Lee has now presented with anaemia and pain in his hips. After several diagnostic tests over a period it was discovered that the cancer had metastasized to his bones, it had spread locally to his lymph nodes and the primary tumour was invading the bladder and partially obstructing the left kidney.

Mr Lee has had several admissions over a two month period. On the last admission Mr Lee was told that he may only have 4–6 weeks (previously it was 6–12 months) to live, after a cystoscopy showed further extensive growth of the tumour. It was determined that any further surgical/medical intervention would not be appropriate in this case and that a palliative care regimen was the next step. At this point the patient reported to the health care team that he had resigned himself to the fact that he was going to die. Mr Lee pulled one of the nurses aside and confided to the nurse that he planned to kill himself. He asked the nurse not to tell anyone else about this. It was his secret. The nurse said she understood.

Source: Adapted from L. Jie (2015). The patient suicide attempt: An ethical dilemma case study. *International Journal of Nursing Sciences*, 2(4), 408–413.

Discussion

What are the ethical dilemmas here? What are the various choices? What is the best ethical course of action, and why? Please use guidelines from the Code of Professional Conduct for Nurses.

After you have discussed this case study, refer to the 'Comments on case studies' section at the end of the text.

Australian Health Practitioner Regulation Agency

The Australian Health Practitioner Regulation Agency (AHPRA) is the amalgamated organisation representing a range of health practitioners including doctors, dentists, chiropractors, podiatrists, physiotherapists, nurses, midwives, optometrists, psychologists and others (over 800 000 members in 2021). Their website (https://ahpra.gov.au) contains a wealth of information and resources. AHPRA works in partnership with 15 national boards to ensure that all Australians have access to safe and regulated health professions registered under the National Registration and Accreditation Scheme. Public safety is their number one priority with every decision made guided by the Health Practitioner Regulation National Law that is mandated in each state and territory.

One of their resources surrounding social media is worth quoting here because it is applicable to so many other professions.

CASE STUDY 7.3 Social media and the workplace

When using social media, just as with all aspects of professional conduct and behaviour, you need to be aware of your professional obligations and other relevant legislation, such as privacy legislation.

Where relevant, National Boards may consider social media use in your private life (even where there is no identifiable link to you as a registered health practitioner) if it raises concerns about your fitness to hold registration.

While you may think you are engaging in social media in a private capacity because you do not state you are a registered practitioner, it is relatively easy and simple for anyone to check your status through the register, or make connections using available pieces of information.

Take care when using apps and sites to ensure you do not inadvertently post or communicate publicly, while thinking you are communicating privately. Make sure you know and understand the relevant security and privacy settings.

The following are examples of when activity on social media could trigger someone to make a notification about a registered practitioner. These examples do not imply or assume that these matters would reach the threshold for a Board to take regulatory action.

Maintain client confidentiality

Take care when sharing information, including comments or photos, that you do not inadvertently disclose patient information. Check what is in the background of a photo before sharing it and make sure that information you share does not unintentionally disclose personal information about individuals (because someone might use available information to work out who you are talking about). Although individual pieces of information may not breach confidentiality, the sum of published information online could be enough to identify a patient or someone close to them.

Example

A mother posts an update about her daughter's admission to hospital, following a car accident. The mother tags her friend, a health practitioner, who happened to be on the ward the night the daughter was admitted. The tag is complimentary about the care received at the hospital. The (nurse) responds publicly to the comment, thinking it was a private message and inadvertently provides information about the daughter's recovery and the status of the other passengers in the car. Parents of the other passengers make a formal complaint about the privacy breach.

Professionalism

The Codes of conduct emphasises that practitioners must always treat patients with respect and communicate effectively, courteously, professionally and respectfully with and about other health care professionals. This applies to any comments made in a social media context. Grievances with work colleagues or *clients* are best resolved privately.

Example

A (physiotherapist) resigns from her job, after feeling she was unfairly treated by her manager and generally dissatisfied with the workplace and level of support provided to staff. That evening, celebrating the resignation with a friend, also a past employee, they post comments about the workplace and the ill feelings they both harbour towards certain work colleagues and the manager. The posts are seen by other staff and a notification is made, claiming that the practitioner's conduct in posting the comments on social media were contrary to the Code of conduct, in that while exercising her right to free speech the statements were not in the ethical interests of the profession and the community.

Maintain professional boundaries

Language and tone used on social media that does not reflect a professional relationship, i.e. is overly personal and familiar or includes suggestive comments, could breach professional boundaries and the Code of conduct.

Example

A practitioner starts a conversation on a dating website and soon identifies the other person as his (patient). The practitioner mentions to (his patient) that it's a 'bit weird' having a conversation on the website but continues the discussion. Because the patient has a bad head cold, the practitioner offers treatment suggestions. The practitioner comments on his patient's physical attractiveness and offers a house-call late at night. The patient makes a formal complaint about the conversation.

Source: J. Purdue & A. Kerr (n.d.). Your responsibilities – Social media. NSW Nurses and Midwives Association. https://www.nswnma.asn.au/wp-content/uploads/2020/05/Social-Media_PPT.pdf

Australian Computer Society

The Australian Computer Society (ACS) is the largest professional body representing the Information technology sector in government, industry and education, comprising over 45 000 members across the country. The ACS Code of Professional Conduct (2014) is summarised in Exhibit 7.8.

The ACS also hosts hundreds of inexpensive events that attract some of the major sectors and stakeholders of the Australian and international information, computing and technology professions. Few other industries have quite so many professional activities available to its members (see https://www.acs.org.au/cpd-education/event-listing.html).

Exhibit 7.8	The Australian Computer Society Code of Professional Conduct

As an ACS member you must uphold and advance the honour, dignity and effectiveness of being a professional. This entails, in addition to being a good citizen and acting within the law, your conformance to the following ACS values.

1 The primacy of the public interest: You will place the interests of the public above those of personal, business or sectional interests.

2 The enhancement of quality of life: You will strive to enhance the quality of life of those affected by your work.

3 Honesty: You will be honest in your representation of skills, knowledge, services and products.

4 Competence: You will work competently and diligently for your stakeholders.

5 Professional development: You will enhance your own professional development, and that of your staff.

6 Professionalism: You will enhance the integrity of the ACS and the respect of its members for each other.

In a situation of conflict between the values, the primacy of the public interest takes precedence over the other values.

Source: Australian Computer Society (2014). Code of Professional Conduct.

CASE STUDY 7.4 Corruption and health services during the pandemic

The following fictional situation illustrates ethical and professional conduct issues.

During 2020 and 2021 most companies in the world lost money, with many having to cease trading via their normal mode. However, one health company made millions of dollars during this period due to the large state government contracts it was awarded, amounting to over $20 million. The contracts were not tendered in the usual fashion, with no competition for the supply contracts for PCR tests, and qualified nurses. It was later found that this company did not have a track record of successful supply of such tests or personnel. In fact, the company had become almost bankrupt over the last decade. The company was also shown to have made political donations in the past, and had existing business relationships with several senior federal government ministers, which raised questions about the reason they were awarded the lucrative contracts.

Discussion

What possible ethical (and legal) issues does this situation highlight? List and explain as many as possible.

After you have discussed this case study, refer to the 'Comments on case studies' section at the end of the text.

Ethical issues in mainstream and social media

Ethical professionals of all kinds are usually respected members of society whose codes of conduct ask them to place public needs ahead of their own personal interests. In order to fulfil this obligation, professional students should be able to understand that not all information in the public sphere is factual or honest. Governments, mainstream media, corporations and advocacy groups have their own agendas for presenting their perspectives. Recognising these sources and understanding their biases is a major ethical issue for all Australian professionals. This section will explore disinformation and fake news, bad science and science denial, and media ethics.

Fake news

Fraudulent information presented as news is not a new phenomenon and has had various names in the past, such as propaganda, disinformation, misinformation or just plain lying and deception. Propaganda in the media landscape has been with us since the beginnings of public communication in ancient times. With the rise of the internet and social media platforms, it has become prolific. Ubiquitous advertising and more recently COVID-19 conspiracy theories and Russia's fabricated explanations for their invasion of Ukraine in 2022, are examples. The term, 'fake news' as a concept became popularised in the lead-up to the 2016 US federal election with Donald Trump's kneejerk use of the label for any critical media views about his improprieties and personal scandals. The label has resonated worldwide with false or deceptive news being so commonplace in the 21st century, that many people cannot tell the difference between what news is fake, and what is not.

Before the Trump election in 2016, a Stanford study by Wineburg et al. (2016) asked American high school and university students to distinguish fake news from real news and were shocked at how gullible students appeared to be. For example, middle high schoolers were asked to evaluate over 7800 tweets, but could not distinguish advertising from credible posts, real accounts from fake accounts, and activism from objectivity. The assumption that millennials are social media fluent does not correspond with their inability to discriminate real from false information. For example, the majority of high schoolers accepted the veracity of photographs without any recourse to the verification process. A strange-looking photograph of a misshapen daisy was accepted as credible by over 80 per cent of viewers because it was called a 'Fukushima nuclear flower'. Results from university students were just as telling when they did not suspect any form of bias from what was clearly an activist group. University students appeared to believe suspect tweets, with less than half bothering to click on URL links within the Twitter posts. Most of the undergraduates could not distinguish mainstream news sources from marginal sources, with 30 per cent believing a fake Fox News account was more trustworthy than a real account.

The same news behaviour is probably true for many other Australians. According to the Digital News Report (Fisher et al., 2019), Australians, on average, have the least interest in accessing and reading news out of the 38 countries included. Australians use fewer news resources, are less interested in news and politics, and are less likely to check the accuracy of a story. These statistics changed in 2020–21 because of the widespread interest in the COVID-19 pandemic and appear to be returning to 2019 figures according to the 2022 Digital News Report (Park et al., 2022).

There is some debate as to the what the appropriate and most ethical response to fake news should be, once discovered. Facebook banned the Hillary Clinton propaganda that appeared on its platform in 2016, and Twitter removed Donald Trump's account because his tweets were deemed to be inciting violence in 2020. Some worldwide government responses to fake news have been creating new laws to prevent the spreading of false online information, blocking of certain social media platforms, increased monitoring and regulation of social media, media literacy campaigns, and promotion of factual content (Buckmaster & Wils, n.d.). In 2018, the European Union (EU) took a much softer approach by stating that any responses to counter the spread of disinformation must not violate the fundamental human right of freedom of expression. The EU recommended targeted, non-regulatory approaches to the problem. However, in March 2022 the EU banned the Russian-backed propaganda news outlets *Russia Today* and *Sputnik* from being broadcast in all 27 EU countries (Council of the European Union, 2022). This has not occurred in Australia so far.

In 2020, the Australian Government requested that a new code be developed to protect citizens from fake news, particularly surrounding the COVID-19 pandemic. The result was the *Australian Code of Practice on Disinformation and Misinformation* (Digital Industry Group Inc., 2021). The code is not legally enforceable and currently has eight major players, Twitter, Google, Facebook, Microsoft, Redbubble, TikTok, Adobe and Apple as voluntary signatories to the code. Signatories are encouraged to use the code to adopt best practices in terms of developing their own approaches to reducing the levels of detrimental disinformation and misinformation appearing on their platforms that possibly affect millions of people.

The eight corporate signatories to the code must fulfil the following key requirements:

- provide safeguards against harms that may be caused by disinformation and misinformation appearing on their platform
- empower consumers to make better informed choices of digital content
- publicise the measures they take to combat disinformation and misinformation. This means that annual reports must be submitted that show user complaints, and individual platform detection and consequences of fake news.

In recent times, the European Commission has suggested two main ways to assuage online fake news. First, it recommended that a colour-tagging system should be established for signalling the credibility of websites (blacklisted for blatant lying, greylisted for occasional false information, and whitelisted for trusted sites). Second, it has recommended that a regulatory body be created to enforce compliance with the EU code. These recommendations have yet to be added to the Australian code as of 2022. For the time being, all Australians are still vulnerable to fake news that seems to be escalating on social media and mainstream media channels. The only way to identify fake news is to verify facts, sources and photographs in a dubious story or suspect website. Additionally, a reverse image search on Google is easily implemented by right-clicking on an image, then select 'Search image with a Google lens' (see **Exhibit 7.9**).

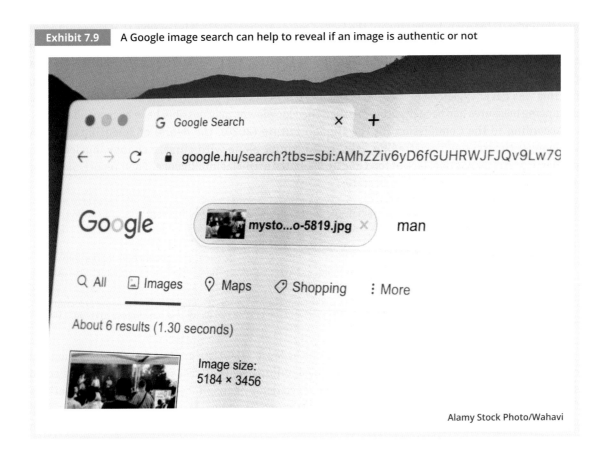

Exhibit 7.9 A Google image search can help to reveal if an image is authentic or not

Alamy Stock Photo/Wahavi

Bad science, pseudoscience and scientific denial

The concept of 'bad science' is not quite the same as fake news. Only a few governments have used bogus scientific results as a form of propaganda. Normally, bad science is the end result of faulty data collection, either intentional or by accident, and includes the use of unethical research methods with human participants. A handful of American psychological experiments in the first half of the 20th century and the horrific medical experiments by Nazi doctors during the Second World War represent some of the earliest examples of bad science, but not everyone understands the scientific method and how results can be found to be flawed or biased, and cause injury and damage.

In the early 1980s Soviet intelligence used a series of scientific papers and news articles to argue that the US government had created the HIV/AIDS virus (Jeppsson, 2017). *Operation Infektion* co-opted two retired Russian biophysicists to write scientific reports that used factual evidence about the rampant disease and attribute its origin to medical experiments on prisoners at Fort Detrick, Maryland. For two years after the initial campaign, the media in over 80 countries had published news stories leading to recurring suspicion that the US government had produced the disease. The campaign effectively persuaded the general public, but it did not convince the scientific community, even within the Soviet bloc. To some extent, the media was culpable for not fact checking or verifying the scientific basis of the fake research. However, the attribution of American involvement would have been impossible to verify, thus the world's media were distributing the disinformation at the time, almost like spreading gossip.

The early COVID-19 advice included a series of unfortunate blunders. Masks were not originally recommended at the beginning of the pandemic. It took six months for the WHO to conclude that COVID-19 was an airborne disease, and another six months for the realisation that the virus was rarely spread by surface infection. Ignorance about the disease led to medical reporting in early 2020 being driven by panic about the dramatically rising numbers of cases in Australia and other countries. The fear was that hospitals and medical services would be exhausted, because of limited intensive care beds. At this point, sick patients would not be able to be treated in hospital and thus die. The overlooked caveat was that case numbers were inextricably linked to the availability of PCR tests. There was a severe lack of the PCR tests in 2020, meaning relatively few people could be tested. The real number of cases was most probably grossly understated each day because of the lack of tests (Archee, 2021). It is possible that these untested infected people simply got better by themselves, but passed the infection on to unsuspecting others. In this scenario, the medical community should have understood that the number of hospitalisations as a percentage of total infections was much lower than the number being reported in mainstream media, but this was never explained to the general public. If strict highly protective mask wearing and social distancing measures had been instituted earlier, then lockdowns may possibly have been avoided.

According to the Commission for the Human Future (2020), the denial of scientific research is amongst the top ten 'catastrophic risks' to humanity along with climate change, nuclear war, pandemics, overpopulation, lack of food and unregulated artificial intelligence. Their report, *Surviving and Thriving in the 21st Century* (2020) states:

> Part of the problem is that there is significant (often deliberate and well-funded) misinformation that contradicts the scientific consensus on catastrophic risk. Delusions, carefully implanted, are difficult to correct.
>
> At the heart of the contemporary global malaise is the erosion of trust, the absence of leadership and the inability of those who govern to create a political narrative that reflects the values on which inclusive, compassionate and resilient societies depend. (pp. 11–12)
>
> Source: Commission for the Human Future. (2020). *Surviving and thriving in the 21st century: A discussion and call to action on global and catastrophic risks*, pp. 11–12.

Science is not always perfect in its conclusions because scientists are human; they occasionally make mistakes, are arrogant, bombastic and biased. But to negate all research endeavour or selected science enquiry as being wrong, or too extreme, or to deploy conspiracy theories to distract others from accepting genuine research findings is simply immoral. Politicians, media commentators, and journalists never use their own scientific data as evidence, instead they manufacture their own narratives about reality, typically ignoring prominent scientists and cumulative decades of research.

Identifying faulty research is a challenging task for ordinary people who may be swayed by statistics and esoteric jargon. Incredible, amazing or 'too good to be true' results are probably best looked at with a critical eye and investigated further as being possible 'pseudoscience'. Karl Popper (1934) popularised this term, which refers to practices or beliefs that that are presented as scientific but lack the rigorous testing, empirical evidence, and methods that are necessary for genuine scientific inquiry. Pseudoscientific ideas often rely on anecdotes, testimonials, or untested hypotheses, and are promoted by people with a vested interest in advocating ideas such as astrology, creationism, some forms of alternative medicine and unsubstantiated claims and theories in any discipline or field.

Media ethics

Mainstream media (which is also embedded in social media) are major players in the ethical infrastructure of all democratic countries. A free press structures public debate, and holds people, governments and institutions up to scrutiny. Newspapers, magazines, online news sites and their journalists need to have the highest ethical standards given the potential size of their audiences and influence of their rhetorical power. Unfortunately, the canon of 'Do no harm' is not observed when parts of the media report on highly controversial topics. Unproven accusations relating to a range of media celebrities, politicians, sports persons and others amount to unsubstantiated hearsay and often result in trial by media, and ruined reputations, despite what the truth really is.

Reflection question: What do you think of the idea that the only way that anyone knows about the world, apart from direct experience, is through mainstream and social media?

The growth of new online media outlets, the search for new audiences and increasing competition across the media landscape has led to a situation where trust in the media is declining in Australia and other parts of the world (Edelman, 2022). To garner audience attention, some media outlets may increasingly offer up provocative stories that may not be able to pass the verification standards of ethical journalism. This ends up eroding trust even further. When a media piece meets ethical standards, you will answer in the affirmative to the questions shown in Exhibit 7.10.

Exhibit 7.10 Discerning if a media piece meets ethical standards

Is the story in the public interest, or just selling stories?

Is the story fair and accurate with information properly contextualised?

Has enough research been expended, including enough people's viewpoints?

Is the story a realistic account of the original report in the case of stories about research findings?

Has the story been verified as being true?

Have news sources been contacted and reported in an honest fashion?

Ethics and moral injury

A **moral injury** is a form of trauma that occurs when someone violates their own ethical code of behaviour (see Williamson et al., 2021). The term was first identified as belonging to returned military personnel who had also been diagnosed with post-traumatic stress disorder. While burnout mainly affects a person's efficacy in a workplace, a moral injury impacts a person's sense of trust in others, and lowers a person's self-esteem. In MRI studies, social pain is processed in the same regions of our brains as physical pain (Eisenberger, 2012). The pain of a moral injury can be just as bad as serious physical pain. Moral injuries are, in fact, ethical injuries and can be characterised by the following symptoms:

- profound feelings of guilt, shame, anxiety or depression
- changes in cognitions and beliefs (e.g., 'I am a failure', 'colleagues do not care about me')
- maladaptive coping responses (e.g., alcohol and substance misuse, social withdrawal, self-destructive acts, sleep problems; Williamson et al., 2021).

Moral injury is often confused with job burnout because the symptoms are somewhat similar; however they are quite different. Burnout occurs when someone is so stressed or bored in their job that they become emotionally exhausted and may experience symptoms such as headaches, skin rashes, depression and anxiety. The psychological effects can include intense feelings of shame, or guilt or disgust.

In recent times, moral injury research has been extended to many other contexts, including health care, education (Sugrue, 2020), social work (Reamer, 2021), counselling and many other workplaces that are high pressure and often poorly funded. Moral injury can be experienced as a kind of panic response to observing or contributing to high-stakes workplace problems. These situations have the potential to cause harm to others in a physical, psychological, or financial manner. A good example is a nurse who has been asked to work long hours in an emergency ward during a wave of COVID-19. The nurse has to triage infected patients, admitting only the worst cases. Those who are not severe enough and accident victims may have to wait longer in the waiting room and might be catching COVID-19 due to the delay. Some may become severely ill, or even die as a result of the delay in attending to them. If the nurse remains in this situation for too long s/he may experience moral injury, and possible psychological harm.

Moral injury
Occurs when someone violates their own ethics, which impacts a person's sense of trust in others, and lowers a person's self-esteem.

Becoming ethical

Unfortunately, there is no single recipe for becoming an ethical professional who can make good decisions in all problematic situations. However, there exists a range of ethical frameworks, or formulas, in the literature, and the process of arriving at an ethical decision varies depending upon the profession, the problem and the individuals involved. There is probably no universal process to solve an ethical problem for all stakeholders, but there are certainly bad or unethical decisions that should be avoided, if possible.

Useful ethics information is available from the Ethics Centre (https://ethics.org.au), a not-for-profit organisation where you can ask difficult ethical questions, and obtain meaningful advice and guidance.

Making ethical decisions

We all make ethical decisions in our jobs, but we are seldom assured that our decisions are always right. A few basic guidelines for making good ethical decisions in our daily lives are shown in **Exhibit 7.11**.

Exhibit 7.11	Guidelines for making good ethical decisions
Locate written policies that might help	In professional settings, locate any written policies from your professional association, other associations or your own company that can assist with discovering an ideal course of action to be decided
Be wary of social media	Social media has become a major stumbling block for ethical violations. If you are using any form of social media, do not mention anybody by name, or by company. Do not believe that you are anonymous – it is not too difficult for another user to guess who you are. It is very easy to commit ethical violations around people or their workplaces on social media
Make sure you understand the problem	The solution to an ethical problem is only as good as your ability to genuinely understand the nature of the problem. One example involved employee anxiety over rush hour lifts impeding people getting to work on time every morning. Solutions could include bigger lifts, faster lifts, staggering employee start times, etc. A real life solution was to broadcast soothing music into the vestibule to allay employee impatience each morning and allow time for socialisation
Create a range of possible solutions	When attempting to create a range of possible solutions to a problem, choose to create more than just two, otherwise you limit your choices and polarise discussion. Greek philosophy would recommend three or more solutions thus allowing exploration of the middle ground
Think about how your solution may benefit others	An almost universal ethical canon is that the maximum number of people should benefit from an ethical decision. Thus, your decision should examine how you can deliver the maximum good, both in the immediate present and in the future
Do no harm	Another ethical canon is the phrase: 'Do no harm'. In other words, the solution should not be worse than the status quo and no stakeholders should be disadvantaged

 CASE STUDY 7.5   Ethics applied to the workplace

Good, ethical behaviour in terms of research is no different to ordinary good, ethical behaviour. We all have a set of rules we must follow when we study at an institution or work for a company. Sometimes these rules are at odds with the moral ethics involved in being a good human being. But issues such as protecting the young and sick, saving lives, not hurting people, looking after the best interests of others, being fair – these are all highly desirable human qualities that are not rules as such, more moral codes that people try to live by.

The following scenarios illustrate ethical problems in a variety of contexts:

1   Dr Smith teaches a first-year writing course at a university. One overseas student, Iriat , struggles with English. Iriat hands in a particular essay that is quite good and ordinarily would receive a Credit,

but it has been submitted one day late – the student is penalised one mark and the essay receives a Pass. Iriat ultimately receives a Pass grade for the unit. The following term, another young woman, Sara, asks to speak with Dr Smith. She tells him that her friend Iriat had borrowed a research paper she had written for another class – 'to see an example of a real essay in English' – and had then just retyped the paper, changing the wording here and there, and handed it in to Dr Smith as her own. Sara then produces her own paper as proof.

2   Michelle is the environmental compliance manager for a small plastics manufacturing company. She is currently faced with the decision of whether or not to spend money on new technology that will reduce the level of a particular chemical in the waste that flows from her factory into a nearby lake. The factory's emission levels are within legal limits. However, if emissions stay at these levels, the fish in the lakes and rivers in the area might soon have to be declared unsafe for human consumption. On the other hand, the company's environmental compliance budget is tight. Installing the new technology would make Michelle's department exceed its budget and could jeopardise the company's ability to show a profit this year.

3   Pablo is the experienced pilot of a medium-sized aeroplane flying between Hong Kong and Madrid. The plane is full of passengers and the weather is awful. A flight attendant informs Pablo that a passenger, a middle-aged man, has suffered a heart attack and that although a doctor on board is attending to him, he will most likely die unless he is taken immediately to a hospital. Pablo radios for an emergency landing in the closest city but is denied because of the terrible weather conditions – gusting winds and heavy rain. He has two choices: travel to Madrid, in which case the passenger will probably die, or perform an emergency landing against international air-traffic control orders, in bad weather and endanger his crew and his passengers.

4   Sebastian is a lawyer working for a large drug company that provides medicine for people in war-torn areas. During his work he comes across a contract involving an agent who seems to be accepting large sums of money to distribute the medicine in one of these countries. He speaks to the executive who contracted this agent, and asks whether this is bribe money. The executive says that yes, it is. He explains that trucks are loaded with medicine in the back and with cash in the glovebox. The cash is a bribe for local militia who set up roadblocks that prevent supplies from getting into the war-torn areas. Sebastian thinks that this deal is highly suspect.

5   In 2016, an American woman was detained for live-streaming personal video footage of police shooting her boyfriend multiple times at a routine traffic traffic stop. The woman bypassed all the gatekeepers of publication and allowed thousands of users to view police violence and brutality. Critics expressed disapproval of such live coverage because viewers cannot be warned about the live depiction of such violence. Advocates have celebrated this new technology which gives power to the victims of systemic violence.

6   Luisa, a registered nurse, protests against her duty to perform kidney dialysis upon a terminally ill patient. She notifies her matron that she 'has moral, medical and ethical objections' against doing so. On two previous occasions, Luisa performed this procedure on a patient and had to interrupt it because the patient suffered cardiac arrest and severe haemorrhaging, causing a great deal of pain and suffering. Convinced that the procedure is more harmful than beneficial to the patient, Luisa asks to be reassigned. The matron reports Luisa to the hospital superintendent and her employment is terminated.

Discussion

In discussion groups, take a scenario and write down (1) the value of the ethical alternatives under consideration, and (2) the best ethical outcomes.

After you have discussed this case study, refer to the 'Comments on case studies' section at the end of the text.

Summary

The Ethics Centre defines ethics as 'the process of questioning, discovering and defending our values, principles and purpose'. Ethics is a universal concept that applies to all individuals living in Western societies and working in all kinds of organisations and institutions. However, ethics is arguably overlooked in training, education and development courses in favour of skills development and career qualifications. While the Ancient Greeks also focused on leading ideal human lives, research ethics and professional codes of conduct are rather different applications of ethical guidelines. Research ethics refer to the specific ethical principles that must be approved for all academic researchers to perform research with humans. Professional codes of conduct are developed by a range of Australian professions with most industries, companies, professions and sports establishing their own codes, some with regulatory powers. The media has its own code of conduct, but individual news outlets often violate these codes without legal redress. Issues such as fake news, bad science and scientific denial are constant problems in the media landscape. We introduce an overlooked form of personal ethics by discussing moral injuries, which are the psychological effects of betraying one's own values, principles or ethical beliefs. Lastly, we attempt to solve possible ethical dilemmas by following six basic rules for making ethical decisions.

STUDY TOOLS

DISCUSSION QUESTIONS AND GROUP ACTIVITIES

1   Plagiarising oneself or using the same material for more than one essay, report, article or assignment is a problem in academia:

    a   What are some 'ethical' recommendations about recycling essays, papers, paragraphs, sentences and ideas that come from previous works?

    b   Who is making these recommendations?

    c   Are these 'rules' fair? Do they coincide with laws regarding copyright, fair use and plagiarism?

    d   How does duplication detection software fit into these recommendations and laws?

2   Create a list of five Australian companies, organisations or institutions that you might like to work for. Do some research to find both positive and negative facts and opinions of each company, institution or organisation. Using this information, consider how these organisations align with your own values and ethics.

3   What are some of the targets of fungal defences? What chemicals do they produce? Does this strengthen the ethical nature of plants?

4   What are the five best breeds of dog for intelligence, loyalty, protection and ethical behaviour? What are the worst breeds? Is there convincing evidence for the ethical nature of animals?

5   A software company is coding a more efficient accounting system that will be used by the government. A manager, who is asked to design the accounting system, assigns different parts of the system to staff. One person is responsible for developing the reports, another is responsible for the internal processing and a third for the user interface. The manager is shown the system and agrees that it meets the requirements. The system is installed, but the users finds the interface so difficult that the system is rejected (Australian Computer Society, 2014). Using the Australian Computer Society Code of Professional Conduct, can you identify some of the problems here, and who might be to blame?

6   Reliable education about sex, alcohol and drugs is arguably a human right, but education on these topics varies considerably depending where you live in the world. What are some of the most successful health education campaigns around the world in terms of alcohol and other drugs, and sex? Choose one and explain why it was so successful.

7   Imagine you are a nurse or family carer, and your job requires you to follow the Nursing and Midwifery Board of Australia Code of Conduct as summarised in the chapter. What is the recommended conduct for the following case study:

    Louise is a midwife working in the community and was making her final visit to a woman who had recently given birth to her second child. Louise delivered the woman's first child five years earlier and had established a good professional relationship with the woman and her family. During the visit, the woman indicated that she would like to continue seeing Louise on an ongoing basis to check in on the baby and the family, or just to have a coffee (Nursing and Midwifery Board of Australia, n.d.).

8   Professor Ruth Morgan has an informative YouTube video, *The dangers of misinterpreted forensic evidence*, located at: https://www.youtube.com/watch?v=xclg8ikPAvI.

    Watch the video and summarise the main points. Have you ever been accused of something you were innocent of doing?

WEBSITES

Butcher, M. (2021). Could supernova be an 'ethical alternative' to the social media giants? https://techcrunch.com/2021/12/20/could-supernova-be-an-ethical-alternative-to-the-social-media-giants

Carucci, R., & Ludmila, N. (2022). Praslova what to do if your job compromises your morals https://hbr.org/2022/04/what-to-do-if-your-job-compromises-your-morals

Fake News Creator https://www.worldgreynews.com/add-news

Governance Institute of Australia, Ethics Index 2022 https://www.governanceinstitute.com.au/advocacy/ethics-index

Khalife, R. How to Spot Fake News https://beconnected.esafety.gov.au/articles-and-tips/how-to-spot-fake-news

Stanford Encyclopedia of Philosophy Ancient Ethical Theory https://plato.stanford.edu/entries/ethics-ancient/

The Ethics Centre https://ethics.org.au

Varkey B. (2021). Principles of clinical ethics and their application to practice https://karger.com/mpp/article/30/1/17/204816/Principles-of-Clinical-Ethics-and-Their

Williams, E. (2017), Australian Business Ethics https://bizfluent.com/info-7829297-australian-business-ethics.html

REFERENCES

AdNews. (2021, December 16). Most complained about ads of 2021 in Australia. https://www.adnews.com.au/news/most-complained-about-ads-of-2021-in-australia

Amnesty International. (2022). *Amnesty International Report 021/22: The state of the world's human rights*. https://www.amnesty.org/en/documents/pol10/4870/2022/en/

Archee, R, (2021). Communication, mainstream media, and Twitter: A summative content analysis of the concepts surrounding the COVID-19 pandemic during 2020. *Global Media Journal: Australian Edition, 15*(1).

Australian Council of Professions. (2003). *What is a profession?* https://www.professions.org.au/what-is-a-professional/#:~:text=A%20Profession%20is%20a%20disciplined,and%20who%20are%20prepared%20to

Australian Computer Society. (2014, May 31). ACS code of professional conduct case studies. https://www.acs.org.au/content/dam/acs/elected-members/pab/EthicsCommittee/ACS%20Code%20of%20Professional%20Conduct%20Case%20Studies.pdf

Barkham, P. (2000, August 30). Website 'discriminated against blind'. *The Guardian.* https://www.theguardian.com/technology/2000/aug/30/internetnews.sydney

Bekoff, M., & Pierce, J. (2009). *Wild Justice.* University of Chicago Press.

Benz-Schwarzburg, J., Monsó, S., & Huber, L. (2020). How dogs perceive humans and how humans should treat their pet dogs: Linking cognition with ethics. *Frontiers in psychology, 11*, 584037. https://doi.org/10.3389/fpsyg.2020.584037 https://www.frontiersin.org/article/10.3389/fpsyg.2020.584037

Buckmaster, L., & Wils, T. (n.d.). *Responding to fake news.* Australian Parliament. https://www.aph.gov.au/About_Parliament/Parliamentary_Departments/Parliamentary_Library/pubs/BriefingBook46p/FakeNews

Commission for the Human Future. (2020). *Surviving and thriving in the 21st century: A discussion and call to action on global and catastrophic risks.* https://www.humansforsurvival.org/sites/default/files/CHF_Roundtable_Report_March_2020.pdf

Council of the European Union. (2022, March 2). EU imposes sanctions on state-owned outlets RT/Russia Today and Sputnik's broadcasting in the EU. https://www.consilium.europa.eu/en/press/press-releases/2022/03/02/eu-imposes-sanctions-on-state-owned-outlets-rt-russia-today-and-sputnik-s-broadcasting-in-the-eu

Digital Industry Group Inc. (2021, February 22). Australian Code of Practice on Disinformation and Misinformation. https://digi.org.au/wp-content/uploads/2021/02/Australian-Code-of-Practice-on-Disinformation-and-Misinformation-FINAL-PDF-Feb-22-2021.pdf

Edelman. (2022, February 16). Trust barometer 2022 Australia. https://www.edelman.com.au/trust-barometer-2022-australia

Eisenberger, N. I. (2012). The pain of social disconnection: Examining the shared neural underpinnings of physical and social pain. *Nature Reviews Neuroscience, 13*(6), 421–434.

Ethics Centre. (n.d.). *What is ethics?* https://ethics.org.au/about/what-is-ethics

Fisher, C., Park, S., Lee, J. Y, Fuller, G., & Sang, Y. (2019). *Digital news report: Australia 2019.* News and Media Research Centre.

Jeppsson, A. (2017). How East Germany fabricated the myth of HIV being man-made. *Journal of the International Association of Providers of AIDS Care (JIAPAC), 16*(6), 519–522. https://doi.org/10.1177/2325957417724203

Jie, L. (2015). The patient suicide attempt: An ethical dilemma case study. *International Journal of Nursing Sciences, 2*(4), 408-413. https://doi.org/10.1016/j.ijnss.2015.01.013

LinkedIn New Australia. (2022, April 5). Top companies 2022: The 25 best workplaces to grow your career in Australia.

Mancuso, S., & Viola, A. (2015). *Brilliant green: The surprising history and science of plant intelligence.* Island Press

Nursing and Midwifery Board. (2018). *Professional standards.* https://www.nursingmidwiferyboard.gov.au/Codes-Guidelines-Statements/Professional-standards.aspx

Nursing and Midwifery Board of Australia. (n.d.). *Case Studies: Code of conduct for nurses and Code of conduct for midwives*. https://www. nswnma.asn.au/wp-content/uploads/2020/05/NMBA_Case-studies_ Codes-of-conduct.pdf

Park, S., McGuinness, K., Fisher, C., Lee, J. Y., McCallum, K., & Nolan, D. (2022). *Digital news report: Australia 2022.* News and Media Research Centre. https://doi.org/10.25916/1xkk-jb37

Popper, K. (1934). *Logik der Forschung. Zur Erkenntnistheorie der Modernen Naturwissenschaft*. Julius Springer, Hutchison & Co. Wien.

Prior, W. J. (2016). *Virtue and knowledge*. Apple Books.

Purdue, J., & Kerr, A. (n.d.). Your responsibilities – Social media. NSW Nurses and Midwives Association. https://www.nswnma. asn.au/ wp-content/uploads/2020/05/Social-Media_PPT.pdf

Reamer, F. (2021). Moral Injury in social work: Responses, prevention, and advocacy. Families in *Society: The Journal of Contemporary Social Services, 103*(3), 257–268. https://doi. org/10.1177/10443894211051020

Stamets, P. (2005). *Mycelium Running: How Mushrooms Can Help Save the World*. Random House.

Sugrue, E .P. (2020). Moral injury among professionals in K–12 education. *American Educational Research Journal, 57*(1), 43–68. https://doi.org/10.3102/0002831219848690

United Nations. (1948). *Universal Declaration of Human Rights*. https:// www.un.org/en/about-us/universal-declaration-of-human-rights

Universum. (2020). World's most attractive employers 2020.

Velasquez, M., Andre, C., Shanks, T., & Meyer, M. J. (1987). What is Ethics? *Issues in Ethics, 1*(1). https://www.scu.edu/mcae/publications/iie/

Williamson, V., Murphy, D., Phelps, A., Forbes, D., & Greenberg, N. (2021). Moral injury: The effect on mental health and implications for treatment. *The Lancet Psychiatry, 8*(6), 453–455. https://doi. org/10.1016/S2215-0366(21)00113-9

Wineburg, S. McGrew, S., Breakstone, & Ortega, T. (2016). Evaluating information: The cornerstone of civic online reasoning. *Stanford Digital Repository*. http://purl.stanford.edu/fv751yt5934

Wohlleben, P. (2016).*The Hidden Life of Trees.* Black Inc books.

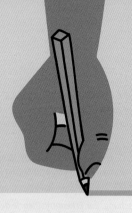

PART 2

Communication in organisations

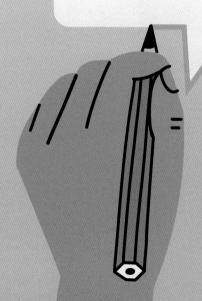

Shutterstock.com/YummyBuum

Concepts and applications in interpersonal communication

'Soft skills': the intangible qualities companies crave

In order to do your job effectively, you need hard skills: the technical know-how and subject-specific knowledge to fulfil your responsibilities. But in a forever changed world of work, lesser touted 'soft skills' may be just as important – if not even more crucial.

These skills are more nuanced, even low-profile: think personal characteristics and behaviours that make a strong leader or a good team member. Especially amid the normalisation of remote work, where collaboration and the ways to innovate have changed, companies are beginning to catch on to the importance of these intangibles when building out diverse, successful teams.

...

[A] major soft-skill area is communication. Effectively communicating with colleagues, clients and management requires dexterity and emotional intelligence. Empathy, teamwork and compassion are also skills that fall under that same umbrella ... Many behaviours – critical thinking, active listening, imaginative problem-solving, to name a few – are also soft skills.

As many of the highly technical parts of work are becoming increasingly automated, or replaced by technological tools, companies are instead looking for workers who can problem-solve, juggle larger responsibilities and work well with others. The ongoing labour shortage also has organisations focused on longevity: employees who have the interpersonal skills and emotional intelligence to grow into leadership positions offer a lot more value.

...

▶

> Additionally, soft skills have become even more important in the post-pandemic, largely remote work landscape. For instance: communication can be much more nuanced and complex when workers don't see colleagues face-to-face …
>
> Source: Adapted from K. Morgan (2022, July 28). 'Soft skills': The intangible qualities companies crave. *BBC*.

Introduction

> Although interpersonal communication is humanity's greatest accomplishment, the average person does not communicate well. One of the ironies of modern civilisation is that, though mechanical means of communication have been developed beyond the wildest flight of the imagination, people often find it difficult to communicate face-to-face. In this age of technological marvels, we can bounce messages off the moon and land space probes on Mars, but we find it difficult to relate to those we love.
>
> **Source: Bolton (2003)**

As humans, we cannot avoid communicating. Earlier chapters noted that not all communication is deliberate or even conscious – our personal life experiences, choice of particular words, non-verbal reactions and cultural biases shape our communication choices. Equally, they shape how we interpret or respond to others. Communication, therefore, can be defined as a process involving both the deliberate and accidental transfer of meaning.

In recent years, the importance of interpersonal communication has been overshadowed by our obsession with new media that have enabled different ways of communicating. However, since the beginning of the COVID-19 pandemic, we are increasingly working remotely from our colleagues, and the 'soft skills' of interpersonal communication are being recognised as highly valuable assets, as the opening chapter article and quote illustrate.

This chapter goes back to basics to reiterate and expand on the key concepts in communication outlined in earlier chapters. The aim is to assist you to be a flexible communicator, whether you are communicating face-to-face, in teams or via a computer. The material will explain how effective interpersonal skills help you to give and receive feedback, handle conflicts and complaints, and express feelings honestly and appropriately. In particular, it will discuss competent communication in a variety of settings, using effective self-disclosure, conversation, listening and assertive expression of your views. Finally, it will address more closely some of the issues related to the relationship between interpersonal effectiveness and the ever-increasing use of new technologies for interpersonal communication.

The importance of intrapersonal and interpersonal communication skills

Well-developed intrapersonal and interpersonal communication skills have been shown to have the following benefits in both personal and professional settings:

- They extend your ability to solve problems and to accept and implement change in modern organisational settings, where competition is often fierce, and the environment is complex.
- They allow you to *contribute* to problem-solving teams, to convince others of new initiatives and to document changes so that appropriate responses can be implemented and monitored.
- They will help you give and receive feedback; handle conflicts or complaints; manage stress; identify the real needs of peers, clients and workmates; and present yourself as a credible expert.
- Most importantly, they enable you to express your thoughts and feelings appropriately and honestly, and give others a chance to do the same.

While this chapter predominantly deals with communication between individuals, it will begin by briefly overviewing the level of communication that exists beneath this; that is, the notion of 'intrapersonal' communication, or 'self-talk'.

Intrapersonal communication or self-talk

Intrapersonal communication (from the Latin *intra*, 'on the inside, within') refers to the communication that you have with yourself. It is your internal communication – the internal voice we all have – which may include self-talk, acts of imagination and visualisation, and even recall and memory (McLean, 2012). It is the sound of our thinking, our cognitive processing, and has been shown to influence how we communicate with other people, as well as how we perform in many situations. The study of self-talk is central to speech therapy, sports psychology and self-motivation, and it underpins cognitive behavioural therapy, a type of psychological therapy that aims to help people identify and challenge unhelpful forms of self-talk that may be impacting on their relationships and lives.

According to Brinthaupt et al. (2009), there are four types of conversations that we have with ourselves, which are shown in Exhibit 8.1. Additionally, our awareness of our intrapersonal communication can be heightened if we monitor our internal reactions to the following:

- *Making plans:* 'How can I convince my boss to support my ideas?'
- *Stressful events:* 'How will I cope with speaking to such a large audience?'
- *Surprises:* 'I didn't expect to be criticised for my initiative.'
- *Non-verbal signals:* 'The customer seemed to hang up rather abruptly.'
- *Emotional reactions by yourself and others:* 'I feel upset because my classmate was so angry' or 'The client seemed confused about the range of options.'

Intrapersonal communication
Refers to our self-talk: the internal voice that we all possess.

| Exhibit 8.1 | Four types of self-talk |

Self-criticism
'I really misread that situation: I should have known better and handled it differently'

Social assessment
'I'll try to anticipate what someone in this position or from this background will say and how I'll respond to it'

Self-reinforcement
'Well I nailed that one. I feel I'm really getting the hang of this and performing well'

Self-management
'OK, this time I have to anticipate the questions and make sure I prepare and practise my presentation'

In each of these sample communication situations, your thoughts (on planning a strategy to deal with the problem, or interpreting other people's motivations) will influence the way you handle the situation and the choices you make about your communication behaviour.

Interpersonal communication or communicating with others

Interpersonal communication

Communication that takes place between two or more people who attempt to mutually influence each other, usually for the purpose of managing relationships.

Interpersonal communication (from the Latin *inter*, 'between, among, amid, in-between, in the midst') refers to the communication that takes place between people – whether one-on-one, small groups or teams, a speaker with a large audience, or even mass communication. According to this definition, the first three types of interpersonal communication involve face-to-face communication. In mass communication, where technological media are used to 'mediate', speakers and writers are removed from direct contact with the audience. We will explore the implications of this further in Chapter 9.

As discussed in Chapters 1 and 2, communication is not merely transactional, it is also about establishing and maintaining personal and social relationships. As such, Hargie (2017, p. 5) observes that recent thinking about the role of communication focuses on the purpose and impact of the '*sharing* of ideas, thoughts and feelings in commonly comprehensible ways'.

Finally, before looking in more detail at specific interpersonal skills and strategies, let's revisit the key elements of interpersonal communication, as shown in Exhibit 8.2.

Exhibit 8.2	The essential elements of interpersonal communication

Elements	Definition
People	The senders and receivers of communication messages. Interpersonal communication requires at least two participants
Messages	The content of the communication encounter; can be explicit or implicit, and verbal or non-verbal
Channels	The medium through which messages are sent; there is often more than one, which always use one or more of our five senses
Noise	Any form of interference in the sending or receiving of messages. This might be due to physiological (hearing, sight impairment), environmental (noisy surroundings, poor phone connections), semantic (misuse or misunderstanding of words), or psychological (attitudes, biases) reasons
Feedback	Information received in response to messages
Context/situation	The context or situation in which the communication occurs
Effect	The outcome or result of the communication

Developing effective interpersonal communication skills, therefore, needs to consider all of the elements in Exhibit 8.2 when diagnosing problems or developing strategies. The following sections examine more closely a range of important factors.

Aspects of interpersonal communication

Well-developed interpersonal communication skills help you to solve problems and to accept and implement changes in modern organisational settings, where competition is often fierce and the environment is complex. In this section we will briefly explore strategies for developing better relationships through conversation and appropriate self-disclosure.

Social penetration and self-disclosure

Our personal experiences would tell us that developing interpersonal relationships requires time and takes place as a series of steps. There are some people with whom we interact that we will feel we have come to know and understand well, and others who we may not know well, despite having known them for a longer period. This is because the depth of any relationship is related to how much we disclose about ourselves, and how much others also disclose.

Social penetration theory, first proposed by Altman and Taylor (1973), relates to the process of developing relationships. It has been called the 'onion theory' because the model looks like an onion (see Exhibit 8.3), and it describes how we develop relationships progressively by peeling back layers of ourselves as trust develops. As we move from public to private information, we make the transition from small talk to substantial conversations and, eventually, intimate conversations. The process of **self-disclosure**, that occurs in this process can be descriptive or evaluative, and can include thoughts, feelings, aspirations, goals, failures, successes, fears and dreams, as well as one's likes, dislikes and favourites (Ignatius & Kokkonen, 2007).

Social penetration theory
The process by which people go from superficial to intimate conversations as trust develops through repeated, positive interactions.

Self-disclosure
A process of communication by which one person reveals information about themselves to another. The information can be descriptive or evaluative, and can include thoughts, feelings, aspirations, goals, failures, successes, fears, and dreams, as well as one's likes, dislikes and favourites.

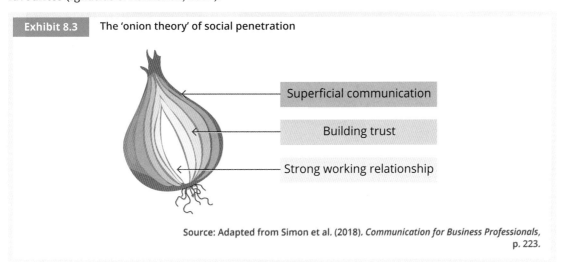

| Exhibit 8.3 | The 'onion theory' of social penetration |

Superficial communication

Building trust

Strong working relationship

Source: Adapted from Simon et al. (2018). *Communication for Business Professionals*, p. 223.

Reflection question: Recall a time when you met someone for the first time and whom you wanted to get to know better.
1 What did you talk about?
2 What sorts of things did you disclose about yourself in this conversation?
3 Were there things that you did not disclose initially? Why?

Conversation: the basic communication mode

We use conversation to make contact with another person and explore our relationship with them (see Exhibit 8.4), in a two-way process of sharing meaning via verbal and non-verbal cues. In conversation, we disclose personal information about ourselves to others and we react to their disclosures. Additionally, the language and tone we use in our conversation with others are subject to interpretation. This interpretation involves trying to work out two dimensions of conversation – the content dimension and the relationship dimension. The content is the possible meaning of your language and tone, and the relationship dimension refers to the level of intimacy or closeness of the interpersonal relationship. What you say and how you say it indicates the type of relationship in the conversation.

| Exhibit 8.4 | Conversation, the basic mode of communication |

iStock.com/Izabela Habur

Learning how to appropriately self-disclose through conversations helps us develop more effective relationship skills. It increases our self-esteem and expands our potential to build working relationships. In conversation, you can represent yourself to the other person by using 'I' statements that reveal your feelings, beliefs, thoughts and ideas. Compare the following two conversations:

Conversation 1

> Mai: I'm really worried about meeting the deadline, and I need your cost estimates to finish the proposal.
> Alex: OK, I'll give them to you at two o'clock. Is that enough time for you?

Conversation 2

> Mai: You make me feel really worried about meeting the deadline because you haven't given me your cost estimates so that I can finish the proposal.
> Alex: Hang on! I've got a lot of work to do for other deadlines. This isn't the only project I'm working on.

In the first conversation Mai expresses an 'I' statement about feelings and concerns and provides specific information needed to meet a deadline. Alex acknowledges Mai's worry and responds by offering a solution to help meet the deadline. In the second conversation, Mai uses 'you' statements that blame Alex for not doing a satisfactory job, and Alex becomes defensive. As a result, nothing is agreed to that will help Mai meet her deadline. Additionally, further communication will be needed to deal with the tense climate created by this conversation.

Double or mixed messages can also be given if your non-verbal demeanour does not match your words. This is referred to as being incongruent. In many Australian and Western contexts, a serious, firm tone of voice and confident gestures and body posture should accompany Mai's request to Alex for it to be effective.

In addition, consider the timing of your conversation. If the other person is stressed or emotionally upset, he or she will probably not be able to give you adequate attention to interpret your meaning as you intended it. It may be more appropriate to wait for another time. Be sure that you listen to what the other person says and observe their non-verbal signals. Also, check your understanding by saying, 'Do you mean that you can't make any progress on the proposal until I give you the estimates?' Keep checking and clarifying until all aspects are clear to both parties.

It is important to be aware of the level of intimacy or distance at which you are communicating; for example, it may be very superficial, friendly or involve deep sharing. Mutual sharing of appropriate personal information and the ability to listen to each other builds friendlier and more respectful relationships. You and your colleagues will then have working relationships based on communication, in which you can decrease the misunderstandings that cause unnecessary conflict, frustration and dissatisfaction. Appropriate self-disclosure is an important interpersonal skill for building working relationships with others.

 CASE STUDY 8.1 The evolving nature of interpersonal relationships in the workplace

Most of us spend more time with our co-workers than with our friends or family members, so these relationships are important to cultivate. Work relationships, like those in our non-work world, evolve, shift and change. Consider the following scenario and then comment on these stages.

Maree and co-worker, Judith started as interns in the company on the same day some years ago, and together have been able to navigate their careers and company politics. They regularly take lunch together and have become good friends outside of work, sharing an interest in theatre, ballet, movies and music. Judith was the first to be told when Maree became engaged to her long-time partner and the only one of Maree's colleagues invited to her wedding. One day, however, Judith is promoted to the position of section manager. She didn't tell Maree at the time that she had been offered the position because it was not confirmed and she didn't know how Maree would react, given that previously they had been on the same promotional level. Additionally, in her new role, Judith will be Maree's line supervisor.

As a result of Judith's promotion, her relationship with Maree starts to change. Judith no longer has time to share regular lunch dates with Maree because she is often out of the office at executive meetings. Judith's new managerial position means that she is now privy to confidential information, and where previously they enjoyed sharing office gossip, Judith is now wary of doing so. While they are still friends, they begin to drift apart. They spend less and less time together inside and outside of work until eventually Judith is just another person in the office with whom Maree has occasional polite conversations.

Discussion

1 From the information in the case study, what are some of the characteristics of the different phases of Judith and Maree's relationship?

2 How might the stages of their relationship be explained using the 'onion model'?

3 Why did Judith and Maree's relationship change once Judith was promoted?

4 How might interpersonal relationships that develop in the workplace differ from those outside of work?

After you have discussed this case study, refer to the 'Comments on case studies' section at the end of the text.

Communication competence

The notion of **communication competence** involves both knowledge and performance (Kaye, 1994). A competent communicator has acquired (and continues to acquire) appropriate knowledge of the principles (norms or rules) of human communication relevant to their experience of communicating in various contexts and cultural settings. In addition, a competent communicator has (and continues to develop) the ability to perform appropriately in these settings, taking a wide range of factors into account. Exhibit 8.5 illustrates the range of interpersonal skills required for communication competence.

Communication competence
A person's ability to choose from among a variety of communication behaviours and strategies in order to achieve effective interpersonal communication outcomes.

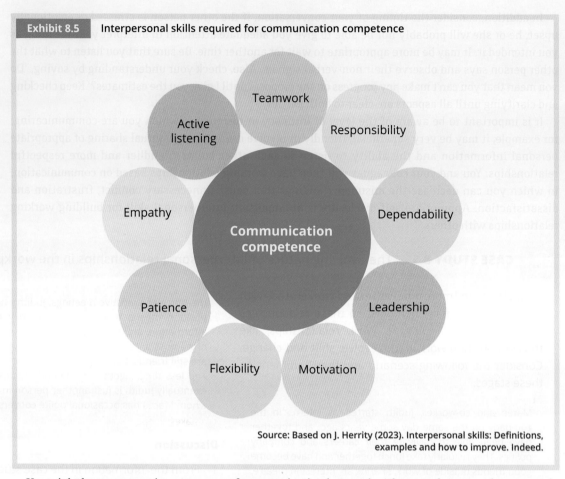

Exhibit 8.5   Interpersonal skills required for communication competence

Communication competence

Teamwork
Active listening
Responsibility
Empathy
Dependability
Patience
Leadership
Flexibility
Motivation

Source: Based on J. Herrity (2023). Interpersonal skills: Definitions, examples and how to improve. Indeed.

You might be competent in some areas of communication but not in others; and you may know certain rules of communication effectiveness but be unable to perform in accordance with these rules in real life. For example, you might know the principles of public speaking but not be able to deliver an effective speech, possibly because you lack practice. As discussed in Chapter 4, communication competence is a Western concept that may not be shared by people from other cultures. Given the priority placed on demonstrating high-level communication skills in many workplaces, you should continue to develop communication competence throughout your life. You can do this by accepting communication challenges, being willing to reflect on your communication performances and asking others for feedback on your communication abilities.

Communication competence and credibility

When you communicate with another person (e.g., as a teacher to a learner, a student to another student, an employee to a customer, or a supervisor to a member of staff), the other person's perception of your credibility can markedly affect the outcome of the interaction. In addition, judgements may be made that will affect future interactions. Assuming that you have adequate credibility in terms of knowledge and experience for a particular situation, how can you use your communication competence to create an appropriate impression in this context? As Kaye (1994, p. 36) explains: 'High credibility occurs when the message source is competent (or expert), trustworthy (or reliable) and dynamic'.

Kaye's comment was based on research conducted in the US and reflects Western values of relating credibility to perceptions of individual expertise, trustworthiness and dynamism. In some communication contexts, credibility may not be demonstrated by behaving as an individual with energy and dynamism, but rather by being quiet, reserved and respectful, and by fitting in with the protocol of a group. A preliminary study carried out in New Zealand, for instance, indicated that in Māori communities, a credible and competent communicator is one who is able to connect with others as a member of a wider group, knows and uses correct behaviours and procedures for the context, uses rich and poetic language including proverbs, tells stories, and attends to the comfort of communicators (Duncalfe, 1996).

A good example of a context in which self-monitoring of appearance and behaviour can indicate communication competence is a job interview. Educators who conduct training for job-selection interviews help their clients 'be themselves' and also to monitor verbal and non-verbal cues in the interview. Training will often involve watching video replays of yourself in a mock interview and practising alternative ways of responding to interview questions. This aims to boost job seekers' confidence in representing their knowledge, skills and experience appropriately, in what is often a very stressful communication context.

For communication contexts in which you are involved, you are the one who will decide how to respond to feedback from others, and even whether you will pay attention to some of the wide variety of communication cues present in any situation. Use the checklist in Exhibit 8.6 to review your communication competence in terms of specific types of interpersonal behaviours.

Exhibit 8.6 Checklist of interpersonal communication skills

PERSONAL PRESENTATION
- ☐ Dress appropriately
- ☐ Monitor personal grooming
- ☐ Use presentation aids: tools, computer and audiovisual technology
- ☐ Monitor punctuality

LISTENING SKILLS
- ☐ Concentrate on what the other person is saying rather than on your solution
- ☐ Demonstrate listening by attentive body posture
- ☐ Express empathy for the other person's thoughts and feelings

QUESTIONING SKILLS
- ☐ Ask open and closed questions to explore and focus
- ☐ Ask enough questions to clarify and check your understanding of the other person's meaning

ORAL-PRESENTATION SKILLS
- ☐ Prepare what you want to say
- ☐ Focus on key information
- ☐ Be sensitive to the cultural context and protocol of the situation

- ☐ State your point of view politely and tactfully
- ☐ Speak clearly with variety and emphasis
- ☐ Monitor feedback and adapt as appropriate

CUSTOMER-SERVICE SKILLS
- ☐ Be accessible and listen to the customer with empathy
- ☐ Create a helping climate and build rapport
- ☐ Acknowledge the customer's point of view
- ☐ Have a good knowledge of products, services and contracts
- ☐ Admit mistakes, as appropriate, and offer solutions

SKILLS FOR WORKING IN TEAMS
- ☐ Contribute information
- ☐ Monitor progress and keep team members informed of developments
- ☐ Clarify objectives
- ☐ Support each other
- ☐ Seek feedback on the team's efforts
- ☐ Give feedback to people who might be supporting the team (for example, administrative staff, colleagues, relatives)

Effective interpersonal communication

In a general sense, there are nine main suggestions for enhancing relationships and helping you to communicate effectively. These apply to many Australian contexts, but cultural and personal preferences should be considered. In other words, the nine suggestions are valued by many in the Australian community but may not be appropriate in a specific communication situation. These can also be considered alongside the principles of emotional intelligence (outlined in the next section):

1 *Openness:* be willing to self-disclose and react honestly and spontaneously to what is said.

2 *Empathy and supportiveness:* try to understand other people's motivations, feelings and points of view in a sympathetic and respectful way. Resist the temptation to rush in with judgements, biased interpretations and criticisms.

3 *Equality:* build an atmosphere of equality that recognises that all people are valuable and worthwhile. Try to solve disagreements rather than 'win'.

4 *Confidence:* feel confident to enable you to deal with others who are anxious or shy, and to convey confidence to them. Be relaxed – flexible in body and voice – rather than stiff and formal, to convey a sense of credibility and trust.

5 *Immediacy:* create a sense of togetherness, of interest in and attention to the other person by:

- using non-verbal cues, such as eye contact, physical closeness, and direct and open body posture
- using the other person's name
- using pronouns that include all parties, such as 'we' and 'us'
- providing relevant feedback; for example, 'That sounds right' or 'I can appreciate that'
- focusing on the other's remarks; for example, 'How would your argument apply to South-East Asia?'
- reinforcing, rewarding or complimenting appropriately; for example, 'I think your comments are really relevant' or 'I've thought that myself'.

6 *Interaction management:* keep the conversation flowing, maintain an equal (or appropriate) share of speaking, and use pauses and silence in a comfortable way for the situation. Use non-verbal cues to support a fluent conversation; for example, smiling, nodding, frowning, or looking puzzled before a request to clarify.

7 *Self-monitoring:* adjust the image you present to others; like openness, self-monitoring should be moderate and selective. Total openness and ignoring feedback from others might be highly inappropriate, just as total monitoring and never disclosing what we really think or feel may be counterproductive to building trusting relationships.

8 *Expressiveness:* be genuinely involved in the interaction – participate instead of watching. Take responsibility for your thoughts and opinions. Encourage openness in others and provide feedback that is relevant and appropriate.

9 *Assertiveness:* recognise the differences between styles of interpersonal communication, including assertive, passive/submissive and aggressive. Be aware that any action is interpreted in terms of the cultural and social context.

 CASE STUDY 8.2   The role of 'communication competence' in health settings

Clear and effective communication is essential for all healthcare professions. Communication skills are required between a healthcare professional and their patient or the patient's family or carers, between different healthcare professionals, and between public health officials and the general public when devising a vital public health campaign, such as during the COVID-19 pandemic. In fact, competent communication with patients has been shown to be central to positive health outcomes, including in cardiac health, cancer survival, and health promoting behaviours, such as quit smoking, weight loss and other health risk avoidance strategies (Spitzberg, 2013).

However, while many health care professionals *think* that they are competent communicators, research has shown that there are often differing perceptions of their effectiveness between the doctor, nurse or other health professional and the patient(s) and/or their family (Dare, 2009; Hurtig et al., 2018).

Discussion

Discuss the following scenarios and, using the nine suggestions for enhancing relationships previously presented, identify where the communication may have gone wrong. Also suggest some strategies that the communicators could have applied to improve the outcomes.

Scenario 1

A nurse in an understaffed ward is attempting to work as efficiently as possible to cover the shortfall. However, a patient who has waited longer than usual for information about their condition interprets the nurse's hurried body language and clipped tone of delivery as lacking in empathy, concern or understanding.

Scenario 2

After a long night shift, the nursing unit manager in a major hospital ward is conducting the regular handover.

The manager of the next shift is new and has not worked on the ward before. While this is a regular event involving routine information and protocols, some important information about a change in medication for a long-term patient is not communicated.

Scenario 3

The communication unit of a major government health department needs to devise pamphlets in multiple languages to explain the need for lockdowns, vaccination, mask wearing and social distancing to minimise the risk of COVID-19 transmission. They decide on a generic set of information points, write the initial pamphlets in English and then outsource these to a translation service to have them replicated into multiple languages. After the pamphlets are distributed among the ethnically diverse population of the major city, many of the government's health prevention messages appear to be ignored.

After you have discussed this case study, refer to the 'Comments on case studies' section at the end of the text.

Values, attitudes and self-esteem

Values, attitudes and **self-esteem** greatly influence communication between people. As such, many breakdowns in communication can be traced to clashes involving these qualities. It is important to be aware of the range of values, attitudes and levels of self-esteem that we hold and that are held by the people we interact with. When you are working in groups or teams, or are making decisions as a committee, issues relating to differences in these areas will be quite common. You will have to be able to accommodate these differences, and perhaps act as a change agent when the differences are difficult to resolve.

It is vital that you are able to monitor your own levels of self-esteem and develop and maintain a positive attitude to the challenges of life and work. By your example, you can motivate others to view themselves realistically and positively. As a trusted colleague, you can encourage the development of positive self-esteem in others by providing skilful feedback on performance and attitude. It is important that you have the ability to recognise, identify and discuss attitudes openly with others. Team discussions on matters relating to attitude have been shown to be a very effective means of changing attitudes among some members of the team. For example, as a team member you might initiate a discussion on attitudes relating to dealing with change in how the team has been working. By encouraging team members who show adaptable and flexible attitudes, others who are more threatened by change may begin to change their attitudes through supportive and collaborative interpersonal communication, including effective listening.

Self-esteem
The positive or negative ways in which a person thinks of themself and the extent that they believe they are able to cope with the challenges of everyday life.

Emotional intelligence

Another important concept in this area is **emotional intelligence** (EI), which was first proposed by Salovey and Mayer (1990, p. 189). They defined EI as: 'A person's ability to monitor their own and other's feelings and emotions, to discriminate among them, and to use this information to guide their thinking and action'.

Following on from that, one of the most comprehensive views of the nature of EI and its impact on the effectiveness of leaders comes from Daniel Goleman (2001). Everyone knows someone who has been promoted on the basis of their technical skills or their intelligence, only to fail in the job. However, Goleman argues that while leaders are often chosen for these reasons, it is their EI which will ultimately determine their success as leaders. Exhibit 8.7 shows the characteristics that Goleman believes make up EI.

Emotional intelligence
'A person's ability to monitor their own and others' feelings and emotions, to discriminate among them, and to use this information to guide their thinking and action' (Salovey & Mayer, 1990).

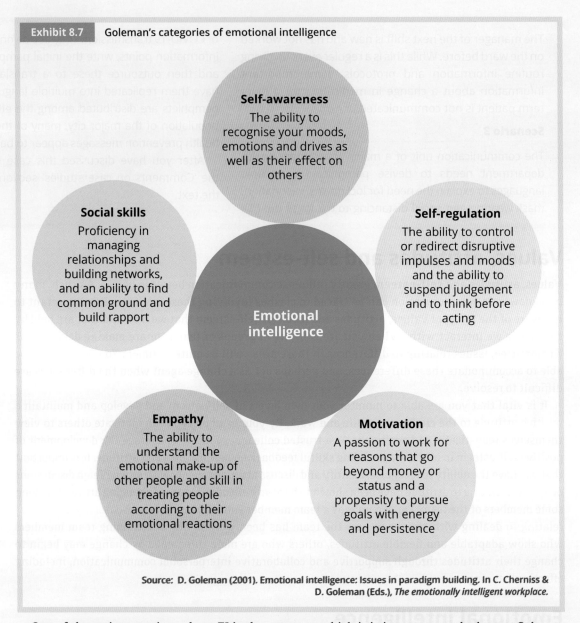

Exhibit 8.7 Goleman's categories of emotional intelligence

Self-awareness
The ability to recognise your moods, emotions and drives as well as their effect on others

Social skills
Proficiency in managing relationships and building networks, and an ability to find common ground and build rapport

Self-regulation
The ability to control or redirect disruptive impulses and moods and the ability to suspend judgement and to think before acting

Emotional intelligence

Empathy
The ability to understand the emotional make-up of other people and skill in treating people according to their emotional reactions

Motivation
A passion to work for reasons that go beyond money or status and a propensity to pursue goals with energy and persistence

Source: D. Goleman (2001). Emotional intelligence: Issues in paradigm building. In C. Cherniss & D. Goleman (Eds.), *The emotionally intelligent workplace.*

One of the major questions about EI is the extent to which it is innate or can be learnt. Goleman suggests that while there is a strong genetic component to EI, nurture plays a role as well. He also notes that EI increases with age, and later research indicates that women exhibit higher levels than men. However, Goleman also argues that it is possible for people to develop their EI by breaking old behavioural habits, such poor listening, and developing their use of empathy. This, however, takes time and genuine commitment.

One concern that has been raised about the focus on EI in management training relates to whether there is a possibility of misusing such a skill to manipulate and deceive people. The argument has been made that the more successful we become at identifying and using subtle communication skills, such as listening, non-verbal communication and so on, the easier it is to fake appropriate responses. However, despite these concerns, ongoing research into management practice and leadership styles and their relationship to productive workplaces indicates that the kinds of perspectives offered by EI are increasingly relevant to professional success. In fact, Edward de Bono (2000) vigorously argued that organisations ignore emotions at their peril because they will lurk in the background and influence outcomes in covert and unexpected ways.

Reflection question: Consider the aspects of EI just described. Think of an example from your own experience where someone in a management or leadership position lacked these skills. What were some of their behaviours? What was the outcome for the team they were leading?

Appropriate assertiveness

Assertiveness offers non-threatening techniques for interpersonal dialogue, as issues are confronted in a straightforward manner. People's views are stated without being rude or thoughtless, and feelings are acknowledged and respected. Assertiveness is a way of expressing ourselves that is solution-oriented and may involve negotiation to reach an agreed outcome.

Assertiveness
The act of getting what you want from others without infringing on their rights.

Researchers, such as Alberti and Emmons (2017), have found it useful to describe people's behaviour as a combination of four communication styles: passive, aggressive, passive-aggressive, and assertive. The characteristics and examples of these styles are shown in Exhibits 8.8 and 8.9.

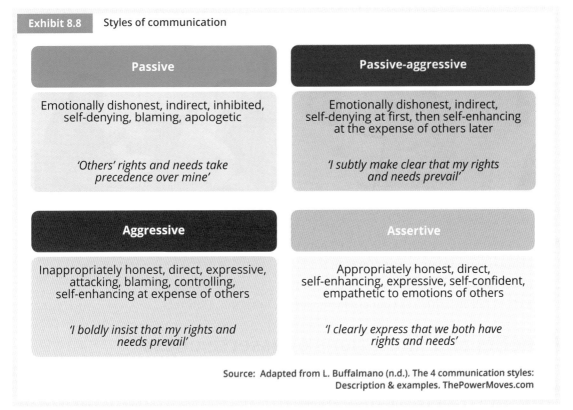

| **Exhibit 8.8** | Styles of communication |

Passive

Emotionally dishonest, indirect, inhibited, self-denying, blaming, apologetic

'Others' rights and needs take precedence over mine'

Passive-aggressive

Emotionally dishonest, indirect, self-denying at first, then self-enhancing at the expense of others later

'I subtly make clear that my rights and needs prevail'

Aggressive

Inappropriately honest, direct, expressive, attacking, blaming, controlling, self-enhancing at expense of others

'I boldly insist that my rights and needs prevail'

Assertive

Appropriately honest, direct, self-enhancing, expressive, self-confident, empathetic to emotions of others

'I clearly express that we both have rights and needs'

Source: Adapted from L. Buffalmano (n.d.). The 4 communication styles: Description & examples. ThePowerMoves.com

The meaning of assertiveness

According to Alberti and Emmons (2017), assertive behaviour is when you can:

- act in your own best interests
- stand up for yourself without undue anxiety
- express honest feelings comfortably
- exercise personal rights without denying the rights of others.

This can be contrasted with passive/submissive behaviour, when a person denies self and is inhibited from expressing actual feelings and thoughts and aggressive behaviour, and when a person expresses their own feelings, attitudes and opinions but does not respect the rights of others.

Some situations where assertiveness may be appropriate include:

- your manager makes unfair comments about your work
- your manager asks you to work back on a report when you have an important family commitment

Exhibit 8.9   Different communication styles

Shutterstock.com/YURII MASLAK

Shutterstock.com/fizkes

Shutterstock.com/Ground Picture

Shutterstock.com/Christopher Willans

- another student fails to do their fair share of the group assignment
- another person claims credit for your work
- a new salary agreement disadvantages you
- a client falsely criticises your product to justify breaking a contract.

Benefits and limitations of assertiveness

Assertiveness offers us non-threatening techniques to present our views and our rights clearly and without blaming other people. The ability to be assertive can greatly assist the process of conflict management. As **Exhibit 8.10** illustrates, the communication style you adopt impacts both the degree to which communication is open and the extent to which your communication style considers others. When we use assertive statements, the other person is more likely to get an accurate idea of where we stand on issues and how prepared we are to negotiate or to work towards resolving a conflict.

One of the major advantages of assertiveness compared to passive/submissive responses is that assertive people feel more in control of their jobs, their lives and their options. Passive/submissive people generally feel frustrated with life and feel that others have the responsibility to take care of them. When this does not happen, the passive/submissive person may feel resentful, and their self-esteem may suffer.

On the other hand, assertive people may not always get what they want, but they feel better about having had a go and taking responsibility for themselves. Their self-esteem is likely to be much more positive. In contrast, although aggressive people sometimes win in the short-term, they do so at tremendous risk. Others who are the victims of aggression may plot revenge and seek to sabotage the 'win'. Aggression often causes defensiveness as well as bitter resentment.

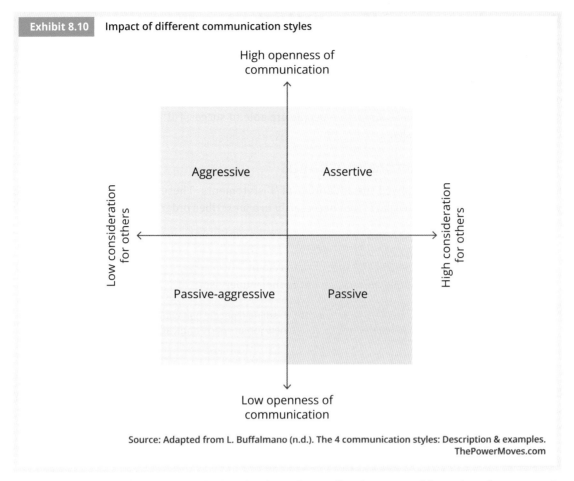

Exhibit 8.10 Impact of different communication styles

Source: Adapted from L. Buffalmano (n.d.). The 4 communication styles: Description & examples. ThePowerMoves.com

Assertiveness, used properly, is designed to be as least offensive as possible to the other person. In communicating our preferences in this way, the other person is more likely to hear what we say. The other person may not always agree to change, but an assertive statement of our feelings and the course of action we would prefer is an honest way of giving feedback.

Don't expect the other person to respond immediately in a positive way to your assertive message. Instead, work together to solve the problem and to reach an amicable solution. Even if the other person ignores your assertive message in the first instance, you will have the satisfaction of knowing that you stood up for your rights. It may be that the other person will respond favourably when they have a chance to think about what you said. People do not always respond straightaway, because they may think they will lose face if they give in to what you have requested.

You can use assertiveness to respond to compliments by saying a simple 'Thank you' instead of a passive/submissive 'It's nothing' or an aggressive 'Leave me alone'. In many cultural contexts, a simple 'Thank you' is an appropriate and assertive way of accepting a compliment that might further enhance our self-esteem and build the relationship with the giver. Discounting the intended compliment – 'It's nothing' – or rejecting the giver – 'Leave me alone' – might lower self-esteem and harm the relationship.

Assertiveness can also be used to make requests in a direct way to express our needs by saying, for example, 'I'd like a refund please, as the product does not work' instead of a passive/submissive 'I'm sorry but this product does not seem to work' or an aggressive 'This product is rubbish'. In many cultural contexts, the chances of receiving a refund or other acceptable outcome would be greater if assertiveness is used to communicate our perceptions of the issues and our needs.

Reflection question: Think of some situations where it is harder to be assertive than in others. Why do you think that is?

Expressing yourself assertively

Assertive behaviour is a means of expressing yourself in an honest, direct and non-destructive way within a given sociocultural context. Assertive behaviour is not intended to hurt the other person, unlike aggressive or passive/submissive behaviour, which may have the intention or the effect of this outcome. If the responsibilities and risks involved in the relationship are too great, you may choose not to take an assertive stance. Assertive people are able to successfully balance their rights with these responsibilities and risks.

Three-part 'I' assertive messages

Earlier in this chapter we showed the advantage of 'I' statements. These assertive messages can be very effective if stated in three parts (not necessarily in a prescribed order), including descriptions of:

- specific behaviour
- your specific feelings
- the tangible effects on you of the specific behaviour.

Here is an example of an employee's statement to their supervisor:

> When you ask me to take on another job with a tight deadline (specific behaviour), I feel pressured (specific feeling) because I don't have adequate time to do the new job properly and carry out the other work I have to do (tangible effects).

These 'I' messages are effective because often the other person has no real idea of the effects of their behaviour or requests on us. If the other person values the relationship, they will respond to a clearly stated and delivered 'I' message. If the other person does not respond and the issue is important to you, you may have to repeat the 'I' message several times.

'I' messages can be extended by clear statements about solutions, options and possible consequences. For example:

> When you ask me to take on another job with a tight deadline, I feel pressured because I don't have adequate time to do the new job properly and to carry out the other work I have to do. I would like to be able to talk about the problem with you. Options might be to reschedule my other work or train more staff. Then we could be more productive and less stressed.

When you have delivered an assertive 'I' statement, listen intently to the response of the other person, and respond with active listening. For example, tell the other person what you understood by their response to your assertive message. This clarification of the other's response will then lead to both of you determining the outcome of the interaction.

Assertiveness is especially useful in conflict management. Conflicts are often complex, and we investigate key interpersonal skills for conflict management in Chapter 9, which deals with communicating in groups and teams.

Using assertiveness to give negative feedback or constructive criticism

You can use assertiveness to give negative feedback or constructive criticism about behaviour that is deficient in some way. Describe the behaviour rather than judge it. Focus on discussing something that the other person is capable of doing something about. For giving negative feedback or constructive criticism consider the following:

- Is the person capable of receiving the negative feedback or criticism now?
- Are you willing to spend time to work to a resolution or to help 'pick up the pieces'?
- How many times has the person heard this negative feedback or criticism before? ('Am I just nagging?')
- Can the person do anything about it? (Consider the present circumstances of the person.)

- Are you sure that the person needs another negative feedback message or criticism? Would the person be better motivated to change by some appreciation or validation instead? (Simon, 1978)

Using assertiveness to respond to negative feedback or criticism

In her book *Self-assertion for Women*, Pam Butler (2011) explains that many people are very threatened when they perceive that they have received feedback that is negative or, in other words, that they have been criticised by another person. She explains that two common irrational assumptions might lie behind these fears:

1 For me to feel good about myself, it is absolutely necessary that I am liked by and approved of by everyone.

2 For me to feel good about myself, I must never make a mistake.

Of course, it is impossible to go through life succeeding in pleasing everyone and without making mistakes. We all receive negative feedback and criticism from other people at some point, and assertiveness can help us to deal with it. Butler (2011) outlines five basic ways in which we can respond assertively to negative feedback or criticism:

1 *Accept negative feedback or criticism:* just accept or acknowledge the feedback and move on; don't apologise or defend yourself.

2 *Disagree with the negative feedback or criticism:* focus on specific aspects of the feedback, try to explain why you think the feedback does not fit, and check the information on which the feedback was based.

3 *Set limits with the person who is giving the negative feedback or criticism:* say how you wish to be treated.

4 *'Fog' away the negative feedback or criticism:* don't agree or disagree but say 'You may be right', 'I can see how you might think that' and move on.

5 *Delay your response:* ask for time to respond if you feel surprised, confused or disappointed by the feedback.

Using assertiveness in these ways helps to maintain and enhance our self-esteem; and healthy self-esteem is fundamental to effective, equitable interpersonal communication.

Reflection question: Explore the notion of assertiveness by completing the following assertiveness questionnaire.

Decide whether the following 18 statements apply to you, using the following categories: 1 Never true 2 Sometimes true 3 Often true 4 Always true Place the number you choose beside each statement.		
		Your number
1	I respond with more modesty than I really feel when my work is complimented	
2	If people are rude, I will be rude right back	
3	Other people find me interesting	
4	I find it difficult to speak up in a group of strangers	
5	I don't mind using sarcasm if it helps me make a point	
6	I ask for more pay if I feel I really deserve it	
7	If others interrupt me when I am talking, I suffer in silence	
8	If people criticise my work, I find a way to make them back down	
9	I can express pride in my accomplishments without being boastful	
10	People take advantage of me	

11	I tell people what they want to hear if it helps me get what I want	
12	I find it easy to ask for help	
13	I lend things to others even when I don't really want to	
14	I win arguments by dominating the discussion	
15	I can express my true feelings to someone I really care for	
16	When I feel angry with other people, I bottle it up rather than express it	
17	When I criticise someone else's work, they get mad	
18	I feel confident in my ability to stand up for my rights	

Scoring

Statement	Score	Statement	Score	Statement	Score
1		2		3	
4		5		6	
7		8		9	
10		11		12	
13		14		15	
16		17		18	
Passive total		Aggressive total		Assertive total	

Note: Your score for each will range between 6 and 24; Low = 0–8, medium = 9–16 and high = 17–24.

Interpretation of the assertiveness questionnaire

A high 'passive' score indicates an unwillingness to confront problems. You are likely to be perceived as one who can be bullied by others. Your desire to please others may result in your being viewed as inconsistent. In the effort to please everyone, the passive person may please no-one. A high 'aggressiveness' score indicates that you are likely to be seen as a dictator. Your desire to take command and dominate others is often interpreted as pushy. Both excessive passiveness and aggressiveness negatively affect interpersonal relations.

The higher your assertiveness score, the more open and self-expressive you are. You confront issues in a straightforward manner. You say what you mean but you are not rude or thoughtless. You are sensitive to the needs of others and receptive to what they have to say. Generally speaking, assertiveness is a desirable quality and tends to facilitate effective interpersonal relations.

The purpose of the assertiveness questionnaire is to increase self-awareness, recognise how you are likely to be perceived by others and identify your strengths and limitations. For example, suppose you are low on assertiveness and high on aggressiveness. If you meet with another person to set goals jointly and collaboratively, you may need to work extra hard to reduce your desire to control the goal-setting session and impose your standards on the other person.

Source: P. Robbins & P. L. Hunsaker (2012). *Training in interpersonal skills* (6th ed.). Pearson, p. 49.

Listening as a vital interpersonal communication skill

Even at the purely informational level, it has been claimed that 75 per cent of oral communication is ignored, misunderstood or quickly forgotten. How often during arguments with significant others in our lives are we accused of 'never listening'? It's been said that at school we have lessons in reading and writing, but we never actually have lessons in listening.

Are we such bad listeners? Can listening be taught or improved? Is listening the same as hearing? Perhaps listening is meaningful hearing – hearing with intention and motivation. Whatever it is, most experts agree that it is a very undeveloped skill (Bolton, 2003; Goulston, 2015). Since we probably spend more time listening than speaking, writing or reading, poor listening habits may be our most serious source of communication breakdown. Hugh Mackay (1998) explains that a fundamental problem with understanding communication in general, but listening in particular, is the 'injection myth' or hypodermic needle model, which assumes communication takes place as long as there has been some response from the audience. He argues that:

> ... communication occurs when the audience does something with the message. The more we look at the way communication works, the more we see that the real power is not in the message, but in the listener. The listener has the power to interpret the message and, in communication terms, that is the ultimate power.
>
> Source: Mackay (1998), p. 25

What Mackay is getting at in this quote is that there is a difference between *hearing* and listening, which the 'injection myth' of communication does not take into account.

Hearing versus listening

Hearing and listening have been defined quite differently. **Hearing** is the physical reception of sound involving an automatic reaction of the senses and the nervous system. It is the physiological sensory process by which auditory sensations are received by the ears and transmitted to the brain. Whereas, **listening** involves a conscious effort to pay attention – a voluntary act involving our higher mental processes to make meaning from sound. The word listen is derived from two Anglo-Saxon words: *hlystan*, which means hearing, and *hlosnian*, which means to wait in suspense. Thus, listening is a combination of hearing what the other person says and a suspenseful waiting, an intense psychological involvement with the other (Bolton, 2003).

Listening is a more complex psychological procedure involving interpreting and understanding the significance of the sensory experience. Receiving and processing the aural stimuli that are heard is an active process that takes energy, time and commitment. This process can be described by the HURIER model and is shown in Exhibits 8.11 and 8.12.

Hearing
The physiological sensory processes by which auditory sensations are received by the ears and transmitted to the brain.

Listening
Actively processing sounds in order to make meaning and understanding.

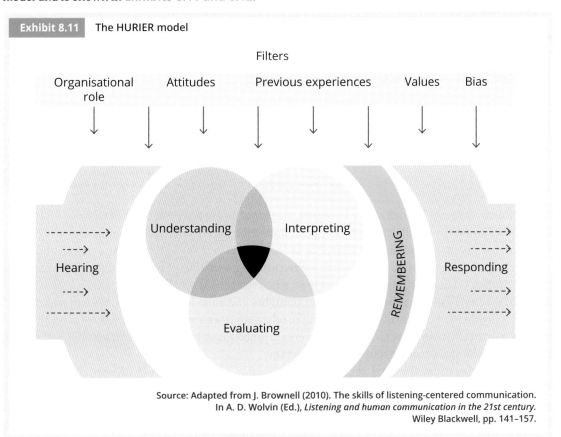

| Exhibit 8.11 | The HURIER model |

Source: Adapted from J. Brownell (2010). The skills of listening-centered communication. In A. D. Wolvin (Ed.), *Listening and human communication in the 21st century.* Wiley Blackwell, pp. 141–157.

| Exhibit 8.12 | Stages of listening in the HURIER model explained |

Stage	Description
Hearing	Physically receiving and processing sounds. Usually, we *hear* what we focus on, meaning that we choose to attend to some aspects in our environment while we ignore the rest
Understanding	Decoding the sounds to make meaning. We attach meaning to the symbols we receive and relate what we have heard to what we already know
Remembering	Retaining what we have heard so that we can act on the message. We cannot remember all of what we hear, so we choose what we commit to memory. Intense feelings or reinforcement increase the likelihood of a message being remembered
Interpreting	Making sense of the physical sounds by considering a range of contextual factors such as our judgement of the speaker, and other visual and aural stimuli, including non-verbal cues
Evaluating	Weighing up the information, distinguishing facts from inferences and making critical judgements about what we have been told
Responding	Reacting to the message by giving feedback to the speaker about our thoughts and feelings

Source: Adapted from J. Brownell (1996). *Listening: Attitudes, principles, and skills.* Allyn & Bacon.

Technology has increased the number of messages we receive and the speed with which they are delivered, requiring listeners to confront a constantly changing and increasingly complex listening environment. You must be able to scan the information you receive, determine where to focus your attention, and make sense of what you hear.

Consider the following possibilities in regard to hearing and listening:

- We hear many things.
- We listen to only a few of the things we hear.
- You can hear without wanting to hear, but you have to want to listen.
- You can be heard accurately by someone who is not listening with understanding.
- Your real friends listen to what you say, whereas other people only hear you talk.

Causes of ineffective listening

Nothing says 'I take you seriously' like attentive listening. Nothing says 'I *don't* take you seriously' like inattentive, half-hearted or 'mock' listening: glancing at your watch, looking over the person's shoulder in the hope of sighting someone more interesting to talk to, or – the worst offence – using the time they're speaking to work out what you're going to say next.

Source: H. Mackay (2019, June 19). The courage to listen. Dumbo Feather. https://www.dumbofeather.com/articles/the-courage-of-attentive-listening/

There are many causes of ineffective listening, and all of us are guilty of some of them at some time. In fact, it is almost impossible to maintain a constant high involvement in listening. There are many physical and psychological reasons why. One is that, while most people speak at a rate of about 125 words per minute, most of us think (when we're thinking verbally) at a rate of about 500 words per minute (Guffey & Loewy, 2014). This means that, when someone is speaking to us, there's a lot of excess mental capacity available to be filled by other thoughts and outside distractions. We can make use of the difference between speaking and listening to relate what we are hearing to what we already know. The discrepancy between the two speeds can create problems unless we concentrate on what is being said and use the spare time to reinforce the message.

As we will see from the final section of this chapter, the proliferation of new communication technologies can make it even harder. We need to 'tune out' to give our minds a chance to rest and be able to synthesise and process what we've heard. But we also need to be able to 'tune in' when we want communication to succeed. The following sections will discuss some of the bad habits that keep us from listening well.

Assuming a topic will be boring

We may assume a topic will be boring, either because it was boring previously or because we have no knowledge of it. We immediately decide that we will get nothing out of the communication, allow our minds to wander and then miss the message the speaker is trying to share.

Allowing the speaker's voice or mannerisms to overpower the message

We may not like the sound of the speaker's voice. Perhaps the tone or pronunciation grates on us. The speaker's physical appearance can also inhibit our listening. We may query the reliability of a speaker with unkempt hair and unfashionable clothing who is talking about marketing skills. We may be more willing to hear some messages from members of our own gender or from younger or older people. We are often guilty of stereotyping people and fail to remember that individuals have their own thoughts and opinions that should be considered.

Poor concentration

Poor listening can also be caused by problems with concentration (see Exhibit 8.13). When we are young children we have very short attention spans but, as we grow into adults, we develop the ability to be attentive for longer periods. However, some of us are more impatient while some are more skilful at concentrating for longer on difficult material.

Exhibit 8.13   Poor concentration contributes to ineffective listening

Shutterstock.com/AF-Photography

Interrupting

The vulnerable areas of bias, prejudice, beliefs and areas that are taboo often stimulate listeners to interrupt. This means that rather than listening to the complete message, we hear only trigger words that prompt us to defend our own viewpoints rather than listen to another's opinion.

Particular topics or the ways in which certain subjects are presented can also affect a listener emotionally. Some subjects, or even words, may be so upsetting that they cause a person to stop listening.

Poor comprehension

Lack of comprehension skills also results in poor listening. We are sometimes unable to grasp the central idea of a speech or argument because we cannot discriminate the important information from the less significant. Some of the skills required for organising written expression are also necessary for oral communication. Listeners, as well as speakers, need to be competent in organising ideas.

A speaker has often had a great deal of time to structure the message carefully, but a listener must be able to follow the ideas instantaneously. We sometimes forget that taking notes or drawing flow charts can help us to see the connections between concepts and thoughts. On the other hand, we sometimes become so involved in taking copious notes that we completely forget to attend to the meaning that may come from the structure of the language or the non-verbal communication of the speaker.

Passive listening

Listening is a complex physical and mental activity that requires energy on the part of the listener. If we are tired, unwell or upset, it becomes difficult for us to concentrate. Even good listeners are not able to function properly if they are not physiologically equipped to be attentive.

If there is background noise or some form of distraction, more effort is required to listen. If the speaker is not skilful, the listener needs to take an even more active role for the communication to be successful. Poor listeners are easily distracted by their surroundings and are unwilling to help a failing speaker.

Poor listening behaviours

A summary of poor listening behaviours is shown in **Exhibit 8.14**.

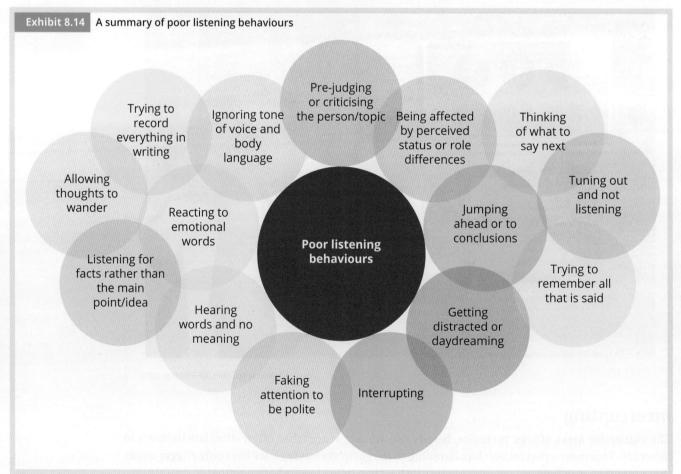

Exhibit 8.14 A summary of poor listening behaviours

- Trying to record everything in writing
- Ignoring tone of voice and body language
- Pre-judging or criticising the person/topic
- Being affected by perceived status or role differences
- Thinking of what to say next
- Allowing thoughts to wander
- Reacting to emotional words
- Tuning out and not listening
- Jumping ahead or to conclusions
- Listening for facts rather than the main point/idea
- Poor listening behaviours
- Trying to remember all that is said
- Hearing words and no meaning
- Getting distracted or daydreaming
- Faking attention to be polite
- Interrupting

Reflection question: Consider your own listening habits. Are there particular situations, topics or speakers where you find it difficult to concentrate and listen? How do these affect your listening behaviour? What are some of the consequences for both the listener and the speaker?

Improving listening skills

As with other ways of communicating, our involvement in listening is influenced by the purpose of the communication. Are we listening for information, or will we be required to make a calculated judgement? Is there an important personal reason or responsibility to listen carefully? Sometimes it is exceedingly important for us to grasp the full meaning of the material the speaker is communicating. Whatever the purpose, improving listening skills will help us to be better communicators. The suggestions in the following sections should help you become a better listener.

Be prepared to listen

Since listening requires physical energy, we need to be prepared both mentally and physically to listen efficiently. We all need sufficient rest and sleep in order to function properly, so that we can participate more effectively and be more involved. In most Western cultural contexts, we need to show a speaker that we are attentive by establishing eye contact and maintaining alert posture and facial expression. Such expressions of interest on our part will have a positive impact on speakers and will enable them to express themselves even more effectively.

Good listeners attempt to minimise distractions by trying to organise their physical environment to be conducive to hearing. This may mean closing doors or windows or moving to a quiet room. It may mean recording or diverting all incoming telephone calls or putting the phone on silent. It could also mean arriving early at a popular lecture to get a front-row seat.

Mental distractions also warrant some attention if we are striving to be effective listeners. It is important to develop the ability to place total concentration on one subject for a period of time. This is a discipline of mind that we can develop with practice.

Listen with an open mind

Condemning a topic as boring will prevent us from gaining anything at all from the communication. To listen efficiently, we need to look for ideas that have some relevance or even minor interest for us, so that we gain something from the communication exchange. All of us would benefit from trying to learn something from each new experience.

Good listening does not imply that we need to agree to or accept what is communicated. However, it does means that we need to try to understand ideas, even if they are alien to us. Practising tolerance towards others will probably also enable us to present our ideas without interruption.

A message is composed of both words and feelings. Effective listeners learn to be in control of their emotions and recognise when prejudice and bias are influencing their perception of the situation. They are also aware of speakers who attempt to stimulate their emotions or arouse their passions, and can discern conflicting messages, such as when someone says they are not nervous but with a hesitant tone of voice. Good listeners are also patient; they try to hear the whole message before commenting or questioning.

Listen with empathy

Another effective listening technique is to put yourself in the speaker's shoes, or listening with **empathy**. When we try to see a situation from someone else's point of view, or feel their hurt or pride, we can come closer to sharing their meaning. We can also paraphrase the speaker's ideas by putting them into our own words to check that we have received the meaning intended. Speakers often have difficulty expressing strong emotions, and a good listener will interpret the speaker's signals and show genuine interest in understanding both the speaker's ideas and feelings.

Empathic listeners avoid making judgemental or dismissive remarks when a speaker is talking about a concern or a problem. In other words, they focus their attention on the speaker, not on themselves or on

Empathy
The ability to understand another person's thoughts and feelings in a situation from their point of view rather than your own.

the direction they would like the conversation to take. Twelve empathy blockers – that is, communications that do not build trust and discourage the speaker from opening up – have been identified and are shown in Exhibit 8.15 (Bolton, 2003). Imagine how you would feel if you expressed a concern and your listener responded with any of these empathy blockers.

Exhibit 8.15	Empathy blockers

Empathy blocker	Examples
Ordering	'Make sure you discuss it with her.' 'This is what to do.'
Warning	'If you do that you won't succeed.' 'You'll regret it if you do that.'
Moralising	'You should contact him more.' 'You ought to get up earlier.'
Advising	'If I were you, I'd apply.' 'Try to organise your time better.'
Arguing logically	'There are many reasons to consider; let's work through them.' 'If you look at the facts you can see that you can't do it now.'
Judging	'You made a real mess of it, didn't you?' 'At last you got it right.'
Praising evaluatively	'You are always such a good team member.' 'You did well, didn't you?'
Name calling	'You union reps are all alike.' 'Another typical management view.'
Diagnosing	'You're just saying that to impress me.' 'What you really mean is that you are afraid of the consequences.'
Reassuring	'You'll be all right.' 'It will be OK, you'll see.'
Interrogating	'Why did you keep doing it?' 'Tell me exactly what you said.'
Distracting	'I've got something else to tell you.' 'That reminds me of another issue.'

Source: Based on R. Bolton (2003). *People skills: How to assert yourself, listen to others, and resolve conflicts* (Rev. ed.). Simon & Schuster.

Instead of empathy blockers, you can use door openers or encouragers, such as 'Would you like to talk about it?' Open questions like 'What ... ?', 'When ... ?', 'Where ... ?' and 'How ... ?' can encourage speakers to expand on issues and explore their ideas and feelings about concerns and problems that may be bothering them. Check your understanding of how to apply empathic listening responses in the following case study, which is based in a workplace.

 CASE STUDY 8.3   Empathic listening in the project team

Tuan is part of a project team and has been assigned the task of collecting the data needed for the next stage and then producing a report. After four weeks of hard work, including unpaid overtime that Tuan felt was needed, Tuan presented the completed report to Lee, the team leader. Prior to the next meeting of the team, Lee said to Tuan, 'I received your report. We'll be using the data you found at the next meeting. You've given a reasonable summary of what we need.' Tuan felt disappointed and let down by Lee's response. The report had taken a great deal of time and effort and Tuan had been hoping that Lee would be very impressed by the quality of the work. Tuan also began to feel resentful about the unpaid overtime.

Tuan spoke separately to four colleagues about these thoughts and feelings. This is what he said to each of them:

You know that report for the new project that I have been working on? It took me four weeks to finish it, including overtime that I wasn't paid for. Well, Lee said I had given only a reasonable summary of the data. I don't know how to improve it and I don't think that I am getting enough credit for the hard work I have done. Perhaps I should be assigned to another project.

Pat's response:

That's not so terrible. You should expect your work to be just up to standard at first. Lee is a very good team leader. You can't expect more than that. You'll get valuable experience in that project team.

Kali's response:

Why don't you ask Lee how to improve your presentation of the data? I'm sure you can sort it out together.

Kerry's response:

You should be pleased that Lee said your summary was reasonable. Others had to do their reports again because they were off track, and one team member was asked to fix up the data in the monthly report, which involved a lot of extra work.

Sam's response:

Sounds like you're saying that Lee said that your summary was OK but you're not happy about it? Seems like you're feeling disappointed that you haven't received more recognition for all the work you did on it and that you're also concerned about your ability to contribute to the team.

Discussion

Consider the responses made by Tuan's four colleagues:

1 How would Tuan think and feel after hearing each response?

2 Are any of the responses identifiable as an 'empathy blocker'?

3 Did any of the responses encourage further exploration of meaningful communication on the issues and feelings involved.

After you have discussed this case study, refer to the 'Comments on case studies' section at the end of the text.

Active listening

Listening isn't an easy task, especially if the material is difficult or the speaker's accent is unfamiliar to you, making it difficult to understand the words. However, like any physical and mental activity, listening can be improved with practice and employing **active listening**. Try to concentrate on the main ideas and pay attention to their development, and look for patterns and organisation in the way information is presented. You should also be conscious that some listening situations will require you to prepare for them by reading or viewing a video or film. If we are more informed about matters, we will be able to get greater benefit from listening to a talk on that subject.

Good listening improves our ability to understand and remember information. One way of accomplishing this is to take brief, meaningful notes when possible. Note taking does not necessarily mean writing down information word for word; it may involve figures, statistics or statements, or just a list of headings and points. It will depend on the nature and purpose of the information. Whatever the situation, note taking skills are very useful, especially if they are flexible and accurate.

Finally, an effective listener is aware that communication is a two-way process. Unless a listener accepts a share of the responsibility for its success, communication is doomed to fail.

Active listening
The practice of preparing to listen, observing what verbal and non-verbal messages are being sent, and then providing appropriate feedback to show attentiveness to the message being presented. Active listening is listening on purpose.

Types of listening

Different listening behaviour is appropriate for different situations, including listening for analysis, comprehension or relaxation. Some listening activity requires a great deal of listener involvement in terms of concentration, whereas other kinds of listening require minimal effort.

Listening for analysis

Listening to something for the purpose of evaluation and analysis requires a great deal of concentration. This kind of listening occurs in board meetings, formal discussions, sales presentations or conferences, in which listeners are assessing the value and credibility of the information being communicated. This requires critical and analytical skills to recognise and assess the quality of facts, inferences, assumptions and observations being communicated in order to arrive at valid conclusions of our own.

Listening for comprehension

Sometimes we listen only for the purpose of understanding and comprehending what is being communicated. Although we need to understand most things that we hear, some messages are more important to us than others. However, even if we do not need to evaluate or analyse all interpersonal oral communication, we should show empathy and understanding so that communication can continue.

People in all sorts of relationships should listen carefully to one another so that they can understand other people's beliefs and feelings.

Listening for relaxation

Listening for the purpose of relaxation and pleasure requires less involvement because it is a part of our everyday experience. In this type of listening we are not trying to remember or understand in an analytical way. Some people are very gifted in the art of pleasant conversation, and it is very relaxing and enjoyable to listen and respond to them. Light music also forms an important part of this type of listening and is capable of creating moods and stirring feelings. Background music in lifts, offices, shops and factories is there for mood-creating purposes. Some people listen for relaxation and enjoyment to the sound of the radio while at home or driving a car, but do not need to listen attentively to the words being communicated.

Listening effort

In all kinds of listening, a listener must know the purpose of listening to the message being communicated. In this way we can focus on what we need to gain from information communicated orally. When we listen to a speech or lecture, there is often a need to shift from one level of concentration and intensity to something less demanding, depending on the relevance of the messages we are hearing.

How and when we listen will affect our understanding of experiences with people and events. Effective listening techniques can remove barriers in communication and increase our knowledge and comprehension. Our listening skills and techniques can always be developed and improved so that we can become better speakers and listeners in the process of communication. Consider the following case study as it relates to listening in an educational setting.

CASE STUDY 8.4 Listening in the classroom

Kim is a first-year university student and is excited at the prospect of entering an 'adult learning environment' where teachers don't check on you every minute of the day and don't contact your parents if your assignment is late. As a reward for graduating high school, her parents even bought her a brand new laptop to use at university. She takes it to uni every day and is excited to find that on campus, Wi-Fi allows her to surf the net, update her social media status and chat with friends. She can even respond to text messages in class as long as she remembers to put her phone on silent. Kim also likes the freedom that if you miss a class, most subjects have an online learning site where the lecturers post podcasts of their lectures for students who are not able to attend. However, the amount of information that you are expected to remember is very daunting.

When Kim receives the results of her first assignment, she is very disappointed. The tutor has commented that Kim obviously did not follow the instructions that were given in the lecture and has not read the required reading, which was mentioned in the tutorial. She is asked to revise and resubmit her assignment.

When she makes an appointment to discuss her grade, her tutor asks if she was attending lectures. Most of the time, she says, but it's often hard to get there for a 9 a.m. class when she has to travel quite a distance. And besides, plenty of others don't bother either. When she has made it on time, she finds that it is often more interesting to check her email and chat online than follow the lecture, especially when the theory seems so dry and she can't see the relevance ... and besides she can always listen to it later. The lecturer also has a European accent and some irritating mannerisms that Kim finds distracting. She prefers to sit up the back of the lecture theatre but finds that other students carry on conversations around her and the low hum of these makes listening even harder.

Kim complains that the assignment instructions were not clearly explained, but the tutor responds that it if Kim was unsure, she should have asked for clarification, and she should have checked the sample assignment that the lecturer had provided online. What example? And how can she ask when she doesn't even remember the lecturer's name?

Shutterstock.com/Ground Picture

Kim goes away to revise her assignment, thinking that she needs to consider her listening behaviour.

Discussion

1 What were some of the listening barriers that Kim experienced?

2 How could Kim have been a more effective listener?

3 What could the university have done to help students like Kim become more effective listeners?

4 What are your own experiences of similar situations? How was your listening affected? What have you learnt about listening from these experiences?

5 Are technologies such as mobile phones and laptop computers in classrooms a help or a hindrance to your own ability to listen?

After you have discussed this case study, refer to the 'Comments on case studies' section at the end of the text.

Navigating 'the human moment': technology and interpersonal communication

A century ago, the world was remade. We synchronised the clocks for the sake of railway schedules, we discovered, through art and literature, new ways to perceive time; the automobile reshaped our notions of distance and adjacency. Now our world is being reshaped again, as a result of computing and communications technology.

Source: Joy (2000)

In the aforementioned quote, American computer scientist and co-founder of Sun Microsystems Bill Joy warns against blind reliance on technologies to replace face-to-face human interaction. This echoes famous Canadian communication theorist Marshall McLuhan (1964) whose seminal work *Understanding Media* coined the famous phrase 'the medium is the message'.

Prior to Joy's warning, the study of interpersonal communication has almost exclusively looked at humans who have met face-to-face and in real time. However, there is increasing ubiquity of ever more diverse forms of mediated communication in both our work and private lives. And research is indicating that technologies, be it smartphones, email or social media platforms, are having a significant impact not only on the manner of communication, but also on the nature of interpersonal relationships themselves (Miguel, 2018; Turkle, 1996, 2017).

An important point to consider, however, is the extent to which these technologies and the way people use them, *alter* both the nature of the communication process and the behaviours of the parties to the communication process, rather than becoming merely another medium of communication. For example, has our preference for email over face-to-face communication changed how we communicate with co-workers in terms of the language we use, the way we interact, the immediacy of communication, our expectation of response time, and how socially connected we feel? It may be that alternative mediated forms of communication, as well as ordinary face-to-face meetings, are equally valid and should be considered for the benefits, as well as the problems, that a particular medium or modality create.

While Chapter 5 examines the specifics of the increasingly broad range of technologically mediated forms of communication, the following sections draw attention to research and perspectives about how these technologies may impact on aspects of interpersonal communication discussed in this chapter.

The importance of 'the human moment'

Chapter 5 outlines three important theories of mediated communication: social presence theory (Short et al., 1976), the social identity model of deindividuation (SIDE; Lea & Spears, 1991), and the hyperpersonal model of interpersonal communication (Walther, 1996). The key assertion of these theories is that the effect of a channel or medium of communication is created by the degree to which it affords its users social presence, which refers to a communicator's sense of awareness of the presence or 'humanness' of the person or people with whom they are interacting (Short et al., 1976).

A large part of social presence is communicated non-verbally, and this is important for the process by which people come to know and think about others, their characteristics, qualities and inner states – in other words, the process of developing empathy or EI. Other researchers have observed that as new communication technologies evolve, there are an increasingly wider range of variables that need to be considered when measuring social presence and its importance (Lowenthal, 2017; Morris, 2020).

So how important is actual physical presence to the state of an interpersonal relationship? In the early days of the uptake of mediated forms of communication, psychologist Edward M. Hallowell (1999) wrote that in his professional practice, he regularly treated executives with anxiety disorders, much of it resulting from what he referred to as the declining 'human moment'. As technologies have become more advanced, despite being more connected with our co-workers via digital means (see Exhibit 8.16), we are also increasingly isolated from them. Hallowell gave the following example:

> At an electronics company, a talented brand manager is increasingly alienated. The problem started when his division head didn't return a phone call for several days. She said she never got the message. Then the brand manager noticed that he hadn't been invited to an important meeting with a new advertising agency. 'What's wrong with my performance?' he wonders. The man wants to raise the question with the division manager, but the opportunity never seems to arise. All their communication is by … email or voicemail, which they exchanged often. But they almost never meet. For one thing, their offices are 50 miles apart, and for another, both of them are frequently on the road. During the rare moments when they do see each other in person – on the run in a corridor or in the parking lot at corporate headquarters – it is usually inappropriate to discuss complex matters. And so, the issues between them smoulder.
>
> Source: Hallowell (1999), p. 1

Hallowell related stories of businesspeople who dealt firsthand with misunderstandings caused by an over-reliance on communication technologies – an email message misconstrued, an email forwarded to the wrong person, and someone taking offence because they were not included in an email circulation list. Was it an accident? While seemingly minor, these misunderstandings collectively resulted in what Hallowell termed 'toxic worry', which over time takes a larger toll on the individual and the organisation in the form of stress, anxiety, depression and loss of productivity. Co-workers, he said, can lose their sense of cohesiveness and connection, and the culture of the organisation can become dysfunctional.

Exhibit 8.16 An increase in digital presence has come at a cost of time spent in physical presence

Shutterstock.com/Andrey_Popov

Sherry Turkle (2017), a researcher who has long studied the impact of technologies on people's sense of identity and how they view the world, notes in her book *Alone Together* that:

> Online connections were first conceived as a substitute for face-to-face contact when the latter was for some reason impractical. Don't have time to a make a phone call? Shoot off a text message. But very quickly, the text message became the connection of choice. We discovered a network – the world of connectivity – to be uniquely suited to the overworked and overscheduled life it makes possible. And now we look to the network to defend us against loneliness even as we use it to control the intensity of our connections. Technology makes it easy to communicate when we wish and to disengage at will.
>
> Source: Turkle (2017), p. 13

Turkle (2015) further argues that the emerging preference for text messages over face-to-face or even phone conversations, even in the most personal and intimate contexts, is spawned by the need to feel in full control of our words and emotions, and to avoid the consequences of spontaneity, which may include uncomfortable silences or unmanageable or unintended conflicts. Digital conversations are often preferred because they are 'low risk' – messages can be edited before being sent to ensure that they are 'right'. The absence of physical proximity with the message recipients also means that the writer is somewhat sheltered from any direct emotional blowback. However, while this may be a convenient short-term solution, she asserts that it has longer term implications for the development of both our individual communication competencies as well as our psychological wellbeing. She writes:

> This new mediated life has gotten us into trouble. Face-to-face conversation is the most human – and humanising – thing we do. Fully present to one another, we learn to listen. It's where we develop the capacity for empathy. It's where we enjoy the experience of being heard, of being understood. ... conversation advances self-reflection ... But these days we find ways around conversation. We hide from each other even as we're constantly connected ...
>
> Source: Turkle (2017), pp. 3–4

So, it seems that the value of direct conversations for self-esteem, enhancing and nurturing relationships, developing of conflict management skills, and creative thinking and reflection, should not be underestimated.

The good, the bad and the ugly of 'digital connectedness'

While the negative impacts of digital interaction have long been the subject of heated media debate and a source of angst for concerned parents in particular, there is a developing body of research, especially in the wake of the extended lockdowns during the COVID-19 pandemic, which is uncovering a range of unexpected impacts on interpersonal communication. Working relationships using mediated communication (e.g., virtual teams) are rapidly expanding in the workplace and social sphere even beyond the 'work from home' mandates.

The presumed lack of physical and social contextual cues can also lead to positive effects. Communicators can gain greater anonymity, since gender, race, age, appearance and indicators of status, position and power are not automatically evident. Mediated communication encourages users to try out different personas and allows shy individuals to gain confidence (see **Exhibit 8.17**). Consequently, in group situations, participation and satisfaction levels appear to be more equitable than in face-to-face settings (McQuillen, 2003).

| Exhibit 8.17 | Mediated communication affords communicators greater anonymity and allows shy individuals to gain confidence |

Shutterstock.com/DedMityay

Some researchers see this as a 'democratising' effect. Others go further and claim that computer mediation makes it difficult for people to dominate and impose their views on others, so women and minorities have a much better chance to contribute meaningfully. The absence of one's physical being (looks, gender, race), which may unintentionally impact on behaviours and perceptions during a face-to-face interaction, may be a positive as meaning becomes more a matter of verbal expression, something which is more likely to be subject to conscious editing (McQuillen, 2003).

The early phase of the COVID-19 pandemic increased the impetus for using technology in ways that both enabled and enhanced our relationships. Teaching, medical consultations, gym sessions, and even funerals and family gatherings had to adapt to the online environment in innovative ways. However, research found that while online connections protected people from psychological distress caused by social isolation in lockdown, the impact did not have a lasting effect as the pandemic wore on (Marinucci et al., 2022).

Even before COVID-19, people met online via social media, dating apps or chat groups. They found friends, formed relationships and even fell in love and got married. As with any new medium, concerns were raised about the depth and sincerity of relationships initiated and evolved online as users made judgements of their online friends on the basis of either limited or misleading information, possibly creating a situation where a partner is not being seen for who they actually are, but for who the other hopes or wants them to be (Walther, 2007).

In the future, new software may be developed that will further facilitate such relationships. Technologies such as virtual reality may lead not only to virtual meeting places, virtual dates and virtual bedrooms, but even to virtual therapists for when a personal relationship breaks up. Some researchers point out that while there are costs associated with online relating, the benefits should not be ignored, and for those who are not socially confident, the internet can be an empowering medium (Whitty & McLaughlan, 2007). For adolescents, especially for those who feel alienated from their parents, the internet can be a valuable safety valve, and can be linked to positive self-esteem and psychological wellbeing (Valkenburg & Peter, 2007). More recently, there have been calls for a more nuanced assessment and distinctions of the relative harms and benefits of social networking sites, depending on the extent to which they are being used actively to make meaningful social connections or passively to pass the time (Clark et al., 2018; Roberts & David, 2022).

Finally, it has been proposed that the sheer volume of information to which we now have access and the ease with which we can be connected is becoming a burden, and this may ultimately impact on the quality of our interpersonal relationships. There is a phenomenon that has been referred to as the 'burden of digital connectedness' (Power, 2011), and is posited to have led to changes not only in our communicative behaviours but also our expectations about other people's communications. In his book *Hamlet's Blackberry*, William Power (2011) observed that:

> Even as the number of people we're connected to rises, so does the frequency and pace of our communications … Today we're in touch by the hour, the minute … It wasn't so long ago that people who received two or three hundred emails a day were considered outrageously busy, figures of pity. Now they're mainstream … The goal is no longer to be 'in touch' but to erase the possibility of ever being out of touch. To merge, to live simultaneously with everyone, sharing every moment, every perception, thought, and action via our screens.
>
> Source: Power (2011), p. 15

These and many other perspectives must continue to be considered in any study of interpersonal communication and measurement of communication competence. From the perspective of our collective experiences during the COVID-19 pandemic lockdowns, consider the questions raised in the following case study.

 CASE STUDY 8.5   Gaming fosters social connection at a time of physical distance

In 2020, as the COVID-19 pandemic seemed never ending, the World Health Organization (WHO) announced its support of gaming as a way of escaping the daily reality of tragic news stories. The following excerpts from a story in *The Conversation* look at this shift in view regarding gaming.

> It wasn't long ago video games were still being blamed for school shootings and real-world violence without evidence … The historical narrative around gamers describes them as anti-social, the lone teenage boy playing in the basement, perched on pizza boxes in the dark, dimly outlined by the glow of the screen.
>
> Now suddenly, video games have become a darling of shelter-in-place and stay-at-home orders. They are a form of social engagement that allow humans to safely follow our instincts to gather together at a time of anxiety. They allow us moments of escape and a sense of agency when we feel we have none [an ability to be a hero or save the world. To experiment and strategise solutions. They allow us to explore, to compete, to solve].
>
> During COVID-19, people aren't playing alone – they are using games to come together. [Multiplayer modes in games like Minecraft and Call of Duty are giving some parents a chance to bond with family members.]
>
> COVID-19 may be the turning point when the world realises playing video games is potentially a form of empowerment that brings people together to solve real world problems. It may be a critical moment when we reflect on the importance of play.
>
> Source: A. M. Phelps (2020, April 14). Gaming fosters social connection at a time of physical distance. Originally published on *The Conversation*.

Discussion

1 Do you agree with the argument Phelps is making that there are positive impacts for interpersonal relationships available via online gaming?

2 From some of the other research cited previously in this chapter, what benefits might online gaming have for those who are isolated?

3 What are the negatives of online gaming for interpersonal relationships?

After you have discussed this case study, refer to the 'Comments on case studies' section at the end of the text.

Summary

As we have seen in this chapter, intrapersonal communication, or self-talk, refers to our private communication with ourselves. Your self-talk affects your attitude towards other people and events, as well as the way you relate to the world. Positive thoughts are usually accompanied by more confident body language that may communicate commitment and enthusiasm.

Interpersonal communication is communication that takes place between people, and in a university or the workplace this can involve communicating face-to-face or via computers, and with other people alone or in teams. Participants need to be flexible communicators, able to apply a range of communication strategies to solve problems and meet people's needs. Effective interpersonal skills help you to give and receive feedback, handle conflicts and complaints, and express feelings honestly and appropriately.

Through conversation you can reveal your thoughts and feelings to build closer, more trusting relationships with others. Take into consideration the level of the relationship (from distant or superficial to more intimate) when you are deciding what to disclose, and watch for signals from others about how they wish to relate to you. In conversation, use 'I' statements to express your opinions, decisions and ideas, and listen to others to share appropriate information about each other. Revealing your thoughts and feelings to others generally builds closer relationships and encourages reciprocal disclosures. Self-disclosure is influenced by culture and usually occurs incrementally in a valued relationship.

Communication competence refers both to having an adequate knowledge of the principles of human communication and to the ability to perform appropriately in a variety of communication settings, taking a wide range of factors into account. Competent communicators establish credibility by being sensitive to cultural values concerning correct behaviours and preferred ways of relating. In Western studies, for example, high credibility has been linked to expertise, trustworthiness and dynamism.

Emotional intelligence refers to the ability to both understand and respond to our own emotions and how they influence others, but also to recognise how to manage these emotions and feelings so that they can be communicated appropriately and effectively.

Effective interpersonal communication in many Australian contexts is facilitated by openness, empathy and supportiveness, equality, confidence, immediacy, interaction management, self-monitoring, expressiveness and assertiveness. *Assertiveness* refers to the ability to confront issues in a straightforward manner, to express your thoughts and feelings appropriately, to listen receptively to the needs of others and to balance standing up for your rights with your responsibilities. Three-part 'I' messages are a way of stating your needs and what is important to you. These 'I' messages mention the specific behaviour that is prompting the message, your specific feelings and the tangible effects on you. Words should be chosen that are describing, not blaming. In many sociocultural contexts, assertive responses can be used effectively to enhance self-esteem and build relationships when replying to compliments, making requests and giving and responding to negative feedback or criticism. There should be less defensiveness and uncertainty between people in communication interactions when assertiveness is used appropriately to express thoughts, feelings and needs.

Listening can be defined as meaningful, attentive hearing. We listen ineffectively when we assume the topic will be boring, allow the speaker's personality or mannerisms to overpower the message, fail to concentrate, comprehend poorly or listen passively. Listening skills can be improved by establishing the right physical conditions, by adopting an open mind, by empathising with the speaker and by listening actively. Different listening behaviour is appropriate for different situations. Analysis needs concentrated listening; relaxed conversation or background music can make listening enjoyable. Listeners need to know the purpose of their listening in order to focus using the correct level of effort.

Mediated communication, although lacking the presence of the five senses used in face-to-face interpersonal communication, can be more democratic because of its anonymity and can lead to strong socioemotional relationships. People's satisfaction with online relationships, whether romantic or at work, appears to be influenced by communication strategies that promote openness, trust and intimacy, and by being willing to spend time using mediated communication. Excessive reliance on or use of mediated communication has its downsides – there are concerns about diminishing empathy, lack of genuine connections and the impact of the sheer volume of interactions on our lives.

STUDY TOOLS

DISCUSSION QUESTIONS AND GROUP ACTIVITIES

For discussion topics and activities in addition to those that follow, please refer to the case studies presented throughout this chapter.

1   Discuss the following questions concerning communication competence at university or in the workplace:
   a   What does communication competence mean in relation to your current or future role?
   b   What strategies and support do you need to practise communication competence?

2   Complete the assertiveness questionnaire (see pp. 223–224), score yourself and discuss your results with a partner.

3   Harika and Lee both live near each other and are studying at the same university. Harika is very interested in a new student club and in persuading other students to join it. Lee is very busy with assignments and is not interested in joining a club. One afternoon they stop to chat near a train station. Harika says, 'I thought you might be interested in joining the new student club. How about coming to a meeting next Tuesday at 10 a.m.?' Three possible types of responses that Lee could make follow. Read them and then answer the following:
   a   What are the possible outcomes of each type of response to Harika's request?
   b   What are the likely long-term effects on the relationship between the two people both at university and socially?
   i   *Passive/submissive response:*
   Lee: (lying) I'm not free to come at 10 a.m. I'm sorry.
   Harika: Can I contact you after the meeting and tell you what happened?
   Lee: Oh, all right.
   ii   *Aggressive response:*
   Lee: The last thing I need right now is to join a club – they're just a waste of time!
   iii   *Assertive response:*
   Lee: I'm very busy on assignments at the moment and I'm really not interested in joining a club. Maybe I can help in some other way when things settle down.

4   Examine the hypothetical situations listed below and then either:
   •   write passive/submissive, aggressive and assertive responses for each of the situations and check your responses with another person; or
   •   form into groups of three, choose one of the situations, write passive/submissive, aggressive and assertive responses for it and present or role-play your responses to the rest of the class.
   a   A team member has borrowed one of the team's procedure manuals and has not returned it for two weeks.
   b   Your manager says something about your work that you feel is unfair.
   c   A colleague is continually late for appointments with you.
   d   A colleague repeatedly drops by to chat when you are very busy.
   e   You are told by a client that there have been delays in the delivery of your company's products.
   f   A team member is not doing their fair share of the work.
   g   The people in the room next door are talking loudly, the walls are thin and the noise they are making is disturbing your meeting.
   h   You have used your credit card to pay for a farewell gift for a previous team member on behalf of all your colleagues. The bill has now arrived, and your colleagues have not asked about how they can reimburse you.
   i   A product that you purchased yesterday is defective and you still have the receipt.

5   Choose one of the situations in question 4, or create a situation of your own, and write a three-part 'I' assertive message. Check the message with a partner. Is the 'I' assertive message specific and non-threatening?

6   Working in subgroups of three or four people, use the five types of assertive responses listed below to devise alternative assertive responses to the following situation. Present your responses to the whole class.
    You have been extremely busy working on a complex project and have not been able to meet your colleagues for lunch or to socialise. One day a colleague, whom you respect and like, says to you, 'You never seem to have time to come and talk things over with the rest of us'.
    a   Accept the criticism.
    b   Disagree with the criticism.
    c   Set the limits with the person who is criticising you.
    d   'Fog' away the criticism.
    e   Delay your response.
    If you have any other examples/situations that you would like to discuss in your subgroup, outline the specific issues and context, then develop alternative assertive responses for dealing with these issues.

7   Imagine that you are the listener in the situations that follow. What factors would determine the way in which you would be listening on these occasions?
    a   You are a student in a large lecture and have no previous experience with the content of this subject, which includes a lot of technical language.
    b   You arrive at a club meeting and in a short time you meet a very interesting, charming and attractive person. You find them very appealing, and they also decide to spend most of their time talking to you.
    c   You are a consultant working on a telephone help desk for computer support and answer a call. The caller immediately launches into a complaint about their computer not working properly.
    d   This is your first day on the job at an electronics factory. The supervisor takes you aside to explain about the work.
    e   A workmate who has been seeking promotion has just heard that the promotion has been given to another colleague and has come to tell you about it.
    f   You are a parent who has been preparing the children's dinner when you have to pause to open the door. Outside is a sales representative who immediately launches into a promotional speech for a floor-cleaning product being sold at a special price.
    g   A relative of one of your closest friends has just died from a drug overdose. You are returning home after having visited the family and turn on the car radio. By coincidence you find yourself listening to a program about drug addiction.

8   Try the following active listening exercise. Work in subgroups of three people acting as speaker, listener and observer. The observer has a sheet listing things to look for and will observe the speaker, who is explaining a topic of interest to the listener. The speaker talks about a topic they are interested in or concerned about for two to three minutes. The listener practises active listening by using:
    •   attentive body language and eye contact
    •   paraphrasing and clarifying
    •   reflecting feelings.
    At the end of the speaker's message the observer will give feedback to the listener. Then, rotate the roles.
    Final discussion
    –   Did the speakers think that they were really listened to? Why or why not?
    –   Were the speakers ever diverted from what they were about to say? Why or why not?
    –   Were the listeners' tasks easy or difficult? Why or why not?
    –   What have the listeners learnt from the exercise?
    –   In the observers' opinions, did the listeners summarise accurately?
    –   How did you feel in each of these roles?

Observer's guidelines
Observe the listener and tick each time you observe the following:

Maintained eye contact much of the time	☐
Used attentive body language	☐
Used encouraging words/phrases ('I see', 'Uh-huh', 'Yes', 'Really', etc.)	☐
Used closed questions	☐
Used open questions	☐
Used paraphrase techniques	☐
Reflected the speaker's feelings	☐
Summarised at various points	☐

Comment on the effectiveness of these techniques

WEBSITES

Conflict Resolution Network – various useful links and resources https://www.crnhq.org

Journal of Computer-Mediated Communication https://onlinelibrary.wiley.com/journal/10836101

Management Library – How to improve your listening skills https://management.org/communicationsskills/listening-skills.htm

REFERENCES

Alberti, R., & Emmons, M. (2017). *Your perfect right: Assertiveness and equality in your life and relationships*. (10th ed.). New Harbinger Publications.

Altman, I., & Taylor, D. (1973). *Social penetration: The development of interpersonal relationships*. St Martin's Press.

Bolton, R. (2003). *People skills: How to assert yourself, listen to others, and resolve conflicts* (Rev. ed.). Simon & Schuster.

Brinthaupt, T. M., Hein, M. B., & Kramer, T. E. (2009). The self-talk scale: Development, factor analysis, and validation. *Journal of Personality Assessment, 91*(1), 82–92. https://doi.org/10.1080/00223890802484498

Brownell, J. (1996). *Listening: Attitudes, principles, and skills*. Allyn & Bacon.

Buffalmano, L. (n.d.). The 4 communication styles: Description & examples. ThePowerMoves.com

Butler, P. (2011). *Self-assertion for women: A new edition*. Nabu Press.

Clark, J. L., Algoe, S. B., & Green, M. C. (2018). Social network sites and well-being: The role of social connection. *Current Directions in Psychological Science, 27*(1), 32–37. https://doi.org/10.1177/0963721417730833

Dare, F. (2009). *The high cost of nurses' communication challenges*. Cisco Internet Business Solutions Groups https://www.cisco.com/c/dam/en_us/solutions/industries/docs/healthcare/Nurses_Survey_Report.pdf

de Bono, E. (2000). *Six thinking hats*. Penguin.

Duncalfe, J. (1996). *Making connections: Implications for teachers of interpersonal communication of some Māori perspectives on good communication*. Paper presented at Australian and New Zealand Communication Association (ANZCA) Conference, QUT, Brisbane, July 1996.

Goleman, D. (2001). Emotional intelligence: Issues in paradigm building. In C. Cherniss & D. Goleman (Eds.), *The emotionally intelligent workplace*. http://www.eiconsortium.org/pdf/emotional_intelligence_paradigm_building.pdf

Goulston, M. (2015). *Just listen: Discover the secret to getting through to absolutely anyone*. Amacom.

Guffey, M. E., & Loewy, D. (2014). *Business communication: Process and product*. Cengage Learning.

Hallowell, E. M. (1999). The human moment at work, *Harvard Business Review 77*, 58–69. https://hbr.org/1999/01/the-human-moment-at-work

Hargie, O. (Ed.). (2017). *Skilled interpersonal communication: Research, theory and practice*. (6th ed.). Routledge.

Herrity, J. (2023). Interpersonal skills: Definitions, examples and how to improve. Indeed.

Hurtig, R. R., Alper, R. M., & Berkowitz, B. (2018). The cost of not addressing the communication barriers faced by hospitalized patients. *Perspectives of the ASHA Special Interest Groups, 3*(12), 99–112.

Ignatius, E., & Kokkonen, M. (2007). Factors contributing to verbal self-disclosure. *Nordic Psychology, 59*(4), 362–391. https://doi.org/10.1027/1901-2276.59.4.362

Joy, W. (2000, March 6). Design for the digital revolution: As computers change the world, we need to make sure the new world works for humans, *Fortune*. http://money.cnn.com/magazines/fortune/fortune_archive/2000/03/06/275229/index.htm

Kaye, M. (1994). *Communication management*. Prentice Hall.

Lea, M., & Spears, R. (1991). Computer-mediated communication, de-individuation and group decision-making. *International Journal of Man-Machine Studies, 34*(2), 283–301 https://doi.org/10.1016/0020-7373(91)90045-9

Lowenthal, P. R., & Snelson, C. (2017). In search of a better understanding of social presence: An investigation into how researchers define social presence. *Distance Education, 38*(2), 141–159. https://doi.org/10.1080/01587919.2017.1324727

Mackay, H. (1998). *The good listener: Better relationships through better communication*. Pan Macmillan.

Mackay, H. (2019, June 19). *The courage to listen*. Dumbo Feather. https://www.dumbofeather.com/articles/the-courage-of-attentive-listening/.

Marinucci, M., Pancani, L., Aureli, N., & Riva, P. (2022). Online social connections as surrogates of face-to-face interactions: A longitudinal study under COVID-19 isolation. *Computers in Human Behavior, 128*, 107102. https://doi.org/10.1016/j.chb.2021.107102

McLean, S. (2012). *The basics of interpersonal communication* (2nd ed.). Pearson.

McLuhan, M. (1964). *Understanding media: The extension of man*. MIT Press.

McQuillen, J. (2003). The influence of technology on the initiation of interpersonal relationships *Education, 123*(3). 616–623.

Miguel, C. (2018). *Personal relationships and intimacy in the age of social media*. Palgrave Macmillan.

Morgan, K. (2022, July 28). 'Soft skills': The intangible qualities companies crave. *BBC*. https://www.bbc.com/worklife/article/20220727-soft-skills-the-intangible-qualities-companies-crave

Morris, M. E. (2020). Enhancing relationships through technology: Directions in parenting, caregiving, romantic partnerships, and clinical practice. *Dialogues in Clinical Neuroscience, 22*(2). 151–160, https://doi.org/10.31887/DCNS.2020.22.2/mmorris.

Phelps, A. M. (2020, April 14). Gaming fosters social connection at a time of physical distance. *The Conversation*.

Power, W. (2011). *Hamlet's Blackberry: Building a good life in the digital age*. Harper Perennial.

Robbins, S. P., & Hunsaker, P. L. (2012). *Training in interpersonal skills* (6th ed.). Pearson.

Roberts, J. A., & David, M. E. (2022). On the outside looking in: Social media intensity, social connection, and user well-being: The moderating role of passive social media use. *Canadian Journal of Behavioural Science/Revue canadienne des sciences du comportement*. Advance online publication. https://doi.org/10.1037/cbs0000323

Salovey, P., & Mayer, J. D. (1990). Emotional intelligence. *Imagination, Cognition and Personality, 9*(3), 185-211. https://doi.org/10.2190/DUGG-P24E-52WK-6CDG

Short, J. A., Williams, E., & Christie B. (1976). *The social psychology of telecommunications*. Wiley.

Simon, D., Grimes, M., & Roch, S. (2018). *Communication for Business Professionals*. eCampusOntario.

Simon, S. (1978). *Negative criticism*. Argus Communication.

Spitzberg, B. H. (2013). (Re)Introducing communication competence to the health professions. *Journal of Public Health Research, 2*(3). https://doi.org/10.4081/jphr.2013.e23

Turkle, S. (1996). *Life on the screen: Identity in the age of the internet*. Weidenfeld & Nicolson

Turkle, S. (2015). *Reclaiming conversation: The power of talk in the digital age*. Penguin Press.

Turkle, S. (2017). *Alone together: Why we expect more from technology and less from each other* (revised edition). Basic Books.

Valkenburg, P. M., & Peter, J. (2007). Online communication and adolescent well-being: Testing the stimulation versus the displacement hypothesis. *Journal of Computer-Mediated Communication, 12*(4), 1169–1182. https://doi.org/10.1111/j.1083-6101.2007.00368.x

Walther, J. B. (1996). Computer-mediated communication: Impersonal, interpersonal, and hyperpersonal interaction. *Communication research, 23*(1), 3–43. https://doi.org/10.1177/009365096023001001

Walther, J. B. (2007). Selective self-presentation in computer-mediated communication: Hyperpersonal dimensions of technology language, and cognition. *Computers in Human Behaviour, 23*(5), 2538–2557. https://doi.org/10.1016/j.chb.2006.05.002

Whitty, M. T., & McLaughlin, D. (2007). Online recreation: The relationship between loneliness, internet self-efficacy and the use of the internet for entertainment purposes. *Computers in Human Behaviour, 23*(3),1435–1448. https://doi.org/10.1016/j.chb.2005.05.003

Communicating in teams to achieve professional goals: group dynamics and negotiation

Learning objectives

After reading this chapter, you should be able to:

- define the meanings of groups and teams
- understand how groups and teams develop and the stages they go through
- recognise the value of diversity in groups and teams
- understand team building and its role in self-directed work teams
- comprehend how problem-solving and decision-making in self-directed work teams occur
- understand how to avoid groupthink
- explain the benefits of creativity in the professional group and team
- identify the key functions of a leader
- understand conflict within groups and how to use conflict management techniques
- identify negotiation strategies and understand how to negotiate solutions
- explain the functions of informal and formal meetings
- describe how teams can review their goals and progress.

Is group communication dead?

Apart from research around mediated groups/teams, there have been few major group communication 'discoveries' for decades. There are no major scholarly conferences and very few academic journals dedicated to group communication. So why should we need to study the behaviour of groups? The first reason is that most organisations function on a daily basis by using group meetings to make decisions. The second overlooked reason is to avoid the phenomenon of groupthink. 'Groupthink' (a term coined by Irving Janis in 1972) is the unconscious process of making bad group decisions because the group is so cohesive and sure of its ability to make the right decision, that it does not waver and does not consider alternatives. The results can be terrible and tragic. There are numerous famous examples of this phenomenon – the Bay of Pigs fiasco came about in the 1960s when US President Kennedy authorised the invasion of Cuba, the decision of Coca-Cola to launch 'New Coke' in 1985, Nokia's lack of vision in 2006, and the US invasion of Iraq to find non-existent weapons of mass destruction. By studying what constitutes good group communication, teams in all professions can successfully brainstorm and discuss issues and problems in order to make smart, creative and ethical decisions.

Introduction

As a student or employee, you will be part of many groups and teams charged with a variety of tasks and responsibilities. A group can be defined as:

> a number of people who know each other by name, share common interests, interact, influence each other, call themselves a group, achieve goals together and are regarded as a group by others.

Researchers have been studying the nature of **groups** for over 50 years, including the influence of groups on individual members and how to improve the experience of working in groups to achieve maximum productivity and member satisfaction. This chapter concentrates on how communication occurs in a group of between three and 15 members. Once the number exceeds 15, some of the characteristics of *groupness* are lost.

This chapter also aims to provide knowledge and skills to assist you to communicate effectively as a member of these groups and teams in order to make decisions, solve problems, manage meetings (both informal and formal), and resolve conflicts. We also explore how to be creative and what leadership means in these group and team contexts. Working collaboratively with others can often be satisfying and sometimes frustrating, or even both. In this chapter you will be introduced to insights and guidelines that explain the advantages and pitfalls of being part of a group or team, and how you can contribute in constructive ways through communicating appropriately. These suggestions should help you to be more satisfied with your experiences of working in groups and teams as a student and in the workplace.

Group
A number of people who know each other by name, share common interests, interact, influence each other, call themselves a group, achieve goals together and are regarded as a group by others.

Communicating in informal and formal groups

In the modern workplace, groups can either be informal or formal, in order to cope with complex technological and human systems. Informal groups arise in a spontaneous way (e.g., a group of students getting together to clarify an assignment, or a group of colleagues interested in having lunch together); while formal groups are established by some kind of authority (e.g., students allocated to a group by a lecturer to complete a group-based assignment, or a decision-making committee established by management for a specific purpose). Communicating effectively in groups requires applying interpersonal skills in a more complex context than that of one-to-one communication. In addition, new technologies allow groups to interact without the necessity of face-to-face meetings. Videoconferencing, using Microsoft Teams, Zoom or some other platform, now frequently replaces traditional face-to-face daily group meetings where everyone sits around a large table, and this adds another dimension to how groups communicate and the skills they need to employ.

Informal groups may be formed voluntarily and spontaneously by people with a common interest. At university, students might become friends and meet as a group after class to give each other support. In the workplace, informal groups might include a group that meets at lunchtime to discuss what has been happening at work, or a wine group that arranges tastings and bulk purchases for its members. There is potential for informal work groups to support and/or subvert organisational workplace culture and working conditions, depending on their communication networks and their ability to influence others inside and outside the organisation.

In contrast, formal groups are usually officially established by organisations, institutions or communities. Such groups focus on specific goals and represent a variety of interests of members who may be either elected or appointed. In this sense, a student club is a formal group, usually with a written constitution, and might receive funding from a body such as a student union. Similarly, a work team is a formal group sanctioned by an organisation and identified as part of the organisation's functional structure, usually with terms of reference or responsibilities. The work team will have designated accountability, and it must be productive in accordance with organisational goals and visions. Therefore, it is essential that the members of a work team know how to manage and develop their team-based way of working. In this chapter, we explore the communication interactions of groups that are small enough to be recognised as a distinct entity and in which the relations between the members are personal.

Groups as teams

Team
A group of people who perform interdependent tasks to work toward accomplishing a common mission or objective.

What kind of a group is a **team**? A group can become a team if the following characteristics are present: an identity (and possibly a designated name), an agreed goal, diversity of members' contributions, interconnected efforts of the members, shared leadership and responsibility, mutual support between members, commitment of members and a larger system in which the team operates (Lumsden et al., 2010). In other words, in a team there is a greater level of team spirit and interdependence of members striving together for a mutual goal than there is in a group. **Exhibit 9.1** shows the main differences between groups and teams

Exhibit 9.1	The differences between groups and teams	
	Group	**Team**
Size	Medium or large	Limited
Selection	Immaterial	Crucial
Leadership	Solo	Shared or rotating
Perception	Focus on leader	Mutual knowledge and understanding
Style	Convergence conformism	Role spread/co-ordination
Spirit	Togetherness/persecution of opponents	Dynamic interaction

Source: Adapted from V. Bird (2018). Groupthink and the importance of behavioural diversity. Belbin.
© Copyright Sabre Corporate Development and Belbin.

The constructive energy, or *synergy*, in effective teams can assist members to maintain their commitment and enthusiasm, so that the results of teamwork can be greater than the sum of what individual members could contribute if they worked on their own. All members need to understand how to participate to build a team, to manage conflicts within the team and to make the most appropriate team decisions (Hartnett, 2011; Hoover, 2005). Effective interpersonal communication is a key aspect of working in groups and teams productively.

> **Reflection question:** Make a list of how many groups and teams you have belonged to in the past and present. What are some of the main differences between these groups and teams?

Communication patterns in groups and teams

Groups and teams develop patterns of communication and norms (or standards) of behaviour for their members. It is important for groups and teams to have productive ways of relating both inside the group or team and with outsiders such as other groups/teams or stakeholders. Communication patterns in the group or team are determined by the way it is structured, the status and kinds of membership, the leadership style and the nature of the task facing the group or team. Five communication patterns commonly found in groups and teams are represented in **Exhibit 9.2**.

While the communication pattern of formal groups and teams, such as a management board, may be imposed by a set of meeting procedures, all groups and teams need effective communication patterns to accomplish the group or team task and support the members. In study groups at university or in work teams, an open, unstructured communication pattern, with all members contributing (like the all-channel communication pattern in **Exhibit 9.2**), should help in group or team problem-solving, even if these interactive communication

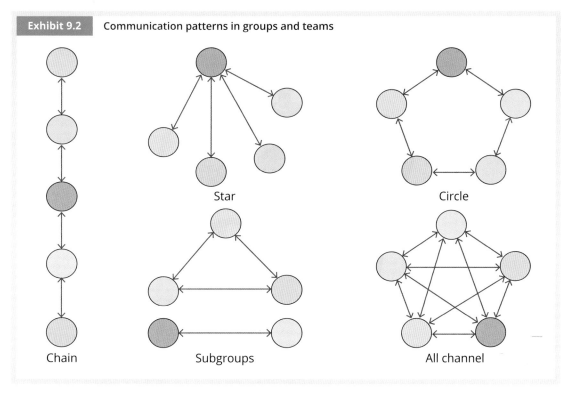

Exhibit 9.2 Communication patterns in groups and teams

Star

Circle

Chain

Subgroups

All channel

patterns take more time and effort. You can help your group or team to monitor the appropriateness of its communication patterns in line with the goals of the group or team and individual members.

Group development: group norms and the life of groups

According to researchers on group dynamics, most groups develop over time in predictable ways (Frey, 2002). Additionally, studies of communication in small groups have shown that groups typically sort out who is accepted in the group and how these members complement each other (Adams & Galanes, 2012). Such research has provided useful frameworks to alert us to potential blocks to group progress, as well as helpful communication interventions that can be used as the group develops or goes through the various stages. (See Jaques [2004] for a detailed comparison of a variety of group-development models in the literature.)

A variety of task and relationship issues are said to be characteristic of the early, middle and later life-stages of a group or team. According to Tuckman's (1965) seminal five-stage model of group development, there are five stages. These are illustrated in **Exhibit 9.3** and discussed further in **Exhibit 9.4**.

Using Tuckman's model of the stages of group development, you can be aware of, and possibly even predict, task and relationship issues, and concerns and problems that might arise in the group or team. You may then be able to assist the group or team to deal with any confusion and uncertainty and to overcome task or relationship blocks to progress.

Group norms

No matter what model is used to explain group development, groups and teams need strategies for maintaining progress and for establishing constructive norms of conduct. **Group norms** are social

Group norm
Social standards of behaviour used by a group's members to regulate the way they interact in the group or team, and serve as guidelines for the kinds of behaviour that are acceptable or not acceptable in a group or team.

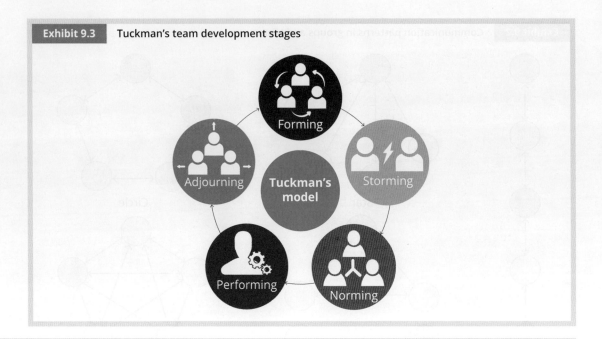

| Exhibit 9.3 | Tuckman's team development stages |

| Exhibit 9.4 | Summary table of Tuckman's team development stages with added task and relationship issues |

Stage	Description	Task issue	Relationship Issue
Forming	Group members try to clarify their concerns about the task or purpose of the group and behave cautiously as they get to know each other	'What is the task of the group?'	'Who are the members?'
Storming	There may be conflict about how the group proceeds with the task and concern about who has authority or status in the group	'How do we want to work on this task?'	'Who is in control of the group?'
Norming	Standards of behaviour emerge that help the group to discuss the task and establish productive communication patterns	'How can we get on with accomplishing the task?'	'How can we communicate to increase trust and respect?'
Performing	The group develops and implements a plan to work together to achieve the task and to build commitment and cohesiveness	'How can we solve problems in creative ways?'	'How can we work together in a supportive way?'
Adjourning*	The group will disband if the task is finished and there is no further purpose or opportunity for the members to continue in the group	'How can we redefine our goals and direction?'	'How do we deal with the prospect of losing the support and security of the group?'

*In 1977, Tuckman added the fifth stage originally named 'mourning' but often re-named as 'adjourning' to be applicable to a wider variety of possible groups.

Source: Based on B. W. Tuckman & M. A. C. Jensen (1977). Stages of small group development revisited. *Group and Organisational Studies*, *2*(4), 419–427.

standards of behaviour used by a group's members to regulate the way they interact in the group or team. They serve as guidelines for the kinds of behaviour that are acceptable or not acceptable in the group or team (see **Exhibit 9.5**). There are two types of group norms – explicit (i.e., open and talked about) and implicit (i.e., hidden and unspoken).

An example of an explicit group norm might be: 'Everyone must be present when we make a decision.' An implicit group norm, one that has never been actually stated, might be: 'We don't pressure everyone to agree'. Hidden, unspoken norms are frequently the cause of group difficulty or conflict, particularly if negative feelings are aroused. Because the hidden norms are not discussed openly, members may

Exhibit 9.5	All groups have norms that guide the expected behaviour of group members

Shutterstock.com/DGLimages   Shutterstock.com/Gorodenkoff

be unaware of these expectations and could break them without realising. It is important for groups and teams to discuss setting up norms that can facilitate and not inhibit their functioning. The group facilitator or team leader can play a valuable role in assisting members to reach agreement on how the group or team will function and work together towards its purpose.

To be most effective, it is recommended that a group knows what its norms are and discusses them openly, and that there are few hidden norms. This will ensure it is easier for the members to recognise when norms are broken and allow discussion as to whether the norms are still appropriate. When the group or team agrees on standards of behaviour, the members can judge effective performance and contributions according to whether the standards have been met. As their working relationships develops, the group or team may also change these standards as required.

Reflection question: Many students dislike working in groups or teams. What is your opinion and why?

Recognising diversity in groups and teams

Recognising the value of diversity in groups and teams at university and in the workplace is essential for these groups and teams to function effectively. Diversity may take the form of differences in gender, cultural background, ethnicity, race, age, language background, literacy levels, personal tastes, religion or sexual preference. Diversity in a group or team can contribute a wealth of perspectives for the members to acknowledge, which may also involve conflict as values and interpretations clash. All members bring different values to the group or team experience, whether these values primarily originate from culture, sub-culture or gender. Effective groups and teams seek to understand individual differences and regard diversity as an opportunity. For example, a person may tend to contribute particular roles or types of communication interactions to a group or team. Groups and teams can encourage members to use their strengths and even to develop a wider range of skills. For example, task or relationship functions may be performed by any person in the group or team with support and appropriate sensitivity, skill, experience and knowledge of group and team processes. When all members are treated with empathy, the value system of the group or team can expand and can increase group or team cohesion, creativity and productivity.

Self-directed work teams

Changing assumptions about what motivates people to work and the restructuring of organisations, or right-sizing, for greater competitiveness has led to flatter organisations with fewer line-managers in supervisory, inspectorial roles. Instead, based on the belief that workers are intrinsically motivated to work given the proper support, encouragement and recognition, organisations are adopting strategies of industrial democracy and empowerment of workers. Organising work to be completed by self-directed or self-managed work teams is a structural mechanism reflecting these changing workplace values. Therefore, effective team communication in the workplace becomes critical for organisational survival.

Self-directed work teams can be responsible for the whole process of production or service they provide, which may involve some or all of the tasks outlined in Exhibit 9.6. They may also be accountable for productivity, quality, costs, and coordination with other work teams and organisational sections. The ability of the work team to manage these affairs is critical to the survival of the whole organisation. These autonomous work teams may consist of five to 15 members who may be multiskilled, learn all aspects of the process or service, and perform the traditional managerial or supervisory roles of monitoring the standard and flow of work. The responsibilities of these self-directed work teams are very broad and require skilled teamwork, underpinned by effective communication and decision-making processes.

Exhibit 9.6	Some of the many tasks that self-directed work teams undertake

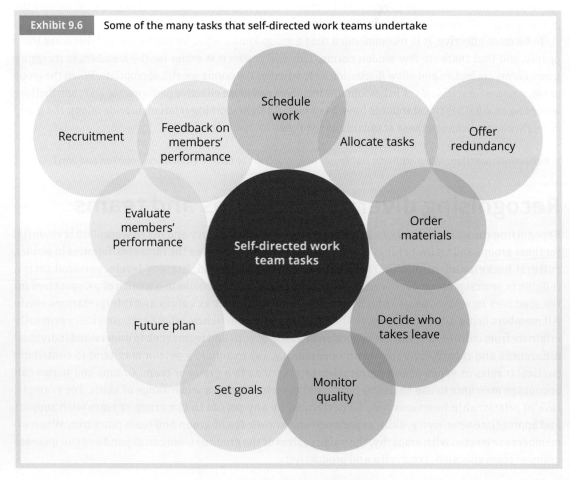

Team building

Have you ever played a team sport? How did your sporting team develop its ability to play? How did it build team spirit? Sports coaches are tasked with managing the process of team building (see **Exhibit 9.7**), and sometimes particular team members play leadership roles in helping to build the team into an effective, competitive unit. However, if you belong to a sports team, you have probably noticed that some individual members care more about their own goals and preferences than they do about the team. Possibly these members did not pass the ball or did not come to team meetings and practice sessions because it was not convenient for them. In cases like this, team building has not been a success.

Exhibit 9.7	Good coaches manage the process of team building

Shutterstock.com/Drazen Zigic

So, what can we learn from these team sport experiences that we can apply in the workplace to build high-performing work teams? The team-building aspects shown in **Exhibit 9.8** are often the focus of sports-team meetings. Such team-building activities help to foster a sense of team identity by providing opportunities for the team members to express personal ideas and opinions, to listen to others and to try to reconcile any differences to achieve the best performance from the team. At university and in the workplace, teams need to be able to structure work patterns so that individual members pool their expertise and coordinate their efforts.

Any problems in personal relations between team members need to be identified early so that ways can be found for everyone to work together constructively. One strategy for managing personality clashes is to focus on the issues, not the person. It may be impossible for us to get on with everyone we are required to work with. Adopting a respectful attitude, treating others politely and courteously, being sensitive to cultural differences, and encouraging an issues-based approach to team problem-solving can help to keep a team on track and build a supportive team atmosphere.

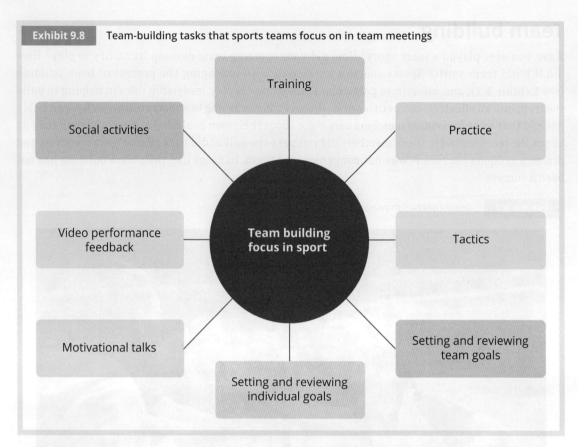

Exhibit 9.8   Team-building tasks that sports teams focus on in team meetings

Training

Social activities

Practice

Video performance feedback

Team building focus in sport

Tactics

Motivational talks

Setting and reviewing team goals

Setting and reviewing individual goals

Some work teams organise to meet away from the workplace, perhaps under the guidance of a facilitator, to explore the team's strengths, weaknesses, opportunities and threats (i.e., a SWOT analysis). These strategies can also be used by student teams at university who are completing team-based assessments. Members' comments and suggestions can be carefully recorded to acknowledge progress and to specify barriers to progress. Members may be encouraged to participate in goal setting and prioritising of issues related to goals. Clarifying unclear goals and testing team goals against individuals' expectations are important outcomes of this process. Team goals may be modified to align with greater commitment from the team members, and the team may explore any dissatisfaction and ineffective decision-making procedures. From these team-building efforts the members may come to agree on a number of realistic objectives, alternatives for organising the work, and strategies for improving resources that the team identifies as necessary to accomplish its shared objectives.

Roles for team building

There are specific task and maintenance roles (or ways of interacting) in the team that contribute to team building, accomplishing the team task, and team cohesiveness. Task roles contribute to getting the job done, while maintenance roles build the team atmosphere and constructive relationships between team members. Individuals can perform more than one role at team meetings. All teams should monitor these roles to check that the team is functioning to meet both the demands of the task and the social needs of the members. Members should coordinate the roles to facilitate team efforts, not damage them. These task and maintenance roles are presented in **Exhibit 9.9**, along with roles that hinder group processes.

Teams should also be aware of roles that hinder group progress by diverting attention to individual needs and introducing behaviour that is irrelevant or counterproductive. Hindering roles should be

Exhibit 9.9	Task roles, maintenance roles and hindering roles

Task roles	Maintenance roles	Hindering roles
Initiating: suggesting ideas, proposing tasks or goals, defining problems, generating options, beginning activities	*Encouraging*: being friendly, approachable, responsive to others, encouraging and accepting others' contributions	*Attacking*: criticising or blaming other group members
Clarifying: asking for needed information, reflecting on ideas and suggestions, clearing confusion, giving examples and elaborating ideas	*Gatekeeping*: facilitating others' participation, and making openings for others to express thoughts and feelings	*Blocking*: rejecting ideas in a stubborn way or for personal reasons
Opinion seeking: asking for feedback from others, seeking clarification of feelings and values and checking on the level of consensus	*Expressing feelings*: sharing your feelings, sensing and verbalising other people's feelings, and commenting on the mood of the group	*Clowning around*: making jokes and not taking things seriously
Diagnosing: determining sources of difficulties, analysing blocks and planning interventions	*Following*: going along with group decisions, and accepting ideas of others	*Dominating*: interrupting others or excessive talking
Information giving: offering facts, providing relevant information and stating beliefs or ideas	*Compromising*: admitting mistakes, and being willing to compromise where conflict is involved	*Diverting*: digressing and avoiding the subject
Summarising: pulling ideas together, summing up areas covered and offering conclusions on decisions	*Harmonising*: reducing tension, clarifying differences, and reconciling disagreements	*Withdrawing*: being uninvolved in what the group is doing
Evaluating: measuring, comparing and focusing on group goals	*Setting standards*: expressing standards for the group to use, applying standards, and evaluating performance	*Special pleading*: lobbying for special interests

Source: Adapted from C. Bundey et al. (1988). *Group leadership: A manual about group leadership and a resource for group leaders.* NSW Department of Health; R. W. Toseland & R. F. Rivas (2013). *An introduction to group work practice: Pearson new international edition.* Pearson Higher Ed.

identified and confronted by the team to deal with personal concerns that may be producing negativity in the group. By recognising behaviours that are blocking the progress of the team, whether in task or relationship areas, members will be setting norms for their team and encouraging members to abide by these standards when the team meets.

Reflection question: Have you ever been in a group where there was one annoying member who did not help the group at all?

CASE STUDY 9.1 **Why groups struggle to solve problems together and have unproductive meetings**

Many professionals, fed up with calendars chock full of long and disorganised meetings, resort to uncharitable and even cynical explanations as to why meetings are unproductive, such as:

- leaders are too lazy to craft thoughtful agendas
- managers hold pointless meetings as a way of flexing their power
- distracted attendees, selfishly preoccupied with their own work, come woefully unprepared.

According to one *Harvard Business Review* article, rather than a cynical answer, the problem lies with a flawed assumption that 'intuitive problem-solving, a highly effective approach for individuals, will, in the context of meetings, prove as effective for groups. But often, it does not' (Pittamapli, 2019).

To understand what intuitive problem-solving is, we need to recognize first that when working out any problem, from picking out a necktie to solving a quadratic equation, we make our way through five stages [as shown in **Exhibit 9.10**].

You might assume that we move through these stages systematically to solve problems, but in the past several decades, psychologists have discovered the opposite to be true. Rather than advance through the stages in order, we tend to do so in a manner that is rather unsystematic.

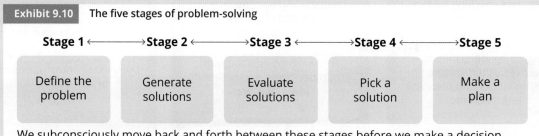

Exhibit 9.10 The five stages of problem-solving

Stage 1 ⟷ Stage 2 ⟷ Stage 3 ⟷ Stage 4 ⟷ Stage 5

| Define the problem | Generate solutions | Evaluate solutions | Pick a solution | Make a plan |

We subconsciously move back and forth between these stages before we make a decision

Source: A. Pittamapli (2019, November 7). Why groups struggle to solve problems together. *Harvard Business Review*.

For example, pretend you're ordering food online. You begin by quickly generating a solution — Mexican (stage 2) — but as soon as the thought enters your mind, you evaluate (stage 3) and remember that you had Mexican the day before, so you generate another solution (stage 2) — Indian. Upon evaluation (stage 3), however, you fear your hefty Chicken Tikka Masala go-to might outsize your appetite. At this point, you take a step back and define the problem (stage 1), asking yourself 'What kind of meal would leave me feeling satisfied but not overly stuffed?' A better question leads to a better answer: sushi (stage 2). You do a quick gut check to make sure sushi is truly what you desire (stage 3), and you move forward with your order (stages 4 and 5).

This is called intuitive problem-solving, and it comes so naturally to us that, when we solve problems in this way, we're wholly unaware that we are doing it. All we have to do is place our attention on the problem and, much like a car's automatic transmission, our brain shifts gears for us. As a result, intuitive problem-solving is remarkably efficient. Magical, even.

… Intuitive problem-solving is so magical for us as individuals that we assume it should fare as well for groups. When we hold a meeting, we gather around a table, place our collective attention on the problem, and let our automatic transmissions take over. But all too often, this turns out to be a mistake.

In order for groups to collaborate effectively and avoid talking past one another, members must simultaneously occupy the same problem-solving stage. But because intuitions are private to their owners, attendees in group meetings are unable to easily discern what problem-solving stage they each are on.

…

The result is a disorganised meeting that traverses many stages, yet conquers none.

Source: A. Pittamapli (2019, November 7). Why groups struggle to solve problems together. *Harvard Business Review*.

Discussion

1 In a small group, discuss some of the experiences and views noted in the article in the light of your own experiences with problem-solving in meetings, whether in the workplace or in general. Do these reflect the experiences of others in your group? What were some of the problems your group noted or identified?

2 What are some of the group interaction problems or behaviours that you have observed in meetings that impact on effective group decision-making?

3   The author argues that, unlike intuitive problem-solving, groups need to be more organised to move through the problem-solving stages: focused agendas, clear direction, strong leadership from the chair and a clear plan. How might these strategies help or hinder group behaviour or creativity in problem-solving?

After you have discussed this case study, refer to the 'Comments on case studies' section at the end of the text.

Problem-solving and decision-making in groups and teams

Working in groups and teams to make good decisions entails harnessing the benefits available from the group or team compared to working alone to achieve the same end. In groups and teams, many of the difficulties faced when solving problems and making decisions relate to how individual members communicate, and how discussions are conducted to arrive at workable decisions to solve a problem. This is where familiarity with problem-solving processes can help a group or team to perform effectively. Some of the advantages and disadvantages of group decision-making are outlined in Exhibit 9.11.

| Exhibit 9.11 | Advantages and disadvantages of group decision-making |

Advantages	Disadvantages
Greater pool of knowledge /experience/perspectives	Some members may feel pressured to conform
Diversity of opinions and viewpoints available	Personal goals may conflict with group goals
Motivation and commitment are increased	A few high-status or more assertive members may dominate
Accountability easier to identify	Chance of conflict and deadlocks
Increased acceptance/ legitimacy of the decision	Riskier decisions can be made due to ambiguous responsibility
Rewards gained from working with others	Reaching a decision can take longer

Whether your group or team meets face to face or virtually, you will need to develop and manage effective processes to solve problems and make decisions. John Dewey (1910) proposed a reflective thinking sequence that has become the model for many recent problem-solving methods, as set out in Exhibit 9.12, with examples.

Exhibit 9.12 Dewey's reflective thinking sequence

Step	Example
1 *Recognise the problem:* clarify the task	The marketing group needs to define the reasons why a new product is not selling
2 *Define the problem:* describe the problem, causes, effects and scope and collect information about the problem	The group needs to look at advertising media, sales data, and other similar product strategies and sales figures
3 *List possible solutions:* as many alternative strategies as possible	The group should prioritise a list of possible solutions to improve current marketing strategy
4 *Select the best solution:* compare pros and cons of possible solutions and use criteria for making the best decision, based on available information and goals	The group works together to decide on the best solution
5 *Implement the decision:* determine details of actions required, by whom and where and when, and then do it	The group decides how to best implement the marketing strategy
6 *Review the effectiveness of the solution:* monitor the implementation process to make adjustments and respond to changing circumstances	The group decides how to best evaluate the implementation

Source: Based on J. Dewey (1910). *How we think*. D. C. Heath.

Reflection question: Identify and remedy these common blocks to effective group work or teamwork:

1 The problem or task was not stated clearly.

2 The needed information was not available.

3 There were inadequate communication patterns within the group or team.

4 Hasty judgements were made and there was poor selection of alternatives.

5 The group or team atmosphere was critical, tense, competitive and evaluative.

6 Members did not realise the scope of the problem and did not pose relevant questions.

7 The group or team was insufficiently motivated to reach a thoughtful decision.

Decision-making methods

At various times, the group or team may find that taking a vote (by open or secret ballot); ranking solutions in order of preference; deferring to an authority, such as a manager or university lecturer; and even flipping a coin, are useful decision-making methods. The most common decision-making methods are as follows:

- *Consensus:* a decision is only made when everyone in the group agrees on it.
- *Consultative:* the nominated decision-maker consults with the relevant team members to gather information before making their decision.
- *Consent:* This method poses the question to the group 'Are there any reasons we can think of not to make this decision'. When no reasons can be found, a decision is made.
- *Democratic:* everyone in the group votes for what they believe the decision should be, then the idea with the most votes wins.
- *Delegation:* the highest authority figure in the group will delegate the decision to other group members but will retain the responsibility for the outcomes.
- *Autocratic:* a top-down style of decision-making where the highest authority figure in the group will decide on behalf of everyone.
- *Avoidance:* this style is the least productive as decisions will often be delayed. It may occur when decision-makers lack confidence in the options or the information available.

Choose your decision-making method carefully to ensure that everyone understands the advantages and limitations of the possible solutions. **Exhibit 9.13** can assist in choosing the right kind of method. The decision-making method should be fair, agreed to by all members and should enhance members' satisfaction with the chosen decision.

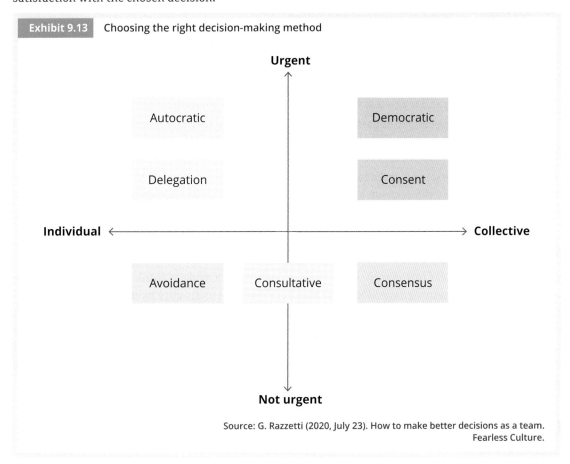

Exhibit 9.13 Choosing the right decision-making method

Source: G. Razzetti (2020, July 23). How to make better decisions as a team. Fearless Culture.

In terms of how to choose one solution over another, groups need to establish the pros and cons for each solution and consider four main criteria (Lumsden & Lumsden, 2010):

1 *Applicability:* Does the solution apply to the whole problem or only part of it?
2 *Practicality:* What resources are needed: costs, time, support?
3 *Risks:* What are possible risks and implications?
4 *Desirability:* How does the solution relate to professional values and ethics?

Reaching a consensus

Making a decision based on consensus is a way of involving all members in the decision. The group or team may not reach full agreement, but striving to share ideas and views in order to reach consensus usually develops greater commitment to the final decision. Note that there can be different interpretations of what consensus means in different organisations and cultures.

Complete unanimity is not the goal of consensus, and it is rarely achieved. Instead, each member should be able to accept a decision on the basis of logic and feasibility. When all members feel this way you have reached a decision by consensus. If a member is not prepared to budge on an issue, then consensus can be blocked. There are significant benefits for commitment and group cohesiveness if groups and teams can make decisions by consensus.

The following guidelines for decision-making by consensus are adapted from Watson et al. (1980):

- Avoid insisting on your own solution. Present your position as lucidly and logically as possible, but listen to the other members' reactions and consider them carefully before you press your point.

- As a group or team, try to arrive at a solution that all members can at least partially agree. Don't think in terms of 'winning' and 'losing'.

- Make sure everyone accepts the solution for basically similar or complementary reasons. The decision should have a sound rationale.

- Avoid using decision-making techniques like majority vote, averages, coin flips and bargaining because such strategies trivialise real decision-making for many participants. Instead, identify common ground and try to test the reality of the possible solutions.

- Encourage all members to express their views, even if they are contradictory. Disagreements can help the group or team decision because, with a wide range of information and opinions, there is a greater chance that the group or team will arrive at more adequate solutions.

Planning by consensus may take more time than some of the other techniques, but you may spend less time implementing the decision because people are inclined to be more committed. There can be a feeling of satisfaction in the group or team when decisions are made by consensus.

Groupthink

Groupthink
A mode of thinking people engage in when they are deeply involved in a cohesive in-group, when the members' quest for unanimity overrides their motivation to realistically appraise alternative courses of action.

Groupthink, which was introduced in the chapter opening, is a mode of thinking that affects people engaged in highly cohesive groups. Here, the members' quest for unanimity overrides their motivation to realistically appraise alternative courses of action, which can lead to rushed and ill-advised decisions (Janis, 1972, 1982). However, the term can only be applied retrospectively, after the decision is made and is judged to be a negative. Obviously, there are good, consensual, unified decisions, and these are never questioned. One can only guard against groupthink by being aware of some of the group processes (listed below) that may be occurring.

Janis (1982) modelled *groupthink* as consisting of several antecedent conditions, which lead to concurrence seeking (or groupthink tendency), resulting in symptomatic observable consequences, yielding a low probability of a successful outcome. The eight symptoms of groupthink are outlined in **Exhibit 9.14**.

Avoiding groupthink

Avoiding groupthink is one of the main benefits of understanding group processes. Groupthink can be minimised by playing devil's advocate and asking experts from outside the group or team to give opinions and ask questions. In general, groupthink can be countered by the group or team being open to all suggestions and critically investigating the pros and cons of possible solutions.

Some solutions to avoid groupthink include the following:

- Encourage each group member to be a critical evaluator of the group's course of action. An open climate of giving and accepting criticism should be encouraged by the leader.

- Leaders should be impartial and refrain from stating personal preferences at the outset of group discussion; they should limit themselves initially to fostering open inquiry.

- Establish multiple groups with different leaders to work the question in parallel.

- Split groups into subgroups to assess feasibility and effectiveness of proposals.

- Each member of the group should privately discuss current issues and options with trusted associates outside the group and report reactions.

- From time to time, bring in outside experts to challenge the views of the core members.

- There should be one or more devil's advocates during every group meeting.

- In conflict situations, devote extra time to interpreting warning signals from rivals and to construct alternative scenarios of their intentions.

- Reconsider the decision in second-chance meetings before going public.

Exhibit 9.14 The eight symptoms of groupthink

The eight symptoms of groupthink are:

1. having an illusion of invulnerability
2. rationalising poor decisions
3. believing in the group's morality
4. sharing stereotypes which guide the decision
5. exercising direct pressure on dissenters
6. not expressing true feelings
7. maintaining an illusion of unanimity
8. using mindguards to protect the group from negative information

The groupthink phenomenon is a useful and cautionary concept that may explain many of the mistakes made in modern-day politics, governments and corporations, as well as day-to-day processes of groups made up of normal people around the globe. Even though the core concepts of groupthink have not been demonstrated in controlled experimental research, there is broad theoretical acceptance of the concept across many fields (Rose, 2011). There is broad theoretical acceptance of the importance of being vigilant and careful in all group decision-making situations. Bad decisions can be avoided by being conscientious group participants and leaders.

 CASE STUDY 9.2 Decision-making in a student group

A group consisting of four students – Ron, Sam, Ari and Jacki – is involved in completing a group report and presentation worth 30 per cent of the assessment in a subject. The group began enthusiastically two weeks ago but momentum has declined as they have tried to deal with the following issues:

- Ari had been conducting telephone interviews on behalf of the group but had not been keeping detailed records of each call.

- Ron agreed to meet Sam at the library, but Sam did not show up.

- Jacki set up a spreadsheet for recording the results without consulting the others – both Sam and Ari saw significant disadvantages with Jacki's spreadsheet.

- Ron is in the process of moving to another suburb where public transport is more limited.

- During the group meetings, Jacki likes to focus on one issue at a time, while Ari likes to chat generally about ideas and presentation strategies.

- Jacki thinks that Ari interrupts Ron and Sam too much and wastes time – Ron and Sam are keen to learn about the topic because it is directly relevant to their future work.

All members are feeling frustrated with their experience of working in the group. There are three weeks left before the report and presentation are due and anxiety is high.

Discussion

1   How can the group facilitate decision-making and build interpersonal relations between the members to achieve the goal of completing the group report and presentation in three weeks? In your answer, nominate specific decision-making strategies and types of communication interactions.

2   Role-play this scenario by holding a small-group meeting. Implement decision-making strategies and communication interactions to build interpersonal relations in the group. Discuss the effectiveness of the decision-making and communication techniques that were demonstrated at the small-group meeting.

   a   As a member of this group, how did you feel after the meeting? Share your feelings about and reactions to what happened at the meeting.

   b   What were you satisfied or dissatisfied with?

   c   Discuss whether you think and feel that the group is now ready to work well together to complete the group report and presentation in three weeks.

After you have discussed this case study, refer to the 'Comments on case studies' section at the end of the text.

Creativity in the professional group and team

Whether your group or team meets face to face or via technology, you need to be able to discuss issues and problems and generate possible solutions for moving forward. How can your group or team be more creative when solving problems and making decisions? How can you generate more innovative ideas for the group or team to explore?

Edward de Bono (1970, 1987) was the famous originator of the term 'lateral thinking' and has helped countless people to think about problems in more creative ways. De Bono emphasises ways of moving from convergent and conformist thinking to more innovative, divergent thinking, also known as 'thinking outside the box'. His techniques include using multiple alternatives, setting quotas, brainstorming, testing assumptions, employing suspended judgement, using analogies and metaphors, examining dominant ideas, re-evaluation of decision-making, and so on. Sometimes we can be more creative if we are able to relax and have fun. His Six Thinking Hats method is a technique to enable teams to consider decisions in novel and inventive ways from different perspectives. His website, https://debono.com is worth a visit.

Creative problem-solving techniques

Complacency is probably one of the most common barriers to creativity because it can be more comfortable to stick to what you know than to take a chance on the unknown. By enlisting imaginative team members and allowing time for innovation, companies may overcome outmoded ideas. To promote creativity at work, you might employ a variety of strategies, some of which are explained below.

Brainstorming

The purpose of the brainstorming process is to enable the group or team to generate as many ideas as possible, without judging such ideas prematurely (see **Exhibit 9.15**). To achieve this level of creativity, it is important to develop processes that encourage members to relinquish their usual mental defences

| Exhibit 9.15 | Brainstorming can help teams generate a large number of ideas to work with |

Shutterstock.com/REDPIXEL.PL

and contribute freely (Johnson & Johnson, 2017). Tyson (1998) suggests that the following procedures may contribute to a successful brainstorming session:

- List all ideas as they come up. A facilitator can do this for the group or team.
- Generate as many ideas as possible.
- Do not evaluate or criticise any idea at this stage.
- Piggyback on or extend other people's ideas.
- Discuss, categorise and prioritise ideas after many of them are listed.
- Analyse the top priorities for feasibility, perhaps using other teams.

The group or team can be informed of the problem to be brainstormed several days beforehand. Brainstorming is most appropriate when problems can be stated specifically and where there is a possibility of multiple solutions. A useful website for brainstorming, if you are interested is https://www.mindtools.com/acv0de1/brainstorming.

Metaphorical thinking

With this technique, the group or team tries to see connections between two ideas and attempts to gain new insights from these comparisons. The group or team suggests metaphors to represent aspects of a problem. One metaphor can be chosen for further exploration and the group or team looks for insights into the causes of and solutions to the original problem. For example, suppose that the problem is to achieve greater team productivity. The metaphor may be conceived as a mountain that the group or team needs to climb. Using the metaphor, the group or team might develop methods to explore the feasibility of a variety of pathways. This process may increase the group's or team's insight into the difficulties and opportunities of such pathways.

Other creative-thinking techniques

Other creative problem-solving techniques include:

- making lists of arguments 'for' and 'against' a proposal, strengths and weaknesses, resources needed or action steps
- going around the group or team systematically, with each member contributing
- using a force-field analysis to identify driving and restraining forces that might be affecting a problem situation
- mapping the problem using a matrix of solutions and assessment criteria such as cost, durability and aesthetics
- making a concept map or *mind map* of the problem by placing the issue in the centre and recording associated ideas from group members as branches radiating out from it (use the term 'mindmap' in Google to see dozens of examples).

These and other creative problem-solving techniques can provide visual processes for a group or team to clarify thinking and suggest priorities for action and decision-making.

Leadership

Whether or not the group or team has a designated leader, effective leadership is provided when a way of working is achieved to accomplish the stated goals of the group or team (i.e., task responsibilities) and when the needs and feelings of members are attended to (i.e., relationship responsibilities). Groups and teams require flexible leadership in these areas to guide and inspire them.

Essentials of group and team leadership

The following 10 essentials of effective leadership may be used by any appointed leader or member to assist the group or team to develop its potential:

1 Encourage every member to contribute, listen and build on the discussion; discourage any members from dominating the discussion.

2 Focus on defining and clarifying the problem and developing criteria for assessing which information is most useful to solve the problem.

3 Help the group or team formulate a series of questions to be investigated, and contribute your own prepared questions if needed.

4 Summarise at strategic points and focus the group or team on answering the questions about the range of issues that have been identified.

5 Be open to fresh perspectives and accept criticism of your own ideas.

6 Keep track of any ideas that are ignored or forgotten and remind the group or team about these.

7 Encourage the group or team to express any concerns, feelings, objections and doubts and to reach decisions thoughtfully, not hastily.

8 Deal with conflict in the group or team by seeking to resolve differences and disagreements and using conflict constructively.

9 Guide the group or team to establish a supportive atmosphere by providing a comfortable working environment, respecting each other and not interrupting when others speak.

10 Help the group or team to realise what has been accomplished and where the group or team might direct energy to make further progress on the task and on building relationships.

Reflection question: Think about teachers you have had in the past. Who was the best teacher? Why was this person a good leader? How did they make the class feel?

CASE STUDY 9.3   Computer-mediated group processes and decision-making

The area of group mediated communication has been highly researched, usually with experimentation using university students. Typically, groups and teams solve problems in a range of different communication contexts, such as face-to-face and computer conferencing. Most early studies regarded lack of non-verbal cues and reduced social context as explanations for observed differences.

In *The New Media*, one of the seminal works in this area, Rice (1984) reported on two opposing schools of thought in considering the effects of computer-mediated communication on decision-making. The first, the *cool* school, is the behavioural or information-processing model that suggests that problems are better served by media that encourage equitable, unemotional discussion of readily accessed information. Here the lack of social presence would be a distinct advantage. The second, the *warm* school, gives priority to human relations inherent in ordinary groups, arguing that trust, group norms and non-verbal communication are all-important ingredients

of quality decisions. Rice (1984) added that the nature of the task might be an important consideration – routine tasks might be better suited to mediated groups, with non-routine tasks necessitating a richer context.

Discussion

1   From your experience with videoconferencing groups, are Zoom or Teams groups better or worse than traditional groups at solving problems or brainstorming solutions?

2   Is the reduced social presence a factor in videoconferencing groups?

3   Social media platforms, such as Reddit, can also be viewed as mediated groups. What do you prefer in your own group communication for problem-solving?

After you have discussed this case study, refer to the 'Comments on case studies' section at the end of the text.

Conflict management

In groups and teams, we can expect **conflict** or disagreement to arise from influences such as interdependence, different perceptions, incompatible goals and interference. Conflicts can erupt in the group or team from emotional reactions, misunderstandings, accidents and mistakes. These disagreements usually cannot be resolved just by finding a mutually convenient time when the group or team can meet. In conflicts there are usually underlying concerns that have to be acknowledged and discussed by the members.

Conflict
Is a protracted serious disagreement or argument. Conflicts can erupt in the group or team from emotional reactions, misunderstandings, accidents and mistakes.

Conflicts can arise in groups and teams because:

- members do not share the same goals
- members have different points of view or ideas about how the goals can be achieved
- there are scarce resources such as time, money, materials and recognition to be shared among the members
- members have different values, attitudes and ways of doing things
- there are misunderstandings where someone feels offended, hurt or angry
- members perceive threats to their egos or identity from something that happens in the group or team.

If a conflict in a group or team involves more than one of these indicators, the chances are that the group or team is experiencing a *mixed conflict*, where there is no single cause. Many conflicts are like this, and mixed conflicts can be especially difficult to handle effectively.

Members' behaviour is a major source of conflict in groups and teams. Have you observed non-functional behaviour in a group or team? Have you behaved in these non-functional ways yourself? One conflict-reducing strategy is to increase self-awareness of your behaviour and the likely impact on other members and the group or team climate. Another way of dealing with the impact of disruptive behaviour or controversy in the group or team is to give constructive feedback to members.

Some signs of conflict in the group or team

When people are experiencing conflict, how do they react in the group or team? Some observable signs of conflict include behaviour changes, individuals avoiding certain other group members, tension headaches, irritability, not achieving as much as usual, speaking abruptly to others, complaining, moodiness, being easily upset, non-cooperation, revenge, absenteeism and hiding feelings so that the conflict simmers.

However, the signs of conflict are not always obvious. You will need to be alert for changes in behaviour that might be quite subtle and non-verbal, such as a change in tone of voice, in manner or look, or in facial expression (which may be more subtle). These non-verbal cues may be important signs of conflict. There might also be hidden agendas that are influencing how members are interpreting things and behaving towards each other.

There is, therefore, a lot to be gained from mastering the skills of effective conflict resolution in the workplace. Nevertheless, it should be recognised that not all conflict between people can be resolved. An assumption often underlying strategies for conflict resolution is that there is a willingness on the part of the parties involved to resolve the conflict. Yet not all people may be willing to resolve a particular conflict – it may be said that some people may even gain satisfaction from bullying others or disrupting group or team processes.

Conflict resolution skills

Many adults are not satisfied with the way they deal with conflict. They may have had unpleasant experiences with past conflicts and start to feel even more uneasy when it occurs in workplace groups. When conflict occurs in a group or a team, members may give up, give in or pretend that nothing is wrong. Destructive behaviours may take over and may continue until something constructive is done to alleviate the situation. A good leader or group member must intervene by announcing there is a conflict and dealing with it on the spot, before the group completely breaks down. A special meeting may have to be timetabled so that the group can start to function as a productive decision-making group again. Early intervention is a very useful strategy.

The *Twelve Conflict Resolution Skills* by Helena Cornelius (2020) of the Conflict Resolution Network provides recommended problem-solving approaches that have proven successful, and are outlined in **Exhibit 9.16**.

 CASE STUDY 9.4   Was the 2003 US invasion of Iraq an example of groupthink?

The 2003 US-led invasion in Iraq should have been short and sweet. Advisors in the US administration were confidently predicting that the war would be over within days. Iraqis would welcome the Americans and the country would become a model free-market democracy for the Middle East. However, the reality was different. The US military was bogged down and incapable of defeating the insurgents. The country lurched towards civil war and the US was unable to control the anarchy. The parallels with Vietnam were striking. The international community was bitterly divided, and the majority of the world's population was deeply distrustful of the Bush administration. How could the most powerful nation on Earth, with access to

sophisticated intelligence and huge military might, have gotten it so wrong? The answer is *groupthink*, a refusal to see reality as it is.

Discussion

Use the internet to determine if in fact the invasion of Iraq was an example of groupthink. Use Janis's list of eight symptoms to test whether the Bush government was guilty of arrogant or rash decision-making. Was there another agenda involved? What of the 'weapons of mass destruction'?

After you have discussed this case study, refer to the 'Comments on case studies' section at the end of the text.

Exhibit 9.16 Twelve skills of conflict resolution

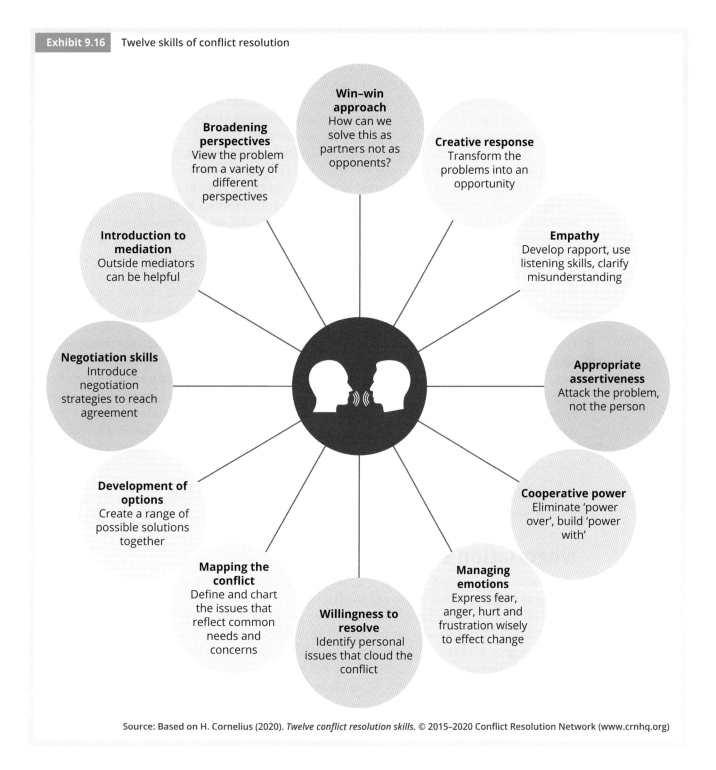

Source: Based on H. Cornelius (2020). *Twelve conflict resolution skills.* © 2015–2020 Conflict Resolution Network (www.crnhq.org)

Negotiation to solve conflict

The word **negotiation** is used in a number of disciplines and contexts and has slightly different meanings depending on the situation. In business, negotiation usually refers to obtaining a price for a product or service, when such prices are not fixed. In politics, negotiation can mean a trade-off in terms of one party offering votes or favours in exchange for other votes or favours at a later date. Negotiation can be seen as the process by which certain pacts or deals are made. Such deals may be short-lived or may last for many months or even years.

Negotiation
The process by which certain pacts or deals are made. A discussion aimed at reaching an agreement.

265

Competitive (trying to always win) and accommodating (always giving in) styles of conflict management are sometimes referred to as win–lose strategies because one party's needs are met at the expense of the other's and, in the accommodating approach, the less dominant party loses out to the other party. In contrast, lose–lose strategies are conflict management styles where neither party's needs are addressed, because one or both parties do not confront the conflict (i.e., avoidance).

Negotiation should be a win–win situation, where conflicting parties attempt to identify a solution where neither have to settle for partially satisfactory outcomes. Negotiation can lead to better outcomes because the act of negotiating can change the positions of the two parties involved. For instance, negotiation can uncover creative solutions when there is a conflict over extremely limited resources or when emotions have hindered the parties' attempts to identify or agree to a solution.

Negotiation is distinguished from other conflict resolution options in that it does not involve the assistance of a third party. This makes negotiation the least formal, most consensual, and least expensive form of conflict resolution option. However, for the very reason that negotiation is not facilitated by a third party, the conflicting parties must have strong interpersonal communication skills if they are to achieve a satisfactory outcome. Indeed, by paving the way for the type of interaction where parties feel they can disclose their likes and dislikes, negotiation can help conflicting parties find an optimal solution for their specific circumstances. Negotiation can also prevent conflict from escalating.

Zartman (2009) states that, for a number of reasons, negotiation brings with it an ethos of equality. The fact that the parties are free to reject each other's proposals means they are forced to recognise their equal standing in the negotiation. This tends to foster behaviour in which the exchanges between the parties are courteously symmetrical (even if there are other asymmetries between them; e.g., due to authority). The ethos of equality is further fostered because the process of negotiation is characterised by an expectation between the parties that concessions will be reciprocated, and is chosen as a conflict resolution method when the parties want a sense of ownership over the outcome. Finally, equality is fostered by the fact that negotiation is used when there is neither a decision hierarchy nor a voting system that the parties can to turn to.

> **Reflection question:** Have you ever negotiated a price at a market or while buying second-hand goods? Did you get a good deal?

Negotiation strategies

The key to being a good negotiator is to understand the other party's interests and tactics. Understanding this allows you to select a strategy that best responds to both party's interests and tactics, so that the best possible outcome can be achieved. A good negotiator will know their own bottom line (what they cannot accept) and also have some inkling of their opponent's bottom line.

According to Makela (2022), there are a range of tactics, including collaboration, neutral and manipulation tactics. Good negotiators will match each type of tactic with a particular type of counter response, as shown in Exhibit 9.17. To use these techniques, you need to be able to identify what kind of tactic is being used. Your chosen response strategy will depend on your opponent and also on the type of relationship you have with them. For example, what level of cooperation and respect already exists between the two parties, and how valuable is the relationship to the future? It will also depend on what you are negotiating, the time frame and the setting you are negotiating within. This could be true of buying a new house, a second-hand camera, or being involved in a divorce settlement. It is equally true of deciding on what to watch on TV, where to go on your next holiday, or how to overcome conflicts in teams.

In some cases, the act of slowing down the decision-making process by 'officially' negotiating a deal or decision sends a signal to one or both parties that they need to adopt a more equitable and reasonable attitude to the entire process.

Exhibit 9.17 Collaboration, neutral and manipulative negotiation tactics and counter responses

Tactic	Explanation	Counter response
Collaboration tactics (always positive)		
Trade-off	Exchanging options of different value and cost to each party	Stress the equality of value; balance offers of equal and greater cost to you
Trial deal	Posing a hypothetical approach	Clarify the offer and level of commitment. Avoid overreacting or underreacting without further research
Shared interests	Reminding the other that their interests benefit both parties.	Be very clear where your interests diverge or converge. Repeatedly weigh the costs and value to both parties
Neutral tactics (can be positive or negative)		
Deadline	Giving a certain deadline for decision to be made	Question the validity of the deadline. Stress the value of the relationship over the timeline
Higher authority	Deferring to someone who is not present	Express your disappointment at the time wasted by the real decision-maker not being involved in the negotiation
Budget limits	Expressing a hard line about budget constraints	Identify the reason for such constraints. Use scaling, timing and customisation to stay within budget
Manipulative tactics (always negative)		
Future promise	The promise of future gain in exchange for concessions made now	Ask for documentation regarding such future promises. Construct advantageous extra terms into the contract if the promises are not kept
Threats	Making drastic ultimatums to obtain concessions	Appeal to the importance of a fair and level-headed process in order to proceed
Precedents and competitor information	Offering up other group decisions, or extra information to elicit a better deal	Know your competitors, and research the landscape so that such tempting offers do not sway your bottom line

Source: Adapted from R. Makela (2022). *Three types of negotiation tactics and how to respond (with examples)*.

Informal and formal meetings

Friends, acquaintances, students, and professionals in a workplace frequently meet in small groups on a regular basis. Such regular events are usually referred to as meetings when there is (1) an agenda (either tacit or explicit) and (2) the agenda results in decision-making outcomes or agreements. In the workplace, such meetings are usually chaired by a senior staff member and include several other members of staff, or they may be meetings between colleagues and clients whose roles are quite different. Informal meetings are those that do not involve formal recording (i.e., minutes) or voting, while formal meetings are more rigorous with a set agenda, and a detailed set of minutes complete with written results of the decisions made.

Professionals often complain about the waste of time involved in poor meetings, and students comment on wasting valuable time in group or team meetings. There are many books and videos to guide you on how to conduct effective formal and informal meetings (see Barker 2011; Bateman 2001; Newton 2001). For example, John Cleese made the famous *Meetings, Bloody Meetings* video in 1976, and it is still a classic training tool (now on YouTube).

Meeting skills

In order to achieve this apparently smooth structure of a meeting, it is very important for members to see that they each must be as skilled in communicating in meetings as they are at writing reports. In fact, effective meetings are more difficult to produce than effective reports because they involve dealing with other people directly.

How should a group or team member prepare for and participate in a meeting? Here are some suggestions that reflect the principles of assertiveness, effective listening and decision-making by consensus:

- *Before the meeting:* get to know as much as you can about the material to be examined. Research necessary information. Analyse the issues leading to critical decision-making and examine the bases of your views.
- *During the meeting:* speak clearly, relevantly and briefly. Be firm but not dogmatic. Be ready to reconsider a position you have adopted. Listen carefully and courteously. Engage in argument, even conflict, but do not personalise the conflict. Do not abuse, ridicule or laugh at an opponent. Use humour to relieve tension, not to belittle others.
- *After the meeting:* check the minutes or your records of the meeting. Note any areas for clarification at the next meeting. Follow up any actions assigned to you.

Role of the chairperson in meetings

A chairperson is the person who assists the meeting to run smoothly by taking on a leadership role in the group or team. In general, they guide the discussion from problems to solutions, maintain the goals of the group or team, encourage general participation and keep the discussion moving. The chairperson may have been nominated (e.g., by management) to take on this role. A team leader, for instance, would normally be the chairperson of an informal team meeting. The chairperson may also rotate due to specific expertise, or members may be required to become chairs to give them experience at this role. In informal groups, leaders can often emerge because of their personalities.

The following are some suggested guidelines for the role of chairperson in any group or team:

- State at the beginning why the meeting is taking place and what problem is to be solved. Ideally the chairperson will provide an agenda for the meeting. If a record of the meeting is needed, organise for minutes to be taken and later circulated to members.
- Guide the discussion from basic problems through to final solutions. Be mindful of keeping the discussion in a logical order without dominating it. The best way to do this is to constantly use questions rather than statements.
- Set the goals for the group or team and keep the group or team pointed towards those goals, discouraging irrelevancies.
- Encourage the meeting to move smoothly from one topic to another, show the logical links between points covered and sum up at key stages so that members can see what progress they are making.
- Achieve balance by encouraging all members, the quiet ones as well as the more outspoken ones, to make useful contributions.
- Deal with disruptive or obstructive members to encourage a democratic process (other members can help with this too).

Conducting and recording formal meetings

The formal meeting is a type of meeting where rules of meeting procedure apply. Formal meetings are conducted by parliaments and councils, companies for shareholders, academic institutions and professional associations. For example, there are public meetings chaired by officials, special government inquiries, and body corporates of apartment blocks hold formal meetings. In organisations, there can be board meetings attended by various stakeholders; for example, see Bateman's (2001) guidelines for company meetings. All of these formal meetings adopt the general rules of meeting procedure.

In Australia, the procedure for formal meetings is subject to official rules and regulations. Two texts that cover these procedures are *Joske's law and procedure at meetings in Australia* (Magner, 2012) and *Guide for meetings and organisations* (Renton, 2005). In these sources you will find specific guidance on features of formal meetings, such as the roles of the chairperson and the secretary, agendas, minutes, order of business, procedural and substantive motions, amendments to motions, points of order, dissent and voting. These rules are summarised in the following section on advantages of formal meetings. One way to become familiar with procedures of formal meetings is to attend a formal meeting; for example, in the area where you live, meetings of the local council are generally able to be observed by members of the public.

Advantages of formal meetings

There are several advantages of formal meetings, the first being that they have rules of procedure that allow conflicting views and vested interests to be stated in front of the whole meeting. Formal meetings are an important part of all democratic countries. There is a tacit agreement by all present that these rules will be followed and that the chairperson has the authority and confidence of the meeting to conduct the business of the meeting in an orderly way in accordance with these rules. Some of the rules of formal meetings are:

- Speakers indicate to the chairperson their wish to speak and must await the chairperson's call to speak. People cannot address the meeting whenever they feel like it, so the process is more orderly.
- Normally, speakers can speak only once in the debate on an issue, so speakers are wise to consider carefully what they are going to say.
- Speakers may not be interrupted, except on a point of order.
- Speakers must address their remarks to the chairperson, not to other members. People at the meeting cannot start addressing remarks to each other.
- Any misbehaviour, abuse, irrelevance or obstruction can be objected to by any member and can be dealt with by the chairperson.
- Importantly, the main points of discussion and the decisions made are recorded by the secretary in the minutes and constitute a record of the meeting for future meetings.
- A decision is made by voting, and the vote is recorded.

Achieving professional goals through groups and teams

Working collaboratively requires effective communication techniques; for example, building trust, using open communication, giving and receiving constructive feedback, sharing leadership, managing conflict and being creative and adaptable. If groups or teams wish to monitor their processes, they can use detailed audit questionnaires, such as the Team Effectiveness Questionnaire (Bateman et al., 2002). This questionnaire has 44 questions organised under six headings: team synergy, performance objectives, skills, use of resources, innovation and quality.

The group or team process review checklist in **Exhibit 9.18** incorporates suggestions by Scholtes (1996) for dealing with common team problems. The questions can be used by groups and teams as a guide for monitoring how the group or team is developing and performing.

	Exhibit 9.18	Group or team process review checklist	
1		Are we reviewing our group or team progress regularly and asking questions if the group or team appears to be stuck or off-track?	☐
2		Are we encouraging everyone to participate according to agreed guidelines by: discussing how much talking is appropriate; giving constructive feedback to overtalkative or quiet members; using methods to structure the discussion to involve everyone, such as brainstorming and 'round robin' reporting?	☐
3		Are we discussing the need for the group or team to agree on limits, the value of balanced participation and focused, relevant discussion?	☐
4		Are we politely challenging opinions, such as by asking for supporting evidence?	☐
5		Are we encouraging the collection of relevant data before decisions are made too hastily?	☐
6		Are we aware of impatience that can lead to premature decision-making by: taking breaks; agreeing on a decision-making process; monitoring the steps and reviewing as necessary?	☐
7		Are we checking perceptions of other people's motives by: describing and listening actively, and not blaming; giving all members attention and respect; helping members to express what is important to them?	☐
8		Are we preparing a written agenda to focus discussion on topics and timeframes by: recording all topics for prioritising; directing discussion to agreed priorities and allocating some topics to other group or team meetings if necessary?	☐
9		Are we selecting group or team members so that known adversaries are not in the same group or team?*	☐
10		Are we aware of conditions of groupthink if the meeting is highly cohesive, possibly with a highly persuasive leader?	☐

*If this is not appropriate, it may be possible to talk to adversaries prior to the group or team meeting to discuss constructive ways of dealing with unproductive conflict. Another option may be to encourage adversaries to discuss some areas of difference outside the team meeting to reduce disruption to the group or team.

CASE STUDY 9.5 How working from home has become the 'new normal' after COVID: what are the impacts for group cohesion?

Pandemic related lockdowns across the world precipitated the directive for many workers to work from home. Three years on, despite the lifting of most restrictions, workers are opting to continue to work from home, preferring to work flexibly two or three days a week rather than commuting to a central office. While some bosses are not happy, they are currently powerless to do anything about it, particularly given the ongoing staff shortages.

But what are the advantages and disadvantages of increasingly flexible work arrangements? Apart from the obvious time and money saved by not commuting and additional flexibility to pick up kids from school, employees report that they get more work done at home, perhaps because there are no interruptions from colleagues wanting to talk about the football or last night's episode of MasterChef.

However, despite companies now referring to their staff as team members rather than staff or employees, it's hard to embed a team culture when members are scattered geographically. Interactions on Zoom with an ironed shirt on top and pyjamas and slippers under the table, and one eye on the baby, are not always conducive to this process either.

This has left some managers lamenting the loss of spontaneous interactions with and between staff in the office environment, and lack of ability to conduct quick meetings or even face-to-face discussions. And, quietly, many bosses are nostalgic for the ability to keep an eye on what their team members are up to.

Source: Adapted from A. Kohler (2022, October 13). Working from home is a proletariat revolution. *The New Daily.*

Discussion

1 Consider your own experience of working during COVID restrictions, and how it has been since. Have you noticed a loss of group cohesion or identity because you no longer see your fellow team members as often?

2 Has team members working from home affected your productivity where you are required to work closely with a regular number of fellow staff members?

3 Has the availability and use of videoconferencing software like Teams or Zoom lessened the impact on group cohesion of working from home?

4 What are the advantages for group cohesion of being able to have casual and impromptu meetings or discussions with colleagues?

After you have discussed this case study, refer to the 'Comments on case studies' section at the end of the text.

Summary

In this chapter we have looked at communication in a range of groups and teams, formal and informal, typically of three to 15 members, where decisions may be made and issues discussed. We have seen that in each situation it is important for the group or team member to be articulate, decisive, controlled, logical and courteous. In many groups and teams, the emphasis is on the constructive exchange of opinion and information. Conflict is a major problem for group decision-making, and using negotiation is one of the best methods to overcome such conflict, and can be used in other contexts. In an informal meeting of a group or team, the emphasis is on the achievement of consensus; that is, all those present agreeing to a decision and being willing to be committed to it. In the formal meeting, emphasis is on democratic discussion and debate and adherence to rules and regulations, ensuring fair play and proper recording of decisions. Groups should always be aware of the possibility of groupthink, which can result in disastrous decisions; strategies should be established to minimise the possibility of overly cohesive group dynamics.

STUDY TOOLS

DISCUSSION QUESTIONS AND GROUP ACTIVITIES

For discussion topics and activities in addition to those listed below, please refer to the case studies presented throughout this chapter.

1   Form a team of four to seven members and discuss how you are going to build the team to work together in a supportive way to plan and prepare a report or presentation on a task that the team must accomplish. Work in the team to complete the task, prepare the report or give the presentation. Monitor your team process during these activities and write a reflective report on the nature and success of team building during this team exercise.

2   Write constructive feedback responses for the following two situations that have occurred in a decision-making group. Explain which feedback skills were illustrated in your response.

   a   You notice that Jason is continually distracting other group members and continues to ignore the chairperson's admonitions.

   b   At two previous group meetings, Isabel has seemed to act in an indifferent manner and at this meeting appears to be bored and withdrawn.

3   Form groups and imagine you are students at a tertiary institution who belong to a student representative association. Select a topic for discussion on an issue that has recently been seriously affecting students. There will need to be some preliminary discussion about the topic and the objectives and purpose for discussing it. The objectives may be to make some recommendations, present a solution to a problem, or simply exchange ideas. The following steps need to be taken:

   a   Elect a group leader.

   b   Make sure the topic for discussion is clear to everyone.

   c   Arrive at a conclusion or recommendation, or provide a summary of what has been discussed.

   At the conclusion of the discussion, each member should write up a short report on how the discussion progressed. **Exhibit 9.18** (see p. 270) can be used to help group members to reflect on their contributions. These views should then be exchanged and discussed among all the participants.

   While one group discussion is in progress, another group can act as a team of observers using **Exhibit 9.19** to monitor types of contributions. After the group discussion, the observers should present their findings to the group for further discussion. The evaluation of the group discussion should be directed towards acknowledging task and maintenance roles demonstrated in the group, and identifying any areas for improvement of the process of group discussion.

Exhibit 9.19	Types of contributions in group discussions				
		Members			
Type of contribution		1	2	3	4
Task roles					
Gives information and opinion Asks for information and opinion Clarifies Summarises Evaluates Takes notes					
Maintenance roles					
Encourages discussion Listens to others Is cordial and pleasant Expresses feelings and mood Reduces tension Facilitates participation in the group					

4   Form a team and hold a team meeting (or meetings) to make a decision, solve a problem or complete a task, and to examine leadership in the team. Examine your team meeting skills using the team meeting skills checklist in **Exhibit 9.18** (see p. 270). Discuss leadership in the team using the following questions:

   a   How do the members provide leadership to accomplish the task?

   b   How do the members provide leadership to build the relationships in the team?

   c   How do the members provide leadership to establish a supportive working climate for the team?

   d   If there is a designated team leader, how does this person lead the team?

5   Read the following scenario and answer the questions that appear after it.

   A small research group of four, in a medium-sized firm, is working on one aspect of a larger project. Two members of the research group, Van Lui (research group leader) and Kip Thomas, have been with the firm for two years, and the other two members, Tom Moss and Kelly Partos, are employed on short-term contracts that expire in about eight months. Kelly, in particular, is a tremendous asset to the research group and is continually coming up with innovative ideas. Kelly's contribution has meant that the group's part in the total project is running smoothly and is well ahead of some of the other areas. The project manager is extremely pleased with the group's work and has complimented the group on its performance.

   Recently, though, Kelly has seemed to lack commitment to the research group. Kelly appears to be restless and has begun to arrive late and leave early. Kelly's contributions, though still extremely useful, seem to be more contained, as though something is being kept back. The other day, Van overheard Kelly talking on the telephone about opportunities interstate and the rights of employees. Kip has been spending a lot of time liaising with another research group and Tom is not meeting agreed deadlines. The working atmosphere is becoming tense, and morale seems to be declining.

   a   What is the nature and likely cause of any conflict in the group?

   b   What strategies can the group use to enhance both task and relationship functions in the group?

   c   How can the group use communication skills to deal with signs of conflict and prevent unnecessary communication breakdown or conflict?

6   Based on the following scenario, roleplay a decision-making meeting using effective communication skills and group decision-making processes. The decision-making role-playing may be conducted as a whole class activity using the following guidelines.

   You are students attending a class at a tertiary institution. You have all seen instructional e-learning systems such as Blackboard and Moodle in your classes and recognise the importance of using such technology to improve your skills as future graduates.

   The lecturer has asked the class to imagine that you are reviewing an e-learning management system to recommend whether the system should be used in the institution and, if so, whether it should be purchased outright or leased.

   The IT department maintains the e-learning management system. The normal charges for such systems are retail purchase price $30 000 or lease charge $10 000 per year. The IT budget, like all budgets these days, is limited, and is carefully scrutinised by other section heads in the institution.

   In order to advise the lecturer, first evaluate the system as a whole class, making individual notes about its content and quality. Then divide into small groups (about six to eight people in each), elect a chairperson and decide on a recommendation from your small group to the lecturer.

   The chair of each small group should structure the discussion so that a problem-solving process is used to make a decision, and the debate moves along logically and constructively. You might structure the small-group meeting according to the following questions:

   a   What is the problem?

   b   What are the issues?

c How well does this proposal (i.e., this e-learning system) solve the problem?

d What alternatives are available?

e Having evaluated the alternatives, what is your recommendation?

Each small-group meeting might begin by discussing the value to students of e-learning management systems. It should ask what qualities to look for in such systems. The small group should strive for consensus, a decision that each member will later be prepared to support in front of the whole class.

After the small groups have completed their meetings, the whole class reconvenes for a plenary session to report their discussions and decisions and move towards a recommendation from the whole class to the lecturer. If the small-group decisions have been different, the chairs of the small groups can meet to try to achieve an overall consensus for the whole class. This meeting can take place with the rest of the class acting as observers. This meeting of the chairs of the small groups should apply guidelines for achieving consensus until a negotiated recommendation to the lecturer can be accepted as representing the whole class.

Each small group should debrief its own decision-making process using the Exhibit 9.18 (see p. 270). The lecturer can also use this checklist to assist the whole class to review communication processes demonstrated in the plenary session and/or the meeting of the chairs of the small groups.

7 Use Exhibit 9.18 in a small group of which you are a member, such as a book club, group of friends, or social media group. What implications do the results have for the purpose of this group and for your contributions as a member of this group?

8 Arrange for a group or team where you are a member to use Exhibit 9.18 as a means of assisting the group or team to assess its goals, development and communication patterns. Together, discuss how the group or team might address any specific results and evaluate the usefulness of this checklist as a method of monitoring group or team processes.

9 The internet has a variety of services that allow for individuals to meet and discuss problems, either in real time or asynchronously. These are usually called 'forums'. Locate one or more of these services, and in groups try to discuss a class topic and reach a consensus or democratic decision. We think Reddit is an under-used social media site for energetic discussions. Students could even use a forum, chat group or the e-learning services of their institution. Discord, originally for gamers, is quite popular in recent times.

10 Open up YouTube, and search for 'Great Negotiation Role Play Exercise 101'. This should lead you to two videos. Play Part 1, and then prepare for Part 2. The videos are about negotiation, and allow you to practise the process, but ask you to elect to be either (A) a person who negotiates from a position of power, or (B) a person who negotiates from a position of weakness. You will need a friend to be your counterpart, and perhaps an observer who can take notes. The videos are useful starting points for further investigation and can be used in a class situation, or externally. You can look up other YouTube videos if you find this topic to be interesting. Doing the exercise/s is the main way to gain benefit from these videos, and lots of practice is the key to becoming a good negotiator.

WEBSITES

Centre for Creative Leadership, The 10 Characteristics of a Good Leader https://www.ccl.org/articles/leading-effectively-articles/characteristics-good-leader

Conflict Resolution Network http://www.crnhq.org

Mind Tools https://www.mindtools.com

New York Times article by Adam Bryant, How to run a more effective meeting https://www.nytimes.com/guides/business/how-to-run-an-effective-meeting

Skills You Need, *Negotiating across cultures* https://www.skillsyouneed.com/rhubarb/negotiation-across-cultures.html

REFERENCES

Adams, K., & Galanes, G. J. (2012). *Communicating in groups: Applications and skills* (8th ed.). McGraw Hill.

Barker, A. (2011). *How to manage meetings* (2nd ed.). Kogan Page.

Bateman, B., Wilson, F. C., & Bingham, D. (2002). Team effectiveness: Development of an audit questionnaire. *Journal of Management Development, 21*(3), 215–226.

Bateman, G. (2001). *Company meetings: What you need to know*. Butterworths.

Bird, V. (2018). *Groupthink and the importance of behavioural diversity*. Belbin.

Bundey, C., Cullen, J., Denshire, L., Grant, L., Norfor, J., & Nove, T. (1988). *Group leadership: A manual about group leadership and a resource for group leaders*. NSW Department of Health.

Cornelius, H. (2020). *Twelve conflict resolution skills*. Conflict Resolution Network. https://www.crnhq.org/12-skill-summary

de Bono, E. (1970). *Lateral thinking: creativity step by step*. Penguin.

de Bono, E. (1987). *Six thinking hats*. Penguin.

Dewey, J. (1910). *How we think*. D. C. Heath.

Frey, L. R. (Ed.). (2002). *New directions in group communication*. Sage Publications.

Hartnett, T. (2011). *Consensus-oriented decision making: The CODM model for facilitating groups to widespread agreement*. New Society Publishers.

Hoover, J. D. (2005). *Effective small group and team communication* (2nd ed.). Harcourt College Publishers.

Janis, I. L. (1972). *Victims of groupthink*. Houghton Mifflin.

Janis, I. L. (1982). *Groupthink: Psychological studies of policy decisions and fiascos* (Rev. ed.). Houghton Mifflin.

Jaques, D. (2004). *Learning in groups: A handbook for improving group work* (3rd ed.). Kogan Page.

Johnson, D. W., & Johnson, F. P. (2017). *Joining together: Group theory and group skills* (12th ed.). Pearson.

Kohler, A. (2022, October 13). Working from home is a proletariat revolution. *The New Daily*. https://thenewdaily.com.au/finance/2022/10/13/working-from-home-kohler/

Lumsden, G., Lumsden, D., & Wiethoff, C. (2010). *Communicating in groups and teams: Sharing leadership* (5th ed.). Wadsworth.

Magner, & Joske, P. E. (2012). *Joske's law and procedure at meetings in Australia* (11th ed.). Thomson Reuters Professional Australia.

Makela, R. (2022). *Three types of negotiation tactics and how to respond (with examples)*. https://www.salesreadinessgroup.com/blog/3-types-of-negotiation-tactics-and-how-to-respond

Newton, C. (2001). *Marvellous meetings: A facilitator's guide*. Gower.

Pittamapli, A. (2019, November 7). Why groups struggle to solve problems together. *Harvard Business Review*. https://hbr.org/2019/11/why-groups-struggle-to-solve-problems-together

Razzetti, G. (2020, July 23). How to make better decisions as a team. Fearless Culture.

Renton, N. E. (2005). *Guide for meetings and organisations* (8th ed.). LBC Information Services.

Rice, R. E. (1984). *The new media: Communication, research and technology*. Sage Publications.

Rose, J. D. (2011). Diverse perspectives on the groupthink theory: A literary review, *Emerging Leadership Journeys, 4*(1), 37–57.

Scholtes, P. (1996). *The team handbook: How to use teams to improve quality*. Joiner and Associates.

Toseland, R. W., & Rivas, R. F. (2013). *An introduction to group work practice: Pearson new international edition*. Pearson Higher Ed.

Tuckman, B. W. (1965). Developmental sequence in small groups. *Psychological Bulletin, 63*(6), 384–399. https://doi.org/10.1037/h0022100

Tuckman, B. W., & Jensen, M. A. C. (1977). Stages of small group development revisited. *Group and Organisational Studies, 2*(4), 419–427. https://doi.org/10.1177/105960117700200404

Tyson, T. (1998). *Working with groups* (2nd ed.). Macmillan Education Australia.

Watson, H. J., Vallee, J. M., & Mulford, W. R. (1980). *Structured experiences and group development*. Curriculum Development Centre.

Zartman, W. (2009). *Negotiation and conflict management: Essays on theory and practice*. Routledge.

Oral presentations, verbal reports and interviews

Chapter 10

Learning objectives

After reading this chapter, you should be able to:

- describe different types of oral presentation purposes and styles
- outline systematic steps for preparing and delivering an effective oral presentation
- explain how to develop and use effective visual aids to enhance a presentation
- describe different strategies for delivering an effective oral presentation.
- understand the purpose of different types of workplace interviews
- develop strategies to effectively respond to common interview questions.

Public speaking: fear and loathing in the classroom

Judith had to give an oral report to her university class and knew from past experience that it was going to be a struggle. She would rather write an extra essay or do an extra exam than stand up in front of an audience and speak. She prepared verbatim exactly what she needed to get across in note form, just in case she forgot what she wanted to say. She had a backup plan for if the data projector did not work. She had even practised the speech several times in front of her boyfriend, pausing at all the right places and using hand gestures for emphasis. As she was waiting for her turn to speak, she became more and more anxious – her heart was beating faster, her hands, armpits and feet were sweating, her stomach clenched, and her breathing was becoming shallow. She thought to herself, 'OK, I am not going to get through this looking anywhere near normal'. Yet, she knew she had to do this in order to pass the class.

When her turn came, she walked to the podium with her prepared paper and slideshow. At that moment she knew there was no way that she could just explain what she had written, so she just looked down at her paper and started reading. She kept forgetting where she was up to in the PowerPoint. She couldn't finish a sentence without taking three or four breaths. Her legs were shaking like jelly. She knew her face was beet red because she could feel all the blood rushing to it. She kept trying to look up to make eye contact with her fellow students, but she would immediately look down at her paper and continue to read from it. At times she felt a strong urge to just quit and run out of the classroom screaming. She barely held on and completed the presentation, but she felt so humiliated afterwards. She couldn't ever recall witnessing anyone who had such a nervous reaction when public speaking; she was convinced she was the only one. Oral reports, she thought, rank right up there as the most horrible, self-esteem draining experiences of her young life.

Source: Adapted from SocialAnxietySupport.com

Introduction

I saw a thing, actually a study that said: speaking in front of a crowd is considered the number one fear of the average person. I found that amazing. Number two was death. Death is number two? This means, to the average person, if you have to be at a funeral, you would rather be in the casket than doing the eulogy.

Source: Seinfeld (1999)

This quote from Jerry Seinfeld might seem funny, but we know some individuals who, like Judith in the opening scenario, would rather risk their lives than speak in public. In spite of such fears, professional people are frequently expected to speak in public in front of groups of people who they do not know. The occasion may be planned, so they have time to prepare, or unplanned and they have to speak impromptu. Many quite competent professionals, happy to chat about the latest information technology, flexitime systems, holiday destinations or futures investments to one or two people, feel very threatened and uncomfortable if asked to present an oral report to a larger audience at a meeting or more formal occasion. During your studies or in your careers there will also be many occasions when you will be required to speak or present to others – to small groups, the whole class, or one-on-one to your boss or a potential client or employer.

This chapter provides specific guidelines to help you improve your **public speaking** ability, and to help you speak effectively to a variety of audiences, such as peers, lecturers or tutors, colleagues in the workplace, members of the community, or potential clients. It also discusses another common form of oral communication, the interview; specifically those that are part of employment, such as job interviews.

Public speaking
The act of preparing and delivering an oral presentation or report to an audience.

Types of oral presentations and verbal reports

A *speech* is a formal talk or address prepared for a special occasion and requiring a fair amount of preparation. For example, well-known professionals in their fields may be invited to give keynote addresses at conferences, or eminent speakers may be invited to graduation ceremonies to give graduation speeches. A *talk* is less formal and is inclined to emphasise the personal relationship between speaker and audience, and may be more likely to lead to a discussion than would a speech or address.

An **oral report** is a special kind of talk, usually work-related or research-based and structured to give useful information about action taken or plans proposed. It resembles a lecture in that it may be illustrated by visual aids and graphics. While a *lecture* is concerned primarily to teach, an oral report is meant primarily to inform.

Oral report
A special kind of talk, usually work-related or research-based and structured to give useful information about action taken or plans proposed.

There are many different types of oral presentations that may be used for different purposes by students and professionals, and some of these purposes are shown in Exhibit 10.1.

Your social life may also offer you challenges that require public-speaking skills. Many professionals accept leadership positions in community organisations. Imagine yourself as president of school council, treasurer of the area scout group or a member of a Rotary club. Such positions often involve giving oral presentations to groups.

When it is your turn to speak before a group, there are a number of guidelines that will help you to succeed. As an initial step, planning is essential. Exhibit 10.2 outlines the steps that you should take to prepare your presentation.

Reflection question: Consider presentations that you've seen that were effective. What were the common characteristics that made them memorable?

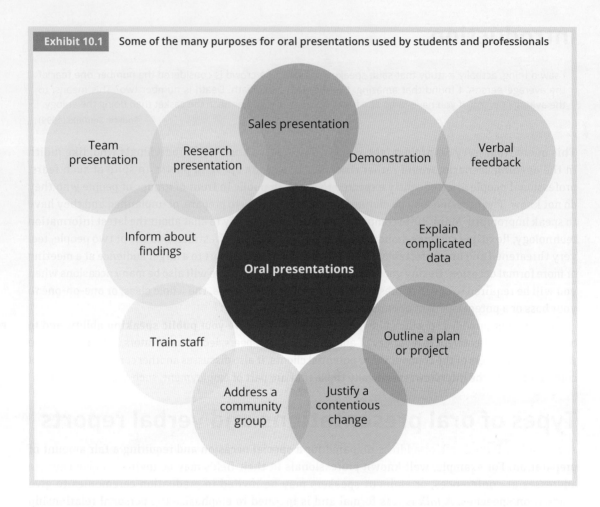

Exhibit 10.1 Some of the many purposes for oral presentations used by students and professionals

- Team presentation
- Research presentation
- Sales presentation
- Demonstration
- Verbal feedback
- Inform about findings
- Oral presentations
- Explain complicated data
- Train staff
- Outline a plan or project
- Address a community group
- Justify a contentious change

Planning oral presentations or verbal reports

Just as with other forms of professional communication, planning is important to ensure that an oral presentation is successful. Planning also helps minimise the onset of nerves or fear of public speaking, which will affect how your deliver your presentation and how your audience receives it. The following section outlines strategies to help you plan a successful presentation, and many of these are similar to those suggested for written communication. They include identifying and anticipating the needs and interests of your audience, and clarifying and identifying your purpose in giving the presentation. Both of these strategies will help you choose the most appropriate information and approach and allow you to consider how different sequences or structures may be used to best fulfil the needs of different audiences and different purposes.

Understand your audience

The audience that will listen to your oral presentation will include people with various backgrounds, knowledge, motivations and needs, so your first tasks will be to consider these aspects (see **Exhibit 10.3**). As with any effective communication, you will be looking for the areas where you can make a connection with the audience. That means you will need to find out as much as you can about them. Some of the questions you will need to ask are:

- Who is likely to be there? How many people will be there?
- What is their background, such as age, gender, education level and cultural background?
- Why will they be coming? What do they hope to gain from your presentation?

Exhibit 10.2   Steps in preparing a presentation

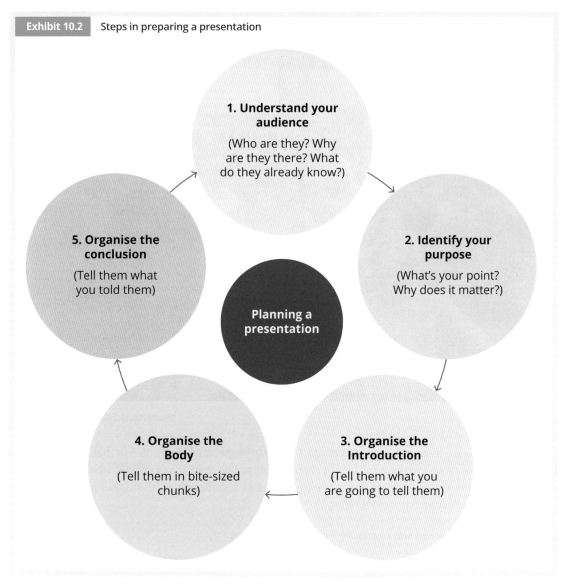

- How much do they already know about the topic? Are they novices or experts?
- What are their likely viewpoints on the topic?
- What are their possible attitudes toward you as a person? What reactions can you expect from them?

A knowledge of the composition and likely viewpoints of your audience will help you organise your ideas, choose your anecdotes and case studies, and define your delivery strategy. It will help you choose the appropriate words and tone for the delivery of your message to this audience. Additionally, considering the characteristics of most listeners and the difference between how listeners process written compared to spoken language (as discussed in Chapter 2) are also important.

Identify your purpose

It is the responsibility of the speaker to make the talk or oral report effective. The speaker must show that the subject has been researched properly and that the information is accurate and soundly based. Knowing your goal or objective is important for deciding how you are going to approach the topic. You should be clear about whether your oral presentation is intended to inform or teach, persuade, or entertain. Exhibit 10.4 summarises the differences between these. Even though a presentation may do all four of these things, one will usually dominate.

Exhibit 10.3	Audiences are varied and need to be considered when planning a presentation

Shutterstock.com/Boris Medvedev

Adequate preparation is vital. Each part of a talk needs to be prepared in advance so that the information holds together and relates to the main idea or theme. The speaker must know exactly what the objectives of the presentation are and should use these objectives as a guideline, so that ideas presented to the audience are logical, coherent and relevant.

Exhibit 10.4	Objectives and strategies for oral presentations	
Communication objective	Purpose and strategy	Example
To inform or teach	An informative speech conveys factual information, using clear examples that need to be tailored to the level of the audience's understanding. It aims to communicate ideas and information, or show how something works or can be performed	University lecture, staff meeting about a procedure change, conference presentation about a scientific discovery, or software use demonstration
To persuade	A persuasive speech addresses a need in the audience and provides reasons and actions to satisfy that need. It aims to bring the audience around to a particular point of view or to take a particular action	Sales presentation about a new car model or investment strategy, or political speech about a new policy
To entertain	An entertaining speech uses a variety of techniques, including humour, anecdotes and interesting examples around a common theme. Speakers aiming to inform and/or persuade often include these elements as a strategy	After dinner speech, or wedding speech

It is also a good idea to ask yourself the question, 'What will the audience say this talk was about?' Look at your planned presentation and analyse the main parts to see if they are contributing to or detracting from the message that you want to convey to the audience.

Consider the context and setting

The context or setting for a presentation will impact on many of these other factors when planning your speech. These include considering the location (where), the timing (when), the audience (who) and the purpose (why). **Exhibit 10.5** outlines examples of some of these and a selection of strategies that a speaker might adopt.

Exhibit 10.5 Contexts and settings for oral presentations

Context	Setting	Example	Strategies
An informal gathering of colleagues	A restaurant or social venue after hours	A short speech bidding farewell to someone who is retiring or leaving the company	Humour, anecdotes, impromptu, casual style
A formal public presentation	Large auditorium or conference hall	Conference presentation, keynote address	Prepared speech, visual aids, strictly timed, inform with researched examples, easy to follow structure, interesting examples
Presentation to the chief executive or senior managers	Boardroom, large corporate meeting room	Presenting the findings of an investigation into an issue or a new development proposal for the company	Focused summary of key points; a longer written report capturing members' key concerns. Well prepared visuals and questions
Sales presentation at a trade show	Conference arena shared with many other exhibitors, possibly noisy	Sales pitch demonstrating a new product or service to interested groups of people	Entertaining, lively, improvised style, using props and interactivity

Reflection question: Have you been in a situation where a speaker has used an inappropriate style of speaking for the audience or the occasion?

The importance of structure: sequence and clarity

In general terms, an oral presentation should have a **structure**; a sequence comprised of an introduction, or beginning; a body, or content; and a conclusion, or summary. These parts represent a 'sandwich approach' to public speaking that has been proven as a good starting point for developing your skills and is explained in more detail in the following sections. Later in the chapter, ways in which you might vary this approach, depending on the situation and needs of the audience, are discussed.

Structure
The order in which parts of a presentation are organised to help the listener more easily understand the points or arguments being made.

Organise the introduction

The introduction is a crucial part of any oral presentation. You need to focus the audience's attention directly on your message and establish your credibility. You must interest them in the topic and show how the topic will meet their needs. For example, you could begin with a startling statement or statistic, a question, a quotation, a story, or a comment on the venue, occasion, or what previous speakers have said. These openings allow time for the audience to settle down and adjust to your style. Whatever technique you choose, it is important that the audience knows what the talk is about from the outset.

Continue the presentation

Your listeners will appreciate it if the structure for the body or substance of your oral presentation allows them to follow your arguments easily, recognise important points, clarify abstract ideas, reinforce critical issues and draw conclusions with confidence. The substantive part of your oral presentation needs to be constructed carefully so that you can emphasise, inform and clarify for the audience as you need to.

Highlight main points

Helping the audience to understand the organisation and structure of an oral presentation is the key to sharing your message and making it easy for listeners to recognise and follow the main points. One of the most effective techniques for highlighting the main points is to number your ideas. This approach not only guides your listeners through the talk but also helps them to take effective notes or write a meaningful summary. In the following example, it only takes two sentences for this speaker to clearly indicates the most important element in their talk:

> There are three main factors that contribute to urban pollution – industrial waste, residential waste and transient waste. The first, and probably the most destructive, is industrial waste ...

Arrange ideas in a logical sequence

Your main ideas will need to be presented to the audience in a sequence that will seem logical to them. You could organise the main points in the following ways:

- *chronologically:* such as from the start to the finish of a project
- *in a spatial order:* for example, following the elements of a flow chart
- *from cause to effect or problem to solution:* for sequencing ideas.

An important issue for any speaker is how to provide a connection between ideas that will make sense and be meaningful to the audience. The use of transition words can help to convey a logical sequence of ideas to the audience. Words such as *however, therefore, consequently, next, then* and *finally* alert the listener to correlate a new idea with one that has already been presented.

Support and clarify ideas

You can support and clarify your ideas for the audience by using case studies, examples, anecdotes, statistics, research findings and your own or other people's personal experiences. Analogies allow the listener to relate a new idea to something already known and develop a mental picture in which the new concept can fit; for example, 'The new system is like an intricate web'. Another technique is to refer to well-known people who agree with the ideas being presented. Sales presentations frequently focus on the testimony of satisfied customers and describe the benefits of the product or service to typical customers the audience can relate to.

If an idea is crucial to the argument, it is wise to present that idea several times during the body of the talk. To do this, you can restate the idea in different words or illustrate it in various ways. Remember that the audience will need more help to understand material presented orally than if they could take their time to read the same material. Careful consideration of the presentation techniques discussed in this chapter will ensure that you can support and clarify your ideas for your listeners and help them remember your message.

Make the structure clear

The ideas of a talk may be clear in themselves but not necessarily clearly linked to each other. You need, especially in an informative talk, to keep reminding the listeners of the structure of the talk. You can use three devices to do this: *previews*, *transitions* and *summaries*.

The preview

In the preview you lay out the points you intend to make, so the audience can mentally tick off the points as you come to them. For example:

> In this discussion of comparable sales, I'd like to deal with three main types of property: commercial buildings, residential buildings and public buildings.

The transition

Suppose you are giving a talk of 15 to 20 minutes that has five main points. Unless the listeners can take notes, they need to be reminded when you are progressing from one point to the next. The transition statement can do this, for example:

> As we have seen, property values in this district have been increasing over the last few years. But what of the future? Will the department's plans to shift to another region mean that more properties will become available so that values fall? My fifth and final point is about this.

The question 'But what of the future?' makes it clear that one part of the talk has finished and the next one is about to be taken up. Notice that the transition technique here is in the form of a question and that a number of key points have been reiterated.

The summary

As you come to the end of each section of the talk it is a good idea to express again the main points. Don't merely repeat what you have already said. Use new words, but make sure it is concisely and directly related to what you have said before. And, of course, the summary at the end of the informative talk also helps the audience retain the overall structure and intended impact of the talk.

Vary the treatment of the subject

One of the guidelines for good composition of a talk is to use variety. Whether the talk is to inform, teach, persuade or entertain, you can add variety by combining different rhetorical modes, such as reporting, narration, instruction, demonstration, analysis, description and illustration. Look at each one of these modes, as outlined in **Exhibit 10.6**, and see how it can make your subject lively and memorable.

Exhibit 10.6 Different rhetorical modes for oral presentations

Rhetorical modes	Description
Reporting	A first-hand account of what the speaker saw, heard or did. Its value is its authenticity because it is an eyewitness report. People are generally more impressed by first-hand accounts than second-hand ones
Narration	Involves telling a story that is not necessarily first-hand. In a narrative, whether fact or fiction, you are answering a number of questions such as: What happened? How did it happen? When? Where? Who did it? Why was it done? (known as the 5Ws and 1H) There is a certain fascination in listening to an unfolding story. Narration is usually organised in time sequence and has a sense of suspense. Notice that the best conversationalists are usually renowned for their storytelling
Instruction	Informing and guiding people about what to do and how to do it is likely to be part of an oral presentation, especially in the workplace. It can be the central purpose of the talk. Clarity of purpose and pitching the instruction to the level of the audience are essential. Tone is important too. It is a good idea to organise instruction in stages and explain potential benefits for the audience
Demonstration	A visual demonstration can be used to add authenticity, variety and interest. For example, using a real golf club to demonstrate putting in a talk on golf is more effective than showing diagrams or pictures, or just describing it. The audience might be given a chance to practise golf putting themselves

Exhibit 10.6	Different rhetorical modes for oral presentations (*Continued*)

Rhetorical modes	Description
Analysis	Analysis means identifying the major divisions or constituent parts of a topic, such as the causes and effects of an event, or the essential characteristics of a program. You might, for example, analyse the causes and effects of the appreciation of property values, the essential characteristics of a successful marketing campaign, or the qualities of a good investment in the share market. The most important question for you to ask and answer in preparing your analysis is 'What are the logical divisions of the subject?'
Description	At some stage in most talks, you will have to explain what something looks like, how big it is, its shape and colour, and other aesthetic qualities it has. The purpose of description is to stimulate the imagination so that the listener can 'see' the object. It may be a substitute for demonstration or could accompany demonstration. Description should focus on the aspects of the topic particularly relevant to the talk. The description of a highway, for example, might focus on safety features, construction materials, traffic flow or scenery. The purpose of the talk should guide selection of descriptive information
Illustration	Giving good examples goes right to the heart of effective informative or persuasive speaking. For every sentence of analysis or instruction, you need at least one sentence of language to 'bring alive' the subject by enabling the audience to paint word pictures before their eyes. See the following example from a talk on 'the rat in history': *Do you know that a rat can swim half a kilometre, jump from a second-storey window, and survive without food for a month? Do you know that rats ate one-quarter of the grain crop in India last year?* You may forget the rest of the talk, but those powerful examples might stick in your mind – the best speakers take some care to think up memorable examples!

Conclude the presentation with conviction and flair

The conclusion is extremely important. There is a great temptation to underestimate its importance and to wrap up quickly. However, a well-presented conclusion can reinforce the central idea, sum up the main points, motivate the audience to action or stir their emotions. It can ensure that the audience leave thinking and feeling just the way you hoped they would.

To begin this section of your presentation, you can simply say, 'In conclusion …' or 'To sum up …' and restate the main points, or you may illustrate the main points by telling a story. A challenging statement or a rhetorical question towards the end of a talk can encourage the listeners to think or act on the ideas presented. When composing the conclusion to your talk, do not forget to refer to both the goal of your speech and its theme.

One useful analogy for the presentation process is that you have opened a series of windows during your report, and you have closed them with your analysis and conclusion. Try to open one more small window that remains half opened, right at the end. Ask a question, draw a comparison, announce a topic that needs attention, or ask the audience to consider a larger question.

 CASE STUDY 10.1 Introducing and concluding oral presentations

Assam, Bryan and Chris are three students who are preparing an oral presentation to the whole class on the topic 'workplace health and safety (WHS) laws'.

During the research phase of their presentation, Assam discovered Australian Bureau of Statistics data from 2021 that showed the majority of work-related injuries were sustained by 15 to 24-year-olds. Bryan discovered that bullying comes under the WHS definition and also composed a question: 'Stress does not count as a WHS issue because people do not suffer physical damage – true or false?' Chris found that there is a new

Act to replace the old *Occupational Safety and Health Act* and this will mean some changes as the Commonwealth seeks to bring all states into line under one 'umbrella' Act. He also found Acts such as the, *Anti-Discrimination Act* and *Human Rights and Equal Opportunity Commission Act* plus the proposed new *Workplace Health and Safety Act*. They decided that their presentation could cover three main aspects:

1. a definition of WHS
2. legislation for WHS
3. obligations of workplaces regarding WHS.

Each student wrote a draft introduction and conclusion to the oral presentation and brought them to the group for discussion.

Assam's introduction

Welcome to our presentation on workplace health and safety. We'll be explaining three main areas of this huge topic: first, what workplace health and safety means; second, what the Acts say about workplace health and safety; and third, what obligations organisations have under these workplace health and safety Acts in their workplaces. It's important to realise that in Queensland, in 2020, 25 per cent of work-related injuries were sustained by 15 to 24-year-olds.

Assam's conclusion

As you can see, workplace health and safety is of vital concern to managers because of the need to comply with the relevant Acts. We would like to leave you with the thought that workplace health and safety is part of professional practice for us all, not just for those directly responsible for its implementation in the workplace. You can find detailed checklists for compliance to risk assessment on the internet.

Bryan's introduction

True or false: 'Stress does not count as a workplace health and safety issue because people do not suffer physical damage'? Well, if stress includes anxiety and mental distress, then the answer is 'false'. Welcome to our presentation on workplace health and safety (which we'll refer to as WHS). We hope you enjoy it and learn a lot.

Bryan's conclusion

In summary, WHS is about protecting resources in the workplace – human, technical and infrastructure. Poor practices in WHS can be costly and must be avoided. In this presentation we have explained a number of obligations that employers must adhere to, and in particular how new legislative changes will impact on them. Thank you very much.

Chris's introduction

In this presentation on workplace health and safety, we'll be explaining three main areas of this huge topic: (1) What is WHS?; (2) Acts relevant to WHS; and (3) obligations for employers. We'll be covering the *Workplace Health and Safety Act*, *Anti-Discrimination Act* and the *Human Rights and Equal Opportunity Commission Act*, in that order. As there is new legislation being enacted as we speak, it is important for all managers and persons conducting a business or undertaking to understand their roles and responsibilities.

Chris's conclusion

In conclusion, there are three relevant Acts regarding WHS: *Workplace Health and Safety Act (2012)*, *Anti-Discrimination Act* and *Human Rights and Equal Opportunity Commission Act*. Obligations for employers can be found on the government websites such as WorkCover NSW and Safe Work Australia, as we have explained. We think it's a very worthwhile topic for us all to know about.

Discussion and activities

From the introductions and conclusions contributed by the three group members, decide which are the best or make changes to create an introduction and conclusion that you prefer. Present them to the whole class for evaluation.

After you have discussed this case study, refer to the 'Comments on case studies' section at the end of the text.

Other structures for organising a talk

While the sandwich approach of introduction (beginning), body (middle) and conclusion (end) is often used as a format for many types of oral presentations, other structures might be useful for certain situations and particular audiences. Examples of other ways of structuring or organising a talk (Blair, 1995), are the sequential argument, hierarchical explanation, question orientation, and pyramid structure, which will be discussed in the following.

Sequential argument

A sequential-argument-type talk is structured as a series of statements leading to a conclusion that takes the audience along as a logical argument develops. This structure might be suitable where the speaker needs to challenge preconceived ideas held by the audience. For example, in a talk on climate change, first establish a definition of the subject. Second, link this definition to practices in industry that may have effects on the composition of the atmosphere. Third, link to examples of extreme weather events around the world. Fourth, project increases in ocean levels and the effects on coastlines. Fifth, offer suggestions for families to implement that can contribute to reversing this trend.

Hierarchical explanation

A talk can be broken into a hierarchy of topics, subtopics and even smaller topics, and be accompanied by explanation of what you are going to cover in the time available. Reinforce your plan by reiterating the hierarchy of topics and subtopics. This keeps the speaker on track and the audience oriented to the whole presentation.

For the oral presentation on climate change, a hierarchy of three topics might be proposed: definition, causes and recommendations. Subtopics could be definition – history, results from scientific papers, report from the IPCC, current Australian views; causes – industry, agriculture, policies; and recommendations – international, national, local. The speaker would indicate the order and detail of discussion of topics and subtopics.

Question orientation

A talk can be oriented to answer a number of questions about a problem or issue. The problem/issue can be introduced, options can be proposed, advantages and disadvantages can be canvassed, a preferred solution may be decided on, or the discussion can be summarised for future decision-making.

In terms of the climate change presentation, the issue can be stated as 'What can we do to help mitigate climate change?' The background and extent of the problem could then be explained. A proposal of options could then be presented, such as changing production methods; reducing the use of electricity; using alternative sources of electricity, like installing solar panels; and introducing recycling. A discussion can then occur regarding advantages and disadvantages relating to costs and company image, and recommendations can then be made or a summary of outcomes presented.

Pyramid structure

The main ideas/conclusions of the talk are all presented at the beginning and are then elaborated on as the talk progresses. As the audience already knows the main features of the presentation, they may be more receptive to listening to further detail on key points. So, a presentation on climate change to a company's board might begin as follows:

> Climate change is a real threat to the earth's environment, and I am advocating that this firm cuts its use of electricity by 20 per cent by reviewing our use of lighting. First, I will explain why climate change is such a threat. Second, I will outline the costs and usage of electricity by this firm. Third, I will explain how the firm's use of lighting can be changed to achieve a 20 per cent reduction in consumption of electricity, reduce our costs and hence contribute to helping to prevent the escalation of the detrimental effects of climate change.

Reflection question: What techniques that speakers use do you find most effective in being able to absorb and remember a speech or presentation?

Creating effective audio-visual and multimedia aids

Once you have a clear idea of the message you wish to communicate, you can give some thought to the various means of conveying that message. Visual or audio-visual aids can greatly enhance the effectiveness of your oral communication. However, if they are not properly designed and skilfully produced, they can be damaging. The main functions of audio-visual aids are shown in Exhibit 10.7.

Remember that all the elements of a visual aid contribute to its success or failure (see a more detailed discussion in Chapter 6). Since communication is the basis for good graphic design, you should ask yourself if the picture, shape, colour, font style, animation effect and medium all serve an identifiable function in your presentation. If the aids do not add to the clarity of the idea, contribute impact or help you to persuade or motivate your audience, then don't use them. Each aid must have a definite function and should not just be used to fill blank space.

Exhibit 10.7   The main functions of audio-visual and multimedia aids

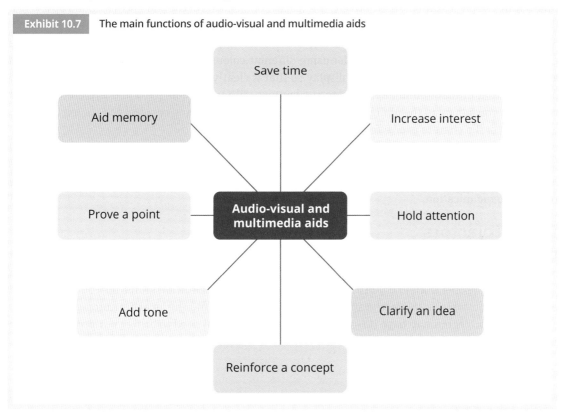

Types of audio-visual aids

You can make your own audio-visual aids or purchase from items that have already been prepared by commercial suppliers. There are countless aids at your disposal, ranging from quite simple models to elaborate and expensive computerised displays. You can consult business magazines and journals for advertisements from the various manufacturers and distributors of communication equipment, and request further information or a demonstration of the latest items that might suit your needs. Thinking beyond visual aids as pictures on paper or projections on a screen, and instead using audio-visual aids, will usually make presentations more interesting and gives a speaker more flexibility in presenting information. Let us begin by considering the most common visual aids.

Whiteboards and flip charts

A whiteboard or flip chart is still a popular piece of equipment to help with oral presentations, particularly during meetings and group discussions. Whiteboards and can be fixed or moveable. Electronic whiteboards allow the presenter to print a copy of what has been drawn on the board as a record that may be given to the participants. Interactive whiteboards (IWBs) are connected to a computer via USB, cable or Bluetooth. They can be touch-based and are connected in a variety of ways including infrared scan (IR touch) or by electromagnetic pen – the technology is rapidly evolving. These days in classrooms they are often connected to a school network and can interact with other online users to allow material to be shared.

Flip charts are moveable and are designed so that a pad of paper can be attached to a stand like an easel. While they may seem old fashioned and low-tech, they can be useful as a point of difference from overused visual aids such as PowerPoint, and an alternative when more high-tech aids are not available. The speaker can prepare the board or flip chart in advance and refer to the material at the appropriate time during the presentation. Alternatively, the speaker or members of the audience can build up a visual illustration on the board or flip chart as the talk or discussion progresses.

To use a whiteboard or flip chart effectively, you need to keep the writing legible, straight, and large enough for the audience to read. Consider using different-coloured pens for visual impact. You should always plan the material you intend to display so that it clearly reinforces your message. One skill to develop is that of maintaining appropriate eye contact with your audience while you are writing or drawing. If you adhere to the principle of keeping visual aids simple and concise, you should be able to use a board or flip chart to good effect.

Regardless of the technology, boards of all kinds are not good for large audiences and can give the feel of a teacher–student interaction. However, the ability to respond in real time and record audience ideas and comments does allow the speaker or presenter to encourage interaction, establish rapport and create two-way communication.

Data projectors

Data projectors are widely used these days to project computer-based presentations such as PowerPoint onto a large screen (see **Exhibit 10.8**). They may be fixed in situ in a room with a lectern or console or be transportable on a trolley. If you are planning on using a presentation stored on your own laptop, ensure that you carry with you the appropriate adaptor to plug into the local data projector. In many cases, a data projector may have its own hard drive and you will need to bring your presentation on a USB.

PowerPoint

Microsoft PowerPoint is the most popular presentation program in the world. It allows users to easily create professional-looking presentations on a computer, laptop or tablet. The application handles text, graphics, video, digital pictures, weblinks and clip art with an intuitive interface similar to Microsoft Word. Coloured backgrounds, text, indentation and slide change animations are easy to construct with practice. Richly coloured electronic slide shows, complete with speaker's notes and handouts, can be designed. PowerPoint presentations can be displayed by connecting your laptop or inserting a USB flash drive to an in-situ data projector.

Avoiding death by PowerPoint

According to Paradi (2019), PowerPoint presentations are becoming the default method of communication in organisations, with an increasing number of people reporting that they see at least two or more each week. Respondents to Paridi's 'Annoying PowerPoint Survey' complained that they are increasingly being used to 'brain dump' documents onto a screen rather than being created with a clear organised purpose or understanding of effective design in mind, leading to information overload, and 'death by PowerPoint' where the audience is overwhelmed and bored.

| Exhibit 10.8 | Using a data projector can make a group presentation more effective |

Getty Images/Helen King

PowerPoint is deceptively simple, but it is easy to make mistakes. The guidelines in Exhibit 10.9 will help you to avoid such mistakes and can also be applied to other kinds of visual displays.

| Exhibit 10.9 | Rules for creating PowerPoint presentations |

1. Use a new slide for each new topic or subtopic

2. Start each slide with a header that summarises the slide topic

3. Limit content to around six to eight lines per slide

4. Avoid large slabs of text, unless you wish to read them aloud

5. Don't use full sentences on slides: use key points only

6. Select easy to read fonts, large enough to be read anywhere in the room (min. 18 pt)

7. Leave adequate space between letters, words and lines.

8. Images should be as large and clear as possible (at least 200 dpi)

9. Use colour with contrast and readability to add interest and aid understanding

Printed text taken directly from a textbook or a typed report is seldom suitable for projection. It is usually too small to read and too complicated to be quickly and easily understood. Instead, provide handouts or design a special-purpose visual that can be projected and read easily.

Finally, don't be tempted to use the PowerPoint slides in place of your notes. The temptation can be to read from the screen, but this will take your eyes from the audience and muffle your voice. Print out your own notes page in hard copy so that you can keep your eyes with your audience at all times. The slides are what your audience sees; they should reinforce your words, not repeat them.

Is PowerPoint 'making us stupid'?

The ubiquity of PowerPoint in both the classroom and business world has led some researchers and technical communicators to question the effectiveness and impact of this over-reliance. One such researcher, Edward Tufte (2003), argues that the widespread use of the template and default settings, the enforced inbuilt hierarchical structures and the animation tools create a number of problems. He contends that they can distract an audience from the speaker, dumb down the content by forcing a simplistic bullet point structure, and mislead an audience by encouraging poorly constructed and misleading graphs, which he calls 'chart junk' and 'conspicuous decoration'. Rather than supporting a presentation, he says, it has become a substitute for one. Other researchers, such as Doumont (2005) and Mackiewicz (2007), while accepting some of Tufte's comments, argue that his evidence is largely anecdotal and that presentation software like PowerPoint can be extremely useful in supporting a presenter. The tool, they argue, should not be blamed for the way people use it, and all presenters should consider the needs and characteristics of their audience when it comes to aspects of slide design such as text, colour, and charts or graphs.

Multimedia

Different forms of multimedia can be used to introduce additional interest to the audience and have the benefit of input from people who are not present. Excerpts can be used to introduce a topic, reinforce a point, present a case study or provide emotional impact. Videos from YouTube can be used for instructional purposes as part of a presentation, and can also be integrated with a PowerPoint presentation. PowerPoint allows direct video links from its screens, but this may be a problem if the internet is security-protected at the location you are using.

Delivering oral presentations or verbal reports

Planning the presentation is the next important stage after preparing the content. Any talk or oral report that you have spent time and effort researching and writing deserves to be presented in a professional and polished manner. The techniques and style you adopt will, of course, vary from situation to situation. However, each element of the delivery needs to be analysed and the most appropriate approach chosen.

Types of speech delivery

There are a number of situations in which a professional may be called on to deliver a speech and so the strategies you use will relate to the type of delivery you are expected to prepare. Exhibit 10.10 outlines the types of speeches; however, most speeches will include a combination of delivery types.

Exhibit 10.10	Types of speeches
Type	**Description**
Impromptu	An unexpected speech that will allow little time for preparation. Examples include welcomes, introductions or acknowledgements. As this type of speech usually takes the speaker by surprise, make it brief and to the point, but have an introduction and conclusion. If time permits, make note of a few key points
Memorised	In this type of speech, the speaker will remember everything that has to be said, and is best suited to shorter, more formal speeches
Manuscript	This is usually researched and structured. It is suited to technical and formal business and conference presentations. Notes are essential but should be used appropriately – use small notes with bullet points to assist memory, don't read from a long manuscript
Extemporaneous	The most common type of delivery, used by most teachers, lawyers or people who speak for large amounts of time per day. Ideas should be memorised rather than specific words, except for key transitions, introduction, conclusion and maybe key examples
Formal	On some formal occasions the speaker may read a prepared speech to the audience that is written in full, and may make a copy available to the press or others afterwards

Using notes

Some oral presentations are written in full, but it is generally best that oral presentations and verbal reports be prepared in outline form. The speaker should write down the main or key points and then expand on these in their own words so that the delivery sounds conversational and personal.

Speaking by reading from a full script is comforting for the nervous speaker – you can't collapse or 'dry up' – but it is very difficult to give a lively and engaging presentation by reading every word aloud (see **Exhibit 10.11**). Using brief notes requires that you know your material fairly well, then your notes serve to simply keep you on track.

Exhibit 10.11	It is difficult to give an engaging presentation by reading every word from your notes

Shutterstock.com/vchal   Shutterstock.com/GobMetha

There are many useful ways of constructing notes for a talk. You can use small cards, half-sheets of paper or a skeleton outline on a single sheet of paper. You should experiment with different methods and choose the one that suits you. Some speakers write their first and last sentences out in full and rehearse them. Keep in mind that there is nothing worse than stumbling over your own notes.

Should your material be lengthy or complicated, such as in a conference presentation or a seminar paper, you may feel the need to have a fully written script for support. In fact, you may need to provide a written paper as well as present orally. In cases like these, it is still a good idea to incorporate an outline approach to allow yourself as much audience contact as possible. You can achieve this by underscoring or highlighting key points, and marking the script to show sections that need emphasis or visual aids.

Print the script in a large font that is easy to scan and read. Other strategies that can help you to deliver your presentation smoothly include careful organisation of how much content is on each page, numbering the points and binding the script. Numbering your pages will also allow you to keep them in sequence, especially if you are nervous.

Writing for the ear

As noted earlier, people process information differently when they *read* it as opposed to when they *hear* it. Some differences are summarised in **Exhibit 10.12.**

Exhibit 10.12	The difference between oral and written presentations and reports
Oral presentations or verbal reports	**Written presentations or reports**
Listeners must understand the first time	Readers can reread if they don't understand
Listeners can provide direct feedback (questions) or indirect feedback (body language)	Readers initial reactions are not known
Listeners' attention span is limited	Readers' attention span is longer
Content is usually shorter, abridged and less dense	Content can be longer, and developed in more depth
Listeners in face-to-face presentations are usually subject to physical restrictions, such as having to stay seated	Readers have fewer physical restrictions; they can choose their location and the pace at which they read
Speakers use pause, inflection, intonation, pitch and pace to aid understanding	Writers use paragraphs, punctuation and page layout and design to aid understanding
Information retrieval is harder unless listeners take notes or record the presentation	Information retrieval is easier
Speakers can help listeners stay interested with activities, audience questions, a variety of multimedia or visual aids	Writers can help readers stay interested with clear paragraphs, use of graphic devices such as illustrations, tables, graphs, colour and layout

When preparing an oral presentation or verbal report, a speaker should, therefore, write their script for the *ear.* An important technique is to practice your script by reading it aloud so that you *hear* any problems with your choice of language, the length of your sentences, appropriate punctuation and perhaps need for pause, inflection, tone or other vocal cues to help the listeners follow your points more easily. Remember that speaking is slower than reading, and where there is a time limit, as in a conference presentation, you may need to adjust your script to ensure that your main points fit within the allotted time.

Other strategies to listen for include:

- Have a clear structure, including a strong and interesting introduction, an organised body, and a clear summary or conclusion that the audience will remember.
- Use active verbs with simple sentences.
- Use concise words or phrases with clear meanings that the listeners will understand and relate to.
- Allow for pauses or breathing spaces so listeners can 'catch up' with your points and arguments.
- Provide verbal signposting so listeners can move through your speech; for example, 'to sum up', 'a case in point is', or 'in other words'.
- Select and use relatable examples to appeal to the interests and characteristics of your audience.

Meaningful non-verbal behaviour

Non-verbal activity certainly has the capacity to help speakers keep the attention of their audience, if used effectively. Chapter 3 discussed the link between verbal and non-verbal communication, especially in oral presentations. The following presents a few more hints about the potential impact on an audience of negative and positive non-verbal cues. Exhibit 10.13 provides some of the non-verbal cues and mannerisms that should be avoided as they detract from a speaker's impact. And Exhibit 10.14 outlines positive non-verbal cues to attend to that help to ensure an oral presentation is successful.

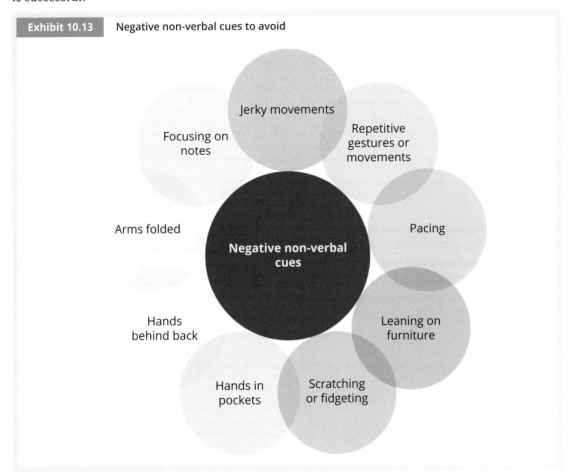

Exhibit 10.13   Negative non-verbal cues to avoid

Jerky movements

Focusing on notes

Repetitive gestures or movements

Arms folded

Pacing

Negative non-verbal cues

Hands behind back

Leaning on furniture

Hands in pockets

Scratching or fidgeting

Using your voice

Chapter 3 discussed the paralinguistic, or vocalic, aspects of communication; that is, everything except the sense of the words spoken. In oral presentations, the audibility, articulation, assimilation and pronunciation, pitch and speed are relevant considerations. Any one of these factors can help or hinder the speaker's effectiveness.

Audibility

Speakers can, of course, be too **audible**. So, if you have a naturally strong voice, don't let it intimidate your audience by becoming too loud. Just make sure you project your voice to fill the room, according to the size of the audience, purpose of the speech and availability of a microphone.

People with quieter voices can get greater force and resonance by dropping their pitch a little. The inaudible speaker may be a mumbler, or a person who allows his or her voice to fall away at the end of sentences so that the most important words are lost. Practise maintaining consistent volume. You could get a friend to listen to you speak in rehearsal and give you frank criticism.

Audibility
The quality or fact or degree of being perceptible by the ear.

Exhibit 10.14	Positive non-verbal cues to attend to

Non-verbal cue	Description
Posture	Stand comfortably erect, weight equally distributed on both feet, with some movement to provide visual variety
Gestures	Practise gestures to ensure they are meaningful and functional: • *Descriptive gestures:* hands used to convey imaginary pictures of sizes, shapes, motions, relationships and directions • *Emphatic gestures:* 'This was not the only problem' (a raised index finger), 'Right here was the crux of the problem' (a two-handed chop, palms facing each other), 'We can do it!' (a pumped fist) • *Enumerative gestures:* one or more fingers used to suggest numbers ('First of all …', 'There are three advantages …', 'The second consideration …') • *Pointing gestures:* to locate points on a visual aid or on an imaginary landscape (but don't point at the audience). Gestures should be natural and spontaneous. Rehearsal helps because fear of public speaking can inhibit normal gesture use
Clothing	Choose appropriate attire for the occasion and the audience. Underdressing or overdressing can alienate an audience and affect a speaker's credibility. Vital first impressions are formed by non-verbal cues, such as a speaker's clothes, grooming, hairstyle, jewellery and even the brands or types of objects and equipment used during the presentation

Articulation

Articulation
The formation of clear and distinct sounds in speech.

Articulation means the way words are formed with the tongue, lips, teeth, and hard and soft palate. The clarity and sharpness of articulation determine the intelligibility of speech. Slow movement of the tongue, lips and jaw may result in mumbled speech that can convey the impression of inexperience or uncertainty. Excessive care in articulation, on the other hand, may sound artificial. The most important thing is to speak as clearly as possible (perhaps more slowly than you would normally), so that the audience does not have to strain to hear your words.

Assimilation

Assimilation is an aspect of articulation; it means running words together. We all do this, saying things like:

> I haftago t'uni.
> He usta be a good driver.

But excessive assimilation can sound sloppy and vague:

> Wassapnin? (What's happening?)
> Emmachisit? (How much is it?)

Make sure that in oral presentations you speak at a rate at which your words are distinct and your phrasing is clear.

Pitch and inflection

Pitch
How relatively high or low a tone is perceived to be.

Inflection
A variation in pitch as indicated by the ups and downs of a person's voice.

The frequency of vibrations in vocal cords accounts for **pitch** and pitch range. Excessively high pitch can sound like whining; excessively low pitch can sound muffled. **Inflection** is variation of pitch and should be used to avoid a monotonous tone. We usually inflect downwards at the end of a sentence; however, a repeated upward inflection at the end of a sentence can suggest tentativeness. Monotony of pitch is the main weakness to avoid.

Rate

Speakers are usually regarded as being more enthusiastic and committed when they increase their speech rate. On the other hand, very fast speech can be tiring to listen to, and may imply a lack of thoughtful consideration. Slow speakers may impress by their apparent wisdom and strength, or conversely may appear to lack confidence. Perhaps the solution is to practise speaking mostly at a normal rate (about 100 words per minute); speed up when you recount a story or explain an incident; slow down when you analyse a difficult idea, define an abstract concept or present a key point.

Pausing and silences

Use pauses to vary rate. Note that you can use the pause immediately before making a key point – or immediately after doing so. In the first case, the audience is alerted to expect something special and will pay attention. In the second case, silence allows what you have told them to sink in.

Combating the 'ums'

Some speakers can distract with their 'ers' and 'ums'. These sounds are, of course, indications of nervousness, so we are all sympathetic. But they can be irritating. If you are addicted to 'ers' and 'ums', try using pauses instead. And speak a little more slowly. This change may need a lot of rehearsal. Try rehearsing your speech to family or friends before the 'big day' of the public talk and practise using the pause while you collect your thoughts or identify the next word you wish to use.

Reflection question: What verbal or non-verbal habits of speakers do you find most distracting or irritating?

Overcoming Murphy's Law: be prepared for all eventualities

Murphy's Law states that whatever can go wrong will go wrong, and this can be disastrous for public speaking, especially if you are nervous to start with. So, consider the following summary when you are planning your presentation:

1 Plan to arrive early. This is especially important if you are unfamiliar with the venue location, or the layout and equipment provided. Are there enough seats? Can everyone see the presentation? Arriving flustered because you couldn't find a parking space or couldn't locate the room is not a good start. Being interrupted as people shuffle for seats is distracting to you and your audience.

2 Check ahead that the equipment works and that you are familiar with how to operate it. Do you have the correct attachment for your computer? Are you familiar with the lecture room console or how to dim the lights? Use a remote to advance the slides as this frees you to move away from the computer and closer to the audience.

3 If your presentation will rely on the internet, check that the network is working or that you have the login code needed to access the wireless in a remote location. Set up software, external links and have demonstrations ready to go so that you can quickly Alt-Tab between your presentation and the demonstration. Be aware of possible internet timeouts.

4 Have a backup of your presentation. USBs can be faulty, data projectors or laptop connections may not work, or display preferences might not be set up properly for the equipment. Always carry a secondary copy on a separate USB or upload a presentation to an online repository, or even carry backup whiteboard markers in case the tech-based presentation equipment does not work.

5 If an audio-visual aid is found to be faulty during a presentation, it is best to improvise and change to some other way of presenting information, rather than persevering with something that might become a strain for the audience and make them lose attention.

6 Finally, practise your presentation so that you are familiar with your material and with the timing. Speaking is slower than reading, so you may need to trim your speech by removing less important information and slides.

Reflection question: Consider presentations that you have witnessed or delivered that have been ruined by equipment breakdowns or other unforeseen events. What strategies did the presenter use to recover? If they didn't, what could they have done?

CASE STUDY 10.2   The end of the lecture can't come soon enough

iStock.com/Wavebreakmedia

Since the internet began its inevitable and relentless domination of our lives, dozens of industries have succumbed to its power: newspapers, books, music, movies, travel planning and holiday rentals. Now, belatedly, it appears the university lecture is about to meet the same fate.

[Several Australian universities] have announced plans to phase out lectures in their undergraduate courses. The reason is simple: it turns out, attendance at most is dismal – about 50 per cent or thereabouts.

[So, what is the problem?] The fact is that lectures are anything but a great way to learn. One expert stands in front of a room of ... students [and] pontificates for an hour or more on a topic while students pay attention or stare out the window, take notes or play hangman with their neighbours.

There's one exception to this rule. On rare occasions, a professor with a performance streak uses the lecture hall for its true purpose: theatre. These exceptions take great care in writing, rehearsing, and performing their lectures, using them to build narratives, suspense, even intrigue, thereby holding students' attention and encouraging them to attend.

...

Source: Adapted from J. Goodman (2015, July 28). The end of the lecture can't come soon enough. Studiosity.

Discussion

In small groups, discuss the following questions with respect to your experiences as attendees or students in university lectures or professional conferences:

1   From the perspective of characteristics of effective oral presentations, why do you think students or conference attendees find presentations boring or non-engaging?

2   What techniques have good presenters used to present material?

3   What are some examples of poor techniques?

4   What advantages do recorded video lectures or 'lecture pods' have over live lectures? What are the disadvantages?

After you have discussed this case study, refer to the 'Comments on case studies' section at the end of the text.

Question time

Oral presentations of a business, informative or technical kind are usually followed by a question time. This is a valuable opportunity for the speaker to connect with the audience. Listen carefully to any questions in order to try to clarify aspects for the audience. Sometimes a speaker can make more impact with effective answers to good questions than through the prepared presentation itself.

You may invite questions at any time throughout the talk. The advantages include the following:

- Confused listeners can be put straight about details and will then understand the rest of the talk.
- Questions provide useful feedback about the clarity of points made by the speaker.
- The talk seems more like a relaxed conversation if the speaker is prepared to be interrupted at any time.
- Questions can allow the audience more direct interaction with the speaker.
- Variety and novelty keep the audience concentrating on the topic.

However, there are also disadvantages to note:

- Questions may develop into debates and take up too much time, breaking the speaker's control of his or her topic development.
- Some questions are unnecessary, being points that the speaker will cover during the talk if the listeners were to wait.
- Questions during a presentation can be distracting, especially for an inexperienced speaker.

So, for more formal reports and speeches it's probably better to let the audience know there will be a question time at the end. But make sure the talk does not go over time and prevent this possibility.

Fear of public speaking

The mere thought of standing in front of a group and making a speech is likely to be quite daunting or even anxiety provoking (see **Exhibit 10.15**). Yet, most of us are experienced speakers in our daily lives. We spend a great portion of each day talking to friends, associates, supervisors, teachers and parents. Sometimes we speak to them in a one-to-one situation, and sometimes we relay a message to them as a group. We may be on the phone for as much as an hour a day. You probably take your skills in these situations for granted yet doubt your competence at proposing a toast at a wedding or presenting your ideas at a staff meeting.

| Exhibit 10.15 | Fear of public speaking is a common experience |

Shutterstock.com/LightField Studios

Most people are nervous about the prospect of talking to an audience. As we begin our talk, we listen to ourselves and become critical of what we are saying, fearing that we will forget what comes next. This fear may become self-fulfilling. The result can be stumbling over words, confusion and eventually panic that results in the 'dry-up' (a situation where your mouth becomes dry and you struggle to speak), which is the worst-case scenario.

What speakers forget, or don't realise, is that most audiences are receptive to a speaker and want the speaker to succeed and have a fair go. If the speaker is not a success, the audience can feel distressed on behalf of the speaker. In other words, most audiences support speakers and share their nervousness.

Why do we feel fear toward public speaking? Why does it occur when we get up to speak, even if we are quite calm about chatting to the same people in a group around a coffee table? The following are some of the key causes of fear of public speaking:

- A strong desire to succeed probably causes us to 'care' a lot about this speech.
- Consciousness of our inadequacies or lack of preparation fills us with feelings of dread.
- We may misinterpret the situation; for example, we may think the audience is very critical of us and can tell that we are nervous.

The following discusses ways in which we can reduce or eliminate fear of public speaking.

Controlling fear of public speaking

The following guidelines will help you to control your fear of public speaking.

1. Realise that nervousness, and even a little bit of anxiety, is normal, and can even be beneficial. Many great stage actors claim to have been nervous every night of their performing careers. Nervousness causes adrenalin to flow, which assist you to make a strong effort and think well on your feet.

2. Remember that the audience is unaware of your nerves and is usually friendly towards you. People are there because they want to hear from you. So, assume their friendliness and behave in a friendly way towards them. Smile confidently and begin the speech with something firm and positive. The audience will mirror your confidence and regard you as one who is not going to waste their time. This empathy from the audience will reinforce your confidence and get you off to a promising start.

3. Understand that there are physiological aspects to all nervousness that can be tackled separately. The adrenalin that is released into the bloodstream results in:
   - faster heartbeat
   - laboured breathing
   - increased perspiration
   - dry mouth
   - minor shaking of the hands.

   You might find it helpful to use some tension-releasing techniques. For example, physical exercise will help drain off the worst of the nervousness. Before the talk, exercises, even just some brisk pacing about (if you can) or pressing your hands or fingers against a table or a chair, may help. As will taking some deep breaths in through the nose and out through the mouth.

4. Use notes; though as a stand-by, not as a crutch. Using your notes too much can distance you from the audience and they might lose interest. This in turn may bring back your nervousness. Other visual aids can also remind you about points you don't want to forget to mention.

5. Use controlled movement. Gesturing vigorously not only helps you to emphasise important points, it also continues the process of calming the physiological symptoms by stimulating blood flow, reducing heartbeat, and so on. Moving about (a little), using the board or flip chart, distributing handouts or operating a projector all serve to relieve fidgeting and shaking and help channel nervous energy constructively.

6. Refer to the pointers in the section on Murphy's Law previously in this chapter. Being well prepared and practised is key to overcoming some of the fears associated with public speaking. Use the checklist in **Exhibit 10.16** to help you plan your presentation more effectively and make you feel assured that you are prepared to give a good presentation, which should help to calm your nerves.

| Exhibit 10.16 | An oral-presentation evaluation chart |

Speaker		Topic				
O = outstanding; E = excellent; G = good; S = satisfactory; NW = needs work						
General evaluation			Specific evaluation			
		O	E	G	S	NW
Content	Well-chosen, interesting, well-researched material					
	Clear, definite purpose and theme					
	Careful selection of detail. Appropriate for audience					
Organisation	Attention-getting introduction. Purpose and outline clearly stated					
	Material signposted and logically organised, main points clearly stated. Clear links between sections					
	Effective conclusion that restates and summarises main points and reinforces opening proposition					
Delivery	Enthusiasm generated. Audience engaged					
	Effective visual aids. Slides clear, easy to read, main points summarised, appropriate for audience and topic					
	Voice clear and pleasant. Appropriate pace, volume, diction, vocal variety and emphasis					
	Appropriate attire					
	Eye contact maintained. Use of confident body language					
	Time used efficiently					
Comments:						

Reflection question: When speakers talk of fear of public speaking, what do they fear?

The interview as a structured conversation

Another common form of oral communication is the interview. Interviews are a necessary function of most professions, but they can be difficult to do well. The main challenge, as both an interviewer and an interviewee, is to combine the effective oral presentation skills that have been discussed so far, with communication principles and skills in language, non-verbal communication, intercultural sensitivity, listening and assertiveness. This section will suggest guidelines for conducting and participating in different types of interviews. This will assist you in using your communication skills to represent yourself well, to enhance your relationships with other people, and to achieve mutually satisfying outcomes.

Communication skills in interviews

The interview format is a good study in the relationship between verbal and non-verbal communication, and all professionals require some interviewing skills. An interview can be defined as a structured conversation, with one person acting as the *interviewer* (i.e., the person who initiates and conducts the interview), and the other as the *interviewee* (i.e., the respondent, or person being interviewed; see Exhibit 10.17). There may be more than two people involved, as in a group job interview, but a larger group will usually be thought of as a *meeting* or an *interview panel*.

Exhibit 10.17   An interview is a structured conversation

Shutterstock.com/auremar

Interview
A structured conversation or meeting between two or more people, either face to face or via some electronic means.

In an **interview**, people get to know each other, seek information, and exchange information, opinions, attitudes and judgements. An employment interview is the most obvious example of this, with the applicant seeking information about the job they have applied for and the interviewer seeking information about the applicant and their suitability for the job. However, interviewing is employed in many and varied situations and professions. For example, a nurse may seek information from a patient about their symptoms and the patient may be seeking feedback on their condition, treatment or prognosis. Additionally, accountants interview their clients about tax minimisation, scientists interview laboratory assistants about experiments, researchers use interviews to gather data for a report, and marketers use interviews to test the quality of a product.

The purposes of interviewing

The objective of any interview is to obtain or contribute information. Even though the respective roles and objectives of interviewer and interviewee may differ from time to time, each party usually has a specific set of aims and objectives that often complement one another, as outlined in **Exhibit 10.18**.

Exhibit 10.18   Examples of how aims and objectives of interview and interviewee complement and differ from one another

Some objectives of an interviewer	Some objectives of an interviewee
• Reveal the interviewee's ideas and feelings • Gather information about the interviewee's experiences • Convey an appraisal of the other person's work or behaviour • Persuade another person to adopt an idea or course of action	• Reveal the interviewer's ideas and feelings • Gather information about the job • Provide an explanation or justification for a particular action or behaviour • Persuade the interviewer that they are the right candidate for the job

The basic reason for conducting an interview from both the interviewer's and the interviewee's points of view is to make a decision or to take an action. The success of any interview depends on the achievement of this objective.

Types of interviews

Interviews are used in many different situations, most follow a similar pattern and, therefore, require similar skills to achieve their objectives. The following sections will focus on interviews that take place in the workplace, including performance-appraisal interviews, employment interviews and client/patient interviews.

Performance-appraisal interviews

Appraisal interviews are common in education and employment (see **Exhibit 10.19**). In education, students may be interviewed by teachers or lecturers about their performance. In such an interview, their progress will be discussed and assessed, and decisions are made about their subjects and areas of future study. In employment, performance appraisals are carried out regularly – usually annually – and discussed with employees in interviews. In organisations with effective human resource policies, appraisals are valuable aspects of training and development, and appraisal interviews are vital to the success of this process. Staff are presented with management's view of their performance and have an opportunity to discuss options for their future development, such as broadening their experience, further their training, possible promotions, and so on.

Exhibit 10.19   Performance or appraisal interviews are common in education and employment

Shutterstock.com/Jeanette Dietl

In this style of interview, the interviewer needs to arrive at an assessment of the interviewee, whether favourable or unfavourable. The psychological climate, therefore, should be open and supportive. Both interviewer and interviewee should aim to explore one another's needs and problems in relation to the job. Both can set goals to achieve common objectives. If a written assessment is required, it should be read and reviewed by both parties. Of course, such interviews may produce anxiety, especially in the interviewee, and may even generate a feeling of defensiveness. But if well handled, appraisal interviews can restore frustrated enthusiasm, inspire corporate unity and stimulate morale.

Employment interviews

Most readers will face a few employment interviews in their careers, first probably as applicants, and later as interviewers. Some employment interviews are informal, and the interviewer or panel encourages the interviewee to talk freely and creates a relaxed atmosphere. Others are extremely formal, with an applicant facing an interview panel of four to six members, each with standard, predetermined questions. The panel will carefully note the answers to each question so that applicants can be compared fairly.

In the employment interview, interviewers are aware that a choice to appoint someone to a position needs to be made on the information that they are able to draw from the applicants at the interview. And in almost all employment interviews, applicants feel nervous because they are conscious of constant evaluation and criticism in the air. And perhaps fear a slip of the tongue will go against them and that they may make a bad first impression.

 CASE STUDY 10.3 The difficult first job interview

Melissa recently completed her teaching degree and was looking forward to her first job in a real classroom. She had always been a conscientious student and achieved excellent grades, including first-class honours in English and History. In her Diploma of Education, she was at the top of her group, and as a result the faculty head had included her name among a select group recommended for a position at a prestigious boys' college.

At the interview Melissa was very nervous. She had arrived early and had dressed in her best silk dress and felt she looked smart. She knew something about the school, yet the sandstone buildings, traditional uniforms and 'old world' style of this school was something she had never personally experienced. Her experience was mostly in the public-school sector where she had both undertaken her teacher placement and received her own education.

The interview took place in the headmaster's office which, like the rest of the school, seemed like a relic from the past – tall bookcases full of dusty first editions, a well-worn, buttoned leather Chesterfield couch and floor-to-ceiling dormer windows that overlooked the school quadrangle. The headmaster himself would not have been out of place at Oxford or Cambridge in his academic gown.

The interview started awkwardly when he asked her to take a seat in one of the deep armchairs – why did she wear such a tight skirt and high shoes? She could hardly get down that far. It didn't get much better after that. She had come prepared with her résumé and had thought carefully about how she would answer questions about her qualifications, teaching philosophy, personal interests, aims and ambitions, but those questions

never came. Instead, the headmaster's first question was to ask which high school she had attended. Her high school was in the Western suburbs, which she never saw as a problem because she was a high achiever – until that moment. She started to feel even more nervous. This wasn't going as planned.

She was totally unprepared for the next question: 'Tell me, what do you know about opera?' "How do I answer this?' she thought. She was interested in contemporary music, loved seeing bands and even played a little guitar ... but opera? Not really her style, and what did that have to do with teaching English? She battled her way through this question and the next couple with brief non-committal answers. Finally, the headmaster put her out of her misery.

'Yes, well, very good', he said, 'but you couldn't teach football.' Football, she thought, as she despondently left the school. That certainly hadn't been listed as a pre-requisite for the job. What had gone wrong?

Discussion

1 Consider Melissa's interview. What had gone wrong in her preparation for this interview? What did she do right? How could she have been better prepared?

2 How did the setting of the interview play a part in the way that Melissa felt and performed?

3 Why didn't Melissa get the job? What should she learn from the experience?

After you have discussed this case study, refer to the 'Comments on case studies' section at the end of the text.

Patient or client interviews

Whether you are a nurse or health professional interviewing a patient, an accountant interviewing a first-time client about their financial needs, or a teacher interviewing a student about their studies, many of the principles of effective interviewing are the same (see Exhibit 10.20).

Exhibit 10.20   Patient or client interviews require special skills

Shutterstock.com/fizkes

In the case of a health care professional dealing with personal information or a case worker enquiring about a sensitive topic, the following tips from Matthew Putts (2010), are helpful:

- *Establish rapport:* while it is sometimes important to gain information very quickly, in many cases you can only spend a minute or two getting to know your patient and the situation.
- *Respect patient or client privacy:* before asking about potentially sensitive things, like the possibility of pregnancy, potential substance use or psychiatric conditions, it is worth considering the environment and the patient.
- *Pay attention to the patient's or client's non-verbal signals, especially their facial expressions:* their facial expressions may provide information that provides additional or confirmatory information. For example, a wince may indicate they are in more pain than they are telling you, or confirm the level of pain they are in. Non-verbal signals can also provide you with information about how comfortable the person is with you and the questions that you are asking.
- *Consider your own non-verbal signals:* consider whether your own facial expressions are conveying openness and any other feelings you wish to convey, and that your non-verbal signals show you are paying attention to what the person is saying. Crossing your arms, impatiently tapping your foot, or not directly facing the patient may convey that you are not particularly interested in what the person has to say.
- *Ask open-ended questions:* you risk missing out on potentially valuable information if you only ask questions that require a yes or no answer.
- *Use common English:* if you must use jargon, explain what it means.
- *Listen:* while this sounds obvious, actually listening to the interviewee's responses to questions is essential. Too often, we are busy thinking about the next step and our next question rather than paying attention to what our interviewee is telling us.

- *Move into the patient's or client's field of vision:* position yourself at eye level so that those who with vision or hearing impairments can see you.
- *Culture matters:* knowing the person's culture and social customs, will allow you to connect with your interviewee and their families, and will assist you in quickly building rapport.

Preparing effective interview questions

As will other types of communication interactions, how you ask and frame a question will often determine how the interviewee responds and how useful or informative their response is. This is relevant to a range of different interview situations including those for academic or professional research, performance appraisal, job selection, or client or patient information gathering. Exhibit 10.21 outlines different types of questions, their application and examples.

Exhibit 10.21	Types of interview questions	
Question type	**Description**	**Example**
Open	An open question encourages the interviewee to speak freely. It also communicates trust by giving the interviewee the freedom to determine the amount and nature of information they give, and it is said in their own words	What have been your impressions of our products over the last few years? Tell me about your symptoms. How do you view recent development in your suburb?
Closed	Closed questions are more limiting as they can be answered with either 'yes' or 'no', or limited sentence. They limit the scope of a response and discourage nuanced explanations	How many staff did you supervise? Have you experienced pain when you walk? Did you vote in the election?
Mirror	A mirror question is non-directive and often involves restatement of an interviewee's response so that they can see how their answers have been interpreted. It also increases rapport. The objective is to encourage the interviewee to respond in more detail. Often used in therapy	As I understand it, then, you were employed for four years in textiles and then moved to product management to get experience with computers, but now you would like to combine both aspects of your experience in this new job. Am I correct?
Leading	A leading question presupposes a certain answer or determines limitation to the answer. It may be useful and proper if you wish to confirm your understanding of something said by the interviewee. In general, however, leading questions should be avoided because they may carry a threatening tone or encourage a misleading response	So, you feel quite confident about operating the new workstation? You like individual, self-directed work, don't you? Are you opposed to the union like most others I've talked to here?
Hypothetical	Also known as the reflective question, this question type tests the interviewee's imagination or ability to think 'laterally' and to put themselves in a hypothetical situation and outline an imagined response	If they made you general manager for a week, what changes would you make? If you had the chance, would you take medication if it meant you would be pain free for the rest of your life?

Many interviewers fail to put enough thought into framing effective questions for interviewees. Sloppy, vague questions fail to bring out the experience and qualities of applicants, may not express the real concerns of the panel, and may discriminate. Some such questions include:

- Have you had enough experience to handle this position?
- Are you able to get people who work for you to extend themselves when needed?
- Do you think that your experience in textile management will be appropriate to this position in insurance management?
- Have you had research experience?

In each case the interviewee may answer 'yes' and say little more, and, therefore, will not elicit specific information about the applicant. In contrast, notice how the following questions are specifically crafted to elicit experience-related information:

- In what ways did you find university different from school?
- What has been your single best piece of work or achievement in the past six months?
- How do you determine or evaluate the success of others around you?
- What qualities do you look for in a manager or supervisor?

The job interviewee's role

This section considers the role of the interviewee: their preparation, participation in the interview, and success in handling questions and leaving the best impression.

Preparation

As an applicant for a position, you have already submitted documents about your qualifications and experience. Now you might prepare to do two things:

1 Find out as much as you can about the company. For example, check the company's website.

2 Prepare a *skills inventory* about yourself to use in the interview, either to answer questions or to ask them and use the criteria stated in the position description for the job to help you to identify relevant skills and experience:

- List your skills that are relevant to the job; for example, computer skills, organisational experience, marketing and communication training courses completed.
- Rank your skills. Make a good case for yourself in the skills closely related to this job and have examples of your work handy to show if needed.
- Recall and make a note of concrete examples of your work and skills. Keep them brief but make them count. When did you last show good leadership, customer service skills, conflict-resolution ability, team motivation or problem-solving strategies?
- Anticipate objections and criticisms. Are you too inexperienced for this job? Are you underqualified or overqualified? Is your experience directly relevant to this job?
- Be ready to discuss salary if the subject comes up. Be prepared to relate your particular accomplishments to what you might be worth to the company if you are asked about a possible starting salary. If the employer does not raise the salary issue, it is probably better to leave it until the next stage, when you have received an offer.
- Keep in mind that you are 'on show' from the moment you enter the building for the interview until you leave. It is not impossible that the interviewer or interview panel will be influenced by comments from other staff who might meet you during this time.

Displaying qualities in an interview

Most applicants for professional or management-level positions are required to offer three main segments of information about themselves:

1 *Qualification:* most professional positions require the applicant to have specific *qualifications*. This may include an academic degree or diploma, relevant and continuous training, and appropriate experience. This information will have been covered in your letter of application and résumé.

2 *References:* as a rule, employers seek reports or *references* from referees nominated by the applicant. These are likely to be about character, expertise and potential. In some fields references are very important and employers may telephone the referees. The most valuable references offer concrete examples of the quality of the applicant, so choose your referees carefully and inform them about the job description.

3 *Qualities:* these are personal characteristics or attributes that the selection committee or interviewer is looking for. Generally speaking, interviewers look for personal qualities, such as:

- *Sincerity*: discuss your achievements modestly but factually. Let the facts speak for themselves.
- *Sociability:* this is an indication of how you will get along with colleagues, so behave naturally, openly and amiably, with courtesy and yet with confidence.

- *Creativity:* this refers to your ability to think originally, so keep your mind alert during the interview and try to look at problems in new ways.
- *Maturity:* doesn't require great age; it's a matter of demonstrating good judgement, clear thinking and balanced reasoning.

Common interview questions

There are many different types of questions that an interviewee might be asked but **Exhibit 10.22** lists some of the most common ones with suggestions for how you might answer them. It's useful to prepare some answers ahead of time so that you're not caught off guard.

Exhibit 10.22	**Common job interview questions and possible responses**	
Question	**Reason for asking**	**Possible response**
Tell me a bit about yourself	A commonly asked first question designed to break the ice and give an overview of you and your professional background, and to see if you will fit into the organisation	Keep it brief. Highlight your strengths, qualifications and general job ambitions. Be sincere
Why do you want to work here?	Designed to reveal your motivation, and knowledge of the company's goals	Give specific examples and try to match your skills, strengths and values to the job position and company. *'I believe being part of this company will give me the opportunity to expand my skill set and make a positive contribution to this program.'*
What do you know about our company?	This question allows you to show that you've done some homework about the company, what it does, its strengths, etc. Has the company won any awards or citations, recent product launches, or been in the news?	*'I read on your website that you're one of the top data security companies in Australia, and that you provide security advice to major corporations like the CBA and Australia Post. I also read a recent news article that you're looking to provide these services to a range of companies in New Zealand and the Pacific.'*
What's your greatest strength?	This is hard to answer without sounding like you're bragging. Choose examples that are relevant to the job position and give examples from your experience of how these have helped you in a position	*'Some of my greatest strengths are my work ethic and management skills. I realised this when I...'*
What are your weaknesses?	The interviewer is trying to assess your level of self-awareness. Focus on one or two areas that you could improve on or what you find most challenging or maybe frame a strength as a weakness	*'One of my weaknesses is I have struggled to delegate because I am somewhat of a perfectionist. However, I have been working on taking a step back and just advising and guiding staff so that they improve their skills.'*
What goals do you want to achieve in the next five years?	This is partly to see if you are a job hopper or a planner	*'I am hoping to obtain more experience and qualifications and to be able to progress to a senior supervisory or management role'*
How do you handle stress?	Can you handle pressure, think on your feet, take initiative without supervision and manage your time? It's a chance to highlight your problem-solving skills. Prepare an example of how you dealt with a relevant high-pressure situation	*'I try to be well organised so that regular tasks don't pile up and if unexpected challenges are presented, be prepared to consult with my colleagues on the best way forward.'*
How do you deal with disagreements or personality clashes with a colleague?	This question is intended to uncover how you deal with situations of conflict at work. Ideally, you should show that you're able to handle these situations with diplomacy and tact and respect for personal differences and styles. Give an example of how you dealt with a relevant situation	*'In any workplace, there will always be differences of opinion and different ways of working. I try to respect other views and make room for other ways of working. If there are differences, I would talk to the colleague and air any differences to ensure it doesn't get out of hand. For example, in my previous job ...'*

Source: Adapted from R. McKenna (2020, July 9). The 38 most common job interview questions: Are you prepared? https://www.training.com.au/careers/interviews/job-interview-tips-questions-and-answers; M. Page (2022, October 10). 20 common interview questions. https://www.michaelpage.com.au/advice/career-advice/interview/20-common-interview-questions

Strategies for dealing with questions

As employment interviews are important communication events, applicants should treat the interview situation with great care. Here is some advice garnered from various experts on winning jobs (Adams, 2010; McKenna, 2020; Page, 2022).

- Don't be defensive if you are asked a difficult question. Answer as positively and honestly as you can. For example, if you are asked a question about not having enough experience, you might reply: 'My experience was limited by doing my degree, but the team I worked with was the most productive in the company.'
- Never speak disparagingly of any previous employers or organisations.
- Don't be too frank or overly cautious. Disclose aspects of your work experience and yourself appropriately and emphasise the positive rather than the negative aspects of each job.
- Anti-discrimination laws invalidate selection-committee questions that discriminate about personal circumstances, such as marital status, carer responsibilities and forms of disability. As the interviewee, focus on asserting your demonstrated abilities.
- Don't talk too little or too much. Most interviewers expect more than 'yes' or 'no' answers, or even answers that merely address the specific question. They look for conciseness in addressing main points, brief but relevant examples and anecdotes, and a confident but modest statement of your feelings and opinions on what you did.
- It is important during your replies to address all members of an interview panel, not just the questioner. Your tone should be a mixture of confidence, thoughtfulness and modesty.
- At the end of the interview the interviewee is usually asked if he or she has questions for the panel. The choice of these questions is very important. They should not be administrative questions on such matters as pay or conditions as these questions can be answered if an offer is made. Suitable questions might be policy-oriented, revealing that the applicant has been researching the company and taking an interest in its future direction. Examples of such questions include:
  - What are the company's plans for diversifying their product?
  - Will the public relations department be responsible for all publicity in the future?
  - Will the company be expanding globally as I read in this week's *Financial Review*? If so, what effect will that have on this branch?

CASE STUDY 10.4 Weird job interview questions and how to handle them

Many interview questions are standard and evoke similarly typical responses … Now, imagine if you are asked this: 'If you were a pizza delivery person, how would you benefit from scissors?'

This question changes the conversation a bit. Suddenly, you've caught your candidate off-guard. They are not sure how to answer, but after a pause, they say, 'I suppose I would use scissors the same way anyone else would. I wouldn't necessarily use it on the job, but I would use it at home to cut things.' Weird unconventional questions like this one allow you to investigate how quick thinking your candidate is and how well they handle stress.

Source: Adapted from C. Forsey (2021, April 27). 15 fun, weird and unexpected interview questions (with sample answers). © Hubspot, Inc.

Discussion

In groups of three or four, discuss this case study. Consider the following questions and how you might answer them. What would an interviewer be trying to gauge by asking these questions?

1 How would you solve problems if you were from Mars?

2 What do you think of garden gnomes?

3 What kind of car would you be?

4 Why are manholes round?

5 You've been given an elephant. You can't give it away or sell it. What would you do with the elephant?

6 If you were a tree, what kind would you be, and why?

After you have discussed this case study, refer to the 'Comments on case studies' section at the end of the text.

Virtual or online interviews and presentations

Traditionally interviews have taken place face to face or perhaps by phone, but with technology advancing, interview may also take place by videoconference or even email (see Exhibit 10.23). In particular, the COVID-19 pandemic has meant that employees and students have had to learn to use tools such as Zoom, Teams or Skype to communicate, and employers have had to use non-face-to-face methods to keep their business communications flowing and to interview potential employees. While Chapter 5 discussed some of the problems of virtual interpersonal communication, the following lists some strategies for using these technologies effectively for presentations and interviews:

1 Choose a video conferencing program that is accessible to all participants and easy to use. Does it have a record function? Does it allow screen sharing and chat?

2 Ensure that you have a reliable internet connection, otherwise lag and screen freezes may distract from the presentation or interview. If the connection is poor, you may need to reschedule.

3 If you are presenting or participating in an interview, choose a quiet place away from background noise or other distractions.

4 If you are recording the interview or presentation, gain the consent of participants.

5 Check your background? Is the room tidy? Have you made the bed? Use an appropriate virtual background, if possible, but be aware that it may impact your bandwidth.

6 Check what you are wearing. Just as with any interview or professional presentation, appearance matters.

7 Ensure that you are using a good-enough quality camera and that it is directed at the right height so that you are not looking up at the interviewer or audience.

Exhibit 10.23	Virtual or online interviews and presentations require special skills

Shutterstock.com/Andrey_Popov

Summary

Public speaking and interviewing require you to apply many of the personal and professional skills that have been discussed in this book so far. Understanding the impact of your non-verbal communication, how you choose and use language and how you apply different types of interpersonal and cultural awareness skills to these different verbal interactions, are central to professional success in these areas.

In the case of public speaking, it is reportedly anxiety provoking for some. This chapter has outlined some skills and strategies to assist you to plan and deliver a professional speech. Experience with oral presentations (i.e., practice, practice and more practice) is the only real cure for fear of public speaking and provides you with vital opportunities to improve your oral reports and presentations. One or two speeches in a communication class only get you started on your speaking career. Try to force yourself to speak at meetings. Do not refuse any invitations to address groups. Get used to the sound of your voice in the speech mode. Do things such as these and eventually you will be much more at ease and more effective as a presenter.

Most important of all, to improve your presenting skills is to move from a speaker-centred mode to a message/receiver-centred mode. Prepare well, absorb yourself in the topic, pay attention to the audience, focus on trying to work out if they are understanding your ideas, and *try to forget yourself*. The oral-presentation evaluation chart in Exhibit 10.16 provides specific criteria for you to reflect on in order to improve your practice as a presenter. You can use the chart to collect feedback on your oral reports and presentations from your audiences, such as peers, lecturers and tutors at university.

Finally, interviews, or 'structured conversations', have been described. How you approach the task as either an interviewer, such as in the case of a patient/nurse interview, or as an interviewee as in the case of applying for a new job, will require that you are well prepared and aware of the needs of the person or people to whom you are speaking.

Ultimately, the abilities to speak effectively in public, and to participate as an interviewer or interviewee, are very valuable and worthwhile communication skills for all professionals.

STUDY TOOLS

DISCUSSION QUESTIONS AND GROUP ACTIVITIES

For discussion topics and activities in addition to those listed below, please refer to the case studies presented throughout this chapter.

1 Below is a list of formal speech skills that professionals are often required to exercise. Tick each of the following skills that you believe you have experience with. Indicate your order of difficulty (on a scale of 1 to 5, where 1 is least difficult and 5 is most difficult) in handling the various situations. Compare notes with others in your small group or in the whole class.

	Skill	Experience with	Difficulty (1–5)
a	Served as leader or moderator of a conference or discussion		
b	Spoke to civic or community groups representing your organisation		
c	Presented a persuasive case to a management group you know to be completely opposed to it		
d	Spoke calmly to a hostile and disruptive audience		
e	Made a speech honouring or paying tribute to someone		
f	Gave an after-dinner speech to amuse and entertain an audience you haven't met before		
g	Answered a surprise question in a meeting, speaking concisely and to the point for some minutes without notes		
h	Addressed an audience of people from higher management		
i	Adapted a difficult technical explanation to the needs of a general audience		
j	Presented a speech organised so that important points stand out and the audience later remembers what you said		
k	Spoke easily and fluently to an audience, being confident enough to involve them in a discussion and mix serious points with amusing anecdotes		

2 Discuss the following statements:

a When it comes to written communication, there are important linguistic rules that we must follow if our communication is to be effective and accepted. However, oral communication provides speakers with almost complete freedom of expression.

b Oral communication is a very complex channel for sending messages because it involves the process of listening, as well as many non-verbal components of communication. It is probably easier to learn to write well than it is to speak effectively.

3 In what ways can the following be used in oral presentations? What qualities must they have in order to effectively contribute to a talk or oral report?

a anecdotes

b questions

c humour

d statistics.

4 Assume that you are to speak to the class next week on 'Censorship of the internet' or 'Are we becoming a "nanny state"?' You wish to know as much as possible about your audience. Form groups of four and try to frame answers to each of the six questions under 'Understand your audience' (p. 278–279). Each group might report its findings to the whole class and consider the need for corrections and adjustments.

5 Discuss the use of notes in oral presentations you have made or are preparing to make. Consider the relative merits of:

a a full script

b a skeleton outline

    c   notes on cards

    d   notes on PowerPoint

    e   no notes.

    What different experiences did members of the group have with each of these? Were some more useful than others? Did it depend on the nature of the audience and/or the subject matter?

6   Search for a televised speech or interview (e.g., during Question Time in Parliament on the ABC or on YouTube). Make notes on the speaker's positive and negative non-verbal cues. Comment on whether these non-verbal cues help to create a favourable or unfavourable impression. If you are analysing a television interview (say with a political or public figure about a controversial issue), comment on both the interviewer's and interviewee's non-verbal cues. How did the interviewee non-verbally handle hostile or difficult questions?

7   Use the same televised speech from Question (6) and comment on the speaker's audibility, articulation, pitch, rate of speech, use of pauses, and 'ums' and 'ers'. Consider whether such vocal features weakened or strengthened the speaker's effectiveness.

8   Based on what you have read in this chapter, write a set of guidelines for a speaker preparing for both of the following situations. How are they different?

    a   A presentation to a group of staff of a large manufacturing company which is being forced to lay off workers as a result of international competition and the high Australian dollar.

    b   A presentation to nearby residents of your chemical plant to discuss rumours that there has been a toxic pollution leak into a nearby river.

    Make sure that you consider:

- the available time
- audience needs, expectations and attitudes
- a clear introduction with definite objectives
- logical development of ideas
- an informative conclusion.

    Select any audio-visual aids and activities relevant to your purpose from the following list and briefly describe how you would use them to complement your presentation:

- a whiteboard
- PowerPoint slides or an online presentation tool
- objects
- models
- charts
- audio recordings
- video recordings from YouTube
- notes or brochures as handouts
- questions and group discussions
- group activities
- class exercises.

9   In a small group of three or four, discuss the issue of how to deal with audience questions in a presentation. For example, does your lecturer ask and invite questions during the lecture, or do they ask students to save their questions until the end? What are the relative merits of each approach? If you are asked by your tutor to prepare questions as part of your presentation, should you ask them as you go through your talk or at the end? Have group members had good or bad experience with these approaches?

10 Using YouTube or the internet, find footage of a politician or company board member fielding questions, preferably from a hostile audience. Write a description and critique of how they responded and what techniques they used to diffuse a difficult situation.

11 As a group, collect recent job advertisements from internet sites or LinkedIn. Establish the necessary criteria and desirable criteria based on one or more of the advertisements and record these on a whiteboard.

Divide the group into three equal groups of interviewers, applicants and observers. The interviewers should write interview questions.

The applicants should write a covering letter and short résumé (use the examples in Chapter 12 as a model) and submit it to the interviewers. Make sure that the letter and résumé covers the criteria outlined in the job advertisement.

- *Applicants:* work out what skills you could contribute to the position in line with the specific requirements. If you are asked why you applied, give an answer that demonstrates your enthusiasm and relevant skills. At the end of the interview, restate your interest in the position.

- *Interviewers:* choose a chairperson for the panel and assign each specific questions. Work out the order of the questions. Conduct the employment interviews and have the interviewers rank the applicants and make a decision. Be sure to include a couple of tricky questions.

- *Observers:* make notes on how the interviewers:

    - created rapport
    - asked and answered questions
    - listened actively by paying attention
    - used non-verbal communication to convey a good impression
    - concluded the interview to establish a satisfactory ending for all.

Report the findings to the whole group.

12 Arrange for your group to view a recent television interview and then rate the interviewer(s) and the interviewee(s).

Also rate the interviewee(s) according to their positive and negative non-verbal cues listed in Exhibit 3.18 (p. 79) in Chapter 3.

13 Form small groups and choose one of the following general topics (or create one specific to your workplace):

a presentation by a contractor of a proposed new IT or accounting system

b annual staff meeting update on successes/challenges during previous 12 months

c staff meeting to progress a new teaching curriculum

d nursing (or other) team meeting to discuss update of monthly roster

e staff meeting to discuss introduction of new work-from-home or WHS protocols

f community residents meeting to discuss a local council development proposal.

In your group, complete the following table to brainstorm the way different audience characteristics might impact the presentation that you are preparing. Explain the reasons for your answers.

Audience questions	Impact on the content, focus, approach of your presentation?	Impact on your presentation strategy
How many people are likely to attend?		
How formal is the event/audience?		
Timing		
Location (small room, large auditorium etc)		
Background: age, culture, education.		
Level of knowledge of the topic		
Likely viewpoints on the topic (support/object)		
Opinion of the presenter (favourable/unfavourable)		

WEBSITES

Fear of public speaking: how to overcome it https://www.mayoclinic.org/diseases-conditions/specific-phobias/expert-answers/fear-of-public-speaking/faq-20058416

How to listen effectively to a speech https://www.forbes.com/sites/nickmorgan/2014/03/18/how-to-listen-effectively-to-a-speech/?sh=2842b44a7602

Public speaking anxiety and fear of brain freezes https://nationalsocialanxietycenter.com/2017/02/20/public-speaking-and-fear-of-brain-freezes

Think outside the slide: tips for effective presentations https://www.thinkoutsidetheslide.com/free-resources/latest-annoying-powerpoint-survey-results

UNSW 10 tips for speaking to an audience https://www.student.unsw.edu.au/speaking-audience

REFERENCES

Adams, S. (2010, June 23). Weird job interview questions and how to handle them', *The Age* http://www.theage.com.au/executive-style/management/weird-job-interview-questions-and-how-to-handle-them-20100623-yxyl.html

Australian Bureau of Statistics. (2021). *Work-related injuries*. https://www.abs.gov.au/statistics/labour/earnings-and-working-conditions/work-related-injuries/latest-release

Doumont, J. L. (2005). The cognitive style of PowerPoint: Slides are not all evil. *Technical Communication, 52*(1), 64–70. http://web.mit.edu/5.95/readings/doumont-responds-to-tufte.pdf

Forsey, C. (2021). 15 Fun, weird and unexpected interview questions (with sample answers). https://blog.hubspot.com/marketing/funny-weird-interview-questions

Goodman, J. (2015, July 28). *The end of the lecture can't come soon enough*. Studiosity. https://www.studiosity.com/blog/the-end-of-the-lecture-cant-come-soon-enough.

Mackiewicz, J. (2007). Perceptions of clarity and attractiveness in PowerPoint slides. *Technical Communication, 54*(2). 145–156.

McKenna, R. (2020, July 9). The 38 most common job interview questions: Are you prepared? https://www.training.com.au/careers/interviews/job-interview-tips-questions-and-answers/

Page, M. (2022, October 10). 20 common interview questions. https://www.michaelpage.com.au/advice/career-advice/interview/20-common-interview-questions.

Paradi, D. (2019). *Key results from the 2019 Annoying PowerPoint Survey*. Think Outside the Slide. https://www.thinkoutsidetheslide.com/free-resources/latest-annoying-powerpoint-survey-results

Putts, M. (2010). *10 tips for a better patient interview*. EMS World. https://www.hmpgloballearningnetwork.com/site/emsworld/article/10319762/10-tips-better-patient-interview

Seinfeld, J. (1999). *I'm Telling You for the Last Time - Live on Broadway* [film]. HBO.

Tufte, E. R. (2003). *The cognitive style of PowerPoint*. Cheshire Graphics Press.

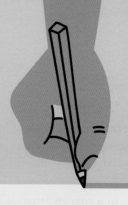

PART 3

Writing skills in professional life

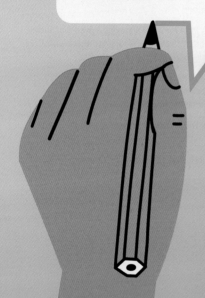

Shutterstock.com/YummyBuum

Writing professionally: process and style

Writing is hard work

Read, read, read. Read everything — trash, classics, good and bad, and see how they do it. Just like a carpenter who works as an apprentice and studies the masters. Read! You'll absorb it. Then write. If it's good, you'll find out. If it's not, throw it out of the window.

> William Faulkner, novelist

Quantity produces quality. If you only write a few things, you're doomed.

> Ray Bradbury, novelist

You do an awful lot of bad writing in order to do any good writing. Incredibly bad. I think it would be very interesting to make a collection of some of the worst writing by good writers.

> William S. Burroughs, novelist

It's not wise to violate the rules until you know how to observe them.

> T. S. Eliot, poet and essayist

Writing and learning and thinking are the same process.

> William Zinsser (2006), journalist, editor, literary critic

Writing is the flip side of sex – it's good only when it's over.

> Hunter S. Thompson, journalist, novelist

One of the really bad things you can do to your writing is to dress up the vocabulary, looking for long words because you're maybe a little bit ashamed of your short ones.

> Stephen King, novelist

Being a good writer is 3% talent, 97% not being distracted by the internet.

> Anonymous

The quotes above are as amusing as they are true. While they are mostly from writers of fiction, professional writers share the same challenges when it comes to different types of workplace writing, including emails, reports, manuals, instructions, letters and blogs. The process is the same. Writers need to write a lot more copy than they need so that they can then edit their work. While storytelling is a large part of fiction writing, it is also a mainstay of workplace writing, in terms of structure (i.e., beginnings, middles and endings) and character development (i.e., persuasion). Writing can be hard work, but it is satisfying when you finish a long, difficult job. And distractions abound for the writer who has yet to start writing, or who does not know how to proceed in the middle of a writing job.

Introduction

> Writing is at the centre of all disciplines and professions. We are often judged on the quality of our writing, so it's essential to strive for professionalism.
>
> Source: Petelin (2022)

The opening quote from renowned Australian teacher of professional writing Ros Petelin, captures our central message about why all professionals need to appreciate and develop good writing skills. While the evolution of the internet and new communication technologies was believed to herald the end of the need to master grammar, punctuation and a professional writing style, this has not come to pass. In fact, new communication technologies, ironically, have spawned the ubiquity of new written forms, such as email, text messages, and a raft of new online publication spaces like websites, blogs and social media platforms. As such, professionals increasingly need to have the skills to compose different forms of text and be able to adapt them to the styles and conventions of different mediums as well as the expectations of different audiences.

On this point, Petelin observes that:

> The rise and rise of the internet in our digital age has dramatically upped the ante. Employers want graduates who are problem solvers ... 'knowledge workers', and 'information architects' – that is, graduates who can research, analyse, write and edit, and who are critical and creative thinkers with technological competence and design sensibility.
>
> Source: Petelin (2022), p. 2

Writing is also a problem-solving process. Sometimes you will write because you need to use your writing to think through a problem. By putting words together as coherent text, you are sorting your thoughts into a logical order, making meaning for yourself. This is one reason why reflective journals have become a popular educational technique. This process of writing is an adjunct to the process of thinking and problem-solving.

Once we have captured the ideas, we can weave them into a variety of compositional styles. In his influential text, *Style: Lessons in Clarity and Grace,* Joseph Williams (2012) notes that successful writing requires us to learn and adapt the style, implicit rules and genre conventions of the **discourse community** or context in which the writing will be read. Most writing, therefore, will require us to identify a specific reader or group as the audience for our work.

Writing has also long been recognised as a form of social practice. Hodge and Kress (1993) have argued with respect to the relationship between language and society that:

> Language is given to the individual by the society in which he or she lives. It is a key instrument of socialisation, and the means by which society forms and permeates the individual's consciousness.
>
> Source: Hodge & Kress (1993), p. 1

Discourse community
A group of people who are united by the way the members communicate and the things they communicate about. This group develops a process for communication, a unique vocabulary or jargon and a common set of rules or conventions by which they communicate.

While this relationship was discussed in more detail in Chapter 2, it is equally important to recognise the implications for the way that language performs this function in its written form.

For all these reasons, we need to continuously extend both our understanding of the influences on how readers interact with our writing, and how this should shape our writing capabilities so that we are better equipped to address the wide range of communication issues we encounter in our professional lives. This chapter explores some techniques focused on the writing process that will help you to extend your writing abilities. It also considers style issues that are appropriate for different genres of professional writing.

Stages of the writing process

Most people agree that the hardest part of the writing process is getting started. It doesn't seem to matter if the task is an email, a report or a thesis – writers seem to experience slight panic each time they take up their pens or sit at their keyboards. Where should I begin? What should I say and how should I say it?

While there has been a great deal of research into the process of writing, there is really no single 'right' way to begin writing. Most of the authorities, however, agree that the pre-writing or planning and post-writing processes are as important as the actual writing process. Through the years most people will develop an approach that suits their own personality and the type of writing they have done. They may have been taught a few 'rules' about writing or may have learnt by trial and error. Some may even be quite comfortable with their approach to writing. However, there are few of us who would not admit that there could be a better, more efficient, less painful way to write. Some of the popular techniques for writers to use are summarised in this following. They are strategies that help writers to be successful in achieving their goals.

The crucial point is to overcome the barriers to your writing and begin to get words into print. It is a good idea to experiment with different models to see if you can enhance your writing. The techniques that we use to brainstorm, research, and edit can greatly improve the final copy. Exhibit 11.1 below suggests three stages.

Exhibit 11.1 Stages of the writing process

1 Planning	2 Writing	3 Revising
Identify the purpose of the writing	Apply plain English, positive and inclusive language, appropriate tone for audience and purpose	Review readability and rewrite where needed for clarity, conciseness, and appropriate tone
Research and collect information	Create a clear reading 'map' using headings, sub-headings, and other visual devices	Proofread for typos, misspellings, grammatical and punctuation errors. Apply any style conventions (e.g., UK or US spelling, referencing, heading style, abbreviation, etc.) across the document
Research your audience: identify their background and reading preferences	Use paragraphs and punctuation to help readers 'digest' the text easily	Ensure design elements are appropriate for the organisation and readers and consistent across the document
Decide on a strategy to organise your content and choose an appropriate rhetorical appeal	Format your document to reflect your organisation's preferred image and expectations of the audience: consider fonts, layout and colours	Have an independent reviewer read through your document for feedback

Some writers, often those who are thoroughly familiar with their subject, find it helpful to plan their writing task fully before they begin. They construct an outline of the main topics and the supplementary and complementary ideas that should be contained in the message. They then organise the outline so that a logical flow of ideas is evident.

Other writers get all their ideas into words in any form or order that is expedient. Next, they make an outline of the composition as it has been written and analyse it for logical flow and organisation. This outline helps them to visualise the key points and their interrelationship. They may rearrange sections or restructure an argument. Then they question whether all the important issues have been included and whether they have been given the treatment they merit. Finally, they thoroughly edit the draft.

More complex writing tasks may require some background reading, investigation or experimentation before the writer can even begin to outline the topic. The approach you choose will vary from task to task and you should not feel constrained to tackle every written communication in a thoroughly systematic manner. It is easy to let the prospect of writing a major composition cause you anxiety. However, as with most problems, the first step is the hardest step. It really doesn't matter where you begin; the important thing is to begin. You will develop your confidence in writing and evolve your own preferred style.

Consider your readers

> A text cannot speak for itself: it needs a reader as well as a writer.
>
> Source: Chandler (1995), p. 5

Earlier chapters discussed the communication process, and you will recall that an objective of communication is to share common meaning between senders and receivers. As discussed in Chapter 2, decoding the meaning of text (or spoken words) occurs in the minds of the readers or listeners, so for writing to be effective, writers need to consider the needs, wants, aspirations and perspectives of their readers.

We may know our readers well – they may be customers or clients who have done business with us for years. We have built up a healthy working relationship of mutual trust and respect and may share goals and aspirations. On the other hand, how can we possibly determine all the readers for our written communication? We, therefore, will need to make judgements about possible readers' perspectives, needs and preferences, based on our understanding of who they may be and what they are likely to want from us. We need to work out how much knowledge they have about the topic we are addressing and also how much interest they have in it. We should try to anticipate how they will react to our words. Will they be in favour of our proposal or strongly opposed to any suggestions we make? Will we cause offence by using a colloquial expression or excessive technical language?

Some readers will read for meaning. They are interested in getting a job done and will overlook many flaws in the writing style in their quest to solve the problem at hand. They are far more concerned with the content, and so long as it is presented in a manner that is clear and easy to decode, they will be satisfied. Other readers will be far more critical of the style of the communication and be more sensitive to errors of tone, punctuation or approach. Part of the learning process is developing the language skills appropriate for the variety of discourse communities we encounter in our professional lives.

A readership model

Not all readers come to a document with the same needs, characteristics or experiences, and not all documents perform the same functions or require the same set of skills from the reader. For example, a novice audience reading a technical document will need more background information, more definitions and explanation of key terms and concepts, and supporting visuals to help them engage with the subject matter. Well-known technical-writing researcher Janice (Ginny) Redish (1993, p. 15) has written widely about the varying nature of audiences or readers. She says there are four critical aspects of how readers work with documents. These are:

1 'Readers decide how much attention to pay to a document': some read in detail, others skim for headings or for critical information. Some prefer diagrams or schematics for explanations, others read step-by-step bullet points.

2 'Readers use documents as tools': most people in the workplace 'read to do' rather than 'read to learn'. They access the critical information or instructions and then get out of the document.

3 'Readers actively interpret as they read': as shown in **Exhibit 11.2**, readers bring their own experiences, skills and expectations to a document and will use different strategies when they read and interpret. These are affected by the physical characteristics as well as the graphic elements of the document itself.

4 'Readers interpret documents in light of their own knowledge and expectations': in order to create a document that will meet a reader's needs, writers need to think about the possible characteristics of the reading audience. What language or style do they prefer? What similar documents may they have had experience with? What is their level of education, existing knowledge of the subject, level of technical expertise and so on?

This model shows that a document's purpose is influenced also by its place in an institutional or social setting. For example, a monthly progress report or budget will be read differently than an email newsletter published by management in head office. Purpose is also influenced by the physical characteristics of the document itself – its layout and design and so on. A writer needs to consider all of these things when researching, planning, writing and producing a document.

Exhibit 11.2   A model of the interaction between readers and documents

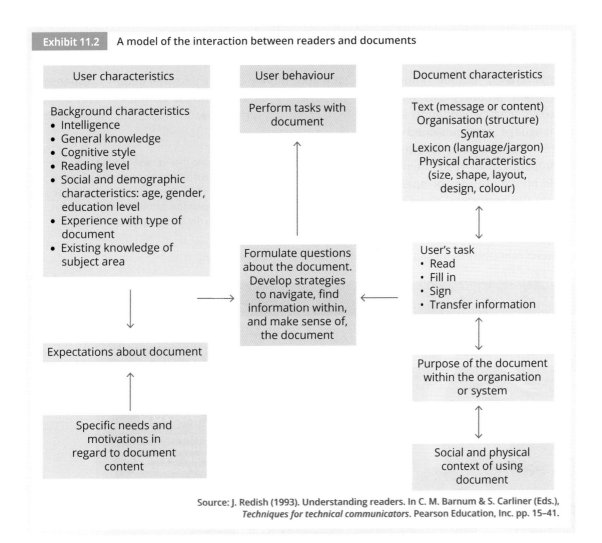

Source: J. Redish (1993). Understanding readers. In C. M. Barnum & S. Carliner (Eds.), *Techniques for technical communicators*. Pearson Education, Inc. pp. 15–41.

A few questions you should address have been listed; however, the more you can discover about your intended readers, the better you will be able to satisfy their needs. This initial focus on your audience will stimulate your thinking about the scope of your writing, including questions shown in Exhibit 11.3. These questions have been applied by a major Australian bank in Case study 11.1.

Exhibit 11.3   Questions to ask yourself about potential readers

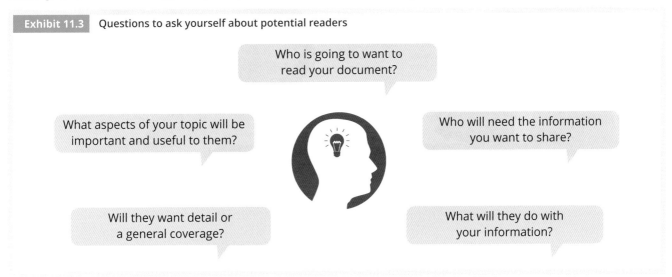

CASE STUDY 11.1 An Australian bank uses visuals to make complex concepts easier to read

Terms and conditions (T&Cs) include important legal information for many products and services. However, they are usually lengthy, written in arcane and complex legal language and published using microscopic font sizes. Research has shown that the majority of consumers fail to read them even when joining a mobile phone provider or opening a bank account: what are the customers' rights? What is the bank or phone company's obligations dealing with your money or your personal data? In response, Bankwest, a subsidiary of the Commonwealth Bank, has come up with a way to make this information more engaging.

[Bankwest introduced a] comic-style version of its T&C in a bid to make convoluted legal clauses simpler and more engaging for customers [see **Exhibit 11.4**]. The graphics are part of an effort to simplify and cut down the amount of text a person needs to digest to sign up to the banking product.

Exhibit 11.4 Bankwest's comic-style terms and conditions: For illustration purposes only

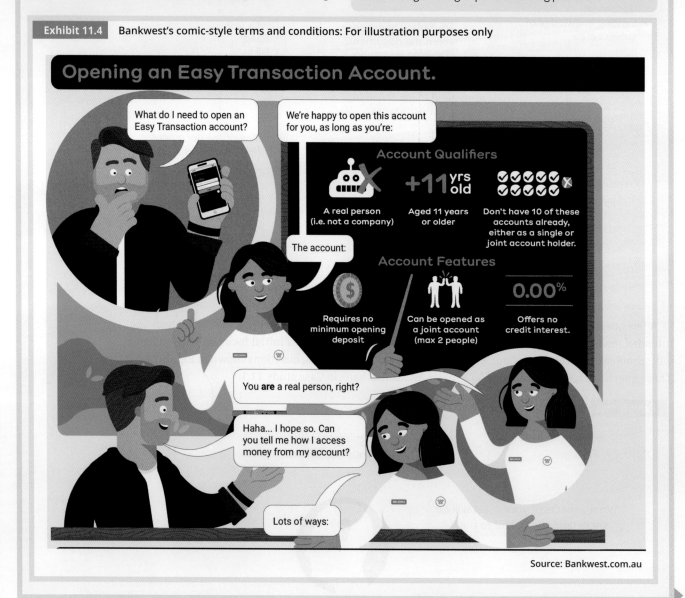

Source: Bankwest.com.au

The new visual contract has been implemented following research conducted by the University of Western Australia (UWA), which found 69 per cent of participants preferred graphics over text-heavy legal documents.

...

UWA law professor Camilla Andersen said the main purpose of the visual contract was to be a document people actually read, which would assist in driving down the risk of potential conflicts and disputes between a customer and the bank. 'Our research has shown that people are far more likely to engage with the comic contracts than the text-based terms, and research in psychology shows that images help people to associate and remember things better' ...

Source: G. Cockburn (2021, February 28). Bankwest to introduce comic-style version of terms and conditions in bid to get customers to properly read contracts. News.com.au. The use of this work has been licensed by Copyright Agency except as permitted by the Copyright Act, you must not re-use this work without the permission of the copyright owner or Copyright Agency

Discussion

1   Why is it important for customers to read T&Cs when signing up for a new phone, opening a bank account or even taking out insurance?

2   Look at a couple of examples of T&Cs (e.g., Facebook, car or health insurance). What aspects of the language, layout and style might make them be difficult to read? What are some possible problems if customers don't read T&Cs?

3   Apply Redish's readership model (**Exhibit 11.2**) to Bankwest's new design. How has the company used visuals to adapt to the reading preferences of its audience?

After you have discussed this case study, refer to the 'Comments on case studies' section at the end of the text.

Reflection question: Find a sample of documents that are all on a similar topic but are obviously written for different readers. Apply Redish's model and identify these differences. How has the writer adapted the style, layout, and so forth, to meet their audience?

Deciding what to say

Many writers complain that they don't know what to say. They have no difficulty with grammar, punctuation or spelling, are capable of composing literate prose, and can research and analyse. But they simply cannot think of how to convey a coherent message. Even established authors may face writer's block; however, in professional settings, just as in university, most managers would not tolerate a feeble attempt to explain why a report was not completed or a letter or email was not sent. Fortunately, there are a few techniques that can help us discover what we really want to say.

The 4Ps strategy

Many writers find that the 4Ps approach helps them to overcome writer's block. The first step is to describe the present situation. What is going on around you that is prompting you to write? The next step is to set out the problem that exists within the context of that situation. This problem becomes the focus for the writing strategies that follow. Step three challenges you to present some possible solutions to that problem and show how each one meets the needs you have identified. Finally, you propose a solution or some action that you feel should occur. **Exhibit 11.5** presents an example of this strategy in use.

Exhibit 11.5	Example of the 4Ps strategy in use
Present situation	Telecommunications technology makes it easy to communicate with people all around the world
Problem	With so many different languages and cultures, it is easy for misunderstandings to occur
Possible solutions	We could develop a common language, or we could develop translation techniques to help cross the language barriers
Proposal	We propose to develop a series of guidelines to help writers communicate with others throughout the world

The 5Ws and 1H strategy

A chapter on the writing process would not be complete without a mention of the 5Ws – who, what, when, where and why. We can also 1H – how. This is a typical tool used by journalists, and as a tool for helping us get started, the 5Ws and 1H strategy is difficult to beat. Exhibit 11.6 outlines the strategy, with examples, from a business or professional context.

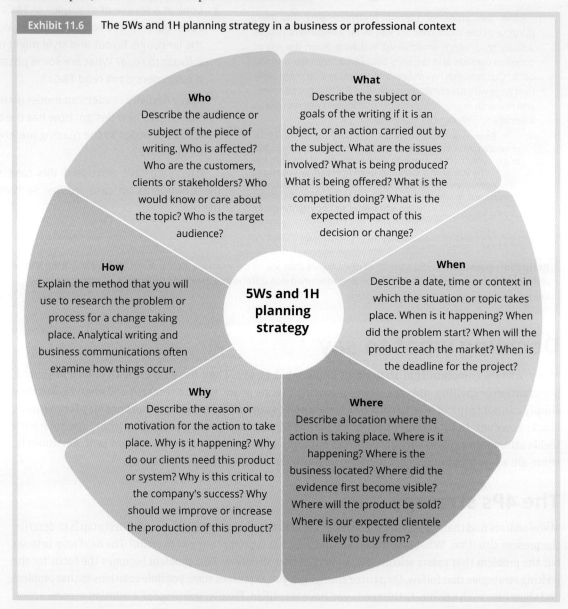

Exhibit 11.6 The 5Ws and 1H planning strategy in a business or professional context

Who
Describe the audience or subject of the piece of writing. Who is affected? Who are the customers, clients or stakeholders? Who would know or care about the topic? Who is the target audience?

What
Describe the subject or goals of the writing if it is an object, or an action carried out by the subject. What are the issues involved? What is being produced? What is being offered? What is the competition doing? What is the expected impact of this decision or change?

How
Explain the method that you will use to research the problem or process for a change taking place. Analytical writing and business communications often examine how things occur.

When
Describe a date, time or context in which the situation or topic takes place. When is it happening? When did the problem start? When will the product reach the market? When is the deadline for the project?

Why
Describe the reason or motivation for the action to take place. Why is it happening? Why do our clients need this product or system? Why is this critical to the company's success? Why should we improve or increase the production of this product?

Where
Describe a location where the action is taking place. Where is it happening? Where is the business located? Where did the evidence first become visible? Where will the product be sold? Where is our expected clientele likely to buy from?

5Ws and 1H planning strategy

Researching a topic

Frequently our writing is an expression of our own thoughts and knowledge, but there are often times when we need to draw on other people's work to help inspire or inform us. The basic skills needed for research are an inquisitive mind and a determined will. Research can be time-consuming, frustrating and tedious; however, it is also exciting when your efforts are rewarded with a fresh piece of evidence or an unusual perspective on an issue. In research, it is as important to ask the right questions as it is to find the right answers, so you will be practising your creative-thinking skills in devising your research strategies. And, importantly, the more you know about a topic, the easier it will be to write about.

The most important point is to avoid procrastination – finding excuse after excuse to prevent you from working on your writing project. Just begin! Often, once you start a writing task, something strange happens ... the writing has a life of its own and it starts to flow from our keyboards.

Chapter 13 gives you specific advice on researching topics for academic papers and professional reports.

Reflection question: What strategy do you use to start writing? What are the advantages? What are the problems?

Choosing the right words

Chapter 2 explored in detail how language broadly works. Obviously, a writer needs to choose appropriate words and compose them in a meaningful way to create the effect that communicates the message. But which words, in what order, and how do we know they are the right ones? For a start, as many of the opening chapter quotes note, wide reading and familiarity with different genres of writing help you develop a large vocabulary as well as an inherent sense of different styles and voices and how these are achieved. We also need to remember that most languages – not just English – are fluid, flexible, constantly evolving and often tricky. A word that means one thing in one context may have the opposite meaning in another: *sanction* can mean 'to allow' or 'to prohibit' depending on how it is used. *Wise*, as in 'a wise man', is a complementary description, whereas *wise* as in 'wise guy' is a negative description.

Petelin (2022) notes that there are three concepts in word usage that are central to good writing: style, voice and tone. Each carries or conveys the meaning of chosen words in different ways.

Style

Style is notoriously difficult to define. It is 'generally judged on a writer's choice and command of words and syntax (sentence structure)' (Petelin, 2022, p. 41). The term can also be applied to a generalised set of conventions that are common to particular *genres* of writing. The stylistic features of genre are explained in detail in Chapter 12.

Voice

Voice refers to the way the writer's attitude to the topic or the reader is 'heard' by the readers. It might be authoritative, reassuring, sincere, humble, knowledgeable or idiosyncratic. Like *style,* it is equally difficult to define. Booth and Gregory (1987, p. 260), state that 'voice in writing is like *presence* on a stage'. With respect to achieving an appropriate voice when writing advertising copy, Felton describes it like this:

> [V]oice can be difficult to talk about for several reasons. For one thing, you can't point to it exactly. It's just there, *among* all the words. For another, it's made up of a myriad of things: the words you choose (and the words you avoid), the sentences you write, the amount and kind of detail you use, what you're talking about, what your point is, how you organise your writing, who you're talking to. Almost every choice you make as a writer plays a part in creating the voice of the copy – the sense we get, when we read it, of living speech.
>
> **Source: Felton (2013), p. 103**

While the concept of voice is more commonly associated with works of literary fiction, it is also important in professional writing.

Tone

Tone of voice is an important part of oral communication. When we speak to someone, we show excitement, interest, anger and power by adjusting the tone we use to express the words we say. In oral communication we can easily see the reaction to our message and can adjust both the message and the tone as necessary. Written communication also carries a tone in the words used. Our words

Style
In writing, is the choice of words, sentence and paragraph structure used to convey a writer's meaning effectively. May refer simultaneously to singular aspects of an individual's writing choices, such as their word choice, sentence and paragraph organisation, or to those that are associated with a particular writing context or genre.

Voice
The mixture of tone, word choice, point of view, syntax, punctuation and rhythm that make up sentences and paragraphs.

Tone
The attitude of a writer toward a subject or an audience. The writer's viewpoint on a particular subject is evidenced by the examples chosen or the perspective from which they approach the subject. It is conveyed by the use of syntax, choice of words, and the level of formality of the writing.

can sound personal or distant, enthusiastic or bored, and witty or dull. How do we create a tone that is appropriate for the message we want to convey?

There is no doubt that vocabulary has an important effect on tone because of the connotative quality of words. Different emphases and effects can be created merely through the choice of words and the way a message is framed, as will be discussed in the following

Consider different word connotations

Consider the differences in meaning in using various synonyms. For example, let us look at the word confusion. We can use this word fairly simply:

> There was confusion during the meeting and, therefore, no decision was reached.

Here we have a straightforward piece of information in a fairly neutral tone. The writer is probably aiming only to convey facts about an event rather than create any special tone, and the word confusion is used for this purpose.

However, consider how the tone of the sentence would be altered if any of the following synonyms were used in place of confusion:

> There was **chaos** during the meeting and, therefore, no decision was reached.
> There was **ferment** during the meeting and, therefore, no decision was reached.
> There was **bewilderment** during the meeting and, therefore, no decision was reached.
> There was **turmoil** during the meeting and, therefore, no decision was reached.

Not only do all of the above words vary in meaning, but this variance also alters the tone of the sentence significantly. The neutral tone achieved through the use of confusion is contrasted to the more dramatic and critical effects created by the other words.

So far, we have only examined the effect that is created by altering a single word within a sentence. However, the range of tone variations is usually more complex and depends on a combination of words rather than on any one particular word. This interplay of words is a determinant of tone.

Take the following sentence:

> It seems that they are unlikely to reach a decision.

Here we have a fairly formal, restrained tone. However, replace this wording, as shown in the following, the result has an entirely different tone:

> They'll never make up their minds.

Not only is the tone emphatic and somewhat critical, it also more clearly conveys the attitude of the writer to the subject. However, the meaning is more direct and less vague. Wording like 'seems that they are unlikely' and 'reach a decision' is less direct, cautious and noncommittal. Using the nominalisation 'decision' rather than the verb 'decide' also increases the formality of the sentence.

As we discussed in Chapter 2, different words have different connotations, usually either positive or negative; some examples are shown in **Exhibit 11.7**. The choice of a word needs to consider its more nuanced connotations, the context in which it will be used and the readers to whom the writing is aimed.

Exhibit 11.7 Words of similar meanings but with positive and negative connotations

Positive connotation	Negative connotation
Generous, unstinting	Extravagant, immoderate
Resolute, dogged	Stubborn, mulish, obstinate
Thrifty, frugal, careful	Stingy, parsimonious, ungenerous
Diligent, industrious	Workaholic, obsessive
Shrewd, astute	Cunning, sly
Sober, serious	Morose, sullen, anti-social
Witty, pithy	Sharp tongued, terse, sarcastic
Tolerant, broadminded	Unprincipled, unscrupulous
Spontaneous, instinctive	Impetuous, impulsive, reckless

Frame your message positively

The tone of any written communication should be appropriate to the subject, the needs of the reader and the situation. Most writers agree that readers respond better to messages that are worded positively. That means that the messages tell the reader what to do rather than what *not* to do. It also implies that you should use words with pleasant rather than unpleasant connotations. The Transport Accident Commission has run 'Drive right' campaigns. The Australian government's 'Tough on drugs' booklet was subtitled 'The right approach for the right results'. These are examples of positively worded, successful advertising campaigns.

Many businesses adopt a personal tone in their correspondence by including the addressee's name within the body of the text or by using informal language. Compare these two sentences:

> Thanks for your order, Mr Lee. We're sure you'll be satisfied with our products.
> Your order has been received. Our products, of course, carry a full guarantee.

The different tones have been achieved by carefully choosing words and arranging them to produce the desired effect. The choice of tone is directly related to the purpose of your communication. Do you want to establish a personal relationship with your reader, or would you prefer to establish an efficient businesslike rapport? In written communication you have the opportunity to reword and restructure until your message sounds and feels just the way you want it.

In summary, here are some basic strategies to improve your tone and, most importantly, get the reader to respond appropriately.

- *Tell the reader what you can do, not what you can't do:* rather than saying 'I'm booked tomorrow morning, so I can't review the proposal until 2 p.m.', write 'I'm available tomorrow at 2 p.m. to review the proposal'.
- *State what you want to happen, rather than frame it as what you don't want to happen:* rather than the negative sounding 'Please do not lock the supply closet', instead ask 'Please leave the supply closet unlocked'.
- *Frame your requests positively rather than negatively:* use 'you' if possible as it is more pleasant. 'Thank you for your request' rather than 'I received your request'.
- *Focus on the solutions, rather than who is to blame:* when you attack someone, they will become defensive and will be less likely to react positively. Rather than say 'you neglected to ...', tell them what they need to do to complete the process correctly.

The way we choose our words, and the tone that we employ in our writing, works subtly on our audience. Remember the old idea of expressing a situation as a glass half full as opposed to half empty? Positive and tactful tone works in this way.

Reflection question: Consider an example where poor word choice in an email, text message or even a social media post has triggered a negative reaction in you, either in relation to the topic or to the writer? What word or expression was the source of your reaction?

Using correct grammar and punctuation

Managers in industry frequently complain of the inadequacies of their staff at grasping the basic principles of English grammar and rules of punctuation. There is a tendency on their part to equate poor English grammar with poor communication. If writers make mistakes in their sentence structure or phrasing, they are sometimes also deemed to be deficient in other professional skills. Managers and teachers are occasionally quite ruthless in this condemnation, however unfair it may seem.

There is an opposite point of view: that grammar doesn't matter. People who believe this maintain that as long as the meaning is clear, there is no need to follow grammatical rules. Some creative writers have employed this approach with great effect. However, in business, academic and technical circles, this method is not widely accepted.

Grammar

In academic and professional contexts, it is important to know the rules pertaining to the writing situation and to follow them. In most cases in Australia, this means employing fundamental principles of English grammar and conventional punctuation. It is recommended that you consult 'style' guides and books on writing and review English grammar as part of your own development program. The newly revised online Australian Government *Style Manual* (https://www.stylemanual.gov.au) is an excellent, freely available resource that is constantly updated to take account of changing conventions. The *Australian Style Guide* is another good resource (https://www.australianstyleguide.com/home).

Those writers who do not feel confident about their skills in English grammar or spelling would probably welcome a computer package to help them. Several quite functional systems exist; for example, Grammarly.com is a free online resource. Software grammar checkers and spellcheckers 'flag' constructions that do not conform to conventional rules, however, it is still up to the writers to decide whether the structure or word is correct or incorrect for the particular message that they are conveying. Spellcheckers are certainly not able to spot all mistakes, as the following popular rhyme shows:

I have a spelling checker,
It came with my PC.
It plainly marks for my revue
Mistakes I cannot sea.
I've run this poem threw it,
I'm shore your pleased to no.
Its letter perfect in its weigh,
My checker tolled me sew.

Punctuation

You can't write without punctuation; however, many professionals fail to take punctuation seriously. To many, attention to punctuation seems old-fashioned. A student in a university writing class, whose assignment had been marked down for poor editing, memorably told one of the authors that it was 'only people like you' who worried about punctuation these days. Here's what English journalist Lynne Truss had to say about that:

> To those who care about punctuation, a sentence such as 'Thank God its Friday' (without the apostrophe) rouses feelings not only of despair but of violence. The confusion of the possessive 'it's' (with apostrophe) is an unequivocal signal of illiteracy and sets off a simple Pavlovian 'kill' response in the average stickler. The rule is: the 'it's' (with apostrophe) stands for 'it is' or 'it has'. If the word does not stand for 'it is' or 'it has' then what you require is 'its'. This is extremely easy to grasp. Getting your itses mixed up is the greatest solecism in the world of punctuation. No matter that you have a PhD and have read all of Henry James twice, if you persist in writing, 'Good food at it's best', you deserve to be struck by lightning, hacked up on the spot and buried in an unmarked grave.
>
> Source: Truss (2003), pp. 43–44

Even if you don't take Truss' extreme view, attention to good punctuation is central to clear writing. It has been described by grammarians as the 'stitching' that holds the fabric of language together. Indeed, punctuation has one main purpose and that is to aid the communicator in presenting ideas clearly. It provides the traffic signals and road signs for writing. A full stop allows the writer to clearly tell the reader that one idea is complete, while a comma lets readers know that supplementary ideas are coming. Punctuation prevents vagueness by indicating pauses, questions, exclamations and quotations.

 CASE STUDY 11.2 Punctuation is important

Consider the following example from Lynne Truss (2003, pp. 9–10). How does changing the punctuation alter the meaning of the two letters?

Letter #1
Dear Jack,
I want a man who knows what love is all about. You are generous, kind, thoughtful. People who are not like you admit to being useless and inferior. You have ruined me for other men. I yearn for you. I have no feelings whatsoever when we're apart. I can be forever happy – will you let me be yours?
    Jill

Letter #2
Dear Jack,
I want a man who knows what love is. All about you are generous, kind, thoughtful people, who are not like you.

Admit to being useless and inferior. You have ruined me. For other men I yearn! For you I have no feelings whatsoever. When we're apart I can be forever happy. Will you let me be? Yours, Jill

Discussion

1   In a small group, read through the two letters and discuss how the different punctuation affect the meaning of each.

2   How do you decide when to use commas, full stops, etc? What are some of the rules or conventions that you apply?

3   What problems do you and your group members have with correct punctuation?

After you have discussed this case study, refer to the 'Comments on case studies' section at the end of the text.

As a quick overview, **Exhibit 11.8** summarises some of the basic punctuation marks and their uses.

Without punctuation we would need to guess where sentences end and begin, and we might arrive at a meaning that was not intended by the writer. There are, of course, rules that pertain to punctuation, and these can be found in references such as the Australian Government *Style Manual* or Martin Cutts' excellent *Oxford guide to plain English* (2020). Expert technical writers might debate the correct way to punctuate lists of instructions. Some would argue that the only punctuation should be a full stop at the conclusion of the list; others believe there should be semicolons at the end of each instruction. Any decision is usually based either on a conventional style manual's approach or on organisational preference. The most important issue is that a consistent method is adopted for the entire document or series of related documents.

Exhibit 11.8 Common punctuation marks and their uses

Punctuation mark	Function	Examples
Period/full stop ●	Ends a declarative sentence. A full stop signals a longer pause than a comma or semi-colon. Further, it marks the end of a thought and signals the beginning of another.	My name is Jim. The dog is a poodle. It is summer.
Comma ،	Indicates a pause in a sentence, either between phrases, clauses, or items in a list. This is what can make them tricky – the points where you'd pause in a spoken sentence aren't always where you'd use a comma in a written sentence. Commas are often misused.	My name is Jim, and I live in Penrith. The dog, whose name was Oscar, was a poodle. It was a long, hot, sunny day.
Apostrophe ،	Apostrophes' jobs include: • creating possessive nouns – Jim's house, the Smiths' car. • combining words into contractions – don't, she'll, weren't • shortening words – government becomes gov't and the 1970s becomes the '70s Apostrophes should not be used to: • pluralise nouns – Fresh tomatoe's, word's fail me. • pluralise pronouns – it's, her's • refer to a decade – 1990s not 1990's	Jim's dog is called Oscar. (possessive) He's a poodle. (contraction) Jim was born in the '50s. Jim called out, 'come 'ere you silly mutt'.
Question mark ?	Indicates that the sentence is a direct question. Indirect questions – 'Mary asked herself why she was always late' – are declarative sentences and end with a full stop, not a question mark.	What sort of dog is Oscar? When will Jim arrive for lunch? When will it stop raining?
Exclamation mark !	Indicates that the statement is exciting! Can be used to emphasise but be careful not to overuse.	Jim is coming for lunch! Punctuation is exciting! Stop!
Colons :	Used to join two independent clauses* when the two clauses are directly related, and there would be no 'and' to emphasise the second clause. Also used to precede a list, either a series of dot points or series of independent clauses separated by commas or semi colons. *An independent clause is a sentence that communicates a complete thought and makes sense on its own.	I love eating spreads on toast: Vegemite is my favourite. Vegemite is my favourite breakfast spread because it is: • tasty • nutritious • spreadable. I eat Vegemite in several ways: I spread it on my toast for breakfast, I eat it with cheese on a sandwich for my lunch, and I add it to hot water for a nutritious drink when I'm feeling unwell.
Semi colons ;	Join two related independent clauses in place of a comma and a coordinating conjunction (and, but, or, nor, for, so, yet). Combine two sentences with a conjunctive adverb (e.g., therefore, however). Is also used to separate items in a list when the items include a comma.	The roads are icy; it's dangerous to drive today. It was a terribly cold day; however, they couldn't get warm because the heater was broken. They ate roasted beef; olive, tomato and basil salad; and orange, cinnamon and chocolate pudding.
Dash —	There are two types of dashes: em dash — can be used to replace parentheses, colons or commas. Often used to indicate an afterthought or to provide emphasis at the end of a sentence. en dash – used for all of the same purposes as an em dash (a stylistic decision but use it consistently). Can also be used to show ranges of numbers, such as times, page numbers, or scores Note: 'em' is a printer's measurement equal to the height of the type size being used. An 'em dash' used in 16 point type would be 16 pts wide. 'en' is half an 'em'. so in 16 point type, it would be 8 points wide.	[Em dash] Freud found the three structures of the psyche—id, ego, and superego. [Em dash] Some small businesses will make it through this hard time—but most will not. [En dash] World War II (1939–1945) resulted in many deaths [En dash] Unfortunately, the team lost – something their fans didn't want to admit.

▶ **Exhibit 11.8** Common punctuation marks and their uses (*Continued*)

Punctuation mark	Function	Examples
Hyphen **-**	Used to join words or parts of words. It's not interchangeable with other types of dashes. Used as a compound modifier (also called a phrasal adjective) to make it clear that the words in a phrase belong together.	face-to-face meeting dog-friendly hotel book-loving student
Quotation marks **" "** or **"**	Used to indicate something that is spoken or to designate a direct quote. That is, they display something that has been said or written (dialogue), or when citing someone's written text word for word. They may also be used to emphasise a word or phrase that may be slang or technical jargon or to indicate the title of a book, movie, television show, play. Double or single quotations marks may be used depending on the style preferred; however, be consistent.	Jim said, 'What time do I come for dinner?' Smith (2007, p. 12) said 'writing is hard work.' An oil-extraction method is known as 'fracking'. Richard Burton performed the song 'Camelot' in the 1960 Broadway musical *Camelot*.
Ellipsis **• • •**	A series of three dots used to indicate an omission from cited text used to remove less relevant material and create space. May also be used as a pause to create suspense in a sentence.	Full quote: 'Today, after hours of careful thought, we vetoed the bill.' With ellipsis: 'Today … we vetoed the bill.' With sweaty palms, I reached out for the knob and threw the door open to reveal **…** a lost puppy.
Parentheses **( )**	Used to add extra information in text that isn't essential, but still useful. Can also be used to define an acronym in a report or essay the first time it is used. Also use where a word can be either singular or plural, add an 's' in parentheses at the end of the word.	Marilyn Monroe (born Norma Jeane Mortenson) was as iconic as her life was tragic. The Bureau of Meteorology (BoM) is a reliable source of information about the weather. Any question(s) you have should be answered in the next chapter.
Brackets **[ ]**	Used to show that text has been added to a quotation often to clarify the subject or add context.	'I read that novel [The Great Gatsby] in high school,' Lisa said. 'I can't believe that he [Brad Pitt] is here!'

Writing effectively

Points of view about writing may have become more liberal, but we can still ask the following questions: What is effective writing? What is poor writing? The short answer is that effective writing narrows or even closes the communication gap between sender and receiver. It does this because it is clear, accurate, concise and coherent. Poor writing, on the other hand, ignores the needs of the receiver and only succeeds in widening the communication gap. It is characterised by ambiguity, vagueness, confusion and wordiness.

So, is correct grammar an outdated concept? Definitely not! Regardless of globalisation, there are rules of correct English expression that do matter, and most of us adhere automatically to them. The trouble is, you can adhere to every rule in the grammar books and still write English that is dull, confused, inaccurate and vague.

So, instead of explaining the rules of English grammar in this text, this text considers effective writing in terms of clarity, accuracy, conciseness and coherence, and joins others in advocating the use of plain English (see Cutts, 2020). If you pay attention to these concepts, your writing should more effectively meet the needs of your readers, no matter what language you use. It is essential that if you do not know the basic rules and norms of English usage, you should continuously work towards mastering them in order to improve your writing.

Plain English: what it is, and what it isn't

Plain English is communication that is designed and structured in such a way that the audience can easily understand the message being conveyed (Cutts, 2020). The plain English movement began in the

Plain English
Communication that is designed and structured in such a way that the audience can easily understand the message being conveyed.

1970s as an active attempt to change the way that people write, and originally focused on changing the way legal and government documents were written. This was to ensure that the information could be understood, not just by lawyers or public servants, but by ordinary people who were either bound by the terms of a contract or whose lives depended on understanding the information.

In Australia, the movement was spearheaded by Professor Robert Eagleson in 1983 when he was commissioned to rewrite NRMA Insurance's policies and the Commonwealth Bank's plastic card terms and conditions in plain English. Some of the unexpected benefits of these revisions were greater productivity, less wastage of employees' time, decreased staff training times, clearer information and fewer questions needing to be answered by senior staff. Eagleson's book, *Writing in plain English* (1990) has since become a classic.

Critics of plain English argue that it is pedantic, dumbs down language, and is not suitable for writing contexts where language needs to be technically precise, such as legal documents. They also say evidence that it works is minimal. This argument has been debunked by Joseph Kimble (2012), whose book *Writing for dollars, writing to please* cites over 40 examples of projects, in the legal profession in particular, where plain English revisions have shown significant improvements, in both the clarity of information as well as in the perceptions of readers towards the publishing organisation.

Similarly, UK plain English campaigner Martin Cutts (2009, pp. xvi–xvii) cites the case of a Derbyshire bus driver who created headlines in 2001 when he took it upon himself to rewrite the company manual in a plainer style. In place of the instruction:

> Ensure the potential impact of non-routine factors and problems and other services are assessed and details notified promptly to an appropriate person.

He wrote:

> Inform the depot if you are stuck in traffic or involved in an accident.

Rather than:

> Ensure that machinery for issuing and endorsing tickets is confirmed as in working order and is set in accordance with approved procedure,

He suggested:

> Check the ticket machine is showing the correct date and price.

Another example is from a report to a local council about the fire safety provisions in a particular building that read:

> The exit doors are not provided with single handed downward action latching devices. This omission will negatively impact on the ease with which persons evacuate the building in an emergency.

Translated, this merely means:

> The exit doors need handles that can be easily opened so that people can escape during a fire.

However, plain English is not just about simplifying complex words and writing shorter sentences, although this is important. It is also about the way a document is laid out to ensure information is both organised logically and its parts are labelled so that a reader can easily find what they are looking for. Strategies to achieve this are discussed in detail in Chapter 12. **Exhibit 11.9** shows a summary of the guidelines for writing in plain English.

Exhibit 11.9   Summary of the guidelines for writing in plain English

1. Plan before you write: group related ideas, order parts in logical sequence. Consider your readers, needs	2. Have a clear core message and reduce unnecessary detail. Present key information first	3. Use language your readers will be familiar with and remove words that add little value	4. Express your points positively whenever you can
5. Break up long sentences; aim for 15–20 words	6. Prefer the active voice to the passive voice	7. Put the central action in verbs, not in abstract nouns	8. Use document design – typeface, line length, white space, headings and lists – to break up text and aid navigation
9. Use examples, tables, charts and graphics	10. Check your material before you publish		

Finally, plain English is not absolute. Cutts (2020) states that there are not 'rules' but 'guidelines'. Most importantly, documents need to be tested with their audiences. What works with one audience, may not work with another. What works in one form of media, such as a brochure or pamphlet, may not work online. The language to convince a middle-aged tradesman to have a regular doctor's check-up may be different to convincing the same person to regularly service his car. The point is that the focus of plain English is on communication, not merely the provision of information.

CASE STUDY 11.3   Enough with the bafflegab. Here's why a Plain Language Bill makes sense

Don't look now, but Kiwis are pivoting. In fact, words like 'pivot' are skating on thin ice in Auckland, along with 'best-practice benchmarking' and 'synergistic growth strategies'. Credit goes to the Plain Language Bill, passed last month in NZ parliament, where plain language is defined as 'appropriate to the intended audience', using words that are 'clear, concise and well organised'.

... the bill seeks to simplify the public sector's paperwork, ditching dense clauses for short verbs, simple nouns, scarce semicolons. Or that's the plan. 'New Zealanders have a right to understand what the government is asking them to do,' says Labour MP Rachel Boyack, who presented the bill. The watchword is inclusion. Bureaucrats must opt for lucid English, the easier for people from non-English backgrounds and varying education levels to grasp.

... Opposition members have scorned the move ... [labelling] the bill as 'a solution looking for a problem', an invitation for 'plain language police' to patrol the halls 'with their clipboards and their little white coats'.

[But how do you] define non-plain language, as English owns three types, for three reasons. The first is officeese, or buzz-talk, often the fodder of bullshit bingo cards. Disrupt. Unpack. Traverse. Seasoned staff will know the dialect well – where every dive is deep, each circle is back, and paradigms are made to shift.

Buzz-talk is a trite shorthand of action and intent, familiar to those who exchange the same phrases: road-testing the optics, aligning the silos, leveraging capacity. Silly-sounding from the margins, office-ese rebounds within an open-plan echo chamber, a tribal affirmation of belonging.

Jargon is the next level of opacity, where English shifts from video chat hubbub to insider tech-speak. Botanists, say, know a spathe as a 'conspicuous bract subtending a spadix'. Coders talk of 'satisficing protoduction' ... The shameless speech of specialists, jargon is distinct from bafflegab, the final frontier of non-plain language.

Bafflegab, the term, was coined by US lawyer Milton A Smith 70 years ago. Our own Don Watson prefers weasel words. This is language contrived to confound, combining office patois with bureaucratic shapeshifting. [W]e wish the Kiwis every strength. Their Plain Language Bill should be a robust, solution-driven, cutting-edge, value-added learning. ...

Discussion

1 Consider your own workplace, what are some of the buzzwords, jargon or expressions that staff regularly use?

2 Are there situations where jargon is helpful? What is the advantage for 'insiders' of a particular profession?

3 Many expressions go in and out of fashion. What are some examples?

4 Australian writer Don Watson (2003) argues that many buzzwords are designed to be 'strategically ambiguous'; that is, designed to be deliberately vague in order to avoid responsibility. What does he mean by this?

5 Is there an advantage to having plain English codified in a law as the New Zealand Government has done?

After you have discussed this case study, refer to the 'Comments on case studies' section at the end of the text.

Clarity

The notion of clear writing implies a relationship between writer and reader. What is clear to one person may not be clear to another, because everyone has different backgrounds and life experiences. You may know all there is to know about outboard motors or mainframe computers; I may be an expert on medieval music or climate change. How can we write clearly for each other? The challenge of communication is to narrow the gap. Clarity has the ingredients shown in **Exhibit 11.10**.

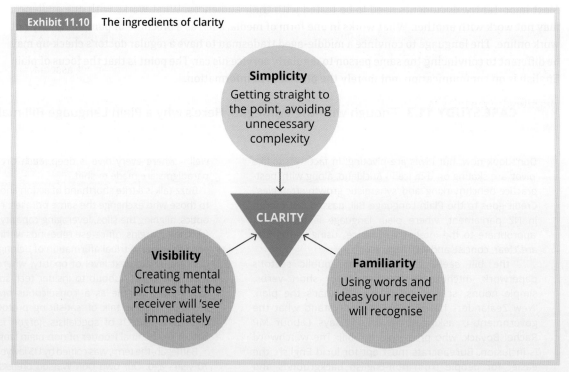

Exhibit 11.10 The ingredients of clarity

Simplicity
Getting straight to the point, avoiding unnecessary complexity

CLARITY

Visibility
Creating mental pictures that the receiver will 'see' immediately

Familiarity
Using words and ideas your receiver will recognise

Ambiguity

Ambiguity occurs when a sentence has more than one meaning. We may sometimes use ambiguity to avoid giving offence or inviting prosecution. Or we may use it ironically. Consider this example of an entry in a visitor's book at a very bad hotel:

We were hungry and they took us in.

This extract from a reference for a poorly qualified applicant for a job that protects the writer from claims of defamation:

> I am able to recommend this applicant with no qualifications whatever. In my opinion you will be most fortunate to get him to work for you. I would urge you to waste no time in making him an offer of employment.

Such ironic use of language is beyond the skill of most of us. Rather, we often fall into the trap of unconscious ambiguity, as the following media excerpt did:

> He was sentenced to a six-month intensive correction order for biting Constable Peter Scott at the intersection of Richmond and Wharf Streets.

Here are some more examples of ambiguity we have collected from students and newspapers. Can you detect the sources of the confusion?

> The building caught fire and the occupants sought refuge in their pyjamas.
> Our expert beauticians will cleanse, tone, moisturise and colour your hair and skin.
> Coming home I drove into the wrong house and collided with a tree I don't have.
> The eggs of the platypus were collected as soon as they were laid by the park ranger.

In each sentence the writer means one thing and the receiver may decode another meaning. This is poor communication and poor writing.

To avoid ambiguity, words should be placed where there can be no chance of incorrect association. Clarify in your own mind the meaning to be conveyed and then carefully construct the sentence so that the intended meaning is clear.

Vagueness

Writing is vague if it fails to give as much precise information as the subject requires. There are two main sources of vagueness: the needless use of abstract nouns and the use of terms that are too general.

The abstract and the concrete

Abstract nouns, such as love, freedom and pride, are necessary in writing about theories, concepts and ideas. Concrete nouns, such as table, tractor and tree, will be found in writing about detailed explanations of activities and narratives. They are usually accompanied by active verbs. The effect is to make a scene vivid, to help the reader 'see' what is going on.

Sentence (1) is an abstraction, while (2) is a concrete narrative.

> 1   Jim loves fishing and gets really excited when he thinks about a big catch.
> 2   Jim hooked a four-pound snapper and drew it up through the clear water, stripping it from the hook and flinging it into the well of the boat with the others.

In a tertiary course of study, you will have to read a great deal of abstract writing, but keep in mind that writing should never make ideas more difficult to grasp than they really are. Beware unnecessarily abstract and vague language. Here are two versions of the same message. Notice that the second one conveys the idea more economically and clearly because it avoids unnecessary abstractions and uses a stronger verb.

> 3   The tendency to make social contacts is a constant factor in the sphere of human relationships.
> 4   People tend to seek the company of other people.

Be careful, though, not to oversimplify an abstract statement so that its meaning is distorted. Consider these sentences:

> 5 Before this era of fabled plenty began, it was widely assumed that prosperity would eliminate or greatly reduce class differences.
> 6 Before everybody became rich, it was thought that prosperity would make everybody the same.

You can see that (5) is a much more careful statement than (6). An 'era of fabled plenty' does not mean that everybody is rich. The expression 'would make everybody the same', though containing few abstract words, is much less precise than 'would eliminate or greatly reduce class differences'.

Nevertheless, even in an abstract argument or explanation you can clarify meaning by introducing concrete details as illustrations.

> The press in a democracy has a circumscribed freedom, a freedom limited by its obligations to vested interests and national security. When John or Betty Average open their copy of *The Daily Gossip*, they would be surprised to find in it an editorial condemning the rotten fruit sold by Michael, who has a full-page advertisement for his 'Fruitique' on page 6. Nor do they expect to read the names of the government's secret agents in Beijing.

In this paragraph the first sentence is full of abstractions: 'freedom', 'obligations', 'vested interests', 'national security'. The reader may struggle to imagine these concepts. But the succeeding sentences give clear 'images' as illustrations of each of the three in action, and we can picture each one. So the concepts or abstractions are clarified and given more impact than if they were not illustrated.

The general and the particular

Vagueness can result from being too general when the specific is called for. Consider the following three sentences.

> 7 A businessman today found that he had to resort to violence to prevent a thief from robbing his office.
> 8 A department store manager at Earlwood fought off a thief who tried to rob him today.
> 9 At 8.45 a.m. this morning, Mr Michael Johnson, manager of the Wentworths Store at Earlwood, grappled with a man who burst into his office and threatened to shoot him unless he opened the store safe.

Of course, sentence (7) is the most general version. Is it vague? That depends on the purpose of the writing. The sentence is adequate as an illustration of the idea that a businessman's life can be hazardous.

Sentence (8) is more specific. It would be suitable as the lead sentence in a newspaper story. Sentence (9) might appear next in the story or be an account of the incident relayed by a friend of Mr Johnson the next day.

Too often, lazy writers fail to search for the precise noun, adjective or verb to identify the idea or piece of information they are describing. As a result, you read this sort of thing:

> The weather was phenomenal last week, and we all felt alarmed. At the peak of the disturbance, communications between our farm and the township were disrupted and it was some days before contact was made again.

This paragraph seems to be giving you vivid information, but what is it about? Rain? Hail? A cyclone? We are not told. There are no concrete details – everything is general.

Accuracy

If clarity depends on narrowing the communication gap, accuracy is about precision, exactness, close observation and using words that convey exactly what we think or have observed. 'Using words' is in fact the key, but it is also a challenge. On the one hand we need to build a vocabulary adequate to the sort of writing we do; on the other hand, we should make sure we use ordinary words properly.

> **Reflection question:** In business letters, technical reports and student essays there is often confusion between words that have a similar function. Which is the more accurate term in brackets in each of the following sentences?
> 1 In 2021 the (amount/number) of projects completed increased by 135 compared (with/to) the previous year.
> 2 This morning's attempt to (elicit/illicit) a response was inhibited by a (deficient/defective) receiver switch.
> 3 The largest item in our (stationery/stationary) is a carton of paper.
> 4 The heat exchanger operates (continuously/continually) throughout the winter, switching on automatically when the temperature drops below 10 degrees Celsius.
> 5 The (principal/principle) need in this company is for a new administrative centre.
> 6 The sales figures (effected/affected) our marketing plans.
> 7 There were (less/fewer) people in the shopping centre today due to the public holiday.
> 8 After the rain, we were able to harvest a large (number/amount) of apples from the trees.
> Noticing errors in using such words will increase your ability to make the correct choice.

Conciseness

Concise writing gets to the point quickly – it is brief and succinct. *Brevity* suggests shortness of time, and *succinctness* implies compression. The pruning process of editing and revising usually involves thinking more exactly about what you really mean.

If when editing your paper or essay you find it possible to scale off 20 per cent of the words, you may do a service to your reader. Consider these sentences:

> 1 The elderly gentleman suffered indigent circumstances at the time of his demise.
> 2 The old man died poor.

There may be a case for writing sentence (1) at some time, but we find it difficult to imagine. Sentence (2) uses five short, powerful words, each contributing clearly to a poignant effect. This is concise writing.

Compare the following two statements:

> 3 At present, our current view of the issue promotes the notion that members of our society are entitled to the possession of facts and knowledge as to the activities being conducted in the field of science and its associated research.
> 4 We believe the public has a right to know what is going on in scientific research.

It is obvious from these examples that statement (4) is easier to read than statement (3). Wordy writing has nothing to recommend it since it only obscures meaning. There are a number of pitfalls to recognise so that conciseness can be maintained. These are discussed in the following.

Tautology

Tautology means needless repetition of an idea in different words. This is different from repeating an idea for emphasis, and it is more likely to weaken the impact or even confuse the reader.

Here are two examples typical of those in student essays:

> This has brought many mixed opinions from different kinds of people, and it is still being debated today, and a final decision has yet to be made.
> The internet has changed somewhat from what it once was to what it has now become.

Do you agree that the highlighted parts of the sentences could be deleted without harm to meaning? **Exhibit 11.11** lists some other commonly used phrases that are examples of tautology.

Exhibit 11.11	Examples of tautology		
around in circles	=	around	
visible to the eye	=	visible	
precedes before	=	precedes	
combine together	=	combine	
I personally	=	I	
make an attempt	=	try or attempt	
reach a decision	=	decide	
true facts	=	facts	
completely filled	=	filled	
advance notice	=	notice	

Verbosity

Officials still tend to pad out their sentences with what Charles Dickens called circumlocution, using three or four words to take the place of one. Its purpose may be to impress or to deliberately confuse the reader or listener, and it is tiring to read. Sometimes students similarly try to 'pad out' an essay to reach the prescribed word limit, but this practice usually produces an unimpressive result. Compare the following two versions from a paper on education.

> 1 The future that lies before those engaged in studies at the graduate school level, seeking advanced degrees from institutions of higher learning, in regard to prospects for desirable employment in teaching positions at best does not have a high degree of certainty.
> 2 Graduate students looking for good teaching jobs face an uncertain future.

Does the first writer say any more than the second? Is there an intention to inflate the author's importance by longwindedness? The second version is clearer and, therefore, better writing, because it is concise.

Phrases for words

In wordy writing, you will probably find that the author has used phrases when a single word would be more effective. **Exhibit 11.12** lists some common 'padding' phrases and their equivalents in simpler English.

Exhibit 11.12	Redundant expressions	
with reference/regard to	=	about
a considerable period of time	=	a long time
in the capacity of	=	as
in the vicinity of	=	near
in some instances	=	sometimes
make an attempt	=	try
reach a decision	=	decide
it would be to your advantage	=	you would benefit
at this point in time	=	now
with the possible exception of	=	except
within the realm of possibility	=	possible
due to the fact that	=	because

Coherence

Coherence is about shaping sentences, emphasising ideas in the sentence, linking thoughts within the sentence, and the ways in which sentences relate to each other. The same concept should be applied to paragraphs, where the subjects of each sentence should be roughly the same.

Coherent means 'consistent', 'logical', 'having a natural or smooth linking of ideas'. Sentences cohere when they follow a logical path. Parts of sentences are coherent if they help the writer produce an effect of unity, balance or emphasis. Entire documents also need to be coherent, but this chapter will consider coherence as a quality within the sentence or paragraph.

Unity

A simple sentence or paragraph should relate one idea, for example:

> Tourism is booming.

Compound sentences link two related ideas. In sentence (1) the ideas are united; in sentence (2) they could cause confusion because they do not really form a united thought.

> 1   Tourism is declining and hotels are vacant.
> 2   Tourism is a major industry in Australia and football is popular.

Some writers let their sentences roll on with long dependent clauses, while others chop sentences into such small bits that they become repetitive in structure. The long sentences are difficult to follow, and the short ones fail to distinguish between major and minor ideas.

The following paragraph is unified and coherent:

> Public transport is a very efficient method of moving from one place to another in a foreign country. It is usually cheap, reliable and efficient. Overseas, *catching public transport* is the only alternative, since hiring a car is not a real alternative due to the prohibitive cost, and possible problems caused by driving on the other side of the road. Trains are usually easier to use in foreign countries because they are often highly developed such as the metro systems of Paris, Rome and London. *Buses,* on the other hand, usually need a tourist to know exactly the right destination and are therefore more difficult to use.

Note the italicised subjects of each sentence above are pretty much the same.

The following paragraph is not unified because the subjects keep changing:

> *Public transport* is a very efficient method of moving from one place to another in a foreign country. Tourists are always having to move around when they travel overseas. *Choosing the right kind of transport* overseas can be a daunting task. *Cars* are usually too expensive and also dangerous due to different driving conditions. *Travelling around in London, Paris or Rome* is easier because they have a developed metro system. *Buses* are also quite difficult to use for a tourist, or even a local person, who does know their way around.

Emphasis

Some writers fail to emphasise their ideas because they place the important point in the wrong part of the sentence so that it is overlooked by the reader.

It is generally agreed that if you place the main idea at the *beginning of the sentence*, you attract immediate attention:

> *The situation in Ukraine is very dangerous,* as you who have witnessed these events will agree.

Placing the main idea at the *end of the sentence* ensures the reader will remember it, as in this sentence:

> As a result of an event that occurred at about this time, *the course of the war and the future of world history was changed.*

If you follow the suggestions that have been presented, your writing should be much more effective because you will have considered your readers and what they need to understand your message. When you keep this in mind during the writing process, you naturally have a picture of some person or group to whom you are directing your ideas. You will have considered their knowledge of your subject area and their language skills. You will have tried to determine their needs or objectives in reading your work and made attempts to satisfy them. This technique helps you write clearly, directly and in an appropriate tone. It also makes the final stage, revising and editing, that much easier.

If you consider yourself an advanced student of writing, you might like to obtain a copy of Joseph M. Williams' (2012) classic book, *Style: Lessons in Clarity and Grace*. This book proposes innovative concepts related to writing and demonstrates how to become a better writer in 10 separate ways coinciding with the 10 lessons.

 CASE STUDY 11.4 Communicating complex ideas

Some science and technical writers have the ability to explain their ideas clearly to non-science readers; others can communicate only with their peers. Here is an excerpt from a NASA website that explains black holes to the general public:

> Black holes are the evolutionary endpoints of stars at least 10 to 15 times as massive as the Sun. If a star that massive or larger undergoes a supernova explosion, it may leave behind a fairly massive burned out stellar remnant. With no outward forces to oppose gravitational forces, the remnant will collapse in on itself. The star eventually collapses to the point of zero volume and infinite density, creating what is known as a 'singularity'. As the density increases, the path of light rays emitted from the star are bent and eventually wrapped irrevocably around the star.
>
> Any emitted photons are trapped into an orbit by the intense gravitational field; they will never leave it. Because no light escapes after the star reaches this infinite density, it is called a black hole. But contrary to popular myth, a black hole is not a cosmic vacuum cleaner. If our Sun was suddenly replaced with a black hole of the same mass, the earth's orbit around the Sun would be unchanged. (NASA, 2010)

Source: NASA (2006). Black holes: What are they?

Discussion

1   What examples of simplicity, familiarity and visibility have been used here to explain black holes?

2   How has the author used plain English?

3   What are some of the possible problems of simplifying a complex subject for a non-scientific reader?

After you have discussed this case study, refer to the 'Comments on case studies' section at the end of the text.

Writing inclusively

As discussed in Chapter 2, words have the power to shape how people see the world and how they see themselves. Today, most workplaces recognise the importance of non-discriminatory language and have inclusive language policies. However, we often use words unthinkingly without considering where they spring from or their potential impact. As we have seen in numerous cases of poorly chosen words by public figures, it is not enough to say, 'I didn't intend any offence' or 'get over it'. Using inclusive or non-discriminatory language is an important part of effective writing style.

Inclusive language can be defined as language that is free from words, phrases or tones that reflect prejudiced, stereotyped or discriminatory views of particular people or groups. The impact is that inclusive language use doesn't deliberately or inadvertently exclude people from being seen as part of a group. Further, the Diversity Council Australia (2016) argues that 'inclusive language enables a diversity of people (e.g., different ages, cultures, genders) to feel valued and respected and able to contribute their talents to drive organisational performance'.

From the perspective of professional writing, it is important to be aware of the impact of language choices. So, what are the issues, and how do writers make appropriate word choices? This is discussed in the following sections.

Inclusive language
Language that is free from words, phrases and tones that reflect prejudiced, stereotyped or discriminatory views of particular people or groups.

Avoid exclusion or invisibility

The first main problem of lack of inclusivity is the issue of exclusion and invisibility of women and gender-diverse individuals. In old English, the word 'man' meant 'human' as there also existed gender-specific pronouns. As English has evolved, these pronouns no longer exist. The use of 'man' as a generic for 'humankind', therefore, merely reinforces the exclusion and invisibility of women. In the case of generic nouns or titles, such as chairman, man-made, manpower, foreman, salesman and so on, historically, these roles or associations related to men, but social changes are not necessarily reflected in title changes. In other words, they act to 'naturalise' a particular way of thinking about the roles and status of particular groups of people and reflect traditional ideas of gender as a 'social construct' – the roles, behaviours, activities and attributes that society at any given time considers appropriate for men or women. Exhibit 11.13 illustrates some issues and suggests ways to correct these.

Exhibit 11.13   Examples of language that enforces stereotypes or invisibility

Issue	Instead of	Use
Gender-specific terms/verbs	Chairman To man	Chairperson/chair/convenor To staff/operate/attend
Generic personal pronouns	Each Dean will determine *his* school's priorities When a student enrols, *he* must ...	Each Dean will determine *the/their* school's priorities When a student enrols, *they* must ...
Words of equal status	Ask the *ladies* in the office	Ask the *staff* in the office
Unequal titles or forms of address	John Brown and his wife Man and wife Dear Sir	John and Jane Brown Husband and wife Dear Sir/Madam or Dear Madam or Sir
Gender role stereotyping	Air hostess/male nurse Actress/poetess/authoress *Mother of three* appointed to Staff and their *wives*	Flight attendant/nurse Actor/poet/author [Name] has been appointed to Staff and their partners
Compliments and put downs	You throw like a *girl* Don't be an *old woman* Don't be a *blouse* *Man* up	These expressions are belittling and act to subtly reinforce gendered stereotypes of women and men

Avoid unnecessary emphasis on difference

Irrelevant information about a person's gender, age, ethnicity, ability, marital status or sexuality may sensationalise and reinforce stereotypes and unnecessarily emphasise difference. Examples include phrases such as young doctor, childless politician, disabled athlete, and so on. You rarely hear about the age, marital or family status of a male company executive. Constantly referring to people with disabilities as 'outstanding', 'heroic' or 'courageous' may act to unnecessarily focus on their disabilities and sensationalise their experiences. Avoid unnecessary detail. If the difference is relevant and appropriate in your communication, use 'person-first' and inclusive language wherever possible. **Exhibit 11.14** gives some examples of appropriate language for respectful, inclusive communication.

Exhibit 11.14 Some examples of inclusive and appropriate language

When referring to:	Examples of appropriate language
People with disabilities or medical conditions	people with disabilities accessible toilet visually/hearing impaired person with an intellectual disability person with a mental illness person living with AIDS
Sexual preference	Only discussed if relevant There are a range of acceptable descriptors for sexual preference: LGBTQI+, gay, lesbian or queer
Gender identity	If you are unsure of a person's preferred gender identity, use plural 'they'. The Australian Style Guide (Plain English Foundation, 2021) suggests the following options: male/masculine: he, his, him female/feminine: she, her, hers non-binary, trans, unspecified: they, them, their, theirs non-binary or trans: xe, xers, xem, xer
Aboriginal or Torres Strait Islander peoples	Always capitalise Aboriginal and Indigenous Use 'Aboriginal and Torres Strait Islander peoples', 'Aboriginal peoples', 'Indigenous peoples', 'First Australians', 'First peoples', 'First Nations peoples' When referring to a specific group of Aboriginal peoples you must check with the local community before using any terms from the local dialect, including the group's traditional name
Age	*Students* in the classroom *Seniors, aged, older Australians* Children and young people *Staff* in the office
Ethnicity	Wherever possible, use specific terms to identify ethnic groups: Lebanese Australian, immigrants, Pacific Islander people

'Political correctness' or good manners?

Finally, deliberate or conscious attention to applying inclusive language principles, as discussed in Chapter 2, is regularly dismissed as 'political correctness' or 'PC'. What this phrase conveniently ignores or dismisses is the role of language in shaping and reflecting attitudes and social mores, which change and evolve over time. If it is true that language use creates meanings and perceptions, and determines what we see as reality, then it may be that language has 'constructed' women as inferior to men, leading to discrimination against them in workplace competition, even in professional workplaces.

The Diversity Council Australia (2016) argues that inclusive language – calling groups by the names they prefer – is a more precise and accurate use of language. 'It is not about being "politically correct" but about using language which is respectful, accurate and relevant to everyone.'

Reflection question: Consider words or expressions that were commonly used in the past that are no longer acceptable. How might these have impacted those at whom they were aimed?

CASE STUDY 11.5 Erasing history or keeping up with the times? The great Roald Dahl debate

Consider the following discussion about recent moves to apply a 'sensitivity lens' to classic texts such as those of English children's writer Roald Dahl.

Is it a matter of keeping classics relevant or political correctness gone mad? That's the crux of the polarised reactions to news Roald Dahl's publisher Puffin, together with Netflix, is changing the language in some of his most iconic works.

Works being examined with a contemporary lens have led to hundreds of changes to the English author's books, including the Oompa Loompas in *Charlie and the Chocolate Factory* being made gender-neutral instead of male, the words 'fat' and 'ugly' being culled, and more inclusive terminology throughout.

What to some seems like benign intervention to keep classic books relevant is damned by others as censorship and revisionism. Acclaimed author Salman Rushdie is incensed by the changes, describing the updated language as blatant censorship.

[According to] Denise Chapman, a lecturer in literacy at Monash University … 'We can't erase it: we have to be able to know our history' … As an African American woman, Chapman says it's a challenging topic, citing *Huckleberry Finn* as an example of a problematic text.

Where The Wild Things Are was also a touchpoint … as people were concerned the character of Max was disobeying his parents.

'We are always going to have books that upset people, that contain ideas that people don't like or don't agree with, that we all agree are absolutely wrong, but if we hide these books it doesn't make it go away. In fact, it prevents us from preparing children to engage with this idea that we agree is wrong and that they will eventually face,' [Chapman] says.

On the other hand, best-selling author Andy Griffiths argues that the changes do not affect the fundamental stories Dahl was telling … He sees the tweaks to the language as logical and indeed justified.

[Others] agree that the changes are minimal and help keep the books relevant, 'while maintaining the irreverence and the spirit of silliness'.

Source: K. O'Brien (2023, February 20). Erasing history or keeping up with the times: The great Roald Dahl debate. *Sydney Morning Herald*. The use of this work has been licensed by Copyright Agency except as permitted by the Copyright Act, you must not re-use this work without the permission of the copyright owner or Copyright Agency.

Discussion

1   Consider the reactions from different sources cited to the changes made to some of the language in Roald Dahl's texts: do you agree 'sensitising' the original language to reflect current language use is 'censorship'?

2   In the case of classic books like Mark Twain's (1884) *Huckleberry Finn* where the repeated use of the 'n-word' is a reflection of the social and language standards of the time, is this a justifiable editorial decision or are we 'sanitising' history?

3   Does raising attention to gendered, non-inclusive or archaic tropes or stereotypes, as reflected in language, work to change attitudes to minority groups? Or is this just 'PC gone mad'?

After you have discussed this case study, refer to the 'Comments on case studies' section at the end of the text.

Editing and reviewing

Some people believe that there is no such thing as good writing – only good rewriting. There is no doubt that most of us will not produce perfect documents instantly. We will probably need several attempts at even a simple letter before we are satisfied that it is correct and appropriate. That process of reviewing, evaluating and adjusting our own text is commonly called revision. Editing consists of calling the writer's attention to flaws in both content and style.

In your workplace, colleagues may ask you to review a document they have just written and give them comments on it. At university, a friend may ask you to help with a difficult assignment. A classmate with difficulties in English may solicit your help in improving their writing. All these situations require you to develop your skills in editing and revising.

It is advisable to consider the editing stage as equally important to the composition stage. Start by getting your thoughts down on paper (or screen) and then go back and edit for accuracy, form and layout. Too much initial worry over correct spelling or grammar may inhibit the flow of ideas.

However, many students and workplace writers are reluctant to go back over work they have toiled so hard to produce, and this is a mistake. In an initial draft, even the best writers miss errors. What may appear to make sense when we first put an idea to paper may read differently after a good night's sleep.

Editing

It is often easier to see the flaws in another's writing than it is to edit your own work. However, several drafts will probably occur before you are ready to allow another to see something you have written. Don't try to achieve everything in one reading. Use a staged approach to your editing. The process of evaluating your own work requires you to hone your language skills and also be critical of your own thought processes.

Once you have a reasonable draft of your composition, you are ready to polish it. Get yourself into a really critical but positive frame of mind and begin. Remember that the objective is not to judge but to improve. You may be tempted to throw the whole composition into the rubbish; however, before you do, try the following editing technique and see if it works for you.

Editing guidelines

1 *Make a point-form outline of your draft.* This gives a clear overview of the coverage of the topic. You can then start to identify what is missing – the areas where you need to do further research or provide supporting information. You will also be able to test if there is a logical flow from one idea to the next and you can reorganise the order if necessary. The outline also indicates whether the hierarchy of headings is appropriate. Are the important points presented as main headings and the lesser ones as subheadings? Are they all expressed in a similar form?

2 *Analyse the introduction.* Does it capture attention, develop interest, define the scope of the topic and critical terms, and indicate your intention to come to grips with the topic?

3 *Review the conclusion.* Does it indicate that you have effectively achieved the goal you set in the introduction? Does it bring all the important points together? Does it leave the reader feeling confident about the reliability of your work?

4 *Bit by bit, work through the body of the paper.* Is each idea clearly presented and have you provided sufficient supporting information? Do your bridging sentences and words lead your reader from one idea to the next? Do the headings describe what is in the section that follows and form a helpful guide to the reader? Are any important points missing? Have you presented too much information and created an overload? Five to seven points are usually all that are needed to explain one section of the work.

5 *Check the references.* All professionals are expected to be able to accurately give credit where credit is due. Chapter 13 gives explicit directions for correct referencing.

6 *Go back to the beginning of your paper for a thorough review of spelling, grammar, sentence and paragraph structure and word usage.* Remember to vary the construction of your sentences while keeping them basically short. Use strong verbs that explicitly indicate the action you are describing in that sentence. Your paragraphs should develop one idea only. It is easier for your readers if you keep the paragraphs limited to five or six sentences, and they may be even shorter for business writing. It is important to focus each paragraph on a strong topic sentence.

7 *Add visual impact.* All written work is affected by its appearance. This doesn't mean that all student assignments need pictures or graphs or various coloured headings. A writer needs to consider the effect that all the visual elements of a paper will have on the reader. If you are using graphs, tables, charts or photographs, make sure they are appropriate to the paper and clearly and neatly presented. Each one should have a title and a figure or table number (e.g. 'Exhibit 6.1' or 'Table 4.1'), and you should refer to them at some point in the text.

8 *Consider all the details of appearance: paper, font, colours, covers and bindings, format and layout.* For some assignments you will spend a lot of time making your paper look good; for others you may consider it unimportant. The essential point is to make that decision in relation to the goals for that particular communication.

9 *Have one last ruthless look through the entire paper.* Reading your text aloud can often help you 'hear' where punctuation should be placed and whether your sentences are too long or poorly expressed. Better yet, have someone else have a look too. Don't be sensitive about critical evaluation from your workmates or friends. Make the corrections you think improve the paper and note the others in case you need to make subsequent alterations.

10 *Keep a backup copy of the finished document and save each version so you can track changes.*

Reviewing

When you are asked to review another's work, your major task is to examine the writing carefully, looking for incorrect spelling and grammar, inappropriate style and inconsistent logic. Writers tend to be defensive about their own work and they may find it difficult not to take your suggestions as a personal criticism of their writing. Therefore, you will need to be sensitive to their feelings and develop your interpersonal communication skills of persuasion. You, as the editor, probably also have doubts about your ability to criticise another's work and may be fearful of offending a workmate. The reviewing process, therefore, should be one of mutual concern. The objective of the exercise is an improved communication. That objective, however, will not come at the expense of the egos or self-esteem of all the persons involved if each accepts the value of constructive evaluation in the process of improving writing.

The following reviewing guidelines will help you in the reviewing process:

1 Think of the writer as someone you are helping, not someone you are judging.
2 Ask what the writer wants you to do.
3 Review first for logic and coherence.
4 Methodically edit for spelling and grammar.
5 Check consistency of style and format.
6 Distinguish between personal preference, corporate style and correctness.
7 Begin your critique by praising the strong points.
8 Phrase your comments positively.
9 Explain your suggestions fully.
10 Give examples to clarify your suggestions.

Summary

This chapter has explored the qualities of good writing, including clarity, accuracy, conciseness and coherence. Clear writing tries to make ideas as simple as possible using language with which the reader is familiar. This is done by searching for the best words, phrases and organisational structures to convey exactly what you mean, and by considering the receivers' needs, perspectives and limitations. The importance of writing inclusively has also been discussed.

One of the most important criteria of the writing process, either at university or in the workplace, is to meet deadlines. Many people, both professionals and students, do not submit their best work because they leave themselves short of time. This requires allowing time to plan, draft, edit and review your writing. Many people submit what amounts to draft work that is full of typographical errors, grammatical mistakes and easily avoided problems, which weaken the impact of ideas on a page either by confusion of meaning or by delaying comprehension. Thus, when industry leaders complain of the lack of writing skills in the workforce, they are also complaining about the lack of preparation that many writers exhibit. Taking in feedback is also important, and most supervisors and managers will discuss your work with you. While there is no universally applicable rule about how to write – it depends on each individual's education and what they value, and the nature of the message and the audience. If you disagree, it is a very good idea to disagree, agreeably. Learn from your feedback, and tailor your next writing job to meet their expectations.

STUDY TOOLS

DISCUSSION QUESTIONS AND GROUP ACTIVITIES

For discussion topics and activities in addition to those listed below, please refer to the case studies presented throughout this chapter.

1 Discuss the characteristics of the different readership groups for the following well-known publications or other similar publications in your locality or online:
   - *Mamamia* [online]
   - *The Australian*
   - *PC magazine* [online]
   - *Australian Women's Weekly*
   - *Australian Financial Review*
   - *NRMA Open Road magazine*

   How would you need to alter an article on reducing pollution from vehicle fumes to appeal to the different readers of these publications?

2 Collect a variety of business communications by asking colleagues, relatives and workmates for interesting samples. Be sure to respect confidentiality by masking specific references to names or other identifying information. Bring your samples to class and in groups of four discuss the differences in writing styles in the various documents.

3 Test your punctuation skills with these sentences. Compare your answers with classmates and discuss any differences.
   a A hard working group these writers can produce a report in a day.
   b Proposals a constant necessity are a major problem for writers.
   c I sat with my boss and his assistant sat elsewhere.
   d This transport company provides its customers with safe reliable and comfortable service.
   e The operator ran the program the disk drive was faulty.
   f The following contractors offered bids Wilsons Sydney Jennings Perth and Sykes Melbourne.
   g The taxes that are reasonable will be paid.
   h The taxes which are reasonable will be paid.
   i How do you know when its its and when its its.

4 Compare the writing style of some of your textbooks and discuss what techniques make them easy or difficult to read and understand.

5 Select the correct word in each of the following sentences. Compare your choice with that of others in your group and check your answers in the dictionary, if necessary.
   a Your action had little (affect/effect) on the decision.
   b You (can/may) take your flexiday tomorrow.
   c I was flattered by his (compliments/complements).
   d Your agenda is different (to/from/than) mine.
   e Perfection is possible, but (it's/its) rare.
   f The (principal/principle) advantage of the word processor is the ability to reproduce material easily.
   g There are (fewer/less) mistakes in this transcription.
   h (Two/Too) of the representatives will be sent (too/to) the conference. Several support staff will attend (to/too).

6   Rewrite the following sentences to improve the tone. Think about how you might react if addressed using these words.

    a   Your stupid mistake is inexcusable.

    b   Unless you improve your keyboarding skills you won't be working here much longer.

    c   I don't know if I will be available if you phone.

    d   I don't care if you did work late last night, I'm not going to do overtime today.

    e   The reasons for the change in policy were too absurd.

    f   Because you misunderstood the terms of the contract, we cannot be expected to pay you more money for the work.

    g   Due to your ignoring our repeated requests for payment, we will begin charging you interest from the first of the month.

7   Read through the following passage and brainstorm a list of words describing the tone.

    a   What is the subject?

    b   Highlight the words or phrases that create the tone.

    c   What is the effect of long sentences and minimal punctuation on the tone?

For the most part they carried themselves with poise, a kind of dignity. Now and then, however, there were times of panic, when they squealed or wanted to squeal, but couldn't, when they twitched and made moaning sounds and covered their heads and said Dear Jesus and flopped around to the earth and fired their weapons blindly and cringed and sobbed and begged for the noise to stop and went wild and made stupid promises to themselves and to God and to their mothers and fathers, hoping not to die.

O'Brien (1990)

8   Working in pairs and using an assignment that you have previously submitted in any subject, review each other's work, being mindful of the guidelines offered in this chapter. Offer suggestions for improvement. Discuss your reactions to the reviewing process and suggest strategies for improving your approach to this task.

9   Edit and revise the assignment used in question (8). Exchange the marked draft with a different partner and see if they can offer further suggestions for improvement. Compile a polished version and compare it to the original. (Perhaps your subject lecturer may be willing to discuss the improvements with you.)

10 Rewrite the following sentences to eliminate wordiness:

    a   It has been my wish for a considerable period of time to gain entrance into the field of accounting. This is due to the fact that challenges of my intellect are what challenge me.

    b   To me it appeared that Smith did not give any consideration whatsoever to the suggestion that had been recommended by the consultant.

    c   At this point in time we can't ascertain the reason as to why the screen door was left open.

    d   My sister, who is employed as a nutritionist at the University of Melbourne, recommends the daily intake of megadoses of Vitamin C.

    e   In the past there were quite a large number of firms located on the West Coast offering us competition. At this present point in time, the majority of those firms have been forced to go out of business by the hardships and difficulties of the present period of business contraction and stagnation.

    f   Dear Mrs Tardy, We are in receipt of your letter of 17 January. It is regretted that we cannot answer in the affirmative to your request. Inasmuch as your policy lapsed on 1 December, be informed that it has been cancelled and that your cheque in the amount of $157 arrived too late and is being returned herewith.

WEBSITES

Australian Style Guide https://www.australianstyleguide.com/home

Australian Style Manual https://www.stylemanual.gov.au

Cambridge Dictionaries Online https://dictionary.cambridge.org

Grammarly guide to punctuation marks https://www.grammarly.com/punctuation

Online Dictionaries and Translators http://www.word2word.com/dictionary.html

Plain English Foundation https://www.plainenglishfoundation.com

The Macquarie Dictionary http://www.macquariedictionary.com.au

WordsAtWork https://www.dca.org.au/research/project/wordsatwork-building-inclusion-through-power-language

REFERENCES

Astle, D. (2022, November 2). Enough with the bafflegab. Here's why a Plain Language Bill makes sense. *Sydney Morning Herald*.

Booth, W., & Gregory, M. W. (1987). *Writing as thinking, thinking as writing*. Harper & Row.

Chandler, D. (1995). *The act of writing: A media theory approach*. University of Wales.

Cutts, M. (2009). *The Oxford guide to plain English* (3rd ed.). Oxford University Press.

Cutts, M. (2020). *The Oxford guide to plain English* (5th ed.). Oxford University Press.

Diversity Council Australia (2016). *WordsAtWork: Building inclusion through the power of language*. https://www.dca.org.au/research/project/wordsatwork-building-inclusion-through-power-language

Eagleson, R. D. (1990). *Writing in plain English*. AGPS.

Felton, G. (2013). *Advertising: Concept and copy* (3rd ed.). W.W. Norton & Company.

Hodge, B., & Kress, G. R. (1993). *Language as ideology* (2nd ed.). Routledge.

Kimble, J. (2012). *Writing for dollars, writing to please: The case for plain language in business, government, and law*. Carolina Academic Press.

Mastrine, J. (2013, August 26). *Thought catalogue*. https://thoughtcatalog.com/julie-mastrine/2013/08/dude-man-up-an-exploration-of-gendered-language/

NASA (2006). (2010) *Imagine the Universe!: Black holes*. https://imagine.gsfc.nasa.gov/science/objects/black_holes2.html

O'Brien, K. (2023, February 20). Erasing history or keeping up with the times: The great Roald Dahl debate. *Sydney Morning Herald*.

O'Brien, T. (1990). *The things they carried*. Flamingo.

Petelin, R. (2022). *How writing works: A field guide to effective writing* (2nd ed.). Routledge.

Plain English Foundation. (2021). *Australian Style Guide*. https://www.australianstyleguide.com/home

Redish, J. (1993). Understanding readers. In C. M. Barnum & S. Carliner (Eds.), *Techniques for technical communicators*. Macmillan, pp. 15–41.

Truss, L. (2003). *Eats, shoots and leaves: The zero-tolerance approach to punctuation*. Profile Books.

Watson, D. (2003). *Death sentence: The decay of public language*. Random House Australia.

Williams, J. M. (2012). *Style: Lessons in clarity and grace*. (9th ed.). Longman.

Zinsser, W. (2006). On *writing well: The classic guide to writing nonfiction*. Harper Perennial.

Writing for the workplace: content and genre

Learning objectives

After reading this chapter, you should be able to:

- understand the range of genres that are commonly used in workplace settings
- describe the content, structure and essential parts of emails, letters, reports and manuals
- describe the stylistic features of writing typically found in workplace communication, including narrative, argument, explanation, description and instruction
- recognise and reproduce standard formatting, layout and design of workplace writing genres
- use a range of graphics typically expected in workplace genres of writing.

Workplace writing with devices in the 2020s

A common question asked by many people is: 'Has technology diminished the importance of written communication in our daily professional lives?' While this probably isn't the case, technology has certainly changed the communication landscape. In particular, writing in workplaces has massively changed from ten years ago, due to the widespread adoption of a range of digital devices for work purposes, such as laptops, tablets and, especially, mobile phones.

These devices have changed the specific audiences and increased the number of possible versions of a range of types of writing, such as reports, proposals, letters, emails and ordinary messages. Reading and writing information is perceived differently on various kinds of devices because of the size of the screen. Thus, the audience's ability to understand or respond to workplace writing depends on the type of device an employee uses. This choice of device is often determined by the location of the employee, whether they are travelling and if they have access to online data at the time.

Workplaces themselves have also been transformed by the COVID-19 pandemic because Australians could not go to their normal place of work. They instead had to work from a home office, and needed to use internet-connected communication systems, such as email facilities, the telephone, videoconferencing and other online digital applications. Working from home is now commonplace with many employees working pro-rata at home and in the workplace.

Introduction

This chapter explores a range of types (or genres) of business and technical writing in detail. To write effective emails, letters, reports, papers or manuals, you need to learn some specific conventions of layout and style appropriate to organisations, but you should also continually develop your general communication and writing skills to keep pace with changing styles and increasing levels of professional development. Above all you should not lose your ability and motivation to read (and read widely) all kinds of materials, both online and offline. You also need to read critically, so be selective about which news sites, social media platforms, books and websites you read.

Genres of workplace writing

There are many mediums or 'platforms' of workplace writing, including email, letters, reports and manuals. Most of these involve a form of mediated communication, where a sender uses a mobile phone, computer or tablet to send text and attachments to other people, either individually or collectively. The following sections will discuss these genres of workplace writing in more detail.

Email

Email has become the most common form of workplace writing, and accounts for the bulk of daily communication in most organisations around the world. Recent statistics predict that in 2023, there will be 347.3 billion emails sent and received globally each day, with this sum anticipated to increase to 361.6 billion in 2024 (Oberlo, 2022). Despite the increased use of messaging apps and other common communication platforms like Slack and WhatsApp, it is clear that email continues to play a major role in workplace lives.

There is a temptation to believe that email messages are casual and informal communications, and for personal correspondence that may be true. However, for all workplace correspondence, fairly formal conventions of traditional letter-writing should apply. To do so, you might consider conforming your emails to the following short business-writing structure:

- Begin with a greeting, such as 'Dear [First name]' or 'Ms [Last name]' or simply 'Hi'; endings can be as simple as 'Best', or 'Cheers' – the rules are not prescriptive.
- Paragraph 1: states the purpose of the message, and sometimes introduces the sender
- Paragraph 2: elaborates on the details of the purpose (usually a request, reply, offer, complaint or information)
- Paragraph 3: asks for some action to occur by the recipient.
- Signoffs with 'Warm/kind regards' or simply 'Best' or 'Cheers' – the rules are not prescriptive.

Typographic errors, missing words and spelling mistakes are usually well-tolerated in Australia. However, an email can be a legal document so do not slander anyone or make disparaging remarks of any kind to be on the safe side. Reread and revise before you press the send button. Put yourself in the receiver's position and imagine how you would feel as you read the email as part of a busy working day. A summary of the qualities of effective emails is provided in **Exhibit 12.1**.

According to workplace email etiquette, it is wise to refrain from forwarding chain messages or jokes, as what may seem humorous to you may offend others. It is also a wise idea to restrict your personal use of the organisation's email or internet system. Keep workplace and personal messages in separate email platforms. Many organisations filter and surveil email messages to ensure an overall quality in correspondence and to safeguard company policies. If you consider that your supervisor may read each email you write, you should be concerned about maintaining an appropriate writing style.

The following case study shows a replica of real email that uses the correct format of many emails: an appropriate subject line, greeting, message, three-part structure, and signoff, but also raises some questions. Chapter 5 provides further details about what is appropriate and inappropriate in electronic mail.

Exhibit 12.1 A summary of the qualities of effective emails

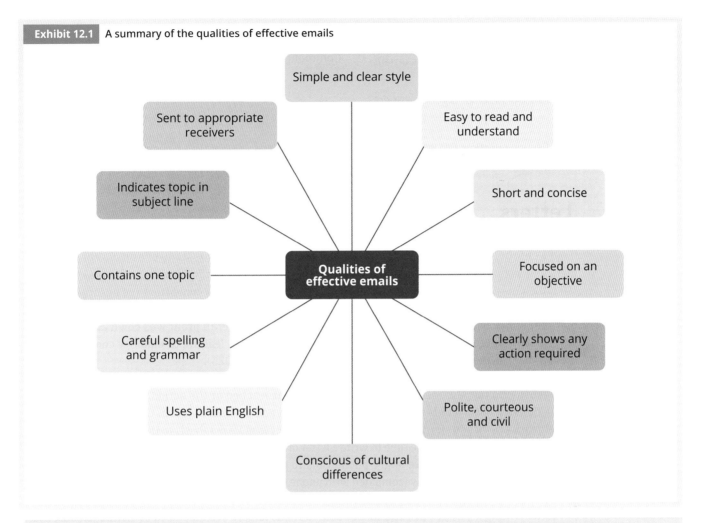

 CASE STUDY 12.1 Email structure and tell-tale signs

[EXTERNAL] Job Offer Available for You

acggroup.hosted.com.au@acme.com.au on behalf of Jessica Palmer <contact@acg.com.au>

Hello,

I hope all is well with you. I am Jessica Palmer , the Recruitment Officer of ACME CONSULTING GROUP, a professional headhunting company. We are affiliated to some recruitment platforms such as Fastjob, Indeed and LinkedIn. We have received your résumé information on one of our affiliated platforms. We reviewed your résumé and we have a suitable job offer for you.

We will be delighted to receive an immediate response with the subject 'Accepted Proposal' and also confirming your AGE and your WHATSAPP number or your Telegram username for fast contact. Currently we have several applications, but our vacancies are very limited. You can get the contact information of the HR manager by replying to this email contact@acg.com,au

and I will forward your contact information to the HR manager of the company where you will be provided with more information about the job you will be matched with, salary and working hours.

After receiving your reply, our HR Manager will contact you immediately. He will take you through a 20-minute online interview during which you will learn about the job details, salary and specific benefits from the company. Looking forward to your response.

Sincerely,

Jessica Palmer

Discussion

1   Can you name the three stages of the body of this email?

2   What is the correct way to address someone at the beginning of the email?

3 What is the correct way to sign-off from an email?

4 What are some of the tell-tale signs that this email might be a scam?

5 How can you check to see if this email is genuine or not?

After you have discussed this case study, refer to the 'Comments on case studies' section at the end of the text.

Reflection question: Can you think of the last email that you wrote? What was it about? Did you follow the three-part structure above? What about the last text message you sent?

Letters

Business letters of all descriptions have become an anachronism for most professions except for highly traditional industries, the legal profession and government agencies. Many of us have not received a personal letter for a long time. While Australia Post remains a profitable enterprise, making nearly $9 billion in the financial year to June 2022, most of this profit has come from the upsurge of parcel deliveries originating in online sales. Letter deliveries to metropolitan addresses have been cut by 40 per cent and now only occur every second day. In 2023 that overall profit was down 2.4 per cent, as a result in reductions in letters (5.7%) and parcels (1.6%) sent, leading to viability concerns for the government-owned enterprise (Australian Associated Press, 2023).

Nowadays, if businesses still choose to send a letter it is usually because it is a formal communication that provides a tangible, dated record of the agreement reached or the action requested. It is also an indication of a particular level of commitment and can add a personal touch. Committing thoughts to paper requires skill and effort, creates permanence and gives more emphasis to those thoughts and ideas. Anyone who has ever taken the time to write a letter of complaint about poor service or an unsatisfactory product will agree that, unlike angry phone calls to customer service lines, letters will always get a response. Their very tangibility (compared with phone calls or email) usually means that an organisation feels compelled to reply and acknowledge the problem or issue.

Letter writing is nowadays a specialised skill that has largely been replaced by writing emails; thus, the focus of this section will be on employment-related correspondence, including employment letters and résumés.

Employment-related correspondence

After weeks of searching, you have may have discovered the perfect job advertised, or you may be sending an unsolicited cover letter and résumé to an organisation. You may then spend hours crafting a tailored application that precisely matches your skills with the essential and desirable requirements of the advertisement. However, a prospective employer will probably allocate a very small amount of time to read each application they receive. In a matter of minutes a decision will be made on whether to read the attached **curriculum vitae (CV) or résumé**, or commit the application to the growing pile of rejects. This demonstrates how important it is to craft .

Curriculum vitae (CV) or résumé
Lists contact details, experience, achievements, qualifications, education, and special interests. It does not need to list demographic details about you, such as height, weight, age, gender or ethnicity.

Cover letters

Although a cover letter alone rarely secures a job, it is the applicant's first opportunity to impress the employer with their skills and professional competence. It is really a sales letter, and its goal is to present the applicant in the best possible light so that the employer will be compelled to then read the applicant's résumé. The cover letter's main purpose is to motivate the recipient to read the résumé. Therefore, an applicant needs to consider not only the impression the letter is likely to create, but also whether it adequately conveys interest in and aptitude for the position.

Even if you are applying for a number of similar positions, the letter should be customised to suit the specific requirements of each position. Every element of the job advertisement should be addressed in the letter and the résumé by explaining how your qualifications and experience meet the criteria that have been specified. You should call attention to the relevant items that detail that experience, while trying to be as persuasive as possible.

Application letters must convey professionalism. So ensure your cover letter is free of spelling errors and flawed use of language. Also be sure to attend to the visual aspects of the letter, as this gives an indication of your personality and work habits, as well as effecting how easy the information is to absorb. An example of a cover letter and its essential parts are shown in Exhibit 12.2.

Exhibit 12.2	Example of a cover letter and its essential parts in brackets

16 Vine Street [**inside address**]
NARWON QLD 4060
Telephone: 07 5555 7777

14 June 2021 [**date**]

Mr G. Sanders, Manager [**recipient and title**]
Highland Regional Development Pty Ltd [**external address**]
GPO Box 160
CANBERRA ACT 2601

Dear Mr Sanders, [**Salutation**]

Application for Position of Town Planner [**subject line**]

I am applying for the above position, which was advertised in the *Weekend Australian* on Saturday, 4 June 2022 [**statement of purpose**]

I believe that my background, experience and educational qualifications, which are described in the enclosed résumé, make me suitable for consideration for this position. The advertisement specified the need for a graduate in town planning with experience in specialised areas of design and supervision. I have recently graduated from Queensland University with a Masters degree in town planning. I have also been employed with the Bainsworth County Council for the last three years and I have had the opportunity to learn a wide range of specialised duties in investigation and design as well as supervise a team of drafters. [**most important information**]

My thesis for the Masters degree focused on subterranean spaces. I chose this field because it enabled me to develop a full range of design skills and gave me experience in the requirements of architectural design and engineering and their effect on town planning. Through my work with local government bodies, I have acquired a keen interest in the need for new visions of town planning to meet demographic change. [**less important information**]

I was able to publish several papers based on my Masters research and have presented two at international conferences on town planning. [**least important information**]

I am more than willing to relocate and would be most interested in an opportunity to discuss my application in an interview. [**statement of need or action**]

Yours sincerely, [**valediction**]

Natalie Proust [**signature**]

Natalie Proust [**name**]

Wherever possible, a letter of application should be addressed to a specific person in the organisation. A telephone call is often all that is needed to discover the name of the person to whom the letter should be addressed. Do not forget to check the spelling and the correct title – Ms, Mrs, Mr or Dr. Where appropriate the cover letter can be followed up with a personal visit or telephone call to present yourself and request an interview. But beware of appearing too pushy.

Curriculum vitae or résumé

The other important part of the application for employment is the personal CV or résumé. This document is a concise summary of a person's achievements, experience and qualifications. It is a portrait of the professional you, so you need to make sure that it shows you in the best light. To help a reader quickly review the contents, it should include appropriate headings to show highlights and details of the applicant's suitability for a job. It may also include special experience and interests if these show motivation and/or unique skills.

Like the cover letter, each résumé should be tailored carefully to suit the job you are applying for. For example, if you have had many casual jobs while studying, you may choose to group them according to the skills you developed, or expand on only those that are relevant to the prospective job. Listing every job you have held distracts attention from those relevant to the application.

Generally, provide details of duties, responsibilities and achievements, since this information lets prospective employers know what you have already accomplished and, therefore, what skills you possess. Information that shows an applicant's interests or positions of responsibility in voluntary organisations may also create a good impression. It is not necessary to reveal your gender, nationality or age.

Applicants should ask work associates or other responsible people to act as referees for them. Choose those who can speak well about your abilities and interests. List their names, positions, addresses, telephone numbers and email addresses on your résumé. Be sure to let them know each time you apply for a position so that they are prepared to discuss your application. In your first few jobs, including your casual jobs, it is also a wise idea to ask your supervisor to provide you with a letter of reference.

As your experience builds, your résumés will expand and change. You should develop a simple one-page résumé and also an extended résumé so that you have an up-to-date version should you need one immediately. Always maintain an up-to-date personal data folder as well, regardless of whether you are currently seeking employment. Keep a list of all the roles and positions you have been in, the tasks you performed and your achievements. Also list any training programs you have attended. Many human resource developers recommend that you keep a personal portfolio where you not only list your progress but also reflect on your development. A number of professions are now competency focused, so you may choose to investigate the models they have set out for you to document your professional competence. Be ruthlessly thorough in managing your own career portfolio.

As you advance in your career, your résumé will be adapted for various functions, both within the organisation and externally. For example, when firms are bidding for contracts, they often need to list the staff who will be working on the project so that prospective clients can verify their qualifications. Your résumé may also be used when applying for recognition by your professional association to highlight those aspects of your experience that are relevant to that organisation.

An example of a simple résumé is shown in **Exhibit 12.3**. For more advanced résumés, consult one of the many career websites and books available that provide a wide range of ways to present your credentials.

Think of the letter of application as leading to your résumé and then your résumé as gaining you a job interview, which in turns gets you the job.

Reflection question: Think of your own job-related experience and current education. What genuine achievements can you think of that will be useful to list in your own résumé?

Exhibit 12.3   Example of a simple résumé with achievements

Résumé

Lee Nguyen

55 East Street

Erewon, Victoria 3258

+61 413 888 888

Email: nguyen.lee@dotcom.com.au

Experience and achievements

Vacation and part-time work:

Dec 2019–Feb 2020	Consolidated Iron – Project Assistant
	Participated in demolition and construction work
	Became familiar with heavy equipment on-site
	Shadowed the project manager
	Supervised a small project measuring and pouring concrete for foundations
Nov 2017–Feb 2018	Colesworth St Kilda Store – Salesperson
	Won employee of the month Dec, 2017
	Responsible for fruit and vegetables
	Maintained clean and fresh displays
	Liaised with customers
Jan 2017–Feb 2017	Pizza Palace – Cook
	Responsible for food preparation and cooking
	Responsible for kitchen cleanliness
	Invented a new pizza for the company

Educational background

2018–present	University of Adelaide
	Bachelor of Science
Achievements	Completing third year with a Distinction average
	City of Melbourne Award for Innovation (2019)
Activities	Leader of inter-faculty sports squad (2018–2019)
	Technical Director, University Review (2019)

Other information

Special skills	Pilot's licence
Hobbies	Underwater swimming, flying and gliding, welded sculpture

Referees

James Soames	Toni Lee
Project Manager, Consolidated Iron	President, Highvale Flying Club
Telephone: (03) 5656 5656	**Telephone:** (03) 5656 5656

CASE STUDY 12.2 Employment opportunity

The following employment opportunity is similar to many that appear on popular online job sites:

Job title: Graduate
Job code: 1234
Location: Brisbane, Sydney, Melbourne
Date: 04-02-22
Job type: Permanent
Description:

A leading international organisation has recently taken on a number of outstanding development projects and is now seeking graduates to join the multidisciplinary teams who will face the challenges presented by these exciting new projects.

The ideal candidates possess a sense of adventure and a consistently positive attitude. They will have outstanding written and oral communication skills and a good work ethic. They should be able to demonstrate that they are team players and can perform under pressure. Most importantly, they need to be quick learners because this role will involve a very steep learning curve.

Candidates must have recently completed an undergraduate degree in any discipline or a Technical College Diploma with outstanding results. Your application must show that you can use your education as a springboard to an exciting career in a multidisciplinary area.

These vacancies are based in Brisbane, Sydney and Melbourne, so please indicate your preference. Candidates must be willing to travel within Australia as well as overseas and have appropriate travel documents.

Candidates can expect a speedy response as the organisation needs to start immediately to build its project teams.

Please send your résumé electronically as directed below. If you have any questions, you can call Marla Gladstone on 02 1234 5678.

Discussion

1 Why would organisations be seeking graduates from a variety of discipline areas?
2 Who are they looking for?
3 How should a candidate apply?
4 What questions could be asked if they rang Marla Gladstone?
5 Develop a résumé that is appropriate to this advertisement.
6 Should there be a cover 'letter' even though it is not asked for? If so, write an appropriate cover letter.

After you have discussed this case study, refer to the 'Comments on case studies' section at the end of the text.

Reports

There are as many different types of reports as there are reasons for reporting. The basic function of a report is to communicate information to someone who needs it. Reports can be defined as structured presentations directed to interested readers in response to some specific purpose, aim or demand. We often report to others orally, briefing them on a situation or supplying them with necessary information. However, as a piece of written communication, a report provides a permanent record of findings, a coherent discussion of alternatives, a logical presentation of conclusions and a detailed list of recommendations that propose the course of action best indicated by the study. Good reports distil and filter a vast amount of data into a straightforward, digestible document that often argues for a definite conclusion or set of recommendations.

There are four main types of reports used in professional organisations:

- *progress report:* shows how things are going at the moment – simply an update
- *informational report:* gives objective facts and figures, with no explanations about causes or the future
- *analytical report:* used for important decision-making, gives information, causes and predictions, and makes recommendations
- *research report:* not commonplace, but used for new products, services. This type of report needs data and other supporting reports, and will be described in detail in Chapter 13.

We may describe an event or detail a process that has been carried out. We may discuss the merits of different items of equipment or suggest what should be done to solve a staffing problem. We may investigate an accident and report our estimate of the damages, or we may survey potential users of a new product and report their opinions to the product-design team. You can see that in all these reports, a common theme is that reports usually result in some decision being reached or action taken. For this reason, reporting is one of the most important communication activities in business, industry, hospitals, research organisations and governments.

While oral reports often provide a quick overview of a situation, the obvious advantages of a written report are that it provides one or a number of readers with a physical copy of the report, and with that the opportunity to study the findings and make frequent reference to the information if required. In an oral report, the listeners will be able to ask questions and demand explanations; in a written report, the writer must anticipate those questions in presenting the information. These differences should be considered when deciding on the format of your report.

Questions to ask when writing a report

When you are commissioned to write a report, begin by listing all the questions that need to be answered if the aim of the report is to be achieved. Then begin the process of answering those questions. Exhibit 12.4 outlines some of the questions you need to explore.

Exhibit 12.4   Questions to explore when writing a report

Why is the report being requested?	Were any reasons given for preparing the report? Are there any additional reasons it might be necessary? For example, should it be an objective presentation of data so that people can make a decision, or a persuasive report to influence a specific decision? Is it simply meant to describe a situation or are you expected to analyse and make recommendations?
What is the purpose of the report?	What are your objectives, or your organisation's objectives in commissioning the report? Is it to stimulate interest in some particular subject, or to prompt readers to take action or make a certain decision? Is the material confidential/sensitive, requiring discreet handling? Market-research reports often need to disguise key elements from competitors while yielding valid information. If possible, write a statement on the aim of the report and check with your supervisor to see if it concurs with the objectives he or she had in mind
Who will read the report?	The report's audience have certain needs and expectations. What will they already know about the subject? Will readers have different degrees of knowledge? Will they be familiar with the terminology? Some executives will prefer a broad overview while technical staff want detailed and concrete data
What is the scope of the information requested?	Should the information be detailed, precise and specific, or broad and general? Is the information requested really the information the client requires, or should you suggest further data be included? Should the information be simply presented or is interpretation and analysis required? Are you supposed to include only existing data or put forward new ideas? How much time and money should you invest in research?
What use can I make of other reports?	Some reports resemble others that have already been submitted and approved. You may be tempted to use the formulas that have worked in the past; however, they should be used as guidelines only because over-reliance on them may blind you to the problems or things that are unique in the new report. On the other hand, departing too much from the routine format of reports accepted in your organisation may raise criticism from senior colleagues, so you need to be able to justify any deviations

Collecting and summarising information

There are many methods of finding and collecting data for a report. The type of information and the way in which it is collected will be determined by the purpose and nature of the report. It will not always be easy to find what you need; however, your responsibility for producing a report that meets your readers' needs will induce you to be innovative and thorough in your research. As you build experience, your reports will reflect this experience, not only because you have met similar problems before but also because your judgements are more mature and accurate than they were in the past. Chapter 13 discusses research methods; these skills are useful for any business reports you are commissioned to write.

Throughout the reporting process you will be summarising information as you condense material to present to others in a useful and informative format. The title of the report is the ultimate summary as it presents in the most concise form the essence of what the report is about. The table of contents is in reality a point-form summary. The complete report is a summary of a much larger body of information, while the section of the report called the *executive summary* presents the report 'in a nutshell'.

In all summarising activities you need to thoroughly understand the material you are shortening and have a clear idea of the audience and the purpose of the summary. Your abbreviated edition should be an accurate reflection of the essential ideas and the emphasis presented in the original work. You should present the key points but omit the details, examples, illustrations and supporting material.

Formal report format

The purpose, nature and scope of a report will influence the final decision about which format or style is appropriate. Choose a format that will best fulfil the aim of the report, be as simple and clear as possible, and be the most useful and timesaving to the reader. Many companies, departments and organisations develop their own special layouts for reports, and their employees soon become familiar with their expectations. However, an understanding of the commonly accepted format for formal reports prepares a writer for any reporting situation.

The traditional divisions of a report help a writer to organise the information into a framework that coordinates or subordinates each piece of data in relation to another. A typical report outline or format usually consists of the parts listed in **Exhibit 12.5**. Some of these parts may be excluded if they are not relevant to the nature, scope and content of your report. Additionally, the order of a standard report can be adjusted to better suit the current report's purpose.

For the structure of the following material, refer to **Exhibit 12.5**.

1 *Title page:* provides instant identification of the contents of the report. In addition to the title itself, which should be a concise and explicit description of the report, the title page should always be dated. Frequently, the name and position of the author and the person or group authorising the report is also presented. Occasionally, some indication of the intended audience is noted and, in some cases, notices or restrictions such as 'Confidential' or 'For internal use only' are clearly stated.

2 *Table of contents:* an outline of the complete report. It shows the section titles and major headings listed in order of appearance and indicates the appropriate page locations. A numbering system identifies each section. The table of contents is useful for an overview of the report and, of course, for quick reference to sections of specific interest to the reader.

3 *List of figures, illustrations and tables:* included if several of these items appear in the report. The figure numbers, titles and page references are listed in order of appearance.

4 *Executive summary:* a concise presentation of the essential elements of the report, including a short introduction to the context of the problem, the aim and scope of the report, the main findings without supporting examples or arguments, and the conclusions and/or recommendations. It permits readers to understand the overall meaning of the report without having to read the entire document.

| Exhibit 12.5 | The structure of a formal report |

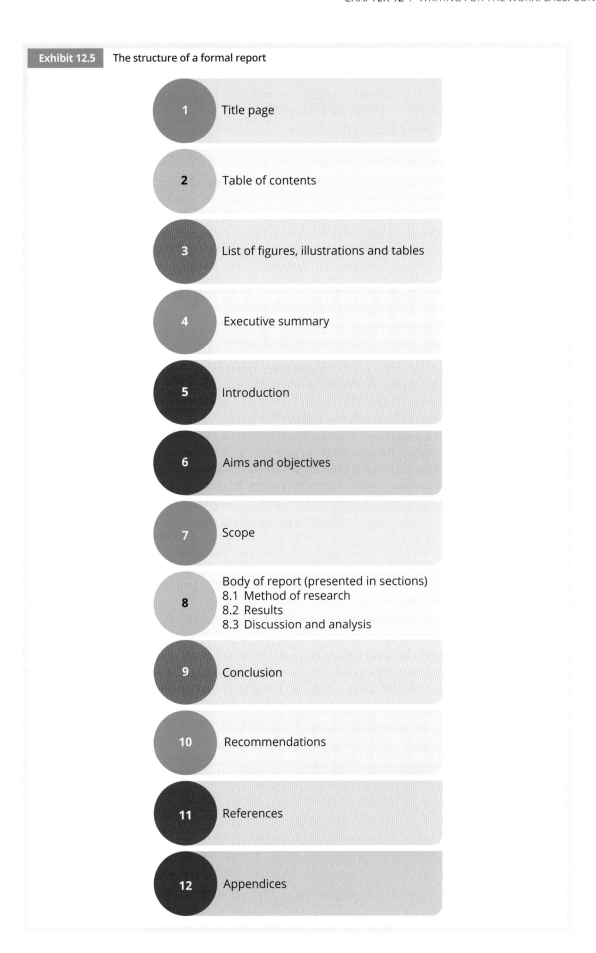

1 Title page

2 Table of contents

3 List of figures, illustrations and tables

4 Executive summary

5 Introduction

6 Aims and objectives

7 Scope

8 Body of report (presented in sections)
8.1 Method of research
8.2 Results
8.3 Discussion and analysis

9 Conclusion

10 Recommendations

11 References

12 Appendices

5 *Introduction:* provides the necessary background of the report. Readers may need some history or descriptive material to fully appreciate the details presented. If specialist terms are employed, it is wise to define these terms so that there is no misunderstanding or confusion throughout the remainder of the report. If extensive technical terminology is used, a glossary could be included after the table of contents or before the bibliography.

6 *Aims and objectives:* clearly outlines the reasons for the investigation and any special instructions that may be useful for the reader. May be included in the introductory section or provided as a separate section to highlight its importance.

7 *Scope of the report:* includes helpful information to be presented as introductory material. The scope should outline what the report covers and what it ignores, why have these boundaries been set. It should also address to whom is the report is directed and who will be affected by it.

8 *Body of the report:* communicates the facts and opinions collected. It should contain headings and subheadings that clearly describe the topics being discussed. One element should lead to the next so that the content is explored in a logical manner. A typical approach is to describe the research undertaken, display the results obtained, discuss the results by considering various viewpoints and perspectives to extract meaning from the data, and then analyse them using your professional judgement and expertise.

   - If a method section is needed, it informs the reader about how the information was gathered and what materials and equipment were used.
   - If you use tables, graphs, photographs or illustrations throughout your report, you should give each one a separate title or caption such as 'Table 1.2' or 'Exhibit 3.5'. Graphs are usually labelled as 'Figure 1.3' or 'Fig. 1.3'.

9 *Conclusions:* the natural outflow of the body of the report. This section usually opens with a brief summary of the report and then leads to the obvious conclusions drawn from the data presented. The conclusion should reinforce the reader's understanding of the report and relate to the objectives stated in the introduction. Some conclusions may simply be summaries of the main points of the discussion, while others may state the results, still others may evaluate the facts presented. However, no new material should be introduced in this section.

10 *Recommendations:* includes clear statements of the action that should result from the report. They often form the basis for motions to be debated and voted on at meetings. They are sometimes included with the conclusions, but if the recommendations are important, or there is extensive text, then a separate section is more functional. For example, analytical reports, in which a writer has been asked to evaluate and initiate change in an area, require a separate recommendations section.

11 *References:* may be included to acknowledge the sources of the information presented. However, many business reports do not use references.

12 *Appendices:* contain any relevant additional graphic, statistical or other supplementary material that may be interesting to the readers. These are placed at the end of the report so as not to interrupt the flow of the main ideas. Each item should be clearly titled and labelled (Appendix A, B, C, etc.), and should be referred to at an appropriate point in the body of the report.

It should be noted that one main difference between business reports and scientific reports is that the method section is usually missing or glossed over in business reports. However, many consultants, managers and outside agencies are employed for their expert knowledge, and so their methods actually represents their expertise or livelihoods. If they show their clients their methods, then many consultants will lose jobs.

CASE STUDY 12.3 The executive summary

The following is part of a university report on maintaining buildings and grounds:

The Henry Hicks Arts and Administration building, which was built in 1955, is probably the university's most recognizable and symbolic structure. Despite its importance to the university, the Henry Hicks building has been not kept up to date with some of the maintenance measures necessary to keep the building in good condition.

According to Marvin Windows and Doors, windows should be replaced every 20 years. This means that the H&H building is 30 years overdue for a window upgrade. This study weighs the costs and benefits associated with replacing the single-glazed windows with three types: the Kohler Energlas Plus, Marvin's Clad Ultimate Double Hung and Marvin's Casemaster.

This report's aim is to analyse the costs and benefits of replacing the building's inefficient single-glazed windows with a more efficient window type.

Each window is compared to the current type to measure energy savings, and carbon dioxide emission savings. These benefits were weighed against the costs associated with the installation using information provided through interviews with the assistant director of Facilities Management and two of the university's main window manufacturers, Kohler Windows and Marvin Windows and Doors. The study results suggest that window replacement cannot prove to be cost effective within 5 years (the university's standard for cost-effectiveness), but the upgrading of windows would produce significant savings in energy costs and carbon dioxide emissions.

It is recommended that in order to promote campus sustainability, the university replace the windows that are overdue for replacement. With this said, the university should choose the Energlas Plus window produced by Kohler Windows and wood rather than vinyl stripping. This window type was not only the most efficient but would be able to reach the point of cost-effectiveness within 17.7 years of installation (sooner than the other proposed window types).

Source: Adapted from N. A. Ahlers, B. M. Campbell, R. J. Cantwell, M. R. Forward & T. H. Spooner (2005). Cost-benefit analysis of outfitting the windows of the Henry Hicks Arts and Administration building with more efficient models to improve Dalhousie University campus sustainability.

Discussion

1 Is this summary written in plain English and easy to understand?

2 Can you identify the introduction, aims, methods, results and recommendations in the executive summary?

3 Do the recommendations follow from the aim of the report?

4 Read the whole report at https://dalspace.library.dal.ca/bitstream/handle/10222/77840/Double-glazed%20windows.pdf and comment on the extraordinary details of the whole report.

5 Does this executive summary provide a good overview of the entire report?

6 What is the main argument forwarded in the 'Introduction' in terms of windows?

After you have discussed this case study, refer to the 'Comments on case studies' section at the end of the text.

Report writing style

Many report writers feel they must write in the third person and use highly formal language. Modern practice, however, recommends using the pronouns *I* or *we* rather than the more formal terms *the writer* or *the investigator*. Others, in an effort to seek variety in their writing, consult their thesaurus to find synonyms for frequently used words, but this can often be unnecessary. Report writing demands precision rather than an elaborate style, so repetition and restatement may be quite appropriate. Also, since reports are often written for others within a specialist area, it is quite appropriate to use the specialist terms and jargon of that profession. If a writer is in any doubt about whether readers will understand a term, it is wise to define that term, either in the text or in an accompanying glossary.

Formatting can help to make information more digestible or noticeable. Many reports list information using bullets (•) or numbers, and others surround sections with a border. This grouping of information is called *chunking* and, although it does not necessarily conform to the usual idea of a paragraph, it performs the same function. Its purpose is to link related ideas into a coherent whole so that a reader will more easily interpret the message presented.

Compare the two versions of a report on building services in the following:

Version 1: Block paragraphing

Quotations are given and sales made under the following conditions. First, prices may fluctuate without notice, either before or during delivery. Second, the whole of the bricks required on the job must be supplied through us from our own yard. Extra payment will be required if carters are required to wait on the job for more than 15 minutes. Delivery is subject to strikes, lockouts, shortage of vehicles or any other cause beyond our control. Face-brick prices are subject to face-bricks being available from yards in this district. In the event of carters having to divide their loads or place bricks on a scaffold higher than their vehicle, extra payment will have to be made. This additional payment will also be required if the carters have to carry bricks over a footpath more than four metres wide or unload bricks over the rear of the vehicle.

Version 2: Bulleting, listing and indenting

Quotations are given and sales made on the following conditions:

- prices may fluctuate without notice either before or during delivery
- bricks supplied on the job are supplied through us from our own yard
- extra payment will be required if carters are required to:
  - divide their loads
  - place bricks on a scaffold higher than their vehicle
  - carry bricks over a footpath more than four metres wide
  - unload bricks over rear of vehicle
  - wait on jobs more than 15 minutes
- face-brick prices are subject to face-bricks being available from yards in this district
- delivery is subject to strikes, lockouts, shortage of vehicles or any other cause beyond our control.

Version 1 is more difficult to read and absorb due to its format, with the solid paragraph prose form making separation of major and minor points difficult. The main problem in version 1 is that every sentence has a different subject. Sentences are totally unrelated to each other. Version 2 recognises this fact and creates a list structure that was the basis of the original.

Headings

Headings, numbering and listing are used extensively in reports to guide your reader towards the information they need. Use headings and subheadings for sections and even paragraphs, to act as signals to the content. Headings can help readers who are skimming the report because they lack time to read it thoroughly, or readers who are scanning for specific information. The headings form the table of contents of a report and, with the addition of page numbers, are a central navigational aid.

Decide on the style you will use to signify your levels of headings. You might use a bold upper-case font for main headings and lower-case words with initial capital letters for subheadings. It is important to be consistent throughout the report. Your word-processing system can help you with the format of your headings so that you can make changes consistently throughout a report.

Numbering is also important in reports to help readers follow and find particular sections. A recommended system is the decimal numbering system, as shown in **Exhibit 12.6**, which is easy to use and does not lead to confusion about the relative levels of letters.

How reports are read

Separating the various sections of the report enables people at different levels in an organisation to read those parts of the report they find interesting or necessary. Senior management may have time to read only the executive summary. Others may scan the executive summary, introduction and conclusions, and these parts should give them a good general idea of the report's main points. Middle-level administrators may wish to concentrate on the conclusions of the report so that they can implement the report's findings.

Exhibit 12.6	Decimal numbering in headings

INFECTIOUS DISEASES

1.0 Summary

2.0 Introduction

3.0 History

    3.1 Local

    3.2 Overseas

4.0 Causes of disease

    4.1 In the home

    4.2 In the community

    4.3 In hospitals

5.0 Conclusions

    5.1 Results

    5.2 Recommendations

Research officers may be asked to read the whole report carefully, especially checking the detailed calculations that may appear in an appendix. If there are a number of tables, charts and graphs in the report, researchers may appreciate the inclusion of a list of illustrations as well as a table of contents at the beginning of the report.

Structuring the body of the report

The structure of the central part of the report, the body of the report, will depend on the subject. Many reports are essentially answers to the question 'What happened?' The answer to such a question might proceed chronologically, dealing with the topic in stages or phases, and bringing the reader up to date.

Another question that might be addressed by the report is 'Why did this happen?' Cause and effect will be the basis of the answer to this question, and again a chronological structure might be used. On the other hand, such a report might begin by discussing the present state of the problem and then move back in time to explain how the problem arose.

If the question is 'What should be done?', the structure of the report is likely to be a sort of debate, comparing solutions to a problem, assembling evidence and making a judgement.

Reports can be broadly classified as either descriptive or analytical. Descriptive reports emphasise facts, figures and descriptions. They say what is happening as concisely and precisely as possible. They might include judgements such as 'The year's trading figures show an improvement month by month owing no doubt to the lifting of the drought in April'. However, in information reports, judgements are of less importance than objective statements of fact. Analytical reports, on the other hand, rely on your professional expertise to examine the information and provide expert opinion on its meaning and relevance.

Many reports are structured according to topic. That is, a number of areas or topics are reported on and the writer must decide the order of the topics. Suppose that you were reporting on the incidence of road-accident fatalities in your state during a particular period. Perhaps your research shows that in order of seriousness the causes of fatalities are drunkenness, speeding, distraction and incompetence. You may decide to treat each cause in the order given; that is, from the most to the least frequent cause of accidents. This order will give prominence early in the report to the most important problems. On the other hand, you may wish to lead up to the most frequent accident cause, in which case you can proceed in reverse order. Yet another method is to classify the types of accident fatality; for example, drunkenness and speeding can be regarded as deliberative behaviour, and distraction and incompetence as non-deliberative behaviour. This structure may enable you to make more interesting points in your analysis and recommendations.

Presenting the final report

The final draft of your report is the copy that will be presented to the reader, and it may take you a number of drafts before you are satisfied that your work meets all of the criteria we have discussed in this text. The usual processes of editing and revising (described in Chapter 11) apply.

Before submitting the document, complete the checklist in **Exhibit 12.7**. You can then be confident that you have achieved the goal of presenting a satisfactory and effective report. If you are satisfied that your report has met all these requirements, then you are ready to submit it to your reader.

Exhibit 12.7   Checklist for report writers

Checklist for report writers	
Does the title clearly show the content of the report?	☐
Is the aim of the report clearly stated in the introductory sections?	☐
Has enough background been given to enable the readers to understand the report?	☐
Does the conclusion leave the reader in any doubt that the goal of the report has been achieved?	☐
Is the structure and sequence of the report logical and appropriate?	☐
Is the information in the report arranged under a set of headings and subheadings that follow a logical hierarchy?	☐
Is the format and layout attractive and visually effective?	☐
Have you planned the placement of illustrations so that they are presented in the best possible way?	☐
Are the graphics interesting and relevant?	☐
Do you make reference to each illustration, figure or table within the text of your report? Do they all have a number, title and, if necessary, an acknowledgement of their source?	☐
Does each section of your report fulfil its function?	☐
Have you included all the necessary examples, details, facts and illustrations? Is there any need for more interpretation and explanation? Are all the major points given sufficient emphasis?	☐
Have the sources of your information been provided?	☐
Is the bibliography complete and has it been correctly set out?	☐
Have all direct quotations been acknowledged? Has this been done in an appropriate manner and correctly set out as references?	☐
Have you carefully proofread the report for any errors in grammar, spelling, sentence structure, punctuation and paragraphing?	☐
Have you presented the report in an appropriate style and at an appropriate time?	☐
Are you proud of your work? Does it reflect your professional competence?	☐
Will your reader be satisfied?	☐

Short reports

In business and industry you often hear the phrase 'time is money'; thus, short reports are often used to describe incidents, such as accidents or faults in a process, or they may recount the results of a test or experiment. They may be called incident reports, progress reports or patient reports, and are often presented in Word or PDF format or in a standardised template or website form determined by the organisation.

No matter what they are called, the process for writing short reports follows the conventional reporting process of answering the 5Ws (who, what, when, where, why; see Exhibit 11.6 on p. 322). With many reports, it may be wise to add an additional question of *what next*? While the 5Ws do not need to be addressed in this order, they do all need attention. You must indicate *who* was involved in the process under review and *who* it affects. You should clearly and objectively describe the accident or incident, including the relevant details of date, time, season and location. *Why* is a more difficult task in technical writing because you must be very careful about attributing blame. Be sure to explain *why* as factually as possible. You can show *what should happen next* as your recommendations for further action.

In terms of layout, short reports are often set out using a custom format or one that requires a professional to fill in text boxes either on paper or on a website form. Unlike long reports, short reports have no title page, executive summary or table of contents. They often include familiar headings and numbering to break up the text and to make it easier to find relevant parts. An example of a short memorandum report is given in Exhibit 12.8.

Exhibit 12.8 **Short report in memorandum format (note: absence of method here)**

To: Margaret Curzon, Branch Manager
From: Jeffrey Blake, Loan Manager
Date: 30 September 2023
Subject: Investigation into processing delays in commercial loan applications

1.0 INTRODUCTION

In response to your request, I have investigated the delays in processing commercial loan applications over the past three months. The following is a summary of my findings and several recommendations on how to improve the current processing timeframe and put in place processes to avoid these problems in the future.

2.0 FINDINGS

2.1 Processing time

The average processing time for a commercial loan application has slipped for the third consecutive month. It now takes approximately six weeks for our customers to get an answer on their loan application. This is more than two weeks longer than our advertised four-week turnaround time and longer than the turnaround time of most of our competitors. The reasons for this slippage include an increase in the number of loans currently being processed, an ongoing problem with the online loan approval system and the impact of staff leave schedules due to mid-year school holidays.

2.2 Commercial loans processed

The total number of commercial loans processed has continued to increase over the past 12 months. During the past three months in particular, these increases have been significant. Table 2.1 below is a summary of this quarter's loan activity.

Month	Total no. of loans initiated	Loan amount
June 2023	50	$350 000
July 2023	68	$598 000
August 2023	86	$843 000

Table 2.1 Loan activity June–Sept 2023

▶

363

> **Exhibit 12.8** Short report in memorandum format (note: absence of method here) *(Continued)*
>
> ### 2.3 STAFF SHORTAGES
>
> The last three months have seen an increased demand for annual leave by key loans staff. This, in addition to two senior staff taking extended long service leave plus one unexpected extended period of sick leave for a member of the conveyancing team, has meant increased workload for the whole section.
>
> ### 2.4 ONGOING IT SYSTEM PROBLEMS
>
> In May 2011, the section underwent an IT upgrade to improve the capacity of the whole company. Unfortunately, glitches in the new system software resulted in unexpected downtime which has had a flow-on effect in terms of staff ability to process applications as quickly as normal. The system manufacturers now appear to have developed a patch to rectify the problem, and the system now appears to be functioning as it should.
>
> ### 2.5 LOST BUSINESS
>
> The length of time that we take to process loans is especially important now that our competitors are becoming more aggressive in their marketing. There were at least five (5) highly rated and potentially profitable loans that were lost last month because customers became impatient with our delayed response and chose to go to another lender. Several of these were long-term customers who took other business such as credit cards and overdraft accounts with them.
>
> ### 3.0 CONCLUSION
>
> As outlined and detailed in this report, processing of loans is currently two weeks behind our advertised four-week turnaround on loan applications for several reasons beyond our control. Unfortunately this is having a significant effect on business, with many customers choosing to apply to our competitors rather than wait. In short, the bank is losing important business due to these delays.
>
> ### 4.0 RECOMMENDATIONS
>
> The following short- and long-term actions are recommended:
> 4.1 Immediately employ an additional loans officer to ease the burden on the department.
> 4.2 Ensure that all staff leave is staggered during the end of financial year period.
> 4.3 Ensure that there is a backup processing system in place when upgrades to the system software are proposed or are necessary.
> 4.4 Advertise an immediate reduction in loan application fees until the backlog of applications has been processed.
> I would be happy to meet with you to discuss these recommendations. If you are happy to approve recommendation 1, I will begin recruiting this additional staff member immediately.

Stylistic features of workplace writing

There are many different styles of workplace writing, which are selected for use depending on the context and purpose of the communication. Workplace writers, in fact all writers, are typically predisposed to write from (1) their own style of thinking and speaking and (2) audience needs. Thus, workplace writing tends to reflect a combination of the writer's thought patterns, their experience and perceived audience expectations. Some common styles of workplace writing options are discussed in the following.

Narrative style

Many sections of documents can be written in a narrative style, in which they tell a story that is composed of facts.

When presenting a report of an accident, a description of a laboratory experiment, or the details of a site visit, your purpose is to give your reader as detailed an account of the situation as they need to appreciate the significance of the event. Many narratives follow a chronological order; that is, they tell of an event from beginning to end in a connected timeline. For simple accounts, this style is usually the most appropriate. However, events are frequently affected by other events and your writing needs to present these diversions clearly and objectively. You should justify why you include them as part of your account and perhaps why you have discounted other influences. You are then employing another important, logical form. You are using your judgement to indicate that one event is important while another is irrelevant. You may also need to argue that there is a hierarchy of importance, from most to least important, or you may indeed be working towards an argument of cause and effect, that one event actually caused the other to happen. You have then moved from a simple narrative to an argument.

Generally, the writing is concise and succinct, but can also be lively and interesting – there is no rule that says that even the most technical writing has to be boring and dull. There is little in the way of 'padding'. The tone is definitive, and the writer knows the topic well and speaks with confidence and authority. Statistics Netherlands (https://www.cbs.nl/en-gb) is one of the best websites of its kind in the world because it uses a good narrative style about really boring facts and numbers. The website does not, however, give any explanations for the national trends that it covers.

Argument style

When using an argument style, you build your case on logical statements. Almost all arguments in workplace writing use a form of inductive logic, known as *inductive reasoning*, where facts are assembled, one after another, until a conclusion is reached. This is shown in the following example:

> **Fact:** Cigarette smokers inhale smoke and vape users inhale vapour, both of which contain nicotine and other toxic substances.
> **Fact:** Cigarette smokers have a significantly higher risk of lung cancer than the general population.
> **Fact:** Vaping has been linked to serious lung disease.
> **Conclusion:** Vaping may eventually lead to lung cancer too.

Some people argue that all writing is argumentative, in that its objective is to influence our thinking and ultimately to persuade us to act in a certain way or to believe certain things are true. The credibility of the argument style is that we rely on our professional colleagues to make appropriate value judgements in the course of their work. Since they are the experts in their fields, they know what is important, threatening or critical, and it is their role to make these judgements explicit in their work. Readers should not have to formulate their own conclusions but should have them presented as professional advice, often in the form of an inductive argument.

Explanation style

Often, your writing needs to be supported with evidence, such as illustrations, examples, research, statistics or expert testimony. You will call on your skills in explanation and also description (discussed next) to present this material. Many of us are probably unaware that we constantly use explanations in daily life to justify our behaviour and decision-making. Statements like: 'I was late arriving home because there was a large traffic jam on the highway' is one justification or explanation for being late. Another could be: 'I was late arriving home because I stayed back to finish off some work'. There are generally five main types of explanations, as shown in **Exhibit 12.9**.

Knowing something about your audience will help you to determine the type and level of explanation required. You may choose to simply enclose the explanation in parentheses following a word, add an explanatory sentence or even add an entire paragraph to ensure that your meaning is suitable or appropriate. Furthermore, the type of explanation will differ according to the context; for example, in the nursing profession, risk-based explanations will predominate. In computer science and scientific contexts, risk explanations will outweigh the others. Academic workplaces tend to rely on expert findings from peer-reviewed journals and books.

Every field of work has its own vocabulary, and each culture attributes different meanings to explanations, which includes a tacit hierarchy of acceptability depending on the culture. This highlights the living nature of language and the recognition that meanings reside in the people who communicate the words, not in the words themselves. Since precision is a critical element in workplace writing, reaching

Exhibit 12.9	Types of explanations that may be used

Type	Example
Value	Buying an annual subscription is much better value than paying month by month
Traditional	The house should retain its original features in keeping with the rest of the dwellings in the street
Risk	The chosen procedure presents the least amount of discomfort for the patient
Scientific	The graph shows that SUVs are the most popular medium-to-large vehicle in Australia
Expertise	The United Nations stated that COVID-19 variants are becoming more infectious and resistant to vaccinations

an agreement on the meaning ascribed to words is an important strategy. We achieve this by defining acceptable problems and explaining solutions at various points throughout our documents. In highly technical papers and reports or in contract documents, we may even include a glossary as a separate section in which terms are formally defined and explained.

Reflection question: What level of importance is the following explanation? Explain why. 'My dying father and I needed to discuss his funeral arrangements'

Description style

A definition tells your readers what an item is and indicates its unique characteristics, but you frequently need to give a much more extensive description of what it looks like and what it does. Specifications that itemise equipment or services include both of these descriptive parts. They tell potential suppliers that you want a machine that has these physical characteristics and can perform these functions. For example, you may want a desktop computer and software that is capable of performing complex mathematical calculations. The description may be general or highly specific. You may include detailed technical drawings with precise dimensions, or you may signify an exact colour, including standard identification numbers.

You may expand your description by including an *example*, for instance 'a desktop computer, such as a Macintosh', or you could use a *synonym* to explain your meaning, as in 'a desktop computer, or PC'. Another technique to help readers derive a clearer picture is to tell them what it is *not*. For example, 'a desktop computer, not a laptop'.

Descriptions are often accompanied by illustration and photographs, particularly when new or old technologies are involved. Leonardo Da Vinci's famous 'aerial screw', or helicopter, invention used his drawing and description shown in Exhibit 12.10.

Metaphor and *analogy* are frequently used in descriptive language, as is the case with Leonardo's excerpt. We have often heard the computer compared to a human brain, or DNA described as 'a chain'. This is a communication technique that helps us to relate an unknown to something that we already know.

Instruction style

Many whole technical documents, user manuals or parts of reports are instructional. For example, a laboratory report carefully details how an experiment was conducted so that other researchers can replicate that experiment to see if they obtain similar results. Similarly, a maintenance manual sets out clear directives so that an operator can keep a machine in peak condition, the method section of a report gives instructions for repeating the study, and quality procedures indicate the processes required to complete tasks. In each case, the material needs to be presented in such a way that a user can complete a task accurately and safely. It is the writer's job to provide clear instructions to achieve this aim.

Some useful techniques for preparing instructional text have evolved. The first step is to use a heading that clearly and precisely indicates what task is to be accomplished. For example: *Programming your phone*.

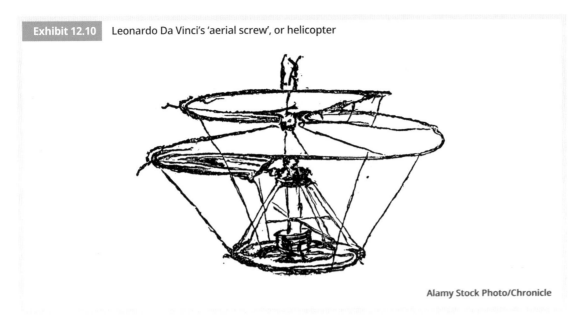

Exhibit 12.10 Leonardo Da Vinci's 'aerial screw', or helicopter

Alamy Stock Photo/Chronicle

Each block of instructions is prefaced with such a heading. The rule of thumb in instructional writing is to keep to seven (plus or minus two) steps within each chunk of text.

You will notice that the term **chunk** has been used instead of *paragraph*. In the jargon of technical writers, the term *chunk* is used to indicate a grouping of words (sometimes with accompanying graphics) that relate to the same topic or theme. Since the words may be presented as bulleted lists, numbered lists or annotated drawings, they do not resemble traditional text paragraphs and may not adhere to traditional punctuation rules.

Instructions tell users what to do, but sometimes a user benefits from knowing a bit about why they will be performing these tasks, and they may even want some background information or company policy as supporting information. This introductory material is usually placed at the beginning of the instructions and separated into a chunk by leaving white space around it or enclosing it in a box, to indicate its role. For example:

> Engine Overhaul (AEO 56) is a routine maintenance procedure.
> Only licensed aircraft maintenance engineers may perform this procedure.

You may also want to indicate the equipment the user will need to have available to perform the task. For example:

> To assemble this component, you will require a screwdriver, pliers and hammer.

Any necessary cautions and warnings certainly need to be clearly displayed at the outset of each chunk of instructions. Use graphic techniques to ensure that your users notice the warning, and skilful writing so that their full meaning is made clear. Compare the following two warning statements:

> 1 Warning. Do not connect red and green wires.
> 2 WARNING! Do not connect red and green wires – you may cause irreparable damage to your machine.

The instructions themselves need to be presented in a simple, precise and logical order. They are presented as clear, step-by-step directives, usually beginning with a command verb such as *turn*, *push*,

Chunk
A grouping of words (sometimes with accompanying graphics) that relate to the same topic or theme. Often presented as bulleted lists, numbered lists or annotated drawings, they do not resemble traditional text paragraphs and may not adhere to traditional punctuation rules.

press, *switch* or *place*. Avoid cluttering up instructions with excess words such as 'you should'; even courtesies such as 'please' can be assumed without the need to include them in writing. For example:

Cluttered: Next, you should press the start button.
Clear: (3) Press the START button.

In the clear example, the number '3' indicates that it is the next instruction following item 2. The words 'you should' in the cluttered example add no value to the statement and slow down the process while the user reads the additional words. Using full capitals highlights the object of the action: the START button. You could even represent the button graphically to reinforce the message.

Your choice of words must be precise and consistent. In the previous example, for instance, you would cause confusion if your instruction used the term START when the actual button on the machine carried the label ON. If you wanted to clarify such an instruction, you could use a qualified directive. For example:

Qualified: (3) To start the machine, press the ON button.

It is important to present your information in the same sequence in which it is going to be used. A user would want to know what they are doing *before* they did it, not after. Therefore, the example above is preferred to 'Press the ON button to start the machine', which would instruct operators to perform an action before they understood the consequences.

Instructions are usually listed with identifying numbers or bullet points. Like all lists, the items should be written in a similar style to achieve *parallel construction*. In the following, Example 1 and 2 are written in different styles:

Example 1: Inconsistent style: Specimen preparation
Remove the specimen from the culture.
You will need to mount it on a slide.
Next, it should be covered with another slide and placed in the microscope.

Example 2: Parallel construction: Preparing a specimen
1   Remove the specimen from the culture.
2   Mount it on a slide.
3   Cover the slide with a sterile slide.
4   Place the stack in the microscope.

When they are presented as a list, such as in Example 1, they appear haphazard and confusing. However, the list in Example 2 is written in a consistent, parallel construction style, and this approach is recommended for writing lists or any text that needs to show cohesion and unity.

All professional and technical writers agree that instructional text needs to be closely integrated with the graphics that support it. All terms should be consistent throughout the graphics and the text. The graphics should be adjacent to each instruction and should be simple and clear. Avoid using complex, multi-purpose graphics. It is far better to have a series of simple, easy-to-identify sketches than one elaborate, beautifully crafted drawing that is so complex that a user would not be able to identify the components.

In summary, instructions should be:

- simple, clear directives for action
- written in the **active voice**
- presented in parallel construction
- consistent in terminology
- clearly identified with an action-oriented heading
- prefaced with warnings, equipment needed and useful background
- integrated with supporting graphics, especially when discussing software.

Active voice
In writing, when the language used discusses a person or thing performing an action.

Standard formats

Reports and technical documents are usually presented in conventional formats because readers need to be able to quickly find the information they need. Each genre or type of document has its own conventions and format. Because the function determines the form in business and technical writing, the way that readers will use the document influences the way it is written and designed.

Organisations have found useful techniques for standardising documents. One popular approach, *information mapping*, was developed by Robert Horn in the 1960s and has influenced the design of corporate documents throughout the world (Horn et al., 1969). The information mapping process identifies different information types and then structures it according to its function. Compare, for example, the same information presented first as a prose paragraph in Example 1 and then in a structured style in Example 2 that incorporates some information mapping concepts. Which do you think is easier to read and comprehend?

Example 1: Volunteer centre – how to enrol a volunteer at the centre

We have volunteers with interests and skills, and we have organisations needing volunteers. Your job is to match them. As many prospective volunteers lack confidence, the interviewer should adopt a calm, friendly manner. You need to get the volunteer's personal details, then supply general information about volunteer organisations and jobs on our files. The volunteer then gives you their preferences so that you can put these into the computer with their personal details. Search in the computer for suitable jobs, then consult the volunteer about these details and get them to indicate their most preferred matches according to time and place. You then decide on three or more jobs you consider most suitable and describe these to the volunteer. You follow this up with some advice to the volunteer about their job interviews, as they will be having interviews with each organisation. You should reassure the volunteer about their suitability for these jobs. If they seem hesitant, suggest they give the matter further thought and contact us again if they need to.

Example 2: Volunteer centre – how to enrol a volunteer at the centre

Introduction	Our mission is to match volunteers who have interests and skills with organisations that need them
Interviewing volunteers	Many prospective volunteers lack confidence and are unfamiliar with interview procedure. Welcome them in a calm, friendly manner to put them at ease. Assure them of confidentiality and that they are under no obligation to accept any position. Briefly explain how we match volunteers and organisations through our computers.
Matching	Open a volunteer file. Complete the volunteer personal data requested. Identify the volunteer's preferred fields. Search the organisational database for three or four appropriate vacancies. Present the volunteer with the details of these vacancies.
Advice on placement	Give the volunteer some guidelines about what he or she can expect in each of these positions. They may also need to know how to approach organisations and how to prepare for interviews.
Caution	If the volunteer seems hesitant, reassure them and suggest that they give further thought to their plans and contact this centre when they are ready.

International perspective

One of the advantages of adopting a standard approach to your writing style is that it assists individuals and companies to communicate with colleagues, clients and customers throughout the world. All the suggestions provided are especially useful when your documents are to be translated into languages other than English. If you have kept your style simple and straightforward, used plain English, provided clear definitions of technical terms, integrated graphics and text in a systematic and consistent fashion, and adhered to commonly accepted formatting styles, your work will be understood around the world and translated quickly and accurately.

Using graphics and layout in professional documents

With the widespread use of word processing and desktop publishing software, writers today are expected to not only to write well, but also understand and use the basic principles of layout and graphics in professional documents. Even though programs such as Microsoft Word and Excel allow writers to produce professionally designed tables and graphics, it still remains important to understand the principles that allow graphics and the layouts you select to effectively communicate.

Graphic material is used to supplement, reinforce and sometimes replace words. Tables, diagrams, charts and photographs should be simple and not require more time and attention to comprehend than the equivalent number of words in a paragraph of text. They should not be used just for aesthetic appeal but should complement and work with the text to allow readers to understand figures, statistics, trend or a complex process more easily.

The following guidelines should help ensure that you effectively use graphic techniques to enhance your communication:

- Determine your objective for using a visual and the message you want to convey.
- Choose a graphic style that is appropriate for your goal.
- Consider your reader – are they familiar with this type of graphic? Will they know how to read it?
- Make sure that the visual message matches the verbal, written or mathematical message.
- Pay attention to detail. Carefully check all the details for accuracy.
- Keep your graphic as close as possible to the text it serves.
- Label each graphic as 'Exhibit', 'Table' or 'Figure' and include an appropriate title.
- Refer to each graphic in the body of the text, e.g., 'As Figure 1 illustrates ...'.
- Acknowledge the source of the graphic and ensure compliance with copyright restrictions.
- Place complex mathematical material, like large bodies of statistics, in the appendix of the report and present a simplified graph or table in the main text.
- Follow the KISS principle – keep it simple and streamlined. Avoid 'chart junk' or fancy effects such as 3D, as this may make the graphic harder to interpret or distract from its message.

Types of graphics and when to use them

Graphics such as tables, graphs, photographs and drawings attract the eye and stimulate the reader to explore new approaches to the subject, as well as the items listed in Exhibit 12.11.

Some professional reports necessitate illustrations, given the content of the report. A report on highly technical subject matter usually requires that content be visually depicted at least in part, so it can be understood by non-specialist readers (e.g., new technologies, industrial equipment or specialist tools). However, not all graphics perform the same function, and they should be chosen wisely to provide and enhance written communication appropriately. Consider Exhibit 12.12, which outlines the advantages and disadvantages of commonly used graphics.

Exhibit 12.11 Some of the benefits of using graphics

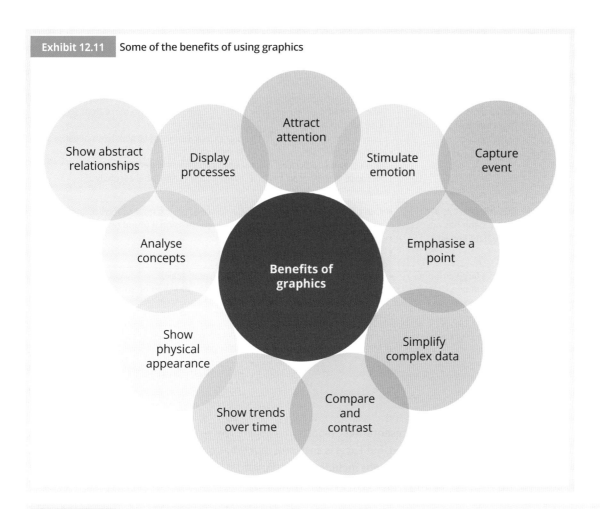

Exhibit 12.12 Uses of different types of graphics

Type	Advantages	Disadvantages	Some rules for use
Table	• Offers comprehensive detail • Allows for comparisons between large amounts of quantitative data	• Difficult to read quickly • Hard to recognise relationships • Sometimes too complex	• Use Word to create tables • Label table accordingly and discuss highlights in the text • Use white space for ease of reading • Be especially careful with financial data
Line graph	• Indicates movement and trends over time • Easy to see differences between variables	• Inappropriate labels and scales can make it hard to interpret information	• Use Excel to create line graphs • Avoid putting numbers on line graphs • Do not place too many lines on the chart • Label the axes clearly • Use colour to differentiate lines
Histogram or bar graph	• Offers clear comparisons between items from one period to the next • The most useful type of graph	• Difficult for the eye to interpret size and proportions	• Use Excel to create bar graphs • Limit the number of columns/bars • Be sure comparisons are clear • Adjust bar widths and space between them equally • Avoid 3D columns/bars • Include a legend

Exhibit 12.12 Uses of different types of graphics (*Continued*)

Type	Advantages	Disadvantages	Some rules for use
Pie chart	• Shows relative proportions and importance of each part to the whole	• Difficult to judge area and size differences • Use for representation only • Use only for non-professional audiences because they are too basic	• Use rarely • Limit the pie 'slices' to no more than six or seven parts • Work clockwise from largest to smallest 'slice' • Use for money and percentages • Keep it simple and label carefully
Photograph or illustration	• Shows subject as it appears and has an immediate impact	• Can be difficult to see the point due to detail • Can be manipulated • Does not show context	• Be aware of ethical implications of choice • Obtain permission if found online
Map	• Shows a large amount of detail in one representation	• Can be difficult to read unless scales, legends and labels are concise and easy to read	• Clearly label scales • Use colour and shading subtly to indicate differences
Technical drawings	• Can simplify a complex concept • Enables a reader to visualise sections unable to be seen	• Representational only • Must be labelled clearly	• Select the proper amount of detail • Label parts carefully • Select the best view or perspective • Use a legend when there are many parts

Most professional graphs for presentations, reports and papers are easily created using Microsoft Excel. Graphics software can be purchased, but Excel is so useful that it has become the de facto standard. Other programs that will produce useful graphs include Adobe Illustrator, Clickcharts (from nchsoftware.com), Microsoft PowerBI (for PCs only), and Visme (from visme.co).

The importance of layout and design

Unless a business document is to be printed for mass distribution, layout and design is generally the author's responsibility. Writers, therefore, need to understand some of the basic principles of graphic design and layout, which are equally applicable to online writing.

Layout is the non-verbal communication aspect of any piece of written communication. Readers use visual cues to navigate a document, so it is useful to think of reading a report or set of instructions like reading a map. That is, layout can be compared to having street signs, legends, icons and other visual signs to help a reader navigate the text. They help the reader find their way, see how the report is organised or argued, or find the parts they are looking for. Headings, subheadings, page numbers and section numbering systems all act as visual signposts for the reader.

Some of the basic layout 'rules' for a traditional document, such as a report or letter include:

• Body text should be between 10 and 12 point. Headings can be larger.

• Use the same typeface, type size and leading (line spacing) for all your body text. The usual rule is to use a serif font like Times for the body, and a sans serif font like Arial for the headings.

• Avoid fancy fonts for text. Choose a font which reflects the nature of the message, the organisation and the audience for whom the text is written.

• Use enough leading (line spacing) to make the text easy to read. Different fonts may require different leading. If using Word, 1.5 line spacing is useful.

• Make paragraph beginnings clear – a (blank) line space is preferable to indentation unless space is tight.

• Ragged right margins with left aligned text make your text more visually interesting and easier to read. Avoid justification of text as it can create uneven space between letters and words.

- Leave more space above headings and subheads than below them. Use subheads liberally to help readers find what they are looking for.
- Use a numbering system to help your reader see the relationships between the sections of your report and to locate sections more easily.
- White space used skilfully can be used to show readers where to start and where to stop reading. It can also isolate important messages.
- Leave only one space after a full stop, comma, question mark or exclamation mark.
- If you choose a design device, use it consistently throughout the document to establish a recognisable pattern. For example:
  - signals used (arrows or numbers)
  - words or terms used for captions
  - format of questions or headings
  - use of screened backgrounds
  - typeface and type size used for text, headings and captions.

These commonly accepted conventions are not the only acceptable approaches to writing. A useful reference is Robin Williams' (2014) *The Non-Designer's Design Book 4e*. There are also a number of useful websites on layout and design for the beginner. Additionally, explore the style conventions for your subject area. You can begin by reviewing the literature published in your field and observing the conventions they have adopted. Textbooks in your subject will signal the correct approach to take.

Summary

This chapter highlighted the range of different devices upon which workplace writing is read and created. This changes the nature of workplace genres of writing, such as emails, letter, reports and manuals. Emails have replaced letters in terms of the medium, but the essential conventions of letter-writing remain largely the same for emails. The same is true for reports, short reports, proposals and manuals, which have mostly all become electronic documents but retain their essential parts and structure from the paper-based era. The stylistic features of workplace writing should be chosen to suit the audience. Thus, writers should carefully select their choice of styles from narrative, argument, explanation, description and instructions. Accompanying graphics are often an overlooked aspect of reports and need to be appropriately selected, created and added to convey interest and clarification to all workplace reports.

STUDY TOOLS

DISCUSSION QUESTIONS AND GROUP ACTIVITIES

For discussion topics and activities in addition to those listed below, please refer to the case studies presented throughout this chapter.

1. Read the following statements. Discuss how a reader might react to their appearance in a professional email.
   a. We can't get onto the guy who sold you the camera.
   b. My secretary informed me that the mistake was definitely not hers.
   c. Payments must be made on time.
   d. You failed to supply the reference number and we can't fill the order until you provide the proper details.
   e. We're terribly sorry about the confused orders but these things do happen from time to time, as we all know, and are probably just meant to try us. We'll have better luck next time.
   f. It is obligatory that any discrepancies in the account be rectified so that the indebtedness will be cleared.
   g. Our interior-decorating service guarantees to give any drab and shabby looking office an appearance of success and prosperity.
   h. May I have an appointment for an interview? You may phone me during business hours between Monday and Friday.

2. Download a variety of employment advertisements from a major online job site. Discuss the different strategies you would use to apply for several different jobs. Choose one advertisement that requests a written application and, using your imagination, write:
   a. cover letter for the position
   b. detailed résumé. (Be sure to tailor the résumé to suit the demands of the position.)

3. Imagine that you work in the market-research department of a large chain supermarket. You have been requested to present a comparative report on the following consumer goods, usually purchased in supermarkets:
   - clothes washing detergent
   - toothpaste
   - margarine
   - bread.

   Your reader wants to know the different brands, types and prices of these goods in the various supermarkets. Present a set of notes explaining your approach to compiling this report.

4. Prepare a report on your suburb or locality outlining the amenities, features, accommodation, house prices, transport, schooling, availability of employment, community activities and any other data you consider to be relevant. (You may even check with local councils for further information.)

   Carefully formulate an objective for your report so that the information is clearly related to that objective. Perhaps the purpose of your report will be to describe a suburb as fully as possible, so that individuals and families may assess its appropriateness and attractiveness as a place in which to settle. Use this idea as a suggestion and modify it or replace it with any other that you feel is suitable.

5. Select a report you have already submitted for one of your subjects. In view of the recommendations offered in this chapter, review the assignment and rewrite it.

6. The manager of ABC Marketing, a small but dynamic organisation that specialises in marketing for technical firms, has requested that Brian, Lee and Ari, who have just joined the organisation as graduate interns,

investigate upgrading the firm's AV equipment and write a report with recommendations concerning the items that should be added to their inventory.

  a Discuss how the team should proceed with this assignment.

  b Compile a list of appropriate equipment for a firm such as this.

  c Compile a report that would be acceptable in this case.

7   Collect instruction manuals for various appliances, medical devices, software or other items. Many such manuals can be found online. Compare and discuss what is effective and what is confusing. Why is it confusing? How could it be improved?

8   Investigate the graphics capabilities of various software packages by visiting computer shops, obtaining brochures, or reading computer and office technology magazines. Discuss the impact that this technology is having on the writing process.

9   Find a PDF version of a report that uses graphics and text to explain a current news story. Write an evaluation of the article, discussing the effectiveness of:

  a the textual information presented

  b the graphic information presented.

10 Company annual reports contain a wide variety of graphic aids. Collect copies of annual reports and discuss the techniques used to supplement the written word.

11 Collect a variety of catalogues for consumer and industrial goods. Compare the graphic presentations. Discuss why there are differences in style.

12 Compare a few websites to decide what you consider to be effective use of visual information for online applications.

13 Write an article for a student magazine, online platform or academic blog on an aspect of your study. Submit it for review and publication.

14 Select a concept used in your field of study and develop an extended explanation of it using the techniques discussed in this chapter. You may include graphics.

WEBSITES

99 designs, Typography design 101: a guide to rules and terms: https://99designs.com/blog/tips/typography-design

Australian Bureau of Statistics: https://abs.gov.au

Society for Technical Communication resources: https://stc.org

Statistics Netherlands: https://www.cbs.nl/en-gb

REFERENCES

Ahlers, N. A., Campbell, B. M., Cantwell, R. J., Forward, M. R., & Spooner, T. H. (2005). Cost-benefit analysis of outfitting the windows of the Henry Hicks Arts and Administration building with more efficient models to improve Dalhousie University campus sustainability. Online document: https://dalspace.library.dal.ca/bitstream/handle/10222/77840/Double-glazed%20windows.pdf

Australian Associated Press. (2023, February 8). Australia Post warns about long-term viability, with letters revenue in 'unstoppable' decline, *The Guardian*. https://www.theguardian.com/business/2023/feb/08/australia-post-predicts-full-year-financial-loss-letters-revenue-decline

Horn, R. E., Nicol, E., Kleinman, J., & Grace, M. (1969). *Information mapping for learning and reference*. I.R.I. (A.F. Systems Command Report ESD-TR-69-296).

Oberlo. (2022). *Number of emails sent per day: 2022–2026*. https://www.oberlo.com/statistics/how-many-emails-are-sent-per-day

Williams. R. (2014). *The non-designer's design book (4 ed.).* Peachpit Press.

Workplace writing: research and reports

Learning objectives

After reading this chapter, you should be able to:

- define *research* and describe the three types of research used in the workplace
- outline the research process from ideas and research questions to the method selection
- understand how to locate information from key sources
- reiterate ethical responsibilities of workplace researchers
- show in detail what the structure of an empirical research report should look like.

Research and confirmation bias

Basic research is usually viewed as research performed to advance an organisation or profession. Such research focuses on research goals and questions that emerge from business requirements or societal needs. Use of formal, scientific and systematic procedures are often employed, but research is not always theory-based and may not utilise a representative or random sample in the case of surveys.

Researchers must be aware of the potential for confirmation bias, which is the tendency to interpret information in a way that confirms pre-existing beliefs or expectations.

Confirmation bias can manifest in several ways during the research process. For example, researchers may selectively choose evidence that supports their hypotheses while ignoring data that contradicts them. Researchers may also interpret ambiguous findings in a way that fits their preconceptions. In some cases, researchers may even unconsciously manipulate data or experiment conditions to produce the desired outcomes.

The formal basic research process often includes scholarship, which includes analysing existing literature, such as books, academic journal articles and conference papers. Scholarship also includes peer review, whereby whole research reports are distributed to experts for their evaluation and approval. Such tasks are not usually a feature of workplace reports or writing.

Introduction

Formal basic research is research that takes place in professional workplaces and results in substantive reports. Professional research spans multiple contexts – marketing, risk, brands, products, finance and settings – that demand different methods and skills of the researcher. There is no single formula to performing this research or writing up the eventual research report which can take weeks or months to conduct. This research is almost always conducted by experienced, senior managers or teams who have specialised skills in specific methods, or sometimes external consultants.

This chapter shows that formal basic research involves a definite process, one that needs to be followed in order to produce good results. After defining the meaning of the word research, a number of issues and contexts that can impact the process will be outlined. The use of the internet as the world's biggest library is considered together with suggestions for locating information. The importance of ethics is reiterated, as discussed in Chapter 7, especially what it means to be ethical in the real world and in the online world. Writing a formal 'scientific' research report is a valuable learning experience, but one that needs to be carefully modelled and explained. Thus, this chapter ends by giving a step-by-step description of this kind of research report and a series of detailed models on which students can base their own report writing. The 'scientific' format can also be used in writing a thesis or dissertation or academic research article.

What is research?

The question 'What is research?' is not easily answered because there are many research methods and many different contexts in which the word research is used. A general definition is:

> Research comprises all those processes by which original investigation is undertaken in order to gain new knowledge and understanding. It includes work of a scholarly nature, such as library research; work that has direct relevance to the needs of commerce and industry, and to the public and voluntary sectors; and the invention and generation of ideas, images, performances and artefacts.

Research refers to the creation of new knowledge and does not include the application of existing knowledge or the expertise to solve specific problems where nothing new is created.

A much longer and more detailed definition is provided by the Organisation for Economic Co-operation and Development (OECD, 2015, p. 44–45):

> Research and experimental development (R&D) comprise creative work undertaken on a systematic basis in order to increase the stock of knowledge, including knowledge of man, culture and society, and the use of this stock of knowledge to devise new applications of available knowledge …
>
> The term R&D covers three activities: basic research, applied research, and experimental development. *Basic research* is experimental or theoretical work undertaken primarily to acquire new knowledge of the underlying foundation of phenomena and observable facts, without any particular application or use in view. *Applied research* is original investigation undertaken in order to acquire new knowledge. It is, however, directed primarily towards a specific practical aim or objective. *Experimental development* is systematic work, drawing on existing knowledge gained from research and/or practical experience, and producing additional knowledge which is directed to producing new products or processes, or to improving existing products or processes.
>
> Source: *Frascati Manual 2015: Guidelines for collecting and reporting data on research and experimental development, the measurement of scientific, technological and innovation activities*. OECD Publishing. https://doi.org/10.1787/9789264239012-en. pp. 44–45.

Types of research

There are many different ways to categorise workplace research, but one of the most common is to differentiate between three types of primary **empirical** research: quantitative research, qualitative research and content methods.

Empirical
Concerned with, or verifiable by observation or experience rather than theory or pure logic.

Reflection question: Did you do any research at high school? Or did you simply use a lot of books and articles and quotes?

Quantitative research methods

Quantitative methods
Research methods that use numbers as a form of measurement.

Quantitative methods are research methods that use numbers as a form of measurement. These methods use systematic investigation with statistical, mathematical or computational techniques. Such methods begin with data collection and then move to statistical analysis using software. The following sections discuss the methods most used to carry out professional research: surveys, correlational research and experimental research.

Survey research

Survey research
Research that involves asking various kinds of questions to participants, and includes polls, questionnaires, interviews and focus groups.

Survey research is probably the most widely used method to collect data for a range of reasons. Surveys comprise asking various kinds of questions of selected participants, and include polls, questionnaires, interviews and focus groups. It also includes observation, usability research and document analysis. Cross-sectional surveys collect data from an audience at a given point of time while longitudinal surveys collect data from an audience over time in order understand behavioural change.

Most major corporations, government agencies and educational institutions employ surveys to gather data and use it to understand their clients and markets and to make appropriate decisions. Online surveys (see Exhibit 13.1), in particular, are commonplace, and can be sent via email or social media or placed on a website. For example, companies can survey people who visit their website with directed questions through an online survey to understand their opinions, gain feedback and hence make appropriate changes to the website to increase satisfaction levels.

Exhibit 13.1	Online surveys are commonly used to collect data

Shutterstock.com/Andrey_Popov

Correlational research

Correlational research
Research that is performed to understand the relationship between two variables.

Correlational research is performed to understand the relationship between two variables. Using statistical methods, researchers can calculate the strength of this relationship. Such research can help understand patterns, relationships, trends and linkages. Sometimes one variable can be controlled to produce a stronger correlation. A causal relationship cannot be concluded on the basis of correlational research.

A company might use a correlational study to understand the relationship between preferences for types of instructions on their packaging and the age of customers. Such results can enable the company to understand the usability of its products.

Experimental research

Experimental research
Research that aims to validate a theory and search for causal relationships.

Experimental research often aims to validate a theory and searches for causal relationships. Such studies can be beneficial for business research as they might reveal certain consumer characteristics that may increase sales. This approach involves running an experiment on volunteers to analyse how different experimental conditions affect their behaviour.

An example of where experimental research has been employed for business research is in the finding that loud music in entertainment venues usually causes people to consume alcohol at a faster rate (Guéguen et al., 2008). Based on this knowledge, owners of bars and pubs worldwide have adjusted the music in their venues and presumably reaped the rewards. The use of other kinds of music could cause advantageous other effects in workplaces, restaurants or shopping centres.

 CASE STUDY 13.1   Why did the political polls get it so wrong … again?

Voter surveys or polls are widely used and reported in elections. But recent examples would seem to cast doubt on their reliability. For example, in the US, the 2016 presidential election widely predicted that Hillary Clinton would beat her rival, Donald Trump. In the 2022 US mid-term elections, there was a predicted 'red wave' or significant victory for the Republican Party. Neither of these outcomes was proven to ultimately be correct.

In Australia, where voting is compulsory, polls tend to be more accurate in anticipating the final result. However, even here there is broad misunderstanding of both the impact of sampling methods as well as how to interpret the results. One example is a misunderstanding of what statisticians call the 'margin of error'.

What's wrong with the polls? The biggest issue appears to be more to do with the questions asked by the polls than anything else – as the old saying goes 'ask a stupid question and you will get a stupid answer'. Another issue is that of sampling: the bigger the sample, the more accurate the result, so smaller samples very well may give misleading results.

Sampling methods are also relevant to consider. Most political surveys, in particular, rely on phone polling, and so in general are impacted by those who are likely to have the time or inclination to respond to a phone call or text, most likely older or retired people as opposed to younger voters. Pollsters try to rectify this by 'weighting' responses

accordingly. Extrapolating from a small sub-sample does, in a sense, increase the margin of error, but that added inaccuracy doesn't, as a rule, get published. As such, the sample will be skewed and often people are unaware.

Source: Adapted from P. Brent (2016, April 8). We're drowning in opinion polls, so here's what to make of them. *The Drum*, ABC News.

Discussion

1   Why does the way a survey question is asked impact on the result?

2   Why is the nature of the survey sample an issue in the accuracy of polls?

3   Why is the survey sample size an important issue in the accuracy of the polls?

4   What do you understand by the term 'margin of error'?

5   Have you ever been polled for your voting intentions or even your purchasing or viewing intentions? If not, would you take the time to answer survey questions if asked?

6   Do you think that politicians and/or marketers place too much emphasis on polling?

After you have discussed this case study, refer to the 'Comments on case studies' section at the end of the text.

Qualitative research methods

In the professional sphere the use of **qualitative research** is also highly valued. Qualitative methods generate non-numerical data and are used to understand peoples' beliefs, experiences, attitudes behaviours and interactions. In qualitative data collection, open-ended conversational methods of communication are often used. This approach enables the researcher to identify the audience's thoughts as well as the reasons behind them. Rich and detailed information can be acquired from participants in this type of study. Qualitative research methods, include interviews, focus groups, ethnographic research and case studies.

Qualitative research
Generates non-numerical data and is used to understand peoples' beliefs, experiences, attitudes, behaviours and interactions.

Interviews

Interviews can occasionally employ similar questions to questionnaires (see **Exhibit 13.2**). The distinction is that the respondent is encouraged to provide a lengthy response to open-ended questions and, depending on their response, the interviewer may follow-up for more details. This is very different to selecting a number on a 7-point scale. Interviews typically provide the researcher with rich and personal knowledge of the respondent that was otherwise hidden from view. Additionally, interviewing subject-matter experts can provide significant information for some researchers.

Exhibit 13.2 — An interview is a common form of qualitative research method

iStock.com/AntonioGuillem

Focus groups

Focus group
A research method that brings together a small group of people to answer questions in a moderated setting. The group is chosen due to predefined demographic traits, and the questions are designed to shed light on a topic of interest.

Focus groups are a research method that brings together a small group of people to answer questions in a moderated setting. The group is chosen due to predefined demographic traits, and the questions are designed to shed light on a topic of interest. Typically, to discuss a certain product or service, a small group of people are asked a series of questions while keeping in mind the characteristics of their target market demographic. This approach allows for a larger sample size than an interview or case study while still utilising conversational communication. In many cases, a video recording allows later analysis of non-verbal behaviours of the group members.

An example of a focus group in action might be when carrying out research about a company's website designs for their current target market. The focus group could be given a range of website prototypes on paper and be asked to discuss the good and bad points of each design. By using this information, the company can make informed decisions about the look and feel of its website to ensure it is well-accepted.

Ethnographic research

Ethnographic research
A qualitative method of collecting data frequently used in the social and behavioural sciences. Data are collected through observations and interviews, which are then used to draw conclusions about how societies and individuals function.

Ethnographic research is one of the most challenging methods to use, but it can produce incredibly accurate results. In order to gather data, the researcher must become part of the target group, to become familiar with the context and surroundings and observe the intended audience. This approach is typically used to comprehend cultures, sub-cultures, or to understand issues or occurrences that might arise in a specific location at a specific point in time.

An early and influential example of ethnographic research involved a study in elderly care wards of hospitals, where nurses attended to those who were dying (Costello, 2001). The author used participant observation and semi-structured interviews to study 74 patients, 29 nurses and eight doctors. Findings showed that the care of patients was characterised by a lack of 'emotional engagement' with patients, and a widespread pattern of non-disclosure about death and dying. Nurses provided physical care for their patients, but emotional and spiritual care was lacking by many staff of the hospital. Such experiential research can be instrumental in institutional reform and can eventually change the entire healthcare system.

Content methods

Content analysis is a research tool used to determine the presence and frequency of certain words or concepts within texts or sets of texts. Texts can be defined broadly as books, chapters, essays, interviews, Twitter posts, newspaper headlines and articles, historical documents, speeches, conversations, advertising or any other form of communication.

Researchers quantify and analyse the presence, meanings and relationships of words and concepts, then make inferences about the text's messages, writer, audience and even the culture of which they are a part. To conduct a content analysis on any text, the text is broken down into manageable categories on a variety of levels – words, phrases, sentences or themes – and then occurrences are counted and relationships examined.

Software is usually used that allows vast numbers of words to be analysed. Programs such as Leximancer, Voyant-tools, and NVivo are used in higher education. Businesses have a range of other data mining software to choose from, including Chattermill, Relative Insight and Thematic.

Because it can be applied to examine any piece of writing or genre of communication, content analysis is currently used in many fields, including marketing, media studies, literature and rhetoric, ethnography and cultural studies, gender and age issues, sociology and political science, education, psychology, cognitive science, artificial intelligence and many other fields of inquiry.

Sentiment analysis

Sentiment analysis is a computational linguistics technique of comparing a sentence with a prepared dictionary of positive, negative or neutral words. A sentence, paragraph or whole passage can be analysed and given a score that indicates the author's sentiment within the unit of measurement. This allows for close interpretation of the emotionality of the text, sentence by sentence, over an entire passage or document. A good free sentiment analysis tool is VADER.

Secondary online research

Secondary online research is convenient, very cost-effective and can yield a wealth of data. When conducting online research, information is gathered from published works that are available in academic databases, Google Scholar, libraries, and other reports. To better understand their own profession or their clients, all kinds of professionals frequently employ this type of research. The only caveat here is that online researchers need to verify the sources of the journal articles they use. Not everything that is published is honest or rigorously created. The problems of confirmation bias, accuracy and pseudoscience need to be considered, and so professionals need to be objective about their searches.

The research process

The formal scholarly research process is a rigorous and highly structured series of events. Schematically, it can be broken up into an iterative set of overlapping parts and is shown in the following model (see **Exhibit 13.3**). The following sections will discuss some of these parts, and then later in the chapter a real research report will be dissected to explain the process in detail.

The following sub-sections will discuss just the beginning stages of a research project without the expectation that students will need to write a complete research report at this stage of their degree. Most undergraduate programs do not ask students to perform genuine research reports until their final years of study.

Ideas

All good research starts with a good idea. This idea may be totally original or, more commonly, may be based on a researcher's experience or the results of previous research or literature review. Good ideas tend to be simple, elegant and able to be investigated further. The next step is to see what other

---

Content analysis
A research tool used to determine the presence and frequency of certain words or concepts within texts or sets of texts.

Sentiment analysis
A computational linguistics technique of comparing a sentence with a prepared dictionary of positive, negative or neutral words. This allows for close interpretation of the emotionality of the text, sentence by sentence over an entire passage or document.

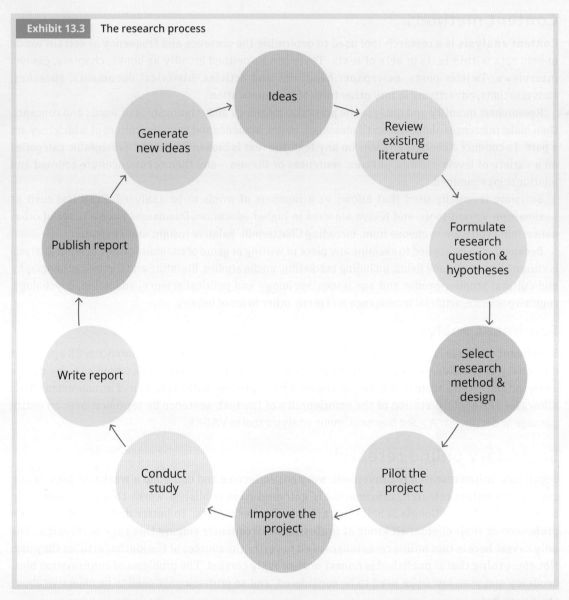

Exhibit 13.3   The research process

people have written about this idea. See 'Locating information' later in this chapter for a discussion on researching secondary sources.

Formulating the research question and hypotheses

The research question guides the researcher through the various stages of the research process. The question encapsulates the research problem and needs to be very clear in the researcher's mind. The research question is the basis on which the study is planned and carried out. It can also include some research objectives but no more than three or four. After researchers have focused on a specific topic of investigation, they formulate a question that addresses a specific aspect of the topic in which they are interested. For example, if a researcher is interested in studying the effect of email on productivity in a company, he or she might formulate a question like the following:

> **Research question 1:** What are the effects of introducing a social media presence on sales in Acme Pty Ltd?

If productivity is defined as higher product orders, the same topic could be addressed through a more focused question:

> **Research question 2:** Will a company social media presence lead to more product orders at Acme Pty Ltd?

In the physical sciences and many of the social sciences, formal research also requires the researcher to formulate a statement of expected results. This is called the **hypothesis**. The hypothesis is a possible response to the research question and is informed by the literature review. For example, two different hypotheses based on the research question in the previous section might look like this:

Hypothesis
A statement of expected results or possible response to a research question.

> **Hypothesis 1:** A company social media presence will lead to more product orders at Acme Pty Ltd.
> **Hypothesis 2:** A company social media presence will have no effect upon product orders at Acme Pty Ltd.

When the hypothesis is stated in a negative way (as in Hypothesis 2), it is called the null hypothesis and abbreviated to H_0.

The purpose of the study, then, is to determine whether the hypothesis can be confirmed or rejected. Most researchers will want to reject the null hypothesis. In this case they would want to measure product orders before and after the social media presence, do a statistical test to try to show a statistically significant difference between the two order rates, and then conclude whether the null hypothesis can be rejected – thus demonstrating that Hypothesis 1 is in fact accurate.

Using the survey method is not easy

The method by which the study is carried out is chosen by the researcher and should be appropriate to the needs of the project, not the needs of the researcher. Different topics and research questions will necessitate different methods of conducting research. However, most students and workplace employees will automatically think of using some form of survey, because survey research is so commonplace. Indeed, questionnaires are very cheap and efficient tools for conducting research and, along with needs analyses, are the best method for studying people's attitudes, opinions, ideas or perceptions about an issue. But, if you are wanting to look at factual material, or even people's behaviour, then a questionnaire may not be the best method of research.

Good survey research depends on three main factors: constructing valid and reliable questions, obtaining a representative sample of participants, and being able to analyse the results using a statistics program, or at least Excel. Questionnaires usually contain three types of questions: demographic, behavioural and attitudinal. Demographic questions ask about participants' age, gender, education and employment status, and normally appear at the beginning of a survey. Behavioural questions are items such as: 'How many times a week do you use email?' These rely on a participant's memory and knowledge. The attitudinal/opinion type questions are probably the trickiest ones to write and should be posed using a bipolar seven-point scale, as shown in **Exhibit 13.4**. Open-ended questions can appear at the end of the survey and are useful for those participants who write well. However, short yes/no questions are too simplistic, and multiple-choice questions (similar to multiple-choice tests) are simply a list of yes/no questions, so these should be used only for basic question to do with demographics.

The odd-numbered option scale allows a participant to enter the midpoint of the scale and thus indicate 'no effect'. Given that Australians (unlike Americans) are hesitant to enter either of the extreme ends of the scale, a five-point scale is, in practice, really only a three-point scale. Using a seven-point (or greater) scale with Australian participants may, therefore, be appropriate.

Exhibit 13.4   Examples (a) unipolar and (b) bipolar attitudinal/opinion Likert scales

(a)

	Strongly disagree	Disagree	Somewhat disagree	Unsure	Somewhat agree	Agree	Strongly agree
Email makes me less verbose in my communication	☐	☐	☐	☐	☐	☐	☐
Email makes me more formal in my communication	☐	☐	☐	☐	☐	☐	☐
I spend a great deal of time attending to daily emails	☐	☐	☐	☐	☐	☐	☐
I do not mind reading all of the emails I receive daily	☐	☐	☐	☐	☐	☐	☐

(b)

Email makes me less verbose in my communication.	1 2 3 4 5 6 7	Email makes me more verbose in my communication
Email makes me less formal in my communication.	1 2 3 4 5 6 7	Email makes me more formal in my communication
I do not spend a great deal of time attending to daily emails	1 2 3 4 5 6 7	I spend a great deal of time attending to daily emails
I do not enjoy having to read all the emails I receive each day	1 2 3 4 5 6 7	I enjoy having to read all the emails I receive each day

Bipolar questionnaire items are arguably the fairest way to ask questions. This is because providing only one (unipolar) statement to agree or disagree with, without presenting the opposite opinion, may bias the survey item. However, you need to be certain that the opposite ends of the bipolar scale really are opposite in terms of the variable you wish to measure.

It is also ideal to place the concept that denotes 'less of' on the left-hand side of the scale, and the concept that denotes 'more of' on the right-hand side of the scale. When dealing with multiple Likert scale items it makes more sense to use small numbers to indicate smaller quantities of concepts or attitudes.

Increasingly, researchers are resorting to online surveys to minimise costs and avoid data-input errors, particularly via websites like SurveyMonkey and others, which have simplified the whole process. Given the widespread availability of the internet in Western countries, using a web-based survey is a quick and seemingly efficient way to do research, but controlling access to a web survey is not always possible, and random sampling is simply impossible. We were taught for paper-based, or email-based surveys a return or response rate of 60 per cent was the rule of thumb for a reliable sample. This figure has dropped over the years to 50 per cent according to Customer Thermometer (2023). Importantly, an online survey does not have a sampling rate because we do not know how many people saw the survey but decided not to participate for various reasons. We believe that most online survey results are influenced by self-selection bias and should be regarded with some degree of caution. The only exceptions to this problem are those online surveys that are initiated by use of a known distribution contact list.

It should be noted that many free online survey websites yield very basic results that cannot be adequately analysed later on. So, depending on the depth of analysis and quality required, a better option might be a paid online platform, such as Qualtrics, which is fairly intuitive.

Reflection question: Have you ever seen a really bad survey? Why was it bad? If not do a Google search for 'bad survey questions' and make some notes.

CASE STUDY 13.2 The case study

This book has many 'case studies', but case studies were not originally a series of boxed scenarios and exercises. Case studies are a form of qualitative research that can be traced back to the French scholar Frederic Le Play in the early 1800s. In the US, from the early 1900s until 1935, the method was closely associated with the University of Chicago's Department of Sociology. Significant immigration to the US took place during this time and a variety of immigration issues concerning different national groups were studied and reported upon (Hamel et al., 1993). Poverty, unemployment, education and other problems were ideally suited to the case study method.

Case studies typically take a single example of a more general problem, such as a family, and then describe, explore, analyse and explain troubles and issues within that family. The case study's main advantage is the special attention to detail in observation, reconstruction and analysis of the subject of study. Case studies may also incorporate the perspectives of the real-life participants of the case under study.

The field of sociology is associated most strongly with the case study. During the decade leading up to 1935, several problems regarding the case study method were raised by researchers in other fields and by sociologists themselves, who wished to make their field more scientific, as quantitative measures were already being used by psychologists, management consultants and educational researchers. Subsequently, the Chicago School was criticised for its reliance on this controversial method. The net result was the denigration of the case study as a valid method of research. In 1935, there was a public debate between Columbia University academics, who championed the scientific method, and the Chicago School and its supporters. The outcome was a victory for Columbia University and the subsequent decline in the use of the case study as a valid research tool.

However, in the 1960s, past criticisms of the case study method were reassessed by researchers looking for more humanistic approaches to research, given certain limitations of quantitative research. There was a renewal of interest in the case study and new support in the guise of the 'grounded theory' of Glaser and Strauss (1967). Qualitative methods found new acceptance in terms of scholarly research, and the case study has since become one of the most useful ways of analysing social issues in textbooks, government publications and research articles.

Discussion

1 Lawyers, marketing consultants and teachers use case studies in very different ways. Use the internet to find some examples and explain their inherent differences.

2 What are the advantages and disadvantages of case studies compared to quantitative (statistical) studies?

3 In what way could you use the case study approach to research a question in your own chosen profession?

4 Have you found the case studies used in this textbook to be useful to your understanding?

After you have discussed this case study, refer to the 'Comments on case studies' section at the end of the text.

Locating information

In the past, locating research information would have involved a visit to your institutional library, or even local library, in order to locate information about your chosen research topic or idea. However, nowadays, not only can you access a raft of information via the internet, but you can also access library catalogues online. Books are the main resources to be found in libraries and can be excellent sources of information. However, peer reviewed material is preferred when researching for formal research, as shown in the hierarchy of research information in Exhibit 13.5.

Therefore, the easiest place to start your research journey is the internet, in particular Google Scholar (http://scholar.google.com). It is also possible to search the electronic journal and periodicals databases that can be found on university library computers, or, if you are registered, on your own computer at home. For communication professionals there are a handful of essential databases where you can locate information, including ABI/Inform Global, Expanded ASAP, PsycINFO, Business Source Premier, EBSCO Online and ERIC, among many others.

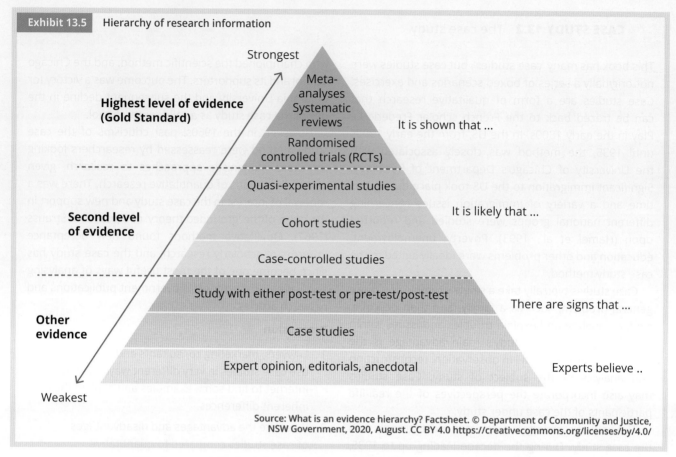

Exhibit 13.5 Hierarchy of research information

Strongest

Meta-analyses Systematic reviews

Highest level of evidence (Gold Standard)

Randomised controlled trials (RCTs)

It is shown that …

Quasi-experimental studies

Second level of evidence

Cohort studies

It is likely that …

Case-controlled studies

Study with either post-test or pre-test/post-test

Other evidence

Case studies

There are signs that …

Expert opinion, editorials, anecdotal

Experts believe ..

Weakest

Source: What is an evidence hierarchy? Factsheet. © Department of Community and Justice, NSW Government, 2020, August. CC BY 4.0 https://creativecommons.org/licenses/by/4.0/

Whether searching for information via database information, Google Scholar, or search engines, many of the same rules apply, which will be discussed in the following section.

At the time of writing, there were more than 25 billion web pages that were searchable on the web. An additional, undisclosed number of web pages also exist within organisational intranets. Search engines, of which there are many, are the best way to navigate the Web's vast resources.

The pre-eminent general search engine in the world today is Google, but there are also other browsers, such as Brave, Opera, Firefox, Safari and other specialist sites.

Tips for using search engines

Let us dispel the myth that finding information on the internet is a simple matter. The internet was never intended to be the world's largest depository of knowledge. Its inventor, Tim Berners-Lee, conceptualised it as a system of sharing information found at different geographical locations. The ease of creating and using the internet has resulted in a body of information that is now larger than the largest libraries. But this comes at a cost – there is no sure-fire, reliable way of retrieving information from the estimated two billion websites, except to use one of the currently available search engines. The following sections provide some tips for better web searching.

Be specific with your search terms

If broad searches, such as *vehicle classifieds*, generate too many results, try more specific words to find what you want: *used car classifieds*, *BMW classifieds*, *Brisbane used cars*, or *used cars classifieds Brisbane BMW*. Choosing your words carefully will narrow down your search and to save time and frustration, regardless of the search engine in front of you.

Use + and – to include or exempt words

Use a minus (–) sign to exclude words you don't want included in your search. For example, type *reports -annual* if you are looking to find examples of reports but not annual reports, or *best movies -comedy* to omit comedies from your search. Do not put a space between the minus sign and the word you want omitted.

You can also add a plus (+) sign to tell the search engine that specific words must be present in the search results and not to show you results that don't have it. For example, you can type *beanies +LED* if you want to see only beanies with a LED light on them.

Put key phrases in quotation marks

Put phrases inside quotation marks to exactly specify the search phrase. For example: use "*business report on hospital services*". If you want to search a certain sequence of words together, use quotation marks on the outside of the phrase or quote (short or long). This works with most search engines, including Google, Yahoo! and Bing.

Use tabs to specify exact content

Most of the popular search engines let you specify the kind of content being searched. After you do a web search for, say, *Federal election*, you can click tabs at the top of the screen marked for Websites, News, Images, Videos, Shopping, Maps and more. Google and some other search engines also have advanced photo search features.

Add medium or file type to search terms

You can add the file type to a search; for example, *PDF* will bring up PDF documents only, the standard file type for any report. This shortcut works for doc (Word), ppt (Powerpoint), xls (Excel) files. For example: *hospitality report Australia PDF* will search for occurrences of all those words that come in PDF format, *Morocco cactus image* will bring up images of Moroccan cacti.

Searching social media sites

If you wish for a person or a topic on sites such as Facebook, Twitter, Instagram or LinkedIn, many search engines can search these social media platforms if you specify the platform. The social media platforms also allow searches, but you need to login to the platform first. For all major search engines, type in the word or phrase and then add @ in front of the platform you'd like to search. For example: *politics @twitter* or *beach photography @instagram*. Or *Putin #ukrainewar* to search hashtags.

Add a website to the search

If you know the website that you need to search, then adding *site:sitename* will tell the browser to only search the site that you specify. If that site is a .com site, you do not need the .com. For example: *refugees site:abs.gov.au* will search the Australian Bureau of Statistics website for the word refugees. A full list of Google's shortcuts and tips can be located at https://www.googleguide.com/tag/special_characters.

CASE STUDY 13.3 Evaluating Google Scholar

Although Google is popular for searching the Web, it should be noted that Google only indexes about half of the available web pages; with the other half indexed by all the other search engines put together. The one exception is Google Scholar, which mainly includes peer reviewed academic papers, such as 'journal and conference papers, theses and dissertations, academic books, pre-prints, abstracts, technical reports and other scholarly literature from all broad areas of research … and index research articles and abstracts from most major academic publishers and repositories worldwide, including both free and subscription sources' (Google, n.d.). Many university libraries permit cross-linking with Google Scholar so that you can click through to access and pay-for-view major academic database articles that come up in your Google Scholar search.

Although Scholar supposedly indexes almost all available scholarly publications in English, users need to be aware that this may also include predatory journals of dubious quality that are not peer reviewed.

Ultimately, Scholar uses Google's algorithms with most popular (not best quality) appearing at the top of the hit list of papers. Make sure to be very careful with your search terms and use the tips discussed in this chapter. Google Scholar can be used in conjunction with Google itself because newspapers, professional research, magazines and other non-academic research are not indexed by Scholar.

Discussion

1   Pretend that you need to find reports that evaluate websites. Use Scholar to search for published reports in the field to see what is available.

2   Use the search terms *website audit* and *website evaluation*. Which phrase yields more useful results?

3   To try to cut down the number of hits that come up when you search, try adding *PDF* to your term. Does this improve your results? Do the same search on Google.

4   Not all of the Scholar results will be suitable – how many appropriate hits are you finding on the first few pages?

5   What are your criteria for suitability? If you can understand what a good-quality report looks like then you can be selective about the hits you should be scanning and perhaps saving.

After you have discussed this case study, refer to the 'Comments on case studies' section at the end of the text.

Other internet sources of information

There are quite a few other sources of information on the internet, including websites, forums such as Quora, the Usenet (or Google Groups) and blogs. Chapter 5 provides a detailed analysis of many of these internet sources of information.

An older, slightly arcane source is the email listserv. Listservs are email distribution lists of people with a common interest. They function to support the information needs of special-interest groups. There are many thousands of these lists, to which users subscribe manually via a simple email message and consequently receive information that others in their group would like to share. Almost every possible professional area of interest is catered for on a listserv. If a particular interest is not available, then it is not too difficult to start your own interest group. Have a look at LSoft's 58 000 email lists (https://www.lsoft.com/catalist.html) or peruse Yahoo!'s extensive range of email and forum lists.

Reflection question: When conducting secondary research, do you always just 'Google' it? What are some of the problems of relying on a general source of information?

Ethical responsibilities in conducting research

Research ethics has become an important topic in itself in recent times (as discussed in Chapter 7), with all higher education research involving human beings subject to national guidelines of ethical conduct. In the past, it was mainly university staff and postgraduate students who submitted ethics-approval requests to ethics committees. Nowadays, all students, even first-year undergraduates, need to carefully consider the possibilities for injury and harm to the participants or the researcher that might occur in conducting any form of research involving human beings. However, the private sector, and some government departments are not subject to ethical oversight apart from professional association policies, which can provide guidelines, but seldom legal sanctions.

The National Health and Medical Research Council has stringent guidelines that must be followed to protect the welfare and rights of participants in research (see also the **National Statement on Ethical Conduct in Research involving Humans**, published by the Commonwealth of Australia, 2007). It is worth repeating the following four criteria of good research ethics:

1   Integrity, respect for persons, beneficence and justice: researchers must conduct themselves in a professional manner at all times, and are expected to be honest and respectful of participants' rights, privacy, beliefs and culture. The rights of the participant are more important than any expected benefits to knowledge.

2 Informed consent: the researcher must provide participants with information at the appropriate level of understanding about the research. They then must obtain participants' voluntary consent.

3 Research merit and safety: the researcher needs to justify that the proposed study has merit in terms of benefiting society and contributing to knowledge. Every possible precaution should be taken to ensure that any risk of harm or discomfort is balanced by the potential benefits of the study.

4 Ethical review and conduct of research: research projects must be reviewed by a Human Research Ethics Committee and not undertaken unless approval is given. The participants' privacy needs to be ensured, and confidentiality and cultural sensitivity exercised.

Ethics is one of those concepts to which many professionals give lip-service but hardly spare a thought for in their day-to-day lives. Neither belonging to the legal profession, taking the Hippocratic oath, nor being able to recite verbatim your company's policy on hiring diverse minorities and the disabled makes you automatically ethical. Only by knowing what is ethically right and acting accordingly can you call yourself an ethical person.

Writing the research report

A research report may take any one of a number of formats depending on the precise field of research and the proposed audience. Organisations will have their own templates for writing a long research report, but all such templates will most probably be based on tried and true report formats from science. We recommend using what has loosely become known as the scientific report format, which is found in academic journals in the physical and social sciences and is widely imitated by government and private business report writers. It usually reports on the investigation of a researcher who uses empirical methods of research (i.e., interviews, experiments, surveys, observation or content analysis). The research report usually reports on primary or basic research, not the results of other researchers whose material is found in library databases. It has a logical structure that is widely practised and recognised. Once you start using the scientific report format you need to follow the style exactly, because departures will be seen as unprofessional mistakes. The scientific report format consists of the sections show in Exhibit 13.6.

Exhibit 13.6 Sections of a scientific report

1 Abstract (or summary)

2 Introduction (sometimes including a literature review)

3 Method (including samples, variables, materials, etc.)

4 Results (including tables and graphs)

5 Discussion, conclusions or recommendations

6 References

7 Appendices

In most cases you will use either a discussion or a conclusion section; however, depending on the discipline or journal, you may be required to use both sections. Appendices are optional and are not included in most academic journal articles. Sometimes sections are combined together, such as 'Results and Discussion'. However, each of the different sections has a separate and distinct purpose and requires careful attention to detail.

Abstract

The abstract (usually written last even though it appears first) is a summary of the research, that can include the research question, hypothesis, and a brief outline of the study, results and conclusions. Typically, the abstract consists of a few sentences that summarise various sections of the report. In practice, many abstracts do not subscribe to summarising every section. This is not a hard and fast rule. Abstracts should be written in such a way that they can be used in a database with searchable keywords, without the rest of the report.

Exhibit 13.7 provides an example of an abstract from a published research report. Note the overview of the topic presented in the first three sentences: the description of the study and the instrument that was used, but missing the results and the conclusion. A reader should be able to understand the main thrust of an article solely by reading the abstract. Once a reader scans the abstract then they will know if they should download the whole report, or not.

Exhibit 13.7	Example abstract

Abstract

For most of 2020 the entire world was subjected to daily breaking news, television forums, health announcements and references to risk about the coronavirus. Australians have been varyingly warned, given instructions, locked down, and unlocked down. Rates of infection, death tolls, social restrictions and vaccines were major topics of conversation with people from all walks of life. The aim of this paper was to identify and explain the main concepts on Twitter surrounding the pandemic during its peak in Australia. Using English language 103 000 tweets surrounding the coronavirus were collected from the Twitter platform, and the most popular themes were identified from Apr to Sept, 2020. Summative content analysis of the data was accomplished using Voyant-Tools software for each month. The main conceptual contexts were then discussed and interpreted in terms of the corpus, mainstream news media analysis and relevant scholarly research findings.

Source: R. Archee (2022). Communication, mainstream media, and Twitter: A summative content analysis of the concepts surrounding the COVID-19 pandemic during 2020. *Global Media Journal Australian Edition, 16*(1).

Introduction

The introduction is challenging for most students and consists of a number of stages. These stages are background, literature review, need for investigation, purpose of the study and the optional justification. **Exhibit 13.8** provides an example of an introduction. In order to better understand the distinct functions within an introduction, the example introduction has been broken into five stages (labelled within the exhibit).

Stage I (background) consists of general statement(s) about the field of research, providing the reader with a context for the problem to be reported. In Stage II (literature review), the writer offers more-specific statements about the aspects of the problem already studied by other researchers. In some reports the literature review is irrelevant and omitted because the research is so specific to the organisation. Try not to use the direct attribution style, such as 'Smith (2001) found …', 'Jones (1999) found …'; you want your own voice to be prominent in the review. Add all references as citations in brackets, usually at the end of sentences, and try not to use quotes. In Stage III, you will include statements that indicate the need for some more investigation of the topic area. This leads into Stage IV, in which you give the purpose and objectives of your study. Hypotheses may also be given at this particular stage. Stage V (justification) is an optional stage; here, statements may be made that explain the value of the study.

Exhibit 13.8 **Example introduction with stages**

Introduction

There is a substantial similarity between the current COVID-19 pandemic and the Spanish flu pandemic of 1918, when 500 million people were infected – representing one third of the world's population – and is estimated to have taken 50+ million lives. In 1918 and most of 2020, there were no effective drugs or treatments. In 1918 citizens were ordered to wear masks, and schools and businesses closed down, anticipating similar policies in today's lockdowns. Most people today have been affected by the influenza virus, but do not die because of effective antibiotics to treat secondary infections, and inherited immunity (Yu, X. et al., 2008).

Stage I: Background – general statements about the field of research

There are several categories of research article surrounding social media data analysis of the coronavirus. Social media search indexes (e.g. the Chinese search engine, Baidu, and the messaging app, WeChat) were supposedly found to be accurate predictors of new cases of coronavirus for 2019 (Qin et al., 2020) and 2020 (Wang et al., 2020). The use of these social media platforms gave health authorities a two-week head start over traditional methods of disease detection.

Stage II: Literature review – specific findings about aspects of the problem already published by other researchers

Warnings about the spread of misinformation and distortion of facts, in other words 'fake news', led the World Health Organization to also declare the disease an 'infodemic' as much as a pandemic (WHO, 2020a; The Lancet, 2020). Kouzy et al. (2020) sampled Twitter tweets on February 27, 2020 from 11 popular hashtags and categorised tweets according to content and tone. Sixty-six per cent of 673 tweets originated from individual or group accounts, followed by journalists (16.5%). Serious tweets (91.2%) were by far the largest genre, followed by informational tweets (81.4%) and humorous tweets (6.1%). The most worrying statistics were that 24.8 per cent of all the sampled tweets contained misinformation and 8.6 per cent contained unverifiable information, or speculation. Misinformation or fake news is reiterated by several other researchers who inspected samples of social media text and photographs (O'Connor & Murphy, 2020; Pulido et al., 2020).

Mental health problems have been found to have increased markedly due to people's association with social media during the period of the pandemic (Gao et al., 2020). Social media are indicted as sources of mental distress, including fear and anxiety, snake-oil treatments, conspiracy theories (Khan et al., 2020), xenophobia and racism against people of Asian descent, and fake news (Ho, Chee & Ho, 2020). Medical advice to combat infection such as physical distancing, self-isolation, quarantine, and social and economic troubles, and misinformation (especially on social media) has been found to be major causative factors of abnormal sadness, fear, frustration, feelings of helplessness, loneliness, and nervousness (Ahorsu et al., 2020). In extreme cases, these factors may trigger suicidal thoughts, attempts and, in some cases, tragic suicide (Mamun & Ullah, 2020).

Paradoxically, such mental health problems might prove to be assuaged by social media because social media messages have been evaluated as an overall positive communication medium and recommended over media such as email as being a faster way of disseminating information from medical authorities and to physicians (Eghtesadi & Florea, 2020; Castadi et al., 2020). Early sentiment analysis of two major hashtags on Twitter – #coronavirus and #COVID-19 - has found that positive tweets (51%) outweighed neutral (34%) and negative tweets (14%) showing the value of Twitter to spread good news (Bhat et al., 2020). By contrast, a more recent study of Indonesian Twitter sentiment found that neutral tweets (93%) far outweighed positive (6%) and negative (0.7%) tweets (Fahmi & Ramadhan, 2020). Kaur & Ranjan (2020) took a different approach and plotted sentiment over 21 days in India, finding that overall negative tweets occurred on only three of the total days sampled. National findings can be seen to be highly diverse and specific from country to country, but few studies have focused on global social media responses as a whole.

Stage III: statements that indicate the need for investigation

There is a definite need for ongoing communication research before, during and after a pandemic in order to understand global impacts including loss of life, impacts on the health system, economic shutdown and anxiety induced by inadequate health information (Lurie et al., 2013).

The primary aim of this paper is to ascertain and explain the main concepts on Twitter from April to Sept, 2020 found in the 103 000 collected tweets that formed a corpus of messages. A secondary objective is to compare the month by month popular concepts to see if these appreciably changed as knowledge of the disease evolved.

Stage IV: Aims and objectives

This study fulfils the need for ongoing communication research before, during and after a pandemic in order to understand global impacts including loss of life, impacts on the health system, economic shutdown and anxiety induced by inadequate health information (Lurie, Manolio, Patterson, Collins, & Frieden, 2013). Research is required to counter biased media responses to emerging infectious diseases both in Australia and overseas that over-emphasise risk, and project worst case scenarios (Holland & Blood, 2013).

Stage V: Justification

Source: R. Archee (2022). Communication, mainstream media, and Twitter: A summative content analysis of the concepts surrounding the COVID-19 pandemic during 2020. *Global Media Journal Australian Edition, 16*(1).

Method

The method section is where you tell the reader what was done, with whom and how data was obtained. Anyone reading this section should be able to replicate a particular piece of research from the information contained in this section. Sub-headings are useful here and could include overview, sample, sampling, instrument(s) and procedures. An example is provided in **Exhibit 13.9**.

Results

The results are the findings, which need to be summarised in tables and/or graphs and can include statistical tests and explanations depending upon the researcher's skills and audience's expectations. The most important findings are usually placed first, followed by less significant findings. Tables, graphs, charts and exhibits present the full findings, while the body text states the most important aspects of the results. In the social sciences, including the Communication field the author/s interprets and explains the results in relation to other research findings. Explanations can include citations to other research in the form of a bracketed author/s and years, such as (Williams & Rice, 2021).

In order to produce tables, an ordinary word-processing program is best for the job. For graphs, probably the easiest program to use is Microsoft Excel, which has quite extensive options in chart depiction. (For more information see Chapter 12.)

Explanation of specific results should occur after every table or graph is depicted in the text of the report. The reader should not have to search for explanations of these charts, nor should the reader be expected to accept results that are not shown in chart format. The following steps will ensure your results are acceptable to the most demanding readers:

1 Insert the particular table or graph and label it clearly.

2 State the most important findings about the chart.

3 Comment on the findings by attempting to explain them, generalising or referring to previous research.

Exhibit 13.9 Example method section (abridged)

Method

Definition

Content analysis is a research method that has found wide usage in health studies and education from the latter part of the 20th century. Early justifications of content analysis often focused on it qualitative vs quantitative benefits. However, rather being seen as a single research method, content analysis can be grouped into three distinct approaches: conventional, directed or summative.

The paper uses the summative approach to understand the main concepts and themes found in Twitter messages. The first stage was data collection of 6 months' worth of tweets that related to the search terms, 'coronavirus' and 'COVID-19'. Using the Voyant-tools text-analysis website, a summative content analysis was performed on the corpus of tweets yielding tables of concepts ranked ordered by popularity for each month and the ability to easily locate such concepts within their month-based sentence contexts.

The method then attempts to elaborate upon, explain, interpret and make sense of the discovered concepts and themes by examining their contiguous contexts. Thus, each of the concepts is not only exemplified by Twitter samples, but also explained in terms of the concurrent risk communication, and health announcements supplied by Twitter news coverage and mainstream media, supported by academic/professional findings during 2020.

Procedure and data collection

The author employed a piece of custom software written by a colleague that exploited the Twitter API, allowing custom searches to be performed. Entitled TwitterSearch, the software was located on a NeCTaR cloud server and was accessed via a website interface. Tweets could be collected using keywords, authors, or hashtags and could be searched at any time of day. Advanced retrospective keyword searches from the Twitter interface were also executed in the early months of the pandemic.

▶ **Exhibit 13.9** Example method section (abridged) (*Continued*)

The two search terms, 'coronavirus' and 'COVID-19' were employed to search Twitter. Other language translations of the virus were not searched, because the returned tweets would be written in languages other than English and beyond the scope of this article.

Each monthly file was uploaded to Voyant-tools.org website, six separate times representing each month and yielding a corpus from April through to September, 2020 in six separate webpages that could be compared and contrasted. The entire corpus of 6 months was also uploaded as a single file.

Analysis

The output of the entire Twitter corpus is shown in five default panels on the Voyant-tools website. Each panel can be exchanged for different tools, or enlarged in its own window for more extensive analysis (see Fig. 1). The URLs for each window are permanent ones and can be bookmarked for future research.

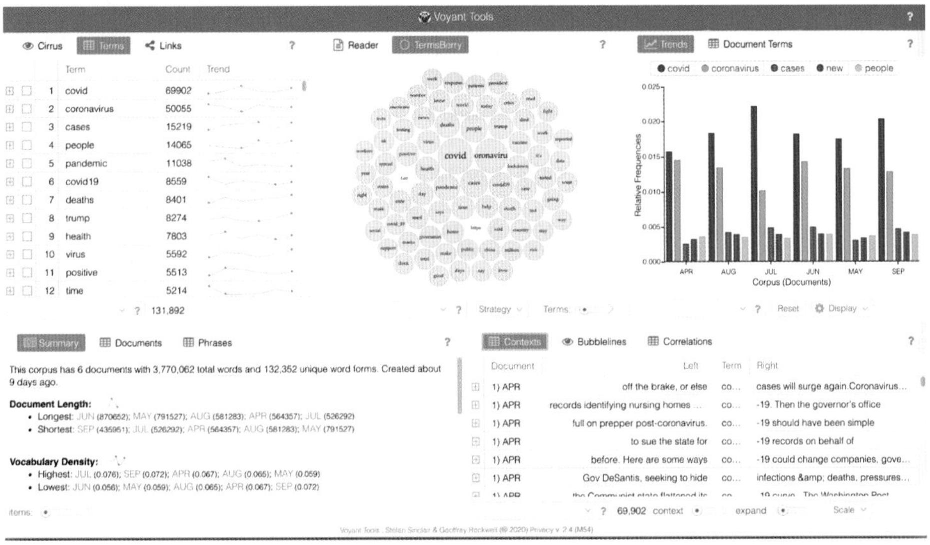

Fig. 1 *Screenshot of the entire Twitter corpus submitted to Voyant-tools.org*

Source: R. Archee (2022). Communication, mainstream media, and Twitter: A summative content analysis of the concepts surrounding the COVID-19 pandemic during 2020. *Global Media Journal Australian Edition, 16*(1).

Exhibit 13.10 is an example of a results section that includes a table, some quotes and two concept maps.

Discussion or conclusions

The discussion or conclusions section (sometimes combined as 'Discussion/Conclusions') is where the reader is told how useful the research has been. If you have very significant and conclusive findings, then then possibly the title 'Conclusions' would be more appropriate; conversely, if you have somewhat controversial findings that require explanation and argument, a 'Discussion' section might be more fitting. We believe that having both a discussion and a conclusions section can sometimes be redundant depending on the protocols of the discipline and the publication.

In the discussion or conclusions section, there are several optional stages:

1 The purpose of the study and any original hypotheses are restated.

2 The most significant findings are reviewed against the original hypotheses, theory and other researchers' findings from the literature review.

3 Speculation occurs as to why the results were found.

Exhibit 13.10 Example results section (abridged)

Results

There were 3 770 062 words in the six-month corpus and 103 566 tweets according to Voyant-tools summary. Table 1 [missing here] depicts the most popular ten concepts, excluding the search terms, that users used in the six month period. The five concepts, cases, people, pandemic, deaths and Trump were the overall most commonly used concepts for the 6 months and were discussed in 50 per cent of the entire corpus of tweets for this period.

The monthly summary of the six-month Twitter corpus can be viewed in Table 2 that shows how the most popular five concepts, excluding 'coronavirus' and 'COVID-19' are remarkably consistent over this time period. The table reveals the ranking and the actual number of instances that the concept was used for each month. It is remarkable that the most popular concepts did not appreciably change from month to month, especially for the concepts in bold type – cases, people, pandemic, deaths and Trump.

Rank	Apr	May	Jun	Jul	Aug	Sep
1	Corona/Covid, 18 516	Corona/Covid, 26 099	Corona/Covid, 30 359	Corona/Covid 19 111	Corona/Covid 20 644	Corona/Covid, 15 486
2	**people, 2 062**	**people, 2 970**	**cases, 4 324**	**cases, 2 549**	**cases, 2 429**	**cases, 2 055**
3	**pandemic, 1 685**	**cases, 2 488**	**people, 3 456**	**people, 1 812**	**people, 2 061**	**people, 1 704**
4	**cases, 1 444**	**pandemic, 2 285**	**pandemic, 2 543**	**pandemic, 1 522**	**pandemic, 1 748**	**pandemic, 1 255**
5	**Trump, 1 215**	**deaths, 1 883**	**deaths, 1 897**	**deaths, 1 063**	**deaths, 1 417**	**deaths, 1 138**
6	health, 1 196	**Trump, 1 809**	health, 1 889	**Trump, 1 058**	**Trump, 1 361**	**Trump, 1 120**
7	**deaths, 1 003**	health, 1 448	**Trump, 1 711**	health, 1 008	health, 1 358	health, 904
8	help, 896	lockdown, 1 266	day, 1 268	positive, 989	positive, 1 141	vaccine, 683
9	time, 867	virus, 1 194	positive, 1 256	day, 792	vaccine, 941	positive, 648
10	home, 847	time, 1 143	time, 1 164	vaccine, 724	day, 798	test, 626
11	world, 776	world, 187	world, 1 162	mask, 691	time, 758	day, 609

Summary evidence is shown

Note: Yellow-highlighted concepts of the 'mask' and 'vaccines' became more prominent at the end of the period.

Table 2: *Most popular concepts and frequencies related to COVID-19 and coronavirus for Apr-Sep, 2020 on Twitter, by month*

The concept of positive 'cases' affecting 'people' was the barometer of the health problem that confronted us all according to the media, government and health announcements, and have become a regular concern for all citizens across the world. Coronavirus cases became the *bete noir* of the news and Twitter reporting in the early months of the pandemic. The concept of 'deaths' was a function of the number of cases since the more cases that a society had, then obviously the more deaths that occurred. Here are some examples of how the concepts appear in context:

Evidence is explained

- The number of new cases per day in the US appears to be peaking (Apr, 2020)
- If people are not serious about COVID-19, what can be done? (May, 2020)
- Really recent information can be really helpful during this pandemic (Jul, 2020)
- The USA has less than 5% of the world's population but over 22% of the deaths from coronavirus (Sep, 2020)

> **Exhibit 13.10** Example results section (abridged) (*Continued*)

In Table 1, it is not immediately clear why these significant preoccupations do not appreciably change. A possible explanation of this finding comes from propaganda research. Rebello et al. (2020) found predictable social media effects with Chinese, Iranian, Russian and Turkish state-controlled news outlets that targeted French, Spanish and German Twitter and Facebook users. The state-backed media outlets spread misinformation and propaganda, reaching tens of millions of users and could be detected in subsequent social media posts as creating chaos, but also endowing the governments of origin as victorious managers of the disease. Such propaganda seems to have been very successful for these nefarious news outlets.

In a similar fashion, risk communication from reliable health agencies and mainstream media could have beneficently persuaded citizen audiences to tweet the same preoccupations over the six-month period. Additionally, the Twitter corpus contains the regular tweets of working journalists, news organisations, health agencies, and other media stakeholders (Moon & Hadley, 2014), all of whom may have submitted the same set of concepts surrounding the pandemic for six months.

Summary evidence is shown

reported • number • **cases** • cure • total • fauci • deaths • died • die • dying • **trump** • **people** • news • calls • like • administration

March, 2020 links

deaths • **new** • reports • positive • reported • **cases** • **people** • died • confirmed • tested • die

August, 2020 links

Exhibit 1. *Voyant-tools link maps for top 3 Twitter concepts (Mar & Aug 2020) re coronavirus tweets*

Evidence is explained

Exhibit 1 shows two relationship maps from March 2020 and August 2020. Twitter's top three concepts surrounding COVID-19 seem to change over time from 'people', 'cases', and 'Trump' to 'people', 'cases', and 'new'. Reading the map shows the concept of cases was linked to the number, deaths and reported cases. It was worth noting that the Twitter corpus was well aware of the difference between reported cases and unreported cases in the early days of the pandemic. Obviously, deaths could only be counted in terms of official reported cases, but unreported cases could easily have occurred creating inaccurate statistics being announced. Six months later, cases of COVID-19 are still high on the Twitter agenda, with new cases, and new reports becoming the overarching concern for Twitter users, who are overwhelmingly American citizens and media outlets. Trump's influence in the pandemic appears to have subsided from March to August, 2020.

Source: R. Archee (2022). Communication, mainstream media, and Twitter: A summative content analysis of the concepts surrounding the COVID-19 pandemic during 2020. *Global Media Journal Australian Edition, 16*(1).

4 Limitations to the current study are given.

5 Implications from the current research are stated and their contribution to the research field explained.

6 Recommendations for further research are indicated at the end.

Exhibit 13.11 is an example of a 'Discussion' section.

References

The references section is essential. Standard referencing procedures should be followed. Reference systems vary from journal to journal and industry to industry, but as a rule the American Psychological Association's (APA) referencing style, in particular the seventh edition (APA7) is commonly accepted

Exhibit 13.11   Example discussion or conclusions section (abridged)

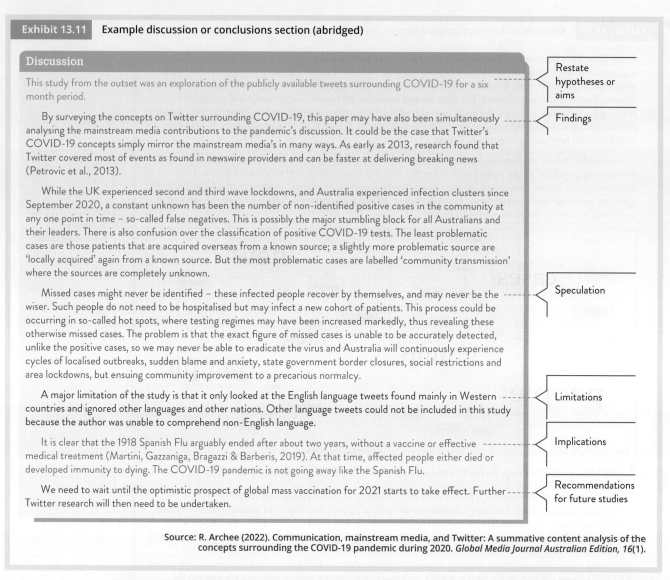

Discussion

This study from the outset was an exploration of the publicly available tweets surrounding COVID-19 for a six month period.
> Restate hypotheses or aims

By surveying the concepts on Twitter surrounding COVID-19, this paper may have also been simultaneously analysing the mainstream media contributions to the pandemic's discussion. It could be the case that Twitter's COVID-19 concepts simply mirror the mainstream media's in many ways. As early as 2013, research found that Twitter covered most of events as found in newswire providers and can be faster at delivering breaking news (Petrovic et al., 2013).
> Findings

While the UK experienced second and third wave lockdowns, and Australia experienced infection clusters since September 2020, a constant unknown has been the number of non-identified positive cases in the community at any one point in time – so-called false negatives. This is possibly the major stumbling block for all Australians and their leaders. There is also confusion over the classification of positive COVID-19 tests. The least problematic cases are those patients that are acquired overseas from a known source; a slightly more problematic source are 'locally acquired' again from a known source. But the most problematic cases are labelled 'community transmission' where the sources are completely unknown.

Missed cases might never be identified – these infected people recover by themselves, and may never be the wiser. Such people do not need to be hospitalised but may infect a new cohort of patients. This process could be occurring in so-called hot spots, where testing regimes may have been increased markedly, thus revealing these otherwise missed cases. The problem is that the exact figure of missed cases is unable to be accurately detected, unlike the positive cases, so we may never be able to eradicate the virus and Australia will continuously experience cycles of localised outbreaks, sudden blame and anxiety, state government border closures, social restrictions and area lockdowns, but ensuing community improvement to a precarious normalcy.
> Speculation

A major limitation of the study is that it only looked at the English language tweets found mainly in Western countries and ignored other languages and other nations. Other language tweets could not be included in this study because the author was unable to comprehend non-English language.
> Limitations

It is clear that the 1918 Spanish Flu arguably ended after about two years, without a vaccine or effective medical treatment (Martini, Gazzaniga, Bragazzi & Barberis, 2019). At that time, affected people either died or developed immunity to dying. The COVID-19 pandemic is not going away like the Spanish Flu.
> Implications

We need to wait until the optimistic prospect of global mass vaccination for 2021 starts to take effect. Further Twitter research will then need to be undertaken.
> Recommendations for future studies

Source: R. Archee (2022). Communication, mainstream media, and Twitter: A summative content analysis of the concepts surrounding the COVID-19 pandemic during 2020. *Global Media Journal Australian Edition, 16*(1).

for scientific writing of all descriptions (see http://www.apastyle.org). Other highly regarded styles include Harvard, Chicago and MLA. Specific style guides are readily available online for these different layout conventions.

A reference list for some of the citations made in this chapter's exhibits, based on APA guidelines, is provided in **Exhibit 13.12**. Note that your reference list should be formatted using hanging indents as the exhibit shows.

Appendices

Appendices include anything that would have detracted from the main text, like large tables, sets of graphs, the survey instrument or large sets of statistical information. Appendices should be labelled 'Appendix A', 'Appendix B', and so forth.

Reflection question: What are the functions of each of the parts of the research or business report? Why is it important to use these parts for a reader?

| Exhibit 13.12 | Example reference section |

References

Ahorsu, D. K., Lin, C. Y., Imani, V., Saffari, M., Griffiths, M. D., & Pakpour, A. H. (2022). The Fear of COVID-19 Scale: Development and Initial Validation. *International Journal of Mental Health and Addiction*, 20(3), 1537–1545. https://doi.org/10.1007/s11469-020-00270-8

Arpaci, I., Alshehabi, S., Al-Emran, M., Khasawneh, M., Mahariq, I., Abdeljawad, T., & Hassanien, A. E. (2020). Analysis of Twitter data using evolutionary clustering during the COVID-19 pandemic. *Computers, Materials, & Continua*, 65(1), 193–204. http://dx.doi.org/10.32604/cmc.2020.011489

Australian Government Department of Health. (2020). COVID-19 Frequently asked questions. https://www.health.gov.au/sites/default/files/documents/2020/03/coronavirus-covid-19-frequently-asked-questions_3.pdf

Baccini, L., Brodeur, A., & Weymouth, S. (2021). The COVID-19 pandemic and the 2020 US presidential election. *Journal of Population Economics*, 34(2), 739–767.

Bentivegna, S., & Marchetti, R. (2018). Journalists at a crossroads: Are traditional norms and practices challenged by Twitter? *Journalism*, 19(2), 270–290.

Bhat, M., Qadri, M., Beg, N. U., Kundroo, M., Ahanger, N., & Agarwal, B. (2020). Sentiment analysis of social media response on the COVID-19 outbreak. *Brain, Behavior, and Immunity*, 87, 136–137. https://doi.org/10.1016/j.bbi.2020.05.006

Bivings Group. (n.d.). The use of Twitter by America's newspapers. https://blog.thebrickfactory.com/pdf/twitter_study_final.pdf

Castaldi, S., Maffeo, M., Rivieccio, B. A., Zignani, M., Manzi, G., Nicolussi, F., Salini, S., Micheletti, A., Gaito, S., & Biganzoli, E. (2020). Monitoring emergency calls and social networks for COVID-19 surveillance. To learn for the future: The outbreak experience of the Lombardia region in Italy. *Acta bio-medica: Atenei Parmensis*, 91(9-S), 29–33. https://doi.org/10.23750/abm.v91i9-S.10038

Source: R. Archee (2022). Communication, mainstream media, and Twitter: A summative content analysis of the concepts surrounding the COVID-19 pandemic during 2020. *Global Media Journal Australian Edition, 16*(1).

Business reports versus research reports

The typical business report also reports on primary research and conforms to the OECD's definition of applied research. Many business reports are typically performed on a smaller scale, or dependent on a single organisation rather than an academic field. There is usually a lack of scientific rigour in a typical business report reflecting tight deadlines and pragmatic considerations. Business reports are usually not peer reviewed since they are not intended for publication. However, they can be very similar to the scientific research report depending on their size, the industry and the purposes of the report author/s. In many cases the research report's subheadings are modified to reflect current practices in particular organisations, industries and government departments. The abstract (or executive summary), introduction and findings are common to both business and scientific formats. Literature reviews and thus references are atypical in business, method sections are often minimal or omitted, and results are subsumed under a variety of subheadings to suit the particular topic/industry. The use of bullet points is a commonplace technique, which allows for a degree of analysis, without verbose explanation.

Summary

For many of us, research is a somewhat daunting, intimidating word that is reserved for scientists in white coats. The chapter began by providing definitions of the word 'research' and then distinguished the three common types of empirical research used in workplaces – quantitative, qualitative and content analyses. The research process was then explained, and ethical responsibilities of the researcher reiterated. The last part of the chapter was devoted to explaining how the scientific format is structured using functional sub-headings. These major sub-headings – summary, introduction, method, results, discussion – have been demonstrated using a real research report. Lastly, it was highlighted how business reports may differ from research reports, depending on the workplace context.

STUDY TOOLS

DISCUSSION QUESTIONS AND GROUP ACTIVITIES

For discussion topics and activities in addition to those listed below, please refer to the case studies presented throughout this chapter.

1   Bad questionnaires and bad survey research is so commonplace that it is the standard that many of us assume is the norm. What should good survey research look like? What are some famous examples of bad survey research? Try to use Australian examples first, then international ones.

2   Do you think that having Google available makes all of us more opinionated about information related to so many professional areas?

3   Locating too many hits is just as bad as finding too few. How can you minimise the number of useful hits for your search term while using Google?

4   Given that there are so many search engines available, what are the advantages of some of the alternatives to Chrome, such as Brave, Firefox, Vivaldi and Yahoo?

5   Test your research skills with the following topics:

   a   Is it ethical for organisations to monitor employees' email and internet behaviour at work? Why, or why not?

   b   What are the privacy laws as they pertain to Australian businesses in the new millennium?

   c   Intellectual property is a serious workplace issue. Discuss whether or not you own the rights to any innovations you might develop while being employed by a company.

6   What is the purpose of each of the five sections of a scientific research report?

7   Discuss the suggestion that different report sections constitute very different genres of writing.

8   Read the following poor examples of overviews of report introductions. Rewrite to improve the structure and tone by being more general (not specific) and more professional (not humble). The sentence/s should not start with the topic. You could use a provocative beginning.

   a   *Drink driving:* I would like to talk a bit about drink driving what happens when drunken men and women get behind the wheel of a car instead of taking public transport or catching a taxi.

   b   *Underage sex:* According to Velasquez (2006) teenagers who have underage sex risk contracting venereal diseases more than those people who are 18 or older.

   c   *Racism:* Looking vaguely Middle Eastern in Sydney can get you stopped by the cops or beaten up in the country. My cousin was accosted by a large gang of guys last month.

9   Using Google Scholar or a library database, find three scholarly articles on the same topic. Compare their literature reviews for length, breadth of coverage, depth of coverage and number of references. Create a table to summarise this comparison. Which is the best literature review?

10 Using APA format, create a table, using MS Word, and a graph, using MS Excel (use 2D graphs not 3D ones), from the following set of data:

   * *Subjects who took Drug 1 had the following average feeling healthy scores on a test:* 22 (baseline), 25 (at 1 week), 26 (2 weeks), 28 (3 weeks), 28 (4 weeks).

   * *No drug:* 22 (baseline), 22 (1 week), 23 (2 weeks), 24 (3 weeks), 24 (4 weeks)

   * *Drug 2:* 22 (baseline), 24 (1 week), 27 (2 weeks), 31 (3 weeks), 34 (4 weeks)

      Compare your graph(s) and your table(s). Label the graph as Figure 1 and the table as Table 1 according to APA format. Write up the text that could accompany the graph and table. Highlight findings and explain highs and lows.

11 Compare scientific reports and business reports. How are they similar and different in terms of their structure?

12 Find some real-life examples of scientific research reports and business reports and contrast their objectives and methods.

WEBSITES

Best research databases https://paperpile.com/g/academic-research-databases

Best software tools for data analysis https://www.datapine.com/articles/data-analyst-tools-software

Google Scholar https://scholar.google.com

Guide to link you university's library to Google Scholar https://libguides.southernct.edu/googlescholar/library

OECD, Frascati Manual, 2015 https://www.oecd-ilibrary.org/science-and-technology/frascati-manual-2015_9789264239012-en

Voyant-tools for content analysis https://Voyant-tools.org

REFERENCES

Archee, R. (2022). Communication, mainstream media, and Twitter: A summative content analysis of the concepts surrounding the COVID-19 pandemic during 2020. *Global Media Journal: Australian Edition*, 16(1).

Brent, P. (2016, April 8). We're drowning in opinion polls, so here's what to make of them. *The Drum*, ABC News

Costello, J. (2001). Nursing older dying patients: Findings from an ethnographic study of death and dying in elderly care wards. *Journal of Advanced Nursing*, 35(1), 59–68.

Glaser, B., & Strauss, A. (1967). The Discovery of Grounded Theory: Strategies for Qualitative Research. Mill Valley, CA: Sociology Press.

Guéguen, N., Jacob, C., Le Guellec, H., Morineau, T., & Lourel, M. (2008). Sound level of environmental music and drinking behavior: A field experiment with beer drinkers. *Alcoholism: Clinical and Experimental Research*, 32(10), 1795–1798.

Hamel, J., Dufour, S., & Fortin, D. (1993). *Case study methods*. Sage Publications.

Marsh, C. 1982, *The survey method: The contribution of surveys to sociological explanation*. Allen & Unwin.

National Health and Medical Research Council. (2007). *National statement on ethical conduct in research involving humans*. Commonwealth of Australia.

Organisation for Economic Co-operation and Development. (2015). *Frascati Manual 2015: Guidelines for Collecting and Reporting Data on Research and Experimental Development, The Measurement of Scientific, Technological and Innovation Activities*. OECD Publishing. https://doi.org/10.1787/9789264239012-en.

Comments on case studies

CASE STUDY 1.1 What is meant by *professional* in *professional communication*?

Answers will vary depending on the specific professions that students are studying. Examples of professional failures at the time of this book's publication include the scandal within the consultancy firm PWC (2023) where a former partner, who had been advising the Australian government on new tax laws targeting corporate tax avoidance, shared confidential drafts with colleagues that were used to pitch for work with other clients. Other examples might include investigations into police conduct regarding the shooting of an elderly woman in Cooma NSW (May 2023) or the behaviour of medical professionals, such as the findings against well-known neurosurgeon Dr Charlie Teo (2023). In the PWC example, many of the directors lost their jobs, but more importantly, the company's reputation worldwide has been damaged, potentially impacting its ability to secure further work from sensitive government bodies. Police in the Cooma case have been stood down awaiting the outcome of various investigation, and Dr Teo had major restrictions placed on his ability to practice in Australia.

CASE STUDY 1.2 Identifying noise in communication

We would classify the sentences as follows:

1 Semantic noise: the tone could be regarded as blunt and offensive. Use of the word 'investigated' creates an overtone of distrust.

2 Semantic noise: this sentence is ambiguous. Does his brother receive 50 per cent or 25 per cent of the estate?

3 Environmental or physiological noise: Joe has trouble hearing because of either too much background noise from the poor acoustics and the loud house band (environmental). It may be that this is made worse by a level of hearing loss (physiological).

4 Semantic noise: again the tone is threatening and accusing. The use of the phrase 'we trust that in future ...' is patronising.

5 Semantic noise: again, this sentence is ambiguous. Whose hands were broken – the surgeon's or Peter's? Or did the surgeon break both of Peter's hands?

6 Psychological noise: even though Melinda has not personally had a negative experience with Acme Insurance, her attitude to the company is shaped by the 'word of mouth' negative experience of her mother.

7 Semantic noise: this kind of jargon often appears in business and policy writing, often because the writer wants to impress the reader with their expertise or their status. The message usually turns out to be meaningless or an inflated version of what the writer is communicating.

CASE STUDY 1.3 Purpose in communication

If the purpose of the notice is to get support and adherence to the request, then (1) is too impersonal and formal, and lacks sufficient detail; (2) is too threatening and also fails to give exact times for the break; (3) is patronising and cloying; and (4) is longwinded and pompous. We think (5) is preferable as it is easily read and understood and gives the exact times. Do you agree? Did any of your group compose a different notice? How was it different?

CASE STUDY 1.4 Supermarket sales tactics cleverly use the way our brains perceive and process sensory information

The human brain experiences the outside world via the five senses and filters and organises the stimuli until it has meaning. In order to deal with the mass of stimuli from the outside world, such as the multitude of colours, smells, sounds, shapes in a supermarket, the brain uses organisational patterns, or schema, to shape interpretation.

Marketers have long studied the psychology of human behaviour to distinguish their products from the many others in a supermarket and this list includes only some of the strategies they use. This illustrates how reality is constructed by the way our brains process sights, sounds, smells and so on, and by how we have learnt to interpret these meanings.

CASE STUDY 1.5 Crime, sex, immigration and climate change: how Australians get it wrong

The annual Ipsos research poll measures the attitudes of people around the world to a range of contemporary issues and then compares them with the actual data. In the examples given, Australians are shown to greatly overestimate the rate of crime, the level of sexual activity of their peers, the number of immigrants from particular ethic groups and the impact of climate change policies. These results are illustrative of a range of factors that illustrate how people's perceptions work:

1   Our perceptions are influenced by both our existing fears as well as the focus of media stories on local crime or terrorist attacks, and often this does not reflect reality and is sensationalised. When people are generally fearful or anxious, as in times of war or economic trouble, their anxieties amplify their perceptions.

2   The extent to which sources of information, such as those on social media, impact these misperceptions is relevant. 'Fake news' is not new, but the unregulated nature of social media means that false and sensationalist information is more easily spread. Research has shown that social media platforms tend to create 'information silos' and 'confirmation bias', where people are attracted to information that confirms their existing views and they reject information that conflicts with these views. This is called 'cognitive dissonance' and is problematic when attempting to overcome long held prejudices or biases.

3   Following experiences with floods and fires, many Australians who were previously sceptical about the importance of climate change policy have shifted their views. The same is often reported when people hold biases against particular ethnic groups; but once they meet people from that group, realise that despite difference in language, dress and culture, people are more similar than different.

CASE STUDY 1.6 Applying communication models to a case study

In the case study, Jane's poorly timed message is problematic. If we apply the elements of the communication models to this example, we can see the following:

1   Jane clearly knew that she needed to advise the change of working hours to her small team.

2   Jane's language indicates that she is both trying to distance herself from the decision ('I've been told to tell you') and downplaying its importance, perhaps to avoid conflict ('Look I'll try not to keep you'). Holding the meeting at the end of the day on Friday means that staff may not be paying attention and will be more eager to leave. She signals this by saying 'I know you are anxious to get away'. There is a lot of superfluous detail in the message, which may distract from the main point of the change in working hours.

3   This message may be problematic for a number of reasons related to staff members' 'frame of reference'. Some staff may rely on public transport or have childcare drop offs that may impact their ability to change arrival times.

4   There are many different channels or combinations of channels that Jane could have chosen for this message. While a face-to-face staff meeting is a good choice as it allows people to ask questions or express concerns directly, holding such a meeting at the end of the day is problematic. Perhaps an initial email sent out with sufficient time for staff to reorganise their schedules would have been more appropriate. This could have been followed up with a staff meeting at a more suitable time.

5   Jane seems very reluctant to allow time for feedback as she says, 'if there are no questions'. She seems in a hurry and is signalling that feedback is not encouraged. This could be problematic if staff are unable to adjust their schedules and may cause tension in the team.

CASE STUDY 2.1 A shutdown, a lockout or industrial action: when is a 'strike' a 'strike'?

The choice of words by the editor of the *Sydney Morning Herald* created considerable debate at the time and he was eventually forced to issue a clarification and an apology. The instance was framed by critics as an example of the further politicisation of the SMH.

The term 'strike' has become highly politicised and negatively loaded over time and has broadly been used in the media to imply that trade unions are making unreasonable demands and behaving thuggishly. 'Industrial action' is a much more neutral term and is far more general in that it can include a range of actions that may be more of an inconvenience to management rather than to the public.

A 'lockout' on the other hand is technically what occurred in this case, as the NSW government pre-emptively shut the rail network down without consultation with the union involved. While workers turned up for their shifts, they were not permitted to enter the workplace and no trains ran that day. The insistence by the editor that 'strike' be the word used on the front page, against the advice of senior journalists, was seen as evidence of the further decline in journalistic standards of fairness and accuracy at the SMH, now controlled by the former Liberal Party treasurer Peter Costello. This was gleefully reported by the rival tabloid *Daily Telegraph.*

CASE STUDY 2.2 The contested language of the euthanasia debate

This is a classic example of the strategic use of euphemism to frame a taboo topic in words that are less confronting with the aim of shifting perceptions. Death has always been shrouded in euphemistic language, largely because most people don't wish to be reminded of their own and their loved ones' inevitable mortality. While *euthanasia* is the technical term, it is cold and medicalised and does not communicate the nuances of what this legislation is proposing. 'Suicide' on the other hand, is equally problematic as a taboo notion

with connotations of mental illness and an inability to cope. It is also problematic for religious reasons. 'Voluntary assisted dying' avoids many of these problems. As Andrew Denton notes in the article, the phrase frames the notion of a deliberate decision made by someone who is already terminally ill, still in control of their mental faculties, and who wishes to end their own suffering. In other words, it connotes a form of ultimate self-empowerment and control over one's own life.

CASE STUDY 2.3 Warspeak

When euphemism moves from the realm of etiquette and social nicety to shifting attention away from the reality of what is being described, it borders on 'doublespeak'. George Lakoff and Steven Poole explain how in political and public speech and writing, parties to disputes use words as slogans, loaded with meaning. Once you have identified an activity or cause in your terms, they say, you have an advantage in the debate that follows, because other parties tend to accept your term. Poole calls this practice 'unspeak', while Lakoff refers to 'framing'. This passage illustrates how military language may act to desensitise the public to the realities of war by framing the actions in seemingly

objective language that filters out the human impact of the war and the weapons being used. Therefore 'soft targets' is a euphemism for human bodies, and the enemy territory and munitions become 'assets'.

It also makes the point that there is a subjectivity behind the labelling of some acts of war as 'terrorism' while others are labelled as 'liberation', with both terms possessing hugely emotive overtones. Some of the terms you are asked to discuss in this case are already well established, but others emerge daily in our newspapers. Read through a week of headlines and you are sure to come across new ones.

CASE STUDY 2.4 Fear of a burning planet: the semantics of climate change

As the frequency of catastrophic weather events, such as floods and fires increases, so does the political battle to motivate more substantive actions to keep global warming within reasonable levels that do not threaten the

survival of the human species. One of the tactics that has been used by both sides of the debate is the appropriation of language that either heightens awareness of the consequences of unrestrained warming or alternatively distracts citizens from the seriousness of the situation by either framing climate change as either something in the future or as a fringe issue taken up for ideological reasons. To some extent the result has been that citizens switch off and ultimately suffer what has been labelled 'apocalypse fatigue'.

However, language is powerful, and as linguist George Lakoff (2010) argues, how we frame the environment in media and politics is hugely important. Frames, Lakoff explains, work by repetition and become embedded in consciousness, evoking often subconscious emotive reactions and a familiar narrative. In the case study, the left leaning *Guardian* news outlet has chosen to move from 'global warming' to 'global heating' and from 'climate change' to 'climate emergency' to more strongly emphasise the seriousness of the consequences of inaction, many of which we are now witnessing. In other examples cited, either removing references to climate change altogether or reframing concepts like carbon in a positive, friendly way ('molecules of freedom'), aims to create the opposite effect.

CASE STUDY 2.5 Medical jargon and the COVID-19 pandemic

Jargon is common in all professional areas as a way of both 'short cutting' conversations about complex, professionally specific concepts and identifying the users as members of a group or 'discourse community'. However, in a public health emergency, as has been the COVID-19 pandemic, public health officials urgently had to find ways of explaining complex phenomena to ordinary citizens in order to minimise death, serious disease and overwhelmed public hospital systems. Clear, unambiguous language was required. The case study proposed more general descriptions such as 'co-morbidities' being recast as 'existing serious illnesses' or similar. Many jargon-heavy professions argue that specialised language is necessary to be able to capture the nuances of the concept, but in the case of a need for mass communication, simpler language is important.

CASE STUDY 2.6 'Not now, not ever': Julia Gillard's 'misogyny speech'

Misogyny is defined as hatred or prejudice against women seeking to keep them in lesser positions within society. As we've discussed, we can examine language choices for the way in which they reflect particular ways of seeing the world. The various examples that the former prime minister Julia Gillard cites illustrate views of women's positions in public life and often the prism through which their actions are viewed and critiqued.

For example, 'witch' and 'bitch' are highly derogatory terms and are applied specifically to women. A 'bitch' is literally a female dog whose primary role is to breed. In more recent usage, the term is applied to someone who serves or is subordinate to another, in a lesser position. The references to a woman's marital status or childlessness as a criticism, something that is rarely done with respect to male leaders, illustrates that this is the primary prism through which these speakers view women. As such, women like Gillard are an outlier. Rather than provide arguments against her policies, they regularly sought to deride her character by questioning her life choices, implying that these were 'unfeminine'.

The responses to the speech at the time were interesting. Many mainstream Australian journalists criticised Gillard for seeking to deflect criticism of her policies by 'playing the gender card'. In contrast, at the time and since, many more people, including former US president Barack Obama and former Secretary of State Hillary Clinton, have lauded the speech as inspiring.

CASE STUDY 2.7 Political correctness versus freedom of speech: do people have the right to be bigots?

This was a highly contentious decision that illustrates very well the power of language to deceive and to influence public opinion. Do a Google search using the terms 'Andrew Bolt' and 'racial discrimination'; you'll find many articles with varying points of view on the court's decision. It might also be useful to look at the words of the judge in this case, which can also be found online. One of the main points of those who defend the decision is that Bolt used incorrect information as the basis of his argument and that this was not only poor journalism but had the potential to inflame racial divisions within society. The fact that Bolt has a large reading audience in a variety of media outlets was also central to the judgment; that is, his free speech was not in fact being impinged on as he was not asked to apologise nor was News Ltd asked to retract. Freedom of speech is not absolute (and never has been), but is always subject to some controls and the laws of slander and defamation enshrine these in law.

Do we have the right to say and publish what we like, even if it is an untruth? Perhaps the words of writer Dr Rosie Scott, cited by one of the applicants in this case, sum this up best: 'free speech is the cornerstone of genuine democracy, but when writers publish disinformation dressed up as fact, lies as truth, slander as objective evaluation, racial discrimination as comment and call it free speech, they are devaluing its very essence and betraying all those who've fought for it.'

Source: Submission to the exposure draft: The attorney-general's proposed amendments to the *Racial Discrimination Act 2013* (2014, April 15).

CASE STUDY 3.1 Non-verbal behaviours: what do they tell us about relationships?

This photo is quite famous because it illustrates the tense relationship between former US president Donald Trump and a group of other important European leaders, led by German chancellor Angela Merkel at the G7 economic summit in 2018. Merkel and to a lesser extent French president Macron to her left are leaning over the desk at which Trump is sitting, while other leaders, including the prime ministers of the United Kingdom and Japan, look on in concern. By leaning into Trump, Merkel is deliberately invading his space to either intimidate or to assert her frustration. By sitting slightly back and crossing his arms, Trump appears to be indicating a stubborn resistance to what is being said. The impassive, and somewhat smug look on his face would support this interpretation. The man to Trump's right is his national security advisor John Bolton, who has an open posture (arms down, holding a folder) and a look of wry bemusement on his face. Bolton was known for his 'hawkish' attitude to foreign dealings and belief in the superiority of US foreign policy. From their facial expressions and stances, other leaders, especially those from the Asian nations, appear concerned at how the discussion is proceeding. This could also be because of a cultural preference for indirect, 'high context' communication approaches rather than direct confrontation, which appears to be happening here.

The background is that while initially agreeing to a joint communique about negotiations on free trade, Trump left the meeting early and refused to sign on to the statement. He then publicly derided leaders such as Merkel and Canadian prime minister Trudeau. In this context, Trump's confrontational and unconventional approach to diplomacy, trade and security would contribute to how you interpret his non-verbal behaviour in this photo. Given that the outcomes of these meetings are normally highly stage-managed for PR purposes, this photo is highly instructive of the level of frustration all round.

CASE STUDY 3.2 How behaviour changes with social distance

There are a number of animated conversations happening in this photo, which are indicated through the subjects' facial expressions, hand gestures and head movements. Most of the facial expressions appear very happy, while others are just intense since they are obviously watching the action. Some are leaning into another's intimate zone, probably to speak above the noise of the crowd.

In a crowd of people, we are forced to inhabit the personal zones, and sometimes the intimate zones, of people we may not know. This is acceptable, even if it may make us feel temporarily uncomfortable. Strategies to avoid excess discomfort include avoidance of eye contact and, if possible, avoidance of touch. Sometimes we may create 'barriers' by crossing our arms or legs or by using a briefcase or book when sitting in a train carriage. In our own homes or offices, we may use furniture or personal belongings to mark our personal space. We need to remember, however, that levels of discomfort and the strategies to deal with them may vary between cultures.

During COVID-19 lockdowns, 'social distancing' became an important public health directive. We were told to stand 1.5 metres from others in public spaces, including supermarkets and shopping centres. Seats on buses and trains were labelled to separate passengers appropriately. Social gatherings of even family and close friends were restricted and discouraged, with many only being able to communicate during lockdowns via video conferencing apps such as Zoom, Skype or Facetime. People reported heightened levels of anxiety, depression and isolation.

CASE STUDY 3.3 Crowd behaviour in the public zone: 2021 US Capitol invasion

In the context of crowded public spaces, people are more likely to behave as a 'mob' as they are less likely to feel they will be individually observed or responsible for their actions, and are more likely to react to the feelings and emotions of those in the larger group. In the case of the January 2021 US Capitol riots, many individuals were carried away in the moment having listened to the former president's address urging them to protest against the outcome of the 2020 election, which he argued had been 'stolen'. They broke into the building and proceeded to roam the corridors looking for lawmakers who were there to certify the results of the election in favour of Joe Biden.

A sense of common identity and purpose is indicated by many of the artefacts that were carried: US and confederate flags, Trump 2020 and MAGA (Make America Great Again) signs. The confederate flag symbolises the secessionist, anti-government movement of the American Civil War and has also come to symbolise notions of white supremacy. Many protestors wore military type uniforms, and others wore balaclavas and hoodies to hide their faces, indicating that they knew they might be breaking the law.

Defacing the symbol of US government by vandalising the building is indicative of the non-verbal expression of contempt for this institution. The protestor with his feet on the desk of House Speaker Nancy Pelosi, was showing his contempt for her personally, for her position and for the government she represents, by literally invading and disrespecting her private workspace.

CASE STUDY 3.4 Are we living through a crisis of touch?

The importance of touching behaviours has been become apparent in recent years. During the COVID-19 pandemic, the need to minimise close personal contact to avoid cross contamination of the virus was amplified.

In healthcare professions generally, such as nursing, there are protocols that guide how professionals touch patients during a medical examination. In particular, clearly communicating the purpose of touching is vital, particularly when involving intimate parts of the body.

In other medical contexts, research in aged care has shown that appropriate touching is vital to communication and to a sense of security for often vulnerable people. However, healthcare practitioners need to be aware of a patient's sensitivities as related to their age, medical issues and culture.

In terms of non-verbal behaviour 'rules', the #MeToo movement drew awareness of the power imbalance of certain touching behaviours in the workplace and how these might be interpreted as forms of intimidation or even sexual harassment. It is, therefore, important for all professionals to constantly monitor their own non-verbal behaviours and to be sensitive to how their colleagues, co-workers and clients may interpret particular behaviours.

CASE STUDY 3.5 Non-verbal communication in a police interview

In this extract, there are many examples of the non-verbal communication cues exhibited by both the defendant, Robert Farquarson, and by the interviewing police. For example, in describing his physical appearance, his 'deflated posture', the possible interpretation is that he has let himself go, that he is ground down by what has happened: 'His eyes are set deep, fatty sockets. He appears not to have shaved. His head is bowed. The slack curve of his spine gives prominence to the plumpness of his belly and chest.'

Garner notes his reaction to the first mention of the fact that his sons have died, 'He closes his eyes for a second in a moment of private pain'. In recounting his story, she notes that he keeps his eyes on the melamine table rather than looking directly at his questioners. She says that he occasionally looks up from under this brow. Generally speaking, we tend to interpret those who avoid direct eye contact as having something to hide.

Non-verbal behaviours also need to be considered in a cluster, not in isolation. Garner, therefore, describes other non-verbal cues that could be read as nervous gestures – rubbing his arms, licking his lips, touching his face and blinking rapidly. This implies the question: 'Why was he nervous?'

From a possible jury member's perspective, the context is important. When considered along with other evidence presented at the trial (detailed in the rest of the book), his non-verbal behaviours could be read as indicative of his likely guilt, and his determination to have the police believe the story that he blacked out before the car ran off the road. 'When he relates the events, he illustrates his account with eager movements of his small, well-shaped, very clean hands.' On their own, these non-verbal signals could alternatively be interpreted as guilt, or as understandable given that his children died in a horrific accident and he is being interrogated by police who suspect that he murdered them.

CASE STUDY 3.6 Mary's crisis: it's often not what you say, but how you don't say it!

This case study illustrates a number of non-verbal factors that exacerbated the problems Mary experienced. It was the changes in her non-verbal behaviour – appearing nervous when suggestions were made, keeping her door closed, using a terse tone of voice – that Mary's co-workers picked up on. Rumours of 'changes' only served to confirm their fears that Mary was not being completely honest and was trying to avoid them, even socially. For her part, Mary should have been more aware of the way her non-verbal communication would be interpreted and perhaps made the connection between her changes in behaviour and the drop in morale.

CASE STUDY 4.1 The Ugly Australian

There is no definitive reason why the terms Ugly Australian or Ugly American were coined. However, many Australians and Americans are very naive and inexperienced with travelling. The requisite big trip overseas for many Australians is the first time they have left their country and is undeniably nerve-racking. Culture shock could result in anxious Aussies resorting to those crass behaviours that were once used when leaving the family home for the first time.

CASE STUDY 4.2 The Meaning of Tingo

The numerous examples in this book illustrate both that languages do not always translate literally and that they often capture extremely culturally specific ideas and customs. For example, the book notes that 'most Americans do not need the 108 words Hawaiians have for different types of sweet potato, or the 29 words the Banuit Tribe of Brazil uses for ants.' From the perspective of cross-cultural communication, therefore, professional communicators need to be aware of the extent to which cultural biases or perspectives are inherent to much of the language they use. As we have said elsewhere, it is always a wise idea to have someone with a working knowledge of a particular culture and its language, advise on the accuracy of a translation.

Source: A. Phillips (2006, April 25). The meaning of Tingo: One man's favourite words from 254 languages. Learning English, Voice of America.

CASE STUDY 4.3 Communicating public health information to culturally diverse communities

The news report in the case study is evidence of the importance of considering culture and the specifics of language when a major government information campaign is undertaken. Using graphics rather than a lot of text, minimising the use of medical jargon and technical terms, and testing the written and verbal messages with groups of the sample audience, would minimise some of the problems identified. In the case of Victoria, the state government sent people door to door in areas with high migrant populations as many of these groups either did not have access to the internet, and were unlikely to watch English language television or read English language news articles. In the case of migrants in some local government areas, their experiences in their home countries meant they may mistrust government information or be fearful of retribution, and so other communication strategies, such as disseminating information via community members, would have been more appropriate.

CASE STUDY 4.4 Customs of other cultures

1   Petra K. explains:

My Indian friend came from a wealthy Indian family living in Nepal. Their house was full of young Nepali girls and boys who lived with them as servants. And now she was in America, on her own, doing her own laundry, tidying up her room, so at least she found someone to bring her a can of Coke, to keep a trace of her old living standard.

People from high power distance, low-individualism countries have no qualms issuing orders to others and being obeyed. People from low power distance, high-individualism cultures are used to helping themselves rather than ordering others around.

2   Raffaella P. explains:

> We realised that Yuko and her friends would not leave unless we did something. So I went to them and gently told them that 'It is OK, now Valentina and I will wait for Paola' and thanked them for their patience. They thanked us profusely (for releasing them from their duty, I suppose) and then they walked away.

Japanese communications patterns are based on understatements and reading indirect messages. Therefore, if you formulate a vague request, a Japanese person may interpret it as an indirect way of issuing a formal command. Add to that possible language problems and the fact that 'waiting' does not have the same connotations universally, and you have the necessary ingredients for this minor but embarrassing intercultural misunderstanding.

3   Omar H. explains:

> In Indonesia, raising our hands to participate in a class discussion is not our custom. However, we are more than willing to answer questions when the teacher points to us or calls our name in class.

In some cultures, a class is mainly a lecture by the professor with the students learning through listening; in other cultures, interaction and discussion is felt to be an essential part of the learning process. Asian cultures in particular respect status and authority, and so asking questions may seem to disrespect the authority of the professor or lecturer.

4   Brad D. explains:

> It seems that a kiss was to her what a handshake is to me; and a hug was too intimate for her, yet I feel that it is less intimate than a kiss.

Codes of conduct that regulate touching, hugging and kissing behaviour are obviously culture specific. Is there any way to know in advance which greeting rituals are appropriate in a given culture? Who should adapt to whom? Is Brad supposed to adapt to the Hungarian girl's habits and expectations, or the other way around?

5   What is polite or impolite is not universally the same in every culture. Would you tolerate Kei's behaviour or would you try to change it? Essay writing is a cultural activity. Westerners learn to write in a linear fashion, usually employing inductive reasoning and ending with a stated conclusion. Eastern cultures and some European cultures employ different strategies, which may resemble a circle or spiral, with the conclusion never stated, only implied. Sources of authority, referencing procedures, citations and quoting are viewed very differently throughout the world.

Source: Adapted from S. P. Verluyten (n.d.).
Selected intercultural incidents.
Retrieved 20 August 2011.

CASE STUDY 5.1 Communication breakdown: emails are the culprit

Emails are quick, easy and less time consuming than organising a face-to-face discussion or even a phone call. They can be sent and read at any time, and today can be managed via multiple devices, including your smartphone.

However, not all emails are the same. They can take the form of a quick, informal reply – 'Yep, see you soon', a sort of substitute for a verbal conversation – or can be more formal, written in the manner of a traditional memo or letter – 'Dear Mr Jones'.

The ease with which emails can be sent means that often we reply unnecessarily, and our inboxes become filled with extraneous responses when colleagues 'reply-all' to a companywide email. The habit of 'reply-all' may also mean that any conversation or off-the-cuff comment can be read by all those in the email chain, sometimes causing conflict or problems when those for whom the comment may not have been intended, can read it. Once an email is sent, it can't be retrieved.

Like the various forms of written communication that they have replaced, emails require skill to both write and to manage. Tone is not always easy to master in writing, and readers can become easily offended if writers do not give enough thought to their language or take sufficient time to write and edit a response.

Finally, the need to register our email addresses for almost anything that we do today means that our inboxes become increasingly overloaded with unsolicited email, often marketing products and services. This may mean that the sheer volume of messages that we receive can cause us to miss an important message hidden among the throng.

CASE STUDY 5.2 Content analysis of Twitter

We expect that the answers to this question will vary considerably within the group. Most people who use Twitter for social purposes post pictures; comments about friends, social events, sport or music; and sometimes post links to humorous websites, YouTube videos or political causes.

The problem is that 'bots' are programs that can pretend to be real people, sometimes liking your tweets and content. But bots can also try to intimidate, bully and persuade you to believe things that may not be true, and act in ways that are fueled by false information. The issue of bots and Twitter is that Twitter has allowed such bots to proliferate. As a response, Twitter has discontinued free access to the Twitter API, from 9 February 2023, meaning that many bots will cease to exist, leaving only the paid-for bots. Ironically, this move badly affects researchers who depend on the free API to detect and monitor misinformation, hate speech and online abuse on Twitter.

CASE STUDY 5.3 The case for turning off your Zoom camera

While Zoom has been a godsend during the enforced lockdowns of the COVID-19 pandemic, enabling employees and students to work from home, the perennial complaint has revolved around the difficulties of communicating to a screen full of blank squares as participants left their cameras off during meetings. The article poses an alternate argument in favour of blank screens.

The main problems of the blank screen are that participants are unable to read the non-verbal facial cues and have a diminished sense of the 'social presence' of the participants. In the case of online learning, in particular, students in online classes are able to 'hide' and use the option to avoid having to engage in class activities or discussions. Others report that they feel less motivated and less engaged than in a traditional classroom, and that this has impacted both their enjoyment and their grades.

The alternative argument as posed by the case study is the need to reduce 'Zoom fatigue' and to allow meeting participants to multi-task while they listen in to discussions in a meeting. You might ask yourself after reading our discussion of listening (Chapter 8) if this discourages or impacts 'active listening'.

Zoom fatigue is certainly an issue, and the research cited (Bennett et al., 2021; Shockley et al., 2021) concludes that the fatigue relates to the higher levels of sustained attention and, in particular, attention required to 'decode' colleagues' non-verbal cues in the online space compared to a physical space. The ease with which groups are able to convene meetings using Zoom or Teams, while a plus, also means that there are potentially more meetings to attend than before.

CASE STUDY 5.4 Find your own case study

This exercise should persuade students that case studies can found all over the internet as well as from individual experiences. Professional misuse of social media is a commonplace occurrence and probably under reported in mainstream media and everyday life. Misusing personal photographs/videos of children, the elderly, the disabled and other vulnerable groups in society needs to be called out and taken off the internet.

CASE STUDY 5.5 The Ashleigh Madison affair

Lying equates with deceptive practices. Examples of these deceptive practices include:

- Some websites or individuals may use false endorsements or testimonials to promote a product, service or website. They may create fake accounts or fabricate positive reviews to deceive users.

- Phishing involves tricking individuals into revealing sensitive information, such as passwords, credit card numbers or personal details, by impersonating a legitimate entity through deceptive emails, messages or websites.

- Spoofing or impersonation occurs when someone pretends to be someone else online, either by creating a fake social media profile or by using other methods to misrepresent themself. It can be used for various malicious purposes, including spreading false information or defaming others.

- Manipulated images and videos can be used to deceive people, spread false information or create fake evidence.

- Some individuals or organisations may completely fabricate content, such as news articles or research papers, to suit their agenda or generate attention. This can be particularly problematic when it comes to disinformation campaigns or propaganda.

- Criminals may create fake online stores or auction websites to trick users into making purchases or bidding on items that do not exist. They may take payments without delivering the promised products or services.

- Clickbait are sensationalised headlines or thumbnails designed to attract attention and generate more 'clicks' (i.e. getting more people to click on the link to find out more). Often, the actual content does not live up to the exaggerated promises made in the headline.

We do not know if all dating websites are accurate or up to date. However we do suspect that many dating profiles of males and females are probably 'enhanced' with younger, more attractive images; higher status professions; deceptive ages; and omissions of important information. This is human nature.

CASE STUDY 6.1 Creating graphs with Excel or OpenOffice for Mac

Neither graph is a perfect example of this data. The data in the original table needs to be edited. Remember that tables have a different function to graphs. Raw scores and percentages are not the same; therefore, an author needs to choose one or the other. You could create two separate tables to use in Excel (or OpenOffice), then choose the most meaningful graph. The rule of thumb is that raw scores are often not fair because of the hugely different numbers of cases. Thus, percentages are the better option. Try the graphing exercise again but remove the raw scores from the table first.

CASE STUDY 6.2 How a graphic design 'disaster' influenced political perceptions

As the case study hints, the context of the controversy is highly important in how the logo was interpreted and the subsequent public reaction. It is very likely that the existing negative attitudes to the Morrison government's perceived attitude to women affected how the logo was interpreted or 'seen'. Do a Google search for some of the examples, including the treatment of female staffers like Brittany Higgins. As with any public communication exercise, designers should have tested the new logo with a sample audience to gauge their reactions. This might have saved them from a politically embarrassing backdown.

CASE STUDY 6.3 Exploring deepfakes

Answers to these questions will vary from student to student. Given that there are no laws or guidelines at present, and that the technology is evolving fast, there are no definitive answers we can recommend. These questions are not just legal issues but also ethical problems. Perhaps ethics guidelines need to be applied first? See Chapter 7, which deals with ethics.

CASE STUDY 6.4 Scary red or icky green? We can't say what colour coronavirus is and dressing it up might feed fears

The choice of red or green to represent the coronavirus has been widely used and is consistent with broader cultural perceptions related to these colours. Red symbolises danger, green in this context symbolises a form of decay, such as you might see in rotting food. The reality, as the article states, is that the virus does not have a colour as colour is created when light diffuses against a substance. The World Health Organization is concerned that the use of these colours might actually feed fear, and that this is possibly counterproductive in persuading people to take appropriate public health precautions against contracting the virus. This is a good example of the power of colour to link to existing cultural and social perceptions.

CASE STUDY 7.1 Accessibility and the internet

David Moradi (2022) states that most companies struggle with website accessibility for disabled users. Moradi cites AudioEye – an industry platform that analyses website data – who found that the vast majority of websites, whatever their size, do not completely cater for users with a range of disabilities. Conservative findings showed that 83 per cent of e-commerce sites, 78 per cent of healthcare sites, and 77 per cent of job sites blocked or hindered screen readers (for blind users) that should have enabled critical tasks for users to be performed. Such tasks included viewing product descriptions, filling in forms and booking appointments.

This is just as true for government websites as it is for universities, hospitals, news organizations, and streaming services. Accessibility is such a challenging issue because the range of disabilities include sight, hearing, colour blindness, cognition, learning, and neurological problems. Website authors must follow a vast list of instructions in order to accommodate disabled users every time they create a new web page. They must also test their solutions and, in some cases, cannot ensure that these solutions will work for everyone, depending on the individual disabled person.

Within a university or school, websites are not the only problem because students need to use a range of software in order to analyse data, submit assignments and read information. Software such as MS Word, Excel, Powerpoint, Acrobat and Photoshop simply cannot be used by visually impaired students (Archee, 2017).

Perhaps making websites accessible is a problem for society as a whole, and for governments that insist that all information be placed online but ignore disabled citizens and do not provide alternate pathways to perform critical tasks. We are living in a world that mandates accessibility, but this same world consists of organisations, institutions, schools and government sites that are not willing or not able to follow the letter of the law and are usually not prosecuted.

CASE STUDY 7.2 An ethical dilemma in nursing

The main ethical issue here is that a patient has informed a nurse that he intends to kill himself. The nurse must comply with the state laws and policies in this case and report this threat to a superior because a suicide threat is equated as a medical emergency. The nurse should not wait to see if the threat was realistic or not.

Some actions that nurses should not take are:

1 Do not say: 'I know how you are feeling'.
2 Do not say: 'Imagine how those Ukrainian war victims must be feeling right now'.
3 Do not ignore this warning sign – people who threaten suicide may be asking for help.
4 Do not leave this patient unattended.

Source: Adapted from C. Marel et al. (2022). *Guidelines on the management of co-occurring alcohol and other drug and mental health conditions in alcohol and other drug treatment settings* (3rd ed.). Matilda Centre for Research in Mental Health and Substance Use, The University of Sydney. https://comorbidityguidelines.org.au/pdf/comorbidity-guideline.pdf

CASE STUDY 7.3 Social media and the workplace

Access the full social media guidelines at https://www.nswnma.asn.au/wp-content/uploads/2020/05/Social-Media_PPT.pdf. The PDF is quite lengthy, but deserves more than a cursory glance. The best way to devise a case study is to recount an actual incident from your own life experience with social media and make it problematic as a health professional.

CASE STUDY 7.4 Corruption and health services during the pandemic

Corruption by health service companies during the pandemic is similar to corruption by many other organisations at any time in history. However, the fact that a company is making money while other companies have had to close down and employees have lost their jobs seems particularly wrong and underhanded.

The fairest way of locating suppliers of any resource is to ask for tenders to be made; that is, to ask for quotes from a range of suppliers. Competition keeps the suppliers from attempting to make too large a profit, thus prices will be as low as they can be because competitors will be attempting to win the tender by having the lowest prices. If the tender system is not employed, then the process is not transparent and other stakeholders may believe that secret deals exist that may benefit both parties. In many cases, corruption occurs when gifts of money, holidays, favours or other benefits are secretly exchanged in order to be selected as the successful supplier.

CASE STUDY 7.5 Ethics applied to the workplace

There are no right or wrong answers here. The most appropriate solutions to these issues are often determined by which side of the fence you are sitting on. For example, the dismissal of the nurse in the last scenario seems to be a clear-cut case of bad ethics on the part of the hospital. However, what if the hospital had a policy in place that stated that nurses may refuse to treat patients only if there are alternative staff available to perform these duties? What if the hospital needed some warning before a nurse could say no to treating a patient? In this case the hospital would be ethically (and legally) justified in dismissing the nurse.

CASE STUDY 8.1 The evolving nature of interpersonal relationships in the workplace

Just like most relationships, Judith and Maree's has gone through a variety of phases. If we consider it in terms of the 'onion theory' of social penetration (Exhibit 8.3), we can see how a work relationship evolved through similar interests in the arts and was cemented through regular workplace contacts. As their friendship developed, they shared an increasing amount of personal time inside and outside of work. Strong relationships are usually based on disclosure of more personal information as there is a strong basis of trust between those involved. This is often indicated by shared experiences in the workplace, a shared status and common experiences.

However, Judith's promotion meant that she no longer shared these common work experiences with Maree, was no longer able to spend the same amount of time with Maree. Also, their altered work status changed as Judith became Maree's boss and so the sharing of information, experiences and even office gossip became more problematic. Maree was no longer Judith's trusted confidant.

Work and personal relationships often show the same evolving trajectories as time spent together, personal trust and shared experiences act to cement friendships and relationships. All of us would have experienced changing relationships, with old friends with whom we were once close moving out of our lives, and new friendships emerging.

CASE STUDY 8.2 The role of 'communication competence' in health settings

Communication competence requires awareness and application of the range of interpersonal communication 'tools' outlined in this chapter. These are verbal and non-verbal skills, listening skills as well as appropriate assertiveness and empathy.

Scenario 1

In this scenario, the nurse is busy and obviously harried, and so has not been as aware of how the patient is feeling during their interaction, leading to a misinterpretation of the nurse's manner. The nurse perhaps could have apologised to the patient for having to wait, and acknowledged their obvious stress and uncertainty related to the medical advice. Initially the nurse could take a few minutes to allow the patient to express their concerns and listen actively to what was said. Even if the nurse was in a hurry, perhaps they could have moderated their body language by smiling, sitting with the patient and once the information was given, offering to check in later to answer any further questions.

Scenario 2

Miscommunication often occurs when we fail to consider what the listener already knows or is familiar with and, therefore, what extra information we may need to give. In this scenario, the nursing unit manager assumes that the next shift is familiar with the protocols and that they can shortcut the information. In these situations, especially given the potential impact on patients' health, a checklist for the shift handover could be useful to ensure all information is covered. Both the nursing unit manager and the incoming shift should look over this and be encouraged to ask questions before they leave.

Scenario 3

As we discussed in Chapters 2 and 4, language does not necessarily translate literally, and different cultures have different communication preferences. It is therefore not sufficient to assume that by merely translating a pamphlet into another language that it will be understood in the same way. In the case of a public health campaign, in particular, the government department should test the translated pamphlet with a sample of the target audience, and take advice about the kinds of appeals or information that the particular cultural group is more likely to react to, before the pamphlet is published and distributed.

CASE STUDY 8.3 Empathic listening in the project team

All responses by the four colleagues were trying to make Tuan feel better but they went about it in very different ways. The first two responses tried to minimise the significance of Lee's assessment. These responses may have been well intended but they do little to foster meaningful communication or to encourage Tuan to talk so that further understanding may be gained. Pat's response blocks empathy by reassuring and consoling. Kali's response has blocked empathy by diagnosing and giving advice. Kerry's response tried to make Lee's assessment seem a little more positive and has blocked empathy by offering facts and avoiding the emotional dimension. The first three responses communicated that Tuan should not have been feeling that way and should be feeling differently – more positively, for instance. The responses denied the validity of Tuan's feelings and put Tuan in the position of having to defend his feelings.

Sam's response used an active (or reflective) listening reply that reflected what Sam thought Tuan meant, in terms of both content and feelings. This response should communicate to Tuan that Sam really had been listening. Tuan's feelings were not challenged; they were acknowledged in an empathic manner. In the first three listening responses, Tuan's feelings are denied without ever actually being identified. By contrast, Sam has given Tuan an opportunity to correct Sam's perceptions of Tuan's meaning and feelings. Also, by acknowledging Tuan's feelings, Sam has made it easier for Tuan to let go of the feelings and identify and explore the issues in a calmer atmosphere. A meaningful and mutual dialogue may follow where Tuan works out a strategy to deal with the issues.

CASE STUDY 8.4 Listening in the classroom

Kim experienced listening barriers associated with a range of environmental and personal factors. Coming straight from school, where learning is extremely structured, into an adult learning environment, where students are expected to be self-directed, is extremely challenging. Information overload often results, especially in the first few weeks of semester when new students are also getting used to a new environment, different routines, new friends and different learning styles.

Listening productively in a lecture or classroom takes some practice. While podcasts and online notes are useful backups, they don't substitute for note-taking skills and attention in a lecture. Even if the lecture seems dry, students can prepare by reading lecture notes ahead of time so that they can practice critical analysis skills rather than having to concentrate just on acquiring 'facts' or information. What argument is the lecturer making? What perspectives are being covered? What is not being said? University lectures are usually structured to overview ideas and concepts rather than provide all the information a student needs, and so extra work from students is always needed.

Allowing yourself to be distracted by technology also doesn't help you to listen effectively. Using a laptop in lectures may seem like a good idea, but if you are easily tempted to surf the net or to chat online, turn off the laptop and mobile phone and use the old-fashioned method of taking notes by hand. Kim could try sitting closer to the front of the lecture theatre if she is distracted by people around her.

Active listening also requires motivation to overcome distractions caused by a speaker's irritating habits or perceptions of the subject matter as dry or boring. Listening to recordings of lectures is very convenient and can often overcome some of these other distractions, including the irritating mannerisms of the speaker, but it requires time-management skills and self-discipline to make sure you keep up to date. It's always easy to put it off until later.

If motivation is a problem, students should ask themselves, what's in it for me in the long term? Often, what seems irrelevant now will make sense later on. How will good grades help me achieve my career objectives? Considering these questions will help you focus your listening and become an active, rather than passive, listener.

Universities and tertiary institutions can help new students by outlining the expectations of each course clearly, by providing flexible delivery and by encouraging staff to be open and friendly so that students feel comfortable with asking questions. Providing an identifiable staff member who is prepared to listen to student concerns in an empathetic manner to act as a first-year coordinator is also a useful strategy.

CASE STUDY 8.5 Gaming fosters social connection at a time of physical distance

The research discussed in the article highlights the way in which technologies have evolved to incorporate and foster social connection, in particular during the COVID-19 pandemic. This has been propelled by advances in the interactivity functions of gaming platforms. Games encourage focus and creativity, and many allow gamers to interact with other players even when the ability to connect with friends face-to-face and in real time is limited.

While 'game addiction' is still a concern, and the impact of desensitisation of vulnerable people to real world violence is still debated, the research discussed in the case study suggests that both the interactive nature of games, the group participation, problem-solving and creativity, has had positive consequences by enabling virtual social interaction.

CASE STUDY 9.1 Why groups struggle to solve problems together and have unproductive meetings

The answers to this will vary among the range of different experiences of members of your group, but we recommend that you write down some of the group's experiences and then, using the five stages of problem-solving shown in Exhibit 9.10, discuss how these problems might have deviated from or missed some of these.

Group interaction issues that might interfere with effective problem-solving might include the possibility of dominant personalities with their own agendas stifling quieter, less assertive members, poor leadership or direction from the chairperson. Identifying and working towards a collaborative and structured process to work through a problem will be more likely to achieve a more satisfying and productive outcome and solution.

CASE STUDY 9.2 Decision-making in a student group

The group can facilitate decision-making by following Dewey's reflective thinking sequence, especially in relation to:
- clarifying the task – what is required for the report
- defining the task – what is needed to complete the report
- suggesting solutions to collect information and write the report
- deciding on solutions about collecting information and report writing
- working out details and allocating tasks to group members
- monitoring how everyone is going on completing their tasks.

The group can use consensus to reach decisions if it is difficult to agree on particular solutions.

Any blocks to working effectively and building interpersonal relations need to be stated by each group member and discussed in an atmosphere of openness and supportiveness. Members can be praised for what they have achieved, and suggestions can be made and agreed to about how to proceed. Group norms can be established and monitored. For example:
- Ari's telephone interviews can be reviewed and a method can be set for keeping records of future telephone interviews
- members can agree on how to contact each other if they cannot meet as planned
- the spreadsheet can be reviewed and modified in accordance with what the group agrees is needed for the report
- the group can agree that only one person speaks at a time and is not interrupted
- Ron and Sam can monitor contributions by Jacki and Ari in order to summarise and focus on what is needed for the report
- the group can agree to meet at locations that are convenient for members or rotate meeting places to be fair.

Members should communicate with respect for each other and avoid being overly critical and judgemental. Every member should be encouraged to share ideas and all ideas should be treated as having value. All decisions on tasks should be made jointly and followed up to give support to members who have responsibility for carrying out tasks.

CASE STUDY 9.3 Computer-mediated group processes and decision-making

The kind of problem addressed by the group or team plays an important role in the process. In early research by Hiltz et al. (1980), two kinds of problems were typically set – a values-laden one and a scientific ranking one, and factors were compared, including participation, leadership, consensus, decision quality and member satisfaction. With the values-laden problem, face-to-face groups tended to be more satisfied, reached consensus quicker and were more likely to have a dominant leader. However, with scientific problems there were no differences in decision quality, nor was there any tendency for leaders to emerge in either face-to-face or computer conference groups.

Contemporary research upholds the importance of the context in which mediated communication occurs. The social context and the interactivity of the whole system all impact on group behaviour. Furthermore, increasingly sophisticated experiences with a range of software and mobile devices, and the growing dependence on email, messaging services, public forums, blogs, and various forms of social media have created a global population of online users who have developed their own norms for communicating in these online spaces. The COVID-19 pandemic has made online spaces a supposedly reliable form of education and workplace. Mediated communication is no longer regarded as an inferior form of group communication compared to face-to-face communication. The medium of choice does not seem to matter at least for initial, short meetings (Han et al., 2011).

CASE STUDY 9.4 Was the 2003 US invasion of Iraq an example of groupthink?

Answers will vary here, but the Bush administration really did think that the Iraqis would welcome their intervention. Here is one set of findings:

1   *Illusion of invulnerability*. 'Everything is going to work out all right because we are a special group.'

2   *Belief in inherent morality of the group*. 'The US stands for freedom and democracy.' Questioning this almost amounts to treason.

3   *Collective rationalisation*. Simplistic statements such as 'Saddam is an evil dictator who possesses WMD' prevent the possibility of rational analysis.

4   *Out-group stereotypes*. 'If you're not with us you're against us.' Opponents to the war are unpatriotic.

5   *Self-censorship*. Intelligence experts got the message from early on that the administration only wanted information supporting a single outcome. The UK's sexed-up 'dodgy dossier' is an example.

6   *Illusion of unanimity*. The course of action was predetermined. The most serious doubter within the administration, Colin Powell, made the dubious case for war to the UN.

7   *Direct pressure on dissenters*. Ambassador Joseph Wilson cast doubt on claims about Iraq's source of uranium. The administration responded by claiming his wife was a CIA operative.

8   *Self-appointed mind-guards*. Karl Rove and a small number of advisors closely guarded access to Bush, ensuring that only like-minded views got aired.

CASE STUDY 9.5 How working from home has become the 'new normal' after COVID: what are the impacts for group cohesion?

During the early years of the COVID-19, most people would have had experience of working or studying from home. How we responded to this varied according to the type of work that we did and our personal circumstances. For many parents, who juggled home learning, their own job and other household distractions, it was stressful; and so for some, going to the office was a relief. For others, not having to waste time in traffic commuting to work was a bonus, and saved time and money. Many people missed the collegiality of their fellow workers in a social and professional sense, and found having to solve complex problems much easier if group members were working in close proximity.

One fortunate aspect of the COVID lockdown for many office workers in particular, was the availability of videoconferencing technologies like Zoom and Teams. While convenient, some workers reported that the very ease with which these could overcome logistical issues of getting numerous team members in a room at the same time, meant that meetings were too easy to convene, which left people with what has been labelled 'Zoom fatigue'. Others reported that while these were convenient, it was harder to solve problems as the minimal number of non-verbal cues meant that communication was more difficult, and decisions and solutions were harder to negotiate. Anecdotes suggest that casual, unplanned conversations around the office often enhanced collegiality, and led to new ideas and creative thinking.

Many first year university students, however, have bad recollections of poor high school planning, missed lessons and improper teaching during 2020–21. Many say that they had to teach themselves the curriculum, while school teachers dithered with trying to use the Zoom or Teams technologies. The situation now is most probably different with the technology becoming more and more reliable and user-friendly.

CASE STUDY 10.1 Introducing and concluding oral presentations

Introductions

Introduce the topic and the three speakers, and indicate what aspect of the topic each presenter will be covering and in what order. Gain attention with an anecdote, statistics or other information that will intrigue the audience and inform them about how your group is approaching the topic. For example, you could start with Chris's question to the audience: 'Stress does not count as a workplace health and safety issue because people do not suffer physical damage – true or false?' Or you could mention Assam's statistics that 'in Queensland, in 2020, 25 per cent of work-related injuries were sustained by 15 to 24-year-olds', especially if the audience is in this age group.

All three introductions gave examples of some of these guidelines, but no one introduction captured the essence of an informative, attention-gaining and structured opening that gives signposts to the listening audience. As the topic was very broad, the audience needed specific information about the scope and structure of what the team members would present. For example, the letters 'WHS' needed to be explained as 'workplace health and safety' at the start.

Sample introduction

Welcome to our presentation on Workplace Health and Safety which used to be called OH and S. We'll be referring to it by its initials WHS. We are Assam, Bryan and Chris. Would you say true or false to the following statement? Stress does not count as a workplace health and safety issue because people do not suffer physical damage. Well, if stress includes anxiety and mental distress, then the answer is 'false'. Here's another one: What percentage of workplace injuries are sustained by 15 to 24-year-olds? It's 25 per cent, according to a study in Queensland in 2020. Obviously, there are huge costs associated with poor WHS practices, for employers, employees and their families, and for governments. We'll be focusing on three main areas of this huge topic and we'll be concentrating on WHS in New South Wales: first, Assam will discuss what WHS means; second, Chris will explain briefly what the Acts say about WHS; and third, Bryan will cover what obligations organisations have under these Acts regarding WHS in their workplaces, in particular how the new Acts will affect workplaces. In particular they will focus on bullying and harassment and will conclude by reviewing the main issues. Assam will start by defining what is meant by workplace health and safety in the workplace.

Conclusions

Signal the conclusion, for example by saying 'In conclusion ...' Sum up what has been covered by each speaker. End on a challenge or action that the audience can follow up. Ask for questions from the audience. All three conclusions attempted some of these guidelines – none ended on a challenge or action for the audience to follow up or asked for questions from the audience.

Sample conclusion

We'd like to finish by reviewing what we have covered. We concentrated on workplace health and safety in New South Wales and divided our presentation into three main areas: (1) What is workplace health and safety? (2) relevant Acts, namely the new *WHS Act, Anti-Discrimination Act and Human Rights and Equal Opportunity Commission Act*; and (3) obligations for employers. Assam defined workplace health and safety to mean identifying hazards, risks and outcomes for protecting human and infrastructure resources in workplaces. Chris summarised the three relevant WHS Acts and referred to government websites, in particular the new umbrella body Safe Work Australia. Bryan focused on risks and obligations of employers under these Acts, including bullying and harassment in the workplace as a form of workplace health and safety. For you to follow up, we recommend looking at the detailed checklists for compliance to risk assessment on the websites that we have mentioned. Finally, what would be your approach to risk management so that workplace health and safety can be managed where you work? At this point we would be happy to respond to any questions of clarification or any comments.

CASE STUDY 10.2 The end of the lecture can't come soon enough

Traditional university lectures have used one-way communication techniques to deliver information to a passive audience. Before the availability of multimedia, data projectors and PowerPoint, lecturers used whiteboards or blackboards to highlight notes, and lectures were not audio recorded. Students were expected to take notes, often verbatim, which made listening and absorbing the lecture difficult. The traditional tiered seating arrangements and often poor acoustics in large lecture theatres, made it difficult for students to interact with the lecturer, to ask questions or to respond to questions.

Today, students expect more sophisticated applications of listening and pedagogical approaches. These include a variety of audio-visual stimuli, information broken into smaller chunks to help retention and attention, and the ability to interact and seek feedback. Also, teachers recognise the need to be aware of their presentation styles and to vary the mix of visuals, video, music, charts, graphs and text, to introduce variety and account for different learning preferences.

While the move to recorded lectures or pre-recorded short videos has created greater flexibility for busy students, allowing them to view a lecture remotely and in their own time requires students to be motivated and organised. Following the enforced online learning during the early years of the COVID-19 pandemic, students and universities are now recognising the importance of physical presence in enabling engagement with learning – remember the notion of 'the human moment' from Chapter 8?

CASE STUDY 10.3 The difficult first job interview

Melissa was reasonably well prepared, but obviously should have done more. She arrived early, and prepared answers to some anticipated questions. While she thought about how she was dressed, conservative rather than smart may have been more appropriate.

What she didn't realise was that in certain situations, reputation and history are important parts of an organisation's culture. Perhaps she could have sought advice from the professor who suggested that she apply for the position, about what the headmaster of such a prestigious school might be looking for in addition to academic qualifications. She needed to know how else she might stand out in the interview. The fact that she had been recommended by her university was obviously sufficient evidence of the fact that her grades were more than adequate. Reading about the school's history, its alumni and so on, could have helped her think more from the point of view of an insider to the school's culture and may have allowed her to answer the headmaster's unexpected questions more easily.

Often, tough interviews are designed to put an applicant off their guard and the location in the headmaster's office was one of these ploys. As we saw in Chapter 3, people use space and artefacts, such as furniture and decoration, to say something about themselves, to reinforce their status and often to intimidate those who enter the space. The headmaster's office was an example of this kind of non-verbal tactic.

Melissa didn't get the job because she wasn't the right 'fit' for the school. The questions about where she went to school and about opera were designed to test this. From this interview, Melissa should learn to research these aspects more thoroughly, know more about the culture of the organisation and be prepared to answer more testing tricky questions without getting flustered.

CASE STUDY 10.4 Weird job interview questions and how to handle them

There will be different answers here to these questions.

1 A candidate might say, 'If I were from Mars, they'd likely have their own problems separate to those on Earth. First, I would so some research to find out the cause and effect and offer some possible solutions.' This displays a thoughtful and analytical outlook.

2 This is a silly question that is intended to loosen up the candidate and see how they respond to a 'curve ball' situation. There's no right answer to this question.

3 This may seem like a similar loosening up question, but it is designed to test an interviewee's intellect. An ideal candidate will think through the question and provide a possible answer such as: 'A round manhole cover can't fall through the round manhole compared to a square cover which could fall through diagonally. Additionally, a round cover fits easily without too much rotating'. This kind of answer shows the candidates ability to think critically.

4 Of course there is no 'right' answer to this funny question, but it allows an interviewer to see how an interviewee thinks, prioritises and solves problems. The candidate might say: 'Since I don't have a place to put an elephant, I'd probably ring up the local zoo and ask them to take it.'

5 This question aims to test your candidate's creativity. It doesn't matter what kind of tree they choose, as long as the answer illustrates their strengths. For example, they might say: 'I'd be an oak because I'm strong and dependable.'

There will be different answers here to these questions.

1 A candidate might say, 'If I were from Mars, they'd likely have their own problems separate to those on Earth. First, I would so some research to find out the cause and effect and offer some possible solutions.' This displays a thoughtful and analytical outlook.

2 This is a silly question that is intended to loosen up the candidate and see how they respond to a 'curve ball' situation. There's no right answer to this question.

3 This may seem like a similar loosening up question, but it is designed to test an interviewee's intellect. An ideal candidate will think through the question and provide a possible answer such as: 'A round manhole cover can't fall through the round manhole compared to a square cover which could fall through diagonally. Additionally, a round cover fits easily without too much rotating'. This kind of answer shows the candidates ability to think critically.

4 Of course there is no 'right' answer to this funny question, but it allows an interviewer to see how an interviewee thinks, prioritises and solves problems. The candidate might say: 'Since I don't have a place to put an elephant, I'd probably ring up the local zoo and ask them to take it.'

5 This question aims to test your candidate's creativity. It doesn't matter what kind of tree they choose, as long as the answer illustrates their strengths. For example, they might say: 'I'd be an oak because I'm strong and dependable.'

CASE STUDY 11.1 An Australian bank uses visuals to make complex concepts easier to read

Terms and conditions are important as they set out for a consumer their legal rights and those of the company. However, they are usually written in complex legal language, printed in minute font sizes and written using lengthy sentences and paragraphs. Research shows that the majority of consumers don't bother to read them unless they have a dispute with the service or product provider, and then it could be too late.

This was the case in 2022 for customers (past and present) of phone provider Optus. The Optus database was hacked and personal customer details were stollen – information that the majority of these consumers had no idea that the company retained.

The example of the Bankwest comic style layout illustrates how the company has used visual formats to make this information more accessible to more customers, and encourage them to read the terms and conditions.

CASE STUDY 11.2 Punctuation is important

While there are specific rules of punctuation use, reading your text aloud and noting where you pause will help you determine where a full stop or comma should go. Are your sentences too long? Do you need to break up ideas with a new sentence or even a new paragraph? Do you need additional punctuation marks to communicate emphasis, possession or even quotations? It's best to check your text before sending to the reader. If in doubt about which ones to use, consult the *Australian Style Guide* (https://www. australianstyleguide.com/home) or even Martin Cutts' *Oxford Guide to Plain English* (2020). Keep in mind that conventions change over time.

CASE STUDY 11.3 Enough with the bafflegab. Here's why a Plain Language Bill makes sense

All occupations or industries use technical jargon to shortcut communication. While this is acceptable if your readers are familiar with a term's meaning, it can confound meaning for those who aren't. Many writers use jargon or 'business-speak' as a form of linguistic uniform – a way of identifying themselves as part of a group or industry. Others adopt buzzwords, weasel words or 'bafflegab' to make themselves sound knowledgeable. Rather than enhance communication, this language makes it opaquer – and often that is the objective. Language that is vague and full of cliched expressions impedes clear communication and should be avoided.

Do we need to legislate that important company communications should use plain English? This has been done years ago in the US and in the UK among others. Maybe it's time Australia did so too.

CASE STUDY 11.4 Communicating complex ideas

Notice that the writer has used simple and familiar language – the online version contains hyperlinks for those who would like to learn more about any technical terms used. By using the term 'cosmic vacuum cleaner', the writer also creates a mental picture of being 'sucked' into a black hole. While there is a problem that complex phenomena are being simplified here, as non-scientists, the readers only need to understand the broader concepts rather than the technical specifics.

CASE STUDY 11.5 Erasing history or keeping up with the times? The great Roald Dahl debate

There will be different 'takes' on this subject and a range of responses. The question is, is this a form of 'censorship' or 'updating' a classic text to reflect modern approaches and concerns about language? In the case of children's literature in particular, the case for moderate updating can be argued; for example, describing Augustus Gloop as 'enormous' rather than 'fat', subtly recognises the modern concern with body shaming and the possible impact on younger readers. In the case of literary texts, such as Huckleberry Finn or even any Shakespearian play, context is important, and the language is a vital reflection of attitudes of the time and an artefact that can be studied. More sophisticated readers can cope with this, and so updating or revising language should be avoided, often because these expressions and terms are nuanced and pivotal to the themes of the piece. Finally, the trope 'PC gone mad', is a convenient catchphrase for those who do not recognise or acknowledge, often for ideological reasons, that language is powerful, and words do matter, and that negative stereotypes of marginalised people are often unthinkingly spread through commonly adopted words and phrases.

CASE STUDY 12.1 Email structure and tell-tale signs

This is a fairly typical employment advertisement and was really sent to one of the authors in 2022. The email shows credibility and gives good news then states that the recipient has a new job waiting, as long as they supply a messaging handle and the recipient's age. If we had chosen to ask for more information, we could have explored what types of projects were expected, what the work might entail, where we may be expected to travel and whether any specific skills were more valued than others. But we had to use email, no phone number was given. A search for the website domain was also inconclusive.

However, this email has some tell-tale signs that it might not be what it appears to be. Why the need to use a messaging platform? Why is age so important?

CASE STUDY 12.2 Employment opportunity

This is an example of a job advertisement that does not specify qualifications or experience. Such advertisements are so vague because the employers are unsure what kinds of backgrounds are needed to work in these positions.

There may be a range of available jobs in a number of locations. The only way to find out about these positions is to make a phone call and ask questions to see if you can work out if sending your CV is worth the time and effort.

CASE STUDY 12.3 The executive summary

This comes from an extensive report and was called an abstract on the original document. We think it is in fact an executive summary, but was located within a university context and, thus, used the academic term 'abstract'. The summary itself is succinct and well-written, but the report is incredibly detailed and long-winded because the recommended new window supplier is not the university's own in-house service department. The in-house quote was substantially higher, hence the need for wide-ranging, in-depth research.

CASE STUDY 13.1 Why did the political polls get it so wrong … again?

The old saying in survey research is 'garbage in, garbage out'. For this reason, how a question is asked or framed, the language used and sometimes the order in which a question is asked, will impact the answer given. A poorly worded question, one that is too general or one that asks something a respondent is unlikely to know, will not elicit a useful response.

To ensure that a survey captures a representative cross-section of opinions, attitudes or behaviours of the group being studied, it is important that a sample includes members of a range of possible demographic characteristics. These will be determined by the research question being studied. For example, if you were to survey a group about their attitudes to the features of a new mobile phone, you would be more likely to get a more accurate or useful answer by asking younger people who are the likely users.

Sample size refers to the number of participants or observations included in a study. This number is usually represented in statistics by n. The size of a sample influences the precision of the estimates and the power of the study to draw conclusions. So, the larger the sample size, the more likely a survey is to capture variations among the sample group.

In statistics, the 'margin of error' is defined as the range of values below and above the sample statistic and is described as the 'confidence interval'. The confidence interval is a way of indicating the extent to which a survey result reflects the population of interest.

The problem with phone polling or even surveys that take place in shopping centre or on the street, is that most people are reluctant to take the time to participate. In some cases (such as student course surveys), only those with a strong opinion (positive or negative) will be motivated to respond. As such, opinion polls are not necessarily likely to capture the views of the 'middle ground' voter whose vote is more likely to sway an election outcome.

It is often said that politicians place too much emphasis on opinion polls in how they govern or create policy. In particular, they are often focused on the views of electors in marginal seats that they need to win to keep government rather than a possible misunderstood policy. Marketing polls are more used by product developers to evaluate attitudes to brands and products and to shape their advertising or promotional activities. Conducted well using representative samples of end users, such surveys will usually get more accurate results upon which to base important business decisions.

CASE STUDY 13.2 The case study

The case study is an important reference for lawyers, allowing them to highlight precedents that may be considered in their arguments. Marketers see case studies or focus groups as possible ways of identifying larger markets. Teachers use case studies to demonstrate certain ideas and concepts.

Case studies are advantageous in that they allow a person's experience to be understood, novel hypotheses to be tested, and much more detail to be assessed than with other methods. Case studies also have disadvantages, however, in that they can be too descriptive, they seldom allow cause and effect to be understood, and it is impossible to generalise the findings to the larger population.

CASE STUDY 13.3 Evaluating Google Scholar

Google Scholar is the best place to begin looking for scholarly peer-reviewed papers, but it is important to be aware that there is no option to tick only peer-reviewed articles results. The following are some extra tips:

- Changing even one search term will substantially change the search hits.

- Constraining the date range to the current year will locate all the newest (and popular) articles on a specific topic.

- You need to add words, use brackets, or use the plus or minus sign to restrict the amount of results you get.

- All kinds of scholarly papers come up in a Scholar search. The reputation of the journal or publication needs to be assessed before being completely accepted. If you are not finding suitable papers, then change your search terms.

REFERENCES

Archee, R. (2017). Accessing the academy: Scrutinizing accessibility problems of disabled students. Paper presented at the International Conference on New Horizons in Education, Berlin, Germany.

Bennett, A. A., Campion, E. D., Keeler, K. R., & Keener, S. K. (2021). Videoconference fatigue? Exploring changes in fatigue after videoconference meetings during COVID-19. *Journal of Applied Psychology*, *106*(3), 330–344. https://doi.org/10.1037/apl0000906

Han, H. J., Hiltz, S. R., Fjermestad, J., & Wang, Y. (2011). Does medium matter? A comparison of initial meeting modes for virtual teams. *IEEE transactions on professional communication*, *54*(4), 376–391. https://doi.org/10.1109/TPC.2011.2175759

Hiltz, S. R., Johnson, K., Aronovitch, C., & Turoff, M. (1980). Equality, dominance and group decision-making: results of a controlled experiment on face-to-face vs. computer-mediated discussions, in J. Salz (ed.), *Computer communications: Increasing benefits for society: proceedings of the 5th International Conference on Computer Communication, North Holland, Amsterdam*, pp. 343–8.

Marel, C., Siedlecka, E., Fisher, A., Gournay, K., Deady, M., Baker, A., Kay-Lambkin, F., Teesson, M., Baillie, A., & Mills, K. L. (2022). *Guidelines on the management of co-occurring alcohol and other drug and mental health conditions in alcohol and other drug treatment settings* (3rd ed.). Matilda Centre for Research in Mental Health and Substance Use, The University of Sydney. https://comorbidityguidelines.org.au/pdf/comorbidity-guideline.pdf

Moradi, D. (2022, April 7). Despite efforts, businesses struggle with accessibility. *MIT Review*. https://www.technologyreview.com/2022/04/07/1048543/despite-efforts-businesses-struggle-with-accessibility

Shockley, K. M., Gabriel, A. S., Robertson, D., Rosen, C. C., Chawla, N., Ganster, M. L., & Ezerins, M. E. (2021). The fatiguing effects of camera use in virtual meetings: A within-person field experiment. *Journal of Applied Psychology*, *106*(8), 1137–1155. https://doi.org/10.1037/apl0000948

Submission to the exposure draft: The attorney-general's proposed amendments to the *Racial Discrimination Act 2013*, (2014, April 15). https://www.aph.gov.au/DocumentStore.ashx?id=acfc7b66-f506-4846-a112-5aeeceb10263&subId=462954

Index